PRAISI

MUSIC
MONEY AND
SUCCESS

"*Music, Money, and Success* acts like career insurance for songwriters, providing the information to protect them against making any career choice that isn't in their best interest. It gives songwriters, composers, and music publishers everything they need to know about making a living in the digital age. *Music, Money, and Success* is so complete, that it is useful to an artist or industry rep at any career level."

ASCAP (American Society of Composers, Authors and Publishers)

"The music business involves a complete set of rights and a complicated landscape of licensing, royalty and income arrangements. Music, Money, and Success explains this in a more concise and useful way than any other book on the market. This book also presents the latest, most up-to-date information from the cutting edge of the business."

Music and Entertainment Industry Educators Association (MEIEA)

"The definitive resource for musicians, record producers, music publishers, industry executives, managers, agents and music attorneys. Remarkable and indispensable— easy to understand and a pleasure to read."

Entertainment and Sports Lawyer

"This industry bible includes a wealth of information about the music publishing industry, explaining the function of the music publisher and the value they bring to the songwriter. It carefully outlines various financial opportunities for music, including sound recordings, TV, movies, commercials, theater, the Internet, and the buying and selling of songs, as well as overall issues of copyright and the roles of managers, agents and lawyers."

The Harry Fox Agency

"Essential guide for any composer, songwriter, or business professional involved in the film and television music industry today."

John Williams (Five-time Academy Award-Winning Composer of Harry Potter, Star Wars, Jaws, etc.)

"*Music, Money, and Success* has more than 500 pages of indispensable information that songwriters, recording artists, music publishers, record producers, and all other music-business professionals can put to practical use. You absolutely need to know this information before considering or negotiating a contract or license. *Music, Money, and Success* is filled to the gills with closely held legal advice geared at optimizing the financial rewards of songwriters, recording artists, music publishers, and producers. It is the most comprehensive and clearly written reference book we've read on the subject."

Electronic Musician

"This book reveals the details of the whole range of music-industry deals, including financial details that could never be gleaned from advance sheets or from books."

Entertainment Law Reporter

"The twins Jeffrey and Todd Brabec, who are entertainment-law attorneys and former recording artists, produce an up-to-the-minute, readable guide through legal swamps of the business. The Brabecs cover all sources of revenue, detailing the exact percentages to be had from each opportunity, be it jingle or karaoke, Broadway or budget record sale. It should hit Platinum in the music industry. Recommended to every songwriter, performer, musician, music lawyer, agent, manager, film and television producer, advertising agency, record company, and music publisher."

The Hollywood Reporter

"This book is a lifesaver and should be on every composer, lyricist, and entertainment industry person's bookshelf. It covers every topic related to the business of film scoring and songwriting. It is the most comprehensive guide to date."

Society of Composers & Lyricists (SCL)

"The leading reference work dealing with the nuts and bolts economics of the music industry. The book provides a detailed analysis of virtually all of the new technologies, including video game agreements, CD and download rates, writer and artist development deals, remix and sample models, the structure of independent label deals, artist website concerns, and the new and different income sources for writers, authors, and publishers. Neophytes, industry veterans, creative

artists, and business professionals alike will benefit from this guide. Clearly and concisely written, thoughtfully structured, logically organized, and aided by numerous tables and charts, *Music, Money, and Success* continues to make even the more complex aspects of music business economics readily comprehensible."
American Bar Association/Entertainment and Sports Lawyer

"The best new book on the music business we've seen in years is *Music, Money, and Success*. One of the most informative features is explaining precisely how much money records and songs should earn in different contexts, such as commercials, movies, stage, TV, foreign, etc."
Billboard Magazine/Nashville Scene

"This is a great resource."
American Songwriter

"This is the most comprehensive and clear book of its kind, explaining the business side of music from recording licenses to advertising jingles, all in plain English, not legalese."
Canadian Independent Record Production Association Journal/CIRPA

"The book is as thorough as *This Business of Music,* the long-established music-industry bible, at explaining the various components of the industry but focuses more on the money aspect. The subjects covered are international in scope."
Society of Composers, Authors and Music Publishers of Canada (SOCAN)/ Words & Music Magazine

"This is an extremely well-written reference book which would be of benefit to any professional in the music business who wishes to improve his/her knowledge of business affairs. It is particularly aimed at songwriters, artists, and their representatives."
British Academy of Songwriters, Composers & Authors/BASCA Journal

"How not to get screwed by the music business. You must not live without this book."
Vibe Magazine

Schirmer Trade Books
A Division of Music Sales Corporation, New York

Exclusive Distributors:
Music Sales Corporation
180 Madison Avenue, 24th floor, New York, NY 10016, USA
Music Sales Limited
14-15 Berners Street, London, W1T 3LJ, UK
Music Sales Pty. Limited
Level 4, Lisgar House, 30-32 Carrington Street,
Sydney, NSW 2000, Australia

Order No. SCH10175
ISBN-13: 978-1-7876-0138-3

Printed in the United States of America

Managing Editor and Production Director: Guy Barash
Copyeditor: Elizabeth Bortka
Cover and Book Design: Fresh Lemon Australia

Library of Congress Cataloging-in-Publication Data

Names: Brabec, Jeff, author. | Brabec, Todd, author.
Title: Music money and success : the insider's guide to making money in the
   music business / Jeff Brabec and Todd Brabec.
Description: 8th edition. | New York : Schirmer Trade Books, 2018.
Identifiers: LCCN 2018037509 | ISBN 9781787601383 (pbk.)
Subjects: LCSH: Music trade--Vocational guidance. | Music--Economic aspects.
Classification: LCC ML3790 .B72 2018 | DDC 780.68--dc23
LC record available at https://lccn.loc.gov/2018037509

NEW AND REVISED 8TH EDITION

MUSIC MONEY AND SUCCESS

THE INSIDER'S GUIDE TO MAKING MONEY IN THE MUSIC BUSINESS

JEFF BRABEC AND TODD BRABEC

SCHIRMER TRADE BOOKS

A Part of **The Music Sales Group**
New York / London / Paris / Sydney / Copenhagen / Berlin / Tokyo / Madrid

*To our parents, grandparents, aunts, uncles, and cousins—
to our loved ones and our friends who have inspired and
supported us throughout our lives—for giving us the
examples of integrity and caring that we have always tried
to follow, our deepest thanks.*
Todd and Jeff

To my wife, Randye, for her love and support.
Jeff

ABOUT THE AUTHORS

Todd Brabec, former ASCAP Executive Vice President and Worldwide Director of Membership, is an entertainment law attorney and industry consultant, a Deems Taylor Award–winning co-author of the best-selling music business book *Music, Money, and Success: the Insiders Guide to Making Money in the Music Business*, now in its eighth edition (Schirmer Trade Books/Music Sales) as well as co-author of the "Music Publishing" chapter in the 2018 Juris Publications multiple-volume treatise *The Essential Guide to Entertainment Law*. He is an adjunct professor at USC where he teaches music licensing, music publishing, film, television, and video game scoring, and song contracts, and a former Governing Committee member as well as Music and Budget Chair of the American Bar Association Forum on the Entertainment and Sports Industries. In addition to the Deems Taylor Award for Excellence in Music Journalism, he is the recipient of the 2005 Educational Leadership Award from the Music & Entertainment Industry Educators Association (MEIEA) and the 2015 Texas Star Award from the Entertainment and Sports Law Section of the State Bar of Texas for Outstanding Contribution and Achievement in the Field of Entertainment Law.

During his 37-year ASCAP career in addition to overseeing and directing all of ASCAP's membership operations in the Los Angeles, New York, Nashville, Miami, Chicago, London, and Puerto Rico offices, he was responsible for signing most of ASCAP's successful songwriter/artists including, among many others, Marvin Gaye, Metallica, Journey, Neil Young, Smokey Robinson, Tom Petty, Sting, James Taylor, Joni Mitchell, the Jimi Hendrix catalogue, ZZ Top, War, Green Day, Jay Z, Bryan Adams, Jeff Lynne (ELO), Steely Dan, Fergie, Donna Summer, Mötley Crüe, Avril Lavigne, Supertramp, Foreigner, Marc Anthony, Bob McDill, America, John Prine, Sting, Rob Thomas and Earth, Wind & Fire as well as the worldwide top-grossing box office feature film score composers James Horner (*Avatar* and *Titanic*—#1 and #2 all-time box office films), Alan Silvestri (*Marvel's The Avengers*), Hans Zimmer (*Pirates of the Caribbean* films), James Newton Howard (*Hunger Games, Dark Knight*) and Randy Newman (*Toy Story 1, 2,* and *3* films) in addition to many of the top television series score composers and theme song writers.

His efforts over his career were instrumental in taking ASCAP from a 20% overall market share to a 52% share of radio and competitive dominance in broadcast television, cable, and worldwide top-grossing feature films as well as an increase in total annual revenue from $60 million to $995 million.

In addition, he significantly changed most of ASCAP's distribution, payment, and survey rules and systems and was responsible for significantly increasing the royalties and payment formulas for successful radio writers and film and television score and theme composers as well as eliminating practically all ASCAP payment and distribution policies, formulas, and rules that were not in the best interests of songwriters and composers or which had a negative effect on their earnings or which financially penalized success. In addition, he was in charge of and responsible for all writer and publisher advances, guarantees, bank loans, financial incentives, and other member inducements.

Past and current board memberships include the L.A. chapter of NARAS (the Recording Academy), the Association of Independent Music Publishers (AIMP), *Entertainment Law & Finance*, American Bar Association Forum on the Entertainment and Sports Industries (Governing Committee as well as Music and Budget Chairs), Academy of Country Music (ACM) and the California Copyright Conference (CCC), among others.

Jeff Brabec is Vice President of Business Affairs for BMG (representing, among others, the catalogues of Bruno Mars, John Legend, Kurt Cobain, Roger Waters, ZZ Top, OutKast, Buddy Holly, David Bowie, Chuck Berry, Bo Diddley, My Morning Jacket, John Lee Hooker, Devo, Hal David, Blondie, Paul Anka, Billy Idol, Jethro Tull, Burt Bacharach, Steven Perry, Tom Waits, Dan Wilson, Paul Anka, and Ray LaMontagne). BMG is the fourth largest music publisher in the world, owning and controling over two million copyrights.

He specializes in evaluating, analyzing, projecting income and negotiating music publishing catalogue acquisitions as well as songwriter, co-publishing, participation, administration, subpublishing, direct license, and joint venture agreements as well as termination rights issues. He also specializes in all music licensing issues including digital media, motion pictures, television, video games, apps, Broadway musicals, and new technology agreements and negotiations.

Previously, he has been Vice President of Business Affairs for both the Chrysalis Music Group and the PolyGram Music Group and Director of Business Affairs for the Welk Music Group and Arista-Interworld Music Group where he represented the catalogues of Elton John, Henry Mancini, Van Morrison, Waylon Jennings, Hall & Oates, Rick Springfield, Richard Rodgers, Jerome Kern, and Oscar Hammerstein II, among others.

Brabec is the co-author of the best-selling book *Music, Money, and Success: The Insider's Guide to Making Money in the Music Business,* now in its eighth edition (Schirmer Trade Books/Music Sales). He has been awarded the Deems Taylor Award for excellence in music journalism and the Texas Star Award by the Entertainment & Sports Law Section of the State Bar of Texas for Outstanding Contribution and Achievement in the Field of Entertainment Law.

Brabec is an Adjunct Professor at USC Thornton School of Music, Business Division, where he teaches music publishing and licensing, is contributing editor to the journal *Entertainment Law & Finance* and is co-author of the "Music Publishing" chapter in the 2018 Juris Publications multiple-volume treatise *The Essential Guide to Entertainment Law.*

The Brabecs lecture extensively throughout the world at conferences, universities, foreign country licensing and collection societies, industry associations, law firms, and management companies, among others. They have appeared on numerous legal and business panels for the Practising Law Institute (PLI), the bar associations of California, New York, Georgia, Texas, Florida, Minnesota, Tennessee, Washington, D.C., and Beverly Hills, SXSW, Midem, the National Association of Television Program Executives (NATPE), the American Bar Association Forum on the Entertainment and Sports Industries, ABA annual conference, NARAS, the Game Developers Conference, Song Summit Sydney, *Billboard*, Americana Conference, DIMA, AFM, MEIEA Educators Summit, the Cutting Edge Festival, Association of Independent Music Publishers (AIMP), Entertainment Law Institute, California Lawyers for the Arts, Guitar Center, Canadian Music Week, Production Music Association (PMA), International Association of Entertainment Lawyers (IAEL), American Film Institute (AFI), NARM, New Music Seminar, Society of Composers and Lyricists (SCL), Volunteer Lawyers for the Arts, ASCAP Expo, and the Irish Music Rights Organization (IMRO), among many others. They have hundreds of published articles on all aspects of the business and law of music and entertainment including the American Bar Association *Entertainment and Sports Lawyer*, the International Association of Entertainment Lawyers' *Annual Handbook*, *Entertainment Law & Finance*, the *Mitchell Hamline Law Review*, the *Entertainment, Publishing, and the Arts Handbook*, *USC Entertainment Law Spotlight*, *The Score* magazine, *Variety*, the *Hollywood Reporter* and many others. Todd's *Entertainment Law Review* article "The Performance Right: A World in Transition" was selected by West/Thomson Reuters as one of the best *Entertainment Law Review* articles of 2016 and was re-published in the *Entertainment, Publishing, and the Arts Handbook*. In addition, they have organized and participated in numerous American Bar Association webinars on music publishing, licensing, contracts, and sources of income in the music industry.

College, university, and law school guest lectures include USC, Harvard, NYU, Belmont, Loyola–New Orleans, Southwestern, Middle Tennessee State, University of Miami, Miami-Dade, Emory, Tulane, Florida State, University of Florida, Berklee College of Music, UCLA, the Trebas Institute, Hastings, Michigan State, University of Colorado, Five Towns College, Thomas Jefferson University, Victoria University, Syracuse University, California State University–Northridge and the Musicians Institute, among others.

Prior to their careers in music and entertainment law, they were legal services attorneys in Chicago for Community Legal Counsel (the U.S. Office of Economic Opportunity). They were also recording artists for Audio Fidelity Records as "The Reunion." Both are graduates of the New York University School of Law.

Website: musicandmoney.com.

CONTENTS

INTRODUCTION

EXPERIENCE + KNOWLEDGE + TALENT + REPRESENTATION + LUCK = SUCCESS

There are many ways to make money in music and these days you better know them all.

In today's world of constant technological changes and innovations, shifting income streams, global concentration of the record and music publishing businesses, the importance of social networking sites and the changing distribution of music models, it is more important than ever that the songwriter, composer, music publisher, recording artist, and record company have the practical, business, and legal knowledge and skills necessary to succeed and exist in the music business.

From best selling music apps to blockbuster movies, from highly rated TV shows to smash Broadway musicals, from the number one song of the year to the most successful video game, millions dream of attaining glamour and wealth through music. For one-hit wonders and lifetime stars, for those who make an everyday living from music and those who never give up even though the chances of making it are difficult, music is a way of life as well as a livelihood, and it is an integral part of the life of many billions of people.

Dollars. Hundreds of dollars. Thousands of dollars. Millions of dollars. Hundreds of millions of dollars. Billions of dollars. This is the kind of money than an individual, a group, a company, or a worldwide conglomerate can make in the worldwide music business. The numbers depend on creativity, talent, persistence, drive, luck, being in the right place at the right time, being associated with the right people and the right organizations, making the right decisions, and most of all, knowing how the business works and where the money comes from in every area of the music and entertainment field.

This book provides the essential information that the superstar, the novice, the composer, the lyricist, the businessperson, the educator, the professional, the aspiring musician, writer, or artist must know to have a shot. How to make it—how much you make—how to keep the money you make—and how to continue to be successful and make a living in a world of changing tastes, short attention spans, rapidly changing technology and complex contracts. It covers in detail the money-generating facets of the music field that you need to know about, showing how things work on a day-to-day basis, who makes the decisions, and how deals are structured and negotiated. It tells you through actual examples and real conversations what to look out for, what to ask for, and how to get it.

Music, Money, and Success is written for professionals and newcomers alike, be they on the creative or the business side of music. It is intended for songwriters, composers, lyricists, publishers, accountants, financial planners, agents, managers, lawyers, advertising agencies, record companies, website operators, motion picture and television studios and production companies, educators, banking and investment institutions, multinational conglomerates, video game developers and publishers, investors, journalists, and individually owned businesses both in the United States and in other countries.

Topics covered include:

- Songwriting and music publishing
- Co-publishing, subpublishing, and administration deals
- Streaming and download royalties
- Recording contracts/major vs. indie
- ASCAP, BMI, SESAC, and GMR
- Major studio and independent films
- Television
- Video games
- Audio visual streaming services
- Advertising commercials
- Broadway musicals and touring productions
- Foreign country rights and royalties
- Buying, selling, and valuing copyrights
- Managers, lawyers, and agents
- Copyright protection
- Putting it all together
- Breaking into the business
- Sampling songs and records
- Artist and publishing company joint ventures
- Apps, holograms, ringtones, e-cards, and new media
- Music-industry organizations

In recent years, the world of music has changed dramatically, and it continues to change on a daily basis. *Music, Money, and Success* has been written to make those changes understandable, as well as to clarify the basic rules that apply to everyone.

Many of the concepts, approaches, analyses, and dollar figures set forth throughout this book are based on the experiences of the authors. As no two situations are alike, and as laws, treaties, court decisions, license agreements, payment practices and rates, new technology, organization rules and policies, business practices, and contract and law interpretations change, current legal and business advice should always be sought from knowledgeable professionals for any situation.

Our gratitude goes to all the songwriters, composers, lyricists, artists, producers, and business people that we have dealt with over the past decades, as all of their experiences in this industry, both good and bad, have very much to do with the reasons this book was written. Particular thanks go to Michael Gorfaine and Richard Perna for their willingness to share their insights, experience, and knowledge. Thanks are also due to Ervin Brabec, Tom Chase, Gaylon Horton, Bob Hunka, Theodore Kaplan, Esq., Leeds Levy, Dennis McCarthy, Ralph Murphy, Paul Sherman, Esq., Jack Wall and the Dramatists Guild, for their help. Finally, a thank-you to the many knowledgeable people that we have dealt with and worked with throughout the years in this industry, as well as all the individuals who have helped us make this book a reality.

Knowledge is power in the entertainment business ... It is essential for success.

SOURCES OF INCOME

Digital Memory Devices
USB Sticks
SD Cards
Production Music
Concert Tours
Movie Theaters
Song Packs
Lyrics on Clothes
Holograms
Performing Rights
Online Instruction
Consumer Products
Sound Recording
  Performance Royalties
TV Syndication
Cable
Catalogue Musicals
TV Websites
Box Sets
Jingles
Cast Show Albums
Soundtrack Albums
Master Recordings
Social Networking Sites
Tethered Downloads
On-Demand Streams
Digital Jukeboxes
DVD Plus/CD-DVD
Slot Machines
Pay-Per-View
Recording Artist Video

Guitar Tabs
Jukeboxes
ISPs
Mash-Ups
Motion Pictures
Television
Ringtones/Ringbacks
Sampling
Home Video/DVD
Greeting Cards/
  Electronic and Physical
Sheet Music/Folios
Dolls, Toys, Music
  Boxes, Cereal Boxes
Interactive Games
CD-ROM
Special Products Albums
Interactive Streaming
Non-Interactive
  Streaming
Streaming
Foreign Countries
Performances
Advertising
Lyric Reprints
Karaoke
Theme Parks
Compilation Albums
Record Sales
Trailers
Limited Edition
  Collectibles

Downloads
Broadway/Off-Broadway
Video Games
Podcasting
Subscription Services
Webcasting
New Media
Video-on-Demand
Radio
Satellite
Mobile Devices
Remix
Cell Phones
Smartphones
Mobile Phones
Tablets
Multimedia
  Configurations
Apps
Airlines
Webisodes
Downloadable Content
Live Music Clubs
CDs
Vinyl

...Many More

CHAPTER 1
MUSIC, MONEY, SONGWRITING, AND MUSIC PUBLISHING

As new technology continues to widen the boundaries of the entertainment industry and create new vehicles of reaching people around the globe, the need for product to take advantage of these opportunities has taken on tremendous proportions.

With hundreds of television production companies churning out thousands of series episodes and specials; more than 700 motion pictures being produced every year in the United States alone; satellite television; audiovisual and audio streaming services; the Internet; billions of dollars of digital recordings, downloads, and CDs being sold annually; the emergence of free, advertising-supported, and pay subscription services; advertisers using hit songs to sell their products; music becoming essential in many apps; Broadway and road shows pulling in more than $2.5 billion yearly; wireless technology taking over the world; the growth of video-on-demand, as well as pay-per-view programming and the success of pay television channels and services; the introduction of VR and interactive media; DVRs, DVDs, Blu-ray, computers, game consoles, mobile phones, smartphones, tablets, handheld game machines, and digital technology having become a staple of every home; and the emergence of high-definition television—with all these developments, music has reasserted its place as a cornerstone of the ever-expanding and enormously profitable business of entertainment. In this world of multinational conglomerates, well-financed entrepreneurs, and million-dollar deals, stand the songwriter, the composer, and the music publisher—suppliers of one of the principal elements that keep entertainment programming exciting and interesting ... music.

Why has the creation and ownership of songs become so valuable? Why has music publishing become the darling of the investment community?

To appreciate fully the increasing value of music operations, you need to know how the business of publishing operates, how songs are licensed, and how the money is made.

This chapter reviews the myriad income-producing areas open to the songwriter, the types of contracts songwriters sign, and the types of protections and guarantees that writers should look for when negotiating their agreements with a publisher.

Many different organizations in the music industry perform essential services for the songwriter or writer/performer. Some, like ASCAP, BMI, SESAC, and GMR license radio and television stations as well as streaming services and collect monies for performances of a writer's songs. Others, such as record companies, make possible the worldwide dissemination of a writer's music through the distribution, sale, and promotion of albums, singles, and other recordings. And still others, such as the Harry Fox Agency, provide licensing services for songs used on recordings or as downloads.

In this panoply of service organizations, the music publisher reigns as one of the most important. For most songwriters, the publisher represents the first step in his or her career, a step that can easily mean the difference between success or failure, between making it or putting those songs back in a drawer forever.

MUSIC PUBLISHERS AND WHAT THEY DO

To many outside and within the entertainment industry, the function of a music publisher is vague and nebulous. In fact, the only knowledge that many people have of the term "publisher" is that it appears on the records, CDs, DVDs, video games, and sheet music they own.

To enhance understanding of the role of the music publisher (which is, in effect, that of an agent, manager, lawyer, and business advisor to the songwriter and his or her original creations), the following represents a brief summary of some of the music publisher's responsibilities:

- Copyrighting musical compositions in the United States and making sure that the songs it represents are also protected in foreign countries
- Securing recording, television, stage, home video, and motion picture uses of songs
- Arranging for the manufacture and distribution of sheet music, folios, songwriter compilations, "how to play" Internet, DVD, and CD packages, and other music-oriented books

- Securing uses of songs in advertising commercials
- Suing infringers of musical compositions and negotiating settlements, when appropriate
- Properly registering songs with the Harry Fox Agency, ASCAP, BMI, SESAC, GMR, and all other representatives and collection agents so that royalties can be collected for record, download, and CD sales, as well as for radio, television, subscription, streaming, live, and Internet performances
- Staying abreast of new developments and formulating relevant policies and procedures so that songs may earn maximum compensation
- Promoting the creation of new songs by helping to support and develop promising writers
- Negotiating fees and issuing appropriate licenses for all uses of music
- Making sure that payments from licensees (Internet companies, record companies, video distributors, ringtone companies, television, and film producers) are paid on time and accurately
- Providing information to representatives in foreign territories so that those representatives remain aware of current developments with respect to a publisher's catalogue
- Giving potential users prompt and correct information on songs being considered for use so that decisions can be made quickly
- Promoting legislation affecting the music and entertainment industries and the protection of the rights of creators
- Promoting interest in songs and their writers through special projects such as commemorative stamps, anniversary albums, single-writer folios, and compilation hit promotional albums for radio stations, producers, recording artists, film producers, television companies, video game producers, ringtone companies, websites, video distributors, subscription services, and all other users of music
- Keeping track of motion pictures, television shows, commercials, and video projects in pre-production, production, or post-production so that compatible songs can be submitted to producers for possible inclusion
- Communicating daily with representatives in foreign countries to ensure that the U.S. publisher has up-to-date knowledge of current developments in foreign territories, and that the foreign representatives have an understanding of what is happening in the United States

SINGLES AND ALBUMS

One of the primary roles of the publisher is to secure commercially released recordings of the songs it controls. The publisher must have an effective staff of professional managers (those who actually promote the songs) who not only know what artists are recording and the type of material needed for a particular session, but also have a good working relationship with record company A&R executives, producers, recording artists, and managers. Considering that most singles and albums never achieve enough sales to recoup their costs of production, the chances of a song's becoming successful are slim enough. Without a record, however, the chances are virtually nonexistent. Exceptions aside (for example, songs written specifically for motion pictures, Broadway musicals, television series, video games, or commercials), the real success and earnings of a song are contingent on its becoming a hit record, or being included on a chart album or performed on a popular website.

After a song has been initially recorded and released, the publisher will try to secure commitments from other recording artists or producers to include the composition on future albums or singles. To accomplish this, the publisher may remix or re-demo the song with a different arrangement to adapt it for promotion in markets other than that in which it had its initial success (for example, changing the sound from pop to hip-hop, or rock 'n' roll to country). Another reason for creating a different version of a hit song is that certain records become the definitive version, and it may be difficult to get a recording by another artist if people feel that the best version has already been done.

The test of a good publisher is not necessarily how many records by other artists it can secure during or immediately after a particular song is on the charts (although that is extremely important), but also the number of new recordings and other uses it can secure during the many years following a song's initial chart activity. It is not unusual for a strong publisher to get hundreds of separate recordings or other uses of a good song. Continual song promotion of both hit and non-hit songs represents one of the real services of a music publisher.

DEMO RECORDINGS

Another important function of the music publisher is the financing and production of "demo recordings" of a writer's new compositions. In the music industry, these recordings or digital files are many times a necessity to secure a commitment to record a song. These demos can range from a simple vocal with piano or guitar to elaborate productions, with the latter becoming more and more prevalent. The costs of making demos (recording session time, musicians, singers, copyists, and duplication) are normally paid by the music publisher and, in many cases, recouped from the song's future earnings.

PROPER ADMINISTRATION

Another necessary and important service provided by the publisher is that of proper administration of musical compositions: registering copyrights, filing necessary information to mechanical and performing rights organizations, reviewing royalty statements and making sure they are correct, auditing record companies and other licensees, keeping track of when income is due and following up when it is not received, bookkeeping, negotiating licenses, and collecting monies due. Considering the complexity of the music industry, the hundreds of thousands of music users throughout the world, the lack of detail on many royalty statements from licensees, and the amounts of money involved $500,000 to well over $1 million in total writer and publisher royalties is not unusual for a worldwide hit song), this service is vital.

TELEVISION AND MOVIE MUSIC

Another important area of concentration is the promotion of songs for television series, made-for-TV movies, and theatrical motion pictures. Standard and contemporary songs are a mainstay of these media, and whether the song is used as a theme, background music, or actually sung or performed on camera, the writer's and publisher's earnings can be substantial.

For example, a song used in a motion picture earns an initial synchronization fee for its inclusion in the film. If the motion picture is shown in a foreign country, the song will earn performance royalties. Since many films have soundtrack albums and hit singles, additional royalties will be generated by download, record, and CD sales, as well as from radio, Internet, and television performances of the songs on the soundtrack. When the motion picture is finally broadcast on one of the television networks such as the "Movie of the Week" or on one of the pay television services (e.g., HBO, Showtime, the Movie Channel), or digital streaming services (such as Netflix, Hulu, Amazon, etc.), additional royalties will be distributed by ASCAP, BMI, SESAC, and GMR. And after its initial network or pay television broadcast, a movie may be shown for years on local or cable television stations as well as on websites, digital services such as Hulu and Netflix, mobile devices and computers throughout the world, with additional royalties being generated.

COMMERCIALS

An important activity for the publisher is the promotion of songs for use as part of advertising campaigns. There has been a growing tendency on the part of advertising agencies to use well-known songs (hip-hop, motion picture and television themes, standards, Broadway music, classic rock, contemporary hits) as important parts of their promotional messages. The initial and option fees paid for the use of such songs range from thousands of dollars to more than $1 million.

VIDEO GAMES

Since the video game and related markets are an important source for not only exposing songs to large audiences but also making money, specific promotions are designed for these areas.

FOREIGN PROMOTION AND COLLECTION OF ROYALTIES

For many songs written by U.S. writers, the foreign market does not represent a major source of income unless the song has been recorded by a recording artist who is successful outside the United States, is in a television series shown on foreign television, is in a motion picture or video game that becomes a hit overseas, is on a worldwide subscription or other digital streaming service, or has attained the status of a standard. When the U.S. publisher and its foreign representatives have a good relationship and communicate effectively, songs can be successfully promoted in foreign territories and generate sizable income—a consideration that should be foremost in making any foreign representation deal.

THE PUBLISHER, WRITER/PERFORMER, RECORD CONTRACTS, AND DEVELOPMENT DEALS

During the past decade, many publishers have taken on the new responsibility of securing recording contracts for their songwriters through record-production affiliates. In many cases, the publisher may be responsible for producing the actual finished recording, or something very close to it. In others, the publisher finances elaborate master-quality demos featuring a number of its writer/performer's songs, so that a record company can hear the commercial potential of the writer as a recording artist, sign him or her to a contract, finance master recordings, and distribute the finished product. Because more and more recording artists write and record their own material, publishers find diminishing opportunities to place songs with such artists. By not only signing a writer/artist or writer/producer to create songs but also trying to negotiate an artist contract or production agreement, a publisher works to ensure a guaranteed outlet and commitment for commercial release of the artist's (and publisher's) songs.

INFRINGEMENT ACTIONS

An important responsibility of the publisher is protecting its copyrights and enforcing the exclusive rights that it has been granted by the songwriter and the copyright laws. Considering the number of actual and potential users of songs throughout the world (record companies, film producers, television companies, subscription or ad supported services, cell phone companies, video distributors, book publishers, sheet music firms, websites, peer-to-peer services, digital distribution companies, magazines, video and audio sing-along booths, jukebox operators, restaurants, retail stores, theatrical productions), this responsibility is both far-reaching and difficult. The good publisher will spend a great deal of time and money to ensure that its songs are not used without permission and compensation.

HOME AND PERSONAL VIDEO

An increasingly important area is that of the inclusion of songs in home videos, whether they be of recording artists, "how to" subjects, television series, exercise programs, sports promos, "the making of" programs, or motion pictures. With hundreds of millions of DVD and Blu-ray players, cell phones, smartphones, tablets, hand-held devices, computers, and game consoles throughout the world, home video represents a significant source of income, and music publishers work hard on song promotion and licensing in this continually expanding area.

THE INNER WORKINGS OF A MUSIC PUBLISHER

Most publishing companies are divided into a number of separate but interrelated departments, all of which are important to the company's success. Each plays an integral part in the success or failure of the operation.

CHIEF EXECUTIVE

The president or chief executive officer brings in many of the deals, determines what acquisitions should be made, and provides much of the direction, insight, and motivation that make every successful company work. In some cases, the CEO's role is that of an overseer charting the direction of a firm and its overall activities; in others, it is a role of intimate involvement with the functioning of virtually every department on a daily basis. In almost all cases, the reputation, integrity, foresight, experience, and drive of the chief executive set the tone for the entire company, as well as for the image of the company worldwide.

CREATIVE DEPARTMENT

The creative department's role is to listen to new material, go to clubs and other venues to see writer/performers live, make recommendations on what writers to sign, help writers with the structure of their songs, and promote or "run with" songs to record producers, recording artists, motion picture companies, video game producers, and television producers. Many of these individuals are also familiar with the ins and outs of recording studios, and produce or help produce many of the demo sessions for new songs. Many of the experienced ones are also able to develop songwriters as recording artists and produce "master-quality" demos for selling writer/performers to record companies as artists.

PROMOTION DEPARTMENT

The promotion department has the responsibility of promoting the catalogue by designing and preparing promotional CD or e-mail packages, songbooks, and other items for distribution to recording artists, record producers, television, motion picture, video game and trailer producers, app developers, ad agencies, and home video, merchandise, greeting card, jukebox, video jukebox, ringtone, and premium companies.

BUSINESS AND LEGAL AFFAIRS DEPARTMENT

Business affairs (which in many companies also serves as the legal department, since most business affairs executives are attorneys) is responsible for negotiating, drafting, and approving all contractual agreements entered into by the company. Due diligence investigations for catalogue or other acquisitions is also a major responsibility. In addition, if any other department requires advice on how to approach a particular situation or problem, the business affairs executive is the one who will be called on to assist because of his or her experience and knowledge of how the industry works. This department can also assist in formulating recommendations on how a firm should deal with the issues related to changing technology, current legal decisions, congressional trends, and the licensing of newly created uses of music.

SYNCHRONIZATION LICENSING DEPARTMENT
Synchronization licensing relates to the use of songs in television programs, commercials, home video, motion pictures, and all other audiovisual projects. Included in the responsibilities of this department are the negotiation of fees for the use of songs, issuing licenses, keeping track of options for additional media (e.g., home video in a television license), making sure that license fees have been paid, as well as following up on all music licenses that have or are about to expire.

MECHANICAL LICENSING DEPARTMENT
This department is responsible for handling all license requests for the use of songs on CDs, records, and downloads. Responsibilities include issuing licenses to record companies or download services, negotiating mechanical rates (if a company is requesting a rate that is less than statutory), negotiating advances, and providing label copy credit. If the publishing company licenses mechanical rights through the Harry Fox Agency in the United States, this department will coordinate licensing activities with Harry Fox personnel and provide all necessary information and direction so that licenses can be issued. The same is true with respect to CMRRA and SODRAC in Canada.

FINANCE DEPARTMENT
The finance department is responsible for the financial affairs of the company, including issuing advances and royalty checks, securing W-9s and other documents required by governmental (state and federal) regulations, budgeting the company's financial year, reimbursing employees for business expenses, analyzing potential acquisitions or deals, paying bills, and projecting income as well as expenses on a monthly and yearly basis. Financial analysis of potential agreements or acquisitions is also part of the responsibilities.

COPYRIGHT DEPARTMENT
The copyright department is responsible for the proper registration of compositions with the U.S. Copyright Office in Washington, D.C. It also provides correct copyright notices for all print and record usages, registers songs with ASCAP, BMI, SESAC, and GMR to ensure that radio, Internet, and television broadcasts as well as other

performances of songs are monitored; and fulfills a wide range of other responsibilities related to the protection of musical compositions in a company's catalogue.

FOREIGN DEPARTMENT

The foreign department is responsible for notifying a company's representatives throughout the world of new record releases, and motion picture, home video, video game, Internet, mobile device, and television uses so that songs can be registered with the local performance and mechanical rights societies. It also informs those representatives about the signing of new writers or recording artists, ownership percentages of songs controlled, and the acquisition of catalogues, and it answers any inquiries received from foreign territories concerning the compositions in the catalogue.

ROYALTY DEPARTMENT

The royalty department is responsible for checking the royalty statements that come in from music users, making sure that the proper amounts are being remitted, crediting all monies to the proper songs, ensuring that all writers and other income participants are paid correctly, tracking income, doing desktop or other audits, and following up with any company that has either not paid or paid incorrectly.

I.T./COMPUTER DEPARTMENT

Because of the complexity of the entertainment industry and the increasing demand to stay competitive and provide myriad services to potential music users, many companies have in-house computer personnel who design and provide programs for all departments. Some major publishers not only have programs to ensure proper royalty accounting. but also have programs that generate song reports by recording artist (e.g., all songs in the catalogue recorded by a certain artist), by type of music (e.g., jazz instrumental, country, rap, rock, pop), by song (e.g., all records of a particular song with the initial release date and identity of the recording artist), by message (e.g., love songs, car songs), and by income (e.g., gross and net income on an annual or monthly basis). Some of the larger publishers, which have affiliates around the world, achieve instantaneous global communication by means of computer link-ups that provide daily, up-to-date sharing of information. For example, information about newly created songs (songwriter identity, ASCAP, BMI, SESAC, or GMR membership, percentage of control, exploitation restrictions such as no commercials without consent, territory controlled, etc.) may be transmitted around the world not only for registration with each foreign affiliate but also for automatic registration with foreign performance societies.

THE ACQUISITION OF RIGHTS BY A PUBLISHER

The rights to musical compositions are acquired by music publishers by means of a number of different agreements. Later in this book we examine each kind of agreement in detail. For now, a brief overview can give a general impression of how publishers assume ownership or control of musical compositions.

INDIVIDUAL SONG AND EXCLUSIVE AGREEMENTS

The most common songwriter-publisher agreements are the individual song agreement and the exclusive agreement. Under the individual song agreement, a writer transfers the copyright to one composition or a selected number of identified compositions to a publisher and, in return, receives a portion of the income earned from uses of that composition or compositions. Under the exclusive agreement, the songwriter agrees to assign all compositions written during a specified term (for example, two years from January 1), once again, with the guarantee of a share of the income generated and usually a proviso for weekly or monthly recoupable advance payments. Included in the rights granted to the music publisher are:

- The right to reproduce the compositions mechanically (license songs for use on singles, albums, downloads, files, interactive digital services, and CDs)
- The right to synchronize the compositions (license songs for use in motion pictures, television productions, video games, DVDs, mobile devices, VR, and other audiovisual works)
- The right to perform the compositions (license the broadcast and other performance of songs)
- The right to print the compositions (license songs or their lyrics for sheet music, folios, magazines, and books)
- The right to represent and license the compositions in all new media created by present or future technology

As part of these agreements, some successful writers are able to negotiate publishing or participation agreements with their music publishers. Under the co-publishing agreement, the songwriter co-owns the copyright in his or her songs (usually through a wholly owned company) and receives a portion of the publisher's share of income in addition to the songwriter's share. Under the participation agreement, the writer shares in the publisher's income similar to the co-publishing arrangement but does not become a co-owner of the copyright.

Publishers also receive rights in compositions through the following types of agreements. None of these actually transfers copyright ownership; instead, they transfer the rights to control and administer the compositions for a specified period of time.

ADMINISTRATION AGREEMENT

Under an administration agreement, the publisher receives the right to administer a composition or group of compositions (i.e., licensing the use of songs in recordings, as downloads, CDs, television series, motion pictures, commercials, ringtones, subscription services, and video productions, and collecting royalties from all music users) for a specified period of time. In return for its services, the publisher usually receives an "administration fee" of 10% to 25% of all income earned during the term of the agreement.

FOREIGN SUBPUBLISHING AGREEMENT

The foreign subpublishing agreement is similar to an administration agreement. The only difference is that the compositions being represented have been written by songwriters from another country. For example, if a U.S. publisher wants to have a publisher in England represent its catalogue in the United Kingdom, or if a publisher in France wants its catalogue represented in the United States by an American publisher, the agreement is referred to as a subpublishing agreement. As with the administration agreement, representation is limited to a specified duration (usually not less than three years), and the fees retained by the foreign subpublisher for its services are negotiable within certain limits.

THE SONGWRITER–MUSIC PUBLISHER RELATIONSHIP

One of the most important decisions that a composer or lyricist will make concerns the choice of a music publisher and the type of contract signed. If the writer makes the right choice, the chances for success in an extremely competitive, complex, and difficult business are increased immeasurably. If the wrong choice is made or the wrong contract signed, the writer may never recover financially or creatively. Also, if the publisher with whom the writer signs does not have the capabilities to promote a writer's compositions effectively, the chances of ever becoming successful, even under a good contract, are minimal.

One must remember that any contractual relationship entered into is usually for the long term, regardless of whether the publishing contract applies to one song or to all songs composed by a writer during a specified period of time. This is so because under almost all publishing contracts, the copyright ownership to the writer's songs is transferred to the music publisher. Under the provisions of the 1976 U.S. Copyright Law, the music publisher owns the copyright to most songs written after 1977 for a minimum of 35 years in the United States and, in many cases, retains such ownership for the full period of copyright protection.

Because of the length of this contractual relationship, the songwriter and his or her representative must be aware of what is a good contract and what is not, as well as what is a fair contract and what is not. Considering that the writer will have to live with the terms of the original publishing contract for many years, one should take into account the present as well as the future when negotiating its terms.

PUBLISHING CONTRACTS

There is no such thing as a standard writer-publisher contract. Each publishing company normally has its own particular contract drawn up by its legal staff to reflect its own particular way of doing business and its own particular view of its relationship with its writers. Although many uniform provisions or procedures will be included in almost every agreement, what is standard for one company is not always standard for another.

We will first explain the provisions that are included in almost every publishing contract. After reviewing the most important of these provisions and their meaning, we will then explain the different types of clauses that may be negotiated (depending on the writer's bargaining power), the varied sources of income of the songwriter, and how much money can be earned.

Of the two basic types of contracts that a writer signs with a music publisher, the first, and most common, is the individual song contract. The second, reserved more for writers who have a successful track record, definite or possible recording commitments, or potential in which the publisher believes, is the exclusive writer's contract.

THE INDIVIDUAL SONG CONTRACT

Under the terms of the individual song contract, the writer assigns to the publisher the copyright to one or more specified songs. For most new writers—at least those without any previous success or future recording commitments—the sale or transfer of the copyright will be for a minimal amount of money, many times for the standard contractual price of $1 or a small advance of from $250 to $1,000.

Because the individual song contract applies only to the song or songs specifically mentioned in the agreement, the writer can go to a number of different publishers with other songs and give each one only those songs that it is really interested in promoting. A number of successful writers who do not have an exclusive writing arrangement with any single publisher have songs published by a number of different companies. When a writer signs an individual song contract, the writer always retains the option to place other material with other publishers. In addition, by transferring the ownership of only certain selected songs to a publisher, the writer is also assured that the songs transferred are the ones that the publisher is really interested in promoting.

Most legitimate music publishers, because of their integrity and the large costs involved in doing their job, will not sign a writer if they do not feel that the songs being assigned are promotable. They may eventually discover that, after signing a writer and trying to promote the songs, they were mistaken about the songs' commercial potential, but they will not sign a writer just for the sake of a signing. To be signed by a major full-service publishing company (whether large or small) is therefore a good indicator that the writer's songs have definite commercial potential. Of course, many things can happen after a writer has signed with a company (change of personnel, the company being sold, change in musical tastes, etc.), which can diffuse the initial enthusiasm and faith in a writer's material, but such things can happen in any business. Such are the chances that must be taken for success.

Because of the nature of the agreement being signed, it is also advisable that every writer, before signing with a publisher, at least look into the publisher's reputation and its ability to promote its material. Sometimes it might be better to receive a rejection from a legitimate publisher than to sign with a company that is not equipped to furnish the professional services required for a song to be placed with a recording artist or otherwise effectively promoted.

THE EXCLUSIVE SONGWRITER'S CONTRACT

The other principal type of publishing contract that a writer may sign is an exclusive agreement with one publisher for all songs written during a specified period of time. The term of the agreement can range from one year to seven years (or longer depending on how the contract is structured), with provisions for weekly, monthly, or quarterly advances whether or not the writer's songs are being recorded or performed. The publisher has the right to publish and own all compositions written by the writer during the term of the contract.

One further point, which we will discuss at greater length later, is that all weekly, monthly, or quarterly payments made to the writer are treated as advances, recoupable from the future royalties of the writer. For example, if a writer is being paid $600 per week in advances, $31,200 will have been advanced in the first contract year. These monies will be deducted from any royalties that become due from downloads, record sales, print, commercials, home video, television, video games, home video and motion-picture synchronization fees, as well as from any other source of income that the publisher controls.

One of the real values of such an exclusive relationship with a publisher—and there are many—is that the writer is guaranteed a steady income, much like a salary, to meet normal, day-to-day financial needs and living expenses while pursuing a career. In addition, because monies from record sales and performances take from six months to more than two years to reach the writer, the weekly, monthly, or quarterly advance payments (sometimes referred to as a "writer's draw") can lend a great deal of financial and emotional security while the writer is waiting for royalties to be collected and processed. The writer is usually given the right to use a company's recording studios to make demos and collaborate and share song ideas with other writers on a daily basis, two factors that cannot be overemphasized in the development of a career.

IMPORTANT PROVISIONS OF SONGWRITER-PUBLISHER CONTRACTS

Even though the publishing contract used by one company is rarely the same as that used by another, certain important terms and provisions are in almost every contract, whether it is one page or 50 pages in length. The following section discusses and explains some of the most important of these standard provisions so that when a company shows interest and offers you a contract, you'll know what to expect.

SALE OF THE MUSICAL COMPOSITION

In virtually every publishing contract, the songwriter (composer or lyricist) sells his or her musical composition to the music publisher. This sale includes the copyright as well as all other equitable and legal rights in the composition. In most cases, the sale is unqualified and unconditional, regardless of whether the publisher is able to secure a recording or other commercial use of the song.

Because the sale is unconditional, it is vitally important that the writer or writer's representative knows the company with which he or she is negotiating and has full confidence in the company's enthusiasm about the material and in its professional capabilities to promote and administer the songs effectively. Too many writers sign with the first company that expresses even a slight interest in the writer or the writer's songs. And too many times, after nothing tangible has happened, the writer has nothing to show except the loss of the publishing rights in his or her material. True, the writer can always try to get a recording on the song, but the writer has lost a good deal of bargaining power by having the ownership and right to publish the song already committed to a third party.

RETURN OF SONGS TO THE WRITER

Some publishers will return songs to the writer if they feel that the compositions are not worthy of further promotion. This is not the general rule, however, since the publisher often has expended monies for a studio demo and incurred additional expenses in protecting and commercially promoting the songs. In such cases, the chances of a writer getting a song back (unless he or she is willing to reimburse the publisher for its expenditures) are minimal. After all, the publisher may still have hope that, in some way, it will not only recoup at least part of the costs but also succeed in making the song a hit or licensing it to a money-generating project.

The prevalent practice in the industry with respect to writers who are not recording artists is for the music publisher to retain ownership of all songs transferred to it by the writer. If a writer is a recording artist with a guaranteed contract with a major record label or successful indie label, however, reversion clauses are many times negotiated so that the music publisher may own the songs only for a specified period of time. Occasionally, these clauses prohibit reversion if the publisher has not recouped its advances, or they restrict reversion only to compositions that have not been commercially exploited by the publisher (e.g., not used in a television program, video game, or motion picture, not released as a commercial download or on a CD, etc.).

THE TERM

The term of an exclusive agreement is usually for an initial period of one year with up to six additional option years at the election of the music publisher. In most cases the publisher has to send the writer a written notice that it is exercising the option to extend the term of the agreement for an additional contract period. In some cases, the options are automatic unless the publisher notifies the writer to the contrary before the end of the current year. A variation, if the writer is a recording artist, is for the term to be coextensive with the artist's current agreement with a record company or, if the publisher is trying to secure such a contract for the writer/performer, coextensive with the agreement that is finally signed. In most of the coextensive agreements, the publisher will also have the option to extend its relationship with the writer by paying additional advances to the writer by turning the contract into a songwriter agreement (with no album release requirements) if a record contract is not signed.

RIGHTS GRANTED TO THE PUBLISHER

In addition to copyright ownership of the composition, the writer transfers the following rights to the publisher:

- The right to license performances on radio, television, the Internet, or other media (with these rights normally assigned to either ASCAP, BMI, SESAC, or GMR for representation and collection of royalties)
- The right to make arrangements of the composition and translations for exploitation in non-English-speaking territories
- The right to dramatize the title, music, and lyric plot of the composition for use in motion pictures or television programs
- The right to license the composition for records, CDs, downloads, home video, streaming, subscription services, and DVDs
- The right to license uses of the composition in motion pictures, television programs, Internet programming, VR, live theatrical stage productions, and commercials
- The right to license the compositions as ringtones, ringbacks, or in video games
- The right to print the composition and its lyrics for use on websites, in sheet music, books, magazines, and folios, and license others to do so
- The right to license the title of the composition as the title of a motion picture, television series, video game, or episode in a series
- The right to exercise any and all other rights in the composition that may then or in the future exist
- The right to negotiate licenses for the use of compositions in both current and future technology

EXCLUSIVITY

Under the exclusive songwriter's agreement, all songs written by a writer during the term of the contract are owned by the music publisher. On rare occasions, exceptions are made; for instance, songs written specifically for motion pictures may be excluded from the agreement, since motion picture companies normally demand copyright ownership when they hire a writer to compose film music or songs. This also applies to the television market when a composition or score is written specifically for a series. Even then, the writer is normally required to use his or her best efforts to retain all or a portion of copyright ownership for the publisher, and only if those efforts are unsuccessful will the exclusion apply. There are a number of alternative approaches depending upon bargaining power and the needs of the parties, such as publishing income participation without copyright ownership or administration.

COMPENSATION

The writer will be paid the following royalties for uses of his or her musical compositions:

Sheet Music. 5¢ to 15¢ for individual pieces of single-song sheet music sold in the United States and Canada (with many contracts guaranteeing the songwriter 50% of the publisher's receipts from such uses).

Folios. From 10% to 15% of the wholesale selling price of each folio or songbook sold in the United States and Canada. Because there are a number of songs in any folio, this 10% to 15% royalty will be shared on a pro-rata basis with all other royalty-bearing songs in the folio. In addition, if a folio is designed exclusively around the songs of a particular writer or writing team, an additional 2% to 5% is usually added. As with sheet music, some writers receive 50% of the publisher's income from songs used in folios or songbooks, and an additional percentage from personality folios.

CDs, Records, Downloads, and Home Video. 50% of the earnings received by the publisher for sales in the United States.

Television and Motion Picture Synchronization Rights. 50% of all monies received by the publisher from licensing songs for use in theatrical films and television programs.

Commercials. 50% of all sums received by the publisher for the licensing of songs for use in radio, television, Internet, and print ads.

Video Games and Ringtones and Ringbacks. 50% of all monies received by the publisher.

Foreign Exploitation. 50% of all monies received in the United States that are earned in countries outside the United States from records, tapes, CDs, downloads, home video, sheet music, television and motion picture rights, commercials, ringtones, video games, and all other sources of income, excepting the publisher's share of performance royalties.

Performances. Because ASCAP, BMI, SESAC, and GMR pay the songwriter and publisher directly and separately for radio, television, and other types of performances of songs and scores, the writer (unless a co-publishing or participation agreement has been signed) will not share in the royalties received by the publisher. In the event that a publisher does receive the songwriter's share of performance income (e.g., if it licenses performances directly to a music user rather than use the services of ASCAP, BMI, SESAC, or GMR), the writer will be paid 50% of those fees.

SHARING OF ADVANCES

On occasion, the songwriter will share in an advance paid to a publisher by a music user if the advance relates exclusively to the writer's song or songs. For example, if a video game company paid a nonreturnable advance as part of its agreement to use a specifically identified composition in a game, the advance would be treated as income and the writer would receive his or her share. In most instances, however, advances are paid on the basis of an entire catalogue and will not be shared with the songwriter, since it is virtually impossible to determine a proper division of such an advance. For example, if a record company wants to do a compilation video of hit songs by a writer/performer and pays the publisher an advance attributable to an identifiable number of titles, the writer of those songs will normally receive a proportionate share of the advance. But if a print company pays an advance to secure the right to print sheet music and folios of all present or future songs in a publisher's entire catalogue (or a ringtone company or karaoke distributor pays a catalogue advance on the signing of the agreement), the songwriters will not share in such "catalogue advance" money, because it does not relate to specifically identified titles.

MINIMUM SONG DELIVERY REQUIREMENT

In many agreements, especially if weekly or monthly advances are being paid, the writer may be required to create a certain number of songs during each period of the contract. In most cases, the requirement is on a yearly basis (e.g., 15 wholly written songs per year, or 20 co-written songs in which the writer has at least a 50% interest, or enough portions of newly written compositions to add up to the equivalent of 10 wholly written songs), but can be on a monthly (e.g., 2 songs per month) or quarterly basis (e.g., 5 songs per quarter), depending on the amount of advances being given, the publisher's policy, and the reputation of the writer.

Such clauses are a necessary incentive for some writers and they provide a safety valve for the publisher if a writer is not actively writing songs. If the minimum commitment is not met, the publisher will have the right not only to suspend all advance payments but also extend the current period (year or quarter) of the contract until the minimum delivery commitment is fulfilled. Many writers may be reticent to agree to such a clause, as they feel that the creative process does not work on a scheduled basis. The minimum commitment required by the publisher is normally a reasonable one, though, and most professional writers exceed the requirement.

If the writer is a recording artist or producer as well, the minimum delivery commitment may relate to commercially released recordings of his or her songs. The provision will function as outlined above with the only exception being that a song is not considered delivered to the music publisher until it is commercially released on an album or single. For example, a sample clause may provide that if 10 newly recorded songs are not released in the United States during any one year of the agreement by the writer as a recording artist or producer, the current one-year period of the contract will be extended until such occurs. If such an extension occurs, all dates at which the publisher can exercise any option rights for additional periods will be moved back accordingly and, in most cases, no further advances will be due the writer during his extension/suspension period. Many times, the songs have to be licensed at a certain minimum mechanical rate (e.g., at not less than a 75% statutory rate) to fully qualify with a pro-rata reduction if a song is licensed at less than the agreed-upon minimum rate. For example, if a song on an album is licensed at 50% of statutory rather than the 75% contained in the songwriter agreement, the song would only count as ⅔ of one song in satisfaction of the release commitment.

ADVANCES

If the music publisher is granted the exclusive rights to all songs created by a writer during a specified period of time, advances are usually paid to the writer on a weekly, monthly, quarterly, or yearly basis. These monies are always recoupable by the publisher from future royalties due the writer for uses of his or her songs. For example, if a writer has been advanced $30,000 during the first year of an agreement and earns $45,000 in royalties, the publisher will recoup its $30,000 and give the writer the excess ($15,000). The publisher will normally not begin to recoup a writer's advances (even if the writer is immediately successful) until the second or third year of the agreement, since earnings (other than synchronization fees) normally take from five months to more than two years to be distributed by the various collection organizations, performance right societies, and foreign subpublishers.

There are many variations on how advances are computed, such as advances based on the achievement of certain earnings plateaus (e.g., an additional $10,000 if a song has earned $20,000 in gross royalties), songs reaching the charts or certain positions thereon (e.g., $10,000 if Top 50, another $10,000 if Top 10, and an additional $15,000 if Number One), the publisher recouping all past advances or a percentage thereof (e.g., $25,000 if the publisher has recouped all prior writer advances, or an additional $20,000 when the publisher has recouped 75% of all advances given to the writer). Each agreement will have its own particular variations dependent on the needs, expectations, and bargaining power of both parties.

MINI-MAX ADVANCES

A number of agreements also use what is known as a "minimum/maximum" advance formula to compute annual advances after the initial period of the term expires. Under this type of clause, the amount of the advance payable to the songwriter during each option year is based on a percentage of the monies earned in the prior year (in some cases, 18 months), but with a "floor" and a "ceiling" provided for, regardless of the amount of earnings. For example, a publisher might offer a songwriter an advance of $50,000 for the first year, with option year advances being based on 66.6% to 75% of the prior year's earnings with the following minimums and maximums:

	Minimum	Maximum
1st Option	$50,000	$100,000
2nd Option	$60,000	$125,000
3rd Option	$75,000	$150,000

To illustrate how these mini-max formulas work, we will take a writer who has a 75% of the past year's earnings calculation with a minimum advance of $75,000 and a maximum advance of $150,000 provided for in the option year. If the writer earns $125,000 in the most recent contract year, the advance for the upcoming option year would be $93,750 ($125,000 × 75% = $93,750). If, however, the writer's share of earnings for the prior year was only $10,000 or $0, the writer would still be guaranteed the minimum of $75,000 for the next contract period. Additionally, if the writer earned $300,000 in the most recent year, the advance for the option year would be $150,000 rather than $225,000 ($300,000 × 75% = $225,000) since there was a $150,000 maximum advance restriction.

One of the values of these types of mini-max advances is that they reward success by increasing future advances, depending upon how much income has been generated in the past by the songwriter's compositions. This type of advance structure also establishes a minimum advance which is payable to the writer during an option year, regardless of the fact that the songwriter's compositions earned very little during the prior year.

One of the major issues in the negotiation of one of these types of so-called "mini/max" advance formulas is what type of income is going to be included in the calculation. Some clauses state that only mechanical income will be included; others add performance income as well; some will include mechanical, performance, and synchronization income; and others will include mechanical, performance, and synchronization earnings but exclude the one-time extraordinary fees paid for the use of songs in advertising commercials or use a percentage of such income versus all such income.

SUBFLOOR ADVANCES

If the "minimum/maximum" formula is used, the publisher will many times provide that the annual advance for an option year will be reduced by any unrecouped advance balance remaining from advances paid in prior years which have not been earned back. For example, "the advance for the first option period shall be a minimum of $75,000 and a maximum of $150,000, but the then-unrecouped prior advance balance shall be deducted from this advance." Under this type of scenario, if the writer has an unrecouped advance balance of $40,000 and the scheduled advance for the next contract period is $100,000, the actual advance payable to the songwriter for the upcoming option year will be $60,000, since the $40,000 negative balance would be deducted from the scheduled $100,000 advance.

When this type of unrecouped advance balance deduction concept becomes part of the agreement, the songwriter many times is able to negotiate a "sub-floor" below which the option year advance will not be reduced, regardless of the amount of the unrecouped advance balance. This type of clause will ensure that the writer will receive a reasonable advance for the next year and protect the writer from having the advance reduced to a minimal amount due to large unrecouped advances. For example, the agreement might provide for a $100,000 advance with a reduction by any unrecouped balance, but in no event shall any such reduction bring the actual advance payable to less than $75,000 for the option year. There are many variations in this area of sub-floors; the final resolution as to how low or how high they will be is dependent on the experience of those negotiating the agreement and the bargaining power of the parties.

PIPELINE INCOME

Some agreements provide that the publisher, when calculating the advance for the just-exercised option year, will take into account monies that have been earned by the activity of the writer's compositions during the prior year but which have not yet been received by the music publisher due to the delays in the transmittal of royalties by the various users of music or industry royalty collection organizations.

There are many variations related to the inclusion of this so-called "pipeline" income in the calculations used to determine option-year advances. Some companies include mechanical income only. Others guarantee a good faith estimate of mechanicals and performance income; some include synchronization income excluding commercials; other companies include monies received by their foreign affiliates which have not yet been paid to the U.S. company; others will count monies that have been received in house but have not yet been remitted to the writer in an upcoming royalty distribution; and some others provide for the inclusion of monies earned and being held for payment by the record company which has had the greatest sales success with recordings containing compositions by the songwriter.

TIMING OF ADVANCES

A number of variations determine when and how advances are paid to a songwriter. The total advance for a particular year may be paid at the commencement of that year (e.g., $50,000 on signing, $60,000 on commencement of the first option year, $75,000 on commencement of the second option year, etc.), on a quarterly basis, in 12 equal monthly installments (e.g., $48,000 per year payable in 12 monthly installments of $4,000 each), on a weekly basis, on achieving certain commitments (e.g., 20% of the annual advance when the writer delivers three new songs, 20% when 6 songs have been written, etc.), or according to a combination of time periods and fulfillment criteria (e.g., 50% of the advance on the later of six months or 50% fulfillment of the song delivery commitment, etc.).

WRITING WITH OTHER SONGWRITERS

Because many writers collaborate with writers who are not subject to an exclusive agreement or who control their own publishing, the publisher may request that its songwriter use his or her best efforts (or, at a minimum, his or her reasonable efforts) to secure the cowriter's share for the publisher. This provision is hard to police or control, because it is difficult to determine whether best or reasonable efforts have been expended. In addition, the legitimate publisher recognizes that collaboration not only is a fact of life in today's music business but also may be a necessary and valuable part of a writer's success. With the exception of fraud or bad faith on the part of the writer, therefore, this provision is usually not strictly enforced.

MOTION PICTURE AND TELEVISION THEME EXCLUSIONS

Under virtually all exclusive songwriter agreements, the music publisher has the ownership (or co-ownership) rights to all musical compositions written during the term of the agreement. But certain songwriters, in addition to writing hit songs, also have a successful track record of writing songs for motion pictures and television series. Because film producers and television companies usually demand that they own or co-own the copyright to any composition written specifically for one of their projects where a writing fee is paid, a number of writers will try to exclude such "written on assignment" compositions from their songwriter agreements, the rationale being that the exposure of such songs in films and television series will enhance the reputation of the writer and the other compositions that he or she may write. This same concept may apply to writing on assignment specifically for video games (as opposed to licensing pre-existing songs). The writer may also argue that the publisher has no right to cut off a source of income that the writer has counted on for many years, since if the publisher demands ownership of such songs, the film and television companies will cease doing business with that writer.

Once again, the resolution of these issues depends on the respective bargaining power of the publisher and writer, with final settlement usually taking one of the following forms:

The publisher retains ownership of all compositions written during the term of the agreement with any "on assignment" song requests being considered on a case-by-case basis.

The writer is able to compose a specified number of songs directly for a film, video game or television project during any one year of the term, provided that such activities do not take a substantial amount of time and do not interfere with his or her songwriting services.

The writer is allowed to write for such projects provided they are for a fee rather than on a "spec" (or speculation) basis and the writer uses his or her best efforts to retain a portion of the copyright ownership for the music publisher.

If a writer is allowed to write for such projects, the music publisher will often demand that all or a portion of the composing fee paid by the film producer, video game company or television company be paid to the publisher (especially where there are outstanding unrecouped advances to the writer) or, in the alternative, have the writer sign a letter of authorization that ensures that the film, video game or television company will send all songwriter monies earned from the composition (soundtrack album and single mechanical royalties, print income, etc.) directly to the music publisher for distribution or recovery of advances. These same considerations and approaches also apply if the writer has a past track record of writing commercial jingles for advertising agencies and wishes to continue such pursuits during the term of the exclusive songwriter's agreement.

If a writer has written a composition prior to signing with a publisher and has secured its use in a motion picture, video game or television series, the synchronization or composing fee paid for the song is usually excluded from the publisher's rights, even if the pre-existing composition is brought into the deal by the writer. In these cases, however, any monies earned from the song after the release of the film or video game or broadcast of the series (performance royalties, soundtrack album sales, cover versions, etc.) are collected by the publisher.

FIRST-USE MECHANICAL LICENSES

Under the U.S. Copyright Law, the songwriter and his or her music publisher have approval rights over the first recorded and released version of a newly written composition (i.e., a "first use" license). After a composition has been released to the general public with authorization on a CD, download, or record, any other recording artist has the right to record and release that composition, subject only to the payment of mechanical royalties to the writer and music publisher. If a writer is a recording artist, he or she will many times restrict the publisher from granting such first-use licenses on any self-written compositions to other recording artists until a decision has been made as to whether or not a particular song will be recorded by that writer. In effect, the writer/performer is claiming the sole right to decide whether to record a song on his or her own album, and the publisher may not promote or license the song to anyone else prior to either the writer/artist's recording being released or the writer/

artist's decision not to put the song on the album. Because writer/artists need the best songs possible for their own albums, such restrictions are very understandable, and most music publishers will agree to them.

There are many variations in the resolution of these types of negotiations, with some publishers giving the writer/artist total approval rights over which songs are to be restricted, and others limiting the number of songs that may be "held" during any one period by the writer/artist. The following is just one example of such a provision: Publisher further agrees that, in the event Writer notifies it that Writer requests that a "first use" mechanical license not be issued for a specified Composition, Publisher shall consult with Writer on such request; it being agreed that Publisher shall have the final decision as to whether such a license shall or shall not be issued. Notwithstanding anything to the contrary contained above, in the event that Writer had entered into a recording artist agreement with a Major Record Company and Writer requests that Publisher not issue a first-use mechanical license to a third party for a Composition being recorded pursuant to said recording artist agreement, Publisher agrees to comply with such request provided Writer has given written notice of such to Publisher, that no more than five (5) such Compositions are so restricted at any one time (unless all such Compositions are to be embodied on one (1) Album in which case up to eleven (11) such Compositions may be restricted), and that such restriction shall not apply to any commitments made by Publisher prior to its receipt of said written notice from Writer. It is further agreed that such a "first mechanical license" restriction shall not be effective for a period in excess of nine (9) months from the date of Writer's notice.

RESTRICTIONS ON PROMOTION IN CERTAIN AREAS

In any negotiation with a songwriter, the music publisher will try to secure as many rights as possible without any restrictions so that it will be able to channel its promotion efforts in a wide range of income-producing areas. For example, it may promote songs not only to recording artists and record producers but also to film and television companies, advertising agencies, video manufacturers, video game producers, ringtone companies, karaoke firms, video jukebox distributors, print dealers, and so on. The songwriter, however, may have concerns, either creative or political, as to how his or her songs are used, and many times will try to restrict the publisher's promotion efforts and ability to grant licenses for certain types of uses. These negotiations usually revolve around the use of songs in commercials, political (or "special interest") radio and television campaigns, and NC-17 or X-rated motion pictures, but can also extend to any use in a motion picture, television series, video game, ringtone, or other audiovisual project that may be seen or heard by the public. Because many writers value the integrity of their songs and have concerns about how and in what context they might be used, the negotiations on these issues can become quite heated and, in some cases, can make or break a deal.

Recognizing that commercials can have the potential of denigrating a song by identifying it with a consumer product, especially when the lyrics are changed, many publishers will give approval rights, or at least consultation rights, to the songwriter, who thus can express his or her objections. Others will ask the writer to list the types of product of concern (alcohol, tobacco, hygiene, bathroom, etc.) and agree that songs will not be licensed for use with such identified "objectionable products" without the writer's consent. Other publishers will demand that such decisions are within their exclusive province and provide for no restrictions on licensing. In film and television the issues are a bit more difficult, because restrictions in promotion and licensing in those media are the lifeblood of many publishers' activities. Because uses in movies and TV rarely hurt songs and have the potential of generating enormous amounts of income, to say nothing of the large media and general public exposure they generate, music publishers try to limit any writer approvals in this area. As for use in X-rated and sometimes NC-17 films, however, writer approval rights are many times accepted by the publisher.

If approvals are given to the writer, the time fuse for the writer to say either yes or no is usually a short one, such as two to five days. Quick answers to producers, especially in the making of television series, where scripts are being rewritten and scenes taped on a daily basis, are essential for getting songs into such projects. For example, the publisher might give the writer 5 days to approve a motion picture use but only 1 or 2 days for a television series request because of the time pressures involved in the shooting schedule. Writer-approval clauses usually provide that if a writer does not respond within the negotiated time frame, the use is deemed approved and the publisher may negotiate the license. In very limited cases, the contract might state that if a response by the writer is not received, the use is deemed denied.

ALTERING COMPOSITIONS

In many agreements, the publisher has the right to make changes in a writer's songs if, in that publisher's good-faith judgment, such changes are justified for the successful promotion of the songs. Even though such unilateral alterations rarely occur, songwriters usually try to limit the type of change that can be made without their consent or, as an alternative, insist on being given the right to be the one to make the changes before someone else is given the opportunity. If a composition is an instrumental, the composer may also secure the right to select the lyricist if a publisher wishes to have words written, or obtain the right to approve or disapprove the final lyrics. A contract may also include restrictions on any reduction in writer royalties to the original writer caused by the addition of a new songwriter to the song; many agreements guarantee that the original writer's share will not be reduced past a certain point.

With respect to translations of the English lyrics to a song for foreign versions, the local performance societies in each country outside the United States have rules that cover the percentage of royalties that any translator may receive for a contribution, and the original writer must adhere to those rules. Before any foreign-language version is written, however, it is imperative that the original songwriter and music publisher ensure by agreement that the non-English-language writer receives a share of the royalties only on the non-English-language version, and not on all versions of the song.

As for changes in the melody of a song or its overall nature, the music publisher virtually always has the right to make different musical arrangements for promotion purposes, but usually is restricted from changing or altering the substance of the composition. This is a very gray area, since determining what is and what is not a substantive change can be difficult; contract language should be specific.

OWNERSHIP AND PROMOTION OF DEMO RECORDINGS

Under most songwriter agreements, when a writer produces a demo session for new songs, the music publisher owns not only the compositions performed at the session but also the actual performance. Occasionally, because many of these demo sessions result in "close to master-quality" recordings, the publisher may be able to promote these demo recordings for use in television programs, video games, and motion pictures—and collect the synchronization and video fees negotiated for their use.

Some songwriters, especially if they are recording artists or potential recording artists, will try to restrict the publisher from exploiting these demos when the writer is also a performer at the session. Where a record agreement already exists, such promotion by the music publisher will always be subject to the rights of the writer/ artist's record company. If the writer is not a performer, or is a performer without a record deal, many of a publisher's activities in promoting demos may be consummated only with the approval of the writer. Alternatively, the contract might list certain specified prohibitions (e.g., licensing to an X-rated film or to a commercial product campaign), with all other exploitation considered acceptable. A songwriter who is able to negotiate co-ownership of the demo performances—usually accomplished by the writer's paying directly for a portion of the costs of the recording session or if advances have been recouped—may also take a cut of any license fees generated by uses of the demo. For example, income from licensing the demo recording might be distributed in the same percentages as provided for with respect to song income in the songwriter agreement. If there are unrecouped advances under the songwriter agreement, a resolution may be achieved with a portion of the master income being paid to the writer performer with the remainder being used for recoupment or a portion used for recoupment and a portion being retained by the publisher, among other variations.

FOREIGN SUBPUBLISHER FEES

Because licensing the use of compositions in countries outside the United States is so complex, virtually all music publishers use local publishers in foreign countries to represent their catalogues. Since these foreign publishers (referred to as "subpublishers") render all the normal publishing services (protection of songs pursuant to local laws, registration of compositions with performance and mechanical societies, negotiation of licenses, collection of royalties, auditing of music users, promotion of local language recordings or cover records, preparation of royalty statements), they charge from 5% to 25% for their efforts. Because these fees are deducted from the gross income earned in any foreign territory before monies are remitted to the United States, they effectively reduce an American publisher's income, and thus a songwriter's income, which is based on a percentage of the publisher's receipts.

Many songwriters try to minimize subpublishers' fees to no more than an agreed-upon percentage of foreign-generated income. For example, if a writer negotiates a "not in excess of 15% foreign retention" percentage and $10,000 is earned in England, the British publisher will not be able to take more than $1,500 for its services, with the remaining $8,500 being sent to the United States. Occasionally, if the songwriter has substantial bargaining power or if the U.S. publisher uses affiliates (as opposed to independent third parties) in foreign territories, an "at source" agreement may be negotiated, which provides that the songwriter's share of income will be computed "at the source" of the income rather than after the subpublisher has deducted its fees. For example, if a writer is to receive 50% of monies earned on an "at source" basis and $10,000 is earned from CD and download sales in England, the writer would be entitled to a $5,000 share of foreign income (rather than 50% of $8,500, as in a non-source or "receipts" agreement). Since foreign subpublishers do provide services and have their own operating costs, many U.S. publishers will reject these "at source" provisions because the subpublisher's fees will be deducted entirely from the publisher's share of income.

It should be noted that the songwriter's share of foreign performance income is collected not by the subpublisher but by the local performance societies, who remit these royalties directly to ASCAP, BMI, SESAC or GMR in the United States for distribution to the songwriter. Therefore, subpublisher fees are never deducted from the songwriter's share of performance income, as that money flows (after deduction of performance society fees) directly to the songwriter.

AUDITS

Some of the most important clauses in a songwriter's agreement are those that outline the songwriter's rights to inspect the books of the publisher if the writer feels that he or she is not being accounted to correctly. Although these rights are rarely exercised, most lawyers, when negotiating such clauses, put a great deal of time and effort into ensuring that the writer may audit a publisher's records. A songwriter's representative usually asks that the writer has at least two or three years to make an objection to any royalty statement. Audits are usually limited to one per year, with a proviso that at least 30 days' written notice be given so the books and records can be organized. Occasionally the publisher will also be able to postpone an audit date for 30 to 60 days. Some negotiations result in provisions that guarantee that the publisher will pay for all reasonable costs of any audit that proves that the writer has been underpaid by the greater of a certain percentage (e.g., if there was an underpayment error of 15% or more) or a certain dollar amount (e.g., if there is an error in excess of $5,000).

In the latter situation, many agreements exclude the costs of travel and per diems of the auditor from the reimbursement of costs provision.

INFRINGEMENT CLAIMS

The infringement clause addresses what happens if someone claims that a songwriter's composition infringes on another writer's composition. Most contracts provide that the writer will compensate the publisher for any costs expended in defending or settling a claim in addition to any monies or profits that must be paid as a result of the infringement litigation or any settlements designed to resolve the claim. For example, if a third party files an infringement claim against a composition that cost $50,000 in legal fees and court costs, and an actual judgment is rendered for another $100,000, the writer will be obligated to reimburse the music publisher for the full $150,000. This is true under most agreements, even if the claim is defended successfully or is dismissed without merit, because the writer has agreed to indemnify his or her publisher against claims regardless of whether or not infringement is proven.

Even though most writers never have to face an infringement claim, their lawyers do spend a great deal of time on these clauses, since if a claim is made, the results can be financially devastating to a songwriter regardless of how successful he or she may be. The writer is virtually always entitled to hire his or her own legal counsel to assist in defending and protecting the writer's interests. Because the stakes in winning or losing can be extremely high, with lawyer's costs alone ranging from $25,000 to over $400,000, the publisher normally retains the right to control the conduct and strategy of the defense—although in most cases, suggestions and input from both the publisher's and writer's lawyers will be shared, because everyone is really on the same side.

Because not all infringement claims have merit, some attorneys are able to negotiate a clause that provides that the writer is liable to the publisher only if the litigation results in a non-appealable judgment against the publisher or a settlement is reached with the songwriter's approval (in most cases, there being language which requires that the writer acts reasonably). Another alternative is to provide that the songwriter will have to reimburse the publisher only a portion of the legal costs if no infringement is found or if the third party withdraws its claim. The value of these alternative approaches for the songwriter is that he or she will not be liable for money spent to defend claims that never should have been made or that were frivolous. Because many of these claims (whether valid or not) result in settlements prior to actual litigation, some writers negotiate clauses that guarantee that the writer must approve any settlement payment over a certain amount (e.g., $5,000), a provision that at least gives the songwriter some control over how the music publisher deals with a claim when it is received.

Since these claims can result in expensive judgments, most agreements give the publisher the right to withhold from the writer's royalties the amount of money that may have to be paid out if the claim is successful. For example, if another writer or publisher is suing for $200,000 plus a transfer of the entire copyright, the music publisher being sued will hold at least $200,000 in royalty income due the writer (plus an additional amount to cover expected legal fees) to ensure that if the case is lost or there is a large settlement, the money will be in house, ready for payment. The writer, on the other hand, will try to limit the withholding only to monies generated by the song in question and not the earnings due from other compositions in his or her catalogue. The writer will also try to limit the time during which the publisher can withhold royalties (e.g., "if a suit is not instituted within one year from the date of the claim, all monies will be released"), or provide that if the writer gives the publisher a surety bond that has sufficient collateral attached to it, all "held monies" will be distributed. Getting one of these protective clauses into the songwriter's agreement, however, depends on each party's relative bargaining strength, as well as the experience of the negotiators and whether the songwriter's lawyer has been able to negotiate such a provision in a previous agreement with the publisher.

WRITER/PERFORMER DEVELOPMENT DEALS

Because so many recording artists write their own songs, the opportunities for music publishers to place songs on new albums have been somewhat diminished. This lack of access to many of the current writer/recording artists has encouraged a number of music publishers to go into the business of developing new writer/performers into recording artists. If a writer/performer is able to secure a recording agreement, most if not all of the songs on his or her albums will be written by the writer/artist and, hence, owned and controlled by the publisher. Many publishers have also taken on the role of developing new artists as part of their business plan.

Most of these development deals begin with one of the publisher's A&R staff hearing a young band in a local club, on a website, hearing a file or CD, or getting a referral from a music attorney, manager, agent, or writer signed to the company. If the publisher feels that the group has potential as writers and as performing artists, a development deal will be offered. This same procedure will take place for individual performers. Under this type of agreement, the publisher usually guarantees that it will finance the production of a certain number of demos so that the group can be presented to record company executives and A&R representatives. The term of these agreements is usually from 12 to 24 months, with further rights based on whether the publisher is able to secure a recording agreement for the group within the development period. For example, a contract might provide that the publisher will have one year to get a group a record contract, and if that happens, the publisher can extend its rights to the group's songs during the full term of the record agreement.

There are a large number of variations in these artist development deals, but most provide for the following:

- A set period for the publisher to secure the writer/performer a record deal (one year, 18 months, etc.).

- A guarantee that a specified number of new songs featuring the writer/performer will be produced in a professional recording studio.
- A guarantee that these sessions will take place within a specified period of time after the signing of the development agreement (two months, six months, etc.).
- A guarantee that a minimum amount of money will be expended by the music publisher for the recording sessions ($600 per song, $1,000 per song, etc.).
- Advances to the writer/performer during the term of the development deal ($2,000 per month, $3,500 per month, etc.).
- A minimum number of newly written compositions to be delivered by the songwriter/performer during the artist development term (10 new compositions, 12 new compositions of which writer has at least a 50% interest, etc.).
- Options on the part of the publisher to extend the development aspects of the agreement if it fails to secure a record deal within the allotted time (e.g., "in the event that the publisher does not secure a record agreement within one year from the signing of the development deal, it shall have one option to extend the term of the agreement for an additional six months provided it pays the songwriter/ performer additional advances," or "if a record deal is not signed within twelve months after the publisher has completed the required number of showcase recordings but negotiations have commenced with an interested record company, the term of the development deal will be extended until the negotiations either result in a recording-artist agreement being signed or such negotiations cease because terms cannot be agreed upon or the record company loses interest").
- A guarantee that if a record deal is secured through the efforts of the music publisher, the songwriter-publisher aspects of the development deal will continue through the entire term of the record agreement negotiated on behalf of the writer/performer.
- Occasionally there will also be a guarantee that, if a record deal is secured and the record company drops the writer/artist or fails to exercise any option for additional albums, the publisher will have the right to secure another artist agreement with a different label.
- A guaranteed minimum recording-artist royalty, recording fund, album guarantee, and advance structure if a recording agreement is secured.

For example, a sample clause might read:
The music publisher shall have the right to negotiate and commit the songwriter/ performer to a recording contract if the following minimum terms are contained in the recording artist agreement:

1. Album Guarantees. A minimum of one album containing at least 10 compositions will be recorded during each contract period.

2. Royalties. A minimum of 12% retail royalty will be paid to the writer as a recording artist for each album sold.

3. Advances. The writer/artist will receive an advance of at least $50,000 per album from the record company.

4. Recording fund. The record company will expend a minimum of $75,000 in recording costs (or recording fund) for the initial album produced and at least $100,000 for each additional album produced.

5. Release guarantees. A minimum of one album containing at least 10 compositions will be commercially released to the general public in the United States during each 18-month period of the recording agreement.

Under these types of minimum-guarantee development agreements, if the music publisher is able to negotiate substantive terms less favorable than those guaranteed (e.g., in the above example, a $50,000 recording fund versus the guaranteed $75,000, a 10% royalty versus the guaranteed 12%, advances of $25,000 per album versus $50,000, or a recording fund of $60,000 versus $100,000), the writer/performer may, in many cases, reject the recording agreement. In the event that the major substantive terms conform with the minimums specified in the development deal, however, the publisher can commit the writer/performer to the record contract.

Record agreements are not that easy to come by, and they are becoming more and more difficult to negotiate. The publisher will try to guarantee as few major areas as possible in the development deal, since "getting a record deal" is the most important goal. The writer/performer's lawyer, on the other hand, will try to secure as many minimum guarantees as possible to prevent the music publisher from committing the writer/performer to a bad record agreement. The reality of these situations is usually that both parties need each other's resources to secure the interest of a record company. The publisher provides financing, direction, and connections, and the writer/performer provides the raw creative talent that will hopefully ensure a marketable product. Because of that mutual need, the negotiations of development deals are usually handled very quickly and reasonably, with only a minimum of the posturing and veiled or unveiled threats that sometimes characterize other types of agreements.

Another approach that is used in the area of artist development deals is for the publisher to guarantee the financing of a set number of master-quality studio recordings so that record companies will be able to hear the writer/performer at his or her best and, if a recording artist agreement is secured, the publisher will receive royalty points on albums and singles released under the deal. For example, the publisher might guarantee $15,000 to $20,000 to record master-quality demos and if a recording artist agreement is secured, the publisher might receive a production or executive producer royalty of 1% to 2% for its efforts.

Other times, publishers might even finance an entire album of the writer's performances and try to sell or license the album to either an independent or major record label. The value of this approach, even though it is more expensive due to the fact that an entire album is being produced, including artwork, is that the publisher is providing the record company with a finished product ready to be released. Many times, this is an easier sell. On occasion, the record company will add some new tracks to the album or further enhance the already-completed master recordings or redo certain aspects of the production. In these cases, the music publisher will virtually always be entitled to royalty points on the album from the record company in addition to many times being repaid its investment or having the right to recoup its recording costs from the initial monies earned.

In all these cases, the publisher may even suggest that the writer/performer record songs written by outside songwriters if these are the songs that show the writer as a recording artist best. Obviously, the music publisher's financial risk is definitely reduced by the writer recording self-written compositions which are controlled by the publisher but the most important object in these cases is to get the writer a record deal, even if it is via songs which were created by someone other than the writer. The optimum situation when a third-party writer's song is used is when that outside writer is also signed to the publisher that is financing the record. But if the best song is controlled by another publisher, good publishers do not hesitate to use that song. After all, getting the record deal is the most important focus and, even if the deal is secured as a result of putting the best compositions forward, regardless of who owns them, there will still be a number of songs on the album written by the recording artist/writer.

DEVELOPMENT DEAL VARIATIONS/EQUIPMENT FUNDS

One of the variations in the area of development deals is to provide for an equipment fund so that the writer/performer can purchase new musical instruments, amplifiers, in home studio equipment, computers, and other accessories. This may be handled either on the basis of an extra advance to the writer who will make the decision as to what is needed (for example, "an additional advance of $5,000 to $10,000 to the songwriter within 30 days after the signing of the agreement which shall be used for the purchase of musical equipment, the choice of which shall be in the songwriter's sole discretion"), a fund which will be spent with the mutual approval of the publisher and the songwriter (for example, "an advance of $5,000.00 which shall be payable by publisher for the purchase of equipment mutually agreed to by both the songwriter and the publisher") or a fund which can be accessed by the writer submitting invoices from the retailers, detailing the amount of the expenditure for each item purchased with the publisher paying the seller directly (for example, "publisher shall pay invoices directly to the music retailer upon submission of invoices for musical equipment selected by the songwriter within the approved budget of $7,500.00"). In addition to new equipment, development deals may provide for additional advances to purchase a van, for voice lessons or rehearsal space and any number of related expenses.

CONVERSION OF THE DEVELOPMENT DEAL

If a recording artist agreement is not secured within an agreed amount of time, the publisher many times has the option to convert the deal into an exclusive songwriter/co-publishing agreement which is based on the writer delivering a minimum number of newly written compositions. If the publisher does turn the development deal into a songwriter's agreement, there will be a schedule of yearly advances (many times with a minimum/maximum formula to ensure that if the writer/performer becomes successful as a songwriter, then the advances will reflect that success) with a clear understanding of the number of songs that the writer or group is expected to write. For example, the term might be 1 year plus 3 options with the advance range being from $25,000 to $75,000 per year, the annual minimum song commitment being from 6 to 10 and, if the advance structure is on the high side, a recorded and commercially released commitment rather than one based only on the creation of new songs, regardless of whether or not they are actually released. There are infinite variations in these conversion deals, but the duration of the agreement will usually match (but not be longer than) the duration of the term of the agreement had the publisher been successful in securing a record deal for the writer. For example, if the original term was 1 year plus 3 contract period options, the term of the conversion deal would not last longer than that contained in the initial agreement.

SOURCES OF INCOME FOR THE MUSIC PUBLISHER AND SONGWRITER

The financial value of a songwriter's and music publisher's catalogue is based on the quality of the songs, the frequency and nature of their use, and how they are licensed. The following section reviews many of the varied sources from which songwriters and publishers receive income.

PERFORMANCE RIGHT PAYMENTS

One of the largest continuing sources of royalty income for writers and publishers is the performance right payments from ASCAP, BMI, SESAC, and GMR as well as from affiliated performing rights organizations in foreign countries. ASCAP, a nonprofit association of writers and publishers founded in 1914, BMI, a nonprofit broadcaster-owned corporation organized in 1939, SESAC, a for profit corporation originally founded in 1930, and GMR a for profit corporation organized in 2013, negotiate license fee agreements with the users of music—radio and television stations, cable stations, streaming services, concert halls, wired music services such as Muzak, etc. The agreements give the user the right to perform the music and lyrics of any member of these organizations. The license fees collected by ASCAP, BMI, SESAC and GMR (in the area of $2.6 billion a year) are then distributed to the writers and publishers whose works are thus performed. This "performance right" is one of the most important rights of the U.S. Copyright Law as well as the copyright laws of most foreign countries. It is based on the concept that a writer's creation is property and that a user must acquire a license in order to perform a copyrighted musical work.

The primary types of music use that generate ASCAP, BMI, SESAC and GMR performance royalties are feature performances (a visual vocal or instrumental on television, a radio or streaming service performance, etc.); underscore on television series, specials, movies of the week, and feature films; theme songs to television series; advertising jingles; production company and network logos; and copyrighted arrangements of public-domain compositions (a new arrangement of a song no longer under copyright). Each type of music use has its own relative value—features are, in most cases, worth more than themes, themes are paid higher than underscore, etc. In addition, ASCAP, BMI, SESAC and GMR have different payment formula schedules, thereby producing different payments for the same type of music use, depending on whether you are a member of ASCAP or an affiliate of BMI, SESAC or GMR. Further, these payment and distribution schedules can frequently change, sometimes without notice to writers and publishers.

As for the approximately $1.4 billion generated each year from foreign performances of U.S. writers' and publishers' works, ASCAP, BMI, SESAC and GMR have agreements with most of the foreign performing rights organizations of the world whereby money collected in the foreign marketplace is forwarded to ASCAP, BMI, SESAC and GMR for distribution to their writer and publisher members. Most of the money distributed by the PROs in the United States is "writer money," (approximately $700 million) as most U.S. publishers collect their foreign performance monies directly from the foreign society through local subpublishers. The foreign performing rights societies generating the most income for U.S. writers and publishers are those located in England (PRS for Music), France (SACEM), Canada (SOCAN), Germany (GEMA), Italy (SIAE), Japan (JASRAC), Australia/New Zealand (APRA), Spain (SGAE) and the Netherlands (BUMA).

CD AND RECORD SALES (MECHANICAL ROYALTIES)

One of the major sources of income for the songwriter and music publisher is the "mechanical" royalties due from the sale of records, and CDs. With the revision of the 1909 U.S. Copyright Law, effective January 1, 1978, a Copyright Royalty Tribunal (which no longer exists) was established whose role is to monitor the mechanical royalties paid to songwriters and music publishers. Rate adjustments were provided for in the legislation based on the U.S. Consumer Price Index. The minimum statutory mechanical royalty payable to songwriters and music publishers was increased from 2¢ to 2.75¢ per song and then, through a series of escalations, to 5¢ in 1986, 5.25¢ in 1988, 5.7¢ in 1990, 6.25¢ in 1992, 6.6¢ in 1994, 6.95¢ in 1996, 7.1¢ in 1998, 7.55¢ in 2000, 8¢ in 2002, 8.5¢ in 2004, and 9.1¢ in 2006.

On October 2, 2008, the Copyright Royalty Judges extended the 9.1¢ statutory mechanical through December 31, 2012. This rate was further extended through

2017. In 2017, the Copyright Royalty Board again extended the 9.1 cent rate through 2022. (There is also a durational formula based on 1.75¢ per minute of playing time for compositions 5 minutes or longer, but we will concentrate here only on the 9.1¢ rate.) Under the current mechanical rate in effect in 2018-2022, a million-selling single would be worth a total of $91,000 per song in combined royalties to the publisher and writer, instead of the $20,000 that would have been earned prior to 1978. As for album, tape, and CD sales, the above royalties, unless agreed to the contrary, would be multiplied by the number of songs on the album, tape, or CD. For example, if 10 songs were included on a CD and each received a 9.1¢ royalty, a total of 91¢ in mechanical royalties would be generated from the sale of each album. If the CD sells between 1 million and 2 million copies, the aggregate writer and publisher royalties for the album would range from $910,000 to $1,820,000.

DOWNLOADS
Songwriter/music publisher royalties for permanent downloads of audio recordings (known as digital permanent downloads or DPDs) are equal to the United States statutory mechanical rate for physical recordings with rates determined by the Copyright Royalty Judges (currently 9.1¢ or 1.75¢ per minute if the timing is more than 5 minutes). These rates are effective through 2022.

MECHANICAL LICENSES
When a record company releases a composition on a recording or makes it available for downloading, a mechanical license agreement will be signed by both the music publisher who owns or administers the composition and the record company distributing the recording. The format is similar in most of these licenses in that they are based on the terms contained in the mechanical license issued by the Harry Fox Agency, Inc., on behalf of its many publisher clients. The license will list the title of the composition, a song code number, the identity of the songwriter, the identity of the music publisher, the percentage payable to the publisher, the name of the recording artist, the name of the album, the record number, the configuration (for example, CD, cassette, digital download, vinyl, etc.), the royalty rate (statutory, 75% of statutory, etc.), and the duration of the composition (4 minutes 11 seconds, 3 minutes 45 seconds, etc.). There will also be "an additional provision" section which will identify the effective territory for the license (for example, "the authority is limited to the manufacture and distribution of phono-records solely in the United States, its territories and possessions and not elsewhere") and will state the credit that will be received ("in regard to all phono-records manufactured, distributed and/or sold hereunder, you shall include in the label copy of all such phono-records, or on the permanent containers of all such phono-records, printed writer/publisher credit in the form of the names of the writer(s) and the publisher(s) of the copyrighted work"). Each license will also have a date and a license number. The license will further provide that royalty accountings be made within 45 days after the end of each calendar

quarter, and that the license covers only the recording and configuration referred to in the license. Additionally, the record company is usually given a 30-day period to remedy any default in the event that it fails to account to the music publisher and pay royalties as specified in the license. If the failure is not remedied within the so-called cure period, the mechanical license will be automatically terminated. There are also bulk licensing procedures established by the Harry Fox Agency to handle requests for permanent digital downloads of thousands of compositions at one time.

It should be mentioned that the per-song statutory mechanical royalty for physical product can be reduced under certain circumstances (for example, if the writer is the recording artist or if the record is sold as a developing artist, midline, record club, television-only, compilation, or budget album) so that the royalty figures can be less than those mentioned above. Such "reduced rates" are voluntary, however, and occur only if the publisher agrees or if the songwriter is a recording artist and has no choice but to accept lower royalties.

Many recording artist and producer agreements contain language that provides that if the recording artist or producer has written or co-written a song, has ownership or control of a song, or has any interest in any composition on the album, tape, CD, or single, the mechanical royalty rate payable by the record company is reduced. Such compositions are referred to as "controlled compositions." Many contracts attempt to establish a 75% minimum statutory mechanical rate (e.g., 6.825¢ in 2018-22) for all controlled compositions computed at the rate at the time a record is produced, the date of the recording contract with the artist, the date that a particular album commences recording, or the date the recording is originally released (regardless of whether the same recording is released again at a later date in another album). Most contracts will state that the so called "long song" per-minute rates will not apply; only minimum statutory rates. Other times, the record company will establish a maximum aggregate mechanical penny royalty limit for an album (for example, 68¢ per album or 11 × 75% of minimum statutory for an album). Under these clauses, the artist or producer guarantees that he or she will secure reduced mechanical rates on all songs on the album so that the maximum penny rate payable by the record company to music publishers and songwriters for all songs is not exceeded. If this maximum aggregate album royalty rate is surpassed, the difference is normally deducted from the artist's or producer's record, songwriter, and publishing royalties (or the per-song royalty rates for the writer/artist or writer/producer will be reduced proportionately). Record companies many times use what is known as an "advice letter," which references the controlled composition clause language to license the songs written by the writer/ artist or producer. These clauses also usually apply to Canadian royalties, subject to a number of pro-songwriter-music publisher improvements established by CMRRA, the mechanical rights organization in Canada.

For example, if a writer/performer has a 10 song × 6.825¢ maximum royalty rate on his or her album (i.e., 68.25¢) and, instead of writing all 10 songs, writes only eight and records two songs written by outside writers who demand the 9.1¢ statutory rate per song, mechanical royalties would look like this:

68.25¢	Album royalty maximum
– 18.2¢	(2 outside songs at 9.1¢ each)
50.05¢	
÷ 8	Number of artist-written songs
6.25¢	Per-song royalty to writer/artist and publisher

As you can see, the writer/artist's mechanical royalty has been reduced to 6.25¢ per song from 6.82¢ per song because of the inclusion of two outside-written songs on the album. As the writer/artist records more outside written songs, the artist's per-song royalties for the artist's own works will be further reduced. In fact, in some cases, where the writer/artist has recorded a substantial number of other writers' songs, the writer/artist has been put in a position of receiving no royalties for his or her own songs, since the aggregate album royalty maximum has been paid out to outside songwriters and publishers. There have also been instances where the writer/artist's mechanical royalties have been in the minus column for every album sold because of the operation of these controlled-composition clauses. Many of these clauses also provide that the writer/artist will receive a mechanical royalty for only one use of his or her song, regardless of the number of versions contained on the album, cassette, CD, or single.

On the other hand, some record companies will give the writer/artist a full statutory mechanical rate for physical product (as opposed to the reduced controlled-composition rate) if the writer/artist assigns a portion of his or her publishing to the record company's publishing company. Such an arrangement ensures that the writer/artist will receive full mechanical royalties and, in most cases, will guarantee the writer additional advance income, since publishing contracts invariably provide for either yearly or per-album songwriter advances. Other times if the artist-writer is successful and has the required bargaining power, the record company will grant a statutory rate formula but with a cap on each album. For example, the record company might agree to pay a 100% statutory rate on an album but limit the amount of royalties that can be paid on the album to 12 times statutory (i.e., $1.09)

TELEVISION SERIES

When a producer wants to use an existing song in a television program, weekly series, special, miniseries, or made-for-TV movie, permission must, with few exceptions, be secured from the music publisher of the song. In this regard, the producer of the show will decide on how the song is to be used (background vocal or instrumental, sung by a character on camera, over the opening or ending credits) and the medium over which the program will be broadcast (free television, pay television, basic cable, pay-per-view, all television, VOD, mobile phones, Internet, airlines, all media, all media excluding theatrical, apps, etc.). The producer or its "music clearance" representative will then contact the publisher of the composition, describe how the song will be used, ask for a specified period of time to use the song in the program, negotiate a fee, and then sign what is known as a "synchronization license." Since home and personal video can be an important ancillary market for television programming, negotiations will usually take place for that medium as well. Considering that some television programs are also released in movie theatres in foreign countries, the producer may also request such rights and negotiate additional fees for such non-television uses. And since many television programs are eventually broadcast in media other than that on which they were initially aired (e.g., a pay television program being broadcast on free over-the-air stations, on air planes, on the Internet, or on smartphones or other digital devices), a producer may also request prices for a wide range of additional options. Synchronization fees vary depending on the distribution media, term and territory being requested by the production company in addition to the actual use in the program.

Program	Song
CSI: Miami	"We Won't Get Fooled Again" (The Who's recording used as the theme to this series about crime scene investigation)
CSI	"Any Way You Want It" (Journey's song is used for the ringtone of a burglar's mobile phone.)

MOTION PICTURES

When a motion picture producer wants to use an existing song in a theatrically released film, the producer must negotiate with the music publisher for use of the composition. Once an agreement is reached, the producer will sign a synchronization license, which will give the producer the right to distribute the film to movie theaters, sell it to television, and use the song in "in context" television promos and theatrical previews. The amount of the motion picture synchronization fee depends on a number of factors, including how the song is used, the overall budget for the film and the music budget, the stature of song being used, the actual timing of the song as used in the film, whether there are multiple uses, whether the uses are thematic or over the opening or closing credits, the term of the license, the territory of the license, and whether there is a guarantee that the song will be used on a soundtrack album or released as a single.

The synchronization fees charged by music publishers are usually between $15,000 and $60,000. In addition, record companies normally charge between $15,000 and $60,000 for the use of master recordings (i.e., the original hit recording) in a motion picture, but, depending on the stature of the artist, the licensing policy of the record company and the nature of the recording being used, these fees can be greater or less than the range referred to above. On occasion, a music publisher will reduce the synchronization fee for a song if the producer guarantees that the song will be on a soundtrack album released by a major label. For example, a publisher might charge $30,000 for use of the song in a film but give the producer a $28,000 alternative quote if the song makes the soundtrack album. Considering the phenomenal success of some motion picture soundtracks and the royalties they can generate, such a reduction in the sync fee may substantially benefit the publisher and the songwriter in the long run. The "alternative quote" arrangement also helps the motion picture producer (especially where a film has a great number of outside songs), as its up-front costs are reduced.

Some film producers will occasionally want to include a pre-existing song in a motion picture only if the music publisher guarantees that the film company will share in the earnings from all or selected subsidiary markets (e.g., soundtrack album sales, single sales, downloads, ASCAP, BMI, SESAC and GMR, radio, television and Web performances, subscription service royalties, foreign theatrical royalties). Other producers will try to secure a portion of the copyright ownership to the song. Most publishers will refuse such conditions, but sometimes arrangements are made on a short-term basis for lesser-known titles to ensure that the song gets into the film (e.g., the producer may receive 25% of the mechanical royalties from the soundtrack or single released from the soundtrack for five years from its release date).

HOME VIDEO/PERSONAL VIDEO/DVDS/BLU-RAY/DOWNLOADS

Because the home and personal video market has become enormous in almost every country in the world, the sale of videos can represent an additional source of revenue for the music publisher and songwriter. Home video licensing is normally handled in one of three ways:

1. A one-time buy-out: Almost all video distributors demand that publishers accept a one-time buy-out fee for all video rights, regardless of how many videos might be sold—a fact of life in today's market that must be faced and negotiated accordingly since the only negotiation is the actual amount of the one-time fee being paid. This approach is used in the motion picture, television and non-music-themed video game area.

2. A per-video royalty: Under this approach, the royalty paid is based on a set rate (usually from 10¢ to 15¢ per song). For example, if 100,000 videos are sold and a particular song has a 10¢ royalty, the payment will be $10,000.

3. A roll-over advance: Under this formula, the producer or video distributor pays a certain advance for a specified number of videos, with additional predetermined

sums paid as additional sales plateaus are achieved—for example, $10,000 for the first 100,000 units and an additional $10,000 for each additional 100,000 units sold or downloaded.

COMMERCIALS

An extremely valuable source of income for the songwriter and music publisher is the use of songs in radio, Internet and television commercials for consumer products. The fees paid by advertising agencies and their clients for commercials can be substantial (e.g., from $75,000 to over $1,000,000 per year for successful songs), depending on, among other things, whether it is a radio, Internet or television commercial, a national or limited-territory campaign, whether there are options for other countries of the world, if the original lyrics are being changed or new lyrics added, and whether all advertising rather than only product category exclusivity is being requested by the agency. On occasion, an advertising agency will ask for a non-broadcast test period during which it will test the commercial in shopping malls, interagency screenings, and the like to see if the pairing of the song and the product is effective. Fees for this off-air testing range from $1,000 to over $10,000, and the term is normally from two to four months. Other times, an agency will request a limited-broadcast test period, during which a commercial will actually be aired in a specified regional market (for example, television in Florida only for two months, or a three-month test in cities that contain not more than 10% of the total U.S. population). Fees for this type of regional-broadcast test period normally range from $5,000 to over $50,000, depending on the duration of the test period, the importance of the song, the product being advertised, and whether there has been a lyric change.

Song Title	Product	Genre
"Purple Haze"	Pepsi	Classic Rock
"Don't Stop Believin'"	Nissan	Pop Hit
"Maniac"	Kia	Movie Song
"Lose Yourself"	iPod/iTunes	Hip Hop
"Welcome Back Kotter"	Mylanta	TV Theme
"Respect"	American Express	Soul Classic
"Dancing Queen"	Visa	Pop Classic
"I Feel Pretty"	Canon	Broadway
"Rhapsody in Blue"	United Airlines	Standard

Certain major advertisers may request total exclusivity from a publisher, but the fees for this type of grant are substantial for a recent hit song or well-known standard (from $250,000 to over $1,000,000), because the song is effectively being taken out of the marketplace. Most commercial licensing agreements provide for restrictions only on licensing for competing or similar products. For example, a beer-commercial agreement may restrict the writer or publisher from licensing the same song for another alcoholic beverage commercial, but it will allow licensing for use in a food or automobile advertising campaign. In addition to the fees paid by the agency or client for the use of a song, the writer and publisher may be eligible to receive radio and television broadcast royalties from ASCAP, BMI, SESAC, or GMR, provided that the performing rights have been reserved and other requirements satisfied. The amount of those royalties would be dependent on whether the song is a past or present hit, the amount of music used, whether the lyrics have been changed and whether the commercial has a national market versus a limited territorial exposure campaign.

BROADWAY MUSICALS

One of the most lucrative markets for a song is its use in a Broadway show, because if the play is a hit, the income from live theatrical performances, soundtrack albums, singles, downloads, ringtones, subscription services, motion picture and television rights, touring productions, video, sheet music, and stock and amateur production rights can mean hundreds of thousands of dollars for the songwriter and music publisher. However, considering that the vast majority of musicals presented on Broadway lose most if not all of the money invested, and that getting a song into a Broadway play is extremely difficult, this is an area with which most songwriters and publishers, unless they are involved with songs actually created for the play, will have little or no contact. With the success of shows such as *Beautiful: The Carol King Musical, Mamma Mia!, The Lion King, Movin' Out, Beauty and the Beast, 42nd Street, Tommy, Jersey Boys*, and *Smokey Joe's Café*, all of which used pre-existing songs, the field has opened up somewhat for writers and publishers.

Music royalties for the Broadway run and first-class national touring productions usually range between a 1.5% and 4% pro rata share of the box office receipts if a percentage royalty is negotiated (which can mean from $200,000 to more than $10,000,000 per year for all songs in a hit show), a fixed dollar amount per week (from $250 to more than $1,000, regardless of the success of the play) if the parties have agreed to a non-percentage royalty or a royalty pool arrangement where all royalty participants share in an agreed upon percentage of a musical's weekly operating profits.

VIDEO GAMES

This is an area which can be extremely important for hit songs and unknown songs alike, both in terms of exposure and money. In most cases, both the composition and the master recording are licensed on a one-time fee buy-out basis, without regard to the number of games that are actually sold. Buy-outs range from $2,500 to over $20,000, with some negotiations resulting in smaller and higher amounts depending upon bargaining power. The music based games, however, do provide for royalties for songs and masters used in the games as well as those that are downloaded after a game's release.

KARAOKE/SING-ALONGS

Certain companies specialize in selling instrumental versions of hit songs accompanied by printed lyrics or lead sheets, so that amateur singers can add their own voices. Some sell equipment (microphones, players with recording, dubbing, and playback capabilities, etc.) to enhance the quality and facilitate the use of such instrumental recordings. Royalties payable to writers and publishers in this area are normally: (1) the statutory mechanical royalty rate per song per version for each tape distributed; and (2) from 4¢ to more than 8¢ for each lyric sheet of the song included with a CD. A number of firms also market home-video versions of the sing-along concept with the lyrics and music contained on DVD. Others market and distribute via the Internet. Royalties paid for such uses are sometimes calculated on the wholesale price of each disc, with all songs sharing the aggregate royalty on a pro rata basis. It is more common, however, for a writer and publisher to charge a set penny royalty (e.g., from 12¢ to 14¢ per song for each sing-along DVD or other recording distributed). In addition, there is usually a one-time fee given to each publisher of between $300 and $350 for the right to include the song in the video—sometimes referred to as a "fixation fee." The licenses in this area normally last for seven to 10 years but can be longer and are usually for the world (or the world excluding Japan). It is also common to receive an up-front advance for the initial 5,000 to 7,500 copies distributed. For downloads and online subscription uses, royalties can be based on a percentage of receipts with a minimum per stream or download.

INTERNET KARAOKE SITES

There are a number of variations and models in this area. One way is to pay the music publisher a percentage of the subscription revenue (e.g., 15%, 20%) with a minimum royalty payment (e.g., 10¢, 12.5¢) for each composition created or streamed by a user. In addition, a share of any advertising revenue may also be paid to the publishers and songwriters whose compositions are used. In the event that a ringtone is created, a royalty of 24¢ will be paid in royalties. And if there are downloads of the customer's audiovisual version, a royalty of based on the greater of a percentage of the revenue or a set penny rate (e.g., 10¢) will be paid. Audio downloads are paid at the statutory DPD rate.

VIDEO JUKEBOXES

Even though the popularity of the video jukebox is greater in Europe, there is a small but growing market in the United States. The video used on such machines is normally a promotional video produced by the record company for its artist, and the royalties to the music publisher come as a one-time $25 fixation or synchronization fee for use of the song in video jukeboxes, plus 10¢ per month per song for each individual video jukebox containing the song. Another formula used is 3¢ per play. The duration of these agreements is normally one year, but can be longer if agreed to by the parties.

LYRIC REPRINTS IN NOVELS OR NONFICTION BOOKS

Another source of income for the songwriter and music publisher is the use of song lyrics in nonfiction books or novels. All fees are dependent on the number of lines being used; the context in which the song is used; the importance of the song; the number of other song lyrics used in the book; whether hardcover, paperback, digital or all are included in the request; the total budget for such clearances; the territory in which the book will be distributed; and whether English or both English and foreign translation versions are being requested. Normal fees for hardcover books are between $100 and $1,500, with additional fees possibly required for paperback, digital, book-club editions if an all in fee was not negotiated. In addition, information on the plot of the book, the publisher, and the context in which a lyric is to be used is normally requested by the music publisher prior to approval and a price quotation being given.

Book	Song Lyrics
You've Been Warned (James Patterson)	"The Circle Game"
Next (Michael Crichton)	"It's All Over Now"
The Power of the Dog (Don Winslow)	"Pancho and Lefty" "Small Change"
Mystic River (Dennis Lehane)	"Pirates"

One example of a lyric use in a book is Thomas Harris' *The Silence of the Lambs* where James Gumb, the psychopathic killer whose murders cause the psychological struggle between FBI agent Clarice Starling and the incarcerated Dr. Hannibal "The Cannibal" Lector, sings the lyrics to Fats Waller's "Cash Your Trash" while in the shower.

Another example of such book use is Joseph Wambaugh's best-selling novel *The Secrets of Harry Bright* (William Morrow and Company, Inc.), which contained portions of the lyrics to 12 songs, including "One for My Baby," "I Believe," "Ain't She Sweet," "Strangers in the Night," "Once in a Lifetime," "Hound Dog," "I'll Be

Seeing You," and "Make Believe." Another example is Nancy Sinatra's *Frank Sinatra, My Father*, which was published by Doubleday & Company and contained portions of the lyrics to many of the songs that the singer made famous.

As in the case of all lyric reprints of copyrighted songs, inclusion of the correct copyright notice is required either on the page containing the lyric or in a separate section devoted to copyright acknowledgments, normally located at the beginning of the book.

LYRIC REPRINTS IN MAGAZINES

Another source of income is the negotiated fee for the use of song lyrics in weekly and monthly magazines. Fees for such magazines range from $100 to over $500 for one issue, but can be more depending on the stature of the composition, the weekly or monthly circulation, and whether it is a special issue (e.g., Valentine's Day or Christmas issues) or supplement. One example of such a magazine use was Valentine's Day article in *New Woman* entitled "Love Songs," which reprinted the lyrics to, among other songs, "My Funny Valentine," "Just in Time," "The Way You Look Tonight," and "Killing Me Softly with His Song." As with novels and nonfiction books, the music publisher will always require that correct copyright notice be printed with the lyrics.

MONTHLY SONG LYRIC AND SHEET MUSIC MAGAZINES

For lyric magazines, the normal fees paid to music publishers are from $100 to over $500 per issue, with additional monies sometimes due if a particular song becomes a Top 10 or 20 pop hit (e.g., an extra $50 if a song reaches Number 20 on the Billboard Top 100 Pop Single chart). For sheet music magazines, the per-song royalty can be a pro rata share of 12.5% of the subscription price of each issue, with advances usually based on the number of yearly subscribers (which in some cases can be as many as 150,000 copies). It is also customary for price reductions to occur for multiple-year subscriptions, and the base royalty for each such issue will normally be reduced accordingly. It is also common for free copies of each magazine to be given to the music publisher and that an additional 2% to 4% of each issue be printed as royalty-free, not-for-sale promotional copies, which may be used for advertising purposes. Set per-composition dollar fee licensing (as with lyric magazines) is also common in this area.

PUBLIC SERVICE ANNOUNCEMENTS

Permission for the use of a song in public service announcements is occasionally given for either no charge or a nominal administration fee of from $200 to over $500 for a limited period of time.

RECORDINGS OF HIT SONGS WITH CHANGED LYRICS

On occasion, publishers will receive a request from a recording artist or producer to change the lyrics to a well-known song so that it can be recorded and released under a new or similar title. Most of these revised versions are not successful, but a few, such as Al Yankovic's "Eat It" (based on Michael Jackson's "Beat It") and Cheech and Chong's "Born in East L.A." (based on Bruce Springsteen's "Born in the U.S.A.") became successful hit records in their own right.

Assuming the music publisher approves the use, the licensing can be handled in a number of ways. Considering that the success of the new version is normally dependent on the popularity and recognizability of the original hit song, some publishers will require that the copyright and publishing rights to the new lyric (and the new song) be owned by them, with the new lyricist receiving no credit or royalties for the lyric. Other publishers will allow the writer of the new lyrics to receive writer's credit as well as a share of the mechanical and performance royalties. In such a case, the royalties due the writer of the original hit song would be reduced for sales and performances of the new revised version, since an additional writer would be sharing in the earnings. In some cases, the music publisher will also give up a portion of the copyright ownership in the new song so that the royalties due not only to the original writer but also to the publisher will be reduced by the same ratio.

As a practical matter, most publishers will refuse any request to change the lyrics of a well-known song. A further complicating factor is that many writer-publisher contracts provide that the original songwriter has approval rights over any changes in English lyrics. In such a case, permissions have to be secured from both the music publisher and the songwriter.

MEDLEYS

Every few years, a single or album containing a medley of prior hits becomes successful. Because this type of album uses a large number of songs with all uses being between eight and 50 seconds, the mechanical licensing is normally handled in a different manner from the usual album or single, where each song might receive a statutory royalty rate. For a medley, each song is usually licensed on a pro-rata basis according to the number of songs contained in the medley of which it is a part, or in relation to its duration compared to other uses on the album. On occasion, a minimum or "floor" royalty (e.g., 4¢) may be guaranteed for each song, regardless of its duration or the number of songs on the album. For example, if a medley album contains 30 songs and all are licensed at 9.1¢, the total mechanical royalties due on the album would be $2.73. Because this aggregate royalty is normally prohibitive to the record company releasing the album, many publishers agree on a formula that computes the normal statutory royalties due on one 12- to 15-song album (between $1.09 and $1.36) and provides that all songs will share in that aggregate royalty either equally or based on their relative durations. In the case of singles, each song in each medley will normally share in either the 9.1¢ that would be due if the medley were treated as one song. In such a case, each of the five songs used in the one-song royalty scenario would receive approximately 1.8¢, unless a minimum guarantee (e.g., 4¢) was agreed to.

Many publishers will give a reduced rate only if they are given a "most favored nations" clause in the license. This clause guarantees that if another publisher or song receives a better rate, they will also get the benefit of such a rate. For example, if one publisher agrees to a 4¢ royalty with a "most favored nations" clause and another publisher's song receives 5¢ from the record company, the first publisher's royalty will be automatically raised to 5¢. The same concept can also apply to all terms of a license if so negotiated by the parties.

A common variation of the medley situation occurs when an original song is recorded that uses a portion of an existing song. In such a case, the two songs can either share all monies earned from the new version equally or, depending on the duration of the use, divide such monies on an agreed-upon percentage basis. There have also been instances where the owners of the pre-existing hit song have received a full statutory mechanical royalty as if theirs were the only song on the single.

For a record producer, it is advisable that reduced-royalty arrangements for all songs be made prior to the recording and distribution of the CD, download, or other configuration containing a medley. If a producer waits until the recording is completed to "clear" reduced rates from writers and publishers, he or she may be obligated to pay a full statutory mechanical royalty for each song recorded, regardless of whether a use is five seconds or 40 seconds.

PROMOTIONAL VIDEOS

All record companies need the right to release a video of their recording artists for website distribution, YouTube, MTV, and similar channels and media, as such exposure is one of the many factors essential for success in today's market. Because these videos are a necessary promotion vehicle and extremely expensive to produce (with costs from $50,000 to over $1,000,000), some publishers will give a free license for this type of use, provided that the record company does not receive any fees or payments for use of the clips. Other publishers, however, negotiate a flat up-front fee, usually a few hundred dollars. Some licenses reference performing rights and royalties; others do not. The terms of these promo video licenses range from 18 months to life of copyright, and the territory of use is almost always the world. In cases where the music publisher will give only a short-term license (e.g., 18 months to two years), the record company will many times negotiate for guaranteed options to extend the agreement for an identical period of time, usually at a set or negotiated fee. If a recording artist is the writer of a composition, however, the recording artist agreement will normally provide that the record company has the right to use the composition in a promotional video for no fee. For example, a clause found in many recording artist agreements reads:

Artist grants to the record company an irrevocable license, under copyright, to reproduce each Controlled Composition in motion pictures and other audiovisual works ("pictures"), and to distribute and to perform those pictures throughout the world for the purpose of promoting Audio Recordings, and to authorize others to do so, without payment.

Once the artist's video leaves YouTube, Facebook, MTV, and similar promotion areas, and is sold for home or personal use to the general public, however, the publisher and record company usually do negotiate a royalty structure for such uses. The fees charged depend on the policies of the companies involved and usually encompass a set penny rate for each song, a pro-rata percentage of the wholesale price of the video, or a percentage of the net profits of each video manufactured and sold. If the writer is also the recording artist, royalties may not be paid until the costs of recording the video have been recouped by the record company.

GREETING CARDS

The greeting card market can, for certain compositions, be a surprisingly valuable source of income. In this area, the major companies prefer to enter into exclusive agreements for the right to use the title or a portion of the lyrics of a song for use on the face of the card, as the inside message, or both. The duration of these agreements are from one to three years, and the rights granted can be for the United States, the United States and Canada, or the world. In addition, the music publisher is usually given the right to approve a reasonable facsimile of how the lyrics will be used and how the card will look prior to its manufacture, sale, or distribution. The music publisher will also require that the appropriate copyright notice be contained on the card itself, normally on the back of the card.

A variety of royalty formulas apply here, with one of the more prevalent being a percentage of the wholesale price of each card, less trade discounts. Assuming that 100,000 cards are sold in a three-month period at a wholesale price of 50¢ and with a lyric royalty of 5%, the calculations would look as follows:

100,000	Cards sold
× $.50	Wholesale unit value
$50,000	Aggregate wholesale value
× 5%	Royalty %
$ 2,500	Gross song royalty
– 1.8%	Trade discount
$ 2,455	Net song royalty

Certain card manufacturers prefer a one-time payment (rather than a percentage per card royalty), and the fees in this area range from a few hundred dollars to more than $2,000 for a one-year period for a specified number of cards (e.g., $750 for the right to print up to 4,000 greeting cards). If the music is also used in a greeting card or used by itself without the lyrics, the card company will pay a mechanical royalty or other negotiated rate for each card manufactured and sold.

MUSICAL GREETING CARDS

Many of the licenses in this area are worldwide and usually limited to five years plus an inventory sell-off period of one year. There is a duration limitation (for example, use not to exceed 2 minutes) and description as to when the music is played (heard when the card or other product is opened or pressed via internal hidden speaker). The consumer is given the right to sample snippets of songs online to determine the actual song that will be placed in the card.

One of the prevalent royalty schemes is 5% of net sales (which is calculated on all gross revenues less returns and customary trade discounts) with all rates being calculated on a most favored nations basis. An advance is also provided.

In addition to e cards and physical cards, some of these licenses also cover gift wrap containers and other recorded accessories such as sound gift bags, gift card presenters, paper CD/DVD sleeves, gift boxes, and other party goods.

ELECTRONIC GREETING CARDS

Electronic cards represent an ever-increasing number of sales in the 5 billion unit greeting card business. The all format song licenses in this area define both the "physical every day and seasonal card" and the electronic card that is "perceived via an electronic device and may be delivered via electronic transmission (e.g., via the Internet, mobile phone, cable television or other electronic delivery media not yet in existence"). Further, the song clip may only be distributed by either secure streaming or other secure file format intended to restrict further distribution or playback.

The territory for these deals is usually the world but can be only the U.S. and Canada with a term of 3-5 years plus a sell off period with a maximum sound duration specified (60 seconds) and a royalty of a % of net sales (e.g., 5%, 6%, etc.) or a per unit royalty (e.g., 12.5¢, 15¢ per card). Many times consumers are given permission to sample the song on an online website to see if they want to purchase it. If an existing master recording of a composition is used, the licensing with the record company which owns the master is usually on a most favored nations basis with the fee paid to the composition. This most favored nations clause will also apply to other co-owners of the composition if there are multiple writers and publishers. There is usually an advance paid to the music publisher by the card company based on a negotiated number of expected units to be sold. Many of these agreements provide that the card company will have the right to prepare derivative works of the composition, reprint or use the lyric and musical notation of the composition not to exceed one complete stanza in the card, synchronize the composition with moving images in the card, and perform the composition in in-context advertising and promotions, but all of the above represent negotiable items with respect to how the composition can be used.

TELEVISION COMMERCIALS FOR MOTION PICTURES

If a song is used in a motion picture, the right of a motion picture producer to use clips from the film in television advertisements and theatrical previews is almost always granted by the music publisher in its synchronization license. For example, if a promo contains a scene from the film and there is music in that scene, there will be no need for a separate license. In the event that a song is used out of context in the commercial (such as a song used in a scene in a film being used over a number of scenes in a trailer), however, an additional fee is negotiated. Many times, a producer will use a song that is not contained in the film as part of its television advertising, preview teaser, or trailer campaign for the motion picture. In such a case, the producer will contact the music publisher and negotiate a fee for television commercial and/or theatrical trailer/teaser use only (usually from $25,000 to over $500,000).

HOME AND PERSONAL VIDEO (TELEVISION PROGRAMS)

Whether the television program is an old collector's item series, a successful miniseries, a hit weekly program, a "best of" collection containing highlights of many shows, a variety special, or a behind-the-scenes look at the making of a show, there is a substantial market for video versions of television programming.

The major television-production companies, however, demand that the music publisher and songwriter accept a one-time buy-out payment for all videos manufactured and distributed (including downloads), regardless of the actual number that may eventually be sold. Such demands originally started with network television hit series but have now been extended to other series, made-for-TV movies, miniseries, and specials and are a fact of life that must be dealt with if you want your songs used in television programs. Fees in this area normally range from $6,000 to over $12,000, depending on whether the song is used as background music or sung by a character in the program, its importance to the story line, whether there are multiple uses, whether it is used over the opening or closing credits, the initial synchronization fee, the home video budget, and the projected success of the video in the marketplace. It should be mentioned that certain successful series pay the combined sync fee and home-video buy-out fee when the initial contract is signed as part of a one-time synchronization/home-video fee or all media fee. In these cases, the producer knows that the series is going to home and personal video and there is no reason to have option language in the agreement.

Although it is not common and becoming rare, if a royalty-based agreement can be negotiated, per-video royalties are usually based either on a penny rate (e.g., 10¢ to 15¢ per song) or on a percentage of the wholesale price. The percentage is shared on a pro-rata basis according to either the number of songs on the video, or each song's duration in relation to the total running time of the entire program, or the aggregate timing of all music on the video.

HOME AND PERSONAL VIDEO (RECORDING ARTISTS)

As in television program video licensing, some licenses are buy-outs, but many provide for song royalties to be based on either a pro-rata percentage of the wholesale price (6% to 8%) or a set per-song amount (8¢ to 10¢) for each video sold. Depending on the video appeal and marketability of a particular recording artist, as well as the producer's video policy, it is not uncommon for a music publisher to receive an advance based on from 10,000 to 25,000 units. If a writer is the recording artist, the recording contract will dictate the video payment formula, which normally ranges from 0% to as much as 50% of the record company's receipts (less a distribution charge, shipping, and duplication costs, as well as union payments) or, in the alternative, a percentage of the wholesale or retail price of each video sold or a set penny rate per video sold. When the writer is the recording artist, the record company may also have the right to recoup from 50% to 100% of the costs of producing the video from these royalties. Some agreements provide that no video royalties are due until all video costs have been recouped.

FOREIGN THEATRICAL ROYALTIES (MOTION PICTURES)

In most countries outside the United States, motion picture theatres are required to pay performance royalties for music used in theatrically distributed films (in many cases, 1% of the box office). These fees are collected by the local performance right society in each country, which in turn remits the writer's share of such monies directly to ASCAP, BMI, SESAC or GMR in the United States, which then pays the royalties to the writer. (The music publisher normally allows its subpublisher representative in each foreign territory to collect its share of such monies for remittance to the United States.) Because of the worldwide appeal of many U.S.-produced motion pictures, it is not unusual for successful films to generate between $50,000 and $300,000 in total foreign theatre performance royalties.

DOLLS AND TOYS

Many dolls and other toys use music via microchips or other technology. Royalty formulas in this area are, because of the merchandising aspects of the license, based on a percentage of either the retail price or wholesale price (the latter being more common) of the product with a set penny rate or "floor" which guarantees the music publisher that the actual royalty that is paid will not go lower than a certain agreed upon amount of money regardless of reductions in the retail or wholesale price of the toy or doll. For example, a representative license request will identify the song (and existing master recording, if applicable), describe the product (e.g., an animated dog in a car, etc.), the territory required (United States, United States and Canada, the world, etc.), the term (3 years, 5 years, etc.), the use (background vocal, one (1) use of not more than 30 seconds), the percentage royalty (6%, 10%, etc.) and, most important, the retail and/or wholesale price of the product on which the per unit royalty calculation will be made. The latter information Is essential in knowing what you are going to be paid as a royalty regardless of any floor that you might negotiate. As an example, a request might state the wholesale price will be $7.00 with a 6% royalty equating to 42 cents payable per unit sold. There is usually a most favored nations clause with the record company royalty if there is an existing master recording being used as well as with other publishers if other compositions are being used in the product.

The needs of the producer to use a particular song that might be identifiable with a particular doll or toy (e.g., a doll based on a contemporary artist singing his or her hit songs, an Elvis Presley doll using "Hound Dog") will dictate the royalty rate that is ultimately accepted. Another emerging market for song use is the area of "interactive toys" that talk to children as well as move their mouths and roll their eyes as they sing famous songs. Although these dolls carry a high retail price, they can sell in the millions each year, and depending on the royalty rate charged, writers and publishers can earn more than $50,000 per year on a successful interactive doll or toy.

TELEVISION PROGRAMS AND MOTION PICTURES BASED ON SONGS

On occasion, a television or film producer will use the title and story line of a song as the basis for a made-for-TV movie, a television series, or a theatrical feature film. The usual negotiation in this area includes:

- Option payments to maintain exclusivity while a script is being developed or financing is being secured (usually from 5% to 10% of the actual acquisition figure, with a portion of such payments sometimes deducted from the final payment)
- A final purchase price, which is usually due at the end of the option period, upon commencement of production, or upon actual first telecast or release
- A percentage of the producer's net profits
- A percentage of all merchandising rights derived from the television show or film (with a restriction on the producer's sharing in any pre-existing merchandising contracts to merchandising unrelated to the television show or film)
- The right to participate in sequels or spin-offs
- Separate synchronization fees for the use of the song in the television program or motion picture
- Possible music consultancy or music supervision during the production of the project
- Possible composing fees for the creation of additional songs for the project
- Approval or consultancy rights on the script

There are no hard and fast rules in this area, however, as everything depends on the importance of the song and its title to the project, the budget for the program or film, the license fees received from the network in the case of a television vehicle, the current popularity and topicality of the song, and the bargaining power and knowledge of the negotiating parties.

BOOKS BASED ON MOTION PICTURES (LYRIC REPRINTS)

On occasion, a screenplay or book based on a popular motion picture will be published after the film's release. If a character in the film has sung a song in a particular scene, the book publisher will request permission to include the composition in the printed edition. The fees for such uses are similar to those for novel reprints and usually range from $200 to more than $1,500 for hardcover rights, with additional amounts due for paperback, digital and book club editions if an all in fee has not been negotiated. The music publisher will require that correct copyright notice be given in the book for each song used and will usually request one or two complimentary books for its files.

An example of a published screenplay for a motion picture is *The Green Mile*, starring Tom Hanks, which was based on Stephen King's 1996 best-selling novel. The final shooting draft written by Frank Darabont had an introduction both by Stephen King and Frank Darabont. The screenplay contains the scene where the former prison guard Paul Edgecombe watches the black-and-white movie *Top Hat* (in which Fred Astaire sings the song "Cheek to Cheek" while dancing with Ginger Rogers) on television in a retirement home. This is the scene that triggers Edgecombe's telling the story of the miracle-working prisoner and what happened on death row in 1935. Two lines are printed from the composition. Near the end of the screenplay, the convict John Coffe watches the same dance scene from *Top Hat* while in the prison auditorium the night before his execution. The same two lines are repeated in the screenplay.

Another example is *The Wizard of Oz: The Screenplay* by Noel Langley, Florence Ryerson, and Edgar Allan Woolf, which contains the lyrics to, among others, E. Y. Harburg and Harold Arlen's "Over the Rainbow," "Ding Dong! The Witch Is Dead," "We're Off to See the Wizard," and "If I Only Had a Brain (If I Only Had a Heart) (If I Only Had the Nerve)."

BOOKS ABOUT A LYRICIST

A book publisher will sometimes put together a comprehensive reproduction of all the lyrics by a legendary writer, such as Sting, Cole Porter, Oscar Hammerstein II, or Lorenz Hart. Because many of these books are coffee table-size, cost from $30 to $50, and sometimes contain 150 to 200 lyrics, the typical licensing formula provides for a set fee per song, or an equal sharing by all songs of either a percentage of the wholesale price or a share of the author's book royalty. For example, one such book, which contained commentary about the lyricist as well as reprints of his more famous lyrics, had all music publishers and songwriters sharing 20% of the book writer's royalty. Since the writer's hardcover royalty was 10%, all songs contained in the book shared a 2% retail price royalty (or 20% of 10%). Thus, if the book had a retail selling price of $40, all songs would share in the 80¢ per book royalty. Simple mathematics indicate that most of these projects are not large income-producing items by themselves, but they often have the potential of re-exposing compositions to the heads of record, motion picture, television, and advertising companies, thus generating new uses. These books, therefore, can be extremely important promotional vehicles, and music publishers should negotiate their royalties accordingly.

REMIXES

Remixes are an important part of the music industry, as they enable recordings and songs to reach different markets and different audiences from the ones for which they were initially designed. For example, an initial recording which may have its appeal to the pop market may need to be remixed to reach additional markets that may not be interested in a pop song. One of the more important markets for remixes is the dance, electronic or club market but there are many more. Obviously, there are recordings that are initially made just for this market but, because of the skills of remixers, songs and recordings that would not be appropriate for these markets become hits and are accepted by music fans who may have never listened to the original.

When it comes to songwriter credit, copyright ownership, and songwriter and music publishing royalties from the remixed version of a composition, however, the remixer does not participate because there is no change in the songwriter-publisher ownership and royalties, unless the original writers and publishers agree in the case of substantial new material. For example, ASCAP, BMI, SESAC and GMR will pay the songwriters and music publishers of the original composition for all performances regardless of whether the performance is of the original recording of the song, a cover version, or a remix version, unless they are notified differently by the original writers and publishers.

Depending on the genre of music, there has been language introduced in agreements that allow the recording artist to give songwriter credit to a re-mixer when the lyrics or music is altered in the new version. Many times this involves not only songwriter credit and a royalty participation but also a copyright interest in the remixed version.

This entire area is many times based on negotiation power with some writers refusing the concept outright and others agreeing to the concept provided certain protections are included. One protective alternative is to make sure that there is language stating that the changes in the remixed version must be substantial (and sometimes approved by all the original songwriters) for the remixer to get a share. Another variation has all writers agreeing that if authorship percentages in a composition are reduced by the share given to the remixer, then each of the original writers' shares will only be reduced on a proportionate basis based on their original percentages.

NOVELTY AND THEME SONG ALBUMS

Novelty and nostalgia albums occasionally become real money-makers for the music publisher and songwriter. One such example is Tee Vee Tunes' Television's Greatest Hits double album, which contains shortened versions of 65 famous themes (sometimes including the voice-over announcer) from television programs from the 1950s and 1960s, including *The Lone Ranger*, *Perry Mason*, *Leave It to Beaver*, and *Star Trek*. As in any such project, you never really know whether such an album will be successful or not but, in the case of Television's Greatest Hits, the results were astonishing: the album made the Billboard Top Pop Album chart, selling more than 200,000 copies in the United States. In addition, the "Jetsons Theme" single made the pop charts, and a number of forgotten themes from old television series were reintroduced to a brand-new audience.

As for the business and licensing aspects of such a project, music publishers usually work with the producer and often accept a reduced mechanical royalty (e.g., 50% to 75% of the statutory rate) on a most favored nations basis because of the large number of compositions contained on such an album, because virtually all uses are between 30 and 90 seconds, and because this type of album is, from an economic standpoint, impossible to produce if a statutory-rate payment must be paid for each composition used.

LYRICS ON ALBUMS, DOWNLOADS, AND CD PACKAGES

Unlike other areas, where fees are usually charged by music publishers for the reprinting of lyrics to a song, it is standard industry practice not to charge record companies for the use of lyrics on album packaging or inserts included with downloads, CDs, or albums. In effect, publishers treat such requests as promotional in nature and do not require any payments. When record companies do ask for permission, however, it should be made clear that proper copyright notice be contained on the lyric sheet.

SHEET MUSIC AND FOLIOS

Best of Motown, Best of Nashville, Movie Songs of the '90s, The Best Christmas Songs Ever—these are but some of the many folios released each year. At one time, the sale of sheet music was a major source of income for the music publisher, but with the increasing monies that can be earned from the sale of downloads, records, and CDs; the use of songs in commercials; the synchronization fees from motion picture and television uses; and the performance royalties received from ASCAP, BMI, SESAC, GMR, and their foreign affiliates, this area has, for many songs, become a secondary income-producing source. It remains a valuable area, though, as it can provide a steady stream of good income for some songs and, for others, a substantial infusion of royalties. For example, successful songs may be distributed in a multitude of arrangements for piano solo, piano duet, guitar, concert band, jazz ensemble, vocal solo, choral arrangement, electronic piano, organ solo, and as part of a "best of" or "songs from a motion picture" series. In addition, sheet music may also be printed in non-music-oriented books such as Merv Griffin's "Jeopardy Theme," which appears in Alex Trebek and Peter Barsocchini's *The Jeopardy! Book*. Guitar tab and "how to play like" combination print and audio or audiovisual recordings have become increasingly important.

TELEVISION AND MOTION PICTURE BACKGROUND SCORES

A substantial source of income for certain writers and publishers is the earnings generated by background music scores to television series and motion pictures.

Although this is a very specialized field normally requiring substantial musical training in composition and orchestration, the field has opened up to many writers initially identified solely as "pop writers" (Trent Reznor, Stewart Copeland of the Police, Tangerine Dream, Jay Gruska, Danny Elfman, Randy Newman, Ry Cooder, et al.) or video game composers (Michael Giacchino). Most composers in this field are not signed specifically to one publisher and normally assign the copyright (or a portion thereof) to whatever film studio or production company is making the film. The publishing and songwriter revenue emanating from background scores includes royalties paid by network, local, public, basic cable, and pay television, as well as by movie theatres outside the United States.

LYRICS AND MUSIC ON SODA CANS

Certain soda companies have utilized the lyrics to well-known compositions on the labels for cans, bottles or on the packaging for soda. In most cases, the use is one line but on occasion it can be more than a line. Many of these agreements are for the territory of the United States but depending on the recognizability of the lyric, the license may include other countries as well. In additional to the actual print rights on the cans or bottles, the soda company may also request the right to use the image in print advertising including in consumer and trade publications, flyers, brochures, in-store advertising, transit posters and signage as well as other product packaging.

In addition, the license might include being part of the Internet and television campaigns promoting the product as well as being part of theatrical, cinematic and/ or industrial exhibitions and other exhibitions to live audiences (for example, on a jumbotron in stadiums). The term will usually be for a set period of time (for example, one year) with the soda company having an option to extend for an additional period. In most cases, fees will be a negotiated sum per period with a sell off period for unsold product. For example, each lyric might receive from $10,000 to $15,000 per year with a sell-off period for product still in the marketplace of two to four months.

Such uses many times occur as part of a limited or seasonal campaign and are licensed on a one-time fee use (much like a television commercial where there is unlimited broadcast rights during a specified period of time), rather than a per-can royalty basis. An example of this type of marketing is Coca-Cola's 2016 campaign which used song lyrics on both their regular and diet cans of soda. Another such promotion was the use by Pepsi Cola of the lyrics and music to "Winter Wonderland." On the Pepsi cans themselves, which were colored a deep blue with white silvery snowflakes, the sheet music was also displayed in white and silver. The names of the writers, Felix Bernard and Dick Smith, were featured near the top of the can, and the copyright notice was displayed near the bottom.

LYRICS ON MERCHANDISE

The use of song lyrics on merchandise continues to be a valuable market depending on the song. The types of merchandise involved are many and include t-shirts, sweatshirts, coffee mugs, mouse pads, etc. Customers can go into stores, buy prepackaged items on the Internet or create their own custom-made versions online.

One royalty formula in this area is a 50/50 equal split of revenues between the company selling the product and the music publisher. This sharing is based on the net after deducting the costs of manufacturing the merchandise as well as a percentage fee for marketing administration and, in some cases, costs directly related to the operation and development of the website. In many of these 50/50 net revenue sharing cases, the actually royalty is the equivalent of between 15% and 20% of the retail price with rates on a most favored nations basis.

Occasionally attached to these agreements is a summary sheet which outlines the type of merchandise being offered (T-shirts, tank tops, mugs), the per unit manufacturing costs of each product, the suggested retail price, the profit per item, the marketing costs (if applicable) and the actual per unit royalty. The value to such an approach is that it provides all the information needed to make an informed decision and eliminates most of the questions involved in how payments are calculated.

LYRICS ON T-SHIRTS, CLOTHING, AND POSTERS

The T-shirt and clothing business can be a substantial source of income for certain compositions with popular lyrics or specific lyric lines. Licenses in this area normally provide royalties on a per-item-sold basis, with royalties calculated on an agreed-upon penny rate, a percentage of the wholesale price, or a percentage of the suggested retail list price of the shirt. For example, a 12.5% to 20% wholesale royalty is not unusual. It is common for an advance to be given and a proviso included that an appropriate copyright notice for the song be printed somewhere on the item. Occasionally, the music publisher may request that a product sample be provided so that it can view the finished product before approving and finalizing the transaction. Posters are handled in much the same way.

LYRICS ON DIRECT-TO-CONSUMER MERCHANDISE

In addition to publishers or songwriters negotiating their own license agreements with apparel and other types of companies that want to use lyrics on their products, there are companies that specialize in selling lyric items directly to consumers on an on-demand basis. These companies will many times request a blanket license from a music publisher to use any lyrics in the publisher's catalogue with certain restrictions placed on certain compositions because of writer approval or type of product issues. The grant may be very broad in that the publisher will grant the company lyric rights for any merchandise of any kind including articles of apparel and accessories (e.g., T-shirts, sweatshirts, caps, etc.) and consumer products (e.g., mugs, writing implements, toys, novelties, trinkets, souvenirs, etc.) which are sold on an on-demand basis directly to the consumer. Other agreements might be more restrictive with respect to the grant of rights.

The territory of these agreements can be the world or the United States only. The term can be for three (3) years with automatic one (1) year extensions unless either party sends a termination notice or can be an agreed upon set period of time (e.g., four (4) years). One formula, among others, being used has royalties to the publisher payable at 33⅓% of the net margin to the on-demand company selling the products after deduction of all manufacturing, fulfillment, and shipping costs as well as monies paid to any third party that engages in printing or other services in connection with the exercise of the applicable lyric merchandising rights.

AUDIO RECORDINGS OF BOOKS

A large number of popular novels and other books are transferred to digital recordings and CDs for listening in autos, on mobile phones, other digital devices or at home. The lyrics to songs used in the print edition of the book are many times contained on the digital copy or CD. In these cases, the licensing is usually handled as if a song is being used on a recording artist's album or single, as publishers view this type of exploitation as an extension of the "mechanical" right. Since a full use of any song is rare in any book, music publishers and distributors normally agree on a reduced mechanical license rate for every recording manufactured and distributed. Another formula provides for a one time buy-out fee to cover all copies. One interesting example is Rupert Holmes' mystery novel, *Swing*, which included a big-band CD with extra musical clues as part of the deluxe edition of the book.

SPECIAL PRODUCTS ALBUMS

A continuing and valuable income source for well-known songs is their inclusion on the various albums, released by the Special Products divisions of the major record companies. Most of these albums are compilations of various songs and recording artists that fit into a special theme. For example, the project themes can be the "best" hits from the 1980s, the "greatest" movie or television themes, the "best of" Elvis Presley, Fats Domino, or the Platters.

These "special products" albums usually contain a large number of songs controlled by several music publishers and, unless they feature only one recording artist, usually contain a large number of master recordings owned by various record companies. Because of the great number of royalty-bearing compositions on these albums, the record company will, many times, ask each music publisher to give a reduced mechanical rate for every song used. In many cases, a 75% statutory rate is agreed to by publishers, but rates can be as high as 100% and as low as 50%, depending on the value of the particular song to the project and the negotiating stances of the other publishers who control songs on the album. It is somewhat standard when these requests are received to ask for a "most favored nations" clause in one's acceptance of a reduced mechanical rate so that if another publisher gets a higher royalty, a publisher granting a lower rate will be guaranteed the same rate. Occasionally, such a clause will relate to all songs on the album with the exception of one or two songs, which demand a statutory royalty. It is also common to receive an advance on a certain number of future sales (e.g., for the first 100,000 units sold) and, in some cases, a minimum guarantee (e.g., a guaranteed sale of 25,000 units).

TELEVISION SALE ONLY ALBUMS

Another variation of the "special products" album is those compilation CDs that are sold by mail order solely through television advertising. Occasionally the recording artist appears in these commercials (if a particular artist is being featured), and there is always a "crawl" showing the titles of many of the songs on the album being advertised. As in special products licensing, mechanical rates are many times negotiated on the basis of 75% of the statutory rate per song. Many publishers will also give a free synchronization license for the television marketer to use the song as part of the commercial. Although many people fail to realize the value of these television mail order packages, they can sell in the hundreds of thousands and generate substantial royalties.

KEY OUTLET MARKETING ALBUMS

Another source of mechanical income is the use of compositions on albums sponsored by a commercial product and sold as part of a marketing plan for a company's retail customers. One example of this type of album is a compilation entitled Pour It On, which was put together and sold by Starbucks. The album included recordings by Judy Garland, Sarah Vaughan, Nancy Wilson, and Chet Baker and sold at Starbucks locations. Compositions used on these special marketing albums are many times licensed at a reduced statutory rate (75%), and it is standard for the publisher to secure an advance on a certain number of units upon signing of the license agreement (e.g., an advance on from 10,000 to more than 50,000 units). On occasion, an advance is only given to those publishers who accept a reduced statutory rate, with the publishers not accepting the reduced rate royalty receiving royalties on actual sales, but without the up-front signing advance. If successful, these albums can experience substantial sales.

BONUS AND HIDDEN TRACKS ON AN ALBUM

On occasion, a recording artist or record company will include so-called "bonus" or "extra" tracks on a physical album. Many times these compositions are not even listed on the album artwork or booklet. Sometimes, however, the titles are listed on a sticker attached to the album.

Mechanical licensing in these situations is many times handled on a statutory basis. Other times, however, the publisher of the bonus or hidden track will agree to abide by the artist's controlled composition clause for physical product (which may be at a reduced statutory rate) or accept some type of reduced rate but higher than what the artist has agreed to accept (for example, 85% or 90% of statutory rather than the artist's 75% rate). Another variation is for the publisher of the bonus composition to agree to some type of reduced mechanical rate but with the guarantee that the reduced percentage will always be computed at the statutory rate in effect when the album is sold, rather than being "locked in" to a rate that is set as of a certain date (for example, a percentage of a "floating mechanical rate" rather than a percentage of the rate which was in effect when the album was released, with no change when statutory rate increases take effect).

LIMITED EDITION COLLECTIBLES

The commemorative plate, rendering, statue, sculpture, or other collectible (such as a hand-painted porcelain egg) represents a growing market and opportunity for songwriters and music publishers, because many of these items include a digital music or musical voice chip which allows the buyer to play a particular song which in some way relates to the subject matter of the collectible. The prices of these collectibles range from $50 to more than $200 and, when music is used, the collectible usually relates in some manner to a particular solo performer or group (e.g., Elvis Presley, Frank Sinatra, the Beatles, etc.) or to a motion picture that has a well known musical theme or song score (e.g., *The Wizard of Oz*). Some examples of this genre are a crystal-domed porcelain sculpture of the Beatles that plays "Sgt. Pepper's Lonely Hearts Club Band," hand-painted Frank Sinatra dolls containing excerpts of the singer performing "Witchcraft" and "My Way," a porcelain clear-domed sculpture of Marilyn Monroe that contains a digital sound chip of the actress singing "Diamonds Are a Girl's Best Friend," a crystal-clear domed structure of Elvis Presley with Graceland in the background that plays "Love Me Tender," a Dorothy from *The Wizard of Oz* musical portrait doll that features an excerpt from Judy Garland's classic version of "Over The Rainbow," and an heirloom collector plate featuring Patsy Cline singing her hit "Crazy."

When a music publisher licenses a composition to the company producing the collectible, the term of rights is usually for a limited period, (e.g., for seven years) or for a set period with an option (e.g., four years with an option on the part of the collectible company to extend the term of the license for an additional three years). The per-collectible royalty is sometimes based on the U.S. statutory rate, but many times the contract provides for a higher negotiated rate due to the merchandising aspects of the license or if the territory is more than just the United States.

MUSICAL TELEPHONES

There are a number of special telephones on the market that play your favorite song in place of the normal ring when someone calls. One such example is a singing Elvis Presley telephone, which has a replica of Elvis in a gold lamé suit holding a guitar on the base of the telephone. When the phone rings, the replica begins to dance while the song "Hound Dog" is heard. There is also a demo button, which you can push to see and hear the performance without waiting for someone to call. Another example is an Elvis phone that plays "Jailhouse Rock." Because this type of use is an audio reproduction, licensing may be handled on the basis of the statutory mechanical rate per telephone, but such rates are usually negotiated higher because of the merchandising aspects involved in the use (e.g., 50¢ or more).

SINGING FISH

Another unusual use of music is in connection with the man-made fish that turns its head and sings a well-known song. One example is a big mouth bass mounted on a wall plaque that sings such compositions as the Bobby McFerrin-penned "Don't Worry, Be Happy" and the more appropriate "Take Me to the River." There are a number of variations in this area, but most are currently battery-operated and can be activated either by a motion sensor or by a manually operated push button. Licenses are many times issued at the statutory mechanical or higher negotiated rate for the territory of the United States, with increased rates for a worldwide license.

THEME PARKS

Music can be used in theme parks in many different ways. One of the more common areas of music licensing for pre-existing songs and master recordings is their use as part of a theme park ride. Obviously, if a song is created specifically for the ride, the theme park owner will usually own the copyright and publishing for life of copyright pursuant to a writer-for-hire agreement where a one-time creative fee will be paid to the writer. The same is true of a master recording. On the other hand, many rides use pre-existing songs and masters as opposed to works created specifically for the ride. In these cases, the contract is very different since it is a license agreement with no transfer of copyright or publishing rights.

The agreement will specify how the song or master will be used (e.g., background vocal), the duration (e.g., up to 40 seconds), the territory (e.g., the identity and location of the theme park or parks), the term (e.g., five years, ten years, life of copyright, etc.), the consideration ($5,000, $7,500, $15,000), any options to extend, and the financial consideration, as well as many times, a most favored nations clause as to compensation with all other compositions and/or master recordings used in the ride.

RINGTONES

The use of songs as ringtones for cell phones was at one time a major source of revenue. In the United States, the publishing royalty rate payable for master tones is 24¢ for each such ringtone made and distributed. This rate was decided by the Copyright Royalty Judges and represents a statutory royalty and is effective through 2022. Ringbacks are licensed as a percentage of the retail price with certain negotiated royalty minimums usually provided.

COMPILATION ALBUMS/MECHANICAL RATES BASED ON PAST SUCCESS

If an album contains separate recordings by different artists, the record company may propose a two-tiered mechanical royalty rate structure, depending on the past or current success of the recording artist or writer/performer who recorded the composition. For example, a statutory mechanical rate might be offered to the publishers of compositions recorded by currently successful artists on the album, and the publishers of compositions recorded by lesser-known artists might be offered a reduced 75% mechanical rate. In such a case, all writer/artists would be treated on a most favored nations basis (i.e., all receiving the identical rate), depending on the tier or category that each was put in by the record company. For example, there might be seven Category "A" writer/artists who receive a full statutory mechanical rate for their compositions on the album and six Category "B" writer/artists who receive a reduced statutory rate for their compositions.

MUSICAL DOOR CHIMES

Another income-generating device for a song is the electronic multi-tune door chime. This device, which is similar to a doorbell, contains a microchip which will play 5 to 10 seconds of a well-known song when the button is pushed from the outside. The homeowner selects the song to be used as the doorbell signal, and everyone hopefully gets to hear a welcoming musical chime. Licensing in this area is either on the basis of a statutory mechanical or higher negotiated rate per composition for each door chime sold, or a one-time flat fee license for a set period of time if a buy-out type of arrangement is negotiated.

MUSICAL CANDLES

There are real candles that actually play music when they are lit. An example is a musical candle which stands on a base where there is a switch which controls whether or not music is to be heard. The music is activated when the candle is lit, continues to play while the candle is burning and, once the candle flame is extinguished, the music stops. The "Love Theme from Romeo and Juliet" is just one of the compositions performed by these candles. These uses are usually licensed at either the statutory mechanical rate per composition per candle or higher merchandising rate.

MUSICAL FLOWERS

Another way music can be used is as part of a musical flower pot. An example of this is a series of battery operated pots with fake flowers that play well known songs when a button is pushed. Compositions such as "I Can See Clearly Now," "California Sun," and "Boogie Woogie Bugle Boy" are performed while the flowers move and dance to the music. These musical pots can also be activated with a motion sensor if the musical gardener so chooses. The licensing of these items is many times handled on a statutory mechanical or higher negotiated royalty rate basis, and there is usually a copyright notice on the packaging.

CORPORATE IN-HOUSE VIDEOS

Many corporations produce videos that feature new products or emphasize the positive aspects of the corporate effort. These videos are designed for employee viewing only and usually are shown for a period of less than one year. Many of these videos contain hit songs as background music, and this music must be licensed from the music publishers which control the compositions and, if the master recording of the artist who made the song a hit is also being used (as opposed to a re-recorded version), with the record companies that own the masters. Fees in this area vary, depending upon the term and territory being requested for the corporate use, the popularity of the song, and the nature of the use.

MUSIC BOXES

A number of music-box manufacturers, in addition to using public-domain compositions, also use copyrighted songs in their product line. These uses usually concentrate on songs whose melodies are very well known or have a seasonal message, such as "White Christmas" or "I'll Be Home for Christmas." These uses are sometimes treated as a mechanical license, with the fee per box being a full statutory but, in most cases, there is a greater rate negotiated since there is a merchandising right included.

SLOT MACHINES

Licensing music for slot machines is usually handled on a fee per machine or bank of machines basis. Fees range from $5.00 at the low end to over $50.00 per machine with reductions sometimes occurring when the license is for a bank of machines rather than a single slot. Some licenses are for a limited term (e.g., 5 years, 10 years) and others as long as the machine is in use.

MUSICAL INSTRUMENT TOYS

There are a number of companies that manufacture and sell guitars, drums and other musical instrument toys that contain built in speakers, earphones or other speaker peripherals. Many of these toys, in addition to being able to be used to create new songs or beats (since they are able to play real chords, drum progressions, etc.), contain existing hit songs in the instrument. The territory is usually for the world, the term 2 years or longer and the royalty based on a percentage of the wholesale price (from 5% to 10%). In many of these agreements, there is a reference to the actual wholesale price ($15.00, $20.00, etc.) so you know what the percentage actually means in dollars and cents terms and a penny minimum (25 cents, 70 cents, etc.) which will be guaranteed regardless of the wholesale price calculation. Most agreements are on a most favored nations basis (other than the amount of any advance). The right to use the song as part of promotion and publicity for the product (demonstrations at tradeshows or as part of a television or Internet program) is many times requested as part of the license for no extra fee but advertisements and infomercials are always excluded unless a separate fee is paid.

BACKGROUND MUSIC SERVICES

There are a number of services in the United States that provide background music to commercial establishments such as small retail or large department stores.

This pre-programmed music (in many cases content designed particularly for the type of store and/or clientele involved) is transmitted digitally to the various locations which have contracted with the service. The royalty payments are many times based on a minimum royalty pool. This royalty pool can take many variations but, in most cases, is calculated as the greater of a set percentage of net music revenue for a particular quarter (e.g., 2%, 4%, etc.) and a set dollar or cents number times the number of actual establishments for that quarter (e.g., $2.50, $6.00, etc. × the actual number of establishments using the service). It should be mentioned that certain services do not have a dollar and cents minimum and the royalty calculations are only based on net revenue.

The next calculation is to compare the number of compositions owned by a particular publisher which were used during a particular quarter with the number of all compositions used and then arrive at a pro-rata royalty based on actual usage. For example, if a publisher's catalogue represented 10% of all the compositions performed during a quarter, then that publisher would be entitled to receive 10% of the total royalty pool. The publisher would then pay the songwriters of the compositions performed their contractual share of such monies pursuant to the terms of the songwriter, co-publishing, administration or other agreement between the parties.

Certain agreements provide for a so called "fixation fee" which covers the initial reproduction of the sound recording containing the composition on the company's server. In many cases, this is a 9.1 cents fee for the first fixation with no additional per-copy fees for additional server reproductions of the same recording containing the same composition.

There will always be a list of limitations on the rights being granted pursuant to the agreement with the following being some of the major restrictions:

- Use in private residences;
- Webcasting to the general public as well as other Internet, radio or television station broadcast and cable transmissions; and
- Physical media such as CDs or vinyl where such are being sold or rented to consumers.

The music publisher will also reserve a large number of rights since the license is very specific as to its intent. Some of the more important (usually contained in an "including but not limited to" clause) are:

- The right to alter the fundamental character of the composition or create a derivative work;
- The right to alter the lyrics;
- The right to exercise synchronization, karaoke and print rights;
- Merchandising rights; and
- Use of the composition in a marketing campaign, product tie-in, game, contest or to directly advertise or promote or co-promote any product or service.

It should be mentioned that in some contracts, performing rights are granted as part of the fee received and the agreements are negotiated accordingly with respect to the rights being granted or reserved. In other agreements, performing rights are reserved for licensing through the applicable performing rights society or via the music publisher but with a proviso that the parties can enter into a voluntary negotiated direct performance license if they so elect.

Accountings will usually be within 45 days following each calendar quarter. If the account balance is less than a stated dollar amount (e.g., $50), the royalties due may be held until a period in which the total amount due (both past and present) meet or exceed the threshold. Audit provisions will be contained in the agreement with certain restrictions such as audits having to be commenced within 3 years after the date that the royalty statement was rendered, after the end of the initial period covered by the statement, time limitations on litigation, etc.

INTERNET MUSICAL INSTRUMENT LESSONS

There is a rising trend of web sites specializing in guitar, keyboard, voice, and other musical instrument lessons. There are numerous licensing approaches in this area, but many will contain the following provisions.

The rights granted by the music publisher to the web site will be nonexclusive and will include the right to synchronize the composition in the video portion of the lesson, the right to create tablatures (or sheet music) or reproduce lyrics and the right to stream the lessons to the purchasing student. Excluded from many of these licenses are the public performing rights as those are usually licensed via performing rights societies (unless a publisher decides to license directly). The term is between two and three years often with automatic 1 year extensions unless one of the parties provides notice of termination 30 to 60 days prior to the end of the initial term or, if applicable, the extended term.

Royalties are structured in a number of ways depending on whether the user selects a one at a time paid-for lesson scenario, or a subscription type of relationship with the web site. If on a one time lesson approach, the publisher will receive a percentage of the price paid for the lesson, on a lesson by lesson basis. The percentages vary but a representative example is 25%. If the royalties are based on a subscription scenario, the royalties will be based on a percentage of the monthly revenue generated by the subscriptions less certain agreed upon continuing expenses needed to run the website. In these cases, there may be deductions for the use of public domain music for which royalties do not need to be paid. The monies which relate to copyrighted royalty bearing music is then distributed to music publishers based on their share of the actual performances of the songs they control. It should be mentioned that most of these agreements have a most favored nations clause to ensure that all publishers are being paid at the same rate for the same or similar type of use.

PHYSICAL COINS

On occasion, a physical coin company will request the use of a portion of the lyrics to a composition and/or the image and likeness to a well known performer or songwriter. The territory of the license is usually the world with a per unit royalty calculated as the greater of a set monetary amount (e.g., $1.00, $2.00, etc.) or a percentage of the net profit or wholesale price of the coin. The term is usually limited to a set number of years and there is virtually always an advance paid upon the signing of the license agreement. Some agreements provide that if a certain number of units are sold during the term (a "threshold"), then the term of the agreement will be automatically extended for an additional number of years. In all these agreements, there is a detailed description of what the coin will look like as well as what it is made of (e.g., physical minted two (2) ounce .999 pure silver coin).

HOLOGRAMS

Holograms represent another source of royalty income which is spread out over a number of different rights encompassing both music related and non-music related licensing aspects. For example, a number of holograms feature performers (usually deceased) singing and performing the compositions which they were noted for … thus the music licensing aspect. Because of the nature of the performance, however, image, name and likeness rights are also involved … thus the non-music licensing aspects.

There are a number of different ways that this media is licensed and the following represent some of the major approaches. The name, image and likeness rights (which many times includes film clips, performances and other existing material from which the hologram company will use as a reference for its production) will be licensed via a royalty percentage of the box office receipts and/or gross revenue derived from the production. The music publishing rights will be licensed in the same manner but with a different royalty scheme much like a Broadway musical where the royalty will start at a certain level and then be increased after the costs of the production have been recovered by the hologram company. The territory can be the world or can be specified territories such as the United States and Canada. The term is many times for a set period of time (e.g., 10 years, etc.) with possible extensions based on certain agreed upon income thresholds having been achieved. There are also usually separate advances paid with respect to the name, image and likeness rights and the music aspects (since such rights might be owned by different parties). In many agreements, there will be a time limitation to ensure that the production is completed by a certain date.

MENU SCREENS

Motion Picture DVDs as well as other entertainment product utilize menus listing what is on the device and where the consumer can go to enjoy the specific features set forth. In cases where music is accompanying the viewing of the menu screen, a license needs to be negotiated for the composition. The following examples of a movie trailer license with an option for a menu and a straight motion picture menu license illustrate the type of agreements and considerations in this field. The movie trailer license with options would set forth the title of the composition being used, the writers and publishers, the usage and timing (i.e., background vocal, 1:30), the trailer license fee, and language as to "broad rights in all media trailers." Various options with additional negotiated license fees would be set forth including a possible option for "all home/personal entertainment media menus up to a full use for life of copyright with the world as the territory." An individual movie menu screen license would contain the composition title, the writers and publishers, the usage (i.e., background vocal up to full length loop in menu screens) with a broad Media clause of "all forms of entertainment media for home/personal use now known or hereafter devised including without limitation audio-visual devices and electronic delivery."

CO-BRANDING VIDEOS

On occasion, two or more companies might create a co-branding video which link their brands together (e.g., a sports car company and a print and online magazine, etc.) and which both companies will use with respect to their various target audiences. A number of these videos will use either a master recording and song or a performer actually singing a live version of the song on camera. There are multiple variations in this area.

The term can be for six months, a year or multiple years. The territory is usually the world if the products are available worldwide. The media is many times concentrated on the product's (or artist's) social media handles such as Twitter, Instagram, Facebook, YouTube, etc. as well as any social media platforms and digital properties owned or controlled by the co-branding companies. Depending on the companies involved, the fees can be lucrative (e.g., $20,000 to $50,000 for a 6- or 12-month license depending on the composition), but the fees depend on the stature of the song, the master, if a master is being used versus a re-record or live performance, the companies involved, the term, the media and the budget.

VIRTUAL REALITY

Because of the nature of this medium, there are multiple approaches to licensing music for such projects. The issues which are addressed in the licensing negotiations included the usual areas such as:

The term;

The territory;

The media; and

How the song is being used.

Because of the expansive nature of the project, however, the issues become more complex because of the nonlinear aspects and inter-activity of the license since the use may not be limited to a static described scene or scenes but may be very fluid depending on the ability of the project to proceed in any number of directions depending on the ability of the end user to manipulate the direction and outcome of the experience and, therefore, the use of the song itself. Because of both the interactive and non-interactive rights being granted, it is essential to secure as much information as possible on the project and the ability of the user to determine the order, outcome and contents of the program including utilization of all or portions of the composition.

The term is many times life of copyright but can be for a limited period (e.g., five years) with options to extend the term for additional fees. Many of the licenses are all media including virtual reality experiences utilizing headsets, specialty glasses, smartphones, location based virtual reality centers, arcades, motion picture theatres, etc.

CHAPTER 2
MUSIC, MONEY, CO-PUBLISHING, AND ADMINISTRATION

In addition to the individual song agreement and the exclusive songwriter agreement, two other agreements—the co-publishing agreement and the administration agreement—need to be discussed. Many of these deals are available primarily to established, successful songwriters who own their own publishing companies and who wish to make use of the greater financial, administrative, and promotional resources of a major music publisher.

The co-publishing agreement is one of the most significant contractual arrangements in the music industry. It gives the songwriter a share of certain rights and income that he or she would not be entitled to under the normal writer-publisher contract. As we have seen previously, industry practice is for the writer to sign with a publisher on a song-by-song basis or on an exclusive basis for all musical compositions written during a specified period of time. Under the terms of such contracts, the writer transfers the copyright of a song or songs to the publisher and is paid 50% of all earnings received by the publisher from those songs. Under the terms of the co-publishing agreement, however, the writer sells and transfers only a portion of the copyright and retains the other portion for his or her own publishing company. More importantly, the songwriter receives not only his or her standard 50% share of all earnings but also a portion of the 50% that normally is reserved to the music publisher. As a general rule, the co-publishing arrangement is usually available primarily to writers who have a successful track record of past hits, writer/performers who have the potential of securing a record deal, or writers who have a current recording artist contract and who have the bargaining power to negotiate such an agreement with a music publisher.

The music-publishing business is highly competitive, and if a particular writer is in demand or has written songs that a publisher feels have the probability of being hits, the publisher may agree to enter into a co-publishing agreement as an inducement for the writer to sign. Obviously, if a publisher realizes that the only way to sign a particular writer is to give him or her part of the future income usually reserved solely for the publisher, that publisher usually will do it. This is a sound business decision: if the writer's songs do fulfill their commercial potential, both the established publisher and the writer will gain substantially and it will be a win-win situation for all parties involved.

There are a number of circumstances that lend themselves to the signing of a co-publishing agreement. One is where the writer has had a number of hits while signed as an exclusive writer to a publisher and the contract is approaching its expiration date. Considering the writer's past success, the current publisher (or another competing publisher) might offer a co-publishing arrangement for all future compositions as an inducement to re-sign or sign as an exclusive writer.

Another situation that often occurs is where the successful writer already has his or her own publishing company and a major publishing company wants to sign the writer and control his or her material. Under such circumstances, the major company will normally agree to a co-publishing arrangement in order to get the right to publish a part of the songwriter's past and future compositions.

A third situation is where a recording artist has written his or her own material and has a recording contract with a label. In such a case, a publisher will virtually always be willing to enter into a co-publishing agreement with the writer/recording artist, since the publisher knows that the recording artist will release self-written material and there will be guaranteed commercial exposure of the songs.

A fourth common situation is where a writer has signed a single-song contract and the song becomes a major hit. Such a writer, because of this success, will have the necessary bargaining power to negotiate not only an exclusive songwriter's agreement but also a co-publishing agreement with a major publisher for all future songs.

A fifth situation, which is similar in some respects to the recording artist example, is where the writer or band has the potential to sign a recording-artist agreement or have interest from a record company. Once again, because of the probability that the writer/performer will record primarily self-written material, the music publisher will offer a co-publishing arrangement.

A sixth situation is where the songwriter is a record producer who has the ability to co-write compositions with the recording artist which he or she is producing or who has access to placing self-written or co-written compositions on an artist's album or individual tracks whether or not he or she is producing the artist.

A major publisher may also offer a writer a co-publishing contract in lieu of high advances to keep the costs of signing the writer at a moderate level. In these instances, the songwriter trades the immediate financial benefit of higher advances for a share of the publisher's income. If the songs are successful, that agreement can mean substantially increased future royalties, which can more than compensate the writer in the long run.

This contractual arrangement is becoming more accessible to many writers and its use is becoming more common in the music publishing industry.

STANDARD TERMS OF A CO-PUBLISHING AGREEMENT

A number of variations on the co-publishing agreement may be negotiated. The basic terms are fairly standard, however. The following section describes both the usual provisions and the principal variations that may be encountered by the writer or the writer's representative in negotiating a co-publishing agreement.

SHARING OF INCOME

The first important aspect of the co-publishing agreement is how the various parties to the agreement share the income that is earned from CDs, downloads, videos, performances, motion picture and television synchronization rights, commercials, streaming, and all other sources of revenue generated by a writer's songs. The most common arrangement to share income in this area is known as the "50/50" split. This equal sharing of income (50% to the writer's company and 50% to the major company) refers only to those monies that represent the music publisher's share of earnings. It does not relate to the writer's share, since the songwriter will still receive his or her songwriter's royalties, regardless of the terms of the co-publishing agreement.

A simple diagram comparing the standard writer-publisher contract and the co-publishing agreement can best explain this sharing of income between the writer's publishing company and the major publishing company. Under the standard music industry publishing contract, the writer usually receives 50% of the net income earned from uses of his or her songs, and the publisher receives the other 50%. For example, if a total of $100,000 is received by the music publisher from the sale of CDs, downloads, or home video, the publisher would be entitled to retain $50,000 and the writer would receive $50,000.

Under the co-publishing agreement, however, the writer receives not only his or her 50% share of songwriter income but also receives a share of the publisher's share. If we keep our previous example of $100,000 received by the publisher from CD, download, and home video sales and assume a 50/50 co-publishing arrangement, the income would be shared as set forth below.

As can be seen, the songwriter receives 50% of all monies received, with his or her publishing company and the major publisher sharing the remainder equally. In effect, the writer and his company receive 75% of all monies earned, and the major "co-publisher" receives the remaining 25%. To illustrate the arrangement once again through the use of actual dollar figures, the sharing of income looks as follows:

Writer Monies (50%)	Publisher Monies (50%)
$50,000	$50,000

Writer's Publishing Company (50% of Publishing Share)	Major Publishing Company (50% of Publishing Share)
$25,000	$25,000

Writer:	
$50,000.00	Writer's 50% share
+$25,000.00	Writer's 50% share of publishing
$75,000.00	Total earnings for the writer

Major Co-Publisher:	
$25,000	Co-publisher's 50% share of publishing monies

If the monies earned are related to performance income, the songwriter will, in most cases, receive his or her songwriter share directly from the performing rights organization with which the writer is affiliated and will also receive 50% of the publisher share of performance royalties which are distributed to the major publisher. The basic 50/50 co-publishing agreement is not the only type of royalty split encountered in the music industry. Another type of co-publishing agreement provides for a 75/25 split of publishing income between the writer's company and the major publisher. Under such an arrangement, the writer will receive his or her full writer's share of income (50% of all monies that are earned) as well as an additional 25% of the publisher's share of monies earned (25% of the remaining 50% of all income). Assuming our $100,000 example, the writer's company would receive 25% of the $50,000 publisher's share ($12,500) and the major co-publisher would receive the other 75% ($37,500). Under this arrangement, the writer and his or her publishing company would receive an aggregate total of $62,500 of the $100,000 earned, and the major publisher would receive the remaining $37,500.

COMPOSITIONS COVERED BY THE AGREEMENT

The agreement will normally cover all future compositions created by the writer during the term of the co-publishing agreement as well as, in some cases, all past songs written by the writer and owned by the writer's publishing company. Sometimes the pre-existing songs are brought into the agreement on an administration only basis where the major publisher does not take a copyright interest but this depends on the negotiation and the bargaining power of the parties. Furthermore, many agreements specify that the contract covers all compositions by other writers that are acquired, owned, or controlled by the writer's publishing company during the term of the agreement.

ACQUIRING SONGS WRITTEN BY OTHER WRITERS

If the agreement also covers outside compositions owned, controlled, or acquired by the writer, most agreements will provide that if the writer must pay an advance or acquisition monies to secure the rights to a composition or catalogue written or controlled by a third party, the music publisher will have the right to control those compositions under the terms of its agreement with the writer only if the publisher contributes its pro-rata share of the monies which were paid for the compositions. For example, if the writer has a 50/50 co-publishing agreement with a major publisher and has to pay $200,000 to acquire the publishing rights to a catalogue of compositions written by another songwriter or songwriters, the major publishing company will be able to include those compositions in its agreement with the songwriter only if it contributes $100,000 of the acquisition price (i.e., 50% of the purchase price). When this occurs, the songwriter's share of the publishing earnings generated by these third-party-acquired compositions will many times not be used to recoup outstanding advances that have been paid under the writer's co-publishing agreement. Depending on the terms of the co-publishing agreement, the intent of the parties, and level of advances paid to the writer by the music publisher, however, the income generated by compositions written by other writers might be used to recoup outstanding advances.

On occasion, if the songwriter is a recording artist, the co-publishing agreement may only control compositions recorded, or recorded and commercially released, pursuant to the writer's recording agreement. Under this type of scenario, all compositions written that were not recorded by the songwriter as recording artist would be excluded from the co-publishing agreement. This type of arrangement is not common, as the music publisher usually has control over all compositions written during the term. When it does occur, the music publisher may enter into an exploitation agreement with the writer, which will bring a non–writer/recording artist composition into the agreement if the publisher is able to secure a new use of such a composition (for example, getting a commitment for a motion picture or television use, or a recording by another artist) or the publisher may control these compositions on an administration-only basis rather than co-publishing.

TRANSFER OF COPYRIGHT AND OTHER RIGHTS

Under the usual 50/50 split agreement, the writer's publishing company will transfer 50% of the copyright ownership of all compositions to the major publisher. In addition, the writer's company will also normally give the major publisher all administration rights, including the right to license the use of the musical compositions throughout the world and the right to collect any monies that may be earned by the compositions. As with songwriter agreements, the co-publishing agreement may also contain certain negotiated restrictions (e.g., no advertising commercial uses without consent) or exclusions (e.g., motion-picture or television dramatization rights with respect to the story line of the song).

TERM OF AGREEMENT

The initial duration of the agreement can vary, but the usual arrangement is for an initial contract term of one or two years, with a number of successive options on the part of the major publisher to extend the agreement for additional one-year periods. The first period of the term may be for one year with three successive one-year options, two years with two one-year option periods, six years with no option periods, or any other variation that may be negotiated. Other agreements may be tied to the release of a minimum product commitment (e.g., for three years or the release in the United States of 24 songs on a major record label, whichever is later) or the recovery of all advances paid under the agreement (e.g., the later of three years or recoupment of all advances).

Options to extend the agreement are of basically two types: the automatically renewable type, and the type that has to be acted on by the major company for it to be effective. The former (or automatically exercised option) needs no affirmative action on the part of anyone for the contract to be extended; the option is automatically exercised at the end of the original term or the preceding option period, unless the publisher sends the writer notice to the contrary. The second type of option clause (which is more common) needs some type of affirmative action by the publishing company for it to be effective: in most cases, written notice given to the writer's company prior to the end of the current contract period.

TERM/RECOUPMENT ONLY DEALS

Some writer and co-publishing agreements do not have a minimum song delivery or release commitment that has to be achieved for the active term to end or trigger an option exercise decision (if options are available). In their place, the term of the agreement will be calculated on the later of a set number of years (e.g., one year, two years, etc.) or recoupment of all advances. For example, if the writer signed a three-year deal, was paid a $100,000 advance when the agreement was signed and at the end of the three years there was still an unrecouped advance balance, the term of the agreement would be extended until the publisher recouped the advance regardless of how many songs were delivered or commercially released (or if the writer had the right to repay the advance or a percentage thereof, the date of repayment which is usually deemed effective at the end of the accounting period during which the repayment was made).

Some agreements may have option periods which provide that the option period, if exercised by the publisher, will not commence until the advances paid during the prior contract period have been recouped or repaid per the terms of the agreement. For example, an agreement might read that there is an initial term that will last until two years or recoupment of advances (whichever is later) with the publisher having an additional two-year option based on the same terms with usually different advances once the initial period and recoupment requirements have been met.

Sometimes the extension of the term is automatic and, other times, the publisher has to send notice to the writer. Obviously, once the date is imminent, the parties will begin to exchange information as to the amount of the actual unrecouped advance balance, when they feel recoupment may occur depending on current activity and earnings (both actual in-house or projected future pipeline receipts) as well as whether the writer has the right and financing or desire to pay off the balance or contractual percentage thereof to effect recoupment.

ALBUM-BASED AGREEMENTS

If the agreement is with a recording artist and is based on the release of albums featuring the writer/artist, options are handled differently from the way they are addressed in a purely songwriter/delivery-of-new-songs type of agreement. For example, an agreement might provide that the term will last for an initial contract period during which one album containing the writer/performer's compositions will be commercially released in the United States, plus three additional option periods with a commitment of one album being released during each of such periods. Under these album-based deals, the current contract period will end only after there is a commercial release of an album. There are variations on this theme that might provide that the album commitment can be fulfilled by a certain number of individual compositions being released on albums by recording artists other than the songwriter, but the norm in these type of album-based agreements with a writer/recording artist is that fulfillment is conditional only on the release of the writer's own albums (and always with a proviso that there must be a certain number of artist written songs on an album for it to qualify).

TWO-ALBUM FIRM AGREEMENTS

Some agreements provide that the initial period of the term will cover the release of two albums rather than the more common one album with options for additional albums. Under this type of "two-album firm" agreement, the music publisher is committing itself to stay with the songwriter/recording artist for a period which will cover the release of two albums; a period that can easily last for in excess of four years. By getting the publisher to agree to commit to two albums, the songwriter is able to count on the financial security of guaranteed advances related to the second album. On occasion, the term of these type of agreements may be for three or four guaranteed albums, but this is not common.

Under this type of scenario, the publisher has committed itself to paying advances for a second album even if the first album is a financial failure. If the term had been structured in the more common manner (a one-album commitment with options on the part of the publisher to extend the agreement to cover additional albums), the publisher would have the choice to end the term without having to pay advances to a writer/artist for an album that the publisher no longer believes will be successful. Because advances for albums are normally high, having an option to pay or not pay can be vital to the publisher's financial well being. On the other hand, the songwriter will usually favor such a guaranteed financial commitment that is not conditioned on success.

Even if the term of the co-publishing agreement is for two guaranteed albums, the music publisher may insert so-called disaster clauses to protect itself in case the first album is a total financial failure. For example, if the first album sells fewer than 25,000 units, or earns less than a stated amount or if the unrecouped advance balance is in excess of a stated figure, the publisher may have the right to turn the second album into an option album rather than a guaranteed album on which an advance must be paid.

Another provision that is usually inserted in the agreement allows the publisher to turn the term of the co-publishing agreement from a guaranteed multi-album agreement to an option agreement if the songwriter-recording artist loses his or her recording artist agreement or changes record labels.

Another variation is to provide that an advance will not be payable to the writer/artist unless the record company has manufactured, or manufactured and commercially distributed, a minimum number of units. (For example, 25,000 albums must be manufactured and distributed through normal retail distribution channels for the commercial release advance to be payable.) This type of provision ensures that advances will be paid only on albums that have at least a minimum commitment from the writer/artist's record company and will many times exclude Internet-only releases.

EXERCISE OF OPTIONS IN ALBUM-BASED AGREEMENTS

One of the major negotiating areas in every writer/recording artist album-based co-publishing agreement has to do with the timing of when the music publisher must exercise the next option period. Obviously, the songwriter would like the publisher to have to commit for an additional period (which means a commitment to pay further advances) as early as possible. The publisher, on the other hand, would like as much time as possible to review the new album and gauge not only the record company's commitment behind the album but also the public's enthusiasm before it has to decide whether to pick up an option.

There are a number of variations as to when an option must be exercised. The following are the more common:

Delivery of the Album: Under this approach, the music publisher is given a certain number of days from the time that the newly recorded album is delivered to and accepted by the record company to notify the writer/recording artist whether it is going to exercise its option to the next option period covering the new album. In this regard, the publisher will normally have at least 30 days from the time that the album is delivered to and accepted by the record company to exercise its rights. During this period, the publisher will listen to the new album, confirm all of the songwriting percentages of the compositions (including the identity of any samples) on the album as well as mechanical licensing rates payable for each song, and try to get some feedback from the record company as to its reaction to the recording, its planned promotion budget and strategy as well as its support for and commitment to the project.

A Number of Days Prior to Release: A variation of the option based on delivery approach is to tie the option exercise date to the later of a certain number of days after the album has been delivered to the record company, or to a set number of days prior to the actual release of the album. This approach usually gives the publisher a bit more time to decide whether it wants to exercise its rights to the new album and ensures that the album is actually put on the record company's release schedule. For example, the agreement might provide that the publisher must make its option decision for a new album upon the later of 30 days after the delivery of the album to the record company or 45 days prior to the commercial release of the album.

Release of the Album: A third variation is to allow the publisher to make its option decision either on release of the album or a certain number of days after the album has been commercially released. For example, the publisher might have 15 days after the release of an album to exercise its option for that album. For a music publisher, this approach is preferable, as this may give it time to see how the album is reviewed by the trades and received by the public, and enable the publisher to do some research as to initial sales activity before it has to make a decision on the option. Because a single is usually released prior to the album, acceptance and activity of the single (which may affect the album) can also be monitored and gauged.

Exercise Based on the Delivery or Release Dates of the Prior Album: Although it is not common, some agreements provide that the music publisher must make its option decision for the next album within a certain number of months after the most recent album has either been delivered to the record company or released by the record company. For example, the publisher might be asked to make its decision to commit to the next album within nine months after the last album was delivered to or released by the record company. The obvious disadvantage to the publisher under this type of arrangement is that it may have to exercise an option (and commit to the payment of advances) for an album that it has not been able to hear or an album that does not yet exist.

NON-EXERCISE OF AN ALBUM OPTION

If the music publisher decides not to exercise its option for the next album, the writer will have the right to make a deal with another publisher, because the term of the current co-publishing agreement will be deemed to have expired. In virtually all cases, the compositions contained on the new album for which the publisher did not pick up the option will be available to the new publisher. There may be an exception to this rule for compositions which are on the new album but which have been commercially exploited by the music publisher (released by another recording artist, used in a motion picture, video game, or television series) prior to the option exercise date. Under these circumstances, such compositions might remain with the prior publisher and not be part of the new publishing agreement, regardless of the fact that they are on the new album that was not picked up. Another variation is to have any unexploited composition written after the release of the most recent album controlled by the publisher revert to the writer if the option for the new album is not exercised. In any event, the prior publisher will have no rights in any compositions created in the future by the songwriter, because the active term of the agreement as well as the exclusive right to the songwriter's services ends when the publisher decides not to exercise the option for the next album.

OWNERSHIP OF SONGS AFTER THE CONTRACT HAS ENDED

Unless there are provisions to the contrary, and subject to any copyright reversion laws, all songs that are subject to the co-publishing agreement will remain jointly owned by the writer's company and the major company for the life of copyright of the compositions.

ADVANCES

Signing Advances. Depending, of course, on the reputation of the writer, the existence of any recording artist commitments, the quantity and quality of the songs controlled by the agreement, and the inclusion of any pre-existing hit songs, the major publisher may make substantial monetary payments to the writer or the writer's publishing company at the time the co-publishing agreement is signed. These payments are treated as advances recoupable from any future royalties that may become due to either the writer or the writer's publishing company. To put it simply, all royalties that become payable to the writer or his or her company under the agreement will be used to reimburse the financing publisher for the monies advanced at the time the contract is signed. For example, if $175,000 is given to the writer at the signing of the contract, then the first $175,000 in royalties due the writer or the writer's publishing company will be used to recoup the advance given. Until that happens, the writer and his or her company will not receive any royalties, although earnings statements with the current status of recoupable monies will be sent.

Option Year Advances. In addition to advances given upon signing, the major company usually pays an advance whenever it exercises an option to extend the duration of the agreement. Such advances can be paid either in a single lump sum at the start of an option period or in several monthly or quarterly payments during each option year of the contract. For example, there might be a payment of $60,000 upon commencement of each option period, or the same $60,000 could be paid out in equal monthly installments of $5,000. If the agreement is for more than one year (e.g., a firm three-year deal) but there are no options, the agreement is often structured so that advances are either paid at the start of each one-year period of the term, on a monthly or quarterly basis, upon recoupment of advances, or upon any number of variables negotiated by the parties.

Advances Based on the Release of Commercial Recordings. If the writer is a recording artist, the co-publishing agreement will guarantee a specified advance if an album containing songs written and recorded by the writer is released during each contract year of the agreement. The amount of this type of advance varies, depending on the writer/artist's commercial success and appeal, the number of songs by the writer that are contained on the album and their mechanical licensing rate, the reputation of the label releasing the album, where the release occurs, how high it gets on the trade paper charts, and whether or not past advances have been either totally or substantially recouped.

The rationale behind record release advances is that a music publisher stands to make a substantial amount of money from a hit single or chart album by an artist performing self-written songs. If the writer is already a successful recording artist, the chances of recouping such an advance are good. Also, a hit record receives plenty of airplay, which in turn can influence other recording artists to re-record ("cover") some of the songs and encourage film, television, and video game producers as well as advertising agencies and video companies to use the songs in their projects—occurrences that will bring the publisher additional income.

RELEASE OF RECORDINGS (MINI-MAX ADVANCES)

Many of the advance formulas for album releases are based on mini-max calculations which provide for advances to be paid in a pre-negotiated range (for example a $100,000 minimum and a $300,000 maximum advance for the next album).

The actual advance is determined by the monetary success of the prior album. Thus, if the most recent album was not successful, the advance for the next option album would be the minimum (i.e., $100,000). If, however, the most recently released prior album generated substantial royalties, the advance payable for the next album could reach the maximum figure (i.e., $300,000), depending on the formula used for calculating the advance. In the event that the earnings from the prior album are so significant that the advance would exceed the maximum, the advance payable will not be more than the maximum stated in the agreement.

As to what is included in the calculation of the mini-max formula, some agreements include only mechanical royalties earned from the prior album, others include performance income, others include mechanical, performance, and synchronization income and some include all types of earnings (or percentages thereof) regardless of source.

Also, there is often included in these min-max calculations a so-called subfloor which will allow the publisher to reduce the current advance by the amount of the writer's unrecouped advance balance but, in no event, to less than a certain stated amount. These subfloors help publishers in limiting their monetary risk on the new album when the prior one has not been successful and allows them to go forward with a writer that they believe in at a more affordable financial risk level. They also guarantee the writer though, that the advance will never be reduced to less than an agreed upon subfloor amount regardless of the amount of the unrecouped advance balance and the lack of success of a prior album or albums.

Many times these subfloor calculations result in an advance for an album which will be somewhere between the subfloor amount and the advance that would be payable under the mini-max formula if the subfloor advance did not exist. It all depends on the calculations and what income is included in the formula, as well as when the formula is calculated. One variable, among many, is whether only actual receipts received by the publisher are included or whether estimates of pipeline income (monies that have been earned but not yet received by the publisher) are somehow added to the mix of what should be recognized in the calculations to arrive at a final number.

ADVANCES BASED ON ALBUM CONTENT

If the co-publishing agreement is an album-based deal, the contract will contain language that calculates advances on the number of compositions controlled by the agreement that are actually contained on the album or, in the alternative, a specified percentage of all compositions on the album. For example, if a $100,000 advance is payable for a newly recorded and released album, the contract might condition payment of the full advance on the writer/artist having written 100% of all compositions on the album. If the album only contains 80% of the writer/artist's self-written compositions, the advance would be reduced by 20%. To put it another way, the writer/artist would receive 80% of the full advance under this scenario.

ADVANCES BASED ON LICENSING RATES

There also are provisions that can reduce the advance if the compositions are licensed and paid at less than an agreed-upon mechanical rate. One such clause might read that "for the full advance to be paid, the compositions written by the writer/artist must be licensed and paid at no less than a 75% of statutory rate for top-line United States normal retail sales of the album." Under this scenario, if the writer/artist's compositions were licensed at a 50% of statutory rate because of the effects of the controlled composition clause in the recording artist agreement, the recording of outside compositions, or the use of samples on the album, the advance for the album would be reduced by 33.33%. This same concept is used in writer-producer deals when separate advances are due when individual compositions are released.

COMMERCIAL RELEASE DEFINITION

Since many agreements base advances on the commercial release of albums, singles or other recordings, one of the more significant issues that is negotiated is the definition of what constitutes a commercial release of a recording. Obviously, depending on the amount of the advance that is payable to the songwriter or songwriter/recording artist, this can be an extremely important issue. For example, if the music publisher is obligated to pay an advance ranging from $100,000 to over $1 million upon the commercial release of an album, the publisher will want an assurance that the album is actually being released on a national basis so that it has a chance to succeed. For example, there might be language mandating that the release be through normal retail distribution channels. Other language may pre-condition the release on the record company distributing the album on a national basis to prevent an advance being paid on only a regional release. There are also provisions which change the advance, depending on whether the release is on a major, non-major, or indie label or available only for download. Occasionally, the agreement will stipulate that the record company must be committed to a certain amount of promotion and marketing money, especially if the artist is on an indie label.

Additionally, the publisher many times will provide that there must be a specified number of albums actually manufactured and distributed by the record company for an album to be deemed commercially released and trigger the payment of the release advance. For example, if there is a $150,000 advance payable on release of an album in the United States, the songwriter agreement or co-publishing agreement might contain a provision which states that in order for a release to occur, the record company must manufacture and distribute at least 20,000 physical units. This type of clause has nothing to do with actual sales. It only ensures that the record company is supporting the artist enough to manufacture and distribute a reasonable number of albums. In such a scenario, if the record company only manufactures and distributes 10,000 albums, no advance would be payable. Or, in the alternative, a reduced advance might be payable. This clause would definitely have an impact on an Internet-only release or where the Internet is the primary distribution platform.

COMMERCIAL RELEASE CONSIDERATIONS

With respect to what releases actually qualify toward the contractual commercial release commitment, there are many variations as to what counts and what doesn't count in a world of both physical and digital releases as well as digital-only releases.

For example some agreements state that a so called "bonus track" that is not contained on all commercially released formats or configurations of an album will not count. Other agreements might disqualify a release from a motion picture or television program unless the recording generates a certain stated amount of mechanical and/or performance income ($5,000, $10,000, $25,000, etc.). In virtually all agreements, a remix of an already released composition will not qualify as a new release.

In addition, there are many provisions dealing with what type of Internet-only release qualifies as a released composition counting toward a songwriter's release commitment. For example, does making a composition available for downloading or streaming on the Internet constitute a commercial release? In this regard, many agreements provide that the composition has to be a featured track from an album. Some contracts stipulate that the record company, other master owner, or distributor has to have a guaranteed marketing and promotion budget behind the Internet-only release with stated dollar amounts included. And other agreements state that there has to be certain stated amount of music publisher/songwriter royalties earned for an Internet-only release to count. There are innumerable variations in this area and the above just constitute some of the directions and considerations taken by publishers to ensure that an Internet-only release is a legitimate commercial release that has a chance of succeeding and earning money (especially since the release may trigger an advance payment or fulfill a commitment which triggers an option pickup or expiration of the active term of an agreement if there are no contractual options left).

NON-ALBUM-BASED ADVANCES

Some agreements provide that the advances will be paid out upon the writer fulfilling a stated portion of his or her minimum song delivery commitment for the particular contract period. These clauses usually contain language that triggers advance payments upon the later of a certain date and achievement of an agreed-upon delivery plateau. For example, if a writer has a commitment to create 12 new compositions during the year, the advance provisions of the agreement might read "$100,000 for the contract period payable $25,000 upon commencement of the period, $25,000 upon the later of the end of three months or 25% fulfillment of the minimum delivery commitment (completion of the third composition), $25,000 upon the later of the end of the sixth month of the contract period or 50% fulfillment of the minimum delivery commitment (completion of the sixth composition), and the final $25,000 upon the later of the end of nine months or 75% fulfillment of the minimum commitment (completion and delivery of the ninth composition). Sometimes the final advance is held until the writer fulfills 100% of the minimum commitment. This type of approach staggers the advance payments to the songwriter over the contract period and conditions actual payment upon the writer continuing to write during the term and meeting the various delivery deadlines negotiated.

This structure is used not only when the minimum delivery commitment relates to the creation of new compositions but is also used when there is a release commitment as well (for example, the writing of 12 new compositions with four of them being commercially released). Under this type of advance approach, if the writer has not achieved 25% of his or her minimum commitment by the end of the third month (which includes both the new songwriting commitment and the release commitment), the advance will not be paid. Payment will be postponed until the 25% plateau has been achieved. In almost all cases, release can be satisfied with a song written during a prior period provided it is the initial commercial release of the composition and the release is in the current contract period.

ADVANCES BASED ON SALES

In addition to the standard advance structures of most agreements, some contracts provide that the publisher will pay additional advances to the songwriter if a composition is on an album which sells an agreed-upon number of digital and physical units. The sales plateaus are commonly between 100,000 albums and 1,000,000 albums, but can be higher or lower depending on the amount of the advances being paid as well as the amount previously paid. For example, the contract might provide that an additional advance of $10,000 will be paid if a songwriter's composition is on an album that sells 250,000 full royalty-bearing units in the United States and an additional $10,000 if the album reaches 500,000 sales during the term. If the writer has more than one composition on an album, the same calculation would take place for each song. The amount of such advances is always conditioned on the composition being licensed and paid at a specified mechanical rate (e.g., 100%, 75%).

"A" SIDE SINGLE CHART ACTIVITY ADVANCES

Another approach to activity-based advances is to provide for the payment of additional monies if a composition is an "A" side single and it reaches certain positions on the national trade paper charts. Because chart activity is a definite barometer of financial success, extra advances are many times negotiated for reaching Top 20, Top 10, Top 5, and Number One. Some agreements provide for a separate advance if the song achieves qualifying positions on different charts (pop, hip-hop, country) and others pay only one advance regardless of the song's appearance on a number of charts.

REDUCED ADVANCES IF UNRECOUPED

If a songwriter has a substantial unrecouped advance balance at the time that a composition becomes eligible for an extra chart activity advance, the publishing contract might provide that the advance that is due the songwriter be reduced by a certain dollar amount. For example, if a songwriter agreement has a clause which provides that the writer will receive an extra advance of $20,000 if a composition reaches the Top 10 on the U.S. Singles Chart, the agreement may also have a clause that states that the chart activity advance will be reduced by 50% if the writer is unrecouped more than $100,000. There are many potential variations in this area, and the previous example is only mentioned to illustrate one of the ways a publisher will try to protect itself when it has advanced substantial monies to a writer and has only recouped a small portion of its investment when a writer begins to have some success.

This same type of clause may also apply to additional advances which are payable if a composition achieves certain sales plateaus (for example, if a composition is on an album that reaches 250,000 sold units). These types of advances are usually based on the songwriter having written 100% of the composition (with pro-rata reductions if the writer's share is less than that) and, if the advance is based on sales, a guaranteed mechanical royalty rate (such as 75%, 85%, or 100% of statutory), with reductions in the advance if the composition is licensed at less than that guaranteed rate. If the writer is known to co-write with other songwriters, the percentage required to receive the full advance is often based on 50% of the composition, with reductions occurring if the writer contributes less than 50%.

FLOW-THROUGH CLAUSES

If a writer has had success with other publishers prior to signing an agreement with a new publisher for future songs, the new publisher will many times request that royalties that are paid to the writer from the prior publisher (known as "flow-through" royalties) be sent to the new publisher even though the royalties are for compositions controlled by another publisher.

This request is many times made in cases where the new publisher is making a substantial dollar commitment to the writer for songs that, in many cases, have not yet been written, and represents a safety valve to help justify the monies being paid for a futures-only deal and help recover its investment in the writer. In some cases, there is a stated dollar figure (e.g., not more than $100,000 may be utilized for recoupment) and, in other cases, the flow-through will continue until all advances (or a percentage thereof) under the new deal have been recouped.

If this occurs, the so called flow-through royalties are many times used for recoupment of advance purposes only (e.g., any monies that are received from the prior publisher will be applied directly to the writer's unrecouped balance) but a publisher might request a small percentage of the flow-through monies as its retained publisher share (e.g., 2%, 5%).

In any event, it should be made very clear what happens when the flow-through requirements have been met (e.g., notice from the writer and confirmation from the new publisher, only one party notifying the prior publisher with proof of recoupment, the submission of a royalty statement indicating recoupment has occurred, etc.) to prevent disputes as to when the prior publisher should stop sending monies to the new publisher.

UNRECOUPABLE PAYMENTS

On occasion, a major publisher will give the writer payments that will not be recoupable from future royalties. Such payments are treated by the publisher as acquisition costs; the publisher is, in effect, buying the rights being transferred. This type of arrangement is not the norm, but it can occur when dealing with major recording artists or record producers who write their own songs. The payments are usually made upon the commercial release of an album containing a certain minimum percentage of songs written by the writer/artist or writer/producer, but are sometimes made at the commencement of the co-publishing agreement as a further inducement for the writer to sign the contract—especially when pre-existing songs are being brought into the agreement.

COSTS OF DEMONSTRATION RECORDINGS

Some of the necessary costs of doing business as a publisher are those incurred in the making of demo recordings that can be played for record company A&R executives, recording artists, or others who are responsible for listening to and selecting material for singles or albums. The costs of such demo sessions are usually 50% to 100% chargeable to the songwriter, recoupable from royalties due the songwriter, or recoupable from the gross income (or net income, in certain cases) prior to distribution of income under the agreement. Since in the co-publishing arrangement the writer's company is also the publisher of any compositions that are produced at a demo session, the costs of such sessions are many times divided between the major company and the writer's company according to each party's percentage of copyright ownership or income participation, with the writer's company's contribution normally being recovered from future earnings of the songs rather than paid up front. A number of agreements also include a maximum cost allowable for the making of such demos. For example, it might be written into the contract that the total costs of any demo session shall not exceed a certain amount of money per song. The limit can be put at a dollar figure, depending on the type of demo to be made and the current rate of making such demos in professional recording studios. Some agreements provide for a stated agreed upon demo fund amount for each composition approved for a demo (for example, $800 in outside costs for each wholly written composition with pro-rata reductions if a song is co-written.) Such a limit on spending will protect the writer against large expenditures that were not anticipated at the time the agreement was originally signed. It also protects the publisher from a writer exceeding the agreed-upon budget if the writer is in charge of the session since any excess will be chargeable to or paid by the writer on a 100% basis. However, many writers have all the necessary recording equipment in their home studios, so these limits are becoming less of an issue (other than how reimbursement is to be handled). The writer is never required to put up any money for the demo recording session, since any cost that may be attributable to the writer for the session will be deducted from future royalties.

ADDITIONAL COSTS

Other costs of doing business are usually shared by the major publisher and the writer's company by means of a deduction-from-earnings approach. These costs include copyright fees, lead sheet preparation fees, and legal fees. Once again, a portion of these amounts is deducted from future royalties due the writer's company (and those of the writer, if provided for in the songwriter's contract which is collected from the writer's performing rights organization) and are not paid by the writer's company when the costs are actually incurred. Normal overhead costs such as rent, electricity, telephones, and such are not charged to the writer's company.

PAYMENT OF ROYALTIES TO SONGWRITERS

The major publisher initially collects all monies earned by the compositions (excluding, in most cases, the songwriter's share of performance income) and distributes the writer's 50% share of income directly to the writer. On occasion, the major publisher will pay such monies directly to the writer's company, which will then be responsible for paying the writer his or her share of songwriter royalties.

SHARING OF INCOME BETWEEN THE TWO PUBLISHERS

Under the terms of most co-publishing agreements, the major publisher will pay the writer's company a percentage of all earnings that are received, minus the following deductions: all songwriter royalties; costs of printing, arranging, and editing printed editions of the songs; all fees of the Harry Fox Agency, Inc., or other collection agencies; administrative charges of foreign collection agencies or foreign subpublishers; and certain agreed-upon administrative, promotion, and copyright fees.

For example, the following clause, in one variation or another, is found in virtually all co-publishing agreements:

Publisher shall pay to Co-Publisher fifty percent (50%) of the net income actually received in the United States by Publisher or credited to Publisher's account against a prior advance from the exploitation of the Compositions. "Net income," as used herein, shall mean the gross receipts derived by Publisher from the exploitation of Compositions, less the following:

a. Royalties and other sums that are paid by Publisher to the author and composer of the Compositions.

b. Actual and reasonable collection or other fees customarily and actually charged by the Harry Fox Agency, Inc., the Canadian Musical Reproduction Rights Agency, Ltd. (CMRRA), and any other industry-wide collection agent which may be used by Publisher and, if applicable, subpublishers which may be used by Publisher.

c. Administrative and exploitation expenses of Publisher with respect to the Compositions, including: (i) out-of-pocket copyright registration fees and costs, (ii) the costs of transcribing lead sheets, and (iii) the costs of producing demonstration records, to the extent not recouped pursuant to the terms of the Songwriter's Agreement.

d. The costs of printing and distribution of the Compositions provided Publisher actually incurs such costs.

PRE-RECOUPMENT VS. POST-RECOUPMENT ROYALTIES

Depending on bargaining power, songwriters may be able to receive increased royalties from a music publisher once all advances paid or payable under the songwriter or co-publishing agreement have been recouped. Such clauses are not that common but are available in certain situations.

For example, if a co-publishing agreement provides for the writer and the writer's publishing company to receive 75% of non-performance income, 50% of the publisher's share of performance income and 70% for synchronization income, these percentages might be increased to 80% of non-performance income, 60% of publisher performance income and 75% for synchronization income after all advances have been recouped.

In most cases, this increased post-recoupment royalty percentage will commence for income received in the accounting period after recoupment has occurred and is usually conditioned on the recoupment of all advances payable under the agreement being recouped to prevent situations where, because of additional advances being paid in the future (e.g., an advance for the delivery or release of a new album or an option exercise, etc.), royalty percentages are constantly changing due to scenarios such as recoupment during one period and non-recoupment during a subsequent period.

ADMINISTRATION CHARGES

Some publishers will occasionally deduct an additional 10% to 15% administration charge on either all gross income or the publisher's share of income (i.e., gross monies less writer's royalties) derived from the songs covered by the agreement to cover general administrative and promotion costs. This administration charge may also be used to cover such costs as copyright fees and the preparation of lead sheets, if recovery of such costs is not provided for in another part of the contract.

THE WRITER'S PERFORMANCE RIGHT INCOME

One major exception to the rule that all monies due the songwriter are collected by the publisher occurs in the area of performance right income, since all monies earned from the performances of a writer's songs on radio and television stations, as well as the Internet, are sent directly to the songwriter by either ASCAP, BMI, SESAC, Global Music Rights, or their foreign affiliated societies. These monies will not be collected by the publisher unless there is an express agreement to the contrary (e.g., a clause that allows the publisher to recoup an advance from the songwriter's share of performance income and the assignment of such royalties or letter of direction to pay is permitted under ASCAP, BMI, SESAC, or Global Music Rights rules) or the music publisher has licensed such rights directly to a broadcaster, Internet site, or other licensee.

THE PUBLISHER'S PERFORMANCE RIGHT INCOME

There are two separate ways of sharing the publisher's performance right income from ASCAP, BMI, SESAC, or GMR. Under the first and more standard type of agreement, the PRO pays the major publisher all the publisher's performance royalties, and the major publisher will then pay the writer's company its share. Under the second type of arrangement, ASCAP, BMI, SESAC, or GMR pays the writer's company as well as the major publisher directly and simultaneously. The latter type of arrangement is not that common and will virtually never occur while the major publisher has unrecouped advances to the writer or the writer's publishing company on its balance sheet.

REVERSIONS AND DIRECT COLLECTION OF INCOME

Most co-publishing agreements last for the life of copyright of the compositions controlled by the agreement. Occasionally, especially where the writer is a successful recording artist or producer with bargaining strength, the compositions may revert to the songwriter's publishing company after a number of years subsequent to the expiration of the term or after all advances have been recouped. Additionally, some agreements provide that, even though the song ownership rights do not revert, the songwriter's publishing company will be entitled, at some specified time in the future, to collect its share of all royalties (including songwriter monies) directly from any users or music-industry collection organizations. The writer's company may also be allowed to administer, control, and issue licenses for its share of each composition, with the major publisher licensing only its respective share pursuant to a co-administration arrangement. For example, under such a reversion of administration rights, a film producer who wants to use a song in a motion picture will request a license and fee quote from both the major publisher and the writer's company, and if the song is used, both companies will issue the license for their respective shares and be paid directly.

REVERSION

In recent years, reversion clauses have also been negotiated in agreements with songwriters who have not had a history of success. This usually occurs when the writer is a recording artist or recording group who has just signed a record contract and there are a number of publishers bidding for the same act. It also occurs when the writer is a record producer. Reversion provisions are also given by some publishers to a songwriter when a song is on the charts or has just been released to good reviews from the trade magazines to secure the song.

The issue of reversion of rights to compositions is one of the most important matters in any negotiation. The response to this issue can, in many cases, either make or break the deal. In fact, a songwriter might take less money in advances if a shorter reversion clause is offered by the music publisher. On the other hand, if the songwriter is demanding large advances or the publisher is offering substantial monies to sign the songwriter, the reversion issue might take a back seat to the money issues. As in every negotiation, resolution of the major deal points depends on the bargaining power, needs, expectations, experience, representation, and perspective of the parties. If, for example, the songwriter's main focus is to secure guaranteed money, that perspective may dominate the negotiations. However, if the main issue is to regain rights at some time in the future, that driving force may influence the give and take on other issues.

Some examples of the many ways that the reversion issue is handled are:

Reversion of Unexploited Compositions. Under this type of reversion clause, the music publisher agrees to re-assign to the songwriter all rights in compositions that have not been commercially exploited as of a certain date. For example, the publisher might agree to give the songwriter back any composition which has not been recorded and released to the general public; been used in a motion picture, video game, television program, or advertising commercial; or been used in any other way that has generated income during the term of the songwriter/co-publishing agreement, or within three years after the term has expired. In this scenario, if a composition was still unexploited three years after the expiration of the active term of the agreement, the songwriter could cause a reversion. In virtually all cases, however, if the songwriter received advances from the music publisher and those advances have not been recouped, the reversion of rights will occur only after all advances have been earned back or repaid. The rationale for this position is that the publisher will not want to lose control of any composition which might have a chance of generating income in the future and allow it to recoup advance monies it paid to the songwriter.

Reversion of the Writer's Songwriter and Co-Publishing Share of Compositions. Some reversion clauses provide that, at some date in the future, the publisher will re-assign to the songwriter both the songwriter's share of compositions plus the songwriter's co-publisher's share of the composition. For example, if the songwriter is the only writer on a composition and has a 50/50 co-publishing agreement with the major publisher, the major publisher would return to the songwriter the full 50% writer's share plus the 25% share owned by the writer's publishing company. The major publisher would retain its 25% interest, and all parties would separately license, administer, and collect monies for their respective interests. In our example, if $1,000 in mechanical or motion picture synchronization income were earned from a composition, the songwriter would be entitled to license the full 50% songwriter's share (i.e., $500) and one-half of the remaining publisher's share of income (i.e., $250). The major publisher would license the other one-half of the publishing income (i.e., $250). Thus, instead of all monies flowing through the major publisher who, in turn, would then pay the songwriter and co-publisher their royalties, all parties would collect their respective shares directly from the user of the composition (in this case, the record company or film producer).

Under this type of reversion, the songwriter will usually sign a co-administration agreement with the major publisher which will establish the specific ground rules for the administration and licensing of reverted compositions, legislate that all users of the compositions be instructed to pay each party directly for their share of each composition, and further provide that if either party receives money due the other party, it will pay such monies to the other within a certain number of days either after receipt or after the close of its next royalty-accounting period.

Reversion of the songwriter's share and the co-publisher's share of a composition is almost always conditioned upon the major music publisher having recouped all advances paid to the songwriter. This reversion will usually take place upon the later of either an agreed-upon number of years after the expiration of the term of the songwriter/co-publishing agreement or recovery of all advances paid to the songwriter. For example, the songwriter might receive both the songwriter's share and co-publisher's share to all compositions upon the later of 12 years after the end of the term of the songwriter/co-publishing agreement or recovery of all advances. In such a case, if there still was an outstanding unrecouped advance balance at the end of the twelfth year, there would be no reversion to the songwriter at that time. In the event all advances were recouped in the fifteenth year, however, reversion would then occur.

Under this scenario which provides that the writer will get the songwriter and co-publisher share of compositions back, the major publisher many times will keep its share for life of copyright (subject, of course, to any copyright law limitations). Other times, the major publisher will retain its share for only a limited amount of time as negotiated in the agreement. For example, in these non-life of copyright situations, the major publisher might keep its share of rights for an additional 5 to 10 years after the reversion of the writer and co-publisher share and will assign its share back to the writer only at that time. This is referred to as a graduated reversion since the rights of the composition are given back to the songwriter in two stages rather than all at one time.

Reversion of All Rights to Compositions. Under this type of reversion clause, the music publisher agrees to re-assign to the songwriter all rights in all compositions controlled by the agreement as of a certain date after the expiration of the term of the songwriter/co-publishing agreement. For example, the publisher might agree to give the songwriter back all compositions controlled by the agreement 20 years after the term has expired. In virtually all cases, if the songwriter received advances from the music publisher and those advances have not been recouped, the reversion of rights will occur only after all advances have been recouped via earnings or a payback by the songwriter. In some cases, however, there can be a full reversion of all rights regardless of whether or not the publisher has recouped its advances to the songwriter, but this usually only happens if the songwriter has extremely strong bargaining power.

Reversion of Compositions Created Prior to the Agreement. On occasion, if the songwriter brought a pre-existing catalogue of compositions into the agreement and the music publisher did not give the songwriter a separate advance for those compositions, the publisher may agree to re-assign those pre-existing compositions which have not been recorded or earned income upon the expiration of the term or a few years after the term has ended. For example, a clause might read that any composition which was written prior to the commencement date which has not been commercially exploited within two years after the term of the agreement has ended will be re-assigned to the songwriter, regardless of whether or not the publisher has recouped its advances. If, however, the pre-existing catalogue was a basis for the advances given to the songwriter, it is rare for such compositions to be re-assigned until all advances have been recouped, regardless of the fact that such pre-existing compositions remain commercially unexploited.

Reversion Notices. It should be noted that when contractual reversion clauses are contained in a songwriter or co-publishing agreement, the reversion to the songwriter is many times not automatic regardless of whether all the criteria for reversion (e.g., all advances having been recouped, a set number of years have occurred after the active term of the agreement ended, etc.) have occurred.

In this regard, some agreements provide that the songwriter or co-publisher has to give the administering publisher actual written notice that everything required for a reversion to occur has happened. For example, an agreement might state that the writer, in order to effectuate reversion, must send a notice upon the later of a set number of years and the end of the accounting period during which all advances were recouped. If the notice is not sent in, the reversion will not take place until, of course, the writer finally sends the required notice. Other agreements provide that if the writer does not send notice within a stated period of time, reversion will not occur.

Effective Reversion Dates. When reversion provisions are put into a contract, the issue of when the reversion will actually take effect will come into play. There are usually two ways of resolving this issue. One is to have the reversion take place on the actual day that is stated in the agreement. For example, if the agreement is dated April 17 and the reversion is to occur ten years later, the effective reversion date will be April 17 and the re-assignment of rights and income will occur on that date.

In many agreements, however, the reversion will take effect at the end of the quarterly or semi-annual accounting period during which the reversion occurred. Using the April 17 example, if all advances were recouped on April 2 of the tenth year, reversion would take effect on June 30 (the end of the next contractual royalty accounting period).

Monies Earned Before the Reversion Date. In most cases, any royalty income that has been earned but not yet paid to the music publisher as of the effective reversion date will still be collected by the major publisher, even though rights to the compositions have reverted to the songwriter. For example, the performance royalties for a television broadcast of a composition will be paid by ASCAP, BMI, SESAC, or GMR months after the performance has occurred. If the broadcast of a composition on a series episode occurred prior to the reversion date, the music publisher would usually be entitled to participate in the royalties generated by the broadcast since the actual use occurred while the publisher still owned and controlled the rights to the composition. The same principle would also apply to CD sales, downloads, and other royalty-generating uses which happen during the term of the publisher's rights. There are usually time limits placed on such collection of income rights which range from 6 to 18 months. A clause might state that the major music publisher will be entitled to receive its share of any royalties that are generated by uses of the composition during the period of its rights, provided it receives such monies within 12 months of the expiration date of its rights to control the composition. In this example, if a use occurred in January for a composition which reverted in February and the royalties were received in August, the major publisher would be entitled to its share of those royalties since the income was received within 12 months from the February reversion date. If the royalty income earned in January was distributed by the user in March of the following year, however, the major publisher would not be entitled to its share of such income even though the use occurred during its term of rights, because the receipt of such royalty income was outside the 12-month period. It should be noted that many agreements provide for a longer collection period for foreign income.

In some cases when a reversion occurs, the major publisher will no longer be entitled to collect monies earned prior to the termination date but will still have the right to share in such income. For example, the contract might provide that, upon termination of a publisher's rights, all monies, regardless of when earned, will be collected by the songwriter's publishing company or its new administrator. The publisher that lost its rights, however, may still be entitled to receive its percentage of income on all royalties earned for uses during the term of its rights which occurred prior to the contract expiration date. In these cases, the monies would be collected by the songwriter's publishing company or new administrator who, in turn, will pay the appropriate share to the major publisher that lost its rights.

There are myriad variations that can be negotiated in the area of reversions (for example, the major publisher's right to receive its share of income from litigation or settlements regardless of when paid), and all depend on the experience and bargaining power of the parties. The prior examples are designed to illustrate only a few of the many approaches.

Repayment of Advances to Cause a Reversion. If the agreement provides that the compositions will revert to the songwriter at a set date in the future, but only if all the advances paid to the songwriter have been recouped, many agreements allow the songwriter to repay the unrecouped balance plus, in a large number of cases, an extra percentage to ensure that the publisher will be entitled to the contractual profit it would have received had the advances been recouped through earnings. For example, if the writer has a 50/50 co-publishing agreement with the publisher and a $100,000 advance has been paid, $133,000 in royalty income would have to be generated by the compositions for that advance to be recouped.

$113,000	Income received
x 75%	Writer/co-publisher share
$100,000	Amount applied to recoupable advance

If the agreement provides that the compositions shall be returned to the songwriter upon the later of 15 years or recovery of advances, the publisher will usually agree to allow the writer to repay 133% of any outstanding advance balance to recoup all advances. This formula guarantees that the publisher will receive its 25% profit margin. If the language provides that the writer may repay only the actual amount of the unrecouped advance balance, the publisher will just receive its money back and forego any profit. It will also incur a loss due to its not receiving what it could have earned by investing the money elsewhere. Depending on the negotiations, compromises are many times made to provide for a payback of between 110% and 120% of the unrecouped advance balance.

ROYALTY DISTRIBUTIONS TO THE WRITER'S COMPANY
Under most co-publishing agreements, the major publisher will pay the writer's company within 45, 60, or 90 days following each semiannual accounting period. This normally occurs between August 15 and September 30 for all monies received during the previous January 1 through June 30 period, and between February 15 and March 31 for all monies that are received during the previous July 1 through December 31 period. A number of companies distribute on a quarterly basis with the same 45-, 60-, or 90-day time limits. Certain publishers also provide their writers and co-publishers immediate access to their accounts via protected Internet portals so that they are able to be aware of monies that have been received by the publisher even before the royalties and statements are sent per the terms of their contracts.

RIGHT TO MATCH AN OFFER OF SALE
Many co-publishing agreements contain provisions which give the major music publisher the right to match an offer that is received by the co-publisher from a third party interested in buying the co-publisher's interest in a catalogue. In these cases, the

co-publisher must send the major publisher a summary of the substantive terms being offered, and the major publisher will have an agreed-upon time period to digest the third-party offer and either match the offer or decline. If the major publisher decides to match the offer within the time period agreed to by the parties in the contract (e.g., within 30 days, 45 days, etc.), the major publisher will buy the co-publisher's share of the catalogue on the terms offered. If the major publisher decides not to match, the co-publisher will be able to finalize the sale with the third party on the terms proposed. If the substantive provisions of the offer change after the major publisher has declined to match, however, and become less favorable to the co-publisher (for example, if the monies for the sale of the co-publisher's share of the catalogue are reduced in the negotiations with the third party), the major music publisher who declined to match the more favorable offer will usually have the right to match the new lower offer.

For example, if a songwriter wanted to put his or her co-publisher's share of the catalogue on the market for sale, received a bona fide offer of $2 million from a third party, presented the offer to the major publisher that owned the other 50% interest, and had the offer rejected by that publisher, the songwriter would be able to sell the co-publisher's share for $2 million. If as a result of the prospective buyer's investigation of the catalogue, however, it was discovered that the income levels on which the purchase price was based were not what was represented by the songwriter, and because of this the buyer lowered its offer for the catalogue (e.g., from $2 million to $1.5 million), the major music publisher would again have the right to match this new offer since the only offer that it had rejected was the $2 million one. This right to match a changed offer also can be triggered by a revision of any substantive term of the original offer and does not only have to relate to the money aspects of the deal. For example, if the original offer was for $500,000 and an ownership term of 10 years, but, in the course of negotiations, the retention of ownership by the new buyer was increased to 20 years, the major publisher would have the right to match the new offer because an important provision had been changed in the offer that it had refused to match.

This right to match usually is exercisable by the major publisher if the offer is received during the term of the agreement and, in many cases, the retention period, if there is one. If an offer is received from a third party after these periods are over, the matching right provisions will normally have lapsed and the major publisher will not be able to match the terms.

It should also be stressed that any sale to a third party of the songwriter's co-publisher's share will still be subject to the rights of the major publisher. For example, if the original co-publishing agreement provided for the major publisher to exclusively administer the catalogue, the new owner would not be able to administer the co-publisher's share that it acquired. Also, if there were still some outstanding unrecouped advances, any earnings related to the acquired share of the catalogue would be used by the major publisher to recoup advances prior to any monies being paid to the new owner.

RIGHT OF FIRST NEGOTIATION

A number of agreements provide the administrating publisher with the right for a set period of time to negotiate with the co-publisher for the right to acquire the co-publisher's rights if the writer is interested in selling. Sometimes these clauses are very formal in their approach and other times very general. They do give the major publisher the first shot at making an offer which is a valuable option even though there is no binding commitment to sell.

The first negotiation period many times lasts for 30 days after a certain agreed upon date or, on occasion, after the original publisher receives the details of an actual offer from a third party for the rights involved in the negotiation (e.g., current rights future rights, etc.). If the original publisher actually makes an offer during this period but the writer or co-publisher rejects the offer, the writer will usually be allowed to enter into an agreement with another party with no constraints after the first negotiation period has expired. Some agreements provide that if an agreement with the third party is not signed within a stated period of time (e.g., 90 days), then the original publisher may be granted the right to enter into an agreement on the same terms of the third party offer which was not consummated (much like a matching right). Other agreements give the original publisher a first negotiation period to see if a deal can be made with absolutely no commitments by either party (other than to act in good faith) if an agreement cannot be entered into within the first negotiation time.

PARTICIPATION AGREEMENT

There is a variation to the co-publishing agreement that provides the songwriter with the same income-sharing benefits but does not provide the writer with an actual co-copyright ownership position in his or her compositions. This type of arrangement is called a participation agreement or income participation agreement. Under this type of contract, the songwriter does not have his or her own publishing company (as occurs in a co-publishing agreement) co-owning the copyright and getting credit on recordings and other uses, but the writer does receive a share of the publisher's portion of income. The financial aspects are exactly the same; the only difference is that the songwriter doesn't have to form a publishing company.

SIGNED DEAL MEMOS

Because it can take anywhere from a number of weeks to a number of months from the time you start to negotiate the songwriter/co-publishing agreement to the time that the agreement is actually signed, many publishing companies use what is known as a "deal memo," "memorandum of understanding," "MOU," or "heads of agreement" to set forth the major points of the overall agreement. These deal memos are usually from five to ten pages long with a few extra pages of exhibits (e.g., copyright assignment, letters of direction to record companies and to ASCAP, BMI, SESAC, or GMR, a list of existing compositions) and are used frequently to commit the parties quickly and enable the songwriter to receive a portion of the advance that would otherwise only be payable after the signing of the long-form agreement. The obvious value of signing a deal memo is that the publisher and writer can commence their relationship immediately and money will be freed up for the writer to get his or her financial affairs in order and take some of the pressure off while the lawyers negotiate and draft all the terms of the contractual relationship. The negative to signing such a deal memo is that you might run into a number of substantive problem areas or issues of disagreement during the negotiation of the long form, so that the short-form deal memo (with its inherent lack of specificity other than the major terms) might be the only document that is ever signed. Obviously, the more specific the deal memo can be on all the major points, the better. It cannot, however, be so specific and cover so many eventualities that it becomes a long-form agreement with the attendant time delays that you are trying to avoid by using the short form.

RECAP

The co-publishing agreement is an excellent way for a songwriter to realize income over and above the normal 50% writer's share of royalties. Yet such an arrangement may not be available to most songwriters during the early part of their careers or, to many, during any part of their careers. It is available to songwriters who have had commercial success either as a writer, as a writer/recording artist, or as a writer/producer, and to writers who have a recording commitment or are about to sign with a record company. The music business has been changing in this area, however, with more and more songwriters being able to retain a portion of their publishing income. For this reason, the co-publishing agreement is taking on an ever-increasing role in a writer's ability to maximize his or her present and long-term income.

ADMINISTRATION AGREEMENTS

Because the music and entertainment businesses are extremely complex, it is in many cases extremely wise for a writer to find a full-service major music publisher to handle the everyday administrative duties involved in protecting and promoting his or her songs, as well as registering, licensing, collecting, auditing, and processing the income those songs generate. One of the main differences between the co-publishing agreement and the administration agreement is that the songwriter (through a publishing company that he or she owns) retains full copyright ownership of all songs. In addition, since the fees charged by the major publisher doing the administrative work are usually not large, the writer will normally be entitled to retain 80% to 90% of all monies earned. This arrangement is usually reserved for established songwriters who have formed their own publishing companies and are not currently under a co-publishing agreement with another publisher, but can be available to others.

FEES CHARGED FOR ADMINISTRATIVE SERVICES

Depending on the bargaining power of the writer and the services being offered by the administrating publisher, the fees charged are between 10% and 20% of all income collected. However, if the writer is a successful recording artist who automatically generates substantial income, or the administered catalogue is a motion picture or television company with guaranteed performance income, the fees charged for administration may be as low as 5% to 7% of the publisher's share of income, depending on the services being provided. For example, if the writer is looking only for the proper registration of songs with performance and mechanical rights organizations, the filing of copyright applications, and the dissemination of necessary information to ensure the proper collection of royalties, he or she should negotiate for lower fees. And since the administrating publisher usually pays royalties on a semiannual basis (although advances of a portion of the monies in the system are many times available), if the catalogue is generating substantial earnings, the interest on the monies being held can certainly cover a large number of costs and ensure a profit. But if the services needed include not only the above but also promotion, the recording of new demo recordings, the drafting of songwriter agreements, the negotiation of licenses, the securing of new usages, issuance of separate royalty statements to songwriters, and counseling as to worldwide trends or developments in the music and entertainment industries, higher fees can certainly be justified.

DURATION

As there is no transfer of copyright ownership in an administration agreement, the duration is always for a specified number of years, normally with all rights (other than collection of monies earned during the contract period) reverting to the writer's company at the end of the term. In most cases, the duration of administration arrangements is between three and seven years, but depending on the needs of the parties and whether advances have been recouped, the term can be shorter or longer.

TERRITORY

There are many variations in the territory covered by an agreement, since this area, once again, is totally negotiable. For example, many agreements cover the United States or the United States and Canada, but an agreement can entail the world or selected countries throughout the world (e.g., all English-speaking territories). If the territory encompasses countries outside the United States, there may be an administration fee (usually 10% to 25%) deducted in the foreign country and, in many cases, an additional percentage fee charged on the foreign monies received and processed by the administrating publisher in the United States. Such a fee is justifiable if the U.S. publisher is performing a real service (for example, servicing foreign countries with cue sheets and performance and record information, organizing the catalogue for proper representation, drafting songwriter and other related agreements, issuing licenses, or preparing royalty statements). If the U.S. publisher is performing little or no real function, however, the fees charged on foreign-generated earnings may be minimal or there may be no fee at all.

ROYALTY STATEMENTS

Depending on the nature of the agreement and the fees being charged, the administering publisher may either prepare and send statements specifying the gross income for each song (which would necessitate writer statements being prepared by the administered company) or compute and prepare both writer and publisher statements for all compositions that earned money. Obviously, since the latter alternative is more costly and time-consuming, the administration fees charged are normally higher.

ROYALTY PAYMENT DATES

As with the co-publishing agreement, accounting statements and royalty checks are usually issued twice per year within 45 days to three months after each six-month period. For example, monies received by the administrator during January through June of any year would be distributed between August 15 and October 1 of that year. Other agreements provide for quarterly accountings within 45, 60, or 90 days after the end of each quarter.

COVER RECORDS AND NEW USES

If a major reason for entering an administration agreement is the use of the established publisher's creative and promotion staff, many contracts provide incentives if a new recording or motion picture/television/video game/advertising commercial use is secured. For example, the writer may agree to increase the fee retained by the administrating publisher from 20% to between 25% and 40% if the major publisher's staff is responsible for convincing a recording artist to release a new version of a song. If that new version reaches the charts as the "A" side of a single, the percentage may be further increased, and if it achieves the Top 10 or Top 5, yet a further increase might be provided. There are innumerable variations in this area, including transfer of a portion of the copyright ownership to a song and extension of the term of the agreement. Such an approach can give the administrating publisher the necessary incentive to expend its total promotion efforts on behalf of the administered compositions.

COVER RECORDS

Some illustrations of increased percentages and extension rights based on what is achieved by the activities of the administrating publisher are:

If the administrating publisher secures a new recording which becomes an "A" side single and reaches the Top 10 on the trade paper charts, the fee chargeable on income from that version is increased from 15% to 25% of gross receipts.

If the administrating publisher secures the use of a new recording of a composition in a motion picture, video game, or television series, the percentage on that synchronization fee is increased from the overall catalogue 10% to 20%.

If the administrator secures a use of a composition in a motion picture and the composition is also included on the soundtrack album from the film, the administrating publisher will not only receive an increased motion picture synchronization fee but also an increase on the mechanical royalties earned from sales and downloads of the album or single from the album.

If the administrator secures a new recording of a composition and that new recording is on an album that sells in excess of 250,000 copies, the administration fee on the mechanical income generated from sales of that album will be increased from 15% to 25%.

If the new recording achieves either 500,000 sales or reaches the Top 10 of the trade paper singles chart, the administrator will be able to control that composition for an additional three years after the end of the term of the administration agreement. If the administrator secures the first recording of a composition which had been previously unexploited, and that recording becomes a Top 20 single or sells over 500,000 copies, the administrator will become a co-copyright owner and life-of-copyright co-publisher of that composition in addition to receiving an increased fee on earnings generated by the composition.

NEW USES

In addition to the securing of first use recordings or newly recorded cover versions by artists other than the performer who originally recorded the composition, it is very common to create incentives for the administrating publisher by increasing the administration fee that is able to be charged on income being collected if the administrating publisher has, through its efforts, secured a new use of a composition. Such new uses can be the licensing of a composition in a motion picture, in a television series, in an advertising commercial, in a video or in any other media which has been secured by the administrating publisher (a Karaoke use, a lyric reprint in a novel, a video game use, a special products recording such as "classic love songs of the '90s," etc.).

In many cases, the whole point of entering into an administration agreement with an established publisher is to get the benefit of the contacts, power, promotion people, and resources of that publisher. It's no secret that certain music publishers are known for their contacts, their ability to license compositions at a competitive rate, their ability to give quick responses to any request and react to the economics of any situation. It, therefore, can be very lucrative to a songwriter or writer/performer to enter into such an agreement with a well-connected publisher because, if the compositions are right for other projects, the short- and long-term financial upside can be very substantial. Looking at the term of years that a composition is protected by copyright, as well as its ability to earn money, the securing of new uses is vital to the continued financial rewards that come from writing a song. For example, if the music publisher can secure a substantial number of new uses (television series, motion pictures, videos, etc.) that have a life of their own for many years into the future, the songwriter has struck gold.

MONIES EARNED DURING THE TERM

Because receipt of royalties for download and CD, radio, and television performances, and other uses can take from six months to more than two years from the date that a royalty-generating use of a song occurs, many publishers provide that they will be entitled to collect all monies earned during the term of the administration period regardless of whether those monies are received after the expiration date of the agreement. These provisions, in effect, guarantee that the administrator will get its fee on all sales, performances, or other uses that occur during the period it has rights to the compositions. On the flip side of the coin, the writer will try to limit the time period that the administrator is entitled to collect. If the concept is acceptable, this issue is usually settled by allowing the administrating publisher to accrued income collection rights for nine to 18 months after the term of the agreement has expired.

For example, if a composition is performed in a United States television series in December of a given year, the performance royalties generated by that broadcast will not be distributed to the music publisher by the performing rights organization for from six to seven months after the end of the calendar quarter during which the performance occurred (in this case, the October through December quarter). If the term of the administration agreement ended on December 31 with all rights reverting on that date, the publisher would not be entitled to collect the royalties for that performance (regardless of the fact that it happened during the term) because the actual royalty distribution by the performing rights organization would be made after the term had expired. The same would be true of album or individual track sales during the last few months of the term, because record companies normally pay mechanical royalties 45 days after the end of each quarter. Having the right to collect, process, and retain its fee on royalties actually generated during the term (so-called accrued royalties), even though payments from uses of the compositions are made after the agreement has ended, enables the music publisher to reap the benefits that occurred during the term of its administration rights.

ADVANCES

As with the co-publishing agreement, advances are many times given to songwriters and their publishing companies, all of which are recoupable from their share of the income generated during the term of the agreement.

As with all other agreements, the amount of the advance is dependent upon many factors, including the past earnings of the catalogue, whether future compositions are included as opposed to a set group of pre-existing compositions, as well as how confident the publisher is that it can secure new uses of the catalogue and generate increased income.

PROS AND CONS OF ADMINISTRATION AGREEMENTS

Songwriters who own the publishing rights to their songs can gain some real benefits by allowing a full-service publisher to handle all the business, licensing, and promotion aspects of their catalogues. But considering the demands on both time and personnel (registering copyrights; registering with ASCAP, BMI, SESAC, GMR, or the Harry

Fox Agency; negotiating and issuing licenses; drafting agreements; preparing royalty statements; filing infringement suits or negotiating settlements; promoting songs for television, motion pictures, video games, and commercials; paying for demo sessions; notifying foreign countries; organizing a catalogue), some publishers are not that interested in certain administration deals. Obviously, if a substantial amount of work is going to be done and all songs will be lost in three to five years, many publishers feel that it is just not worth the trouble, especially since time and effort are being taken away from handling the songs that they own for the life of copyright. Additionally, the profit margins on many of these agreements are so small that they are not worthwhile.

On the other hand, if an administered catalogue is earning substantial monies (e.g., a hit recording artist's songs or a motion picture or television catalogue), the administration fee as well as the interest earned on the monies generated might be well worth the efforts expended, regardless of the limited duration of representation. In addition, if an administering publisher is weak in one genre of music (e.g., rock, soul, pop, hip-hop, standards, or country), it may enter into such an agreement just to get a foothold in that area. There are also some catalogues that are so prestigious by their very nature that many publishers will accept a short-term administration relationship because being associated with such a catalogue will enhance their reputation and, more than likely, generate additional business from other sources.

And if a music publisher knows that the catalogue has been underexploited in the past and feels that its promotion department can secure new cover recordings or film, television, video game, cell phone, and soundtrack uses, an administration arrangement may be attractive, especially if the fee is increased on new uses secured by the publisher's activities. In addition, if the past business practices of the people who ran the catalogue were not good, a major publisher may enter into an agreement because it knows that it will be able to track down and collect a substantial amount of missing or unpaid royalties via audits, litigation, and business acumen—a factor that can make an administration agreement very lucrative, despite its short-term nature and smaller profit margins. In many cases, if the administrating publisher increases the income of the catalogue, the contract may be renewed for continuing periods, which can turn a short-term relationship into one that lasts for many years of profitability for all parties.

CHOOSING THE RIGHT ADMINISTRATOR

Since an administration agreement, by its very nature, is usually not a commitment for an extended period of time, many writers do not undertake the necessary research to find out which publisher is best suited for their needs. After all, many feel that if they make a mistake, it can always be rectified by going to an experienced publisher when the current agreement ends. But a great deal of damage can be done in a very short period of time and a substantial amount of money can be lost by being with the wrong administrator—whether it be a publisher, lawyer, manager, or other representative. A writer must be aware that two or three years can, in the wrong hands, create a lifetime of problems and that any decision should be made only after extensive research on the reputation, personnel, and capabilities of the company being chosen to act as administrator, regardless of the amount of up-front advance money that may be offered to secure the deal.

CO-ADMINISTRATION AND JOINT ADMINISTRATION

When a composition is co-written by a number of songwriters, all of whom are signed to different publishing companies, the various publishers many times enter into what is known as a co-administration or joint administration agreement. This type of agreement will define the rights of all the parties with respect to licensing the composition and collecting royalties from uses. It is also many times used to document the percentages of all publishers when a song is sampled. The agreement has a number of variations, but in most cases it will provide that each publisher may only negotiate for and license its respective share of the composition to ensure that any licensee must go to each publisher for permission to use the composition. For example, if a motion picture producer wants to use a composition in a theatrical film and there are three publishers, each of which owns 33⅓% of the song, each publisher can only negotiate a fee and license its 33⅓% share of the composition. If there is more than one music publisher of a composition, they usually agree on an overall fee to charge the producer (for example, $35,000 for 100% of the composition) and split it according to their respective percentages. This type of agreement prevents one publisher from licensing another co-publisher's share of the composition without that company's knowledge and approval.

The co-administration and joint administration agreement will also provide that each of the music publishers will collect their share of all royalties directly from the source of the monies (for example, directly from the record companies, performance rights organizations, etc.) and will be responsible for paying the songwriter signed to them his or her respective songwriter royalties from the monies received. There will also be an agreement that if a publisher receives another publisher's share of royalties, it will remit such monies to the other publisher within a set period of time. If demo recordings are made, the publishers will usually share the costs according to their respective interests; provided that all publishers have approved a demo session for the composition and the cost budget related thereto. The agreement will also guarantee that, outside the United States, each of the publishers will be able to have its own foreign representative administer, license, and collect royalties on its respective share of the composition.

SONGWRITING COLLABORATION WITH A PERFORMER

When two or more songwriters write with each other to create a new composition, there are various forms of agreements that are signed which define the relationship between the various co-writers.

In most cases, they are fairly short documents which list the title of the composition or compositions, the identity of the songwriters, their performing right affiliation (ASCAP, BMI, SESAC, GMR, etc.) and the names of the music publishing companies which control each writer's share of the composition. In addition, they many times contain language which explains the administration rights of the writers and their music publishers in the composition.

When dealing with very successful writers who are also performers/ recording artists, though, a number of other provisions may be included in the collaboration agreement which are designed to protect certain rights of the writer-performer. One such clause prohibits the co-writer from disclosing information and other material acquired by the co-writer in the course of or in connection with the parties' creative collaboration since such information is to be deemed confidential unless it is disclosed by the successful artist to the public (e.g., to a news reporter in an interview). In effect, the collaborator is being asked to sign a confidentiality agreement.

In addition, if the collaborator is exposed to and is able to listen to unreleased recordings embodying the writer/performer's musical performances and/or unpublished musical compositions written by the performer, the collaborator may be asked to agree not to make any reproductions or copies of such unreleased materials (or authorize others to do so). This includes permission for others to listen to the materials or to broadcast or use or exploit those unreleased materials in any medium including radio, television, Internet, print, and electronic data transmission without the consent of the writer/performer.

Such agreements may also contain a provision for liquidated damages in the event of a breach by the collaborator of the confidentiality clause without the performer's having to prove actual damages.

Additionally, the agreement will many times have a provision which requires the collaborator to return any copies of files, discs, or other material containing the performer's vocals to the performer and erase all such vocals upon the performer's request and provide an affidavit of such destruction.

The writer/performer will also virtually always be given the right to issue a "first use" mechanical license for the composition. If there is co-administration by the parties, each party will usually have the right to approve any non-compulsory use of the composition including any synchronization license unless another arrangement is agreed to. In some cases, though, the recording artist will have the right to license the composition when the performer's master recording is also being used subject to the collaborator receiving his or her share of the fee or other income derived from the use.

PLACEMENT DEALS FOR NEW RECORDINGS

There are a number of companies or individuals whose sole job is to secure cover recordings by additional recording artists after a song has been initially recorded and released. Since most major music publishers have people on staff who provide this service, these placement companies are usually hired by smaller publishing companies or writers who do not have publishing deals, although a songwriter signed to a publisher may occasionally bring in such a company to assist in the combined efforts to secure new versions.

In some cases, the territory of the services agreement concentrates on the United States, but many times the emphasis is on getting new recordings in countries outside the United States.

The term of these agreements may be for a minimum of one year and a maximum of five years with usually a right to terminate the term if no results have been achieved in a negotiated period of time. For example, if a new recording is not secured within __ months, the contractual relationship can be terminated. Obviously, if a song is "on hold" by an artist or producer for recording on a future album or digital single track release, the term can be extended for a reasonable period of time to see if the release for which the song is being held actually happens. Some of the issues involved in these "on hold" situations revolve around whether the hold is exclusive and the duration of the hold (3 months, 6 months, etc.) or whether it is a nonexclusive "we are interested in the song for the next album" situation, etc.

If the placement company secures a new recording because of its efforts, compensation can range from 10% to 25% of mechanical royalties (which can be based on publisher income, writer income or both), but the percentage is negotiable. Some agreements also provide for a participation in the publisher's share of performance income directly related to the new recording only.

To put it mildly, the language in this part of the agreement is really important since it may have a real impact on income. In addition, the language which relates to what was secured by the efforts of the placement company and what was not secured or what use happened outside of the efforts of the placement company is also extremely important. There is always the possibility of more than one party claiming to have been responsible for the recording so the language in the placement agreement should be very specific as to how the words "secured" or "procured" are defined.

For example, if the writer, manager, current publisher and placement company have all sent the song to the record producer, artist, or other representative interested in recording a new version, who is to get the credit for the placement? This scenario is just one of many conflicting fact patterns that can and do occur and which are the basis for disputes.

Clarification of the roles and rewards from promotion efforts, therefore, is good for all parties involved and the old axiom "the clearer the better" should be the rule of the day in this area.

These agreements are many times nonexclusive, but some companies demand exclusivity. Again, this aspect is usually negotiable depending on the bargaining power and needs of the parties involved.

CHAPTER 3

MUSIC, MONEY, CO-VENTURES, AND JOINT VENTURES

One of the more common ways for an artist/writer, producer/writer, successful songwriter, or smaller record company to grow their publishing assets, through financing or co-financing from a third party, is to align with a major music publisher under what is known as a co-venture or joint venture publishing arrangement.

The value to the major publisher of such an agreement is that the publisher gets the benefit of the creative expertise of the artist/writer, producer/writer, songwriter, or record company, and the publisher will be able to participate in the songwriters and songwriter/performers discovered by its partner. In effect, the major publisher is hiring an additional A&R source, which will enhance and complement its own creative staff and, hopefully, introduce opportunities that the publisher may not have a chance to be involved with. The value to the artist/writer, producer/writer, songwriter, or record company of the arrangement is that, because of the support, administrative expertise, promotion abilities, and, in many cases, financial contribution, of the major publisher, they will have a source of financing and administrative support to take their creative dream and business plan to a level that they may not necessarily be able to achieve by themselves.

Under this type of agreement, the major publisher many times guarantees that it will provide a certain level of financing on an annual or per individual writer deal basis that will be used by the writer/artist or writer/producer to sign other songwriters (which, in most cases, will be writer/performers). The copyrights to the compositions will be co-owned by the co-venture parties, but the major music publisher will usually administer the compositions throughout the world. The major publisher will also many times be responsible for the payment of the advances required to sign the songwriters selected by the writer/artist or writer/producer.

TYPES OF JOINT VENTURE/CO-VENTURE AGREEMENTS

There are a number of variations in these types of joint venture/co-venture agreements, and some of the major structural points follow.

TERM

The term of the agreement can be for a set number of years (for example, a firm two-year, three-year, or five-year term) or a one-year period with a number of option years (for example, one year plus two one-year options to extend the agreement exercisable on the part of the major publisher).

CO-PUBLISHING

The major publisher and the writer/artist or writer/producer will co-own all compositions written by writers signed with the copyright ownership, and the income split being usually in equal shares. For example, if a songwriter is signed to an exclusive songwriter agreement, those compositions would be co-owned 50/50 by the major publisher and the writer/artist-writer/producer-co-venture party. If, however, the writer is signed to an exclusive songwriter/co-publishing agreement where the songwriter owns a portion of the publishing rights, the major publisher and co-venture partner would own that portion of the copyright and publishing rights which is able to be retained by the major publisher under the exclusive songwriter/co-publishing agreement. For example, if the songwriter signs a standard 50/50 co-publishing agreement and owns 50% of the copyright, the other 50% would be shared equally—25% to the major publisher and 25% to the co-venture writer/artist or writer/producer.

In some joint ventures, each party to the agreement will have its own publishing company, both of which will be listed as co-copyright owners. Another approach is for both joint venture publishers to form a new limited liability company that will own the copyrights. Under this scenario, there would be a separate operating agreement that would define the rights and obligations of the joint venture parties.

ADMINISTRATION

During the term of the co-venture agreement, the major music publisher will be the party who performs all the administrative functions related to the songwriters signed to the co-venture. For example, the major publisher will collect all royalties earned by the compositions, issue all the licenses, audit users, litigate infringements, and prepare all accounting statements being sent to the songwriters and other third party royalty participants. The major publisher will also prepare all the accountings to its co-venture party covering all the monies being generated by the deals signed.

There are a number of variations that can occur once the term of the co-venture agreement has expired. One variation is for both co-venture parties to begin to administer their respective share of each composition upon expiration, or at a stated number of years after expiration, so that both parties will begin to issue licenses and collect monies for the share that it owns. This co-administration variation many times occurs only when all advances given to the songwriters signed to the co-venture have been recouped. Another variation might provide that the major publisher will have the right to acquire the co-venture party's share at a specified time in the future, calculated on an agreed-upon multiple of the net earnings from all the compositions. An additional variation is for the major publisher to have the right to match any offer from a third party received by its co-venture party for the sale of its share of the compositions controlled; this matching right usually being exercisable for offers that are received either during the term or a negotiated number of years after expiration of the term.

ADVANCES

Under many of these agreements, the major publisher is the party that pays all the advances due to the writers who are signed. For example, if a songwriter agreement signed by the co-venture provides for $75,000 in advances for the initial period, the major publisher would fund the entire advance. Under some agreements, the major publisher and the co-venture partner will co-finance the advances required by the deals that are signed. For example, if the writer agreement provides for $100,000 in advances to be paid to the songwriter during the initial contract period, the major publisher and the co-venture partner may each contribute 50%. If there is such a shared financing responsibility arrangement, the major publisher may agree to pay slightly more than its co-venture partner (for example, 60% of the advances rather than 50%) in recognition of the added value being brought to the deal by the creative expertise of its partner.

Even when the major publisher is the party that has the initial funding responsibility for the writers that are signed, some agreements provide that the joint venture partner must co-fund any options (e.g., via an equal sharing responsibility or other negotiated percentage) that are exercised in order to continue to participate in compositions created or controlled during the option period. If the joint venture partner elects not to contribute, then the major publisher will continue with that writer outside of the joint venture.

Some agreements will provide that the major publisher will fund all agreements during a stated period of time (for example, the initial two or three years of the venture) without having the venture partner being required to participate in the funding of advances or other payments related to options which occur during that period. But any options that are mutually exercised after that stated period must be co-funded for the parties to mutually participate in the earnings resulting from compositions written during the option period or subsequent option periods.

ADVANCES TO THE CO-VENTURE PARTNER

On occasion, the major publisher will pay the co-venture partner a separate advance or advances (over and above the advances it pays to the songwriters signed by the co-venture) that will be recoupable from the co-venture partner's share of the net income generated by the compositions controlled. For example, if $100,000 was earned by a composition and the songwriter was entitled to $75,000 of those monies in royalties under his or her co-publishing agreement with the co-venture, the remainder would be split between the major publisher and co-venture partner on a 50/50 basis (i.e., $12,500 each). Under this scenario, the co-venture partner's $12,500 allocation would be used by the major publisher to recoup any separate advances given directly to the co-venture partner. For example, if the co-venture partner had been advanced $100,000, the major publisher would apply the $12,500 against the unrecouped advance balance (thus reducing it from $100,000 to $87,500).

SCOPE OF THE AGREEMENT

The co-venture partner usually guarantees that the major publisher will have the right to be involved with all third-party songwriters whom the co-venture partner wants to sign to its publishing company. In effect, if the partner wants to sign a writer, the major music publisher will be given the first opportunity to participate in the deal (and, in many cases, must participate). Exclusivity as to third-party signings or at least a right of first refusal on the part of the major publisher is almost always an essential part of the agreement.

SONGWRITING SERVICES OF THE CO-VENTURER

If the co-venture partner is a songwriter, his or her services may also be covered by the agreement but this does not have to be the case. On occasion, the co-venture partner is a songwriter who is either signed to another publisher as an exclusive songwriter (but with the ability to acquire outside songs or sign outside songwriters who will not be controlled by the exclusive songwriter agreement) or is a songwriter who controls the publishing rights to his or her own songs and does not wish to be affiliated with a major publisher for the self-written catalogue. In these cases, the co-venture arrangement may only cover the compositions written by outside songwriters who are discovered and signed by the co-venture partner.

SHARING OF INCOME

In many cases, the net income of the co-venture is split equally between the major publisher and the co-venture party regardless of which party funded the deal. Depending upon bargaining power, the income splits can be different. At other times, the net income is shared proportionate to the amount of money each party has contributed to the advances paid to the songwriters signed by the co-venture. For example, if the major publisher paid 75% of all advances to songwriters and the co-venture partner paid 25%, the net income of the co-venture might be split 75% to the major publisher and 25% to the co-venture partner. In these cases, the rewards follow the risk.

DEALS THAT EXTEND PAST THE TERM OF THE CO-VENTURE AGREEMENT

Since the term of the co-venture between the major publisher and its co-venture partner is for a set number of years (for example, from one to five years), a number of the songwriter agreements signed by the co-venture will last beyond the expiration of the formal term of the co-venture agreement. For example, if the term of the co-venture agreement is for three years, a one-year plus four one-year-option songwriter agreement signed in the third year of the co-venture will last far beyond the expiration of the co-venture term if all options are exercised. In these cases, the term of the co-venture would be extended past its termination date for that particular songwriter agreement only provided that both parties to the co-venture continue to exercise the various options available in the songwriter agreement.

GUARANTEED FUNDING

In many of these agreements there is usually a guarantee by the major publisher that it will contribute a specified amount of money during the term, which will finance all or a portion of the songwriter agreements signed by the co-venture. For example, there might be a guarantee that the major publisher will provide a minimum amount of advance funding on an aggregate term basis (e.g., $500,000 over a three-year period) or on an annual basis (e.g., $150,000 per year during each year of the term of the co-venture agreement).

There will, as a fiscal safety valve for the major publisher funding the agreement, also be limits on the amount of money that the co-venture partner is entitled to commit to a particular deal. For example, the co-venture partner may be able to sign deals without the approval of the major publisher if the annual advances for such agreements are under $75,000. If an agreement with a songwriter provides for advances in excess of the $75,000 annual limit (for example, $125,000 per year), the deal could only be entered into with the approval of the major publisher.

Additionally, if the co-venture partner exceeds the annual aggregate guaranteed advance fund, no further agreements may be entered into without the approval of the major publisher. For example, if the aggregate advance fund for the signing of all deals during a particular year is $150,000 and the co-venture partner is allowed to enter into $75,000 deals without the approval of the major publisher, if separate $75,000 and $50,000 songwriter agreements ($125,000 total) had already been signed during the year and the co-venture partner wanted to sign another $75,000 deal, approval would be needed since the yearly $150,000 maximum would be exceeded even though the individual songwriter agreement was not above the $75,000 limit that needed approval.

There are also certain standards that must be met by the co-venture partner for any agreement to fall under the "without approval" category. For example, the qualifications might require that the compositions be owned for life of copyright or at least have a 20-year retention term, that there be a commitment that there will be a certain number of released compositions per contract year, or that the publisher have the ability to grant television, motion picture, video game, and other synchronization licenses without the permission of the songwriter, among other terms. If these qualifying terms are not included in the songwriter agreement, the co-venture partner will not be able to sign the deal unless the major publisher approves the deal despite the fact that the individual agreement is under the advance limit.

These guaranteed funding provisions are also usually part of the type of co-venture agreement that provides that the co-venture partner must pay a portion of the advances due songwriters (in contrast to the co-venture arrangement that has the major publisher responsible for 100% of all advances due). For example, the major publisher may guarantee that it will be responsible for up to $210,000 per year in signing advances, provided that the co-venture partner is responsible for the payment of 25% of the total advances paid to songwriters. In this case, the co-venture partner would be agreeing to pay $70,000 in advances to writers if the major publisher paid out $210,000 in advances. The schedule would look as follows:

Year	Annual Advance Total	Major Publisher 75%	Co-Venture Partner 25%
1	$280,000	$210,000	$70,000
2	$280,000	$210,000	$70,000
3	$280,000	$210,000	$70,000

CARRY FORWARD ADVANCES

Some agreements provide that if the minimum funding guarantee is not used during any one year period of the co-venture term (for example, if the major publisher agreed to finance $200,000 in advances to songwriters per year but only $100,00 was actually spent due to not enough writers being signed), the difference between what was guaranteed by the major music publisher and what was actually spent will be added to the advance minimum funding guarantees for the next year. Under our example, the $100,000 in potential advances which was not used during the year would be added to the $200,000 in guaranteed annual funding advances due for the next year (resulting in the major publisher agreeing to an annual guarantee of $300,000 for that year). On the other hand, the major publisher will want each year to be treated separately, and if the co-venture partner does not find enough deals to expend the amount guaranteed during a one-year period, the advances for the new year will not be increased because of any advance-spending shortfall in the prior year.

ARTIST DEVELOPMENT BUDGET/JOINT VENTURE

If the joint venture concentrates on the ability of the venture partner (whether the partner is a recording artist or producer) to discover, nurture and develop new artist/writers, there may be provisions which will guarantee an aggregate yearly fund for all writers signed or an individual per writer fund which can be used by the partner to accomplish those goals. In this regard, a representative clause might read that there will be a stated negotiated fund (e.g., $5,000, $10,000, etc.) to be used for instrument purchase, studio rental, out-of-pocket travel, per diem and lodging expenses or other marketing expenses which are designed to develop the writer/artist to the next level. Sometimes there is a guaranteed dollar amount available to the co-venture partner to use without permission (usually with a caveat that the amount must be reasonable or there is a cap) and other times these monies are only allowed to be spent with the approval of the major publisher funding the deal. In virtually all cases, these monies will be recoupable from the developing artist/songwriter royalties (many times whether as a songwriter, co-publisher and recording artist but this is subject to negotiation) and will usually be included in the calculation of when the co-venture partner begins to share in the net publisher share of income which is generated from the income by the compositions and/or recordings of the artist/writer being developed.

EXERCISE OF OPTIONS FOR SONGWRITER AGREEMENTS

Because most of the agreements signed with songwriters have option periods, a major issue in the co-venture negotiations establishing the joint venture rights and responsibilities is which party can decide whether or not to exercise an option to extend the songwriter agreement for another contract period. Since virtually all of the songwriter agreements will provide for the payment of advances when options are exercised, this issue can have an important financial impact on the co-venture parties. In many agreements, the major music publisher will give the co-venture partner the right to determine whether an option is to be exercised, provided that the maximum advance cap is not being exceeded. In most cases, however, both co-venture parties have to agree on the decision. In those cases, if there is a disagreement between the major music publisher and the co-venture partner, the party who wants to exercise the option will be allowed to do so, but the compositions written during the exercised option period (and any option periods exercised thereafter) will be totally controlled by the party who exercised the option. If this occurs, all compositions by the applicable songwriter owned by the co-venture prior to the commencement of the option period shall be controlled by the co-venture. Any compositions written during the exercised option period will be controlled by the party who exercised the option, and the party who did not want to exercise the option will have no rights in future compositions.

When the term of the co-venture agreement has expired but the term of a songwriter agreement extends past the end of the co-venture term, options are usually exercised only with the mutual approval of both co-venture parties; with the proviso that if either of the parties does not want to exercise an option, that party would not have the right to participate in the compositions written commencing with the start of the applicable option period.

If the active term of the co-venture has expired (sometimes it might be two or three years) but there are still songwriter agreements with future exercisable options controlled by the joint venture, some joint venture agreements provide for the major publisher to continue to pay the songwriter advances for mutually approved option pickups. However, many agreements provide that if the parties elect to go forward with an option exercise on a writer after the expiration of the joint venture term, each party must contribute according to their respective publisher interest to the advances that must be paid. For example, if the advances to a songwriter will be $50,000 if the option is exercised, each of the co-venture publishers would be responsible for paying or contributing $25,000. Under this scenario, if one party does not want to contribute financially to the going forward aspect of the songwriter agreement, then that party will not be able to co-own or participate in the income earned by the compositions written during the exercised option period for which it did not contribute its share of future advances.

TRAVEL AND OTHER EXPENSES

In some joint ventures, there will be a set travel and hotel accommodation fund which will be provided to the creative partner. The fund will be utilized for trips involved with talent scouting. In addition, there may be funds guaranteed for the purpose developing the writers signed to or intended to be signed to the venture. In many cases, these expenses must be approved by the joint venture parties. Other times they are spent at the discretion of the creative partner provided they are within certain parameters. On occasion, the creative partner whose role it is to discover new writers will be paid a separate fee for each writer signed to the venture; such monies usually treated as an advance recoupable from that party's share of the net income generated by the venture.

PUTS AND CALLS

In some joint venture agreements, there are options known as "puts" and "calls." A "put" entitles the party exercising the option to force the other party to buy its remaining interest at a specified price (many times a multiple of the earnings over a set number of prior years). A "call" option is when one party can request the other party to sell its share back to the party exercising the call (once again, at a predetermined price or formula).

PUBLISHING PLUS VENTURES

There are also some joint venture agreements that provide that the music publisher and songwriter share in a number of sources of income (such as touring, merchandising, and recording artist-related income) that are traditionally not part of the publishing deal. These types of arrangements are sometimes entered into when the music publisher has been the party who has secured the recording artist agreement for the songwriter/performer (sometimes having financed all or most of the initial album released by the record company). These partnership agreements many times guarantee the songwriter certain monies during the term of the deal (either as nonrecoupable payments or advances against monies that may become due) in addition to providing that certain things will occur during the active term of the venture (for example, that three albums will be recorded and released within six years of the signing of the agreement). There are also provisions that detail how the net profits will be shared by the writer and the music publisher (for example, 50/50, 75/25), how decisions of the venture are made, who manages the assets once the term has ended, and whether one of the parties has the right to buy the other party's interests once the deal is over or if someone receives an offer from a third party to buy their respective share.

CHAPTER 4
MUSIC, MONEY, AND COPYRIGHT

T he copyright law of the United States and those of other countries form the basis of the lifetime and worldwide earnings of creative works. Though the rules in this area can be quite complex as well as technical, there are some basics that every writer, publisher, representative, record company, and user of music should understand.

Once a writer creates a work, the basic questions that need to be answered are: What qualifies a work for copyright protection? What formalities does one have to follow? What rights does one have? How long does one own those rights? What can one do with those rights? And what happens when someone violates those rights?

The concept that a creative work is a property right was first recognized in the United States in 1787 in Article 1, Section 8 of the U.S. Constitution. Under the article, Congress was given the power to "promote the Progress of Science and useful Arts, by securing for limited Times to Authors and Inventors the exclusive Right to their respective Writings and Discoveries." The basic ownership rights for musical compositions as well as the remedies for the infringement of those rights are set forth in the 1909 U.S. Copyright Law; the 1976 Copyright Revision Act, which took effect January 1, 1978; and the 1998 Sonny Bono Copyright Term Extension Act.

In the music field, the basic types of work that are copyrightable are musical works, including any accompanying words; dramatic works, including any accompanying music; motion pictures and other audiovisual works; and sound recordings. The two primary elements that a work must have in order to enjoy statutory copyright protection are: It must be an original work of authorship, and it must be fixed in a tangible medium of expression that is now known or later developed.

EXCLUSIVE RIGHTS OF COPYRIGHT

The exclusive rights that a copyright owner has in a work are:

1. "The right to reproduce the copyrighted work in copies or phonorecords." This right includes the ability to authorize copies of a work that are fixed in practically any form, including tapes, records, CDs, and sheet music.
2. "The right to prepare derivative works based upon the copyrighted work." This very important right allows a copyright owner to authorize arrangements, motion picture adaptations, abridgments, translations, sound recordings, and so on that are based on the copyrighted work.
3. "The right to distribute copies or phonorecords of the copyrighted work to the public by sale or other transfer of ownership, or by rental, lease, or lending." This right gives the copyright owner initial control over the first authorized record or copy of the work. After the first "copy" is authorized, all others may record the work simply by complying with the compulsory licensing provisions of the act.
4. "The right to perform the copyrighted work publicly." Financially, this is one of copyright's most important rights, as it forms the basis of all ASCAP, BMI, SESAC, and GMR licensing, as well as the direct and source licensing of music users.
5. "The right to display the copyrighted work publicly." This right authorizes individual images of a work such as projecting an image of the copyrighted work on a screen.
6. "In the case of sound recordings, the right to perform the copyrighted work publicly by means of a digital audio transmission."

The limitations and exemptions on these exclusive rights include "fair uses" of the work, certain reproductions by libraries and archives, certain educational uses, certain face-to-face teaching activities, performances in the course of religious services (but not if the service is broadcast to the public at large), charity and other nonprofit performances (but not if an admission is charged or there is a profit motive or anyone involved is paid a fee), performances in the home, and other uses that do not require the authorization of the copyright owner.

All of these exclusive rights are initially owned by the creator of a work, and they may be individually or totally transferred to others by a written and signed document. Any transfer should be recorded in the U.S. Copyright Office by submitting a signed document of the transfer as well as the Copyright Office recordation fee.

WORKS MADE FOR HIRE

The "work made for hire" is a special category of copyright that affects primarily film and television underscore composers as well as songwriters writing songs specifically for film and television series. The duration of protection, the ownership, and the right to "recapture" a copyright are all affected if a composition or score is so categorized.

A work made for hire is defined as "a work prepared by an employee within the scope of his or her employment or a work specially ordered or commissioned for use as a contribution to a collective work, as part of a motion picture or other audiovisual work…if the parties expressly agree in a written instrument signed by them that the work shall be considered a work made for hire." The employer, not the writer, becomes the "author" and the copyright owner for the entire term of copyright.

COMPULSORY LICENSES

A very important notion of U.S. Copyright Law is the existence of compulsory licenses. These "licenses" give certain types of users (e.g., cable systems, jukebox operators, and public broadcasters) the right to use copyrighted musical works without the permission of the copyright owner, provided they follow certain procedures and make payment of royalties. Copyright owners and users are still permitted to negotiate their own agreements if they so choose, and such agreements supersede the statutory rates.

Compulsory licenses include the retransmission by cable systems of distant non-network programming, the right to make recordings of copyrighted non-dramatic musical works once the first authorized record is made and distributed in the United States, and the right of public broadcasters to broadcast copyrighted works. Jukebox performances, once the subject of a compulsory license, are now covered by negotiated agreements between the copyright owners and the jukebox operators. If the parties cannot agree, Copyright Royalty Judges decide the fee for the compulsory license.

Prior to January 1, 1978, jukeboxes were exempt from copyright liability. The Revision Act changed that and set fees at $8 per box in 1978 with increases each year to $50 in 1987. A 10-year agreement was reached among ASCAP, BMI, SESAC, and the Amusement and Music Operators Association (AMOA) that provided for a 1990 rate of $275 for the first jukebox plus lesser amounts for additional boxes. A 2001–2005 agreement provided $350 for the first box plus $59 per additional box for AMOA members and $79 for non-AMOA members with a CPI increase each year. For 2008–2112, AMOA members paid $405 for the first box and $68 for each additional box with non-AMOA members paying $405 and $93 respectively. The 2018 license fee is $495 for the first jukebox and $84 for each additional box for AMOA members with non-AMOA members paying $114 for each additional box. Video and digital jukeboxes are covered under separate agreements.

For phono-records (CDs, records, vinyl, tapes, etc.), once the copyright owner authorizes one recording that is distributed to the public in the United States, anyone else may make recordings of the composition regardless of whether they have permission from the copyright owner. The Copyright Act requires that, prior to the distribution of records, a "notice of intention to obtain compulsory license" be given to the copyright owner containing, among other things, the work being recorded, the name of the new recording artist, the names of the original writers of the work, the name and address of the person or company taking the license, and the date when the phonorecords are set to be distributed. The compulsory license applies only if the primary purpose in making the phonorecords is to distribute them to the public for private use and includes the right to make an arrangement of the work as long as it does not change the basic melody or fundamental character of the work. If the names and addresses of the copyright owner are not on file in the Copyright Office records, the notice must be filed with the Copyright Office rather than directly to the copyright owner. The act requires monthly as well as annual summary accountings to the copyright owner as well as the timely payment of statutory fees. The rates for 2018–2022 are the greater of 9.1¢ per composition or 1.75¢ per minute of duration. In reality, most mechanical licenses that are issued in the United States are not compulsory licenses but variations of the compulsory license, with terms that are somewhat less stringent than those dictated by the Copyright Law. For example, if a record company uses the mechanical licensing services of the Harry Fox Agency in New York, the licenses issued are modifications of the compulsory license provisions and contain terms that are acceptable to virtually all major and smaller record companies. Additionally, if the songwriter is a recording artist signed to a record company, the mechanical licensing terms will be specified in the recording agreement, and such terms will supersede the compulsory license provisions of the Copyright Law.

THE AUDIO HOME RECORDING ACT OF 1992

In 1992 the Audio Home Recording Act was passed, requiring equipment, tape, and disc manufacturers of digital audio recording devices and media (recordings and blank tape) to pay royalties to creators for the loss of revenue that occurs from home taping. The royalty to be paid by the manufacturers to the Register of Copyrights is 2% of the transfer price, with a minimum royalty payment of $1 per device and a maximum royalty of $12 for certain types of devices. The royalty on blank tape and other media is 3% of the transfer price.

The act divides all of the royalties received into two funds. The Sound Recording Fund receives $\frac{2}{3}$ of the money, with 4% of that money allocated to non-featured musicians ($2^5/_8$%) and vocalists ($1^3/_8$%) who have played on sound recordings distributed in the United States, and the remaining 96% of the fund to be distributed 40% to featured recording artists and 60% to record companies. The second fund, the Musical Works Fund, receives $^1/_3$ of the total royalties received and is split 50% to writers and 50% to music publishers. The royalties in the Sound Recording Fund are to be distributed on the basis of record sales, with the Musical Works Fund having the option of being distributed either on performances, on record sales, or a combination of both. Royalty claims can be made to the Copyright Royalty Judges by agents of interested parties (e.g., ASCAP, BMI, SESAC, GMR, the Harry Fox Agency, the Songwriters Guild, RIAA) or by individuals themselves. The distribution of royalties within each fund can be voluntarily agreed to by all of the interested parties within that fund, but if no agreement can be reached, the distribution goes to the Copyright Royalty Judges for determination as to the claimants who should receive royalties as well as the amounts to be paid to each claimant.

COPYRIGHT ROYALTY JUDGES (THE COPYRIGHT ROYALTY BOARD)

The 1976 Copyright Act created a tribunal to determine reasonable terms and rates of royalty payments under certain sections of the new law, to adjust those rates over time, and to distribute the royalty fees that come into the Register of Copyrights under these sections. The primary royalties covered are the compulsory licensing areas of the mechanical rate, secondary transmissions by cable systems, jukebox royalties, the copyright fees to be paid by noncommercial broadcasting (PBS), and the distribution of royalties under the Audio Home Recording Act. The Copyright Royalty Tribunal received claims to royalties and distributed those fees to copyright owners or the agents for those copyright owners. If the CRT determined that a controversy existed regarding deposited funds, it conducted a proceeding to determine the correct distribution of royalties. All final royalty determinations by the CRT were published in the Federal Register and could be appealed to the U.S. Court of Appeals. In 1993, the CRT was replaced by Copyright Arbitration Royalty Panels (CARPs) consisting of three arbitrators per panel. The Copyright Royalty and Distribution Act of 2004 (which became effective in 2005) replaced the CARPs with the Copyright Royalty Board, which has three full-time Copyright Royalty Judges. The Chief Copyright Royalty Judge's term is for six years with the two additional Judges having initial terms of four years and two years. Subsequent terms for all Judges are six years.

COPYRIGHT NOTICE

The notice that should appear on all copies of a published musical work includes the symbol ©, "Copyright," or "Copr."; the year of the first publication of the work; and the name of the owner of the copyright. For example, "© 2018 Todd Brabec" or "Copyright 2018 Brabec Music Company." Prior to March 1, 1989, this notice was mandatory, as its omission could, and did in many cases, result in loss of copyright.

Since that date, however, the placement of the notice on all copies of works first published on or after March 1, 1989, is optional, although highly recommended, particularly to combat claims of "innocent infringement" of the work by others. For unpublished works, the copyright notice is not required, but it is recommended to have it on all copies.

FEES AND FORMS

The U.S. Copyright Office charges different fees depending on the types of registrations and recordations involved as well as the services being provided. Since these fees do change, one needs to check the official site to secure the most current information as to both fees and practices. The Copyright Office forms applicable to music use are Form PA for all published or unpublished works, Form RE for any remaining renewal copyright claims under the 1909 law, Form CA for any supplementary information to be added to a work already copyrighted, and Form SR for sound recordings. The Copyright Office also provides, free of charge, many informational circulars on various aspects of copyright, including international copyright, and investigating the copyright status of a work.

DURATION OF COPYRIGHT

The number of years that copyright protection lasts for a work has been increasing steadily over the past 300 years. From 14 years of protection under the 1710 English Statute of Anne and a maximum 28-year protection under the U.S. Act of 1790, the 1909 Copyright Law established for most works a 28-year initial term of protection with an additional 28 years if the copyright was renewed. The 1976 Copyright Revision Act increased the term of protection for most copyrights created after January 1, 1978, to the life of the author plus 50 years after the author's death. The 1998 Sonny Bono Copyright Term Extension Act increased the 50-year term to 70 years after the author's death. Therefore, in the case of a work written by two or more authors, the term for most copyrights is 70 years after the death of the last surviving author. Although the 1976 act continued the rule that compositions written prior to January 1, 1978, must still be renewed after 28 years to receive extended protection, a 1992 change in the law provided for an automatic renewal for works first copyrighted between January 1, 1964, and December 31, 1977. For works written on or after January 1, 1978, the concept of renewal of copyright no longer applies.

EXAMPLE. A song is written by four writers in 2011. Three of the writers die in the year 2035, and the fourth writer dies at the age of 100 in the year 2075. The copyright for this work (assuming it was a joint work and not a work made for hire) would last until the year 2145, which is 70 years after the death of the last remaining author. The publisher of this work would also have copyright protection until 2145, as the duration of copyright protection depends on the length of the author's life and not who the author has assigned or transferred the copyright to.

RULES GOVERNING DURATION OF COPYRIGHT

The rules affecting the duration of copyright protection for a work fall into a number of categories, depending on when the work is written and what type of work it is. The rules in this area can be somewhat complex and technical, but the following categories of works should provide most of the basics that every writer and publisher should be aware of:

Works Written Prior to January 1, 1978. Total copyright protection under the 1909 Copyright Law was 56 years (28 years plus a renewal of another 28 years). In the early 1960s Congress enacted a series of laws extending the duration of copyrights in their renewal term that would have fallen into the public domain in the years 1962-1977. In effect, an additional 19 years of protection was added to copyrights in their renewal term, giving them a total of 75 years of copyright protection. Works still in their initial term of copyright (the first 28 years) at the time of the effective date of the 1976 Copyright Revision Act (January 1, 1978) were given an additional 47 years of protection, provided they were renewed in the 28th year of copyright. The 1998 Act added 20 more years for a total of 95 years of protection.

Works Written on or after January 1, 1978. The copyright protection for these works lasts for 70 years after the death of the author. If a work was written by more than one author and the work is a "joint" work, the term of protection is 70 years after the death of the last remaining author.

Works Made for Hire. The duration of copyright protection for works made for hire written on or after January 1, 1978, is 120 years from the writing of the composition or 95 years from its publication, whichever date is earlier. Under the 1909 law, works for hire were treated similarly to other types of musical works (28 years plus a 28-year renewal), with the exception that only the employer had the right to apply for renewal.

REVISION OF COPYRIGHT RENEWAL PROCEDURES

On June 26, 1992, Public Law 102-307 was signed into law and drastically changed the renewal provisions of the U.S. Copyright Law with respect to musical compositions initially copyrighted between January 1, 1964, and December 31, 1977.

In effect, the new law made the need for actually filing a formal renewal application to extend copyright protection for an additional 47 years optional, as it would be given automatically whether or not any affirmative action was taken.

Under the 1976 Copyright Revision Act, the copyright term in a pre-1978 musical composition mirrored the provisions of the 1909 Copyright Law in that it continued to be an initial period of 28 years. There was established, however, an additional 47-year renewal term, which would become effective only if a renewal application was filed in the U.S. Copyright Office prior to the end of the twenty-eighth year. In the event that such a renewal application was not registered, copyright protection in the musical composition was lost at the end of the twenty-eighth year. For example, a musical composition that was copyrighted in 1970 would be eligible for copyright renewal in the year 1998. Provided that the renewal registration was filed in the U.S. Copyright Office by the end of 1998, copyright protection would be extended for an additional 47 years. If timely renewal was not made in 1998, however, a loss of copyright protection would commence on the first day of 1999.

Because of innumerable instances of copyright owners inadvertently failing to register timely renewal claims, and the resultant loss of protection and benefits (which, in some cases, amounted to hundreds of thousands of dollars), it was considered to be in the best interests of all parties involved to guarantee continuing protection without any formal action on the part of the songwriter, music publisher, or any other copyright owner. In effect, the new law gave copyright holders automatic entitlement to an additional 47 years of protection after the initial 28 years, thus guaranteeing a 75-year copyright term for 1964–1977 copyrighted compositions. This was increased to 95 years by the 1998 Act.

These renewal provisions do not apply to any musical compositions written on or after January 1, 1978, since copyright protection for such compositions lasts for the life of the creator plus 70 years or, in the case of a work made for hire, the shorter of 95 years from publication or 120 years from creation. Additionally, the new law did not affect pre-1964 compositions that had been lost owing to a failure to renew their copyrights.

Even though the filing of a formal renewal registration is now unnecessary to secure copyright protection for a full 95 years (i.e., 28 years plus 67 years), there still remain certain advantages to filing. For example, having a formal renewal registration filed in the U.S. Copyright Office will constitute prima facie evidence (i.e., a presumption by the court) of the validity of not only the information contained in the renewal certificate but of the copyright itself—a factor which can be very important in a court of law in the event of a copyright dispute. If there is litigation, the burden of proof will be on the party disputing the validity of the copyright to a musical composition and not on the creator of the composition.

As for the renewal process itself, both the Form RE renewal application and the filing fee must be received by the U.S. Copyright Office within one year prior to the expiration of the initial 28-year copyright period. The initial 28-year copyright term is computed on a calendar-year basis, rather than measured from the date that a musical composition is actually copyrighted. For example, if a composition was copyrighted on June 20, 1977, the initial 28-year copyright period would expire at the end of 2005 rather than 28 years from the actual copyright registration date (i.e., June 20, 2005), and the renewal period would commence on January 1, 2006. Thus, the proper period to renew such a copyright would be from January 1, 2005, through December 31, 2005 (i.e., during the one-year period prior to the commencement of the renewal period).

RENEWAL CLAIMANTS

The persons entitled to claim renewal rights in musical compositions are as follows:

The author, if living

The widow or widower of the author, or the child or children of the author, or both, if the author is deceased

The executor of the author's will if the author is deceased and there is no surviving widow, widower, or child

The next of kin of the deceased author in the event that there is no surviving widow, widower, or child and the author did not leave a will

If a writer granted the music publisher renewal rights to a composition in his or her songwriter's agreement and the writer survives into the renewal period, the music publisher to which he or she assigned the renewal rights will continue to be the copyright owner of the composition.

TERMINATION RIGHTS

Under the 1976 Copyright Revision Act and the 1998 Term Extension Act, creators and their representatives were given new rights to terminate grants that were made not only on or after January 1, 1978, but also prior to that date. In effect, the act provided authors, their estates, their heirs, and other duly authorized representatives the opportunity to recapture rights in and to musical compositions, provided they complied with certain formalities.

TERMINATION OF THE EXTENDED COPYRIGHT RENEWAL TERM

The 1976 Copyright Revision Act not only increased the duration of copyright protection from 56 years to 75 years—thus allowing the writer and publisher of musical compositions to continue for a longer period of time to benefit financially from being able to license such works—but also gave the author the right to recapture rights in the musical compositions during the extra 19-year extension period.

WHEN THE TERMINATION NOTICE MUST BE SENT

In order for an author or his or her duly authorized representative to terminate a music publisher's right to continue to control a pre-1978 composition, written notice must be sent to the publisher not less than two years nor more than 10 years prior to the effective date of termination. In this regard, termination of the extra 19-year renewal period can take place only during the fifty-seventh through sixty-first year of copyright protection (i.e., during the initial five years of the 19-year extension period). In other words, termination can occur only during the five-year period commencing with the end of the fifty-sixth year subsequent to the initial copyright date, and notice must be sent not less than two years before that five-year period nor more than 10 years before the same five-year period.

WHAT THE TERMINATION NOTICE MUST CONTAIN

The termination notice should include the following information:

The name of the musical composition

The name of at least one of the writers

The date of initial copyright

The original copyright registration number, if available

The date on which termination is to take effect

Identification of the agreement or grant of rights to which the termination applies (e.g., songwriter agreement between [writer name] and [publisher name] dated [day/month/year])…

The name and address of the music publisher or other company (or said party's successor-in-interest) whose grant is being terminated

If the writer is deceased, the notice should also contain the names of the successors to the deceased writer and their relationship to the writer. And if the termination notice relates to a contract signed by someone other than the writer, the name of the surviving person who signed the contract should be included.

SERVICE OF THE NOTICE

The notice must either be served by personal service or sent by first-class mail to the last known address of the original music publisher or its successor-in-interest. The terminating party should make a reasonable investigation to determine the address of the party that currently owns the composition. It is also vital to record a copy of the termination notice in the U.S. Copyright Office prior to the date on which the termination is to take effect.

PERSONS ENTITLED TO TERMINATE THE EXTENDED RENEWAL TERM

The original creator, if alive, is the person who is entitled to terminate the additional 19-year period of the 47-year renewal term. If the creator is deceased, the right to terminate vests in the surviving spouse. If there are children or, in the event a child is deceased, grandchildren of such deceased child, the spouse will own a 50% interest in the termination rights and the children or grandchildren will divide the remaining 50% interest in equal shares. For example, if there is a surviving spouse and three children, each of the children would be entitled to $1/_3$ of a 50% interest. If the original creator is dead, termination can be effectuated only if those persons entitled to more than 50% of the termination interests execute the notice. Executors, trustees, etc. come next.

TERMINATION RIGHTS UNDER THE 1998 TERM EXTENSION ACT

This law gives most authors or successors another opportunity to terminate a transfer for the added 20 years of protection given by this Act (95 years total rather than 75). The author has the opportunity effective during the five years following the 75 years of protection to terminate such a transfer, provided the work was in its renewal term at the time of the law and where the rights had previously been transferred before January 1, 1978. If the old law termination right had expired and if that termination right was never exercised, then the new termination right would be available. Any termination notice must be recorded in the U.S. Copyright Office prior to the effective date of the termination. This new right does not apply to works for hire.

TERMINATION OF AGREEMENTS MADE DURING OR AFTER 1978

In addition to the termination procedures established with respect to the extended copyright renewal period, the 1976 Copyright Revision Act also established termination procedures for compositions written on or after January 1, 1978. The act gives authors, their heirs, or duly authorized representatives the right to terminate a grant-of-rights contract effective during the thirty-sixth through fortieth year after the agreement was signed. If the grant-of-rights agreement covered publication of the work, the right to terminate can occur during the five-year period commencing at the end of 35 years from the date that the musical composition was published or at the end of the fortieth year after the signing of the agreement, whichever occurs first.

WHEN THE TERMINATION NOTICE MUST BE SENT

The termination notice must be served not less than two years nor more than 10 years before the effective date that is stated in the notice.

SOUND RECORDINGS

Sound recordings are considered original works of authorship under the 1976 act and are able to be copyrighted. The copyright protects the actual sounds on the record, disc, or tape and not the physical object of the record itself. The protection for sound recordings also applies to nonmusical works. The 1976 act recognizes the "authorship" notion of performers and record producers, and sound recordings are therefore fully protected. This copyright is separate from the copyrights issued for the songs being recorded. The ownership of a record's copyright is many times transferred to the record company as part of the negotiated artist contract. In non-work-for-hire 1978 and beyond recordings, a right of termination vests 35 years after delivery of the album.

The copyright notice that should be placed on all publicly distributed records, tapes, discs, etc., consists of the symbol (P), the year of first publication of the sound recording, and the name of the owner of the copyright in the sound recording or an abbreviation by which the name is generally recognizable or known. The notice should be placed on the surface of the record or on the label or container in such way as to give reasonable notice to others of the claim of copyright. The sound recording copyright applies only to original works in a fixed form (the sounds on the discs, records, tapes, etc.) that were fixed on or after January 1, 1978 (the effective date of the 1976 act) or fixed and able to be distributed on or after February 15, 1972 (the effective date of the federal law recognizing a copyright in sound recordings).

INFRINGEMENT OF COPYRIGHT

Copyright infringement occurs when someone violates any of the exclusive rights of the copyright owner (subject to certain exemptions and limitations) as set forth in the 1976 Copyright Revision Act. As any or all of these exclusive rights may be transferred by the copyright owner to others, normally through assignment or an exclusive license, each separate owner of an exclusive right can initiate an infringement suit, as each is entitled to all of the protection and remedies accorded to the copyright owner. Infringements in the music area come up most frequently in cases where one song is, or appears to be, very similar to another song or where users of music perform copyrighted compositions without permission. Some of the remedies for infringements include attorney's fees and court costs, the actual damages suffered, a wide range of statutory damages ($750–$150,000), criminal jail terms, profits of the infringer, and injunctions. Increased penalties and damages apply to willful infringers, with reduced damages applicable to innocent infringers.

As registration in the U.S. Copyright Office is not mandatory under the 1976 Act, the act included certain provisions regarding the filing of infringement suits that strongly encourage registration. In order for a copyright owner to file an infringement case in the federal courts, a work must have been registered for copyright. For any transfer of any of the exclusive rights of a copyright, the new owner of the right must record the transfer in the Copyright Office before initiating an action. For published works that are registered subsequent to an infringement, statutory damages and attorney's fees are not available. The same non-availability of certain remedies applies to published works that are not registered and where the infringement occurs after publication. Statutory damages and attorney fees are available, provided that the published work is registered within a three-month grace period after it is published.

A second type of copyright infringement involves the importation into the United States, without the authority of the owner of copyright, of copies or phonorecords of a work that have been acquired outside of the United States. Exceptions to this infringement include items brought into the country for the personal use of the person bringing them in. The main thrust of the clause has to do with "pirated" recordings.

The basic issues in an infringement case involve one's ownership of a copyright and whether someone else copied that original work. As for the copying issue, the court looks at whether the defendant had access to the work in some way and whether there was a substantial similarity between the two works.

An argument raised in some infringement cases is that the new work is a parody of the original work, that the doctrine of "fair use" applies, and that the new work therefore does not infringe upon the old work. The 1976 act states that "notwithstanding the provisions of 106 and 106A [the sections of the law that apply to the exclusive rights that a copyright owner has in a work], the fair use of a copyrighted work, including such use by reproduction in copies or phonorecords or by any other means specified by that section, for purposes such as criticism, comment, news reporting, teaching (including multiple copies for classroom use), scholarship, or research, is not an infringement of copyright." In determining whether the use made of a work in any particular case is a fair use, the factors to be considered include the purpose and character of the use, including whether such use is of a commercial nature or is for nonprofit educational purposes; the nature of the copyrighted work; the amount and substantiality of the portion used in relation to the copyrighted work as a whole; and the effect of the new use on the potential market for or value of the copyrighted work.

The decisions of different courts regarding fair use many times conflict. The specific circumstances of each case go far to determine whether something is or is not a "fair use" of another's copyrighted work.

INTERNATIONAL COPYRIGHT PROTECTION

U.S. copyrighted works are, in the main, protected in most countries of the world through individual treaties between the United States and foreign countries as well as U.S. participation in the major international conventions, primarily the Universal Copyright Convention, the Berne Convention, and the WIPO treaties. An important point of all of these treaties and conventions is that with certain exceptions (e.g., duration), U.S. works basically receive the same protection in a country that the country gives to its own nationals. Many of the positive changes that have occurred in U.S. copyright law over the years are the result of the U.S. having to conform its law to the copyright laws of other countries and conventions in order that U.S. copyright owners may receive adequate protection in foreign countries.

PRE-REGISTRATION

For certain types of works which have had a history of infringements prior to their authorized commercial distribution (musical compositions, sound recordings, motion pictures, etc.), the Copyright Office offers preregistration of a work. To qualify, the creation of the work and fixation in some tangible medium must have already begun though not yet complete. Preregistration allows an infringement action to be brought before the actual authorized commercial distribution of the work. It applies only to unpublished works, is not a substitute for registration as you do have to still register the work when complete, and has a filing fee of $140.

THE DIGITAL PERFORMANCE RIGHT IN SOUND RECORDINGS ACT OF 1995 DPRSRA) AND THE DIGITAL MILLENNIUM COPYRIGHT ACT OF 1998 (DMCA)

The 1995 DPRSRA created a public performance right for artists and record companies in certain sound recordings when they are performed by digital audio transmissions. Previously only songwriters and publishers enjoyed the performance right. This new right is a limited one and covers subscription (statutory license) and on-demand transmissions. Webcasting (audio streaming of recordings over the Internet) was included under this limited right by the 1998 DMCA. FCC-licensed broadcast station Web transmissions are also covered. License rates and terms are to be decided by voluntary negotiation or compulsory arbitration. The first CARP royalty decision for the fees for non-exempt subscription digital services was 6.5% of gross revenues resulting from residential services in the U.S., with 50% of the royalties going to artists (45%), non-featured musicians (2.5%), and non-featured vocalists (2.5%), and the remaining 50% going to record companies.

The 1998 DMCA implements the WIPO Copyright Treaty and the WIPO Performances and Phonograms Treaty, which deal with copyright protection for works in a digital form and require countries to give protection to foreign works no less favorable than the protection afforded to domestic works. The DMCA also creates civil and criminal penalties (up to a $1,000,000 fine and 10 years imprisonment) for the circumvention of the technological measures used by copyright owners to protect their works as well as for the tampering with copyright management information (title of work, author, copyright owner, conditions or terms, etc.). Limitations on the copyright infringement liability of online service providers is also included with the steps set forth that Online Service Providers (OSPs) must follow when they either detect or are notified of infringing transmissions. These include disconnecting repeat offenders; removing infringing material on the Internet and identifying infringers to copyright owners based upon subpoenas.

CONCLUSION

The copyright area is a complex, technical, and changing field affected by legislation, court decisions, treaties, foreign laws, and different interpretations of all the copyright acts. Consultation with an attorney versed in copyright law is essential for any inquiry or action in this area.

CHAPTER 5

MUSIC, MONEY, AND THE RECORDING ARTIST

MAJOR RECORD COMPANY 360 DEAL

(SCENARIO 1) (THE PHONE CALL)

RECORD COMPANY EXECUTIVE: We'd like to enter into a relationship with your artist which is more encompassing than the traditional major record company contract.

ARTIST ATTORNEY: In other words, a "360 deal."

RECORD COMPANY EXECUTIVE: Yes, as it will be an arrangement that will cover a number of aspects and income sources of the artist's career. For example, we will not only be involved in recording and distributing albums but we will be involved and participating in the monies earned from touring, branding, and merchandising as well as the artist's songwriter and music publishing career.

ARTIST ATTORNEY: These rights and the income generated from these sources have always been kept separate by my client, but we will listen to your proposal.

RECORD COMPANY EXECUTIVE: That's good to hear. I do want to emphasize that we need these other income sources to be part of the deal since it is company policy not to go forward unless we have them.

INDIE RECORD NET PROFITS DEAL

(SCENARIO 2) (THE PHONE CALL)

RECORD COMPANY EXECUTIVE: As you know, we're an indie label and our deals are net profit split agreements which are different from your standard record deal.

ARTIST LAWYER: I realize that so let's cut to the chase. I'm assuming it's a 50/50 split of profits after costs and expenses related to the album have been recovered. Let's first discuss the types of expenses that the record company expects to get back before the artist gets paid their 50% of net income. I also want to make sure that the artist's mechanical income from Internet downloads and physical sales are paid whether or not the record company has recovered its costs. We also need some pass-through of license fee income for television, film, advertising commercial and video game uses secured or created by the artist. I also want to make sure that each album is treated separately as to profit and loss and that there is a guaranteed marketing fund as well as tour support.

MAJOR RECORD COMPANY TRADITIONAL DEAL

(SCENARIO 3) (THE PHONE CALL)

RECORD COMPANY EXECUTIVE: Hello, this is the vice president of business and legal affairs for _____ Records. As you know, our A&R people are very interested in signing your client to a recording artist agreement. Before I send you a summary deal memo of our proposal, I'd like to go over the main points of the offer so we know whether or not we have a deal.

ATTORNEY: That sounds good to me. The more issues and areas we can define and agree to before you draft a deal memo, the better for everyone.

RECORD COMPANY EXECUTIVE: We'd like to sign the artist for one album, and we need to have options for six more albums after the first. We'd also like to have the right to issue a "greatest hits" album over and above the option albums. The royalty rate will be 15% of retail for albums and 12% for singles with a 15% new technology/media reduction. We'll pay on 90% of all recordings sold and will reduce the artist royalties by 60% for sales outside the United States. There'll be a guarantee that one video will be produced per album, the cost of which will be cross-collateralized with both the artist's audiovisual royalties and audio, download, CD, and ringtone income. We'll advance your client $150,000 on signing the agreement, with an escalating advance payable for each new album that is recorded and released. The amount of each option album advance will be based on 66⅔% of the earnings from the most recent past album. As your client is a songwriter, there will also be a 75%-of-statutory mechanical rate, with a 10-song cap payable as songwriter and publisher royalties for sales of each physical album released, and with 25% reduction for developing artist releases. The mechanical rate will be the one in effect when the artist starts to record the album. As to digital, the songwriter/publisher mechanical royalties will be paid at the 100% statutory rate. Those are the basic terms. What do you think?

ATTORNEY: I'll discuss the offer with my client and will get back to you with our counterproposal. I do want you to know that, in its present form, the proposal is unacceptable. However, if we can get a 16% album rate on 100% sales without producer royalty deductions, with percentage escalators based on the achievement of sales plateaus as well as option years, increased royalties in at least the major foreign territories, a release guarantee for each album in not only the United States and Canada but also in the United Kingdom, an understanding that only 50% of the video costs will be recouped from the artist's audio-recording royalties, guaranteed independent promotion and tour support, minimum guarantees as to album advances regardless of the earnings from the most recently released album, a 13-times-statutory mechanical rate cap for physical albums, 100% statutory for downloads, no packaging deduction for downloads or other digital distributions, market value for new configurations, and an effective mechanical rate determined by the U.S. release date of each album, we'll at least have something to talk about. I also want to make sure that the artist will own the official website.

NET PROFITS LICENSING DEAL FOR FUTURE RECORDINGS

(SCENARIO 4) (THE PHONE CALL)

RECORD COMPANY EXECUTIVE: As an alternative to the type of deals you've been offered from other record companies, I'd like to suggest a different approach to you which I think you'll find beneficial. We'd like to have you sign with us for future recordings under a license arrangement where the ownership and copyright in your recordings would remain with you and not be assigned to us. The term would be ten (10) years from the release of the last album under the agreement. At such time all rights would revert back to you. We will fund the recording costs and the marketing budget; both of which will be approved by you after consultation with us. Additionally, you will be entitled to 50% of the profits after the recording and marketing costs as well as a distribution fee have been recovered. The advance per album will not be as large as you may receive from another company but what we're offering with respect to reversion of all rights plus our belief in you makes us a more beneficial place for you to be.

ARTIST LAWYER: Thanks. I appreciate the approach as the thought of retrieving control of the recordings created during the deal is attractive. A number of things to be worked out but I'll go back to my client and their manager to start the conversation and gauge interest.

MARKETING AND DISTRIBUTION DEAL

(SCENARIO 5) (THE PHONE CALL)

ARTIST LAWYER: We came to you because my client is looking for a situation where the artist will have creative control over the album and tracks but recognizes the need for a partner who has marketing, promotion, and distribution expertise in both the traditional and digital marketplace. We do not intend to transfer any ownership to the master recordings but we are willing to give the right partner sufficient leeway to ensure that the album and its individual tracks will be successful and commercially exploited in the right manner.

RECORD COMPANY EXECUTIVE: Appreciate your thoughts, perspective, and letting us know what you are looking for. We will come back to you with a detailed marketing plan which will include how we intend to promote not only the album and its individual tracks but also your artist's brand which will help with re-energizing your artist's back catalogue even though we will be only controlling new recordings. We will need pre-approval for certain of our promotion approaches and will need certain assurances that, if our efforts are succeed, that we will be able to be involved in at least one (and hopefully more) future album. We will provide you with a guaranteed marketing budget of $_____ for the album and tracks and we will discuss the distribution plan every step of the way including certain minimum expenditure commitments for agreed upon promotion areas.

One of the most complex and important relationships in the music industry is the one between the recording artist and the record company. It is a contractual relationship that controls virtually every aspect of a performer's career, from how much he or she makes to whether or not there is even a chance of becoming the next superstar.

The cornerstone of this part of the entertainment industry is the record contract—a 25- to 100-page legal document prepared by high-priced lawyers designed, in many cases, to do one thing and one thing alone: protect the record company at all costs. For the average person, it is virtually impossible to understand. In many instances, even attorneys who are not versed in the jargon and hidden meanings of this specialized area find themselves negotiating what seems to be a good contract only to discover, after their client reaches the top of the charts and is considered the industry's next superstar, that the contract is a total disaster. For example, it is not unusual for two recording artists to sign contracts at identical royalty rates with the same company and have their actual earnings for the sale of the same number of downloads, CDs, streams, and videos be totally different because of the interaction of the other provisions negotiated.

INSIDE THE BUSINESS

In a world where Rolls-Royces, airplanes, yachts, art masterpieces, and million-dollar estates are bought on whims, and where one word in a 50,000-word agreement can mean the difference between success or failure and ultimate financial security or bankruptcy, it is absolutely essential that the performer and his or her representatives understand not only the basic provisions of the recording contract but also what the document actually means in terms of "real" money. With this in mind, the present chapter outlines the most important provisions of the record contract and explains the hidden meanings, pitfalls, and industry practices that really determine the amount of money you earn from the sale of CDs, digital downloads, vinyl, MP3s, other recordings, streams, and videos, as well as whether you really have a chance as a recording artist. In addition, many of the important variations that can be negotiated (both from the artist's and the record company's point of view) are explained, so that when a record company says it's interested, you'll know what to do.

THE MOST IMPORTANT POINTS IN EVERY RECORDING CONTRACT

Before signing a record contract, every performer must know the answers to the following questions, because they will have a substantial effect on not only the direction of his or her career and the amount of money that is earned but also on whether or not the artist will ever be on the charts or receive a Grammy.

1. Type of Agreement: Is it a "360 deal," a net profits deal, a standard artist deal, a license agreement, a marketing and distribution deal or a variation of the five?
2. Time Limit: How long will the contract last?
3. Options: How many times may the contract be renewed, for how long, and by whom?
4. Recordings and Releases: How many sides will a performer record, and does the record company have to release the finished recordings commercially?
5. Royalty Clauses: How much money does an artist receive from the sale of singles, albums, CDs, downloads, mastertones, and videos?
6. Reduced Royalty Clauses: How much does an artist receive for sales in foreign countries, or television album collections, promotional copies, and low-priced budget albums and new technology?
7. Record Company Deductions from a Performer's Royalties: What expenses do record companies deduct from a performer's earnings?
8. Escalating Royalty Clauses: Are there ways to guarantee that as an artist becomes more successful, royalties will be automatically increased?
9. Costs of Packaging a CD, or Other Recording: How much money do record companies deduct from an artist's royalties for the cost of album covers, special inserts, download services, and CD or video containers?
10. Free or Discount Recordings: How many recordings can a company give away for free or at a discount without paying royalties to the artist?

11. Returns and Reserve Accounts: Since an artist is not paid for CDs and other recordings that are returned for credit, how much money can be withheld from royalties in anticipation of such returns?

12. Advances: When do record companies give cash advances to artists? What criteria do they use?

13. The Recording Artist as a Songwriter: Do record companies pay lower songwriter royalties to artists who perform their own songs? Can a million-seller or successful "best hits" album mean financial disaster to a writer/performer if other songwriters on the album don't agree to reduce their writer and publisher mechanical royalties?

14. Foreign Releases: After the album is released in the United States, is there a guarantee that it will also be released in foreign countries?

15. New Technology Formats: What type of royalty reductions occur when a record company releases a recording via a new technology format? How do you protect yourself and your income to make sure that these reductions stop when new technology becomes old technology?

16. Videos: Will the record company produce a video of each single from the album? How much is the record company obligated to spend?

17. Audits: What rights does the artist have to audit the record company's books to check sales and royalty figures?

18. Tour Support: How do record companies handle the all important issue of tour support when the performer is on the road, and who really pays in the end?

19. Advertising, Marketing, and Promotion Support: What type of guarantees can you get that the record company will commit monies to marketing and publicizing the performer and the album?

20. New Equipment Funds: Will the record company agree to buy new, state-of-the-art musical instruments or recording equipment for the performer?

21. Sampling: If the performer samples another recording or composition, whose responsibility is it to get permission and negotiate the terms of the deal? Most important, how does use of a sample affect royalties paid by the record company to the writer/recording artist who uses the sample?

22. Websites: Who owns and controls the artist's website?

23. Net Profit Deals: How do artists and record companies share the costs and income under these agreements? What happens when an album is upstreamed?

24. "360 Deals": What type of income streams are included (publishing, touring, merchandising, etc.)? What percentage is the record company taking? What is the record company doing to justify its percentage?

25. Sponsorships and Branding: Does the record company participate in these areas and, if so, what rights do they have?

THE TERM

The term of the recording agreement is usually structured around either the artist's recording and the delivery of a long-playing album, or the record company's commercial release of the album. For example, a representative contract will state that the initial period of the recording artist agreement will commence on the date that the contract is signed and will expire six months after the commercial release in the United States of the initial album recorded under the agreement. Another alternative is for the initial period of the term to last until nine months after the artist has delivered his or her minimum delivery obligation (e.g., enough individual master recordings to constitute one long-playing album of at least 35 minutes of playing time), regardless of whether or not such recorded material has been released. Variations in this area depend on the policies of the record company involved and the negotiating strength of the artist, but most provisions calculate the term on a certain time period after either the artist has recorded and delivered the album to the record company or commercial release of the recording. Occasionally, depending on the artist and the expectations of the record company, the initial period may cover only a single, a number of singles, or an EP, with options for long-playing albums, but that is all subject to negotiation.

In addition to the initial period, which usually covers the artist's first album, the record company will always have a number of options to extend the recording agreement for additional periods and additional albums. Most recording agreements will give the record company the right to exercise from four to nine separate options, each of which will control a newly recorded separate album.

For example, a sample clause might read:
Artist grants to the record company six (6) separate and consecutive options to extend the term of the recording artist agreement. The record company may exercise those options by sending the artist notice at any time prior to the expiration of the then-current contract period of the term. If such notice is sent, the agreement shall be extended for an additional option period. If such notice is not sent, the recording agreement shall terminate at the end of the current contract period of the term.

Another variation of when an option must be exercised is the earlier of a set number of months after an album is delivered (for example, 12 months, 15 months, etc.) and a set number of months after the last album has been released. For example, an agreement might read that the option can only be exercised prior to the earlier of 16 months after an album has been delivered or 12 months after it has been released.

Because there have been instances where a record company has mistakenly not sent the requisite option pickup notice and has, because of such failure, lost the recording services of an artist that it wanted to keep, many recording agreements provide that even if notice is not sent, the record company will still have the right to the artist's services unless the artist sends a termination notice and the record company does not formally exercise its option to renew the agreement within a certain number of days after it receives the notice.

On occasion, the term of the recording agreement is based entirely on the recording and release of a specified number of albums and does not include options. For example, an agreement might state that the term of the recording agreement shall expire upon either the delivery or commercial release of the fourth album recorded under the artist agreement. Another alternative is for the term to be for a set number of albums, with options for additional recorded product (e.g., two albums firm, with separate options on the part of the record company for four newly recorded additional albums).

ARTIST ROYALTY CLAUSES

The Artist shall be paid a royalty of 15% of the applicable suggested retail list price in respect of all long-playing albums manufactured and sold for which payment has been received.

The royalty clauses represent some of the most important parts of any recording contract, because these provisions determine how much money an artist will receive from the sale of records, CDs, downloads, other audio recordings, and videos. The figures used in almost all contracts are expressed in terms of percentages rather than in actual dollar figures, and are usually based on either the suggested retail list price or wholesale price of each recording, depending on the business practices of the particular record company.

The royalty percentage provisions cannot be treated in isolation from the rest of the contract, but must be read in conjunction with a number of other clauses that effectively reduce the base on which the royalty percentages are computed. For example, if a 20% artist royalty read in conjunction with all other contract provisions and reductions, such as producer royalties, packaging costs, free goods, and new technology deductions, actually equals 12%, ecstasy may turn to depression when the first royalty statement is received.

RECORDING ARTIST ROYALTIES

The royalty that an artist receives for the sale of downloads, CDs, and other configurations ranges from a low of 7% to a high of 25%. New artists usually receive a 10% to 12% royalty, whereas very successful artists receive from 17% to 25% of the retail-selling price of each download, CD, or other recording sold. Royalties for singles, long-play singles, and EPs are often lower.

RETAIL PRICE BASE

The artist royalty percentage is usually based on the suggested retail list price of each recording that is sold. For example, if the price of an album is listed $16 and the artist had a 10% royalty, the artist would theoretically receive $1.60 from the sale of one download or CD. As will be seen in subsequent sections, other contract clauses will reduce that amount in practice.

WHOLESALE PRICE BASE

A number of major companies use the record's wholesale price as the base on which artist royalties are computed. Because the wholesale price is roughly one half the amount of the suggested retail list price of a recording, the artist should (if the company pays on the wholesale price) receive twice the royalty that would be received if the record company used a retail price base. For example, a 15% retail royalty would normally be the equivalent of a 30% wholesale royalty.

CHANGES IN THE COMPUTATION FROM THE RETAIL PRICE TO A WHOLESALE PRICE OR FROM A WHOLESALE PRICE TO A RETAIL PRICE

If an artist royalty is based on a percentage of the retail list price and the record company changes to a wholesale-based royalty for all of its artists, most contracts will guarantee that the same dollars and cents royalty amounts will still apply (including the monies due for escalations in the artist rate based on the achievement of sales plateaus, etc.). The same principles will apply if the record company changes to calculating artist royalties from a wholesale price to a price based on the suggested retail list price of an album or single. It is, however, vital to have such a guarantee in the artist agreement.

FACTORS THAT DETERMINE AN ARTIST'S ROYALTY

The royalty percentage is completely negotiable, but as already indicated, the standard figure for new artists is between 10% and 12% (which does not include producer royalties). In this regard, the following chart summarizes some of the main factors considered by a record company when deciding how much it will pay the artist. The factors listed in the chart represent only some of the basic considerations weighed by the record company in its determination of how much it will pay a particular artist. High royalty percentages for well-known artists can easily be justified, since the company is almost assured of recouping its costs and making a substantial profit. Newer groups, however, do not have a guaranteed audience and rarely sell enough records to recoup even the recording costs of their first or second album, to say nothing of the substantial costs involved in the pressing, packaging, advertising, marketing, and promotion of each release. Therefore, until a recording act establishes a certain guaranteed sales level and consumer acceptance base, its artist royalty will usually remain low. If the A&R staff at the label really believe in the artist and feel that the artist has the potential of becoming a superstar, higher royalties can and have been negotiated.

Low Percentages	High Percentages
New group	History of sales
Unknown national reputation	Artist celebrity status with broad market appeal
Inexperienced in live performances	Good live performances Experienced record attorney
Unknown manager	Bidding war
	Good video act
	Substantial social media presence Known manager

GRADUATED-INCREASE ROYALTY PROVISIONS

A number of recording artists, recognizing that their initial royalty percentages may be low, negotiate escalating royalty clauses that increase their royalties proportionate to their success in selling albums. Such "sales success" clauses are not necessarily used only in new artist agreements; they also appear in the contracts of more established artists.

In addition, if the record label renews the artist contract for additional option years, it is often agreed that the performer's royalty percentage will be increased during each successive option year.

SALES LEVEL INCREASES

Example:	Number of Albums Sold	Artist Royalty
	1 to 149,999	10%
	150,000 to 299,999	11%
	300,000 to 499,999	12%
	500,000 and over	13%

Graduated royalty percentages normally become operative when the recording artist achieves certain stated sales level plateaus. For example, if an artist has album sales over an agreed-upon number of units, the artist royalty might be increased. If sales reach an additional level, there may be a further increase in the artist royalty. And if certain additional higher sales marks are achieved, there may be additional increases.

Such escalating royalty percentages normally apply only to the number of recordings sold in excess of the stipulated sales plateaus. In addition, these escalating royalty rates usually apply only to album sales as well as to non-reduced-royalty sales (i.e., top-line, full-priced product vs. midpriced or budget albums). Occasionally, graduated royalty provisions are written into contracts that apply to the sale of individual single tracks, but the plateaus that must be reached for increases are usually higher than in the album agreements.

In the above example, as an artist sells more albums, the album sale royalty is progressively increased. If sales are only 100,000 albums, the royalty is 10%. But if sales achieve the 150,000 mark, the artist receives an 11% royalty on every sale over 150,000 up to 299,999, where the next increase becomes operative. The escalating royalties apply only to sales that occur after a certain sales plateau has been reached. The higher royalty is virtually never retroactive to sales achieved before a plateau is achieved.

It should be mentioned that the escalating royalty provisions and the sales thresholds for artists signed to indie labels will be much lower. For example, there might be a royalty increase if sales levels reach 10,000 or 15,000 and another at 25,000.

CONTRACT OPTION YEAR INCREASES

Another variation on the theme of escalating royalty provisions is to increase the artist's royalty percentage when the record company picks up an option for another year. A number of recording agreements provide that the artist will receive a certain royalty for the first two contract periods and an increased royalty if the company extends the contract for additional option years (e.g., 12% for the initial period and first option period, 13% for the second option period, 14% for the third option period, and 16% for any subsequent option period). Under these types of option-year increase provisions, the new increased royalty percentage will apply only to those albums or singles recorded during the particular option year and will not be retroactive to albums or other configurations recorded and released during prior years, when a lower royalty rate was in effect.

ROYALTIES FOR SALES OUTSIDE THE UNITED STATES

Most record contracts contain provisions that reduce the artist royalty for sales of recordings outside the United States. The actual rates many times are dependent on whether or not the U.S. company has an affiliate in the foreign country or licenses the manufacture, distribution, and sale of its recordings through a third-party record label in the territory. A sample artist royalty schedule for foreign sales might grant 85% to 90% of the U.S. rate for Canadian sales; 75% to 85% of the U.S. rate for United Kingdom, the EU, Japan, and Australia sales; and 66⅔% of the U.S. rate for all sales in the remainder of the world. Depending on the record company, the reductions in artist royalties for nondomestic sales may be expressed in actual royalty percentages rather than as percentages of the U.S. rate. For example, a representative foreign royalty clause for an artist receiving an 18% U.S. royalty might list a 16% royalty for Canada, a 14% royalty for the United Kingdom, and a 12% royalty for all other territories.

Some record companies will agree to increased royalties for the artist in the event that certain aggregate sales plateaus are achieved in a combination of certain specified foreign territories. For example, a record company may agree that in the event that either 250,000, 500,000, 750,000, or one million full-priced albums are sold in a specified group of identified foreign territories (e.g., United Kingdom, Australia, Japan, France, Germany, and Canada), the artist royalty on all sales after the plateau has been reached in those territories shall be increased by 1% or 2%.

ALBUM PRICE LINES AND ROYALTY RATES

Record companies sell recordings under a number of different suggested retail price points, depending on the status of the artist, the nature of the product recorded, and the length of time a particular album has been in commercial release. It is important to know the various designations used and corresponding retail price ranges, since an artist's royalty will usually be different depending on the price line under which an album is sold. For example, almost all record labels have what is known as the "top line," "full-priced line" or "highest-price line," which relates to that company's prime artists and releases. As the name designates, albums in this category have a suggested retail list price at the top of the price guidelines. Most companies also have a midpriced line, which usually carries a suggested list price range of between 20% and 40% lower than the price of the top-line product. Many companies also have a new or developing artist line, which is less than full price. Companies also have a budget line, which usually covers albums in the lowest suggested list price range.

Midline and Budget Line Royalty Rates. The highest artist royalty rate is applied to the so-called top-line product, with reduced rates usually applicable to midline and budget albums. In most agreements, the record company will pay the artist a 75% rate on midprice recordings and from 50% to 66⅔% for budget albums. For example, if an artist negotiated a 15% album royalty in the recording agreement, and an album was sold as part of the midpriced line, the artist royalty would be 11¼ % (i.e., 15% × 75% = 11 ¼%). If the suggested list of the same album was eventually reduced for sale as part of the record company's budget line, the artist royalty for such budget sales would normally range from 10% to 7.5% (i.e., 15% × 66⅔% = 10% or 15% × 50% = 7.5%).

Other Reduced-Royalty Albums. In addition to midline or budget albums, there are a number of other recordings on which the record company will reduce the artist's royalty due to the nature of the product being sold and the type of distribution outlet handling the sale. The recording contract should contain specific provisions dealing with these reduced royalty rate albums.

Mail Order and Television-Only Packages. The mail-order business can be a moderate profit center for many record companies. For example, the "Best of..." television albums have proven that this area can be a decent source of income, even though the profit margin on each album is much smaller than for sales at the normal retail level. The standard clause for such mail order or television-only albums provides for an artist to receive one half of the top-line royalty rate based on either the net sales of such records or the suggested retail price of such albums. For example, if a record company markets such a television album and the artist has a 15% royalty percentage for normal retail sales, that artist will receive a 7.5% royalty for the television record sales (or one half the normal royalty). If, on the other hand, an artist is one of a number of artists on one of these albums, the artist would receive the applicable one-half royalty based on the number of that particular artist's performances on the album in relation to the total number of performances from all artists contained on that album.

PACKAGING DEDUCTIONS

One of the single largest items deducted from an artist's royalty base before computation of the actual physical album royalty is the cost of the covers, sleeves, and containers in which the recording is packaged. These packaging deductions (also known as "container deductions" or "container charges") are always expressed in percentage terms rather than actual dollars-and-cents figures. The percentage ranges from 15% to 25%, varying from company to company depending on the type of configuration being sold. Because of their impact on an artist's royalties, packaging deductions should be a major consideration when negotiating the artist's royalty computation provisions of any recording agreement. For example, it is more than possible for an artist with a high royalty rate and a high packaging deduction percentage to make less in royalties than an artist at another record label who has a lower rate but also a lower deduction.

Actual Packaging Percentages. Packaging deductions usually range from 10% to 20% for vinyl records, 20% to 25% for analog cassettes, and 25% for CDs and other nonanalog configurations, which in some record company contracts include new technology distributions. The actual percentage is usually based on and deducted from the suggested retail list price of the particular recorded configuration that is sold. Other variations may specify the type of price point and definition on which the container deduction is applied (e.g., the actual selling price, the list category price, the advertised price, the constructed price), but for the purposes of this discussion, we'll focus on the suggested retail list price calculation.

Operation of the Packaging Deduction. To illustrate how the packaging deduction works and how it affects the royalties paid to the recording artist, Table 5.1 sets forth the calculations under the scenario of an artist having a 20% royalty with a 25% suggested list price packaging deduction.

The same formulas can be used for each type of physical configuration (e.g., vinyl, etc.) that is sold, the only differences being the suggested list price of the specific audio format and the container deduction percentage applicable to that type of configuration.

PACKAGING DEDUCTION FOR AN ALBUM

Table 5.1

Without Packaging Deduction	
$12.98	Suggested list price
× 20%	Artist royalty
$2.60	Artist royalty

With Packaging Deduction	
$12.98	Suggested list price
× 25%	Packaging deduction %
$3.24	Actual deduction
$12.98	Suggested list price
− $3.24	Packaging deduction %
$9.74	Reduced royalty base
$9.74	Reduced royalty base
× 20%	Artist royalty %
$1.95	Artist royalty

FREE GOODS/DISCOUNTED GOODS

In addition to not receiving royalties on recordings that are returned for credits, the artist will also not be paid on recordings that are given away for free as part of merchandising or discount programs. For example, the record company may, rather than putting a discount on recordings that are shipped to its retail customers to make them cheaper and more attractive to purchase, give the retailer or wholesaler a number of free or bonus recordings instead—a strategy that in effect discounts all recordings purchased. To illustrate, rather than discounting the per-unit price of every 100 albums ordered by a retailer, the record company may only invoice the customer for 80 or 85 albums, with the remainder being distributed as "free," "promotional," "no charge," or "bonus" recordings.

Because this type of marketing and sales incentive plan is extremely common and the principle of nonpayment on such free recordings is well established, most artists try to negotiate a limitation on such giveaways. Some clauses will limit such free goods to the "standard merchandising program" or "standard free goods" guidelines set by the record company for the majority of artists signed to the label. Under this type of provision, the record company will often specify its current policy (e.g., 15% on albums, 20% on singles) so that all parties know to what they are agreeing. Other protective clauses will set an actual percentage limit, which cannot be exceeded without the consent of the recording artist. For example, the record company may agree that no more than 15% of all albums distributed will be treated as free or bonus recordings. Additionally, if an album is a major hit, the artist may be able to negotiate a lower percentage for that particular album.

THE 90% TO 92.5% SALE PROVISION

Certain record companies structure their artist agreements to provide that royalties will be paid on only 90% to 92.5% of physical recordings that are actually sold. For example, if an artist had a 20% album royalty and the record label sold 100,000 full-priced CDs, the artist would receive a royalty on only 90,000 to 92,500 units. Some artists are able to secure a higher royalty rate when signing with a "90% of sales" label because of the differential between an actual sales royalty base vs. a 90% sales royalty base, but this is a subject left to bargaining power and negotiating strategy.

NEW-TECHNOLOGY ROYALTY RATE REDUCTIONS

Most recording agreements will provide for a reduced royalty rate on new-technology recordings. For example, a sample clause might state that the artist royalty rate for albums sold in the new technology format would be from 80% to 90% of the otherwise applicable rate. Under such a new-technology, reduced-royalty provision, if an artist received an 18% royalty on top-line albums, the artist rate on albums sold in the new format would range from 14.4% to 16.2% (i.e., 80% × 18% = 14.4%, and 90% × 18% = 16.2%).

To prevent the artist's royalty from staying at the reduced new-technology level long past the time when the new configuration has become an accepted format, many artists will either negotiate a cutoff date for the reduced rate (e.g., five years after the introduction of the new format to the general public) or include a proviso that the lower rate will end if the record company starts to give other artists higher rates. If the cutoff date approach is selected, many of the clauses will contain language that provides for good-faith negotiations between the artist and the record company to arrive at a mutually agreeable rate, with the negotiations usually taking into account not only the industry practices at the time of the cutoff date but also what other artists of comparable stature are receiving.

Another approach to such new technology royalty rate reduction is to provide that, if during any calendar year the revenues generated from the sales of records in a particular new technology format exceed a certain agreed upon percent of the total United States recorded music revenues (e.g., 15%, 20%, etc.) as reported in a reputable published industry source, then, with respect to sales of records in any subsequent calendar years, such particular new technology format will no longer constitute a new technology format and will be paid at 100% of the otherwise applicable royalty rate rather than the reduced new technology rate.

WHOLESALE PRICE CALCULATIONS WITHOUT DEDUCTIONS

A number of record companies have switched from using retail price-based deductions for packaging and free goods to a wholesale or published dealer price-based formula, which deletes the packaging deduction as well as the free-goods deduction from the royalty calculation. With the proper guarantees and protective language, there is many times no difference in the final monies paid to the artist.

CUT-OUTS AND SURPLUS COPIES

All record company contracts have provisions that stipulate that once a particular album is either deleted from the catalogue and sold as discontinued merchandise (a "cut-out") or is sold as scrap, surplus, or excess inventory at less than from one third to one half of the record company's subdistributor price, no royalties will be paid. The same nonroyalty payment provisions also apply to recordings distributed to reviewers for critiques and to radio stations for airplay. Many artists are able to negotiate a time limit prior to which the record company may not sell a particular recording as a cutout (e.g., no album may be sold as a cutout until two years after the initial release of the recording). And in some cases, the artist is even given the first opportunity to purchase all of the cut-out recordings at the cut-out price.

ROYALTY PAYMENTS AND ACCOUNTING STATEMENTS

Royalty payments and statements to artists are made twice per year, usually in May for the six-month period from September through February, and in November for the six-month period from March through August. Certain record companies set the semiannual periods two months earlier so that the accounting periods run from January through June and July through December. Some agreements provide for quarterly accountings. As with most royalty accounting clauses, the contract will provide that each payment be accompanied by a royalty statement, with some contracts providing that a statement need not be sent if royalties have not been earned, charges have not accrued, or the artist does not specifically request one. During the active term of the recording artist agreement (while the artist is recording new albums for the label as opposed to the period after the artist has fulfilled the entire album delivery commitment), however, statements are normally sent even though no sales have occurred.

Many agreements provide for specific time limits during which the artist may object to a royalty statement, audit the record company, or sue the record company for either nonpayment or incorrect payment of royalties. For example, some agreements provide that a royalty statement is binding on the recording artist unless the artist objects to the statement in writing within one to three years after the statement has been either sent by the record company or received by the recording artist. Many contracts that provide for the time limit to commence on the receipt of the statement will also provide that a royalty statement will be deemed to have been received by the artist from 30 to 90 days after the statement has been mailed.

The artist who wishes to audit will usually have to first object to a statement within certain time periods and then, if the artist intends to hire an accounting firm or other representative to conduct the audit, give advance notice to the record company, usually at least 30 days before the artist's auditors intend to commence their audit. The record company usually has the right to postpone the audit at least once by giving notice to the artist within a specified number of days prior to the audit commencement date. For example, a sample provision might give the record company the right to postpone an audit for one to two months provided that it gives the artist notice at least 10 to 20 days prior to the scheduled commencement date. There also may be limitations on the amount of time that the audit may last (e.g., if the audit is not completed within two months from commencement, the record company may have the right to end the audit period upon notice to the artist), provided that the record company has been cooperative with the auditors.

There are usually restrictions on what the auditors can examine (e.g., manufacturing records or other records that do not relate to actual sales reports or other distributions of the artist's recordings are normally unavailable), when they can examine the records (e.g., only during regular business hours), who the auditors can be (e.g., certified public accountants from a firm that is not currently examining the record company's books), and where the audit is to take place (e.g., only at the record company's regular place of business).

ADVANCES

In virtually every recording agreement, the record label will guarantee the artist a series of advance payments throughout the term of the contract. There is usually an advance to the artist upon the signing of the record agreement, with additional advances payable on the occurrence of a number of various events, such as commencement of recording of an album, completion of the recording of an album along with its delivery to and acceptance by the record company, commercial release of an album, and commencement of an option period. Additionally, advances may be due the artist if certain sales plateaus are achieved during a certain period of time after the release of an album in the United States (e.g., $_____ if album sales reach 250,000 units within 18 months after release) or if the actual recording costs are less than those allocated by the record company for the completion of a particular album (e.g., the artist receiving the difference between the $150,000 spent in recording an album and the $200,000 in costs budgeted for the album). Table 5.2 illustrates the artist's advances under a recording agreement that has a one-album guarantee plus options for five additional albums.

RECORDING AGREEMENT ADVANCES TO ARTIST

Table 5.2

Initial Period:	
$200,000	upon signing (to cover the initial album recorded under the agreement) Option Periods:
$225,000	for the second album
$250,000	for the third album
$275,000	for the fourth album
$300,000	for the fifth album

Payment of Option Album Advances:	
10%	upon commencement of the option period
10%	upon commencement of recording of the option album
20%	upon delivery to and acceptance by the record company of the completed option album
60%	within 10 days following U.S. release of the option album

MINI-MAX FORMULAS

A common advance formula that is used in many recording agreements to calculate the monies due the artist for option albums is one that is known as either the "minimum/maximum" formula or the "floor/ceiling" formula. Under this type of provision, the record company will compute its actual advance for an option album based on a percentage of the earnings generated by the most recently released prior album, the percentage usually being from 50% to 75%. There will also be a "minimum" or "floor" to prevent the advance from being less than a certain figure and a "maximum" or "ceiling" to prevent the advance payable to the artist from exceeding a certain dollar amount. In many cases, the earnings used in the computation will be limited to full-priced sales in the United States and Canada and further limited to a specified period after the commercial release of the particular album being used in the calculation (e.g., 12 months to 18 months after the release date of the most recent album).

A sample "floor and ceiling" advance clause might read:
With respect to the second through sixth option albums, the advance payable to the artist will be 75% of the royalties earned by the artist from sales of full-priced albums during the 12-month period following release in the United States of the prior album with the following floor and ceiling amounts:

Album	Floor	Ceiling
2nd	$150,000	$250,000
3rd	$175,000	$275,000
4th	$200,000	$300,000
5th	$225,000	$350,000
6th	$250,000	$400,000

Some record contracts provide for the payment of additional advances to the artist based on the achievements of agreed upon sales plateaus. For example, if an album sells over 500,000 units in the United States within a set period of time, an advance of $1.00 will be paid for each unit above 500,000. If the album sells over 1,000,000 units, an additional advance of $2.00 per unit for each album in excess of the 1,000,000 figure might be paid. Both digital and physical sales are counted in the calculation with the sale of individual tracks from the album equal to the number of tracks on the particular album being counted as the sale of one album. These types of advances will also be reduced by royalties previously paid for such sales.

The advance provisions of a recording artist contract are subject to countless variations, depending on a number of factors including but not limited to the past success of the artist, the desire of the record company to sign the artist, the projected sales base throughout the world, the percentage being used in a minimum/maximum formula, and the expertise and experience not only of the artist's representatives but also of the record company's business affairs and legal departments. Regardless of the amount of the advances being paid, how the computation is structured, and the actual timing of payments to the artist, it must be remembered that these monies are advances; by their very nature they are totally recoupable and deductible from the future earnings of the recording artist. They are, in effect, a prepayment of royalties that may or may not be actually earned. For example, if an artist receives a $100,000 advance and eventually earns $150,000 from sales of albums, a check would be remitted for $50,000. If the artist only earned $40,000 from album sales, however, no monies would be forthcoming because there still would be a debit balance of $60,000 in the artist's account. In addition, once multiple album advances have accumulated without substantial earnings, it is more than possible for an artist to have a hit record and not receive a royalty check or even clear the negative balance in his or her account.

EQUIPMENT FUND ADVANCES

Especially in the case of newer bands and usually in respect of the first album being recorded only, many record companies will agree to pay additional advances to enable the band members to buy new musical equipment. For example, a clause might read that the record company "will make available an additional advance of up to $35,000 for the purchase of new musical instruments and/or other musical equipment." Payment is many times made directly by the record company to the retailer on an invoice basis for the instruments selected, but payments can also go directly to the band as reimbursement upon the submission to the record company of the receipts substantiating that the equipment was actually purchased. Equipment advances are treated in the same manner as recording costs and are fully recoupable from royalties due the recording artist.

ALBUM RELEASE OBLIGATIONS

One of the most important guarantees that any artist can secure is the guarantee that the record company will release the recorded album to the general public in the United States. In most cases, if a record company spends the requisite $60,000 to $500,000 to record an album, it will release it, since without such a release, the project will become a total write-off. However, it is not that uncommon for a record company to lose faith in an artist (perhaps because the finished recording does not meet the company's expectations, there are financial problems at the company, the company has been sold, or the A&R executives who were behind the act have left the company) and shelve an entire album without releasing it. The adage about "not throwing good money after bad" does come into account in such situations, as record companies do cut their losses occasionally, even if it means taking a total loss on the project. This is especially true if the record company feels that it will have to expend in promotion, advertising, marketing, and video production monies at least as much as it has spent in recording the album and paying advances to the artist. After all, if the record company has paid the artist $75,000 in advances for the album, spent $200,000 to record the album, and is looking at future expenses of $75,000 for a video and an additional $200,000 in manufacturing, promotion, trade advertising, and marketing costs, it is no wonder that certain albums are pulled from the release schedule if the faith of the company's creative, business, and financial executives is not there. The reality of the situation is that sometimes it is better to retreat and fight another day, a conclusion that might be disastrous for an artist's career but that might make perfect sense to the record company.

If an artist can negotiate a release guarantee, it is to his or her benefit.

A sample guaranteed release clause might read:
Record Company agrees to release each album recorded pursuant to the product commitment provisions of the recording agreement through normal retail channels in the United States within four months after delivery of each such album to the record company.

Because Canada is an important market closely related in geographic location and musical tastes to the United States, this territory may also be included in the release guarantee.

In addition to the United States and Canada, there are a number of other important territories for which artists try to negotiate guaranteed release schedules of their albums. For example, the United Kingdom, Australia, New Zealand, Germany, Japan, France, Benelux (Holland and Belgium), Italy, and the Scandinavian countries can all be important album sale territories and, depending on an artist's bargaining power and international sales base, such guarantees can be vital to an act's chances of succeeding overseas. If such nondomestic release guarantees can be secured, the release date obligation is usually within one to three months after the U.S. release date. Additionally, certain major recording artists are able to secure guaranteed release commitments in many of the so-called minor territories as well as those countries that represent major sales territories. Some agreements provide for a release in certain foreign territories if the album reaches the Top 50 of the U.S. album charts.

Now that the release guarantee concept has been discussed, the realities of the record industry must be introduced into the equation. Even if an artist has a guaranteed release clause in the recording agreement, other provisions in the agreement will almost always modify this obligation. For example, some agreements may provide that if an album is not released within a certain period of time (e.g., 30 to 90 days after the so-called guaranteed release date), the artist can send the record company notice that the release commitment obligation has been breached. If such notice is sent, the record company usually has from 60 to 120 days to release the album. If it does, the breach will be deemed to have been cured and the artist will have received what was denied—the commercial release of the album. If the release does not occur within the extra time period, however, the artist may have a number of different options ranging from termination of the recording agreement to being able to license the release of the album to another record company. In most cases, if the third-party licensing remedy is taken, the artist can require his or her recording company to enter into an agreement with another record company selected by the artist but usually within certain agreed-upon business and legal parameters (e.g., that the royalty will be within certain percentage guidelines, that 50% of the receipts will be credited to the artist's account, that all union fees will be paid, that audit rights are provided for).

RECORD COMPANY EXPENSES

VIDEOS

Since videos can, in many cases, be as important to a performer's career as audio recordings, this entire area is of benchmark importance to both the performer and the record company. Additionally, since the sums of money that can be expended in the planning and production of audiovisual performances are enormous and the chance for recovery of expenditures is a very speculative proposition, the provisions relating to the making of videos represent one of the most contentious areas in any recording agreement negotiation.

In most contracts, the record company not only will have the option to decide how many videos it will produce on a particular artist but will also have the final decision as to how much money will be spent. During the negotiations and depending on one's bargaining power, however, a number of inroads can usually be made that will guarantee at least certain commitments from the record company. For example, a minimum amount of money may be guaranteed to be expended on each video produced (e.g., the record company will allocate a production budget of not less than $75,000), and a minimum number of videos produced for every album the artist records. There may be additional commitments for single releases, such as the record company guaranteeing a video for each single that is released or a guarantee of further videos if a single reaches the Top 25.

As for the choice of concept, script, storyboard, the composition being recorded, choreography, director, producer, production personnel, and other creative and business aspects of the video, control over these items depends once again on the track record and bargaining power of the recording artist. If there is little bargaining power, the record company will normally exercise total control over all of these aspects, usually after consultation with the recording artist. If the performer is somewhat successful, the creative aspects will be many times handled on a mutual approval basis, whereby both the record company and the artist have to agree on the concept, planning, and production of the video, with the record company usually having the final decision in the event of a dispute or disagreement. And if the artist is an extremely successful superstar, most if not all of the creative and business issues will be within the hands of the performer, with possibly some consultation or limited approval rights held by the record company, especially with respect to actual costs exceeding budgeted amounts. For example, in a superstar's contract, the concept, planning, story line, script, shooting dates, and location are determined by the writer/artist. The selection of the composition being used in the video, however, will almost always be a mutual decision between the record company and the recording artist. Additionally, in a superstar contract there will always be a minimum amount of money guaranteed for each video—a minimum that, in most respects, is usually in excess of the entire advance and recording budgets for most performers. For example, it is not unusual for "deemed approval" per-composition video budgets for superstars to be in the $400,000 to $750,000 range.

Recouping Video Costs. Since the monies expended on an artist's video are virtually always treated as additional advances recoupable from the artist's royalties, there are a number of ways that recouping the money is handled by the record company. The preferable approach for the recording artist is for the expenses of videos to be recouped only from the income generated by the video. Most record company contracts, however, provide that the company can use monies received from other areas to recoup the costs expended on videos. Initially, the production cost of each video (which usually includes flat-fee payments to music publishers and unreimbursed duplication and delivery expenses, in addition to all the costs related to the planning and making of the video, but usually excludes overhead costs and service costs of the employees of the respective record company) is charged to what is usually referred to as the recording artist's video account. In most contracts, however, the record company can transfer from 100% to 50% of the video account to the recording artist's audio account so that the record company will be able to use monies due the artist for the sale of CDs, downloads, and other audio product ("audio account royalties") for reimbursement of the monies expended for the production of videos, with a large number of contracts using 50% as the limit.

Because the monies spent on videos can range from $50,000 to more than $750,000, the negotiations relating to how the record company can get its money back can be very intense. Large recoupable items such as videos can easily wipe out a record company's profit margin or an artist's entire royalty account. Occasionally, recording artists are able to get the record company to agree that the audio account and the video account will not be cross-collateralized, but in most cases, at least a portion of the video account expenses will be recoupable from the recording artist's CD, download, streaming, and other audio product royalties. Certain writer/performers are able to exclude songwriter and publisher mechanical royalties from the equation, but some contracts provide that mechanical royalties can also be used by the record company to recoup all or a portion of the video costs.

Video Royalties. Since many recording artists' videos are released for sale to the general public (as opposed to serving as "promotion only" vehicles and sent to music channels, websites, social networking sites, etc.), it is important for every writer/ artist to negotiate a royalty structure in the recording agreement that will cover videos sold on the commercial market. Certain record companies, at least with respect to new and unproven artists, do not pay royalties on videos that are sold at the retail level. Most companies, however, will negotiate and provide for a royalty (either on a to-be-negotiated good-faith basis or actual set penny or percentage royalty basis) in the recording artist agreement.

Depending on the policy of the record company involved, a number of different formulas can be used to determine how much a recording artist/writer gets paid for the sale of videos, whether they be single-composition, promotion-only videos or, more likely, multi-composition video projects. Some record companies will pay the artist a percentage of the wholesale price of the videos; others will pay on the basis of net receipts received by the record company; some will pay on the basis of a percentage of the list price; and others will pay a set penny rate (e.g., 8 to 10¢, etc.). In addition, if a writer/artist is a superstar, the record company will more than likely provide in the agreement that if other artists signed to the label receive higher royalty rates than those negotiated in the current agreement, the superstar will automatically get the benefit of such higher royalty rates (i.e., a "most favored nations" clause).

One example of how video artist royalties are computed is to provide for a 10% rate based on the wholesale price (the price to dealers) of the video configuration pro-rated based upon the timing of the controlled compositions in relation to all musical compositions used, including the controlled compositions. Under this scenario, if the wholesale price is $10 and the artist-writer's compositions represent 80% of the timing of all musical compositions on the video product, the royalties would be 80¢ (10% × $10 = $1.00 × 80% = 80¢).

There is often a royalty cap for all writer-publisher royalties. If this cap is exceeded because of the inclusions of noncontrolled outside compositions, the excess will be deducted from the writer/artist's share of royalties or, if not sufficient, the recording artist royalties. These royalties are payable many times starting with the semi-annual accounting period after the audio-visual recording costs have been recouped.

TOUR SUPPORT

If the recording artist is an accomplished live performer or if the record company desires that a new group go on the road to establish an audience and sales base, the record company will many times provide a certain amount of money in tour support. Occasionally, a lump sum may be guaranteed (e.g., $100,000 for a three-month U.S. tour) or a certain amount of money allocated to each live performance (e.g., $4,000 per performance), with certain limitations on the maximum amount of money it will be obligated to pay (e.g., $2,500 per performance but not in excess of $30,000 during the entire length of the tour). In most cases, a record company executive must approve a written tour budget confirming the concert dates and itemizing how the money is to be used—a safeguard that record companies do not want to give up. The monies expended in this area are normally treated as additional advances to the recording artist and are recoupable from any royalties due the artist under the recording contract. On occasion, mechanical income due the performer is excluded from this formula, but this is a matter always left to negotiation.

In some cases, the record company may approve the tour because certain guaranteed major markets have been included and, because of the inclusion of such markets, will guarantee any losses suffered by the group up to a certain limit. For example, if a tour includes 10 major record business markets, the record company might guarantee the group that it will reimburse them for the difference between the actual out-of-pocket costs of the tour and the revenue received. Under this type of scenario, if the tour earned $400,000 in income but cost $550,000 to produce, the record company might reimburse the group the $150,000 shortfall. Obviously, if the tour is successful and either covers its costs or generates a profit, the record company will not have to pay anything. If the tour is not successful or is successful artistically but doesn't pay all the bills, the terms negotiated in this area can be vital for an artist's financial survival.

TRADE NAME SEARCHES FOR GROUPS

Most recording agreements will contain a warranty by the artist that the group or professional name being used is actually owned by the artist and that no other performer has the right to use that name in the record business. In this regard, many contracts will give the record company the right to conduct a trademark search investigation to find out whether or not the group name is being used by anyone else. The record company is many times also given the right to file a federal trademark registration for the name in favor of the group if protection has not already been secured. The record company may treat the expenses of the search and the filing of the application as advances recoupable from any royalties due the recording artist. If this is the case, it is prudent to negotiate a limit to such costs so they won't exceed a certain amount of money (e.g., $500 per name).

PROMOTION EXPENSES

Since independent promotion can be an important aspect of establishing an artist or making a particular recording a hit, record company contracts will usually provide that all or a portion of third-party promotion expenses will be treated as additional advances to the recording artist recoupable from royalties due under the recording agreement. Such costs are usually 100% recoupable with respect to newer and less powerful artists, and 50% recoupable for more established artists. The record company will often agree to consult with the performer as to the actual promotion and marketing plans designed for a single or album but almost always will have the right to make the final decision.

In recent years, music publishers have tended to contribute guaranteed monies to their writer/recording artists for promoting their albums and singles, over and above monies expended by the performer's record company. Occasionally, such guarantees are part of the music publishing contract (e.g., the music publisher committing a minimum of $25,000 in independent promotion and marketing for each album released); at other times, they represent voluntary decisions on the part of the publisher either of its own volition or at the request of the writer/performer's management, attorney, or record company. Sometimes the record company may be able to commit only a certain amount of promotion money for a newer artist, and the monies expended by the writer/artist's music publisher can make the difference in pushing the writer/performer or recording over the top. Most promotion-related monies paid out by music publishers are, as in record contracts, treated as additional advances that are recoverable from publishing royalties due the songwriter/performer from sales of CDs and downloads, interactive streaming mechanicals, film, video game and television synchronization uses, publishing performance monies, print licensing, and other income-generating sources controlled by the publishing agreement.

MARKETING AND PUBLICITY PLANS

Some record company contracts are very specific about the marketing and publicity commitments and others are very open ended. The types of items included are the production, creation and placement of ads, including ad subsidies for trade partners, trade flyers, main page positioning (nonphysical distribution) and point of sale material, print, television and radio campaigns, online (including banner creation, banner campaigns, E-cards, wallpaper, etc.), artist biography, press photos, press kits, promotional CDs, vinyl or other configurations, artist website materials, artist presentations via various promotional websites, upload of recordings and videos to online communities, app involvement as well as press, television, radio, online and street promotion.

RECORDING COSTS/RECORDING FUNDS

Depending on the stature of the artist and the type of contractual relationship entered into between the record label and the performer (e.g., artist signing directly to the record company, artist being signed through a production company, artist signed through a third party by means of an inducement letter), the costs of recording an album are paid directly by the record company, by the artist, or by the artist's production company.

If the artist is signed directly to the label and does not have an established sales base, is recording a first or second album, or has not had great success, the record company will control the purse strings and retain control of all payments relative to the recording and delivery of the album. If the artist is established and has prior experience in the financial aspects of recording albums, however, the record company will many times provide the artist or the production company with an album fund from which all recording costs will be taken. This fund, which usually takes the form of an up-front advance (e.g., $250,000 payable 30 days prior to the commencement of recording) but which can be structured on a reimbursement basis, enables the artist or production company to pay all recording costs. In most cases, if the artist's expenses do not exceed the recording fund (e.g., if the artist spends $175,000 out of a $250,000 recording fund), the amount left over is kept by the artist and treated as an additional advance recoupable from the artist's royalties.

The costs of recording an album, single, EP, or any other recorded configuration designed for commercial release are always treated as advances to the recording artist and recoupable from royalties due that artist. Such costs are recoupable not only from royalties derived from the album for which they were incurred but also from royalties due the artist from all other recordings produced during the term of the agreement. In other words, recording costs are cumulative during the term of the recording contract, and the record company will be able to recoup royalties due from any recording released during the agreement to cover any recording costs expended during the agreement. For example, if the costs of the initial album were $100,000 and the artist earned $50,000 in royalties, there would be a debit balance of $50,000 in the artist's account. If the costs of the second album were $125,000 and the artist earned $150,000 in royalties from that album, no royalties would be distributed, because there still would be a recording costs debit balance of $25,000 from both albums, even though royalties earned from the second album exceeded the recording costs for that particular album (e.g., $100,000 + $125,000 = $225,000 in recording costs, less $50,000 and $150,000 in royalties = $200,000 in earnings, resulting in a $25,000 deficit for the two albums). It is more than possible, therefore, that an artist can have three unsuccessful albums and a major hit on the fourth album and still receive no royalties because of the overall debit balance incurred from the unrecouped recording costs of the initial three albums.

Recording costs under most agreements include all direct costs relating to the making of the audio recording. They include all costs for arrangements, orchestration, and copying; all union scale payments to the recording artists and all others who perform on the recording, in addition to all payroll taxes or other taxes required to be paid on such earnings; all instrument rental, cartage, hall rental, studio, and engineering charges; mastering, remastering, mixing, and remixing fees; recording costs; digitization expenses; transportation, hotel, per diems, and living expenses; immigration clearances; all costs of trademark and service mark searches and registrations; all costs related to delivery to the record company of the fully edited master recordings; all monies that may be due from any collective bargaining agreements based on union scale payments; any payments made or required to be made for "sample" clearances of other compositions or recorded performances owned by third-party writers, music publishers, record companies, producers, or artists; and any advance payments, fees, or royalties payable to personnel and companies rendering services with respect to the recording of the compositions on the album.

The record company expects that the artist will stay within the recording budget. In the event that costs exceed the maximum budget amount, the record company will usually take responsibility for payment of any such overage expenses, usually after notice to the artist. If the record company does assume responsibility for such over-budget items, it will normally either deduct the overage from any future advances due the artist or recoup the money from recording artist royalties and, in many cases, writer and publisher mechanical royalties.

THE ARTIST'S OBLIGATIONS

THE MINIMUM RECORDING OBLIGATION

The minimum recording obligation (sometimes referred to as the "minimum delivery obligation") refers to the number of individual master recordings that the artist will record during each contract period of the term of the recording agreement. For example, a contract may state that during each period of the term the artist shall record enough songs to constitute one long-playing album of at least 35 minutes in duration. In some cases, the record contract will refer to the number of individual sides; in other cases, the contract may refer to a minimum number of individual sides plus any additional recordings deemed necessary by the record company for satisfactory completion of the album (e.g., 10 recorded sides plus up to an additional five sides at the record company's discretion).

Under all recording agreements, the current period of the term will be extended until the artist actually delivers to the record company the minimum recording obligation. For example, if an agreement states that the artist will deliver to the label a minimum of 12 newly recorded sides within six months from the commencement date of the contract, with the same guarantee applicable to each exercised option period, the agreement will always have a provision that extends the current period of the term for a certain period of time after actual delivery, to cover the eventuality that an artist might take longer than expected in the studio and deliver the requisite recordings after the contract deadline. Because timely delivery of recordings according to the schedule outlined in the recording agreement is vitally important to the record company and can be considered a serious breach by the artist, the record label will, if there is a substantial delay, many times be able to demand reimbursement of all monies paid to the artist that are related to the sides being recorded, suspend the agreement, or even terminate the agreement.

On occasion, a record company will not allow a recording artist to go into the studio to record the minimum recording obligation. This can occur for a number of different reasons, with some of the primary ones being loss of faith in the artist, the departure of the A&R executives who signed the act, a change in musical tastes at the label or by the general public, financial difficulties at the label, and negative attitude or discipline problems with the artist. When this occurs, the record label is usually obligated only to pay the artist the union scale payments that would have been due had the artist been allowed to go into the studio and record the minimum to meet his or her obligation for that period—a provision that is referred to as the "pay or play" clause.

In the event that the record company elects to go this route and does not allow the artist to record the minimum delivery obligation, the artist will often have the right to terminate the agreement so negotiations can commence with other labels. In most cases the artist must send the record company written notice demanding that it allow the artist to record sufficient master sides to fulfill the minimum recording obligation within a specified period of time (e.g., within 60 days after receipt of the notice). If the record company does not allow the artist to commence recording within that time period, the term of the recording agreement will be deemed to have been terminated at the end of the period.

SATISFACTION OF AN ARTIST'S DELIVERY COMMITMENT

In many contracts, clauses define what can or cannot be recorded by an artist to fulfill his or her album-delivery commitment. Some companies will structure the record agreement so that an artist can record only in a certain designated style or styles for an album to count toward the delivery commitment. For example, a sample clause might provide that the artist's performances will be in the rock, pop, metal, hip-hop, or rap genre for them to be acceptable. Or a provision might have the artist guaranteeing that the style of any new recordings will be similar to the performances contained on previously released albums. Obviously, this type of clause can lead to major disputes between the performer and record company, as most artists have a tendency to grow in their musical tastes or change their style of performance to place themselves in the midst of a popular new musical trend. Consequently, the wording of such clauses is important to each side of the negotiating table, especially when millions of dollars in recording costs, video costs, promotion commitments, marketing expenditures, and album advances are at stake.

Other restrictions in this area include re-recordings of material previously released, live performances, instrumental recordings (where the artist is a vocalist), and special themed albums (e.g., a Christmas album). Having such restrictions in an artist's contract does not necessarily mean that a performer may not record such compositions, as such recordings may be made with the approval of the record company. Whether or not such approval is given, however, depends on the relationship of the company and the artist, whether there has been past financial success, and the nature of the album.

"GREATEST HITS" ALBUMS

Virtually all record contracts give the record company the right to compile and release a "greatest hits" album. For most recording artists, such a right is never exercised, because only a select number of artists ever have enough hits to justify the release of such a recording. Occasionally, the sides to be included on a "greatest hits" package must be approved by the performer; the agreement usually contains certain provisos of what type of compositions are automatically deemed approved. For example, a sample clause may provide that the "A" side of any single that reached the Top 40 is deemed approved by the artist; such a proviso ensures that all hits will be put in the "greatest hits" album, regardless of how the artist feels about certain compositions artistically. Should there be disputes over which recordings to include on the album, some contracts provide that the artist and the record company may each select a certain number (e.g., the record company selects 60% of the album and the artist 40%).

In certain instances, the record company may ask the artist to record new songs for inclusion on the "greatest hits" package. Sometimes these new recordings are mere "filler"; other times, the record company hopes that one of the new recordings will become a hit single and further enhance the album's sales. The bargaining power of the parties negotiating the record contract will determine how such newly recorded material will be approved. In any event, along with such a "new recordings" clause will always be a parallel provision that mandates that such new recordings must be delivered to the record company within a certain number of days after a formal request is made (e.g., within 60 to 180 days after a request). Such provisions are designed to ensure that the scheduled release of the "greatest hits" album will not be delayed because new material scheduled for inclusion on the album has not been delivered. Additional advances are usually paid for the new compositions.

RECORDING SESSIONS AND STUDIOS
In many cases, the studio to be used for recording an album is chosen by the record company after consultation with the recording artist. Established performers, however, are able to select the recording studio (provided it meets certain technological specifications) after consultation with the record company. The same principles and considerations also apply to the selection of recording personnel, arrangers, and other creative personnel at the recording sessions.

ALBUM ARTWORK
In the case of new or less-established artists, the record company will usually have final approval rights over artwork, as it will want to reserve the right to determine how a particular artist is presented and marketed. This right will always encompass photographs, photographic settings, and likenesses, since the matter of establishing the right image for an artist is of utmost importance to the record company, whose vision and checkbook are definitely at risk. In many cases, the budget for the album artwork is totally discretionary with the record company; in other cases, specific provisions are made in the record agreement guaranteeing certain minimum artwork expenditures. In the case of well-established artists, the record company will many times leave the album artwork totally up to the recording artist—subject, of course, to certain reviews by its legal department to prevent potential litigation on issues ranging from right of privacy, libel, copyright infringement, criminal law, and civil rights.

The record company will many times, in the case of well-established acts, provide not only a specific approved budget for album artwork but also give the artist the right to prepare all the materials for delivery to the record company. A sample clause might read that the artist will be given an agreed-upon amount of money (e.g., $35,000) and, in return, present color-corrected negatives, camera-ready artwork, and proofs that will provide the record company with sufficient materials to prepare the album cover and inserts for the upcoming release. Additionally, the record company will usually demand that all liner notes and other credits be supplied by the artist simultaneously with the delivery of the album artwork.

Budgets for album artwork can range from $10,000 to over $100,000, depending on the elaborateness of the project. In cases where the artist has been given the responsibility of providing all artwork elements, if the costs exceed the approved budget, the excess is many times treated as an additional advance to the artist, recoupable from recording artist royalties or, if the artist is also a songwriter, from the songwriter and publisher royalties due the performer for sales of the album. How the record company is reimbursed for excess artwork expenditures is a matter of negotiation, though, with the outcome, as usual, dependent on the bargaining power of the parties.

WARRANTIES AND INDEMNITIES

Some of the most important clauses in any recording artist agreement are those dealing with the warranties and indemnities made by the artist, whether as a performer or a songwriter. The initial warranties relate to the right of the recording artist to enter into the agreement and fulfill its obligations. Secondly, the artist usually warrants that his or her recorded performances will not violate or infringe upon the rights of any third parties. Additionally, the artist represents that no other person or company has any rights that will in any way interfere with the services being provided under the recording agreement. If the artist is a songwriter, the warranties will also run to the originality of the compositions that are created under the agreement and embodied on the albums released by the record company. The warranty sections of the recording agreement are always accompanied by the indemnity sections, provisions that dictate what happens either when a claim is made that a warranty has been breached or when a breach of warranties has been proven through a court judgment or settlement.

Some of the major arguments between opposing lawyers occur when the warranty and indemnity provisions are negotiated; the issue of who is ultimately responsible for payment of the expenses related to a claim can have monumental financial implications. Considering that the legal fees expended even in infringement cases that are won by the artist and record company can easily exceed $400,000, these provisions are hard-fought, especially by experienced attorneys who have seen profits from a hit record fly out the window from even a "crackpot" claim.

Many record contract indemnity clauses provide that the artist will hold the record company harmless from any loss or damages (including attorneys' fees) that are related to any claim or action that is inconsistent with the warranties made by the recording artist. Under such provisions, the artist is held responsible for reimbursement of all the record company's expenses in defending itself and the artist against a claim from a third party, whether or not the artist has actually breached his or her warranties under the agreement. For example, if another record company sues the artist's current record company, alleging that the artist is still under contract to it (a breach of representation by the artist, if proven), the artist would be responsible for all monies expended in defending the action, since this would be a claim inconsistent with the artist's representation that he or she was free and clear to sign a new recording agreement. It doesn't matter who wins the litigation; all that is needed to trigger indemnification by the artist under such a clause is for a claim to be received, since whether or not a claim is proven to be true is immaterial to the issue of who has the responsibility for the fees expended in defending the claim.

Because of the financial implications inherent in such clauses, the artist's lawyer will try to negotiate provisions that base indemnification by the artist only on claims that actually result in a judgment against the artist and record company. Such a proviso insulates the artist from paying out monies in instances where the artist has not in fact breached any warranties, since it distinguishes financial responsibility for the defense of claims alleging that a breach has occurred but that are never proven, and claims that actually result in a judicial finding or settlement establishing that a breach by the artist has occurred.

An additional issue that always comes up in the negotiations concerns what the record company can do when a claim is received. In virtually all instances, the record company will be able to hold an amount of royalties due the artist that is consistent with the amount of money that might be lost if the claim against the company and artist is successful. For example, if the record company determines that $150,000 might be lost if a suit is lost, it will have the right to withhold $150,000 of an artist's royalties to cover such a possibility. On occasion, the record company may also be able to withhold the payment of future advances to an artist (e.g., an upcoming album advance), but such remedies are always a matter of negotiation.

Since the record company will always have the right to withhold a portion of the artist's royalties in the event of a claim, the attorney for the artist will usually request that the monies being withheld be placed in an interest-bearing account (sometimes segregated from the record company's other funds) so that the artist will, if the monies are eventually released, receive the benefit of the interest that would have been made had the monies been paid and placed in the artist's bank account. Record companies will many times also agree to release the monies being held if litigation is not commenced within a certain period of time (e.g., if a suit is not filed within one to two years from the date that the claim letter was received), if the litigation is dismissed or claim withdrawn, or if the artist is able to post a bond with collateral securing the recovery of the monies being released.

The record company will almost always have the right to select the law firm that will control the defense on its behalf. In most cases, the artist will be able to retain independent personal legal counsel, provided that such counsel will not be able to interfere with the conduct and direction of the defense. The artist's lawyer, however, will usually be able to advise as to strategy and provide input to the legal staff retained by the record company.

BACKUP MUSICIAN PROVISIONS

In many recording agreements, the record company will allow its artist to perform as a backup musician or "sideman" on the commercially released recordings of other recording artists. Such clauses are usually a courtesy to the artist, a goodwill gesture that represents an exception to the contract's "exclusivity of recording services" provisions. If the record company agrees to such a clause, the artist's ability to perform as a sideman is usually conditioned upon the other record company's not being able to feature the photo or likeness of the sideman artist on the album cover or in any advertisements or promotions of the album. Additionally, there are always guarantees that a courtesy credit on the album liner notes will be given to the sideman's record company, that any credit for the sideman will not be larger than the credit afforded other sidemen, that any credit for the sideman will only be as a sideman, and that the recording sessions using the artist as a sideman will not interfere with the requirements of the artist's primary agreement.

SIDE ARTISTS

Side artist agreements are used when a vocalist performer contributes to a specific track but is not treated as a featured artist. There are a number of variations as to the type of provisions contained in these agreements but the following represent some of the major ones. Although this is negotiable, the side artist will, in most cases, not receive a credit for his or her services other than for songwriting services, if applicable. The performance will be created under a writer for hire agreement so that the featured artist, producer or record company will be the copyright owner. If the side artist is signed to a record company as a featured artist, that record company will have to provide its approval as well as a waiver of exclusive recording services.

There will, in most cases, be a recoupable advance paid and a royalty based on the terms of the featured artists' recording agreement with the record company releasing the track. For example, the side artist might receive 10% of the royalties due the featured artist calculated in the same manner as the artists' record contract. For example, if the featured artist is receiving a 15% royalty, the side artist would be entitled to a 1.5% royalty under the above scenario. In these cases, a separate account will be set up that relates specifically to the track on which the side artist appears so that only the costs and expenses specifically attributable to that one master shall be considered for purposes of recoupment and payment. Since there can be substantial royalties collected by SoundExchange, the side artist may be acknowledged as a "featured artist" for the purposes of being entitled to participate in monies generated by the public performance of the master. In these cases, the side artist would register his or her share with SoundExchange and collect the royalties directly.

Included in any side artist agreement will be indemnification clauses as well as royalty accounting provisions. In addition, the side artist may have to agree not to perform the composition on the track for a period of time after the release of the initial side artist recording (much like a re-recording restriction in a recording artist agreement). If the side artist wrote or co-wrote the composition recorded, the agreement will also contain controlled composition clauses detailing the percentage of writer and publisher shares, the mechanical rate and what party has the right to issue licenses relating to the use of the composition contained on the track (e.g., synch licenses, etc.).

RE-RECORDING RESTRICTIONS

If a recording artist changes record labels or is dropped from one label and signs with another, there are always certain restrictions placed on the artist by his or her previous company as to what songs can be recorded for the new record company. Almost all contracts prohibit the artist from re-recording any selection for the new company that had been recorded while under contract with his or her former record company. These re-recording restrictions are not open-ended in duration, however; they always contain stated time limitations after which restrictions no longer apply. Many contracts take the approach of prohibiting any re-recording of past material for the later of (1) from five years after a particular recorded performance has been delivered to or released by the record company, or (2) three years after the expiration of the artist's featured recording contract. Under such a proviso, if an artist recorded and delivered a composition in December 2012 and the artist's contract with the record company lasted for two more albums until November 2016, that artist would not be able to re-record that same composition for another record company until November 2019, three years after the contract ended (i.e., not December 2017, which is five years after the song was delivered).

Other record companies have longer re-recording restrictions. For example, some companies prohibit the artist from re-recording for five years after the expiration of the contract. Occasionally these restrictions apply not only to the recording services of the artist as a featured performer but are extended to the services of the artist as a producer. For example, if an artist is also known as a producer for other acts, a restriction in the contract might prevent the artist from producing another artist who is re-recording a composition previously recorded by the producer/artist. If such a clause is contained in the recording agreement, the restricted period is usually shorter than that imposed on the artist for re-recording as a featured performer.

SOLO ALBUMS (FOR MEMBERS OF A GROUP)

The individual members of a group may have plans for eventual solo careers, or at least for recording solo albums. Provided that the desire for a solo album does not interfere with the group's recording and touring schedules or with the record company's album release and promotion and marketing plans, contracts often allow the various members of the group to make solo recordings.

In most cases, a member of a group must give the record company written notice before beginning a solo project. If the record company consents, and provided there is no conflict with any plans it has for the group, the company usually has the right to control and release the solo album if it so desires. In some cases, a specific advance is payable if the record company picks up such an option (e.g., $75,000 to the individual artist, one third of which is payable upon commencement of recording, one third upon acceptance of the solo album by the record company, and one third upon release of the solo album in the United States). In other cases, a good-faith negotiation clause may give the record company the exclusive right to negotiate with the solo artist as to the terms of an agreement (e.g., advance, recording budget, royalties) for a period of time (usually from 30 to 90 days) or the right to match an offer from a third-party record company. In the latter instance, the individual artist will be obligated to supply the record company with all substantive terms of the bona fide third-party offer, and the record company will usually have from 15 to 60 days to match the offer. If the offer is not matched, the solo artist will be free to enter into the proposed third-party agreement. But if the terms of the agreement eventually negotiated by the solo artist with a third party are less favorable to the artist than as originally presented to and rejected by the group's record company, that company will usually get another opportunity to match the final offer.

PROVISIONS FOR NEW BAND MEMBERS AND DEPARTING BAND MEMBERS

The record company will always demand that any new member of a contracted group ratify and sign the existing recording agreement before becoming part of the group. This is true whether the new performer is replacing a member of the group who has left or is being added to the group without any current member leaving. The ratification form that is signed by the new member can take a number of different forms, but usually will provide that the new member has read all the provisions of the recording agreement, has received independent legal advice from outside counsel, and agrees to be bound by all the terms and conditions of the recording agreement as if the new member were an original signatory to the agreement. The effective date of the new member's acceptance of the contract is usually the earlier of the date of his or her signing the ratification agreement or the new member's actual rendering of services to the group.

In the case of a band member's leaving the group, the recording agreement will always provide that the leaving member must send written notice to the record company. Within a certain number of days after receiving the notice, the record company will usually have the right to elect a number of different options relating to not only the leaving member of the group but also the remaining members of the group. These options include the right to terminate the recording agreement with the group, the right to require the remaining members of the group to provide a substitute performer for the leaving member, and the right to have the remaining members perform as a self-contained act without replacing the leaving member.

The record company will also have the right to negotiate with each performer of the group with respect to the signing of a new recording agreement. For example, the company may have the right to acquire the individual services of any member of the group by sending that member notice of such within 30 to 90 days after a leaving member has given notice. In many cases, if the record company elects to sign an individual remaining member or a leaving member, a provision will bind the parties to good-faith negotiations concerning the terms of the new agreement. If within a certain time period (e.g., 60 days or 90 days) negotiations do not result in an agreement, the artist will normally be able to negotiate with other record companies, with the proviso that the current record company will have a certain number of days (usually 30 to 45) to match any offer from another record company. In other cases, the record company, if it so chooses, will elect to have the leaving member sign an identical contract to the one that he or she signed as a group member, the term of which usually consists of the remaining balance of the group contract.

In addition, some record companies will require any leaving member to go into the studio to record a number of demonstration recordings pursuant to either a budget approved by the record company or one that is mutually approved by the artist and label within certain previously negotiated guidelines. The record company will then usually have a specified number of days after it receives the finished demo recordings to decide whether or not it wants to exercise its right to sign the leaving member as an exclusive recording artist. Under this type of provision, the record company is giving itself the opportunity to listen to what the leaving member can do as an individual artist and make a decision only after it is able to review newly recorded performances.

RECORDING AND DELIVERY OF ALBUMS

Virtually all contracts provide for a specified outside date by which the initial album must be delivered to the record company. For example, if an artist agreement commences on January 1, the contract may provide that commencement of recording will start no later than March 1 and that completion of the album be satisfied not later than July 1. Other agreements may not refer to a commencement of recording date but only refer to a guaranteed completion and delivery date for each album. For example, a delivery provision may provide that the initial album be delivered within 90 to 180 days after the recording agreement is signed and that each option album be delivered within 90 to 180 days after commencement of each option period of the term. Some agreements compute delivery dates for option albums from the delivery or release of the previous album (e.g., each subsequent album being delivered no earlier than nine months and no later than 18 months after delivery of the prior album, or no earlier than six months and no later than 12 months after the U.S. release of the prior album).

When an artist changes record labels, restrictions in that artist's contract with the old label may restrict the timing of album releases by the new label. For example, the new record company may not be able to release a newly recorded album until a specified number of months after the old record company has released (or, per contract, should have released) the last album recorded under its agreement with the artist. These restrictive clauses can also be tied to the delivery of an album (e.g., the artist agreeing not to have an album released by the new record company until six months after the delivery of the last product commitment album to the old record company).

DELIVERY OF THE FINAL MASTER RECORDING

In cases where the recording artist is responsible for all aspects of the recording project or in instances where the artist is being furnished by a production company that is acting as producer of the album, the record company will normally require that the producer/artist furnish the record company with all consents and clearances necessary for the release of the completed album and its cover and liner notes, correct writer and publisher information on all compositions recorded, timely submission of all musicians union contracts and W-4s, clearance of any sampled recordings or musical compositions, and mechanical licenses for compositions that are not written by the artist or controlled by a company owned or controlled by the artist or producer.

Most record companies will, once the album is completed, require that the artist or producer deliver the master recordings in an acceptable format. A representative clause will state that the artist will deliver to the record company in a format(s) reasonably requested by the record company fully recorded, edited and mixed master recordings which are technically satisfactory to the record company and are determined by the record company to be in proper form for the production of the parts necessary for the manufacture of records and for dissemination of electronic transmissions. Occasionally, the record company will also require an additional reference copy. In many contracts, the record company will have a specified number of days from its receipt of the master tape of the album to approve or disapprove of the completed recording. For example, a sample acceptance clause may state that if the record company does not notify the artist/producer that a particular album is unacceptable within 20 days of receipt, that album shall be deemed to have been accepted. In some cases, there may be a warranty that all outtakes will also be delivered to the record company, but such a requirement is always subject to negotiation and agreement by the parties. Additionally, record companies will usually agree not to release any outtakes without the permission of the recording artist. Included in the delivery requirements are all original session multi-track masters (including any audio files that were not part of the final mix) which, in quality, reflect the then current state of the art recording techniques (with a safety copy); flat and equalized mixes of each master; additional mixes such as a television track (instrumental and background vocals only or instrumental only), album mix, a cappella mix and any other specialty mixes requested by the record company. All data files, tapes, and work parts will be submitted as well.

Considering the amount of time, effort, and money involved with the recording of an album, the issue of "what is or is not acceptable" is of paramount importance not only to the record company but to the artist as well. After all, the record company may easily have a commitment of from $200,000 to more than $3 million on the line, and will therefore demand as much perfection as possible in the final master recording, in terms of both technical competence and creative expression. The artist, on the other hand, will try to limit the record company's approval rights to the technical acceptability of the album (the domain of engineers and experts involved in the "sound" aspects of recording) as opposed to the artistic expression or creative direction taken by the performer on a particular recording. Established recording artists usually succeed in securing language that guarantees acceptance by the record company as long as the master recording is technically satisfactory for commercial release to the general public and the compositions have not been previously recorded by the artist, provided that the style of such performances is not adverse to the past performances of the artist. Less-established artists and new performers must accept language that usually gives the record company more leeway in accepting or rejecting an album (e.g., the record company may require that the performances be of a contemporary nature, etc.), language that can many times enable the record company to become involved in the creative focus and expression of the recorded project. The record company will almost always have the right to require the artist to re-record any master that is deemed unacceptable.

OWNERSHIP OF THE RECORDINGS

Unless the contract contains other provisions, the artist agreement will usually state that the record label is the copyright owner of the performances recorded during the term of the recording agreement. In many cases, the ownership will be termed a "work made for hire" under the U.S. Copyright Act, and, if upheld, there may be no reversion of rights to the recording artist or record producer. The general grant-of-rights clause of the recording agreement gives the record company the right, among other things, to manufacture and distribute audio and audiovisual recordings of the performances of the artist under the record company's trade name, to perform such recordings, and to package and exploit such recordings, all such rights being subject to the other terms of the agreement, including those provisions that guarantee royalty payments for most types of commercial exploitation. Depending on one's bargaining power, a number of restrictions can be negotiated by the artist (e.g., initial release of any recording to be on the record company's "top line" label, no inclusion of a master on "compilation" or "television-only" albums until a certain amount of time has elapsed after the initial release of the recording, or approval over certain motion picture, video game, or advertising commercial uses), but in most cases, the record company will have fairly unrestricted rights to exploit the master recordings in the manner that it sees fit to promote the artist.

In cases where the artist is able to cause a reversion of ownership of his or her recorded performances contractually via negotiation (an occurrence that usually happens only with the biggest superstars or in the case of a licensing of pre-existing masters agreement), that right is often subject to the record company's having recouped all advances paid to or on behalf of the artist. Such reversion provisions normally refer to a grant of rights that will last for a certain number of years after the expiration of the term of the recording artist agreement, with an automatic extension of time if the record company is still in an unrecouped position at the time of the agreed-upon reversion date.

For example, a sample clause might read:
All rights in and to the recordings shall revert to the recording artist 15 years after the expiration of the term of the recording agreement, said agreement to expire upon the commercial release in the United States of the fifth album recorded during the term of the record contract. Notwithstanding the above, however, in the event that the record company has not recouped all of the advances previously paid to the artist (e.g., signing advance, commencement of option advances, album delivery and acceptance advances, commercial release advances, etc.) or paid to others on behalf of the artist (e.g., audio and audio visual recording costs, per diems to performers, musician union fees, etc.), the rights to the master recordings shall remain with the record company until either all such advances and direct costs are recouped or until the artist repays the record company the total outstanding unrecouped advance balance related not only to the most recent album but all albums recorded under the artist agreement.

In the event that such a "repayment of any outstanding advance balance" provision is included in a recording agreement, the effective reversion date will usually be the last day of either the calendar quarter or semiannual calendar period during which the repayment by the artist is made. For example, if the artist repays the unrecouped advance balance on July 14 of a particular year and there is an "end of the semiannual calendar period" reversion date, the transfer of ownership of the recordings to the artist would not occur until December 31 of that year. If an "end of the calendar quarter" reversion date had been used in the above scenario, the reversion date would be the end of September.

MOTION PICTURE, TELEVISION, VIDEO GAME, AND COMMERCIAL USES

Considering that the use of a master recording in a motion picture can generate from $15,000 to more than $75,000 in licensing fees, the use of a master recording in a television series from $1,750 to more than $30,000, the use of a master in a video game from $2,500 to over $20,000, and the use of a master recording in a national television consumer product commercial from $75,000 to more than $1,000,000, income from these sources can have a substantial impact not only on the record company's bottom line but on the artist's earnings as well. In addition to the licensing fee received by the record company, these uses can also open up a number of other opportunities, such as being included on a soundtrack album, being placed in a video game, or being introduced to a new audience by means of increased exposure to the general public, all of which will usually have the potential of positively affecting sales and other uses of the recording.

Most recording agreements will provide that the artist will receive 50% of the net license fee received by the record company for the motion picture, television, video game, or commercial use. As to the definition of what is "net" in a licensing situation, duplication costs, out-of-pocket charges, and all third-party payment obligations such as union payments and, if applicable, songwriter and publisher royalties will be deducted from the gross monies received to arrive at the net. For example, if a master recording is licensed for use in a motion picture at a fee of $30,000 and it costs the record company $1,500 in duplication costs and union fees, the net licensing fee would be $28,500 (i.e., $30,000 − $1,500 = $28,500). Under the 50% sharing formula, the record company would retain $14,250 with the remaining $14,250 being paid to the recording artist. In the event that the artist is in an unrecouped-advance position, the monies will be used by the record company to reduce the outstanding negative advance balance. Streaming income is often shared this way.

In many recording agreements, the record company will have sole discretion in deciding whether to license a certain master recording for use in a particular motion picture, television series, video game, or commercial. Depending on the artist's bargaining power, stature, and quality of legal representation, the negotiations may result in the record company's having to secure the approval of the artist before entering into any such licensing agreements. Unless one is a superstar, it is not common for an artist to have total approval over all film and television uses, as most record companies try to retain as much discretionary power in this area as possible. On the other hand, a large number of artists are able to secure consent rights over the use of their recorded performances in certain types of motion pictures (e.g., X-rated or NC-17-rated theatrical films) and consumer product commercials, especially with respect to certain types of products, such as alcohol or hygiene products.

SHIPPING AND RETURN POLICIES
(PHYSICAL RECORDINGS)

Record companies normally extend to their distributors, rack jobbers, and other customers the privilege of returning all unsold physical recordings for credit. Considering that the vast majority of albums do not recover their costs, this "return privilege" can become a major problem to the record company. In addition, if a record company has a policy of consistently overpressing and shipping more albums than can realistically be sold, this problem can be further aggravated. For example, in the case of a company that overships, the artist may be initially ecstatic about the number of records out in the market. What the artist does not realize, however, is that out of a shipment of 100,000 physical albums, 25,000 might be bought by the general public, with 75,000 returned as unsold goods. Fortunately, most record companies adopt a more judicious approach in the pressing and shipping of recordings, especially in the case of new artists without any established sales pattern or base. With these companies, the return rate is usually lower than that of a company that overships just for the sake of having large numbers of recordings in the stores. But even in the case of companies with more selective and modest shipping policies, the number of physical recordings that might be returned can still be substantial.

RETURNED RECORDINGS AND THE ARTIST'S ROYALTIES

In every recording contract the artist and the record company agree that royalties will be paid only on physical recordings that are actually sold or distributed to the general public, not on records that are manufactured and shipped but eventually returned. For example, if 100,000 albums are shipped and only 50,000 are actually sold at the retail level, with the remainder being returned for credit, the artist will be paid only on the 50,000. If for some reason a performer is overpaid because the record company's accounts indicated more sales than eventually occurred, the record company will always have the right to deduct such "excess royalties" from future sales due the artist and, in some cases, demand immediate reimbursement.

Reserve Funds and Anticipated Returns. Recognizing that there are always going to be returns as to physical product (regardless of the artist) and that unsold recordings may continue to come back for years after the initial release date of an album, single, or EP, record companies normally withhold a certain percentage of an artist's royalties in anticipation of such returns. These withheld royalties are referred to as "reserves" and are designed to ensure that the record company will not overpay an artist based on the initial sales figures from its distributors instead of actual sales to the general public. For example, if a record company ships 100,000 albums to its distributors, who then sell those albums to a number of retail stores, the initial sales figures to the record company will indicate that all 100,000 records have been sold. Let us also assume that during the following 12 to 18 months 50,000 of those albums are returned to the company for credit because they could not be sold. If the record company had based its royalty computations on the original sales figures from its distributors, it would have already remitted royalties to the recording artist on a full 100,000 albums sold, resulting in an overpayment on 50,000 albums—a costly mistake for artists making $1 to $2 per album.

Reserve Fund Holdback Percentages. Under the reserve clause provisions, therefore, the record company is allowed to hold back a certain percentage of the artist's royalties to protect itself against large numbers of physical returns. In effect, the company is paying only on recordings that have actually been sold to the public and not those that it anticipates will be returned for credit. There are many times no stated limits as to how much the record company is thus allowed to hold back. Each company has a different policy, usually with lower percentages for established artists and higher percentages for newer groups. Some companies even hold as much as 50% of an artist's royalties pending a final accounting as to how many records have actually been sold. The vast majority of companies, however, have lower reserve percentages, which range from 20% to 40% depending on the past track record of the artist. Different configurations may have different reserve percentages because of the history of returns for that particular type of recording. For example, the reserve percentage on a long-playing album may be 25% to 30%, but on EPs the reserve may be 30% to 40%. It is, therefore, important to secure the actual policy in writing.

Liquidating the Reserve Fund. The reserve fund can pose real problems for many recording artists, because it substantially reduces the artist's initial royalty payments and postpones the date when he or she will finally be paid all royalties due. In addition, if a company's reserve percentage is much higher than the actual number of returns (for example, a 50% royalty holdback where only 25% of the recordings are actually returned), the artist might be penalized unjustifiably. Because most reserve clauses are open ended, many artists try to negotiate a limit on the amount of time that a record company can withhold such reserved royalties. For example, some agreements guarantee that the company will liquidate the reserve within a "reasonable amount of time." Other contracts are more specific and put an actual time limit of from 12 to 24 months for a complete accounting of any monies being held in anticipation of returns. Still others will actually recite the record company's current reserve policy (for example, "no withholding in excess of 35% of all recordings sold and paid for") or, in the alternative, provide a returns history for a particular recorded configuration at the artist's request so that all parties know what to expect. And others will base the reserve for a particular album on the actual return percentage of the prior album plus an additional "safety net" percentage (e.g., 30% + 5% = 35% reserve). Many record companies will also have a provision in their contracts that if they become aware of any facts concerning the artist that might indicate that returns on a particular album in excess of the contractual limitations may occur, a larger reserve may be put into effect for that album.

INSURANCE POLICIES

Because the record company is making a substantial investment in a recording artist, the record contract will usually have a clause that permits the label to purchase insurance covering the performer's life or any disability suffered due to illness or accident. The record company will be the beneficiary under the policy and will pay the premiums. In the event that the record company elects to take out insurance, the artist will agree to be available for any medical examination that is required for the issuance of such a policy. It is common for both the record company and the artist to have mutual approval over the physician chosen to do the examination.

CONFIDENTIALITY CLAUSES

The record contract may limit both the artist and the record label from disclosing the major negotiated provisions to the press or the general public. Such a clause enables the record company to protect information about what it gave to one artist from the legal and business representatives of other artists who may already be signed or who will be signed in the future. There are exceptions to the disclosure rules (e.g., disclosure of information being allowable to legal, financial, and investment advisors of the artist, to governmental agencies, etc.), and occasionally the record company and artist will agree to consult with each other over a mutually agreed-upon press release about the signing or renegotiation of a recording agreement. In many cases, the record company will have the right to issue the press release and the "final say" as to its wording.

ARTIST–PRODUCTION COMPANY AGREEMENTS

It is common in the recording industry for the artist to be signed to a production company, which in turn signs with the record company as the provider of the performing services of the artist. This arrangement is extremely prevalent in the case of superstars and established artists, especially when these performers not only produce or coproduce their own recordings but also take on the responsibility of many of the creative and business aspects surrounding the conception, creation, recording, and delivery of their albums.

The production company will always warrant that it has a binding agreement with the performer that guarantees that the artist not only is required to perform exclusively for the production company but also will comply with all the terms of the record company-production company agreement. The record contract will further provide that if the production company does not fulfill its obligations or enforce its rights with respect to the recording artist, then the record company will have the right either to fulfill an obligation or to remedy a default on the part of the production company. For example, if the production company defaults on a royalty payment to the artist, the record company may step in to assure proper payment to the artist. The record label will demand to see a copy of the contract between the artist and the service or production company, and will secure guarantees that no revisions or modifications will be made in the production company-artist agreement without the approval of the label.

FLOW-THROUGH CLAUSES

Because of the enormous investment on the part of the record company in the recording, distribution, manufacturing, promotion, and marketing of albums (to say nothing of the monies expended to sign the artist and secure the rights), the record label will always demand that the artist sign a "flow-through clause" that will guarantee that, if the production company furnishing the services of the artist defaults on its obligations, the artist will fulfill his or her obligations directly to the record company. Under this type of arrangement, the record company effectively protects its investment and rights to the artist's services, since the artist is in reality agreeing to be obligated directly to the record company.

The record company will use its flow-through rights to the artist in a number of situations, the most common of which are the liquidation or dissolution of the production company, a bankruptcy or insolvency filing, an assignment of rights for the benefit of creditors, a failure by the production company to fulfill its obligations under the recording contract, and a breach by the production company of a term of its contract with the recording artist that jeopardizes the record company's rights.

PUBLICITY

Many record companies will agree to hire a publicist whose major responsibility will be to garner positive publicity for the artist. If the record company agrees to hire a publicist, the publicist's activities will normally be coordinated with the company's promotion and/or publicity departments, and all activities will be subject to a mutually approved budget. The monies expended by the record company in this area are often 50% recoupable from royalties due the recording artist.

RESPONSIBILITY FOR PAYMENT OF PRODUCER ROYALTIES

Many recording artist agreements provide that the recording artist is responsible for paying the record producer his or her producer royalties from the artist's gross royalties or, in the alternative, provide that the producer shall be paid directly from the record company after all recording costs of the album have been recouped by the record company from royalties due the artist. Under this scenario, the record company will begin paying the record producer royalties starting with the next quarterly accounting date after all recording costs have been recouped. These producer royalties will be paid retroactively to the first album sold subject to the recovery of any advance that might have been paid to the producer, as well as any over-budget recording costs or other charges that may be contractually deductible from the producer's royalties.

PRODUCER CREDIT

If the artist is the party who is choosing and contracting with the producer, there may be a provision in the artist's recording agreement that will guarantee the producer credit on all album packaging and/or labels, and in paid trade advertisements in the United States when the record company places ads that are of one-half page or larger and that relate exclusively to the album.

PRODUCER ADVANCES

If the artist is paying the producer, the record company will many times limit the amount of advances paid to the producer. For example, a clause might read "the aggregate producer royalties payable to producers supervising the recording of masters on an album shall not be less than $25,000 or greater than $75,000." In the event that there is more than one producer on the album, clauses in the artist agreement may put limits on the individual master recordings that make up the album. For example, the contract might put a dollar limit on the advance payable on any one particular track when there are multiple producers on an album.

PRODUCER ROYALTIES

When the artist is responsible for the payment of producer royalties, the record company will accept a letter of direction from the artist which will provide that the record company, on the artist's behalf, will have the obligation to pay the producer his or her share of advances and royalties. The record company will many times provide the artist with its standard-form record producer agreement and letter of direction if the artist requests such.

Many artist agreements will also contain language setting forth the type of producer terms which are deemed to be approved by the record company and which may not be exceeded in the producer agreement. For example, a 3% producer royalty (which is paid in the same manner and at the same times as the artist royalty) will be provided for. This royalty rate will be reduced, computed, and otherwise determined at the same base prices, subject to the same deductions and reductions (for example, packaging charges and free goods), as are the royalties paid to the artist for the applicable album or singles. Of course, if there is more than one producer for a master recording, the aggregate producer royalties will not exceed the maximum royalties that would be paid if there were only one producer. If the record company is accounting to the producer directly, then the artist may grant the producer the right to conduct an independent audit of the record company on terms no more favorable than those that the artist has.

PRODUCER-CONTROLLED COMPOSITIONS

Additionally, the producer will many times guarantee that any compositions written or controlled by the producer which appear on the album will be subject to the terms of the controlled composition clause contained in the artist agreement.

CONTROLLED-COMPOSITION CLAUSES

One of the most important areas in any recording artist agreement negotiation is the area related to how the performer gets paid for self-written compositions ("controlled compositions" in industry lingo) on an album, EP, single, video, or combination of audio plus audiovisual configuration released by the record company. A controlled composition is defined in a number of ways depending on the record company, but it always includes musical compositions written by the performer and musical compositions that are either owned or controlled by the performer's publishing company. These provisions (known as "controlled-composition clauses") tend to be as hotly negotiated as any clause in the contract (including artist royalty rates, advances, video budgets, and deductions), because they can and do have a major impact on how much money a performer can make as a songwriter and, in many cases, how much money the performer will not make because he or she wrote a song. These clauses also apply to the songwriter/producer.

MECHANICAL RATES

Most record companies will try to reduce the amount of mechanical royalties (i.e., songwriter and music publisher royalties due for the sale of recordings) that they have to pay to their songwriter/recording artists. For example, most record companies will pay the writer/performer (with the exception of downloads which will usually be at statutory) only 75% of the minimum statutory mechanical rate per musical composition written by the artist for each CD or record sold in the United States. The contract almost always states that the so called "long song" per minute rate will not apply in any calculation of album, single, or EP rates.

To illustrate, the mechanical royalty computations for one copy of a 10-song album would look as follows:

9.1¢	Statutory rate
× 75%	Controlled rate
6.825¢	Per-song royalties
× 10	Songs on album
68.25¢	Aggregate mechanical royalties

Under the above scenario, if 100,000 physical albums are sold in the United States, the record company would pay $68,250 in mechanical royalties, rather than the statutory $91,000.

SALES PLATEAU INCREASES

Occasionally, these controlled composition rates can be increased based on a recording artist's success in the marketplace (e.g., an album or single achieving certain predetermined sales levels), but such increases are always subject to negotiation and are rarely given voluntarily. To illustrate, if the writer/performer has to accept a 75% rate on all self-written compositions, some agreements will provide for the record company to pay a 75% rate for sales of each album up to 100,000 units, increase the royalty to 82.5% or 85% for sales between 100,001 and 250,000, and further increase the mechanical royalty rate to full statutory or 100% for all albums sold after 250,000.

A sample sales incentive/royalty increase clause may read as follows:
With respect to the writer/performer's self-written compositions that appear on any album recorded hereunder, the controlled composition royalty rate shall be increased from 75% to 82.5% for all full-priced sales in excess of 100,000 but not in excess of 200,000. For full-priced sales in excess of 200,000 but not in excess of 400,000 units, the 82.5% rate shall be increased to 90%. For full-priced sales in excess of 400,000 but not in excess of 500,000 units, the 90% royalty rate shall be increased to 97.5%. And for full-priced sales in excess of 500,000 units, the mechanical royalty shall be 100% of the minimum statutory rate.

INCREASED ROYALTIES FOR LATER ALBUMS

If a writer/performer has to accept a 75% mechanical rate in the recording artist agreement, it is often possible to negotiate a higher rate for subsequent albums. For example, if a writer/performer has signed a seven-album recording agreement with a record company (e.g., one album plus options for six more), the mechanical rate might be increased from 75% to 82.5% or 85% for compositions on the fourth and fifth albums, or even to 100% on the sixth and seventh albums. Variations in this area depend on one's bargaining power and the experience of one's representatives. All are based on the principle that if a writer/artist has recorded more than three or four albums for the same record company, the albums must be fairly successful and thus be generating profits for all parties. That being so, the writer/recording artist should not be penalized for being a songwriter. A sample clause might read:

Notwithstanding the 75% controlled-composition statutory-rate provisions of this Agreement, it is agreed that all musical compositions written by the writer/artist which are embodied on the fourth and fifth albums recorded hereunder will be paid at 85% of the minimum statutory rate. For musical compositions written by the writer/

artist that are embodied on the sixth and seventh albums, payment of mechanical royalties for musical compositions written by the writer/artist shall be paid at 100% of the statutory rate.

CANADIAN SALES

In addition to covering sales in the United States, the controlled-composition reduced-royalty rate provisions of the recording agreement also apply to sales of albums and singles in Canada. The clauses relating to Canada usually provide that the 75% rate will be based on the compulsory mechanical rate established under the Canadian copyright law or, in the event that the law does not provide for one, on the rate established by the major record companies and major music publishers. On occasion, the clause will mention an actual penny royalty that would become effective if either of the other two alternatives does not exist.

"LOCK IN" RATE DATE

Because the compulsory statutory mechanical rate has gradually increased over the past years, most record company contracts will provide that the royalty rate for a particular composition on a particular album or single will be frozen at the rate in effect on a particular negotiated date. In this way, the record company's mechanical royalty costs for songs written by its writer/artists will be fixed and will not be subject to increase if the compulsory statutory rate goes up at some time in the future.

For example, some contracts provide that the rate will be the one in effect when the recording of an album commences; others calculate the effective date as the year in which the album is released; and still others fix the mechanical rate as of the date that an album is delivered to the record company. Sometimes the contract will provide that the earlier of either the actual delivery of an album or the date on which the album should have been delivered is the date that should apply. Occasionally, the controlled rate will be based on the statutory royalty rate in effect on the date of manufacture of a particular album, but this is not common.

"GREATEST HITS" ALBUMS

One area where a writer/artist can often negotiate an exception to the lock-in rate date provisions of the recording agreement has to do with "greatest hits" packages. Because "greatest hits" albums take recorded performances from a number of different albums (with many of the compositions being paid at differing mechanical rates because the albums were released during a wide span of years), some artists are able to get the record company to agree that the mechanical rate payable for all self-written compositions on such an album will be that in effect when the "greatest hits" album is released to the general public in the United States. For example, if a number of the compositions were being paid at 75% of a 6.25¢ rate because they were initially contained on albums that were recorded in 1993 when the statutory rate was 6.25¢, the mechanical payments for these compositions for sales of a "greatest hits" album released in 2019 (when the statutory rate had increased to 9.1¢) would be calculated on the 2019 rate rather than the lower 1993 rate.

MAXIMUM ROYALTY CAP

In addition to the controlled-composition rate and the lock-in date for a particular album, the other important clause in the record company's controlled-composition provisions is that which determines the maximum amount of mechanical royalties a record company is willing to pay on a particular album. Here a writer/performer's lawyer must be not only a proficient negotiator of the legal aspects of an agreement but also an accountant and mathematician, because all these clauses work in concert with each other and cannot be considered independently of one another. If they are dealt with in isolation, financial disasters can, have, and will continue to happen.

The way these clauses usually work is that the record company dictates that no more than 10 to 13 times the controlled writer/artist rate of 75% times minimum statutory will be payable in mechanical royalties on any one album regardless of how many compositions are on the album or when sales actually occur.

A sample clause might look as follows:
Notwithstanding anything to the contrary contained in this Agreement, with respect to net sales of albums in the United States and Canada, the maximum aggregate mechanical copyright royalty rate payable by the record company in respect of any particular album (excluding multiple albums), regardless of the number of selections embodied therein or the playing time thereof, shall be ten (10) times the Controlled Composition rate (hereinafter the "Maximum Aggregate Album Rate").

To understand how this type of clause works in a recording agreement, we will first illustrate what the cap means in dollars-and-cents terms. The record company is taking the position that it will not pay more than 68.25¢ per album in mechanical royalties for physical sales in the United States. The calculation is as follows:

9.1¢	Statutory rate
× 75%	Controlled rate
6.825¢	Per-song royalty
× 10	Maximum songs per album
68.25¢	Maximum album royalties

If the writer/artist records 12, 14, or even 16 compositions on the album, the maximum album cap will still be 68.25¢, the same as for 10 songs.

In the case of the writer/artist recording only self-written compositions, the royalty calculation is a straightforward procedure. The tricky part occurs when the writer/artist writes a portion of the album and elects to include compositions by other songwriters. Even though choosing the best songs for an album (whether or not they are created by the writer/artist) is a justifiable and commendable aesthetic decision, it can have a disastrous effect on the writer/artist's songwriting income.

For example, if the writer/artist records 12 compositions for an album, five of which are self-written and seven of which are by outside songwriters, the writer/artist might receive only a minuscule mechanical royalty for each self-written song because of the mechanical payments made for the outside songs. If we make the assumption that the music publishers of the seven outside songs all demand a 100% statutory mechanical rate (i.e., 9.1¢ per song), the record company will be obligated to pay 63.7¢ in mechanical royalties for all the outside songs each time an album is sold. Since the maximum amount of aggregate royalties that the record company has agreed to pay per album is 68.25¢, there remains 4.55¢ that can be paid to the writer/artist for the five self-written compositions, which means that the writer/artist will be receiving less than one cent (0.91¢) per composition each time an album is sold.

68.25¢	Royalty cap per album
− 63.7¢	Outside songs royalties
4.55¢	Remaining royalties
÷ 5	Writer/artist songs
0.91¢	Per-song royalties

If the album sold 100,000 copies in the United States, the writer/artist would receive $910 in mechanical royalties per song—a far cry from the $9,100 earned by each outside song licensed at the statutory rate. Because of the inequities involved in how these maximum royalty rate caps operate on the writer/performer's mechanical income, it is not unusual for a writer/artist to try to convince the writers and publishers of the outside songs to accept a 75% rate so that all songs will receive the same royalties per album sold. Depending on the relationships between the various parties, sometimes this is accepted by the writers and publishers of the outside songs and sometimes it is not. Occasionally, a writer/artist may not record an outside composition unless an agreement is reached for a reduced rate, a position that sometimes succeeds in getting acceptance of the reduced rate and sometimes doesn't.

Even worse, some situations can put the writer/artist in the unenviable position of owing the record company money each time an album is sold. As absurd as it may seem, this is not an uncommon occurrence in the case of writer/artists who do not write all the songs on their albums. Clauses in virtually every recording artist agreement provide that in the event that the mechanical royalty cap for a particular recording is exceeded, the excess can be deducted from the writer/performer's recording artist royalties.

For example, if an album contains nine songs by outside songwriters and one song by the recording artist, and all of the outside songs are licensed at the minimum statutory rate of 9.1¢ per composition, the record company will be obligated to pay 81.9¢ in mechanical royalties to the publishers of the nine outside songs (i.e., 9.1¢ × 9 = 81.9¢). If the recording artist's contract specifies a 68.25¢ mechanical royalties cap, the record company is paying more than 13¢ in excess of the maximum that it agreed to pay, and will reduce the mechanical royalties due the recording artist or take that overage from any recording artist royalties due the writer/performer.

A modification that has been negotiated in this area is to have the royalty cap per album calculated on a rate of either 11 to 13 times 75% of the statutory rate or 10 times the statutory rate (rather than 10 times 75% of statutory)—or 12 to 13 times the statutory rate. There are a number of variations in this area, all of which give the writer/artist more leeway to pick outside songs without being financially penalized for such a decision.

DOWNLOADS, SINGLES, AND EPS

When individual tracks are downloaded from iTunes or other sites where consumers can purchase permanent downloads, songwriter and music publisher royalties are paid at the statutory mechanical rate. With respect to physical audio configurations that are released to the general public, the royalty cap is usually two times 75% to 100% of statutory for singles, and five to six times 75% to 100% of statutory for EPs. If a writer/performer is an established recording artist, it is possible to negotiate caps based on the statutory rate.

ONE-USE-ONLY MECHANICAL ROYALTIES

Many record contracts provide that only one mechanical royalty will be payable per composition, regardless of how many times that composition appears on the album or single. For example, if the same composition is repeated a number of times with different mixes, the record company will usually pay mechanical royalties only for the first use of the composition on a particular recording, with the other uses being deemed non-royalty-generating uses. To illustrate, if a recording company put two versions of the same song on an album in 2019 and the song was licensed at the statutory rate, the record company would pay only 9.1¢ per unit sold, not 18.2¢. It is possible to negotiate better terms (e.g., payment for up to two uses of the same composition), but it is very difficult to receive mechanical royalties from the record company on a per-use basis for unlimited uses of a composition on an album, single, or EP.

FREE AND DISCOUNTED UNITS

Since record companies have free goods and discount policies which can result in 10% to 20% being either given away for no cost or discounted, the writer/artist and writer/producer will ask for a guarantee that they be paid mechanical royalties on at least 50% of those units.

MIDPRICED AND BUDGET REDUCED ROYALTIES

In addition to the 75% or other reduced-rate clauses that affect a writer/artist's mechanical royalties, virtually all record contracts will further reduce the mechanical rate when the artist's albums are sold as part of its midprice or budget lines. In most cases, rates for this type of sale are calculated at from 75% to 50% of the controlled composition rate. For example, if a writer/artist receives 75% of the statutory rate for compositions on full-priced product (6.825¢ in 2018-2022), the mechanical rate per composition for midpriced and budget sales might be 75% of the 75% rate (i.e., 75% × 9.1 = 6.825 × 75% = 5.12¢). Many of the very successful writer/recording artists are able to raise some of these rates (e.g., 80% to 90% for midpriced albums, etc.), but virtually all recording artist agreements contain some form of reductions for lower-priced products.

INCREASED ROYALTY RATES FOR COMPOSITIONS THAT ARE PUBLISHED BY THE RECORD COMPANY

A number of record companies guarantee a full statutory mechanical rate to writer/performers who allow the record company's music publishing firm to own or co-own the compositions. Restrictions attached to this guarantee may include an aggregate royalty cap of from 10 to 13 times the statutory rate for each album, a limitation of one royalty payment per composition despite the number of times a composition appears on the album, a minimum statutory-rate calculation versus a "Long Song" durational statutory-rate formula, and a proviso that the 100% statutory rate applies only to top-line, full-priced product or that the rate is fixed as of the delivery or release date of the recording. Even with these restrictions, receiving a full statutory royalty rather than a reduced-rate royalty can mean a substantial amount of extra money for the writer/performer. If the record company is able to guarantee a full statutory rate, this can be a factor in choosing one publisher over another, especially if the services, promotion and administrative staff, advances, royalty splits, and other terms being offered by competing publishers are close.

CO-WRITER/RECORDING ARTIST ACKNOWLEDGMENT FORMS

Many recording artists request that their co-writers sign agreements detailing each writer's contribution to a song. Many times these are much more detailed than a co-writer agreeing to a certain authorship split to a song (such as 50% or 25%) and go into many areas outside of who wrote what portion and how much each is to receive in royalties.

Some of the areas that may be covered in these 4 to 6 page side agreements are indemnification for infringement claims, warranties of originality, guarantees that a writer's mechanical rate will not go below a certain percentage (for example, the co-writer being guaranteed that his or her mechanical rate on a particular song will not go below 75% of statutory regardless of the number of songs on the album), most favored nations assurances as to rates being received by other writers of the songs, who has the right to license synch uses as well as any so called "making of" or "behind the scenes" bonus DVD uses when bundled with the album, actual royalty rates for uses in videos relating to the artist (such as a tour performance video), approval of any samples used in the released composition and how much the sampled writer and publisher will own of the composition as well as whether or not a re-mixer will be allowed to receive songwriter credit and royalties for the particular remixed version.

Because these acknowledgment agreements can become very complex and cover a large number of areas (which many times refer directly to clauses in the artist's recording agreement which the co-writer has not seen), it is always advisable to get professional advice before signing.

SYNCH RIGHTS WHEN CO-WRITING WITH A RECORDING ARTIST OR PRODUCER

In addition to agreeing to accept the provisions of the artist's controlled composition clause with respect to mechanical royalty rates, the co-writer is many times asked to go along with any provisions relating to licensing of the song for audio visual uses. For example, if the artist has agreed to a set penny rate or percentage of wholesale royalty formula for videos, the co-writer will be asked to accept the same terms.

More and more artists are also making sure that co-writers agree in advance to license their songs or their share of songs at the same rate and under the same terms that the artist licenses his or her share of the song. For example, if the artist agrees to a $1,000 television license, the co-writer will be bound to that fee without a chance to negotiate something different even if the fee is lower than normal for a particular series.

In many of these cases, the artist guarantees that the co-writer's license fees will be on a most favored nations basis with the artist's share of the song or on the same basis as co-writers of other songs on the album written with the artist. Other times, the co-writer will only agree that he or she will negotiate fees for synchronization licenses in good faith or in accordance with accepted industry standards without being bound by the artist's rates. These same issues many times apply when a writer co-writes a song with the producer of the track.

SUCCESSFUL OUTSIDE WRITER EXCEPTION

When a recording artist co-writes songs with a successful outside writer, or has a successful writer write songs for the album, the record company may, depending on the bargaining power of the parties, provide some leeway in the reduction of mechanicals if the album royalties exceed the maximum cap. For example, if the successful co-writer demands a full statutory rate for his or her songs, the record company can increase the album royalty cap to compensate for the rate demanded by the successful writer so that the writer-recording artist is not penalized by having any overages deducted from his other royalties.

In these situations, however, there will be some type of royalty cap on the album. For example, the record company may agree to pay the outside writer a full statutory rate but with the provision that the total album mechanicals do not exceed 12 or 13 times full statutory. This type of solution benefits everyone because recording artists are able to bring in the best outside writers possible without having to worry about their own songwriter royalties being reduced because of the outside writer's mechanical rate.

Under this type of scenario, the actual definition of who is to be considered a successful writer to trigger use of this clause is important. One definition has this type of arrangement being used when the successful writer is one who has written a song that achieved Top 40 on the best selling singles charts published by Billboard during the two or three year period prior to the initial release in the United States of the current album. Definitions using other criteria are also possible.

VINYL/DIGITAL REDEMPTION PROGRAMS

A number of record companies offer a redemption reward program which allows the consumer who buys the vinyl version of an album to get a free digital version of the same album. In most cases, the publishing and songwriter royalties will be waived on the digital version but this is a voluntary decision unless such is specifically contained in the writer/artist's recording agreement. It should be emphasized that in many of these arrangements, the publisher will put a limit on the number of royalty-free redemptions. This same concept can be used in other album configurations.

CHANGING MECHANICAL RATES

The statutory mechanical rate has changed over the years and will continue to change after 2022, based upon either a negotiated agreement between the representatives of writers, publishers, and record companies, or a decision by Copyright Royalty Judges.

Because statutory mechanical rates are subject to change, it is possible for a writer/ artist to have complied with the maximum album cap at the time a particular physical product recording is released but be penalized for recording outside compositions at some time in the future, depending on how those outside compositions are licensed. For example, if a writer/artist had a 10-times-statutory album cap for a recording released in 2019, 91¢ would be the allowable maximum for that album. If the album contained seven compositions written by the artist and three outside compositions, each would receive 9.1¢ for every album sold. In the event that the statutory rate is increased to 10 cents, the three outside compositions would begin to generate 30¢ in aggregate royalties for album sales (rather than 27.3¢), leaving 61¢ to be shared by the seven artist-written compositions (instead of the 63.7¢ previously paid).

The reason that such a changing statutory rate is able to reduce the monies earned by the artist-written compositions is explained by the way outside compositions are usually licensed. Most music publishers license their compositions on what is known as a "floating statutory rate," which enables the rate to fluctuate depending on the current rate in effect when the recording is manufactured and distributed rather than the rate in effect at the time when the initial recording was either manufactured or distributed. How an outside composition is initially licensed can therefore affect a writer/artist's earning capacity on any album recorded during the term of the recording agreement. A recording artist must accept the reality that, depending on the terms of his or her controlled-composition clause and how such provisions interrelate with the maximum album cap limitations, royalties for artist-written compositions can decrease due to increases in the statutory rate for outside songs.

COPYRIGHTED ARRANGEMENTS OF COMPOSITIONS IN THE PUBLIC DOMAIN

A number of limitations are placed on recording artists who record a song that is in the public domain (a song no longer protected by copyright). Granted, not much public domain material is recorded in comparison with original material, but if such a song becomes a hit or is on a successful album, the royalties can be substantial provided the writer/arranger (who is many times the recording artist or record producer) has copyrighted his or her version and registered it with the performing right society with which the writer is affiliated.

In the artist's record contract or the producer agreement (if the writer is the producer) there is almost always a clause that deals with how mechanical royalties are paid if a public domain song is contained on the album or released as a single track. Some record companies refuse to pay any writer or publisher mechanical royalties for public domain compositions. Others pay a reduced stated penny rate.

The most common approach (one accepted by most record companies), however, provides that the record company will pay the songwriter/arranger on the basis of the percentage that ASCAP, BMI, SESAC, or GMR determine what they will pay the writer/arranger for performances of the copyrighted arrangement.

ASCAP will treat an arranger as a writer and pay royalties according to the amount of new material that has been added to the original public domain composition. The percentages range from a low of 2% to a high of 100%. Below is a summary of ASCAP's guidelines in the crediting of public domain works for royalty purposes.

If the arrangement is separately published or separately copyrighted, there will be a 10% royalty crediting (i.e., the royalties payable for performances will be 10% of the royalties that would be earned by an original song). If it is included in a copyrighted collection (but does not qualify for 10%), then the royalty crediting is 2%. If the composition contains public domain lyrics and new, original music, it may receive up to 50% crediting, depending on the extent and treatment of the lyrics within the context of the entire work.

If the copyrighted arrangement contains lyrics, it is deemed to be a vocal arrangement and can earn up to 100% depending on the extent to which it embodies changes in the underlying composition as follows: (a) new lyrics, up to 50%; or (b) changes in the music, up to 50% (in addition to any % received in (a) above). If the work is primarily an instrumental, it can be accorded up to 100% of the % given to an original composition as follows: (a) a transference from one medium to another, up to 35%; or (b) a development of a composition, which exhibits creative treatment and contains original musical characteristics and is identifiable as a set piece apart from the source material, up to 100%.

BMI, on the other hand, will pay the writer/music publisher 20% of what an original newly written song would earn. Unlike ASCAP, where there is a review process if the writer requests such to increase the percentage from the initial 2% to 10% that is initially allocated, this is a flat rate determination which is applied to all copyrighted arrangements of public domain compositions across the board. SESAC treats public domain works in a manner similar to BMI, as arrangements of songs that are in the public domain are paid at 15% of the otherwise applicable income that would have been earned by an original song. GMR provides full credit for performances of copyrighted arrangements of public domain works and pays the same per-minute royalties as any background music use.

To illustrate with an example as to how the procedure works in reality, let's assume that a writer/artist or writer/producer is an ASCAP writer member who records a contemporary arrangement of a song that is in the public domain. In the artist's record contract there is a provision that the artist will be paid the 9.1 cent United States statutory royalty for the sale of every composition that the artist writes and records. There is a 13x statutory cap on physical product but such does not apply due to the fact that the album does not exceed the cap (i.e., the album has only 13 songs on it). In addition, there is a provision in the controlled composition clause of the artist and/or producer agreement that states that mechanical royalties on any arrangement of a public domain work will be calculated in proportion to the percentage given the writer's copyrighted arrangement by ASCAP, BMI, SESAC, or GMR.

The single is released, is successful, and sells 100,000 downloads. The album goes to Number One and sells 200,000 units in the United States. The recording artist/writer (or writer/producer if applicable) submits the recording and a copy of the new arrangement to ASCAP, where the composition is analyzed in-house and a % determination made. For the sake of this example, ASCAP and its Special Classification Committee gives the composition a 50% royalty rating because of significant additional new material, creativity, etc.—in effect, making the new composition worth one-half of an original newly written song.

The record company is sent a copy of the ASCAP determination (the same would occur with BMI, SESAC, and GMR with their flat fee rates) which then gives the song a 50% mechanical royalty payout rate. In other words, the song will receive 50% of the "original song" 9.1 cent statutory rate per composition mechanical royalty. Certain agreements have a time limit on when the determination and supporting evidence has to be received by the record company but this discussion is not intended to concentrate on whether such type of provision is enforceable or not. One should, however, be aware of such.

The mechanical royalty calculations for sales in the United States would be:

Single	$9.1 \times 50\% = 4.55 \times 100,000 =$	$4,550
Album	$9.1 \times 50\% = 4.55 \times 200,000 =$	$9,100
	Total	$13,650

Such a clause may not seem important to most recording artists and producers who write their own material, but a good recording or producer contract should anticipate and provide for all contingencies. It may not seem likely that the artist will be recording any public domain compositions. But if it happens, the artist (or writer/producer) should be guaranteed some type of fair formula for payment.

It should be emphasized that songwriter and music publisher performance royalties will be based on that same percentage so if a public domain song becomes a radio or Internet hit, the % allocation received from ASCAP, BMI, SESAC, and GMR can really have an effect on the amount of money that can be earned. For example, if a song is a major radio hit, earnings in the area of $300,000 to $700,000 in songwriter earnings are not unusual in performance royalty income for an original song during the period of chart activity. One just has to do the math to see the monies at stake depending on the % given by the writer's performing rights organization for the public domain work arrangement. For example, an ASCAP 50% public domain crediting would generate $150,000 to $350,000 in writer earnings if one were to use the above original song payments. A BMI 20% crediting would generate total songwriter figures in the area of $60,000 to $140,000. A SESAC 15% crediting would generate $45,000 to $105,000. And a GMR writer would be credited with the full amount of royalties. Another good example would be a successful public domain Christmas song where substantial airplay continues every year for many decades. And since the music publisher is paid at the same rate as the writer/arranger, this is not only a songwriter issue but a publisher issue as well.

NEW ARTIST/DEVELOPING ARTIST PRICING

A number of record companies will further reduce the mechanical royalties due to the new artist/writer when they sell the album at a lower list price than that of albums by more established artists. For example, the contract may provide that if the list price of the album by the new artist is between 80% and 66.66% of the top-line suggested retail price of a particular album, the mechanical rate for controlled compositions might be 75% of the already-reduced controlled rate. And if the actual retail list is less than 66.66% of the top-line suggested retail list, the new controlled rate could be reduced to 50% of the applicable mechanical rate. Many companies will limit the number of albums sold under this pricing structure or will put a time limit on the reduced pricing policy.

NET PROFITS DEALS/INDIE LABELS

Many indie record companies structure their contracts so that the recording artist and record company each receive 50% of the net profits from each album and other recordings controlled by the agreement. In most of these agreements, the recording artist does not receive a separate non-cross-collateralized accounting of mechanical royalties for the sale of albums or singles since profits include mechanical income as part of the net monies jointly shared by the artist and the record company.

This is unlike most major record company or traditional artist agreements, which guarantee that the artist-writer will receive his or her songwriter/publisher mechanical income for album and single track sales regardless of whether or not the record company has recouped all recording costs, artist advances, and other recoupable costs. There may be controlled-composition clauses in these major record company agreements that reduce the mechanical income due the artist-writer, but the record company does not share in this source of income.

Net profits in these contracts are usually defined as gross receipts less expenses. As to how gross receipts is defined, in most cases, the term includes all income received (or credited to) the record company from the sale of the master recordings as well as all licensing income (e.g., the use of a recording in a television series, video game, or motion picture). Gross receipts for mail order sales and sales from the website of the record company may be calculated on the basis of its standard wholesale price.

Expenses may be defined as all monies payable to third parties in connection with the masters including, but not limited to, recording costs, manufacturing and packaging, jackets, booklets, shipping, storage, distribution, advertising, marketing, and promotion directly attributable to the recordings. One should be careful not to include costs associated with the general overhead of the record company (salaries and benefits, rent, etc.) as these are not expense items to be considered. As with any agreement, much of the negotiation relates to how much can be spent by the record company without the approval of the artist and how much money the record company is willing to guarantee to spend on recording budgets, advertising, and marketing.

Many of these agreements also provide that the record company is entitled to produce a T-shirt for each album recorded and that the artist will split the profits equally on T-shirts that are sold through the record company's website, the Internet, or mail order, as well as through wholesale or retail outlets. Some of the other contract issues covered in these agreements include "work for hire" status of the masters (the label becomes owner of the masters), option clauses/or additional albums as well as delivery and release commitments, selection of a producer and studio (mutual), recording fund budgets, videos, accounting dates, rights to audit, and approval of samples, among others.

In addition to the net profits type of recording artist agreement, which is favored by many indie labels, some record companies request that they share in the copyright and music publisher income to the compositions via a co-publishing agreement and also ask for a share of the net profits from touring and merchandising.

There are also a number of indie recording contracts which contain two types of deals in the same agreement. Both are based on a net proceeds type of sharing arrangement but there are differences in the approach, percentages, income streams that are included in the mix and costs that can be deducted or recovered by the record company in calculating the actual royalties payable to the artist (and, in many cases, the artist as songwriter).

In these dual scenario type of deals (e.g., pure indie vs. indie album distributed through a major record label via an upstream or other similar arrangement), royalties can be either the standard 50/50 split of net revenue under the indie distributed label or increased up to a 75% share of the net proceeds under the indie via major distribution model.

It is important to realize that net proceeds or net revenue (the words on which the artist royalty is based) is defined differently in each case and the artist and his or her representative must focus in on the distinctions as well as the real world dollars and cents economics of the language since there are not only creative and career decisions involved but business and legal ones as well.

As to how the artist royalty is calculated, if it's a purely indie situation, all income from digital and physical rates, licensing (film, television, video games, etc.), touring (if included), and music publishing income including the songwriter's share of nonperformance income (if included and only to the extent included) will usually be included in gross receipts.

As explained previously, the indie label's costs are then deducted to arrive at the net revenue (which costs include advances to the recording artist, recording costs, mechanical royalties paid to third parties for songs not written or controlled by the artist, marketing, promotion, and publicity costs, and manufacturing and shipping costs or, in the alternative, a packaging/container charge to cover such manufacturing/shipping costs). The royalties to the parties are then computed with the net revenue figure used as the basis on which the split is made.

As to the second scenario which focuses on major distribution of the album, the elements of how an artist gets paid and on what basis are different.

Under this scenario, the artist's royalty may be paid on a net proceeds basis which consists of all advances and royalty payments which are paid by the major distributor to the indie label after deduction by the indie label of all recording costs, producer advances, fees and royalties, plus royalties paid to any other third party. The artist-writer will many times receive mechanical royalties as a separate income stream (as opposed to the indie label 50/50 split of profits arrangement where mechanical royalties are encompassed by the net receipts definition without being a separate payable line item). There are a number of variations in this area due to the different business models of the many types of indie record labels and the above represents just some examples of how the deals work and the issues/considerations involved in the royalty calculations.

With respect to publishing rights, the indie label may request a copyright ownership and/or publishing interest with administration rights for the songs recorded and released under the agreement. In many cases, the indie label will not be entitled to income from cover versions of the compositions by other artists or users which do not use the indie controlled master recording with such exclusions being part of the negotiations. In some cases, the indie label will collect the monies and pay the artist 100% of the monies collected from these excluded uses and, other times, the artist's publishing company will be able to negotiate such uses and collect all the publishing monies directly from the user. In any event, virtually all such agreements will exclude the songwriter's share of performance income from ASCAP, BMI, SESAC, or GMR.

NET PROFITS LICENSE AGREEMENTS/NEWLY CREATED RECORDINGS

An additional approach outside of the various types of recording artist and/or master agreements being entered into is the net profits license agreement, which entails a profit participation royalty scenario for the artist without transferring the copyright ownership of the master recordings to the record company which is releasing the albums and single tracks.

Many of these agreements will use a 50/50 net profit split, but there are many variations depending on the bargaining power of the parties, the structure of the deal, the policies of the record company, whether publishing rights are involved as well as the concessions that the parties have agreed to in the negotiation resulting in a final agreement so that the following represents an explanation of the types of resolutions that can occur.

As to copyright ownership of the master recordings, the recording artist remains the copyright owner since there is not a transfer of such to the record company as the contractual arrangement is only a license.

Since the agreement is a license arrangement, there will be a set term during which the record company can exercise its rights and a set date when the master recordings will revert to the recording artist. There are a number of formulas with one being a set number of years after the release of each album, a set number of years after the last album under the agreement has been released, the longer of a set number of years after release and recoupment of all recoupable costs, etc. The territory might be North America, the world or various selected countries. North America is essential if the agreement is with a U.S.-based record company emphasizing a U.S. release. The term can be for only one album but usually has at least one if not more options for additional albums.

As to recording costs, the record company will be responsible for such and guarantee a certain dollar amount budget for the first album with a scheduled payment formula. For example, it might be $_____ in the aggregate payable $_____ on execution, and $_____ on delivery of the final original master recordings which constitute the album.

As to option albums, the recording fund can either be a set amount or can be a formula based on the sales of the prior album with a mini-max formula to ensure that the recording fund will not be less than a certain amount nor be greater than a certain amount. For example, there might be a set dollar amount per album sold multiplied by the number of albums sold with a minimum dollar amount (e.g., $75,000) and a maximum dollar amount ($200,000), a formula which protects the artist's minimum recording budget but also protects the record company's financial commitments as well.

As to how the recording artist gets paid under such a net profits formula, the definition is many times, with variations, a percentage of gross receipts received from the sale or exploitation of the master recordings (including many times the artwork for the albums, which may include the photographs, created for the master recordings) as well as music videos less, in some cases, a distribution fee for services which will be negotiated at the time of signing. In some cases, the mechanical royalties payable to the songwriter/recording artist will be excluded from the definition of net profits so that the mechanical income from downloads, physical sales, and interactive streaming shall be excluded and paid directly to the songwriter/recording artist or the artist's music publisher. Other times such mechanical royalties will be treated as a cost recoverable before the net profits calculation is finalized.

In many of these agreements, the marketing plans in connection with the marketing of the albums will be subject to the mutual approval of the parties. In addition, the record company will usually agree to a number of restrictions as to its activities which will be subject to the approval of the recording artist. They may include the use of the masters in a television program, motion picture, commercial, or video game, use as a sample, release of outtakes or demo recordings, resequencing of an album, re-mastering or remixing, editing either for timing purposes or the creation of ringtones or ringbacks, and the sale of the masters as a premium or in connection with the sale or promotion of any other product (other than the label's records), among other things. There will usually be an agreement that the logo as well as trade name of the artist or the artist's label will be included as part of the packaging of each album released.

DISTRIBUTION AND MARKETING SERVICES AGREEMENT

This type of agreement represents an alternative approach to the normal recording artist contract as it focuses on the distribution and marketing expertise of a record company with no transfer of ownership of the master recordings recorded and released under the deal.

The term of the agreement may be for one album with an option by the record company to secure additional albums if certain criteria are achieved. For example, if a certain specified number of albums are sold within eighteen (18) months of the release date, then the record company will have the right to an additional album since conceivably the activity on the first album met everyone's expectations. If the criteria were not achieved, however, the artist would be free to go elsewhere with respect to future albums. For informational purposes, these formulas can rely on a specified number of actual downloads, a combination of single track and album downloads, a combination of downloads and streams, or a stated dollar amount in earnings, among other things.

The artist, or artist's company or owned label, will guarantee the delivery of the album as well as a number of mutually agreed upon official music videos in addition to artwork and related marketing assets all pursuant to a mutually agreed upon budget and marketing plan.

There will be provisions which provide that the album will be first class, fully edited, mixed and mastered newly recorded studio master recordings of at least a certain number of individual tracks which will be sufficient to comprise one long-playing recording. There will also be a qualifier which provides that "live" recordings, holiday or "specialty" recordings, instrumental recordings, and recordings of compositions previously released (except for single tracks that were marketed as part of an upcoming album) will not be part of the album unless the record company and artist agree in writing. On occasion, previously released tracks (such as from a motion picture soundtrack) will be allowed but there usually is a limit on the number of such recordings that can be included on the album.

In addition to the album commitment, the record company may also require the artist to deliver a number of additional recordings as reasonably requested by the record company for use as "B" sides and non-lead tracks for singles and a certain number of bonus tracks for retail partners exclusive programs (e.g., iTunes, Amazon, etc.) as well as a reasonable number of special versions of the master recordings (e.g., so-called instrumental tracks) for purposes of the licensing of synchronization rights for motion pictures, television, apps, video games, and advertising.

Depending upon bargaining power and track record, the artist may be granted complete creative control in the creation of the masters including choice of recordings, studios, producers, mixers, single releases and artwork. In other cases, many of the decisions will be by mutual approval of the parties. On the business side of things, the artist or artist's company will have the responsibility to deliver the album within a stated time period from the commencement of the agreement including all clearances and licenses (e.g., side artist agreements, sample agreements, if applicable, artwork, first use mechanical licenses, producer agreements, etc.).

Even though there is not a transfer of ownership to the master recordings, the record company supplying the distribution and marketing services will have exclusive exploitation and licensing rights. Included will be the right to manufacture, distribute, broadcast, publicly perform and otherwise exploit the masters with, depending on the negotiations, certain agreed upon restrictions or limitations to said rights.

The territory of the agreement can be the universe, the world, the United States and Canada or wherever the parties decide. The duration of the record company's rights (sometimes referred to as the "exploitation period") is many times computed as the later of a stated number of years (e.g., 10, 15, etc.) or recoupment of all chargeable costs. The artist is also usually given the right to repay the negative balance or a percentage thereof to cause recoupment so that the artist can elect to end the term and recover the rights to the recordings at the end of the stated number of years.

As with virtually all agreements, there will be a release commitment which, in many cases, encompasses both a physical and digital release unless the parties agree to the contrary. With respect to payment to the artist, one formula that is used is to pay the artists 100% of the net proceeds from the recordings; net meaning gross income received or credited to the account of the distributing record company less a service fee (20%, 25%, etc.) which will represent the compensation to the record company for its marketing and promotion efforts.

As for budgetary commitments by the record company, there will, in many cases, be an advance in a negotiated amount which will be spent for marketing, promotion, A&R and manufacturing for the initial album and, if there are option albums involved, either an agreed upon amount or a fund based on the sales and/or success of the prior album. If the artist owns a label, the released album will many times be released referencing not only the distributing label's name but also the artist's label name and logo as well. Accountings will either be semi-annual or quarterly with negotiated audit rights for the artist. The distributing record company will also have the right to license the master recordings for use in motion pictures, television programming, video games, etc. subject to any restrictions negotiated by the parties.

QUICK VIEW OF TWO INDIE RECORD DEALS

1. **Agreement between Artist and Label regarding Artist's Albums and Master Recordings.**

Services: Label shall perform all services customarily performed in the record industry including incurring costs associated with mastering, manufacturing, promotion, distribution, and marketing in good faith consultation with the artist. Label agrees to physically release in the territory (the World) within __ months of delivery and make __masters available online through major digital retailers. Minimum duration is __ minutes of music and the album must be technically and commercially satisfactory.

Copyright Ownership/Grant of Rights/Term: Artist is the copyright owner. Label has an irrevocable exclusive right and license to reproduce, manufacture, market, and advertise, license, and distribute the masters and album in digital and physical format for a period of __ years after the commercial release date with automatic __ year extensions unless notice given with a __ year sell off period of inventory.

Revenue Split: 50% of net proceeds to Artist. Net Proceeds defined as Gross sales less all documented out of pocket costs paid or incurred by label in connection with…. (list of all areas included).

Advance/Reserves/Payment Dates: $___ recoupable with reserves not to exceed __% of net proceeds with distributions to artist made twice a year.

Approvals: Artist has approval rights over _____(list all areas, e.g., synch, etc.).

Warranties/Representations/Cure Periods, etc.:

Legal Counsel: All parties have had the benefit of legal counsel as regards all aspects of the agreement.

2. **Joint venture between Label and Artist with Artist licensing the album and master recordings for the 1st album with the 2nd album owned by the Label if they, rather than the Artist, pay to make the record.**

Territory and Term: The Universe with a 2 year term with the Company having the option to renew for an additional 2 year term.

Grant of Rights: Exclusive, unlimited and perpetual rights to manufacture, advertise, sell, lease, license, and distribute records throughout the world.

Income and Royalty Splits: Exclusive joint partnership between the Company and the Artist to participate in all forms of income including a 50/50 split for synchronization licenses, merchandise, performance royalties, among others areas. Company will pay mechanical royalties to the Artist's publishing designee at 100% of the statutory rate with a 10 song cap.

Net Receipts: Company will pay Artist 50% of the Company's Net Receipts defined as any and all monies actually received in respect of the sale and exploitation of records in any manner, merchandise, sponsorships, and endorsements less any and all costs and expenses incurred by company including marketing, mechanical royalties, recording costs, video production, and any other expense related to Artist's recordings. All royalties to be paid quarterly.

Company Commitment: Company will provide funds for album and artwork, manufacturing, merchandise, and video production costs with all funds spent upon a mutually agreed upon basis.

UPSTREAMING

Without getting into a discussion as to the pros and cons of signing with an indie, one of the values of being with an indie label is that it may provide the opportunity to be noticed by a major. A number of indies have contractual relationships with majors (sometimes called "upstream agreements"), which allow the major to contribute monies for marketing and promotion for acts that achieve certain sales levels. In addition, if the major elects, the act may also be transferred from the indie to one of the major record company's labels. The value to the indie of one of these deals is that it retains certain rights to its successful artists via its co-venture agreement with the major (rather than have the artist leave and sign with a major after the indie term has ended). The value to the artist is that the act will more quickly receive larger advances and a better royalty rate, and will be guaranteed national promotion and marketing of its albums (provided, of course, the artist wants to be with a major).

"360" DEALS

"360" deals involve a contract between a recording artist and a record company or other entity in which that entity shares not only in record royalties and master use licensing but also many of the artist's nonrecording sources of income. The headline deals in this area involved very high end artists—Robbie Williams and EMI, Madonna with concert promoter Live Nation, Korn with EMI Music, etc.—and involved, in many cases, guarantees, large advances, high artist royalty percentages, partner type sharing arrangements, and ownership involvement. But with the decline in CD and traditional recording sales not being offset by digital sales, record companies have attempted to expand the concept to other artists, both new and old. Other types of non-record label entities have also seen an opportunity to create new business models in partnerships or joint ventures with appropriate artists and are making similar type deals.

The nonrecording revenue areas covered could include a share of merchandising (T-shirts, bags, etc.), touring monies as well as all live performance fees (a major concert venue, corporate events, etc.), sponsorships, brand associations, film, television, and videogame projects, books, media rights, songwriting and music publishing royalties, any types of song or master licensing (musical toys, advertising commercials, lyric reprints on clothes, etc.), web store sales, fan club info, and more. In a sense, a 360 deal could also be a "270" or a "180" deal depending on the number of additional income producing areas covered.

These type of deals take a number of forms but the main purpose is to involve a record company or other entity in as many aspects of an artist's career as possible and recoup or share in all or many of them. Under these deals, record companies or other entities could provide extra tour support, a higher advance to sign, additional monies upon the release of an album, an ability to cross market products better, and a better percentage of the label's profits from an album rather than the standard recording artist royalty from record sales.

The size of advances, nonrecoupable payments and the revenue split between the artist and the company on record sales, merchandise, touring, and all other affected areas as well as what each party brings to the table would be among the factors determining the feasibility or desirability of these type of deals. The experience, strategies, and budget allocations in each area involved in these deals represent major selling as well as negotiating points.

If you are signing one of these types of arrangements, it is essential that you understand the types of deals as well as the economics of everything that is being shared by the parties. These include all aspects of the licensing process (placement of songs in films and television episodes, a song in a singing doll, or musical toy, a song being placed in a regular video game as well as a music simulation type game, use of a song in a theater production, foreign royalties, etc.), the live performance and merchandising aspect, as well as the value of the artist's "brand" both now and in the future. It is also important to determine if a company has the expertise to actively take charge and manage an area of income or is just going to be a passive participant in the income being generated from a particular revenue area.

ADDITIONAL RIGHTS SECURED

Some of the areas that record companies try to participate in under the 360 deals include endorsements, sponsorships, strategic partnerships with third parties, name and likeness rights, artist logos, trademarks, merchandise, video games, dramatizations using the artist's name or likeness, live performances and touring, television, webcast and radio performances, books or other publishing materials created by the writer/ artist, and musical compositions written by the writer/artist.

In most cases, the artist has the exclusive right to negotiate the terms of these additional rights agreements but all may be subject to the record company's right to participate in the income according to the terms of the recording artist agreement.

RECORD COMPANY PERCENTAGES

The record company's share of income is based on monies paid to the artist from the additional right sources but is usually calculated after deduction of applicable commissions which are paid to the manager, talent agent, business manager or other advisors (including lawyers). Many times, there is a provision that limits the total amount of commissions that are able to be deducted by the artist to arrive at the base on which the record company share is calculated. For example, a clause might read that no more than 30% may be deducted by the artist from monies earned from a particular income producing area. Record company percentages range from 10% to 20% of income generated from these additional sources but can vary depending upon the bargaining power of the parties. For example, a deal might give a 20% income participation in publishing, sponsorships, and endorsements with a 10% share of merchandise and tour earnings.

Many of these income obligations may continue after the term of the recording artist agreement ends if the exploitations covered occurred during the term of the record deal provided that the terms of the additional rights agreement were agreed to during the active term of the recording artist agreement. This is true regardless of whether the income is paid to the artist after the recording agreement has ended.

The record company will also try to make the artist include a clause in any agreement covering these additional rights that enables the record company to audit the third party company directly or, at least, be able to exercise the artist's audit rights.

When computing the record company's share of artist's earnings from additional rights, the cost to the artist of the merchandise sold plus direct selling expenses will be deducted prior to the calculation. In addition, there might be a mutually agreed upon production expense allocation applicable to certain live performance concerts and this will be taken off the top as well provided that this deduction is also taken by the artist when commissions to the manager and booking agent are computed. In this regard, the record company will ask for a copy of the pertinent provisions of an artist's management and booking agent contracts.

SONGWRITER PERFORMANCE INCOME

There are a number of variations in this area, from the record company receiving a portion of the music publisher share of income, to a share of the songwriter ASCAP, BMI, SESAC, or GMR share of income if the writer/artist already has a publishing agreement. For example, the writer/artist might have to pay the record company 20% of the writer's share of performance income received from ASCAP, BMI, SESAC, or GMR. This can be limited, in many cases, depending upon bargaining power. For example, the payment may only apply to individual tracks that are so called "A-Side Singles" or songs that are promoted to radio or the streaming services as singles (versus album cuts).

Another variation limits the record company's right to this type of income only after the writer/artist has achieved a stated income threshold from all nontraditional record company sources. For example, the performance income payment might only become effective when the writer/artist has earned in excess of a specified amount of income in touring, marketing, or endorsement income, and then only on a prospective basis. These criteria can also be computed on a calendar year–by–calendar year versus multi-year basis as a protection for the writer/artist.

Many agreements also put a time limitation on the record company's right to continue to be paid on performance royalties after the active term of the recording artist agreement ends. For example, the record company's right to a share might end two years after the end of the term or its rights might only encompass royalties earned during the term of the recording artist agreement.

Another important aspect of these arrangements which needs to be considered is at what point, based on the number and scope of rights being included, do these deals go beyond strict contractual relationships and enter into the realm of a "fiduciary relationship" between parties; a relationship of much stricter standards, obligations, and duties.

CHAPTER 6
MUSIC, MONEY, AND SAMPLING

One of the more significant issues in today's music industry is that of sampling. It is a term that crosses all areas of music from songs, records, films, television, theater, commercials, and beyond. There are many definitions of the word "sampling"; in briefest terms, it is when a songwriter, recording artist, or record producer takes a portion of an existing song, existing recorded performance, or both, and integrates it into a newly recorded performance.

OVERVIEW

Sampling can take a number of different forms; the following are the most common.

The Song Itself. The recording artist or record producer uses a portion of an existing song as a bridge, insert, or portion of a new song.

The Master Recording. The recording artist or producer uses an instrumental portion (e.g., a guitar or bass line or full instrumental track) of an existing master recording and inserts it into a newly recorded master.

The Master Recording and the Song. The recording artist or producer transfers an existing master recording and vocal performance of the song directly into the newly recorded master.

In cases where the producer supervising the session, remixer, or recording artist samples without permission from the music publisher (the owner of the underlying song sampled) or the record company (the owner of the pre-existing recorded performance sampled), the publisher and record company will contact the recording artist or record company that releases the unauthorized sampled performance and advise that such use constitutes an infringement of copyright. A demand will also be made that the infringing party cease and desist all activities related to the sample, that all product be recalled from the market, and that damages and profits be paid immediately.

In these instances, the matter will either proceed to litigation or, if a settlement is negotiated, will be resolved through a continuing monetary or copyright participation on the part of the sampled publisher and/or record company, or a release of claims and settlement that results in a monetary payment by the sampling party to the sampled party and, many times, an agreement that the sample will be deleted from any and all recordings made and distributed in the future.

In cases where the recording artist, producer, or record company requests permission prior to the actual sampling or release of the recording which incorporated the sample, the applicable music publisher, record company, or both will, if the use is approved, usually negotiate a settlement of the matter. If the sample is not approved, the sample can be deleted from the recording before it is released without any harm to the recording artist, record producer, and recording company. In this regard and as a piece of practical advice, if permission to utilize a portion of an existing composition or recorded performance is requested by the sampling party prior to a sample being recorded or released, the owner of the sampled composition or sampled recorded performance is more likely to view the new recording in a positive manner and be amenable to a non-litigation resolution.

If the sample is approved, resolution is handled in a number of different ways, including a one-time "buy-out of all rights" fee, the payment of a percentage of income received from either the new recording or the new song, or the transfer of a portion of the copyright of the new composition (plus the income generated). As a part of any negotiations, the music publisher or record company owning the sampled composition or master recording will request a copy of the new recording for review, time the duration of the sampled section, review how the sample has been used, and determine its importance to the new version. There are no hard and fast rules in this analysis, and final resolution is usually based on, among other things, the bargaining power of the parties, the duration of the sample in comparison to the duration of the entire new recording (although timing may have little relevance if a key element or recognizable piece of the original composition or recording has been used), the nature of the sample (i.e., whether a core portion has been utilized or just an incidental portion), whether it re-occurs during the new recording or is only used once, the content of the nonsampled elements (for example, the theme and/or other lyrics of the new song), the actual sales of the new version if it has been released, whether the new version has reached the charts, and whether the sampling party requested permission prior to the commercial release of the new recording.

If the sample has been approved, negotiations can take a number of different forms. For example, the publisher can grant the owner of the new composition a worldwide license to use the sampled composition for an agreed-upon share of the mechanical royalties generated by sales of CDs, downloads, and other audio configurations embodying the new composition. Under this type of arrangement, the publisher and writer of the sampled composition normally receive from 10% to 75% of the royalties generated, but such percentages can be higher or lower, depending on the facts of a particular case. Occasionally, these payments will be made on a so called "rollover" advance basis (e.g., $2,000 for the first 50,000 recordings sold, $2,000 for sales between 50,001 and 100,000 units, an additional $2,000 for sales between 100,001 and 150,000, etc.) or an advance against a specified number of units will be given to the publisher of the sampled composition. For example, if the sampled publisher secured a 50% interest at a statutory rate, an advance of $4,550 might be requested to cover the initial 100,000 units sold. At such time that sales reached the 100,000 level, the sampled publisher would start receiving mechanical royalties on a per-unit basis for future recordings sold because the prepayment advance had already covered all royalties that were due for the initial 100,000 in sales. On the other hand, if the recording never achieved the 100,000 sales plateau for which the advance was paid, there would be no reimbursement required since most advances, by their nature, are nonreturnable unless negotiated to the contrary. Sometimes non-recoupable fees may also be paid for use of the sample.

If a share of the copyright ownership is negotiated, the publisher of the new composition will transfer a portion of the copyright (e.g., usually from 10% to 75%, but it can be as much as 100%) to the publisher of the sampled composition. In addition, the names of the songwriters who wrote the sampled composition will be added as writers and will receive credit on all uses of the new composition. Under this type of arrangement, the publisher and writers of the sampled composition will receive a portion of all income generated by the new version whether it be from CD sales, downloads, ringtones, video games, film and television uses, commercials, print, or any other commercial exploitation of the new composition. For example, if the new composition is licensed for use over the opening credits of a major motion picture, the publisher and songwriter of the sampled song would not only receive a portion of the synchronization and video buy-out fee negotiated for the use but would also receive their proportionate share of all income generated from all other uses generated by the film (e.g., mechanical royalties from sales of the soundtrack album or, if applicable, soundtrack single, performance royalties for television broadcasts of the film, radio and television performances of the song from the film, foreign theatrical royalties, advertising commercial fees, sheet music and folio use, interactive media, lyric reprints in novels, karaoke, streaming royalties, etc.). The screen credit for the new composition will also mention the title of the original composition, its writers and, in some cases, publisher information.

Even if permission for the sample is approved, restrictions may sometimes be placed on how the new composition and/or recording can be used. For example, in some settlements the new composition may be restricted from being placed in a motion picture, television program, or video unless the writer and publisher of the sampled composition give their approval. There also may be restrictions on the use of the new composition in commercial advertising campaigns as well as new technology uses.

Many times, the writer and publisher of the sampled composition will, in the case where the sampling writer is either a recording artist or record producer, agree to be bound by the terms of the controlled composition clause of the recording artist or record production agreement. For example, if the sampling writer/artist has agreed to a 75% mechanical rate for all physical albums sold in the United States, the publisher of the sampled composition may also agree that its share of royalties will be calculated on the same reduced rate. In many cases, however, the publisher of the sampled composition will demand that its share of royalties be based on the statutory mechanical rate regardless of the reduced controlled composition rate agreed to by the recording artist or producer.

This latter arrangement is very common and can have a significant negative impact on the royalties due the writers and publishers of the nonsampled portion of the composition. For example, if a writer/artist is subject to a controlled composition clause that dictates a 75% reduced rate mechanical license for a composition contained on physical product (6.825¢ in 2018–2022) and the publisher and writer of the sampled composition demand not only 50% of the copyright and income but also a 100% statutory rate for their share (9.1¢ × 50% = 4.55¢), there would only be slightly more than 2¢ remaining in mechanical income for the writer/artist who sampled (6.825¢ – 4.55¢ = 2.275¢). And if the publisher of the sampled composition licensed its share via a "floating" statutory rate basis (which would get the benefit of any future increases in the statutory mechanical rate), the writer/artist's mechanical income would continue to decrease as the sampled composition's mechanical rate increased. This is because the writer/artist's 75% controlled composition rate is "locked in" as of a set date and does not change regardless of any industry-wide mechanical rate increases.

As to performance income, the performing rights organizations will follow the percentages agreed to in the sampling agreement and will remit royalties accordingly. For example, if the parties agree that the sampled composition was entitled to a 60% copyright and income share of the new composition, the performing rights organizations would remit 60% of the songwriter royalties due from performances of the new composition to the writer of the sampled composition, and 60% of the publisher's share of all performance royalties to the publisher of the sampled composition. The remaining 40% writer's share and corresponding publisher's share of income would be paid to the writer and publisher of the new composition. These splits are set forth in the song registrations submitted to the performing rights organizations ASCAP, BMI, SESAC, or GMR by the music publisher. Since worldwide radio and television performances for chart songs can range from $400,000 to over $1,000,000, the negotiations as to royalty shares between the sampled composition and the new composition can have a very significant financial effect on all of the writers and publishers involved.

In most cases, the publisher of the sampled composition will administer its own share of the new composition throughout the world with direct collection of royalties from all sources.

FORMAT OF THE SAMPLE AGREEMENT

A sample clearance/permission agreement can take many forms but the major areas of concentration which are dealt with are as follows.

COPYRIGHT REGISTRATION

If a portion of the copyright in the new composition is being transferred to the music publisher of the previously existing sampled composition (an occurrence which is the norm and not an exception to the rule), the parties will provide for the registration of the new composition in the Copyright Office of the United States via a registration that reflects the mutually agreed upon ownership percentages. For example, if the ownership split is 50% to the publisher of the existing sampled composition and 50% to the publisher of the new material, such will be stated in the sample agreement. If the publisher of the new material has already registered the new composition in its own name, an assignment will be prepared to transfer the appropriate share to the publisher whose composition was sampled. The publisher of the sampled composition usually has the right to sign such an assignment on behalf of the sampling publisher as its attorney-in-fact if the sampling publisher does not do so within 10 to 20 days after request to do so by the music publisher of the composition sampled.

ADMINISTRATION OF THE NEW COMPOSITION

In many cases, each of the publishers will have the right in the United States and Canada to administer and exploit the new composition as well as enter into license agreements for the new composition provided no such licenses are exclusive and no mechanical licenses are issued at less than the statutory mechanical rate (with reduced rates being permissible only for those types of sales for which music publishers customarily grant reduced rates to nonaffiliated record companies).

The sampled publisher usually demands that there will be restrictions placed on certain agreed-upon types of commercial exploitation of the new composition and will provide that its share of the new composition not be subject to or adversely affected by any controlled composition clause in the sampling writer/artist's or writer/producer's recording artist or producer's agreement with a record company, and that synchronization licenses, advertising commercial licenses, and other such licenses only be issued jointly by the sampled publisher and sampling publisher (with approval to be withheld in either party's sole discretion). Under this common scenario, if a motion picture producer, television producer, or advertising agency wants to use the new composition in a motion picture, television series, or commercial, they must negotiate with both the sampled publisher and sampling publisher for the right to use the new composition. In addition, the sampled publisher and sampling publisher will agree to instruct all licensees that the licensee will remit each party's respective share of monies directly to that party, and that a copy of the signed license will be sent to both the sampled publisher and the sampling publisher. For example, if the negotiation of a motion picture license fee for the new composition results in a fee of $40,000 and the agreed-upon money split is on a 50/50 basis, the film producer will send $20,000 directly to the sampled publisher and $20,000 directly to the sampling publisher.

COLLECTION OF MONIES/PAYMENT OF SONGWRITER ROYALTIES

Each of the publishers (both the publisher of the sampled composition and the sampling composition) will agree to collect its share of income directly from the source (or through their respective subpublishers as to foreign income), including mechanical royalties from both physical and digital distribution, the publisher's share of performance income, streaming income, synchronization fees, video royalties, print income, and all other miscellaneous royalties generated by the new composition. In turn, both the sampled publisher and the sampling publisher will guarantee that each will be responsible for the payment of songwriter royalties to the respective songwriters signed to them.

On occasion, if an affiliate or subsidiary of one of the publishers is a print company, there will be a stated royalty which will be deemed to be the gross royalties payable for various print configurations. For example, all parties might agree that the royalty for each copy of regular sheet music will be 20% of the suggested retail list price, the royalty for folios or songbooks which contain the new composition and other compositions will be a pro-rata share of 12.5% of the marked retail selling price, and the royalty for fake books and educational, orchestral, choral, or band arrangement editions will be 10% of the marked retail selling price.

ADDITIONAL SAMPLING

The writer and publisher of the new material will guarantee the original songwriters and the publisher of the sampled composition that no other existing compositions have been sampled in the new composition. The sampling writer and publisher will also indemnify the sampled publisher against any claims from a third party that its composition was sampled as well, and will agree that, in the event another composition was sampled and a share of the new composition has to be assigned to the publisher of the additional sample, that such share will only be deducted from the sampling publisher's share of the new composition. For example, if one sample takes 50% of the copyright and income of the new composition and it is discovered that there is an additional sampled composition contained in the new composition, the copyright and income percentage given to the publisher of the additional sample will only be deducted from what remains after the share of the other sampled composition has been deducted.

The obvious danger in these situations when more than one pre-existing composition is sampled in the new composition is that the publishers of both sampled compositions might demand 50% of the new composition (leaving the writer and publisher of the new composition with 0%) or, even worse, a demand by each of the sampled publishers for 75% or more of the new composition (leaving the writer and publisher of the new composition with, at a minimum, a minus 50% interest and an obligation to ensure, at a minimum, a payout of 50% more than is actually earned). In these situations, the irony is that it is sometimes better to have a failure rather than a hit since as more royalty-generating albums, singles, and other recordings are sold, the payout to third parties gets larger and larger.

The variations in this area are innumerable and the calculations as to who owns what and who is entitled to what and where the money is going are limitless. Suffice it to say that one needs a calculator at all times when dealing with the issues involved in sampling as it is relatively easy to give away more than you get if you are the writer/artist or writer/producer doing the sampling.

CONCLUSION

One of the main financial and copyright dangers of sampling to the party who is doing the sampling, and this is not an exaggeration, is the possible loss of 100% of the income from the new composition as well as 100% of the copyright ownership in the material newly created by the artist/writer or producer/writer that is part of the new composition. For example, some writers and publishers of existing hit songs demand 100% of all rights in the new composition that has sampled an existing hit song. This includes the copyright, administration rights (the right to license the composition and collect all royalties), all songwriter royalties (including performance income from radio, Internet, and television airplay) and all publisher royalties (including record sales, download earnings, advertising commercial fees, motion picture use fees, television synchronization income, and video game and ringtone payments). This worst-case scenario for the writer/artist or writer/producer doing the sampling does occur, and you have to be aware of the fact that the bargaining power in the negotiations is totally in the hands of the owner of the composition being sampled. Clearance of samples prior to a recording being released or otherwise used is essential.

CHAPTER 7
MUSIC, MONEY, AND TELEVISION

E ach year, well over 4,000 individual series episodes are produced for the ABC, CBS, and NBC television networks; the Fox, CW, and other networks; Netflix, Amazon, Hulu, Apple, Google, Facebook, and other streaming services as well as Internet connected devices; first-run syndication, pay television, cable services, the Web, apps, and PBS. In addition, many movies of the week, miniseries, and one-time specials add to the annual total of television production. This multibillion-dollar business is a lucrative field for composers, theme writers, songwriters, and music publishers. Whether it is a brand new network, streaming, cable or local television series, a series that has been running for years, or a series that was a hit years ago and runs forever in U.S. and foreign syndication, a single TV series can provide composers and songwriters with royalties that provide a substantial, life-long annuity.

THE TELEVISION INDUSTRY

The producers of television shows include most of the same studio production companies and independents that are involved in the feature film area, plus many more. With more than 1,000 commercial television stations operating in the United States, many thousands of broadcast outlets outside the United States, the presence of many cable systems and services, and the increasing importance of the Internet, smartphones, mobile phones and tablets, the demand for programming is at an all time high.

Despite the increasing need for programming, production companies are dealing with an initial loss on every show produced. As the per episode budget for many shows runs into the millions of dollars—some high profile shows have broken the $10 million mark—and the fact that the network license fees normally cover between 60% to 80% of these per-episode production costs (e.g., a show that costs $3,000,000 to make receives a license fee of $1,800,000 resulting in a deficit of $1.2 million), production companies must look to future local television syndication, cable, streaming, and foreign television sales, DVD and home/personal video, downloads, and in certain cases, foreign theatrical distribution merely to recoup their initial production investment, much less to make a profit.

THE MAKING OF A TELEVISION PROGRAM

Practically all television programs are produced by either major production companies affiliated with a studio (Paramount, Warner Bros., Universal, Disney/21st Century Fox, Sony/Columbia, etc.), streaming services (Apple, Netflix, Amazon, Google, Hulu, Facebook, etc.), independent television production companies, production arms of the various broadcast and cable television networks, or a combination of these. In many cases, the networks have ownership stakes in the weekly series that they air because they are part of an entertainment conglomerate that has both broadcast as well as production facilities.

The first step for getting a new show on the air is many times the production company's "pitching" a script or an idea to the network, with the network assuming the costs of a final script if there is interest. If the script is accepted as a possible series, the network and the production company negotiate a fee for the making of a pilot episode. If the pilot goes to series, the parties will negotiate a per-episode license fee, which the network will pay the production company for each episode. The production company will use these license fees to defray part of the costs of production of each episode, with the remaining costs of production borne by the production company. Many of the larger production studios have put under contract a number of successful writers and writer/producers who develop much of the new programming ideas for the studios. Studios are also oftentimes informed as to the type of programming that the network may want for the new season. In those instances, the in-house writers come up with ideas and write the treatments, and the studio pitches them to the network. Many studios create new shows based upon the "holes" in a network's schedule (canceled shows) as well as the type of image the network is trying to project (e.g., under-30 audience).

As the number of new full-scale pilots has been reduced in recent years, some studios approach the networks with short "presentation" films of a prospective new series rather than a full-length pilot. If the network shows interest, it might either order one additional full-length episode or pay a certain amount of financing dollars to finish the "presentation" episode. Live "showcases" of new series ideas are also being tried in an effort to cut the costs of producing pilots.

THE MARKET

For many years the primary initial market for any series was the ABC, CBS, and NBC television networks. In the 1980s a major change occurred whereby many shows started to be produced for initial airings on individual local television stations rather than on the networks. The success of this concept of the "first-run syndication" of shows (e.g., *Star Trek: The Next Generation* and *The Simpsons*) drastically changed the viewing habits of many households and eroded the networks' share of viewing. Also, new "networks" were formed (Fox, UPN, WB, CW, My). The emergence and success of cable and pay cable also created substantial new markets for the production of original programming. What once was a straightforward progression of an initial network run plus subsequent sales to specific other types of users has now become a world of original programming everywhere.

As to the traditional big three networks, their standard episodic TV deal usually involves a maximum 22 episode season with the right to broadcast repeats as well as multicast, multiplex, repurpose, download, and stream the show. After a sufficient number of episodes have been produced, the show will be syndicated to local television stations or cable systems for either once-a-week airings or "stripping" (broadcast five times a week or more). Assuming the show is successful and translates well to the foreign marketplace, the show will be sold to foreign country television stations, cable systems, and streaming services.

Under this type of scenario, it was relatively easy for a composer to predict income. If you had 22 episodes of 10 minutes of score in each and the ASCAP, BMI, etc. performance monies were $170 a minute, the composer income would be $37,400. If half the shows received network primetime repeats, an additional $18,700 would be earned. Local television or cable "strip" syndication could, depending on the number of broadcasts and license fees paid to the PROs, equal or surpass the network run. Successful foreign sales could add substantial additional royalties assuming the show was broadcast in countries with societies that had significant license fee deals with the broadcasters in their territories (e.g., France, Germany, the U.K., etc.)

With the emergence of the audio visual streaming services (Netflix, Amazon, Hulu, Apple, Google, YouTube, Facebook, etc.) as well as premium cable services into the "television" production area, the standard deal as outlined above has undergone changes. One of the biggest changes involved the number of episodes in a series where 10 or 8 became the norm for a full series or season in the streaming or premium cable area rather than the 22 episode standard of the traditional television model. This change resulted in many more series being produced with an increased demographic reach by these subscription services but with fewer episodes produced for each series. Another change involved a primary focus on the need to increase subscriber numbers for these services rather than a reliance on traditional media's need for advertising dollars and instant ratings. A major factor in the success of this new type of programming is the very high quality of the productions—the result of many billions of dollars being allocated to the production budgets of shows being produced by these "new" players in the television business.

For the composer and songwriter though, some of these changes have not been financially beneficial—particularly when it involves the "backend" performance royalties emanating from original series being created for the audiovisual streaming services or first-run network or cable shows airing on these services. The music performance license fees paid by the streaming services to the PROs in the United States (ASCAP, BMI, SESAC, and GMR) are significantly less than those paid by broadcast television and cable networks and stations resulting in performance royalties well below what composers, songwriters, and music publishers are used to from traditional media.

Some of the other markets for television series include DVD, Blu-ray and home video rentals as well as video-on-demand and downloads. As to the home video market, it is rare for royalties to be generated for composers as most contracts, when dealing with home video, provide no additional compensation for these uses and are many times worded as a buy-out or included in the "all in" composing fee. There are exceptions with respect to existing songs that are licensed to certain television programs (such as music and dance centric series where there are home and personal video options exercisable by the producer) but video monies are almost always formulated as a one-time negotiated fee regardless of the number of videos sold or downloaded. The home and personal video market continues as an income source for old and new TV series where entire seasons or the "best of" still sell but not in the large numbers that were enjoyed prior to streaming becoming the norm. Incidentally, some reality shows, which at one time had few repeats and little syndication value, now enjoy some home and personal video sales.

TYPES OF TELEVISION MUSIC AND HOW MUSIC IS USED

The television field, by its very nature, provides composers and songwriters with a broad spectrum of music uses: the series theme song, the underscore, the song written for a specific scene in a television show, the use of a pre-existing song in a television show, the hit song used as a theme for a series, the network and production company logo, promo music for upcoming or current shows, bumpers in and out of a program, and the commercial jingle. Each of these types of music may be heard continually throughout the broadcast day of any television station. Moreover, each type generates not only a different initial writing fee (or synchronization fee if it is a pre-existing piece of music) but also very different amounts of performance royalties from ASCAP, BMI, SESAC, GMR, and foreign country performing rights organizations.

THE TELEVISION MUSIC BUDGET

One rule of thumb used by some studios and production companies to estimate and arrive at the music budgets for series as well as for movies of the week is to allocate $20,000 to $25,000 per hour for all music-related costs. If a show is a one-hour series or a two-hour movie of the week, the initial rough music budget would be $20,000 to $25,000 for the series episode, and $40,000 to $50,000 for the movie of the week. Miniseries would be handled in the same manner. The budgeted music costs include the composer's creative fee, studio rental time, tape, engineers, musicians, instrument cartage and rentals, music-licensing fees, and miscellaneous other music-related costs.

After the initial allocation figure, the actual costs of each project are discussed and calculated more accurately. Some factors that affect the cost are whether it's an electronic home studio recording or a live orchestra (rare these days), the amount of music to be composed, and the number of pre-existing songs that are to be licensed. If live musicians are needed and two or three hit songs are used in the show, the costs of musicians, studio time, and synchronization fees could substantially raise the $25,000-per-hour figure. On the other hand, if very little music is needed for the show and no outside songs are being licensed, the music costs could be substantially less than the initially allocated $20,000 to $25,000 rule of thumb. For example, a first-season half-hour show containing only two to three minutes of music might be completed with a $3,500 to $5,000 composer "package deal."

Another budgeting approach involves preparing an initial generic budget from a "read-through" of a script. The music supervisor looks at a show and determines whether it needs a full orchestral score or suits itself to an electronic or small-ensemble score. One then determines whether "outside" songs as well as master recordings are necessary. After completing all of the cost estimates, there is a discussion with the producer to see if the figure allocated for music fits into the total budget and to find out if the producer is in agreement with the necessity of all the items included.

One factor that affects the budgets of shows that have been on the air for three or four years is a change in the way production companies negotiate the terms of the synchronization licenses for outside songs. For shows still in their initial seasons, producers many times negotiate five- to six-year free television synchronization licenses for between $2,500 to over $3,500 per song. When shows go into their third or fourth seasons, a number of production companies negotiate "all television, in perpetuity, worldwide" synchronization licenses for outside songs at substantially increased fees ($7,500 to over $12,000, for instance). Although this total buy-out approach increases the music budget for shows in the third or fourth season, it is necessary, as the company now knows that it has enough episodes to go into syndication and prefers not to renegotiate five-year licenses each time they become due. In some cases, this occurs in the first year. For successful shows many studios automatically request "worldwide in perpetuity or life of copyright" all media excluding theatrical licenses, since this type of television release almost always promises a home video release, a foreign television release, and other platform releases. Although the synchronization costs will be initially higher, money and time will usually be saved by the production company in the future by paying for long-term licenses up front. These life-of-copyright licenses are sometimes handled on an option basis with respect to each different medium.

TELEVISION UNDERSCORE

The great majority of the music heard on television, whether on an episodic one-hour or half-hour show, a movie of the week, or a miniseries, is underscore. This is the music underneath action or romance scenes and in portrayals of emotion. It is the music that accompanies, enhances, and explains much of the visual elements of television. At one time, symphonic training and the ability to conduct an orchestra was necessary for many shows. In today's world though, the economics of the business make the home studio, electronic, or small ensemble scores the norm.

Although television composers may have differing styles, they all agree on the type of show for which they would like to score: a successful series. To be the primary underscore composer of a long-running series represents not only very steady work but also substantial domestic and foreign royalties long after the series is canceled.

An extra benefit of being the initial score composer on a series is that many television theme songs are written by the composer of the underscore as part of the initial composing contract. Many others are written by composers who have had past successes with themes, whether or not they are the primary composer for a new show. In some cases, feature film composers write the theme to a show and leave the underscore to others. Whereas the score needs to be composed anew for each separate episode of a series, the theme needs to be written only once, and the performance royalties for this one-time composition can sometimes be more substantial than the underscore composer performance royalties.

THE TELEVISION UNDERSCORE CONTRACT

Most terms in contracts for television music are fairly standard, with the primary differences being whether the composing agreement covers the series pilot, a series pilot plus a commitment for subsequent episodes, a single show within a running series, or multiple episodes of the same series. Other factors include the stature of the composer, the power of the composer's agent, or a "package deal" where the composer bears most of the costs related to the production of the music.

The basic areas covered in every television series underscore contract are the type of services to be performed by the composer, the compensation for those services, the type and placement of on-screen credit, the length of the agreement, the delivery requirements, the ownership of the copyright, and whether the composer or the production company will bear most of the costs of producing the music.

Composer Services. The standard agreement will provide that the television underscore composer is hired to compose, arrange, orchestrate, record, and produce original music for use in an episode of the television series. The composer shall deliver to the producer a master-ready score in addition to lead sheets, and session contracts no later than the date specified by the producer. The composer must also consult with the producer of the show as to the music and must comply with the recommendations, directions, and requests of the producer in all areas, including those regarding artistic taste and judgment. In addition, the composer is required to make any changes, modifications, or additions to the score when requested to do so by the producer. Many of these contracts also contain an all-purpose clause stating that the composer is to "perform all services and duties customarily performed in this field by a composer, scorer, conductor, arranger, and orchestrator."

Starting and Completion Dates. With time being very much of the essence in the television industry, starting and completion dates must be strictly observed. It is not uncommon for a writer to compose, score, and record an episode in five to seven days (two or three days is sometimes necessary), with dubbing of the music taking place a day later and actual television broadcast occurring within a week after the dubbing. Many series allocate more time for this process, but the nature of the business requires the ability to produce on a moment's notice.

A typical scenario after a composer is hired is for the composer, the picture editor, the music editor, and the show's producer or director to come together for a viewing of a work video of the program. This is the "spotting" session. At certain points, the video of the show will be stopped to discuss where the music should begin and end, as well as the style or "feel" of the music. After all of the ideas are discussed, the video progresses to the place for the next music cue. At the end of this session, the composer goes home and makes his or her own notes. The music editor will send the composer specific notes as to the location and length of the music cues. For many shows, the time between the spotting process and the dub is less than one week. The dubbing process is where the edited picture, the sound effects, the finished score, and the dialogue are mixed together. For larger orchestral scores, more time is allocated for composing and recording.

Composing Fees. The composing fees paid to television composers are unlike those paid to film composers, both in terms of the initial writing fee as well as the range of composing fees separating the "top-end" composer from the "bottom-end" composer. Budgets are the primary driver of fees rather than who the composer is.

Package composing fees for episodic series range from $9,000 to $20,000 for a one-hour dramatic series, and $5,000 to $10,000 for a half-hour series. For a top end composer, $35,000 would be a top fee for a one-hour show. As to movies of the week, a reasonable package would be double the one-hour show fee but could be higher. For miniseries, one could negotiate a package fee for each episode or negotiate an entire music budget for the whole series. These fees vary, based on the amount of music the episode needs, the type of orchestration necessary, and the music budget. In package-deal situations, the writer must be exceptionally careful to determine what music costs he or she is undertaking, and what costs are excluded from the deal and are borne by the producer. Non-package deals (composing fee only) would be considerably less than the package dollar figures.

Under a package deal, the composer undertakes all of the costs of producing the musical score with certain items excluded. Included will be all costs for composing and conducting, all studio costs, all copying, orchestration, and attendant music costs, including musicians, etc. A composer who undertakes a package deal needs not only to exclude certain items from the deal (costs of singers and lyricists, synchronization rights for outside songs and existing master recordings, re-scoring or re-recording subsequent to the acceptance of the score, re-use payments to the A.F.M., SAG-AFTRA, etc.) but also to be able to "control" a hands-on producer or director who either has difficulty explaining what he or she wants or constantly changes his or her mind. When possible, a composer should always try to show a producer in advance what he or she is doing, an approach that helps slow the ticking of the financial clock at the session. A composer should also know the studio where the score is being recorded (if a home studio is not being used) and be assured of a good technical staff and professional engineers.

The following clauses provide a feel for the types of arrangements as well as dollar amounts that composers receive for episodic television scores:
EXAMPLE 1. A network television one-hour episodic series/package deal
  1. $15,000 for the pilot
  2. $12,500 for each of the next 12 episodes, provided that the composer's services are required.
  3. $12,500 for each episode aired during the second half of the television season in which the composer has written the music
  4. $15,000 for each new episode scored by the composer and aired during the series' second season.

Assuming that the show is picked up for an entire first season of 22 episodes and the composer scores all 22 episodes, total composer compensation would be $277,500.

EXAMPLE 2. Individual episode of a half-hour network primetime comedy series/package.
  1. $4,000 upon completion of all of the composer's services.

The most sought-after type of contract is the network pilot and series contract, as it ensures that a composer will score not only the pilot episode but also all or many of the series episodes. If the show becomes a hit, the writer can earn hundreds of thousands of dollars a year in domestic and foreign performance monies in addition to the composing fees generated by each new episode. As many successful series also generate spin-offs (e.g., *CSI*, *Law and Order*, etc.), the original composer often times is given a shot to score the new series.

The producer hires the composer to compose, orchestrate, and conduct for the first 13 episodes of the series, with an option on the composer's services for any episodes produced for the second half of the initial television season on the same terms and conditions as the first 13 episodes. The producer's notice to pick up the option on the composer's services must be given to the composer, in writing, within 10 business days of the show's producer being given an unconditional network commitment for the production of additional shows.

In recent years, many of the "full series" contracts have come to be handled as a continuing sequence of options on the producer's part, whereby the composer is paid an amount for each episode for which he or she "renders and completes" services, and continues to receive the contract money each time the producer exercises its option for the composer's services for each subsequent series episode.

Another recent variation on a pilot/series deal is a step deal whereby a composer is asked to sketch out a score that he or she thinks is appropriate for the non-broadcast version of a new pilot. The fee paid is lower than the composer's norm. If the pilot does get picked up, additional monies are paid to produce a broadcast dub-ready score. A separate "all in" deal for the theme is also offered.

An example of this type of deal is as follows: $7,000 for the non-broadcast "sales presentation" version of the pilot; $14,000 for the broadcast version of the pilot; and $15,000 per episode for the series. The fees would be paid 50% on the commencement of services and 50% upon completion of services and delivery of the masters. A separate main title theme fee for a demo could be in the area of $2,000 and if accepted, an additional $10,000 to $15,000 might be paid to the composer. Top-end film and television composer theme fees are significantly higher than the figures mentioned.

It is important to note that many original series being produced for the audiovisual streaming services (Netflix, Hulu, Amazon, etc.) are in many ways similar to the network deals as to compensation and packages with the main exception being the backend performance royalties which are significantly lower than traditional broadcast media.

THEME SONGS

For some series, the "opening" theme is part of the scoring contract where the fee is either incorporated into the total music score fee or separately allocated in the agreement. Closing themes are generally considered as part of the music score agreement and usually result in some additional monies. For example, a pilot and potential theme deal for a one-hour series might read: "To compensate and package the music score (with listed exclusions) for $17,500 with a $2,000 all-in payment for theme demos. If the Producer accepts the composition for use as the theme, the Composer will receive an additional $8,000. Payment would be 50% upon commencement of services and 50% upon completion."

In situations where the production company hires a composer or songwriter just to write the series theme song, the writer would furnish his or her services on a nonexclusive basis to compose and package the main title theme and end title themes in various lengths with end title separate card credit of "Theme by _____." Payment (in this case, $15,000) would be 100% upon completion and delivery of the masters.

A "theme only" deal for a top film composer or songwriter might also include, in certain situations, 100% (or a portion) of the publishing with the production company owning the masters. The writer would provide an irrevocable grant to the producer to use the song in the series in "any media now known or hereafter existing in perpetuity throughout the universe." When themes are incorporated into the music score contract, the package amount is typically in the area of $10,000 to $20,000. Where a top-end composer or songwriter is hired just to write the theme, the package fee could be in excess of $50,000.

SCREEN CREDIT

The composer's screen credit for episodic television will be in either the show's opening or closing credits. The type and placement of the composer credit is a negotiable item. The following are sample clauses:

"Composer shall receive credit in the form of MUSIC BY [name of composer] in the opening titles on a separate card."

"Composer shall receive credit on a separate card in the end titles in the form of MUSIC BY [name of composer]."

"Composer shall receive credit of MUSIC BY in such place and size as Producer may elect or "an appropriate credit shall be negotiated in good faith."

EXCLUSIVITY OF COMPOSER'S SERVICES

Although many television music contracts merely state that the composer must perform all of the services required according to the production schedule and the producer's direction and instructions, some contracts directly specify the exclusive nature of the agreement:

"Though the Composer's services are on a nonexclusive basis [the Composer can work on other projects during the term of this agreement], this project is to be considered as 'first priority.'"

"Composer agrees not to render services of a similar nature to anyone unless the Producer's specific written consent is received."

OWNERSHIP OF THE COPYRIGHT

Practically all television underscore contracts fall under the rubric of "employee for hire" or "work made for hire," under which the producer becomes the author and copyright owner of the work. The grant-of-rights clause that the composer signs is normally similar to those contained in feature film composing contracts, in that the producer becomes the owner of "all now or hereafter existing rights of every kind and character whatsoever throughout the world, whether or not such rights are known, recognized, or contemplated." The term "producer" in this context normally means the studio or production company making the television series.

MUSIC PUBLISHING

The standard contractual arrangement in the television industry gives all of the music publishing rights to the producer by means of the employee-for-hire contract. As the owner of the copyright and all of the rights that flow from that ownership, the producer is not only allowed to collect income generated by the musical work from most sources but also is able to license to others all of the rights of copyright, rights that can generate millions of dollars of royalty income.

Occasionally, writers with substantial past success may be able to negotiate some retention of partial publishing rights to their work. In doing so, though, the up-front composing payment may be reduced as part of the negotiation with the production company. Other times, a writer may keep all or a portion of the publishing if the production company is a small one or one not knowledgeable about the "value" of owning music copyrights. Those situations, however, are the exception rather than the rule.

MEMBERSHIP IN A PERFORMING RIGHTS ORGANIZATION

"The Composer must be a member in good standing of a performing rights organization as well as any other applicable labor organization, guild, or union that may have jurisdiction" or "Composer's public performance royalties throughout the world are to be paid directly to Composer from Composer's own affiliated performing right society" are variations of the standard clause whereby composers are assured of receiving the writer's share of performance royalties whenever the series is broadcast anywhere throughout the world. This clause is essential to any contract, as the U.S. and worldwide performance royalties represent, for most composers, their main source of composing income.

The following example of the possible composer earnings from a successful show should help put the importance of this clause into perspective:
EXAMPLE. A composer has 15 minutes of underscore in each of 66 episodes (three seasons) of a one-hour primetime network television series. All 66 episodes are repeated once (132 airings), and the show is sold to foreign countries and eventually

widely syndicated on U.S. local or cable television stations and streaming services. Possible composer royalties might be as follows:

U.S. network television airings:	$336,000
Foreign television performances:	$140,000
Initial-year U.S. local or cable television performances:	$85,000
Streaming Service:	$3,500
Total performing rights income:	$564,500

Although the performing rights clause was a fairly standard one during the 1960s and 1970s, attempts to modify and condition the clause emerged in the 1980s. The modifications in these contracts involved primarily the instances where the producer could license a show's music directly to a user, thereby bypassing the performing rights organizations completely.

Although composers have had for decades the right to license their music directly to a user, the new wording of these clauses became a concern, because most did not provide any specific amount to be paid to a composer when a show was broadcast, nor did these provisions make any specific mention of the all-important principle of continuing writer royalties for the life of copyright based on continuing performances of the work.

Two variations on this clause follow:

"In the event that the Society does not license the performing rights in the background score, the Producer may license the score directly and negotiate a reasonable fee according to industry standards and shall divide such negotiated fee between Composer and Producer."

"In the event that a broadcasting station does not have a blanket nondramatic performing right license with ASCAP, BMI, SESAC, or GMR and the station's agreement with the Producer states that a license must be provided, then the Producer may license the score directly. Once the license is issued, the Producer has to negotiate with the Composer in good faith as to what the fee should be. If no agreement can be reached, the negotiation will go to arbitration."

As new variations on the standard clause continue to be introduced during the negotiations, many writers and their representatives have expressed concerns that not only are many of the clauses vague as to what the performance fees would be but many also seem to provide for a one-time-only fee with no reference to any entitlement right to continuing writer royalties when the show is rebroadcast.

One variation of this clause actually spells out the factors that should be taken into account in negotiating the direct license fee, with the listed considerations being the amount and type of music use, the stature of the composer, and other "relevant factors of custom and practice in the industry." Although this type of contract actually includes a list of items to be considered in negotiating a fee, some of the items listed continue to be very vague.

Many composers are concerned about the effect that these clauses could have on a composer's foreign royalties. The foreign television market is now larger than the U.S. market, and this profitable source of composer royalties may be given up entirely if a composer agrees to some of these clauses. The best course to take in handling this type of clause is to talk to one's lawyer or representative, so that he or she can advise as to both the short-term and long-term ramifications of signing such a document, and negotiate accordingly.

The top countries for performance income for television uses are the United Kingdom (PRS), Japan (JASRAC), Canada (SOCAN), Netherlands (BUMA), Germany (GEMA), Italy (SIAE), France (SACEM), and Australia (APRA), among others.

SUSPENSIONS AND TERMINATIONS

Suspensions come into play when either the writer cannot perform his or her services or the production company has to put a halt to production for any of various reasons. The key triggering terms of "disability," "default," and "force majeure" are covered in the section on feature film contracts in Chapter 8, "Music, Money and Motion Pictures," and those same definitions apply to the television world.

In the event that any disability, default, or force majeure occurs during the term of the agreement, the composer's services are suspended for the period of the occurrence. If the suspension is due to composer disability or default (e.g., the composer's mental or physical inability to compose or the composer's failure, refusal, or neglect to compose), no compensation is paid to the composer and, in many cases, the composer is prevented from working for anyone else. If the suspension occurs owing to a force majeure (e.g., the production of the show has to cease due to labor disputes, fire, an act of God, or war), the composer is normally allowed to work for others as long as he or she is able to resume work immediately on the original production when it again commences. If the force majeure situation continues for a certain amount of time (five weeks, for example), the composer can terminate the agreement, with payment due for all of the composer's work completed prior to the force majeure. The producer can also terminate the composer if the composer suffers an illness or incapacity (disability) continuing over a stated amount of business days or a force majeure situation lasting more than a set number of weeks. In such a situation the producer is obligated for all composer payments due up to the time of the suspension. If the composer's default results in termination, the producer is under no obligation to the composer for any payments due prior to the default situation.

Some contracts provide for the absolute right of the producer to terminate a composer's services. These provisions normally refer to the producer's "sole discretion" and provide for composer termination at a stated period of time (three weeks, for instance) after receipt by the composer of the producer's termination notice. Some contracts even provide for a similar composer right to terminate the contract with the producer.

DISPOSITION OF THE SCORE

As with feature films, the producer has no obligation to use the background score in the program or to exercise any of the rights granted to it under the agreement. If the producer does not like the score for any reason and decides not to use it, the producer can do so, with the only obligation to the composer being the payment of all of the compensation provided for in the contract. A corollary to this clause is the provision whereby the composer waives "moral rights," with the producer retaining the right to rearrange, edit, cut, and add to the score any time the producer may so choose. Though this is not a heavily negotiated clause, composers should be aware that an occasional practice in certain countries is to replace the U.S. composer's original episode score with a local composer's score when the show is aired in that country. Such a replacement score, if used with permission, can have a profound effect on a composer's foreign earnings, and negotiations should bear in mind this possibility.

TRANSPORTATION AND EXPENSES

Because most television scoring and recording occurs in the cities where the main production facilities are (Los Angeles and New York), most television composer contracts do not provide for transportation and living expenses. Owing to the increasing production and studio costs in those cities, though, a trend has arisen toward producing shows and occasionally scoring and recording the music elsewhere (e.g., Vancouver or Toronto). In instances where the composer is required to score and record the music away from his or her home base, business or first-class transportation, hotel, and meals are contractually provided for.

SHARE OF ADVANCE PAYMENTS

Most contracts state that the composer will not share in any advance or guarantee payments for the music that the producer may receive from making a subpublishing, licensing, or other collection type of agreement. For example, if the producer of a television show makes an agreement with another publisher for representation in a specific territory and receives an advance against future royalties generated in that territory, the composer will usually not share in the advance but will receive composer royalties as they are earned.

WARRANTIES AND INDEMNIFICATIONS

The composer represents that he or she is free to enter into the agreement, that the music will be totally original to the composer, that the music does not infringe upon any other copyrighted composition, and that no rights in the music have been previously conveyed by the composer to any other party. The composer also agrees to indemnify the producer "from and against any liability, loss, claims, costs, and expenses arising from" the material that the composer has provided for the show. If a claim does arise and the producer takes on the responsibility to defend it, the composer will usually be liable for many of the costs expended in fighting the claim or litigation as well as the amount of any adverse judgment in the case.

ASSIGNMENTS

The producer usually has the right to assign or license the rights to the agreement to any other party.

ROYALTY PAYMENTS

Most score agreements contain an attachment or exhibit that specifies the various types of royalties that will be paid should the music be exploited beyond the broadcasting medium. (These royalty figures are covered in depth later in this chapter.) A typical exhibit would cover the composer's share of earnings derived from licenses covering the sale of sheet music, band arrangements, mechanical rights for recordings, synchronization rights for uses of the score in other projects, and foreign uses. Soundtrack album royalties would also be specified including artist and producer royalty percentages, if applicable.

THEATRICAL VERSION RELEASE

A fairly common clause in two-hour television movie as well as television miniseries contracts is the theatrical version clause, which provides additional composer compensation if the movie or miniseries is released outside of the United States as a theatrical (movie theater) release. Though there will be a definition of what actually constitutes a "theatrical release," a sample clause might provide for an additional one-time composer payment of $15,000 if the movie is released in two or more international territories. The amount of this additional compensation is an item subject to negotiation. Some of the factors taken into account include the amount of the original composing fee as well as whether or not the movie or miniseries was a "package" deal.

TELEVISION SERIES SONG DEMO DEALS, SERVICES, AND OTHER PROVISIONS

A number of television producers will enter into agreements with outside songwriters which give them the opportunity to write new songs for possible use in the producer's television series. These opportunities are usually geared to an individual series in production but can apply to any series controlled by the producer.

This can be a great opportunity for a songwriter and there are numerous ways that these submission agreements are handled. A representative agreement will usually cover all or most of the following areas.

Services/Projects. The songwriter will agree to create a new song for an identified series and deliver a demo recording by a certain date.

Compensation. A fee is set ($5,000, $10,000, $20,000, etc.) which will cover the creative contribution compensation for all writers of the song. This is not a buyout of future songwriter royalties (performance royalties, mechanical income, etc.), only a fee for creating the song.

Demo Recording. The agreement will usually provide, if the television producer has interest in the song, for a recording fund to enable the songwriter to have the song professionally recorded. This aspect is many times structured as a record production agreement with the fee (e.g., $2,500, $5,000, $10,000, etc.) payable when the recording is accepted by the television producer. This fee is in addition to any producer royalties that maybe negotiated for uses of the recording outside of the series' episode.

Reassignment. If the composition and demo recording are not approved by the production company within a set time period after the composition was written and/or submitted (e.g., one year, etc.), the composition may be returned to the songwriter. This reassignment of rights would not include any materials, concepts, or ideas related to the series, its characters or any other part thereof.

Ownership. If the composition is accepted or approved by the television producer, the ownership of both the composition and demo recording will be in the name of the television producer. The copyright will almost always be termed to be created under a "writer for hire" relationship which is intended to prevent any reversion of the copyright in the future.

Use of the Composition. The grant to the television producer will allow use of the composition and recording in any and all media, subject to the payment of songwriter royalties as provided in the royalty schedule attached to the agreement.

Short Form Agreements. The majority of these song and demo submission agreements are in the form of signable deal memos (as opposed to long form contracts), a format which enables the parties to quickly negotiate the essential terms of the deal without going through weeks or months of negotiation. These deal memos are binding agreements which cover the major points (e.g., services, compensation, royalties, re-assignment if not accepted, use rights if accepted, copyright ownership, indemnification for claims, remedies for breach, and choice of law in the case of litigation) so, even though short in length, it must be taken seriously.

Other Major Points. Since the initial agreement is a short form which anticipates a longer formal and more encompassing agreement, there is usually a "catch all" clause which deals with a number of items not specifically covered. For example, there usually is a clause that states that until a more formal agreement is signed which will specify the actual songwriter, producer royalties and, if applicable, artist royalties (which shall be in accordance with certain standard, or specified terms and conditions such as the producer shall receive at least a 3% royalty or that the composition will be licensed at not less than 75% of statutory for physical product and 100% for digital), the short form is binding.

ADDITIONAL IN-HOUSE SYNCHRONIZATION FEES FOR OTHER PROJECTS

An issue that may occur when negotiating an agreement for writing an original composition for a television series is whether or not there will be any additional compensation paid to the songwriter or composer if the work is used in another project controlled by the producer. There are a number of approaches in this area depending upon bargaining power and the policies of the producers. One approach is to have a schedule attached to the writer for hire agreement which contains in very specific details the amount of additional fees that the songwriter and/or composer will receive if the composition is used in projects other than which it was written for.

An example of this detailed additional fee approach is:

a. Television/Motion Picture	
i. Non-Title:	$
ii. Title:	$

b. Theatrical Motion Picture	
i. Non-Title Single	$
a. Non-Charting:	$
b. Charting:	$
c. Top 40:	$
d. Top 5:	$

ii. Title Single	$
a. Non-Charting:	$
b. Charting:	$
c. Top 40:	$
d. Top 5:	$

There can be many variations that may result from the negotiations as to this area but the above is an example of something that captures a definitive understanding between the parties so that everyone knows what the future holds if there are additional uses of a composition in projects other than the original project for which a composition was written.

TELEVISION SYNCHRONIZATION RIGHTS (GETTING SONGS INTO SERIES, SPECIALS, AND MADE-FOR-TV MOVIES)

THE IMPORTANCE OF SONGS

In contemporary television, music has taken on a significant role in the success or failure of a series, miniseries, special, or made-for-TV movie. Because of this significance, producers and their music supervisors put a special emphasis on selecting hit songs, recognizable standards, newer songs, and other compositions that are right for a particular scene or project. Granted, the premise, writing, and acting all have to be there for a program to make it, but if a television program has these basics, good music can add that final touch to the elusive formula of what makes a hit.

THE PHONE CALL FROM THE TV PRODUCER

Setting:
Office of the vice president of business affairs for a major music publisher.

The Phone Call:
MUSIC SUPERVISOR: Hi, this is the music supervisor from [Name of Television Series]. We'd like to use the song [Name of Composition] in a scene for an episode in which two of the characters find themselves in a singles bar.

PUBLISHER: How would you like to use the song and what rights do you need?

MUSIC SUPERVISOR: The use will be a two-minute background vocal, as we'll be using [Name of Performer]'s record on a jukebox. There is a possibility that one of the characters may also sing a few lines either while the record is being played or a couple of scenes later. For your information, I'm getting a fee quote from

[Name of Record Company] so we can use the master recording with his actual performance. For the use, we'll need a worldwide price quote for the following media:

1. A five-year all television license
2. An option for Internet streaming/one month
3. An option for a life-of-copyright all television license
4. Options for a pay television license for life of copyright, as well as an airline option
5. An option for all media rights excluding theatrical, for life of the copyright
6. An option for a home and personal video buy-out including mobile phones
7. An option for theatrical use outside the United States
8. An option to use the song in out-of-context promos for the series
9. An option for digital downloads for one year until the all media option is exercised

PUBLISHER: That's quite a laundry list. When do you need the quotes?

MUSIC SUPERVISOR: Well, we're really under the gun. The scenes are being filmed tomorrow, and I need your confirmation whether we can use the song and how much it will cost almost immediately, so we can know whether we'll have to go with another song.

PUBLISHER: Okay. Let's go through the list: $5,000 for the five-year all TV license, and $1,000 for Internet streaming. Life-of-copyright all television will cost $10,000. Pay TV for life of copyright will be $7,000. Home video will be $10,000. Foreign theatrical will be $12,000. Airlines will be $4,000. All media excluding theatrical will be $24,000. Out-of-context television promos will be an extra $2,000 per week. And the one-year digital download rights will cost $3,000.

MUSIC SUPERVISOR: Thanks, as the fees all fit in with our budget considering the stature of the song. I'll send you an e-mail confirming our understanding and, if the song is used, I'll request a license.

With more than 100 television companies in the United States and usually more than 400 series, specials, and made-for-TV movies actually in production at any given time, the previous call occurs more than 100 times a day, virtually 365 days every year. It is a call that can take on many variations and consist of many twists. It is a call that everyone hopes for. It is a call that can produce hundreds of thousands of dollars in future income. It is a call that requires an immediate answer. And it is a call that you had better be ready to take. It should also be noted that a large number of requests are initially received via e-mail. With 4 million viewers watching even the lowest-rated network series and more than 100 million tuned into the best, television can be the answer to a songwriter's prayer. Because of its importance, this chapter reveals what you need to know about getting your songs on television and making the right deal.

NEGOTIATING THE TELEVISION LICENSE FOR A SONG

When a producer wants to use an existing musical composition in a television program, weekly series, special, miniseries, or made-for-TV movie, permission must, with few exceptions, be secured from the music publisher who owns the song. The producer or music supervisor of the show will decide what song he or she wants to use in the program and the scene in which it will appear, how the song will be used (e.g., background vocal or instrumental, sung by a character on camera, over the opening or ending credits), and the initial media needed (e.g., free television, pay television, subscription television, streaming, pay-per-view, Internet, video-on-demand, satellite-on-demand, closed circuit, basic cable, all television, all media, all media excluding theatrical, etc.). The producer or its "music clearance" representative will then contact the owner of the composition, describe the context of the program and particular scene in which the song will be used; ask for a specified period of time to use the song in the program (usually from three years to life of copyright), negotiate a fee, and then sign what is known in the television business as a "synchronization license." On occasion, the producer may also want to alter the original lyrics of a song to make a scene work better or add a laugh, and such a request will always be a part of the initial negotiations.

In many cases, the "synch license" is signed after the first broadcast of the program, but the negotiations and securing of permission to use a song virtually always occur prior to the inclusion of the song in the program or, at the latest, prior to the initial broadcast date. Some series and made-for-TV movies have quite a bit of lead time before their actual air date, and then the song permission negotiations take place at a reasonable pace. Most television programs secure price quotations from music publishers for the use of songs either during the scriptwriting stages of a project or immediately after a final script for an episode has been approved. Many weekly series and some miniseries and specials, however, clear music while scenes are being shot or, because of impromptu ad-libs during taping, last-minute additions, or editing delays, a few days prior to actual broadcast and sometimes even after the airing.

Because home and personal video is an important ancillary market for television programming, negotiations (many times on an option basis unless the license includes all media) will take place for home and personal use as well. Considering that some television programs (normally miniseries, made-for-TV movies, and two-hour episodes of certain series) are also released as films to motion picture theaters in countries outside the United States, the producer may also request rights and negotiate additional fees for such nontelevision theatrical uses. And since many television programs are eventually broadcast in media other than that on which they were initially aired (e.g., a series originally made for and broadcast on pay television being subsequently shown in the free over-the-air syndication market, etc.), a producer may also request option prices for a wide range of additional media, such as pay television for the world outside the United States, public broadcasting stations, nonpay cable in the United States and Canada, and pay cable in certain foreign countries, mobile phones, streaming services, as well as any number of variations and combinations of these.

ACTUAL FEES CHARGED FOR SONGS USED IN TELEVISION PROGRAMMING BY BROADCAST TELEVISION (ABC, CBS, NBC, FOX, CW, MY, INDEPENDENT LOCAL STATIONS, AND SYNDICATION)

The standard synchronization fees charged by music publishers usually range from $2,000 to more than $7,000 for the use of a song in a television series for unlimited television distribution of the program for five to six years throughout the world. Certain producers occasionally request that the term of such licenses be for longer periods (for example, 10 to 15 years at either double or triple the aforementioned rates, or guaranteed options after expiration of the initial license period at specifically agreed-upon or "to be negotiated in good faith" fees). And others sometimes request life-of-copyright synch licenses for songs used in certain hit series, with fees ranging from $7,500 to more than $12,000 depending on a number of factors, including the music budget for the program, whether the song is a well-known standard or current hit as opposed to a new song in need of exposure, the song's importance to the series episode and the particular scene in which it is performed, how many times it is used in the program, the manner of the use (e.g., background music from a jukebox or sung by a character on camera), and the song's remaining copyright life.

Free Television. Under a free television synchronization license, the music publisher gives a series producer the right to include a musical composition in a particular television program and to sell that program to any station in the world without any further payment. For example, the series can be sold to a television network for early-morning, primetime, or late-night airing and unlimited repeats; to syndication; or on a station-by-station basis during the term of the license, with the only conditions being that the television stations showing the series do not charge their viewers a fee to watch the program and that they have a valid performance license, which permits them to broadcast the music contained in the episode or series.

In addition to the length of the term of the license, the actual timing of the song's use is also important in negotiating a fee. For example, if the duration of the song used in the program is less than a full or substantial usage (30 seconds or less), then the fees charged by many publishers may be reduced. But if the song is a recognizable hit or standard and the use is important to the context of a particular scene (such as a main character singing the song on camera or a background mood use that is essential to the plot of the episode or series), there is usually no reduction in the synchronization fee even if only 15 to 30 seconds are actually used. One example of a show that usually merits reduced synchronization fees is *Jeopardy!*, because only 10 to 30 seconds of a hit song are usually broadcast as part of one of the audio question-and-answer categories. One example from the show was the use of the theme from the motion picture *Jaws* as a clue to the category of "Scary Movies." Alex Trebek asked, "What monster would you expect to meet after you've heard this music?" The *Jaws* theme was played, the answer of a great white shark was correctly given, and the game moved on to a new category.

The synchronization fees to use master recordings (the original hit record of a song) can be more costly, depending on the type of license request, with such monies paid to the record company that owns the rights to the single or album cut being used. The reason that such "master fees" can be more expensive than those charged for the song itself is that there are no performance royalties paid to the record companies or performers for the broadcast of recordings in the United States. The existence of such broadcast performance royalties for songwriters and music publishers, which continue as long as a particular television program is broadcast, enable music publishers to keep their synchronization fees at a low or moderate level. Record companies, however, do not receive any such royalties based on how many times a program is broadcast; therefore, they may charge more for the use of a master recording because their only income will be the one-time payment for the master use synchronization license although many licenses are on a most favored nations basis.

Pay or Subscription Television (HBO, Cinemax, Disney Channel, Showtime). The prevalent fees charged by music publishers under a five-year license for the use of a song in a program on pay television (which includes pay-per-view, video-on-demand, and subscription video-on-demand) range from $3,000 to over $12,000 but, as with network or syndicated programs, can be increased or decreased depending on the length of the use, the stature of the song, whether it is background music or sung on camera, its importance to the plot of the show, and whether it is used more than once in a given episode. The territory for such licenses used to be the United States and Canada, but with the emergence of pay and cable television in most foreign countries, producers are more and more frequently requesting worldwide rights. For many programs, the term of the synchronization license is from three to five years, but it can be shorter or longer depending on the popularity of the program and distribution needs of the producer. For example, some producers ask for only two to three years, as they may feel that the pay television life of the project may be short. Others request terms of from five to 15 years, and many request life-of-copyright licenses, with fees raised accordingly.

There is a growing trend for producers to request guaranteed options at set fees to ensure that if a program continues to be broadcast after the initial license term has expired, the procedures for renewing the license will be predetermined. For example, a 25% increase may be negotiated for each successive renewal period, or there might be an actual dollar schedule for all possible option periods in the initial contract (e.g., $_____ for the first five years, $_____ for the second five years, $_____ for the tenth through fifteenth years, etc.) to prevent any chance of a misunderstanding between the publisher and producer as to the music cost of a show's future distribution. Obviously, these guaranteed option clauses are extremely important to a television producer, as they assure that any song put in a series will remain in that series regardless of any future changes in the copyright ownership of the composition (e.g., the song reverting to the writer) or changes in the personnel at the music-publishing company that gave the initial permission—an important guarantee if the program is a hit. After all, it could get very expensive if a major star in an episode of a hit series sang a song on camera and there was no guarantee that the song could be used in repeats of that series after the five- or 10-year term of the initial synchronization license expired. Because of this, many of the major television producers license all outside songs for the entire term of copyright of the particular composition (or at least have a one-time option to turn the license into a life of copyright term) rather than dealing with multiple extension option agreements—a much more expensive approach, but one that guarantees that a song will not have to be taken out of the program at some future date.

Basic Cable Television. Many television programs appear only on basic cable, the type of nonpay system that many viewers use to get better reception, pick up distant signals, or receive programming not available from the over-the-air free television stations. The definition many times includes all forms of nonpay cable television, including wired and nonwired media (including HDTV). The synchronization fees charged by music publishers for the use of songs in programs distributed via basic cable are in the range of those charged for free television. Depending on the actual number of subscribers for a particular system, however (for example, an area where only 1 million households receive cable), fees can be lower. Many times, basic cable is included in the free television price quote without any increase in price.

The Old World. At one time, television synchronization licensing was a very simple process. In many cases, the initial request was a five year (or less) free television or similar pay television license with options for an extension in those areas if the program was successful in addition to home video distribution.

The Changing Landscape. In a world of ever-expanding media options, distribution platforms, marketing plans, divergent audience viewing patterns, advertiser preferences, current and expectant markets, new technology distribution methods (known or which will be developed in the future), monetization of ancillary profits, etc., licensing music for television has taken on, depending on the program or type of series, a new simplicity for some shows and a new level of complexity and intricacy for others.

It's an area of new concepts, new demands to respond quickly, new types of structures, new relationships and new types of considerations. Because of its value with respect to not only present and future income but also exposure, television licensing is an area that you have to know the current state of affairs and deal accordingly. If you don't or are not able to, success will be hard to achieve.

The New World. Many network series (especially the successful ones that have been on the air for years) have fairly simple licensing schemes (e.g., "all television," "all media excluding theatrical," "all television with a home/personal video buyout option," "all television and home/personal video combined license without the option").

All Television Media. Rather than request separate licenses for free television, basic cable, satellite, subscription, video-on-demand, and pay television, a number of producers will ask for an "all television" or "all forms of television" synchronization license, usually for the life of copyright of the composition being used. Pursuant to the terms of such a license, the producer is able to distribute the program via any television medium without having to resecure permission from the music publisher. Because this type of license is all-encompassing, fees are fairly expensive and range from $7,500 to over $12,500. This approach is many times used for successful series.

All Television Media with Home and Personal Video Options. A number of producers will ask for an "all television" or "all forms of television" synchronization license, usually for the life of copyright of the composition being used. Pursuant to the terms of such a license, the producer is able to distribute the program via any television medium without having to resecure permission from the music publisher. In most of those licenses the producer has the right to extend rights to home and personal video via an option for an additional fee. The home video option can range from $5,000 to more than $15,000 for known compositions.

All Television and Home/Personal Video. Some successful series use an all television and home/personal video combined license without any option language which pays for all rights when the agreement is signed. Fees range from $15,000 to over $25,000.

All Media Licenses Excluding Theatrical. Some studios are requesting "all media" licenses, excluding theatrical, for certain programming—a license that includes, television, home video, the Internet, mobile phone use, and any other media over which television shows can be distributed. Such licenses include all TV transmissions such as free, pay, cable, satellite, subscription, hotel/motel to any type of monitor or receiver; all digital or broadband transmissions including streaming and downloading rights; all audiovisual devices (linear formats) such as DVDs, Blu-ray, cassettes, and other digital media; all other nontheatrical uses (including common carriers); and "in context" trailers, ads or promotions. Some licenses are for life of copyright, and others are for shorter periods (e.g., five to seven years) with an option to extend the term to life of copyright. Fees can range from $17,500 to over $30,000 for the life of the copyright.

All Media (Short Term) with Options. Another variation, many times reserved for newer series, is an all media excluding theatrical license which has a shorter duration than life of copyright (and a lesser synchronization fee) but with options to expand the nature of the license if the producer so elects.

One such example is to request an initial term of five (5) years for all media excluding theatrical, license now or hereafter devised but with the following options:

Option 1: All forms of home and personal video/DVD/Blu-ray/EST rights now known or hereafter devised regardless of the means of delivery including in-content promos in all media/worldwide/in perpetuity (life of copyright).

Option 2: All media now known or hereafter devised via any distribution method or means of transmission, excluding theatrical, but including in context promotional rights in all forms of media now known or hereafter devised/worldwide/in perpetuity.

Option 3: In the event the initial term payment has been made to extend such rights to a term of perpetuity (life of copyright).

Another example, if the program is a music-driven dramatic series, the license request may have a number of different media distribution variations and then contain additional options for further distribution channels which can be exercised by the producer at any time between 12 to 18 months after the initial broadcast of the episode.

The initial areas of focus are:

a. All Media (excluding theatrical) now known or hereafter devised, worldwide in perpetuity.

b. 5 Years All TV Media now known or hereafter devised, including Internet streaming (linear only) worldwide.

c. Perpetuity All TV Media now known or hereafter devised, including Internet streaming (linear only), worldwide in perpetuity.

d. Digital Downloads—Unless or until the All Media option is exercised, an option for digital downloads of the entire episode (linear only) for sale or promotion. (For clarity, commercial DVDs and other forms of physical home video devises are not included), worldwide, one year commencing from the initial download availability.

Then there are the additional options which cover the following:

1. All Media (excluding theatrical and All TV Media previously licensed in perpetuity) now known or hereafter devised, worldwide in perpetuity (exercisable within 24 months after initial broadcast of the episode).

2. Out-of-Context Advertising and Promotion—U.S., its territories and possessions, All Media up to 0:30; $_____ for 30 days or $_____ per week; exercisable no later than 12 months after the airdate of the final episode of the production.

Additional Theatrical Option. Since certain television programming is being shown in motion picture theaters (e.g., episodes of *Game of Thrones*), this can become an extra option in television licenses or may be included in an all media license.

Synchronization Plus Direct Performance Licenses. There are certain producers who request a direct performance license as part of the synchronization request. In effect, the producer is requesting that the performance of the composition be licensed outside of the writer's and publisher's performing rights organization (e.g., ASCAP, BMI, etc.).

Under the agreements of ASCAP, BMI, and SESAC, writers and publishers have the right to license performing rights to compositions to a user directly since the grants to those organizations are nonexclusive. If the decision is made to issue a direct performance license to a producer, broadcast network, or streaming service, an additional fee will be negotiated for this right, which will be in addition to the synchronization payment. In virtually all cases, it is a one-time fee without any continuing backend performance royalties which would otherwise result from multiple performances if licensed via a PRO.

An example of this type of license is one that has been requested by ESPN. Sample terms are:

Program(s): ESPN branded programming in December

Term: A set term (e.g., December through March)

Airings: Unlimited

Type of use: Multiple background TV and separate Internet edits in teases, bumps, and montages

Credits: On-screen credits, when applicable; title, artist

Duration: Up to three (3) minutes cumulative timing, each airing

Territory: Worldwide

Media: ESPN owned, produced, or branded programming on all linear media and free TV on ABC, includes streaming TV, Internet, mobile/wireless devices, and simulcast media, excluding theatrical

Performance Rights: Direct performance is granted to ESPN (owned or branded) television U.S. only.

Fee: $ _____ (sync), $ _____ (perf.)

It should be noted that if the producing entity has a performance license with one or more of the U.S. performing rights organizations but not all, it may just request a direct performance license for the portion of the composition affiliated with the nonlicensed organizations.

Music/Performance/Dance–Based Series. On the non-drama side, series such as *The Voice, American Idol, Dancing with the Stars, So You Think You Can Dance, America's Got Talent,* and similar shows will have numerous options which cover a large number of different types of uses, timing of uses and distribution media.

For example, a series in this genre may ask for the following terms and options:

Initial Term: Five (5) Years, United States, Canada, Bermuda, Caribbean, Latin America, Asia and Disney Cruise Lines in All Television Media, including but not limited to free, basic cable/satellite/HDTV, pay, subscription, broadcast-on-demand, including video-on-demand and direct-by-satellite (DBS) and Internet/mobile streaming (including in-context promotion in all media).

Options:
1. Extension of initial All TV/streaming term to Worldwide, Perpetuity;
2. World Perpetuity, All Media, now known and hereafter devised excluding theatrical; and
3. Clip Streaming.

In addition to the above, each license will further divide the options and fees depending on the actual use of the composition. For example, the following separate use categories are included in the license, and all with different dollar fees.

Use:
a. Visual Dance: up to 2 minutes;
b. Short Recap: single recap up to 25 seconds in future episodes;
c. Single/Multiple Recaps: up to full repeat in future episode;
d. Bumpers and Rejoin (various timings): single/multiple recaps up to full repeat in a future episode;
e. Last Dance/Closing Credits: up to 2 minutes;
f. Extended Dance: over 2 minutes;
g. *The View, Good Morning America,* and *LIVE with Kelly* Performances.

Another series may request that the territory be the U.S. and Canada plus Internet for the world, the term be for two years, and the media being all forms of television, mobile, Internet streaming, nonpermanent downloads, in context trailers and promos and the right to pan lyrics and lead sheets during rehearsal packages with options to review the rights for two years, renew for life of copyright, extend the territory to the world outside the U.S. and Canada and to extend the distribution channel to include electronic sell-through (EST), among other things.

As to another popular series, the initial license request may be as follows:

Use:

1. U.S., its territories and possessions/Canada
One (1) year commencing with each original airdate of episode.

Free, basic and pay cable/satellite/telco television (and all linear simulcasts thereof and VOD via any and all means of distribution (including Internet and mobile streaming) and in-context advertising and promotion rights up to 0:30 (in all media).

1. Rest of World
Two (2) years commencing with each original airdate of episode.

Free, basic, and pay cable/satellite television and VOD via any and all means of distribution, including Internet/mobile streaming and in-context advertising and promotion rights up to 0:30 (in all media).

Options:

1. Electronic Sell-Through or EST (audio and/or audiovisual download offered via official show website and all other associated branded websites, and iTunes and/or other download partners, as well as all wireless and mobile platforms, but excluding downloads of realtones/ringbacks): World/5 Years.

   a. Audiovisual: The greater of (a) 10% of the actual retail price or (b) ___ cents per download.

   b. Audio-only: The prevailing statutory mechanical rate in effect at the time of download.

2. Realtones/Ringbacks (up to 0:30 audio for realtone download and/or ring back stream offered via all wireless and mobile platforms through AT&T): U.S., its territories and possessions. Commencing on signature below and continuing throughout season finale. Rights granted per composition including the right to

reproduce and distribute by means of transmissions to subscribers of AT&T in the territory. For realtones, the prevailing statutory mechanical rate in effect at the time of the download/For ringbacks (answer tones), the greater of (a) 10% of retail price; or (b) ___cents per purchase.

3. Audiovisual Streaming of Clips: World/Terms and Fees Below:

   a. Internet/Mobile Streaming served via one website and/or app:

4 months:	$
6 months:	$
1 year:	$
3 years:	$
5 years:	$

   OR

   b. Internet streaming served via two or more websites/apps:

4 months:	$
6 months:	$
1 year:	$
3 years:	$
5 years:	$

4. Out-of-Context Advertising and Promotion Option: U.S., its territories and possessions/All Media up to 0:30. $_____ 30 days or $_____ /week. Option exercisable commencing on the date of signing but no later than 12 months after the airdate of the final episode of the production.

Another variation is:

License Terms:

1. Term: Perpetuity

   Territory: Worldwide

   Media: Basic Cable and Satellite, including in-context promo

2. Options:

	Media	Territory	Term
Option 1	Free television now, known or hereafter devised, including in context promotion advertising	Worldwide	Perpetuity
Option 2	All forms of television	Worldwide	Perpetuity
Option 3	All forms of home and personal video/DVD/EST rights regardless of the means of delivery	Worldwide	Perpetuity
Option 4	All media now known of hereafter devised via any distribution method or means of transmission for any viewing device excluding theatrical	Worldwide	Buyout/ Perpetuity

One final variation follows:
Possible Uses in Show:

    a. Portions of recordings that contestants can hear;

    b. Prove-outs (a longer version of the song is played if a contestant questions the answer);

    c. Impromptu singing of the song after the recording is heard;

    d. Host, contestants or guests impromptu singing of a song at any time.

Media: All forms of television media including video-on-demand, "Over The Top" (OTT) streaming rights on a simulcast/near simulcast basis and Internet and mobile streaming.

Territory: Worldwide
Term: Three (3) years
Timing/Fees:

Up to 6 Seconds	$
7–15 Seconds	$
16–20 Seconds	$
21–30 Seconds	$

31–45 Seconds	$
46–65 Seconds	$
66–80 Seconds	$

Options:

a. Renewal of initial right for three (3) years (initial fees + 5%)

b. Nontheatrical media, limited to: all common carriers (airlines, ships, buses, etc.), libraries, educational facilities, military bases and other places of display where no admission is charged specifically for viewing. (i) Three year term and (ii) six month option.

c. Electronic Sell-Through (EST). Three (3) year term with fees based on timing.

d. Out-of-context trailers of $____ for 30 days or $____ per week.

Thirty-Second Promotional Audio Streams. Certain programs will request a no-fee, 30-second audio of the recording and composition used in each episode of the series which would be accessible on the program's official website. The license is for streaming only with no download capabilities and is designed to help viewers identify the music on the program since such information is not available in the closing credits. The name of the artist and the song title will be listed and there may be links either to the artist's website or to another site where the viewer can purchase the track.

Internet Streaming. Certain series require options for a short period of time (one month to one year) to stream the episode over the Internet in nondownloadable format. Fees range from $500 to over $2,500.

Official Website-Only Audiovisual Streaming. This request many times includes temporary (time-out) downloads. Fees for this option, which encompasses use by affiliated and associated websites as well, vary but can range from $500 to over $1,000 depending on the duration of the license.

Audiovisual Linear Downloads. Music centric series may also offer audiovisual linear permanent downloads of the performances from the program. Per song rates range from the greater of 10% of the actual retail price to the consumer or 20 to 30 cents.

Limited Period Downloads. Some series request an option which covers worldwide permanent downloads for a limited period of time (e.g., one year). Fees may range from $1,000 to over $2,000.

Audio-Only Downloads. Many music centric programs offer permanent audio only downloads of the performances from the episodes. Royalty payments to the music publisher will be the statutory rate at the time of the download (currently 9.1 cents).

Ringtones. Many music based programs request an option to cover ringtones and ringbacks. Fees for ringbacks are in the 10% of the retail price range with a floor from 12.5¢ to 20¢. Audio-only ringtones are licensed at statutory in the U.S. (24 cents for the period 2018 through 2022).

Extended On-Camera Performances. A number of series, whether they are music/dance centric performance shows or dramatic shows which feature on-screen performances by the actors, request the right to stream extended versions of on-camera performances (which may be newly recorded depending on the request) on certain web streaming services or on the show's website and/or social media page for a period of time after the date of first use. This can be part of the rights granted in the overall synch fee or may be on an option basis.

Shorter Term Licenses. Certain programs which do not have a projected long audience shelf life since they focus primarily on contemporary events and issues (such as *The Late Late Show with James Corden*, Conan O' Brien's *Conan, Access Hollywood, Ellen DeGeneres Show, Jimmy Kimmel Live, The Tonight Show Starring Jimmy Fallon*, etc.) will many times only request short-term licenses, limited-territory licenses, many times with options.

For example, one such show requests:
License Terms: Guest Artist Performance (Includes in-context advertising and promotional rights):

1. World 1 Year, All Television Media, including but not limited to Free, Basic, Cable/Satellite, Pay, Subscription, Direct-by-satellite (DBS), and Internet streaming/mobile/wireless (including video on-demand and Internet streaming inclusive of temporary cached on device)
2. Option to renew the initial term for one (1) year.
3. Option to extend the term for five (5) years.
4. Option to extend worldwide, one (1) year, Internet streaming. Inclusive of temporary cached on device, standalone excerpt via on-demand Internet streaming limited to [Name of Network] and show's websites, the show's official YouTube page, and authorized 3rd party PRO-licensed websites.
5. The show also has a separate synchronization fee request for use of the compositions as bumpers or play-ons with fees payable for a one (1) year term plus options for an additional (1) year and five (5) year renewals.

Another show requests:
Buyout for all television media (including, without limitation, pay-per-view, video-on-demand and subscription video-on-demand) and streaming via any digital media (including, without limitation, on a free pay-per-view, and subscription-on-demand basis, the Internet, social media, and wireless devices, irrespective of the form of delivery); including in-context advertising and promotional use or other clips (in media).

Additional options in the request include:
1. One (1) year worldwide buyout for streaming via any digital media of clips of guest band/artist performances.
2. One (1) year extension of the initial all television media and streaming license.
3. One (1) year extension of the guest band/artist performance clip streaming via any digital media rights.
4. One (1) year worldwide electronic sell-through (i.e., downloads-to-own) irrespective of the form of delivery; including context advertising and promotional use.
5. One (1) year extension of the sell-through rights

A final variation of many is:
Media: All forms of television (on all platforms, including without limitation, basic cable/satellite television, pay cable/satellite television broadcast and video-on-demand) and any digital exhibition of the program including without limitation streaming wireless, streaming Internet (strictly limited to nonpermanent download exhibition), and in-context trailers in all media.

Territory: Worldwide
Term: One (1) year
Options:
a. Renewal of license for one (1) year.
b. If the composition is used in a sketch or performance and the television producer wishes to exploit the sketch or performance on a stand-alone basis, on the Internet/wireless (whether in streaming, nonpermanent downloadable or other formats) including in-context promos; worldwide for one (1) month (renewable).
c. Video-on-demand, the nonpermanent exhibition of audiovisual programming by a consumer at times selected by the consumer (with or without the ability to pause, fast forward, or rewind), regardless of whether or not the device is

ad-supported or the consumer is charged a fee for such capability; worldwide; one (1) month (renewable).

Educational and Public Broadcasting Television (PBS). Section 118 of the Copyright Act establishes a statutory license for the use of certain copyrighted works in connection with noncommercial television and radio. Because of the noncommercial, listener supported nature of public television and lack of substantial government funding for its programming, the following "reduced" synchronization fees have been established by the Copyright Royalty Board to cover the use of music in PBS-distributed shows.

Programs First Broadcast from 2018 to 2022:
Three-year license for the use of a song in a program
$118.70 per feature performance
$59.99 per background performance
$35.65 per minute for a concert feature usage
$59.99 per theme (single program or first series program)
$24.36 per theme (other series program)

For the same period, the Copyright Royalty Board accepted a confidential settlement agreement between ASCAP, BMI, and SESAC as to the royalty rates to be paid by the primary PBS, NPR, and other public broadcasting entities for the over-the-air broadcasting of feature, theme and background music. Separate rates were established for two other categories of public broadcasting entities with formulas based on the number of full time students, population counts and Percentage of Feature music use. The fee allocations in these latter categories were 45% to ASCAP, 45% to BMI and approximately 10% to SESAC. For the performance of any other such compositions in 2018–2022, $1.00.

Multiple Uses of a Song in a Show. In many cases, a song will be used a number of times during a made-for-TV movie, miniseries, special, or series episode. For example, it may be used as background music to a scene and sung on camera by one of the characters, used as background music in a number of different scenes, used as the theme in addition to background mood music, or used once in a scene and also under the closing credits. The initial fee quotation should take into account that a song is used more than once, and the price is almost always increased accordingly even though the actual cumulative duration of the use may be less than a full version (e.g., three background uses of 10, 25, and 40 seconds or a nightclub performer singing partial versions of the same song in two different scenes of the same episode). In most instances when a television producer requests a song, he or she will specify that there will be more than one use, and a publisher will be able to quote a fee that reflects such multiple uses. Portions of the script or scene descriptions will also be provided on request. Because of the time constraints involved in shooting a network television series, continuing script revisions, and the likelihood that changes will be made while a scene is being shot, the experienced publisher will check the actual music cue sheets (or watch the program) to make sure that the song was used in accordance with original request from the producer.

A number of approaches are used to price multiple uses of a song in an episode, with some publishers charging what one full use of three minutes would have cost (regardless of the number of shortened versions, as long as the three-minute total is not exceeded), but most charging extra for additional uses regardless of the aggregate timing (e.g., $10,000 for all television for the first use and between $1,000 to more than $3,000 for each additional use). As in other areas, however, each licensing negotiation is somewhat different from the others that have preceded it, and each must be dealt with on a case-by-case basis after weighing all the factors involved in the particular request.

Additional Payment Formulas for Television (When There Are Numerous Songs Used in a Show). Certain television programs such as specials or anniversary shows use large amounts of existing songs. If these shows were to be licensed at a free television five-year rate of $3,500 per song, the costs would be prohibitive. For example, many of these shows use clips of five to 15 seconds of each song, and if 50 such uses occurred, the producer would have to spend $175,000 for the music synchronization rights alone—a figure that doesn't take into account the additional fees paid to a composer for new music written specifically for the show, option fees for different media, or payments made to record companies for the use of master recordings. Since such an aggregate music budget is in almost all cases unaffordable, music publishers will normally agree to reduce their fees and negotiate a payment formula based on the duration of each performance and how such timing fits into certain negotiated categories (e.g., less than 10 seconds, between one and two minutes, or in excess of one minute). For example:

Timing (Seconds)	Points	Synch Fee for Each Song
1 to 30	1	$400
31 to 60	2	$500
61 to 120	3	$600
over 120	4	$750

Foreign Theatrical Distribution. For most television shows (because of their half-hour or one-hour duration and subject matter), the possibility of release as a motion picture in countries outside the United States is nil. Capsule versions of miniseries are sometimes released for foreign theatrical distribution, however. In addition, major television producers are increasingly securing options from music publishers to cover possible foreign theater release for two-hour made-for-TV movies and series episodes (usually as part of a two- or three-episode combination). The fees charged for this type of license are normally between $4,000 and $20,000 but can be more depending on, among other factors, whether there are multiple uses throughout the miniseries or television movie. The term of such foreign theatrical release licenses are usually for the life of the copyright of a song (like the standard motion picture synchronization license).

Television Performance Royalties (ASCAP, BMI, SESAC, and GMR). One of the reasons why synchronization fees are low is the future income that can be generated from broadcast of a series or program on television stations in the United States, Canada, and other countries around the world. This entire area is a complex one, but the following examples should give the reader a basic grasp of the type of money that songwriters and music publishers earn from ASCAP, BMI, SESAC, and GMR) when music is broadcast on a primetime network television series.

How Music Is Used	Combined Royalties to the Writer and Publisher for One Primetime Network Television Broadcast
Sung on Camera	$5,000
Background to a Scene (three minutes)	$1,100
Theme of Program	$2,000

Promotional Spots for Television Programs. Occasionally, television producers will ask for the use of a song in a television, radio, or Internet advertising campaign designed to promote an upcoming series or bring attention to an important event in a current program. The licenses for such uses are normally very limited, and the synchronization monies paid to the music publisher and songwriter are usually between $1,500 and $4,000 per week. In addition to the synchronization fees, these uses can also be very valuable in terms of re-exposure of the song to millions of viewers as well as in performance income. Consequently, many publishers license these uses at prices that are very affordable to the producers, television stations, or streaming services requesting permission.

Airlines and Common Carriers. Many television licenses also contain an option to distribute the series to common carriers, which include airlines, ships at sea, trains, and buses. Fees range from $3,000 to $4,000 for a worldwide life of copyright license.

Songs Used as Episode Title of Television Series and as Theme or Underscore. On occasion, a television series producer will want to use the title of a famous song as the title of a particular series episode and employ the song in various scenes for dramatic effect. In such cases, the music publisher must find out whether the series episode is a dramatization of the story of the song or if the producer just wants to use the title and song because it helps the mood of an already written script. In such cases, the fees charged are normally between 50% to 200% above those quoted for the use of a song in a television show but can be more, depending on the stature of the composition being used, the uniqueness of its title, and whether it has ever been used before in such a manner.

HIT SONGS USED AS TELEVISION SHOW THEMES

Show	Theme
CSI: New Orleans	"Boom, Boom"
CSI: NY	"Baba O'Riley"
CSI	"Who Are You"
CSI: Miami	"Won't Get Fooled Again"
Married…With Children	"Love and Marriage"
Parenthood	"Forever Young"
True Blood	"Bad Things"

Rather than hire a composer to write a theme song for a new television series, many producers will use a well-known song as the show's opening and closing theme. This is also true for revival series where the new producers do not have the rights to the theme song used in the original series. When presented with such a request, a music publisher may take one of a number of different approaches to handle the licensing, the most prevalent being a per-show fee for each series episode. It is becoming common for a life-of-copyright all television license to be negotiated for use of the song in the series, with the fees ranging from $5,000 to $20,000 per episode. Each case, however, must be treated on its own merits, recognizing the stature of the song being requested (e.g., current hit, well-known standard, or prior hit in need of new exposure), the budget for the series, the policies of the production company producing the show, the performance monies that will be earned from ASCAP, BMI, SESAC, or GMR and the possibility of a television series soundtrack album or hit single coming from the program.

In addition to the initial synchronization fee negotiation, all of these agreements provide for an additional fee to be paid when each episode goes to home video unless, of course, an all media license was agreed to. And many times there is a guarantee that a certain number of series episodes will use the song as the theme (and payment made), even if the series is unsuccessful and the guaranteed number of episodes are not broadcast or even produced. Most agreements also provide that the song and, if applicable, the master will be available for uses as the theme to the series for a number of seasons into the future via options with fee increases normally provided for each new season. On-screen credit is also one of the issues negotiated. There are also a number of series which use existing songs and masters that were not major hits as themes. The issues involved in the negotiations are the same as in the hit song scenario, with the exception that the initial fees may not be as high.

MUSIC CLEARANCE (GETTING PERMISSION TO USE SONGS IN TELEVISION SERIES)

Most television producers do not have the resources to find out who owns the rights to the vast number of musical compositions that they may want to use in their productions. Because the job of tracking down rights can be monumental (close to 25 million songs are registered with ASCAP and BMI alone) and has been made even more difficult because of the reversion laws in many countries and an emerging trend toward two or more copyright owners of a single song, producers who do not have the finances for in-house staffs rely on a number of independent service organizations to assist them in their investigation, negotiation, and clearance of rights to use existing songs in television series. Granted, producers can contact ASCAP, BMI, SESAC, GMR, the Harry Fox Agency, and CMRRA for information on the ownership of selected compositions, but producers then have to follow up and negotiate licenses, a process than can be expensive and time-consuming. Consequently, a large number of them use independent "clearance" organizations to fulfill this need. The following section discusses a number of alternative ways of finding out who owns a song.

Independent Music Clearinghouses. A number of independent agencies represent certain television producers who do not have in-house researcher/negotiators. These agencies' sole purpose is to find out who owns a song, explain how a song is to be used, and request (and many times negotiate) fee quotes for television synch licenses. The television producer pays the fees for such research, negotiation, and licensing services on a per-show, per-song, or flat-fee series basis.

In-House Television Production Staffs. Many producers have personnel on staff to "clear" (i.e., get permission for a negotiated fee) existing outside music that will be used in a television program.

Law Firms. On occasion, synch requests will be handled by attorneys or paralegals. Some of the major entertainment law firms now have separate departments (usually composed of paralegals) dealing with this area for the firm's television producer clients. At one time, the licensing of music for television was a fairly straightforward and uncomplicated business. In recent years, however, because of the many reversion laws in countries such as England, Australia, and Canada, the need for a producer to secure options to extend its rights into new media, the potential inclusion of broadcast rights as part of the negotiation of the synchronization license, the somewhat complex determinations involved in the issue of who really owns the rights to license the extra years of U.S. copyright protection added to all songs written prior to 1978, termination rights in the United States under the U.S. Copyright Law, and the increasing trend of having two to ten separate publisher owners of a song (many of which have no knowledge of the music industry), the business of licensing hit songs and famous standards has become extremely complex. Consequently, the trend to use law firms and specialized clearance agencies to negotiate synchronization rights will more than likely continue to grow.

ASCAP, BMI, SESAC, and GMR. ASCAP, BMI, SESAC, and GMR have "index" or repertory information departments that assist producers trying to locate the owner or owners of a song. These performing rights organizations have information on virtually every song that has ever been performed and are many times the first stop for producers or music-clearance services. ASCAP, BMI, SESAC, and GMR do not assist in any negotiations, though, and are purely a resource point for finding out who owns a particular song. The PROs have online, searchable, repertory databases with the two largest, ASCAP's ACE Repertory and BMI's Repertoire Search, in the process of merging.

The Copyright Office. If all else fails, a producer can request the U.S. Copyright Office to do a search of its registrations to find the current copyright owner of a song. This service costs $200 an hour with a two hour minimum. It should be mentioned that one can search the Copyright Office's online database for records created between January 1, 1978, and the present.

Websites. A number of music publishers have established online synchronization sites where the potential music user (whether it be a motion picture producer, television production company, advertising agency, or video producer) can access and search the catalogue of the music publisher. The search engines usually are accessed by song title or songwriter identity, but some sites have enlarged the information field by allowing the potential user to find titles that fulfill a particular need or fit a particular theme (for example, love songs, drinking songs, or songs about trains). Audio samples of compositions can also be heard. Additionally, many of the sites provide an online licensing capability which enables the potential user to select the desired composition, complete the use request form (type of use, television series name, background vocal, term, territory, media, etc.) and have the request transmitted immediately to the synchronization licensing department of the publisher that owns the composition for processing.

SHARING OF PAYMENTS

Pursuant to all so-called standard songwriter agreements, where the publisher owns 100% of the copyright, the writer (or writers, if applicable) receives 50% of any synchronization fees and the music publisher will retain the remaining 50%. The writer who has a co-publishing agreement with the music publisher will also receive a share of the income traditionally retained by the publisher. In almost all cases, the music publisher is the one who is paid the entire television synch fee, with the songwriter receiving his or her portion of the monies on the accounting dates specified in the songwriter's agreement with the publisher.

THE PERFORMANCE RIGHT

A synchronization license historically has not included permission to broadcast the composition on television. It is purely a license that gives a producer the right to include a musical composition in a film or taped program. A producer will normally have to rely on a broadcast station's performance license with ASCAP, BMI, SESAC, and GMR for the right to broadcast the program or series. Most television synchronization licenses provide that the program or series can be broadcast only over stations that have valid performance licenses with ASCAP, BMI, SESAC, GMR, the music publisher, or its duly authorized representative.

In the past few years, some producers have requested performance fee quotes (usually a one-time payment vs. ASCAP, BMI, SESAC, and GMR's per-broadcast royalty procedures) to cover the possibility that a broadcaster may not have a valid performance license or that ASCAP, BMI, SESAC, or GMR might, at some time in the future, be prevented by law from licensing music broadcast on television. Publishers and songwriters (because of their nonexclusive agreements with ASCAP, BMI, and SESAC) have the right to make such arrangements and, at times, issue such performance licenses to television producers. This complex area has been troubled by a great deal of past litigation between the broadcasters and the performing rights organizations, as well as legislative efforts that would have eliminated continuing payments to writers and publishers of music used on television. It is imperative that one knows the ins and outs of the performing rights business and the monies that can be earned or lost before negotiating such a license.

TELEVISION LICENSE RENEWALS.

As previously indicated, some television producers initially request a five-year world television license for first-run series because this will usually give them sufficient time to see if a show is a hit or has a chance for syndication. Once the five-year period has expired and if there is no option language in the agreement, the producer must renegotiate another license with the publisher for a further period if the series is still being broadcast in any country of the world. Because of the failure rate of many television series, many of these licenses are never renewed. For successful syndicated series, however, producers do negotiate license renewals. The same is true for primetime network series that are airing simultaneously in local syndication, for hit series that have been running for at least five years, and for series that become popular in foreign countries.

In the case of popular series that are broadcast through syndication, the requested renewal term is many times from 10 to 15 years. There continues to be a trend for the producers of extremely successful older syndicated series to request life-of-copyright renewal licenses so that they won't have to contact the publisher every five, 10, or 15 years for additional renewal licenses. For most songs, such a request could mean a 30-, 40-, 50-, or 60-year license; therefore, the fees charged are substantial.

For this reason, the well-organized publisher will have an extensive "tickler" system (in many cases, completely computerized) that will bring up reminders that a television synchronization license for a specific program is about to expire so that a renewal notice can be sent to the producer and negotiations commenced. For example, if the initial synchronization license is for five years commencing January 15, 2018, a notice will be sent to the television producer in September 2022 reminding it that the license will expire on January 14, 2023, and that a new license will be needed if the program is still being broadcast after that date. In some cases, reminder letters are automatically generated by computers without anyone at a publishing company having to draft a notice or look up a file. Even though some of the larger television producers do keep track of when their synchronization licenses expire and either call or send out notices, a good publisher will not count on a producer's voluntary notification that a new license is needed.

BLANKET SYNCH AGREEMENTS FOR OLD PROGRAMS

Occasionally, a television producer will plan to redistribute a number of old series or specials to the television syndication and streaming markets but, because of the weakness of the programs due to age, subject matter, or noncolorization, the producer will want reductions in the normal fees charged for music rights. In such cases, the producer will many times go directly to music publishers with a fee formula covering all songs owned by a particular publisher regardless of the show. Such an approach not only reduces a producer's actual cost of licensing songs but also lessens its music-clearance costs, since individual negotiations do not have to take place for each song.

WHY SYNCHRONIZATION FEES ARE LOW

You might think it strange that music publishers who control major contemporary hit songs as well as time-tested standards might allow a television producer to use a composition in a series or special for affordable prices. The answer is very simple. The use of a song on television leads to performance (broadcast) income, home video monies, and in many cases, re-exposure of a song to millions of people, including motion picture producers, record producers, recording artists, game developers, advertising agencies, and other potential users of music.

As for performance income, many series continue to be broadcast for decades after their initial run not only in the United States but in foreign countries as well. And since ASCAP, BMI, SESAC, GMR and their affiliated societies in countries outside the United States collect money from broadcasters and streaming services and distribute royalties to the writers and publishers of the music used in those programs, the performance royalties can be substantial for songs used in popular series. As for video income, more and more television series (or certain selected episodes or specials) are being released to home/personal video, with the royalties or one-time buy-out monies being in many cases very lucrative. As for re-exposure of a song, many fine compositions need new life breathed into them, and a television series can be the perfect vehicle for reintroducing a good song to millions of viewers (including people who choose the music used in motion pictures, commercials, and other television series). In addition, television can generate increased interest in newer songs, as in the case of "I'll Be There for You" from the *Friends* television series; "Woke Up This Morning," which was the theme to *The Sopranos*; and "Smuggler's Blues," which was the centerpiece for a *Miami Vice* episode and a hit record because of it.

Because television is such a powerful medium, with millions of people watching even the lowest-rated shows (for example, Nielson estimates that there are more than 289 million potential viewers in the U.S.), and because television will still be watched for many years to come, it is extremely important to get songs into series at prices that are not only fair to the writer and publisher but also affordable to producers who normally deficit-finance the network run at significant per episode losses. The long-term royalties that result from having a song in a hit series can mean a guaranteed annual annuity for the publisher and writer as well as his or her family and heirs.

MUSIC CUE SHEETS AND THEIR IMPORTANCE

After a television program has been produced and there is a final edited broadcast version, the producer will prepare what is known as a "music cue sheet," which lists all the music used in the show, including how each song was used, its timing in seconds, and the identity of the writers and publishers as well as their performing rights affiliation. Since ASCAP, BMI, SESAC, and GMR use the music cue sheets for each episode of a series to determine how music was used, who owns the music, and how royalty payments should be made, it is essential that the writer and publisher secure a copy for review. Mistakes on cue sheets as to timing, whether a song is background music or sung by an actor on camera, and writer and publisher identification and performance rights affiliation are not unusual, and it is vital to correct any inaccuracies before the cue sheet is sent out by the producer. On rare occasions, a song may even be left off the cue sheet altogether. Since a good publisher will forward all cue sheets of television shows to its foreign representatives (who then register them with their local performing right society to ensure that royalty payments are made for foreign broadcasts of the programs), a correct cue sheet takes on added importance—especially since most foreign societies will not distribute royalties without proper ownership information, but will instead put the royalties in a suspense account or, in the worst-case scenario, distribute the royalties to someone else.

A final reason why it is important to have copies of cue sheets is that they indicate the original broadcast date of an episode, a fact that can be used to check whether or not the performance has been logged by ASCAP, BMI, SESAC, or GMR. For example, if you know that the initial broadcast of a show containing your song was on ABC on January 14, you can look at the ASCAP, BMI, SESAC, or GMR royalty statement for the January through March quarterly period of that year to see if the network television performance showed up. If the use did not appear on your royalty statement or the performance was not credited properly (for example, if monies were paid for a background instrumental use rather than a more profitable "on-camera song sung by an actor or singer"), you can contact the show's producer and ASCAP, BMI, SESAC, or GMR to rectify the mistake and make sure that you receive your correct royalties.

Music cue sheets take a number of different forms, depending on the company preparing the cue sheet, with some indicating who sang the song, others giving brief scene descriptions, and some reflecting the mood of a scene. All, however, give the identity of the television network or streaming service broadcasting the series, the first air date, the title of the compositions, how the music was used (background vocal, visual instrumental, etc.), the timing of the use, the number of uses during the episode, and complete writer and publisher information for each composition use in the particular episode, including performing rights affiliation for each songwriter, composer, lyricist, and publisher.

TELEVISION PROGRAMS PRODUCED IN FOREIGN COUNTRIES

If a television program or series is produced in a territory outside the United States by a foreign producer, the music publisher's representative in that country usually has the right to grant a worldwide synchronization license for a U.S. composition. For example, if a series is produced in England, one's subpublisher in the United Kingdom will be able to grant the local producer the right to use a song in a particular episode in every country of the world. In such a case, if the series is broadcast in the United States (as many British series are), the U.S. publisher will not be able to charge an additional synchronization fee for the use of the program. Even though an additional fee is not paid for distributing a series outside the territory in which it was produced, all synchronization licenses guarantee that the U.S. publisher and songwriter will be entitled to the performance royalties generated by the broadcast of the foreign-originated program on television stations and streaming services in the United States—a provision that can mean thousands of dollars to the U.S. writer and publisher. For example, if the BBC or Granada Television in England produces a program using an American song and that series is broadcast in the United States, the U.S. writer and publisher will not be able to charge an additional synch fee (as this was done by their representative in England), but they will receive royalties from ASCAP, BMI, SESAC, or GMR when the program is shown. Because ASCAP, BMI, SESAC, and GMR also have contractual relations with performance societies around the world, broadcast royalties will also be collected for the U.S. writer and publisher in virtually all major foreign countries.

MOTION PICTURES SHOWN ON TELEVISION

When a theatrically released motion picture is finally broadcast on television or streaming service, no additional synch fee is paid to the music publisher and songwriter, since these rights are always included in the overall fee initially paid by the film's producer when it secures the right to use the song in the motion picture. The music publisher and songwriter will receive performance royalties through ASCAP, BMI, SESAC, or GMR (or their foreign affiliates) for such television broadcasts, however. That guarantee can mean thousands of dollars each year if the film is a television favorite.

GUARANTEED SYNDICATION

When a series airs on network television during its first or second year, all that a music publisher and songwriter can usually hope for, other than the initial synchronization fee, is the ASCAP, BMI, SESAC, or GMR performance income for the initial broadcast and possibly one repeat. And with the high failure rate of network series (most programs never reach the minimum episode mark at which a program may be considered commercially viable for weekly syndication by local TV and cable stations as well as streaming services), that is normally all you will get.

When a series is in its third, fourth, or fifth year of first-run production and a producer wants a song for a particular episode, however, a whole new set of negotiating considerations come into play. First of all, the series has been popular enough to interest syndicators and has enough filmed episodes in the can to play five days per week across the country, back to back episode showings on certain days, or on an unlimited access streaming service. Sometimes a syndication deal has already been negotiated with stations or streaming services around the country (as in the cases of Law & Order, CSI, and Cheers, which were being aired simultaneously on the networks and in syndication), a factor that guarantees additional performance money long after the series has left network television.

THE IMPORTANCE OF WRITTEN CONFIRMATION

Since requests for songs are often made over the telephone (although most are received by e-mail), with the producer or its representative and the music publisher taking notes on the particulars of the conversation and agreement, it is vital to summarize the terms and send them to the other party as soon as possible after the phone call or e-mail. By following such an approach, both parties will know if there is a misunderstanding within a couple of days, which is usually ample time to work out an agreement prior to a song's actually being put in an episode. If an episode has a short time fuse (e.g., it's for a scene being shot that day or the next morning), the producer will e-mail the publisher a confirmation letter asking for a countersigned copy or corrections by return.

At one time, these confirmation notices were very short and simple (e.g., $4,500 to use "Title of Song" in "Title of Series" as a background instrumental for two minutes for a period of five years from the initial network broadcast of the episode). In this day of expanding markets and media, however, the telephone conversations and e-mails are becoming more complicated, making confirmation letters or e-mails an absolute necessity. For example, if you give a price for the use of a song in a television series and option prices for both domestic and foreign home/personal video, pay TV, cable TV, mobile phones, smartphones, video-on-demand, pay per view, VR, educational stations, foreign broadcast, airlines, promotional uses, U.S. theatrical, website, and foreign theaters, all commencing on different dates, both parties had better be sure that they understood the conversation.

It is also imperative that if there is a mistake or a point that needs to be clarified in these confirmation notices, the clarification should be done by phone and in writing immediately by letter, or e-mail. Nothing should be taken for granted. If you find yourself thinking, "Well, that's not exactly what I meant but it's fairly close," or, "I'll fix the mistake later," correct the misunderstanding or clarify the choice of words at once. Doing so will save a lot of hard feelings and ill will in the future, to say nothing of preventing litigation because a so-called minor issue all of a sudden becomes a major one after the television program has been aired or used in another entertainment medium.

GETTING SONGS INTO TELEVISION PROGRAMS

Music publishers play an important role in convincing television producers and their music supervisors to use past hit songs in their programs. The good ones vigorously promote their catalogues with e-mail catalogue samplers, sampler albums, full-version CD packages, individual files, instrumental versions, remix ideas, new signing information, catalogue lists, and songbooks. Many publishing companies have film and television departments whose sole purpose is to secure uses in these areas. Because of the increasing use of past hit recordings as well as current or future new releases in television shows, record companies can also be invaluable when they push the use of their recordings (and consequently the song and writer) with producers. Good working relationships with and proximity to the Los Angeles-based television company music department heads and music supervisors (because of their knowledge and instincts of what is right for a scene and what makes a successful soundtrack album) as well as independent music consultants is extremely important. Music clearance companies can also play a role, as some of these firms have expanded into the field of music consultancy. Websites are extremely important because they allow music supervisors 24-hour access to music publishing catalogues as well as audio samples of many compositions.

It is also vital to know what the needs are for series in production. Contact with producers or music supervisors to suggest ideas can help, as television companies appreciate constructive promotion. In this regard, never use the shotgun approach of suggesting every song in one's catalogue for a particular series (unless you are sending a hit sampler album); good relationships and respect come from selectivity and good judgment in your submissions. For example, if a series has a 1970s setting and the producer is looking for period songs, it would be unprofessional and unproductive to submit 1980s or 1990s material. Depending on the project, however, there may be scenes that call for pre-1970s songs (for example, a flashback or a scene that might have some "oldies" on a record player or jukebox), and 1950s submissions would then be acceptable and, many times, appreciated.

Many music publishers are also able to secure a plot outline or script of a made-for-TV movie or miniseries from the producer or music supervisor (either during the pre-production or actual shooting stage) and thus give specific suggestions for the use of compositions as either background music or visual vocals for use in individual scenes. Such an opportunity gives the inside track to any music publisher with a variety of songs in its catalogue.

Producers and the Selecting of Songs. Prior to making the final choice of which songs will actually be used in a television program, some producers select a large number of possible songs and secure fee quotations from various music publishers. As in the motion-picture field, the rationale behind such a "laundry list" approach is to ensure that a producer will have an extensive list of songs in various price ranges to choose from, with the final decision many times being made as a result of budgetary rather than creative considerations. For example, if a producer, director, or music supervisor has a specific song in mind for a particular scene but the fees quoted by the music publisher are too expensive for the music budget of the series, it is sound business practice to have commitments on a number of alternate, less-costly songs. If the song is being used as a visual vocal (i.e., being sung on camera by one of the characters in the film), however, the producer obviously does not have the luxury of waiting until post-production to make a decision, as it must be made prior to the scene being rehearsed and shot. For visual vocals, the producer will usually secure price quotes for only a few compositions and make a decision quickly.

In this regard, most of the major television production companies know which publishers are flexible in their pricing policies and are easy to work with. Many television producers and their music supervisors also have a good knowledge of the types of songs certain publishers control, as many of the large producers have extensive music libraries and reference materials, which they review when making selections. The music publishers who continue to be successful in the promotion of songs for use on television, however, are those who promote their catalogues day in and day out, since the constant personnel changes at many television production companies make it vital continually to let people know what you have. Good working relationships with the people at the various production studios cannot be overemphasized; this is the factor, provided you have the songs to license, that many times gets your songs on television and gives you the edge over other companies.

Blanket Synch Agreements for Current Series. One of the methods used by many of the larger music publishers to secure more uses of their songs in television series is to enter into blanket agreements with producers whereby their entire catalogue is offered up front at set rates, with certain monetary incentives built in if the producer uses a specified number of songs during any one-year period. For example, a publisher may guarantee a producer that all songs chosen for a particular series will be licensed at a certain mutually agreed-upon rate until such time that the series has used eight compositions during a year. For all compositions used in excess of the eight-song minimum, the fee might be lowered. Under such an arrangement, the producer is provided some incentive for using a certain publisher's catalogue, as it knows that if enough songs are used, the overall price will be reduced. There are a number of variations in this area; the above example illustrates only one of the ways that publishers deal with producers to promote their catalogues.

Precleared Compositions. Another method of promotion used by music publishers is to provide a series producer and music supervisor with a list of songs that can be used without any problems. Because many compositions may be somewhat difficult to clear for television use (because the songwriters or their estates have approval rights over television uses, reversions have occurred or are about to occur, or a large number of copyright owner/music publishers control a song and all have to be consulted for a license to be issued), producers will many times discourage the use of such songs in favor of songs for which they can receive immediate permission. Consequently, if a producer has been provided with an extensive list of "precleared/no-problem" songs, a preference is many times given to such songs, if only because of the immediacy of the approval process—an important factor in a business that, unlike the choosing of songs for motion pictures, is under substantial time restraints to get quick and definitive answers. Certain series not only have a list of precleared compositions and masters, but also have precleared prices from the music publishers and record companies.

The Experience Factor. Because of the time pressures placed on producers and music supervisors of most weekly television series, there does many times exist a preference for dealing with music publishers who have experience in negotiating television synchronization agreements. Since nothing is more frustrating than to be discussing a television license with someone who has no experience or real knowledge of the contractual status of a song in a catalogue, or is uncooperative, producers have a tendency to deal with people who know the rules and are flexible and competent enough to find a quick way to arrive at license terms that are fair and equitable to all parties concerned. Having experience, understanding, and flexibility in the music-licensing department, therefore, is an essential element in successfully placing songs in television programming, an element whose importance cannot be overemphasized.

LIFE AFTER A SONG GETS INTO A TELEVISION PROGRAM (WHERE THE REAL MONEY IS MADE)

For many songs used on television, the real money comes from sources other than the fee paid for their inclusion in the television program. (See Table 7.1 for the possible royalties of a song in a television program.) Granted, that initial payment can be substantial; still, the major royalties for many television songs will come from the sale of downloads and CDs (if the song hits the Top 40), radio and television performances, commercials, uses in other television shows and motion pictures, soundtrack album sales, streaming, ringtones, ringbacks, sheet music and folios, television broadcasts throughout the world, cover recordings, home/personal videos, electronic sell through, and the Emmy Awards show. Because of the importance of this "after television synch license" income and what it means to the song, its creator, and the music publisher, the following sections review the major revenue-producing areas and the type of money that television songs can earn.

TELEVISION SONG ROYALTIES

Table 7.1

$7,500	Synchronization option fees
$8,500	Home/personal video buy-out fee
$800,000	U.S. radio and television performance royalties for a hit single
$9,100	"A" side of a single (U.S. download sales, 100,000 units)
$9,100	U.S. album sales (100,000 units)

$10,000	Sheet music and folios
$23,000	Television broadcasts of the program on pay, subscription, network, and syndicated television
$200,000	Advertising Commercial
$26,000	Motion picture use
$8,000	Foreign "A" side single CD/download sales
$10,000	Foreign album sales
$600,000	Foreign radio and television performance royalties for a hit single.
$20,000	Miscellaneous royalties including Internet streaming
$1,731,200	Total writer and publisher royalties

OPTION FEES

As previously indicated, some television producers will request only a five-year worldwide free television/basic cable license (sometimes the request is for six years) when they initially contact a music publisher for the use of a song. Options will usually be built into the initial request (e.g., an option for an additional five years or for successive five-year periods, an option to distribute the program to all television, an option for Internet distribution, an option for home/personal video use, an option for an all media excluding theatrical media, an option for out-of-context promo uses, an option for foreign theatrical release), but in some instances, the music publisher and writer will receive only the initial synchronization fee for free and basic cable television.

At such time that the producer is able to distribute the program in areas other than on free television, the appropriate option will be exercised and additional monies will be paid to the music publisher. For example, if the program or series episode is initially licensed only for pay television and the producer enters into a distribution agreement for the series with a basic cable service, an additional fee will be paid to the music publisher for this additional medium. If the series is eventually distributed to the home or personal video market, another fee will be paid. And if the program is distributed to any other area not covered by the initial synchronization fee, additional monies will be paid.

If all the various options normally included in a television synchronization license are exercised by a producer, the monies can be substantial and stretch out over a long period of time. Because of that ultimate dollar total, many producers will initially bite the bullet (or at least provide an option to do so) and license a song for a one-time fee either for "all television for the life of copyright," "all media excluding theatrical," "all media excluding home/personal video and theatrical," or on a "broad rights" motion picture-type basis, which will involve all rights, including video. Either type of license can usually be secured for a price that will be cheaper in the long run. With the option type of license, moreover, the options are usually not open-ended, but have to be exercised by the television producer within a specified period of time (e.g., within 24 months from the initial broadcast date of the television program).

DVD, DOWNLOADS, PERSONAL USE VIDEO, AND DISCS

The market for home/personal video distribution of television programming represents an additional source of income, whether the program is an old collector's item, a successful miniseries, a hit weekly series, a "best of" collection containing highlights of many shows, a variety special, or a behind-the-scenes look at the making of a show. As with television synchronization, there are a number of things that you have to know before negotiating a license agreement for the use of your song on a DVD, Blu-ray, smartphone, or other home-use/personal use technology including downloads (sometimes called videograms) and electronic sell through. Much of it has to do with your experience in dealing with this field on a day-to-day basis, as you eventually learn how far you can negotiate with each individual company and where you should draw the line. For those who don't have the necessary experience, however, the following section explains the most important principles that underlie every request.

Duration of the Home and Personal Video License. The producer of an extremely successful television series will commonly demand "life of copyright" or "in perpetuity" agreements. When faced with a life-of-copyright agreement, always remember that you may be granting a license for more than 100 years, since the U.S. Copyright Law protects new songs for 70 years past the songwriter's death. Unfortunately, most times the fee will be dictated by how much the television producer can afford to pay for music in a particular series episode (i.e., the music budget).

Video Royalty Rates and Fees for Songs. The following (with buy-outs the most common) are the different video approaches used by television producers in this area.

Video Buy-Outs. All of the well-financed Hollywood television producers and most of the major independents who regularly produce series programming demand one-time worldwide buy-outs on home video rights for television series. If a publisher elects to give a worldwide buy-out on permanent downloads, cassettes, DVDs and discs, the fees charged many times range from $7,500 to more than $12,000 for a life-of-copyright home/personal video buy-out of a song. Rather than securing a worldwide home video buy-out for one price, some studios provide for two separate options: one for the U.S. and Canada, and the other for the World outside the U.S. and Canada. Many times, the producer has 24 months from the initial broadcast date to exercise its home video buy-out option with the fee being paid when the option is exercised. For many successful television series, the home video buy-out fee is paid at the time the synchronization license is signed, because the producer knows that the episode is guaranteed to be sold in the home video market. The same is true under the "all media excluding theatrical" license which, by its definition, includes home/personal video in the fee.

Penny Rate per Song for Each Video Sold. Although this is not at all common, some independent television producers accept the per-unit penny rate formula for songs used in television programs, since the up-front costs to get the program into the home video market will be sizably reduced if payments are restricted to actual sales. For example, many small producers can't afford to buy out a song for $7,500 to over $12,000 when there are no guaranteed sales, and instead prefer a simple royalty based on actual sales figures payable every three or six months. If a penny rate is used, a royalty of between 10¢ and 15¢ per song is not uncommon, with additional monies due for multiple uses or if a song is used as the theme of the program. These per-unit royalty formulas are becoming extinct, however, and have already become a thing of the past for songs used in all major contemporary television series.

Roll-Over Advances. Many of the smaller producers who license on a "penny rate per video sold" basis prefer what is known as a "roll-over advance" home/personal video license because it alleviates quarterly or six-month accounting obligations. Under such an approach, the publisher receives an agreed-upon advance that covers a set number of videos at the time the agreement is signed (e.g., $1,000 for the first 10,000 units sold). Then, as each 10,000-unit sales plateau is reached, an additional $1,000 is paid in advance for the next 10,000-unit block of sales. It should be noted that this type of payment formula is not common.

Percentage of the Wholesale Price. Although this approach is not common, video royalties may be based on 4% to 10% of the wholesale price and shared on a pro-rata basis according to the number of songs on the program, each song's duration compared to the aggregate timing of all music on the video, or each song's duration in relation to the total running time of the entire program (music and nonmusic portions combined). For example, if 10 songs are used on a video that has a wholesale price of $10 and each music publisher agrees to a 6% pro-rata royalty formula, the per-song royalties will be 6¢ (6% of $10 = 60¢ divided equally among the 10 songs). Occasionally, a minimum per-song royalty (or "floor") is also negotiated by the publisher so that the actual music royalties received cannot fall below a certain amount. For example, a song might be licensed under a 6% wholesale royalty formula, but in no event may the actual royalty be lower than 5¢ per video. As with many of the per unit royalty based formulae, this has become less common since the one-time video buyout is the prevalent manner of payment by producers.

Deleting Songs from Consideration for a Television Series Because of Home Video Policies.
As in the motion picture industry, if a television producer has a "video buy-out or nothing" policy and a music publisher or writer does not agree to license on such a basis, the song will usually not be used, even though it may be perfect for a particular series episode, and another song will be substituted.

Deleting Songs from Videos of a Television Series. A producer's "video buy-out only" policy may not only apply to the initial consideration of whether a song will be used in a series but also extend to the inclusion or deletion of a song in the home video version. For example, if a producer cannot negotiate a video buy-out with the music publisher of a song used in a broadcast episode, it may take the song out of the home video version of the series. On occasion, if a song was not originally cleared for home video use (i.e., the original synch license was for television use only), the producer may not even contact a publisher to negotiate a fee but will simply insert new music into the home video version. Since video rights are nowadays almost always negotiated simultaneously with the synchronization license, the deletion of a song from the home video version commonly occurs only with respect to older programs. It also occurs with new series because of budget reasons since some producers replace the music that was in the original episodes when the series goes to home video because the replacement songs are less expensive (regardless of whether an option price was available).

HIT SINGLES FROM TELEVISION PROGRAMS

Even though television songs do not become hits with the frequency of motion picture songs, the hit single nevertheless represents an important source of income for the composer, lyricist, and publisher of television songs.

Hit Song	Television Series
"I'll Be There For You"	*Friends*
"The X-Files Theme"	*The X-Files*
"Moonlighting"	*Moonlighting*
"Miami Vice Theme"	*Miami Vice*
"Welcome Back"	*Welcome Back, Kotter*
"Peter Gunn Theme"	*Peter Gunn*
"Happy Days"	*Happy Days*

"Hill Street Blues"	*Hill Street Blues*
"Mission Impossible Theme"	*Mission Impossible*
"Batman Theme"	*Batman*
"Suicide is Painless"	*M*A*S*H*
"Those Were The Days"	*All in the Family*
"Love Boat Theme"	*The Love Boat*
"Falling"	*Twin Peaks*
"Where Everybody Knows Your Name"	*Cheers*
"You've Got Time"	*Orange is the New Black*
"Bad Boys"	*Cops*

Mechanical Royalties. The writer's music publisher (usually the television company, when the song is written specifically for the series) will normally license a television song to a record company for the statutory mechanical royalty for every record, download, and CD sold. For example, if 100,000 singles of a song are sold in the United States, the mechanical royalties to the writer/music publisher would, under the statutory rate of 9.1¢ per song, be $9,100. And if the song is covered by other recording artists on albums, singles, downloads, or CDs, the mechanical income from the sales of those other versions can add up to hundreds of thousands of dollars long after the song's initial popularity. Mechanical royalties are also earned when a song is streamed on an interactive digital service with the rates being set by the Copyright Royalty Board.

ASCAP, BMI, SESAC, and GMR Royalties. In most cases, the principal immediate source of a writer's and publisher's income from a hit single comes from the royalties earned for radio, television and streaming performances of the song. Depending on a number of factors, including the amount of quarterly airplay a song has received on broadcast radio or streaming services, the song's past history of performance, the types of stations on which it is broadcast, its eligibility for award or bonus payments, and its genre, the writer and publisher performance royalties normally range from $500 to $750,000 for a Top 10 song and can run as high as $2,000,000 for a Number One across-the-board hit. In addition, there are also increased royalties for hit songs as well as for songs that have been past hits and that are used as background or theme music on radio or television shows, or in highly rated television shows.

If a song from a television program becomes a standard, is recorded by many different artists, or is used by television and motion picture producers in other films or series, it has the potential of generating hundreds of thousands of dollars in performance income for years after the initial television broadcast. For example, it is not unusual for a popular song to earn from $25,000 to $100,000 per year in "catalogue" performance royalties after its initial chart activity as a hit single.

Foreign Performance Royalties. Foreign radio, television, and online songwriter and publisher earnings represent the least-understood area of music and lyrics income, even though for many writers and publishers it is their main source of royalty income. One needs only to look at the amount of American music on the foreign pop charts as well as the television series aired in England, Canada, Australia, France, Germany, Italy, and Japan, among others, to appreciate the importance of the foreign marketplace as a substantial and continuing source of royalty income. Pursuant to reciprocal agreements that ASCAP, BMI, SESAC, and GMR have with all of the foreign performing right societies throughout the world, those foreign societies license performances of U.S. writers' and publishers' works, collect the money, and forward it to ASCAP, BMI, SESAC, and GMR who in turn pay the appropriate writers and publishers. Most of the incoming money is writer money as many publishers collect this money directly from the foreign society via a subpublisher or by direct membership. For songwriters with a song in a television series, the areas that can generate foreign performance royalties include radio, broadcast television, cable, streaming, mobile phone, wired music, and live performance.

THE TELEVISION SERIES SOUNDTRACK ALBUM

Because of the international appeal of many American-produced television programs and their music, soundtracks have the potential of being a significant source of revenue for television companies, record companies, recording artists, and the writers and publishers of songs in television series.

As with singles, the composer and the lyricist through their music publisher will normally license the U.S. mechanical rights to their songs for the statutory rate per song. Since some television series soundtracks can sell over 100,000 copies, the aggregate royalties can be substantive from the United States alone. And because some television soundtrack albums do very well outside the United States, the foreign market can be another gold mine for writers and publishers.

TELEVISION COMMERCIALS PROMOTING THE PROGRAM

Virtually all series, made-for-TV movies, miniseries, and specials use commercials to advertise the broadcast date of the program. On occasion, payments are made for the use of songs in those commercials, but normally these rights are given as part of the license to include the song in the program. For example, the television producer usually gets the right to include the "in context" use of the song in any television commercials. If, however, the song is being used other than as it is used in the program (for example, being used as thematic background throughout the commercial and over a number of scenes), additional fees are usually negotiated. Occasionally, a television producer will also use a song that is not in the television program as part of the advertising campaign. In these cases, additional fees will be charged.

SHEET MUSIC FOLIOS

Songbooks that contain classic television songs such as the themes from *The Simpsons*, *I Love Lucy*, *The Brady Bunch*, *Cheers*, *Happy Days*, *Gilligan's Island*, *Friends*, and *All in the Family* generate good sales. The standard royalties for such folios are between 10% and 15% of the retail selling price, with all copyrighted compositions sharing equally in the aggregate amount.

ROYALTIES FROM MOTION PICTURE THEATERS (WHEN A TELEVISION PROGRAM IS RELEASED AS A MOTION PICTURE)

Occasionally, U.S. television programming (usually made-for-TV movies or capsulized versions of miniseries) is released in the foreign theatrical marketplace. In most countries outside the United States, motion picture theaters are required to pay royalties to the local performing right society for the music used in films.

BROADCASTS OF THE SERIES, SPECIAL, MADE-FOR-TV MOVIE, OR MINISERIES

Whether or not a television program has a theatrical exhibition and home/personal video release, it will usually continue its life after its first broadcast throughout the world on streaming services, subscription or pay television, basic cable, and over-the-air free television stations. In the United States, ASCAP, BMI, SESAC, and GMR monitor such broadcasts and distribute royalties to the writers and publishers of songs contained in the programs actually broadcast. Through their arrangements with affiliated performance societies around the world, broadcast royalties are collected in virtually all territories outside the United States for television showings of programs. Because of the continuing need for programming to fill the schedules of television stations and digital audiovisual streaming services, recognized series remain a valuable source to fill air time and attract viewers. And for programs that consistently earn high ratings, the performance royalties from television broadcasts throughout the world can represent a lifetime annuity for the writers and publishers of the songs contained in them.

TELEVISION SONGS IN COMMERCIALS

Another source of income for the television song is its use in radio or television commercials advertising consumer products. The fees for such commercial use can be substantial (e.g., from $75,000 to more than $1,000,000 per year for successful songs), depending on whether it is a radio, television or Internet commercial, a national or limited-territory campaign, whether there are options for use in foreign countries, if the original lyrics are being changed or new lyrics added to an instrumental hit, and whether total advertising vs. product category exclusivity is being requested by the agency. Some examples of television songs used in consumer product advertising include the *Cheers* theme for Michelob-Ultra and for UPS, *The Odd Couple* theme for Subway, the *Star Trek* theme for Hummer, the *Welcome Back, Kotter* theme for Pringles, *The Beverly Hillbillies*" theme for Velveeta, the "Final Jeopardy! Theme" for Allstate, the *Bonanza* theme for Taco Bell, *The Love Boat* theme for Princess Cruise Lines, and the *I Dream of Jeannie* theme for Lexus and Tropicana.

TELEVISION SONGS USED IN OTHER TELEVISION PROGRAMS

The use of well-known television themes as either background music or visual vocals in other series can be extremely valuable in terms of synchronization income, performance income and re-exposure of songs to millions of people. Unless an "All Media Excluding Theatrical" license has been granted for the use of a composition in a different television program, there may be additional synch fees if the series is successful since more and more series are requesting options for additional media (pay or subscription television, foreign theatrical release, home/personal video, mobile phones, all media, etc.), with extra monies forthcoming as the programs are purchased by different suppliers. Since ASCAP, BMI, SESAC, and GMR pay royalties for television broadcasts, as do their affiliated societies in foreign countries, substantial performance monies can also be earned by the writer and publisher for years after the program has been initially aired.

TELEVISION SONGS USED IN MOTION PICTURES

Another lucrative source of income is the inclusion of television songs in motion pictures as theme, background (often from a TV set within a scene), or visual vocal. Because of the various royalty-generating media involved in motion pictures (the initial synchronization and home/personal video/electronic sell-through buy-out fee, television broadcast, foreign theatrical distribution, soundtrack album, etc.), this area can mean hundreds of thousands of dollars in long-term income to the writer and music publisher.

TURNING A SONG INTO A MOVIE OR TELEVISION PROGRAM

Although it is not common, a movie producer or television production company may express interest in using the storyline of a song as the basis for a theatrical motion picture or television program. In most cases, the interested producer will contact the music publisher of the song (who is usually the copyright owner) for permission but many times the writer of the composition is contacted as well, especially if the writer owns the publishing rights or has contractual approval rights for this type of use in the publishing agreement.

When the request is made, there will be a full description or outline provided of the actual project so that the publisher and songwriter will know the creative direction envisioned by the producer. There may also be a projected budget but this may be difficult without knowing whether the commitment might come from a major film company, independent film company, broadcast television network series, cable series or Internet series.

If approval is given, the producer will have a certain agreed-upon time to commence the production and secure a broadcast commitment.

In most cases, the actual license agreement will cover many if not all of the following areas:

a. An option period during which the producer will have exclusive rights to develop the project. It should be mentioned that there may be multiple options, all of which have a fee attached.

b. A purchase price for the project (with different amounts dependent on whether the final product is a motion picture or television program).

c. A synchronization fee if the song is used.

d. A consultancy fee if the final project is a television series.

e. A per-episode rights royalty if the final project is a television series.

f. A profit participation (usually based on "adjusted gross receipts") if a motion picture release.

g. Additional fees if there are sequels, remakes, spin-offs, or prequels based on or connected to the original project.

h. Appropriate credit many times on a separate card in the form of "Based on the Song by (Writers)" either in the opening or closing credits.

PRODUCTION MUSIC/LIBRARY MUSIC

An increasing trend in the audiovisual production world is the use of production music in television, films, advertising commercials and other media. Production music, sometimes referred to as library music, is pre-recorded music (as well as songs) which is precleared both for synchronization and master licensing for use in any type of audio video or audio production. In short, it's a "one stop shop" source for music to fit "any occasion." Production music libraries, which include the major entertainment conglomerates, medium to small size companies as well as individual composer owned entities, provide music at a cost that is many times less expensive than score and songs commissioned for a project. It is theme-based music (i.e., car chases, love scenes, drama, comedy, mood, etc.) available on practically every format including hard drives, CDs, DVDs, downloads, vinyl, and searchable online data bases, among others, where the producer or the user can choose the type of music they want to insert into the production. In most cases, users can preview tracks and sort needs by instrument, genre, tempo, mood, era, region of the world, voices, lyrics, style, and length, among other factors. In other cases, newly created music can be requested to fulfill the needs of the production company. Price, easy access and "all rights" included are major selling points of production music.

Based on the growing importance of this field to practically every type of audio visual medium—television, film, video games, audio books, to name just a few—it is essential to understand the various types of contracts, business arrangements, and compensation packages being offered. They run the gamut from work-for-hire buyouts and work-for-hire agreements with limited or full backend royalty participation to non-work-for-hire arrangements where the copyright is not transferred and sharing of some or all income is the norm. Many agreements state that the production music company bears the cost of producing the sessions whereas others require the composer to undertake or share the costs.

The following should give you a good idea of the range of the deals in this area:

1. Work-For-Hire/Limited Compensation

Services: Company engages Composer to compose and deliver to company for exclusive representation, all of the Composer's interest in and to new and original music cues (compositions) and to record, perform, produce, and deliver to Company new and original master recordings.

Territory: The Universe.

Grant of Rights: The works are specifically ordered and commissioned by Company as "works made-for-hire" with the Company as the sole author for purposes of copyright and the exclusive owner of all rights in and to the work. If for any reason, the work is not deemed a work-for-hire, Composer irrevocably assigns, transfers, and grants to company an undivided 100% of all rights and interests now known or hereafter discovered or established.

Compensation: Upon full and faithful performance, Company will pay Composer a fee of $_____payable 50% upon the execution of this agreement with the balance paid on the satisfaction of the delivery requirements as set forth in the agreement.

Composer is entitled to the writer's share of all PRO performance income with the company receiving the publisher's share of such income. The fee represents the full compensation for the composer.

2. Work-For-Hire/50% of Receipts:

Compensation: Company shall pay Composer an advance against all future royalties and monies in the amount of $____ payable 50% on execution of the agreement and the balance upon the satisfaction of the delivery requirements.

Subject to the full recoupment of the advance and any and all mixing, mastering, and musicians' costs incurred by Company in connection with the works, Company will pay composer 50% of the Net Receipts received by Company for the exploitation of the works. Composer will receive the full writer's share of performance monies.

3. Composer Retains the Copyright:

Services: Writer will deliver to Company original master recordings and musical compositions based upon the delivery specifications as set forth in the agreement (lyric sheets and key signatures, beats-per-minute for masters, alternative mixes as requested by Company, stems, masters requirements, etc.).

Term: Full term of copyright.

Territory: Exclusive right to exploit the compositions in any medium in the territory during the term. Right to grant public performance licenses, including "direct" or "source" licenses. Right to grant exclusive and nonexclusive licenses for synch into any audio or audiovisual production including games, audiobooks, ads, movies, television, etc. License to make "mechanical" copies and the right to sublicense all rights to subpublishers. Writer retains the copyright with the Company registering the compositions with the writer's PRO and naming the Company as administrator of writer's publishing company.

Compensation: All synch fees to be split 50% to the writer and 50% to the publisher with all public performance fees to be split 50/50. If the company issues any "direct" or "source" licenses, company will pay the composer the writer's share. Company will advance writer $____ upon receipt of each CD of material accepted.

4. Assignment Agreement/Revenue Sharing:

Rights: For good and valuable consideration, Composer irrevocably and absolutely assigns, transfers and grants to company an undivided 100% of all rights, titles and interests of every kind and nature. Company shall have the right to utilize the works in such manner as company shall determine including the right to make changes and the right to exploit the works by any and all means in any and all media. Company has the exclusive right to issue licenses including, but not limited to, mechanical reproduction, public performance, synch uses, subpublication, merchandising and advertising.

Compensation: 50% of all Net Receipts received by Company in connection with the exploitation of the works. Company has the right to recoup from the Net Receipts payable to Composer some or all of the production costs. Writer and company will receive their respective shares from performing rights organizations. No obligation on the company's part to any additional compensation other than as set forth above.

Accounting: 90 days after June 30 and December 31.

Representations/Warranties/Indemnities: Works are original and contain no samples, no rights having been granted to others, etc.

5. Work-For-Hire/Fee Plus Limited Backend Royalties:

Fee and Compensation: $___ payable 50% upon signing the agreement and 50% upon satisfactory delivery of the masters. Composer is entitled to receive 100% of the PRO writer monies with company receiving the full publisher's share. Company will receive the Composer's share of mechanical royalties as well as a percentage of sheet music, band arrangements, and orchestration fees.

Other Provisions: Nonexclusive agreement. Composer to comply with all reasonable instructions, directions and requests as well as rewrite, revise, and change if requested.

PER TRACK VERSUS BLANKET LICENSE PAYMENTS

Production music libraries make their money either on a per-track fee basis or on blanket licenses which allow a user to have access to the entire library of works for a negotiated fee. In some cases, the blanket license does not impose reporting requirements where the user is not identifying the works used.

Under the blanket agreements (sometimes referred to as annual usage agreements), the composer, assuming he or she is sharing in the Net Receipts formula, is entitled to receive a portion of the blanket fees on a pro-rata basis based upon the fraction of the total number of uses of the composer's works by such blanket license over the total number of works used in the blanket license. As to licenses that do not impose a reporting obligation, the nonreporting percentage shall be the same as the percentage received from licenses that report.

ADMINISTRATION/DISTRIBUTION AGREEMENT

Parties: Administrator is engaged in the exploitation of background music libraries throughout the territory. Publisher is the owner of a library of musical compositions.

Exclusivity: Administrator has the exclusive right to license and/or sublicense all of the production music library's rights during the term.

Term: Specific number of years with an option to extend for an additional period or if there remains an unrecouped advance balance at the end of the term.

Rights Granted: Exclusive rights to exploit in the territory during the term all compositions in the library. Rights include the granting of licenses in the performance area as well as "direct" and "source" licenses, the right to grant nonexclusive licenses to third parties into any and all forms of audio or audiovisual productions now known or hereafter devised. Right to make copies of the works, both digital and analog, and the obligation to register all new works for copyright and for PRO purposes.

Delivery Commitment: Company agrees to supply a certain number of new fully mastered and mixed tracks each year at its sole cost and expense.

Advances and Royalties: Fully recoupable advances against synch income will be paid during the term based on specific deliverables and conditions. As to blanket or "annual usage agreements," percentages will be negotiated as to reporting and nonreporting licensees. Administrator will pay to the company 50% of all fees received.

Additional Clauses: Representation, warranty, indemnity, termination and other clauses included.

CONCLUSION

As one can see, having a song in a television series, made-for-TV movie, special, or miniseries can open up an unlimited number of opportunities and prove to be a lifetime annuity for writers and music publishers. From hit records, commercials, and videos to motion pictures, apps, foreign theater performances, other television shows, dramatization rights, and option fees, the financial life of the television song can last well beyond the initial broadcast.

CHAPTER 8
MUSIC, MONEY, AND MOTION PICTURES

E ach year, the major Hollywood studios and hundreds of independent film
production companies release over 700 feature films for U.S. theatrical
distribution. Hundreds more are being produced by the audiovisual streaming
services (Netflix, Amazon, Hulu, Apple, etc.), university film schools, and budding
filmmakers throughout the United States. Outside the U.S., many thousands of
additional films are produced and released by foreign companies. Practically all of
these films use music as an integral and necessary part of the production (see Table
8.1 for examples). And for the writers of this music, a single song or underscore can
generate a lifetime of substantial earnings.

OVERVIEW

THE MOVIE INDUSTRY

Most feature films are produced either by the major studios (Paramount, Universal,
Sony, Disney, 20th Century Fox, Warner Bros., and Metro-Goldwyn-Mayer, etc.)
or by the hundreds of U.S. and foreign independent production companies. The
independents range from major companies just below the rank of the well-financed
all-purpose studios to medium or small ongoing companies to firms that fold up their

tents after just one production. Although the feature film industry was once primarily the domain of U.S. companies, the industry has significantly changed in recent years with the acquisition of major U.S. studios by foreign companies. (Matsushita of Japan bought MCA/Universal in 1990 and sold it to Seagram of Canada in 1995, with a sale to Vivendi of France in 2000 and to General Electric (NBC) in 2004 and Comcast in 2011. Sony of Japan purchased Columbia in 1989; News Corporation of Australia acquired 20th Century Fox in 1985 and sold it to Disney in 2017). There have also been an increasing number of joint ventures between U.S. and foreign companies, partnerships between film companies and nonfilm entities, and partial ownerships through public stock acquisitions.

Filmmaking costs have skyrocketed in recent years. The average cost to produce, market, and advertise a major film is in the area of $200 million. Compare that to a 1980 figure of $16 million. Out of necessity, films are now financed in a variety of complex ways, including major studio backing, joint ventures, outside private or public investors, limited partnerships, and presales of ancillary and distribution rights. Regardless of how a film is financed, though, all parties involved normally have a good idea of the principal revenue-producing areas from which their investment will be recouped and, they hope, a profit made. They are usually also familiar with the various stages of production that ultimately lead to the release of a finished motion picture.

Though the stakes are high, the returns for a blockbuster hit can be monumental. Up until 1976, only one film had generated more than $100 million in U.S. and Canadian box office receipts; by 2018, more than 700 films had reached the $100 million mark. Considering the fact that foreign markets can equal or surpass the U.S. and Canadian gross (the 2009 film *Avatar* grossed $2 billion in foreign receipts, with the 1997 *Titanic* at $1.2 billion, the 2015 films *Star Wars: The Force Awakens*, *Jurassic World*, and *Furious 7*, and the 2017 *The Fate of the Furious* all over $1 billion with others on the brink), the profit potential for a hit can be astronomical despite the high cost of producing a film and the odds against box office success.

The same factors that affect the film producer also affect the composer and songwriter. A film's budget determines the amount of the initial writing fee (whether it be underscore or a song), and the success of the film in various types of markets determines the total amount of short- and long-term earnings the writer and music publisher receive.

THE MAKING OF A FILM

The film producer (studio or production company) acquires a property (a book, short story, or play; an outline of an idea; a developed treatment of a story) and orders a script to be written. Based on the script, the producer determines what the production will cost and then negotiates for particular actors, a director, and other personnel; chooses locations to shoot; secures financing for specific budgets; and orders completion of a final script. Principal photography—the actual shooting of the movie—commences next. The final element is post-production: underscore and songs, editing, sound effects, and so on. When post-production is complete, prints of the film are made and the movie is ready for distribution to U.S. and foreign theaters.

SCORES AND SONGS IN FILMS

Table 8.1

Music	Film	Scene
"Theme from Jaws" (classic John Williams background score)	*Jaws*	The fin of a great white shark cuts through the water while bathers play at the beach in the Number One film of 1975.
"My Heart Will Go On"(song written for the film by scorer James Horner and songwriter Will Jennings)	*Titanic*	The Number One box office movie of 1997 with this Number One song featured in the closing credits.
Psycho (Bernard Hermann's chilling and unforgettable score)	*Psycho*	The shower scene.

THE MARKET

The initial market for most films is exhibition in U.S. and foreign motion picture theaters. Films are then released for download and to home and personal video for purchase and rental, and to video-on-demand and streaming services with subsequent sales to pay-per-view, pay cable services (HBO, Showtime, the Movie Channel), television networks, local television stations or basic nonpay cable services (USA Network, Lifetime), and to foreign television and cable stations. The exclusivity windows—the period of time that one has the right to exclusively show a film in each area—are getting shorter and shorter. Soundtrack albums and singles are sometimes released, with many of them becoming major chart hits, and in turn creating additional income from such ancillary sources as ASCAP, BMI, SESAC, GMR, and foreign country performing rights organizations (PROs), mechanical royalties from CD sales, downloads, commercial advertising fees, and ringtones, among many other areas.

TYPES OF MOTION PICTURE MUSIC

Three types of music are primary to any film: (1) the underscore; (2) the song written for a film; and (3) the previously existing song, or song and record. Underscore is the music you hear under the dialogue, in chase scenes, in romantic settings, and throughout the picture. It creates or sets the mood, underscores the action, and is the primary music in practically all films. Songs, on the other hand, can be used as visual vocals (a character singing on camera), as visual instrumentals (an orchestra playing on camera), as background music, or as the opening or closing theme to the film. The way that each of these three types of music is used within a film is important, as the particular usage not only determines the initial writing or synchronization fee but also affects the lifetime writer and publisher earnings that result from the composition's use.

THE FILM MUSIC BUDGET

A starting point for any discussion of film music is the music budget. Though in years past the music budget was usually a specific percentage of the total cost of the picture, recent years have shown that no formula is typical and that the music budget really depends on what role music plays in the film and what price the producer is willing to pay to achieve what he or she wants the music to accomplish. Certain films contain only underscore, whereas others combine underscore with new songs and pre-existing songs as well, frequently using the original recordings of those songs. For major studios, total budgets can range from $150,000 to more than $2 million, depending on the stature of the composer, the type of score required (large orchestra, synthesizer, etc.), the number of pre-existing and new songs being used, and the commitment that the producer or director has with respect to the role and purpose that music plays in the overall product.

USE OF PRE-EXISTING HIT SONGS IN FILMS

Many successful motion pictures use hit songs to create a period flavor, establish a mood, give an actor a chance to sing, make people laugh, make people cry, elicit emotions, and create interest in the movie through successful soundtrack albums and hit singles. A film producer who wants to use an existing song in a motion picture must secure the permission of the music publisher to use the composition in the film. Once an agreement is reached as to a fee, the producer will sign what is known as a "synchronization" or "broad rights" license, which will give the studio the right to distribute the film theatrically, sell it to television, use the song in motion picture theater trailers or television and radio promos, and sell videos.

THE PHONE CALL FROM THE FILM COMPANY
Setting:
The office of the vice president of business affairs at a major music publishing company.

The Phone Call:

MUSIC CLEARANCE SUPERVISOR: Hi, this is the music clearance supervisor on a film that is going into post-production.

PUBLISHER: Hi, how can I help?

MUSIC CLEARANCE SUPERVISOR: As you know, we're finishing up our film and need some additional music for certain scenes. We've already shot the footage of scenes where songs are sung by the actors, but we have some important scenes which need music behind them. For your information, the film is about [description of plot].

PUBLISHER: Do you have any songs in mind?

MUSIC CLEARANCE SUPERVISOR: Yes, I'd like to use [name of recording artist]'s version of [name of composition]. Here's a brief description of the use, and I'll send over the script pages if you need them. I've also contacted the record company that owns the master recording, and it looks like we'll be able to get permission.

PUBLISHER: What kind of rights do you need?

MUSIC CLEARANCE SUPERVISOR: We'd like to get worldwide synch rights, including theatrical release, television broadcast, use of the song in trailers and promos, website use, smartphone and tablet distribution, video-on-demand, download, and home/personal video rights.

PUBLISHER: Before I give a price quote, I'd like to make sure that we receive a royalty for every video sold.

MUSIC CLEARANCE SUPERVISOR: Like the other major studios, we need a one-time buy-out price for all videos sold.

PUBLISHER: In that case, the total fee for all rights will be $45,000. I hope that fits into your budget, as I think the use is good for both the film and the song.

MUSIC CLEARANCE SUPERVISOR: I'll check the remaining budget, but I think the price will be acceptable.

PUBLISHER: That's good. Also, is there a chance that the composition could get on the soundtrack album? Maybe I could lower my price if we could get a guarantee.

MUSIC CLEARANCE SUPERVISOR: I'll check to see if a soundtrack is being contemplated and get back to you.

Another Call:

HEAD OF MUSIC AFFAIRS: Hi, this is the head of music affairs at a major studio. The director and music supervisor of [Name of Actor]'s new film have heard your song and would like to use it in a scene that is being shot next week. The song will be played in the background in [Name of Actress]'s apartment during a party when they first meet and begin to fall in love. It might be played for about a minute, but it could be longer, depending on the final cut.

If the scene works, we might also reprise the song sporadically throughout the film and possibly use it over the opening or closing credits or both. There is also a good chance for a soundtrack album and an "A" side single release.

Because time is short, we need separate price quotes for use of the song for:

1. A 60-second or less one-time use
2. A more-than-60-second one-time use
3. Up to five uses of various lengths
4. Over opening and/or closing credits

Since you could also make quite a bit of extra money if a soundtrack album is released and if your song is released as an "A" side single, we'd like to see if you can reduce your synchronization fee in the event that these possibilities occur.

For your information, we need all the "standard broad rights," including:

1. Worldwide synchronization
2. Worldwide free, pay, cable, and subscription television
3. In-context and out-of-context television advertising and film trailer use, including promos on other film videos plus website and mobile phone use
4. Performance rights for U.S. theater distribution
5. Theater distribution outside the United States
6. DVD, download, video-on-demand, and all home and personal video rights on a nonroyalty one-time buy-out basis
7. All future technology rights, whether now known or not

We also need to have you agree to a reduced CD mechanical royalty if your song makes the soundtrack album (downloads will be at statutory), and I'd like a separate price if we decide to use the title of the song as the title of the motion picture.

I'd like to get back to the director almost immediately, so I'd appreciate it if you could give me the price quotes right away. For your information, we are considering a number of other potential songs for the same scene, so I need your fees to be competitive.

Unlike the television industry, where hundreds of series, specials, and made-for-TV movies may be in production during any given week, only about 700 feature films are released in the U.S. each year. And because the majority of music in each film is original underscore, the competition to get existing songs into motion pictures is intense. Because of the larger monies involved and the possibility of getting a hit single or being put on a multimillion-selling soundtrack album, the ability to handle a call from a film producer intelligently is the key to success. Because of the importance of what you say during that conversation, how quickly you respond, and how well you are able to "read" the other person, the following pages will reveal what you need to know about getting your songs into movies and making the right deal. There is nothing worse than seeing a film open to rave reviews with a hit soundtrack and an Oscar nomination and know that your song could have been in it...but wasn't.

DETERMINING HOW MUCH TO CHARGE FOR A SONG

When the call comes in from the music supervisor of a motion picture and you are trying to decide how much to charge for the use of a song, a number of factors must be considered, including:

The rights being granted

How the song is used (vocal performance by an actor on camera, instrumental background, vocal background, visual performance by a band in the background of a scene, theme, under the opening and/or closing credits)

The overall budget for the film, as well as the music budget

The stature of the song being used (current hit, new song, famous standard, rock 'n' roll classic)

The duration of the use and whether there are multiple uses of the song

The term of the license (two years, 10 years, life of copyright, perpetual)

The territory of the license (the world, universe, specific foreign countries)

Whether there is a guarantee that the song will be used on the film's soundtrack album and the stature of the recording artist and power of the record company releasing the album

Whether there is a change in the original lyrics

Whether deferred payments are being offered if a film breaks even or makes a profit

Whether the producer requests an exclusive hold on the song or places restrictions on its use in other motion pictures

Whether the producer also wants to use the hit recording of a song, rather than re-recording a new version for use in the film

Whether the motion picture is a dramatization of the events described in the song

Whether the motion picture uses the song as its musical theme as well as its title

Whether the motion picture is over-budget at the time a song is requested

Whether a number of songs from the same publisher are contained in the film

Whether the film producer wants a share of the publishing income or a co-ownership interest in the song

ACTUAL FEES PAID FOR EXISTING SONGS

The synchronization fees charged by music publishers are usually between $15,000 and $60,000 (with the majority being between $20,000 and $55,000), but they can be lower if the music budget is small, or higher if the song is used several times in the motion picture (e.g., sung by one of the actors and used as background music or as a reoccurring theme), if the use is under the opening or closing credits, if the song is a major hit, or if it is vital to the plot or particular scene of the motion picture. There are no hard and fast rules in this area, and anyone who advises that there are lacks experience. The fees are negotiated in the context of each individual film; the same song may be licensed at different rates for different projects. It's not a guessing game, though. By carefully considering the myriad factors discussed here, you will be able to say to yourself, "I did the best that I could under the circumstances."

It should also be mentioned that record companies normally charge between $15,000 and $60,000 for the use of existing master recordings in a motion picture, but depending on the stature of the artist, the length of the use, the music budget, and how the recording is being used, these fees can be greater or less.

OPENING AND CLOSING CREDITS

Because the songs used over the opening credits of a motion picture many times reflect the theme or ambiance of the film, they are often more important to the film than other songs used for background. The same is often true for use of a song over the end credits, although it is becoming more common for songs to be run during the closing credits in order to complete the requirements for a soundtrack album. The fees charged by publishers are almost always higher than other uses of music in a film and usually range from $30,000 to over $70,000 for synchronization and video rights, but each negotiation and final price depends upon many of the factors mentioned earlier (e.g., budget of the film, music budget, importance of the song, whether there are replacement songs available, etc.). If the title of one of these opening-credit songs is also used as the title of the film (but the film's plot is not based on the story line of the song), the fees are increased further (e.g., from $75,000 to over $500,000).

MULTIPLE USES OF A SONG

If a producer uses a song more than once in a motion picture, the fees charged by music publishers will be higher than if the song is used only once. The duration of each of the uses is also important, as four uses of less than 20 seconds each is usually less costly to a film producer than four uses of one minute or more. The importance of the song to the plot development or movement of the film (e.g., if it becomes a signature song for an important character or if it becomes thematic of a certain reoccurring point of the film, such as the first time two lovers saw each other) can also be a factor that raises the price. Obviously, it is important to secure from the film producer an overall plot summary and specific scene descriptions when negotiating fees for multiple uses of a song in a film, as you must be aware of how the song is to be used before you can give an intelligent price quote.

LYRIC CHANGES

Occasionally, a film producer will request permission for a lyric change in a song that will either be re-recorded for the film or sung by one of the characters in the motion picture. In most cases, the changes will be of only a few words to fit a particular point in the plot or help a scene comedically, but in some cases, substantial lyric changes will occur. When such a request is received, a music publisher should ask for a copy of the new lyrics, a plot summary of the film, and a scene description including script pages so that it knows exactly how the song will be used before making a decision. Because certain lyric changes can live with a song for a long time—especially if the film is a hit or if the song is used in trailers and television advertising for the film—it is vital to know all the particulars before approving or rejecting the use.

A publisher may have certain restrictions in its agreement with the songwriter (e.g., all changes in the English lyrics to a composition must be with the approval of the writer) that require additional consents from the songwriter or from his or her estate. Because of the possible negative effects that lyric changes may have on a song—especially a standard or well-known contemporary hit—a publisher must be careful in these situations, and if approval is given, an additional fee is virtually always added to the price that would have been charged had there been no change. The scriptwriter who revised the lyrics will virtually never get credit on the song nor be entitled to receive any royalties generated by the revised version.

DURATION OF LICENSE

The term of the license is virtually always for the entire copyright life of the song, unless the film is a documentary or other noncommercial film intended for only limited theatrical release. Many times, the producer will demand "perpetual" rights, but whether or not this language is contained in the contract, the music publisher can guarantee rights only while the song is under copyright protection (i.e., "life of copyright and any and all extensions thereof that are under the control of the publisher").

RIGHTS GRANTED TO THE FILM PRODUCER

The motion picture synchronization fee paid to the music publisher for the use of a song includes the right to distribute the film to network, local, syndicated, pay-per-view, video-on-demand, pay, satellite, cable, Internet, and subscription television stations; the right to show the film in motion picture theaters in the United States; and the right to include the song in "in context" trailers, previews, and advertisements of the motion picture. U.S. television performance and broadcast rights (which are normally licensed through ASCAP, BMI, SESAC, and GMR) are usually excluded, but some major producers try to include such rights in the license agreement, or at least to provide for negotiation, set fees, or arbitration in the event that a broadcast station does not have an ASCAP, BMI, SESAC, or GMR license or if ASCAP, BMI, SESAC, or GMR are legally prohibited from licensing television performance rights. Foreign theatrical distribution rights (i.e., the right to show a film in motion picture theaters outside the United States) are also given to the producer, but such rights are subject to the payment of performance fees by theaters to the various performing rights organizations in countries outside the United States. These societies usually collect a percentage of the box office receipts or a per-seat charge for music performing rights and then send the songwriter's share of such theater monies to ASCAP, BMI, SESAC, and GMR and the music publisher's share to the publisher's representative in each country. The same procedure is used for foreign writers and publishers: each foreign society around the world collects monies for films distributed in its territory and remits the income to the society that represents the songwriter and the local publisher that represents the foreign publisher (e.g., PRS for Music in England sends money to ASCAP, BMI, SESAC, and GMR).

HOME AND PERSONAL VIDEO

As will be described later, there are no royalties payable for the music used in motion pictures when the film goes to home/personal video, regardless of how many units are sold and regardless of whether the distribution channel is physical or digital.

TERRITORY

The territory of the license is normally the universe or world, but in the case of certain television miniseries, made-for-TV movies, and weekly series that are broadcast on television in the United States and shown as features in foreign theaters, the territory may be for the universe or world excluding the United States. In the latter case, synch fees are usually reduced to between $5,000 and $15,000 depending on the duration of the agreement, since the large U.S. theatrical market has been excluded from the license.

LIMITED THEATRICAL DISTRIBUTION

Depending on the nature of the film (normally in the case of documentaries or art films that do not have mass-market appeal), the license may be for a limited duration and apply to the distribution of a film on a limited theater engagement or "film festival" basis. In addition, the territory may also be limited to the United States or to certain specified countries such as England, Australia, and other English-speaking countries. Fees for this type of license are lower than those charged for commercial theatrical features with wide distribution. In many cases, the producer will also have the option to distribute the film theatrically on a broader basis for an additional fee and then to home/personal video for another pre-negotiated fee—important rights if a film is well received or receives an award from an important film festival competition and goes into national distribution. For example, a "film festival" license may give the producer the right within 18 months after the initial showing of the film to extend the territory and the duration of the license for an additional fee.

SOUNDTRACK ALBUM GUARANTEES

On occasion, a music publisher will reduce the motion picture synchronization fee for a song if the producer guarantees that the song will be on a soundtrack album released by a major label. Sometimes there are even guarantees of an "A" side single release, but these usually occur only when a successful recording artist on a major label records the song for the film. In this case the publisher will many times give two price quotes: a higher figure if the song does not make the soundtrack album or if an album is not released and, because of the possibility of additional ancillary album income, a lower quote if the soundtrack provision actually takes effect. For example, if a publisher gives a $35,000 quote for the use of a song in a film, it also might agree to reduce the price to $32,000 if there is a guarantee of a nationally distributed soundtrack album and may even further reduce the fee if the song becomes an "A" side single from the album.

Considering the phenomenal success of some motion picture soundtracks and the hit singles released from the albums, such a reduction in the synch fee may pale in comparison to the mechanical royalties earned from sales of the soundtrack album and singles, not to mention over-the-air radio, audio and audiovisual streaming services, and television performance monies received from ASCAP, BMI, SESAC, GMR, and foreign societies (e.g., $500,000 to more than $2,000,000 for a Top 10 worldwide pop single). Each situation must be decided on its own merits. However, many film soundtracks are not huge money-makers, and a music publisher or writer may wind up reducing the synch price to get on an album that has no single releases and only sells 10,000 copies. Still, such reduced-fee arrangements are valuable incentives to motion picture producers, as they do help reduce up-front production costs (especially where a film uses a great number of pre-existing hit songs) and many times make the difference between a song getting into a film or being left out.

MOTION PICTURE PRODUCER CUT-INS
Some film producers occasionally try to condition the use of a song in a motion picture on a guarantee from the music publisher that the film company will co-own the copyright in the composition or share in the earnings from all or selected subsidiary revenue-generating music markets (e.g., a percentage of the monies derived from the soundtrack album or single royalties).

Most publishers refuse such conditions for pre-existing compositions, but sometimes, when a song is not well known, arrangements are made on a short-term basis to ensure that the song gets into the film (e.g., the producer may receive 10% of the mechanical royalties from the soundtrack album for five years from the release of the movie or for 10 years if a song is an "A" side single). Other publishers may give the producer a copyright interest in the song or a total monetary participation, which means that the producer will share in all income from the composition regardless of whether the income is generated by the film version of the song. Others will grant the producer a life-of-copyright participation in income generated by the song's use in the film only (e.g., a percentage of the earnings derived from the sale of soundtrack albums and singles, foreign motion picture theater royalties, television performances of the film, and radio and television performances of the song itself if it is released as an "A" side single and becomes a hit because of its inclusion in the film). Obviously, such arrangements can substantially benefit the music publisher and songwriter if the song is unknown or has a weak track record and the movie becomes a real hit. But if the song is already a hit or has an income-generating life of its own outside the film and the movie is not successful, the publisher has cut someone else in on a song's future earnings for nothing in return.

Because no one can say what makes a movie a blockbuster or a bomb, most publishers feel that the proposal to allow a motion picture company to share in a pre-existing song's income is an affront to the publisher's integrity and business ethics (much like a recording artist or producer cutting himself in as a co-writer or co-publisher for recording a song). Such proposals usually elicit a negative response from the publisher. In the event, however, that such an arrangement is made as a condition for including a song in a film, the motion picture company will never share in the initial synchronization or video buy-out fee; instead, its interest will only cover income generated after the film is released.

There is a growing trend for film producers to contact songwriters and/or songwriter recording artists who are signed to exclusive agreements with music publishers to write a song or songs for an upcoming motion picture. The request can come during the pre-production scripting stage, the actual filming, or during post-production, when the producer is looking for songs either to fit into certain scenes or to fill out a soundtrack album. In virtually all of these cases, the songwriter (who is usually a recording artist) and his or her music publisher will give the motion picture company a 50% interest in the copyright to the newly created composition. In some cases, the film company will administer the entire composition, and in others the writer's music publisher and the film company will separately administer their respective shares of the composition. In virtually all instances where the writer is a recording artist, the terms of the soundtrack album will also be negotiated, including artist/producer royalties and mechanical licensing arrangements.

In some cases, the film company will provide the writer with a demo budget so that the producer will be able to hear the newly created composition, with further payments due upon delivery of the final composition to the film company and inclusion in the motion picture. For example, the film company might pay the writer $1,500 to produce a demo recording, make an additional $10,000 payment upon completion of the composition, and pay another $10,000 to $60,000 if the composition is actually put in the motion picture. In the event that a song does not make the final cut of the film, the motion picture producer will often have the right to use the song in another of its films, but this is a matter of negotiation. On occasion, the writer is also given the right to reacquire the composition if it is not used in the film by reimbursing the film company for the monies expended.

As many successful songwriters and songwriter/recording artists are signed exclusively to publishing companies and/or record companies, motion picture companies must receive waivers of exclusivity from these companies before going forward on any deal. Basically the waivers acknowledge the exclusive nature of the songwriter or artist agreement with the publishing or record company and that the company agrees to waive such rights of exclusivity for this particular project.

FIRST-USE RESTRICTIONS

If an outside song is chosen by a film producer and the song has not been previously recorded and released as a single or album cut, the producer will sometimes ask the music publisher not to promote or license the song to any other company until the film or the soundtrack album has been released or for a period of time after release. Some publishers will agree to this, and others (especially when a song is considered a possible hit regardless of whether it is included in the motion picture) will not. Once again, such requests are decided on a case-by-case basis, with the publisher treating them more favorably if there has been little outside interest in the song, or if the songwriter is a recording artist and is performing the song in the film, or if there is a commitment that a well-known or up-and-coming artist will perform the song.

TRAILERS FOR MOVIES

The synchronization license usually grants the producer the right to use all music in the film in theatrical trailers (previews of upcoming films that are shown in movie theaters) as well as in television, social media, website, cell phone, and radio promos. In most cases, an extra fee is charged for promos that use the song out of context (e.g., that use a song throughout the entire commercial over many scenes, as opposed to just the scene in which it actually occurs), because these rights are usually not included in the overall synchronization fee charged by the music publisher.

There are also many options contained in motion picture trailer agreements which provide the producer with additional marketing platform rights in case they are needed.

Some of these options, and there are many, are:

- Non-trailer use on the motion picture's website on a worldwide basis in perpetuity.
- Out-of-context use in "making of" or "behind the scenes" productions based on the film in all media known or hereafter derived, including DVDs in connection with the film.
- Blu-ray, DVD or other configuration menus, worldwide, in perpetuity.

All require separate fee quotes and are almost always in the original license quote request which is sent by the film producer's licensing representative.

INDIE FILMS/STEP DEALS/DEFERRED PAYMENTS

On occasion, producers of independent films, documentaries, lower budget films (e.g., from $500,000 to $6 million), or films that have substantially exceeded their production budgets at the time music is being selected, will ask a publisher to reduce its up-front synch fee for a song and, in return, guarantee an additional payment at some time in the future if the motion picture turns a profit or exceeds a certain agreed upon gross or net dollar plateau. The experienced publisher or other representative knows that such a guarantee (considering the sometimes unorthodox accounting practices of some film companies and the unsuccessful track record of most low-budget films), is usually pie in the sky, and will many times refuse such a request. However, if the publisher has a good relationship with a particular producer or director, knows how profit-and-loss accounting works in the motion picture business, believes that the company will remain in business or has an affiliation with a financially stable firm, has fairly strong audit rights, or simply believes in the project, such arrangements can be and are made. In these cases, step deals are many times agreed to because they provide additional payments if a film is successful. For example, if a film reaches certain agreed-upon box office receipts plateaus (e.g., $10,000,000, $15,000,000, etc.), additional payments will be made to the music publisher of the songs in the movie.

Since a number of film festivals offer video-on-demand distribution to enlarge the audience for indie films being shown, this distribution platform represents an additional plateau that can be included in the step deal scenario. In many cases, VOD is limited to a specified period of time after the initial theatrical premiere of the film (for example, 30 days) and may be restricted, at least, initially, to the film festivals' branded distribution channel although there are many variations in this area including streaming and downloadable distribution to cell phones or other personal devices. In any event, it is an area to be considered in the negotiation of the type of "step" that will contractually trigger additional payments.

RESTRICTIONS ON THE USE OF SONGS IN OTHER FILMS

Occasionally, a motion picture producer will try to restrict the use of a song being licensed for other motion pictures so that the song's impact will not be diminished by its use in another movie. This usually occurs when the song has an essential role in the film (for example, as its theme or signature) or is being used as the film's title, or when major promotion monies are committed to a future soundtrack album and the producer wants the motion picture and soundtrack album audience to feel that the particular use is special to that motion picture. Additionally, most record companies will not want to commit hundreds of thousands of dollars to a song when the same song may be released by another artist or record company in competition with its soundtrack album or single. If the publisher agrees to such restrictions, they normally last for a period of from a few months to not more than two or three years. Sometimes the restriction will last only until the release of the motion picture—a commitment that is usually treated more favorably by the music publisher if the film receives major distribution, if there is a firm release date in the not too distant future, and if there is a guaranteed soundtrack album. In the case where a song's title is being used as the title for a film produced by a major studio with guaranteed national distribution, such restrictions, as long as they are not onerous in duration, are usually acceptable to music publishers because of the substantial monies payable in such circumstances.

EXCLUSIVE HOLDS

Some film producers will request an "exclusive hold" on a song that has been used in an unreleased motion picture. In effect, they are asking the music publisher for a guarantee that it will not promote or license the composition in any medium (which usually can be limited to other motion pictures or national advertising campaigns) until the film is released and, in many cases, for a number of months or years thereafter. Such a request (or, in some instances, demand) is handled on a case-by-case basis after weighing both the benefits of getting a particular song in a motion picture and the disadvantages of putting a song on the shelf for a number of months or years. A variation of the exclusive-hold request often occurs when a producer is doing a film about a well-known performer or recording artist (e.g., Johnny Cash, N.W.A, Elvis, the Doors, Kurt Cobain, Janis Joplin, Ray Charles, or Tupac Shakur) and wants to make sure that the music publisher of one of the performer's "signature songs" does not license the song to another film company contemplating the same type of project. In these cases, there is always a fee given to the publisher (usually in the form of an option, such as "$5,000 to $10,000 for each six-month exclusive-hold period, with such hold period lasting for no longer than 18 months"). On occasion, a portion of these option payments is deducted from the final synch fee paid when the film is produced (e.g., "one-fourth of all option fee payments up to $8,000 may be deducted from the final fee payable") but in most cases they are not.

REDUCTION OF FEES DUE TO THE USE OF MANY HIT RECORDS

A film producer who wants to use the original hit recording of a song in a motion picture must not only negotiate a synchronization license for the song itself but also go to the record company that owns the master recording for permission to use the pre-existing recorded version. Since the motion picture company must pay two separate fees in these "master plus song" licensing situations (e.g., one to the music publisher for the use of the underlying musical composition and one to the record company for the use of the existing recorded performance), it will often try to negotiate a reduction in the aggregate monies paid for both the song and the recording under the rationale that the film's music budget cannot justify such a large payment for one piece of music. In many cases (e.g., if the quote for the song is $40,000 and the price for the use of the master recording is $40,000, with the producer having to pay an extra $2,000 in reuse fees to the musicians' union, for a combined total of $82,000), such a request is justifiable, since certain producers simply cannot afford such aggregate fees. In other cases, however, such a negotiating tactic by a producer is merely an attempt to get the cost of music down with little or no real justification.

Obviously, there is a fine line in determining when to hold firm and when to compromise on a fee, but the expert negotiator, because of past experience with the licensing procedures of various film companies and knowledge of how the business works and what the real music budget is for a particular film, knows when to hold the line on a fee and when to compromise. Knowing the people you are dealing with is also extremely important, since if you know someone has been straightforward with you in the past about the real financial restrictions on a film project, that trust can make decisions easier. Without experience, though, you will more than likely come out the loser, either because your song was not used when you refused to compromise on your fee or because you gave it away.

A PUBLISHER HAVING MORE THAN ONE SONG IN A FILM

Occasionally, because of the promotion efforts of a particular music publisher or its relationship with a motion picture producer, an up-front agreement will be made that guarantees lower synchronization fees to the producer if it uses a specified number of that publisher's songs in a film. For example, a publisher might agree to reduce its per-song fees by 10% to 30% if a producer uses more than four of its songs in a film, the publisher might guarantee a set fee (e.g., $20,000 per song) if a certain number remain in the final version. Such arrangements can be vital to a film company's ability to secure the best possible songs for a price that is within its music budget and can also help the music publisher (and its writers) because of the guaranteed theatrical exposure of its songs. In effect, this helps everyone concerned, even though the immediate per-song synchronization and video fees may be somewhat reduced, because all parties gain from the immediate use and resulting ancillary uses of songs in a motion picture. Such arrangements really work only if the music publisher has a large number of well-known songs that fit the needs of a particular film. For example, if a film has a 1950s setting and you have a wealth of 1950s hits in your catalogue, this type of deal can be most attractive.

STUDENT-PRODUCED FILMS/STEP DEALS

Because student-produced films have limited chances for commercial success and small budgets, many music publishers will license their songs for substantially reduced fees. In such cases, most publishers recognize the importance of assisting young filmmakers, since they are an integral part of the future of the entertainment industry. Songs will sometimes be given to these young producers for free or for a nominal cost so that their projects will be realized and their careers advanced. Most publishers, however, will provide that if the project has any type of commercial success or secures more than just film festival or art house distribution, an additional fee or fees will be paid as certain criteria are achieved—a proviso that not only helps young producers get their projects off the ground but also ensures adequate compensation to the publisher and songwriter for their generosity if the film realizes national distribution, availability on a streaming service, or achieves some kind of financial success. This type of arrangement is called a "step deal."

RESCORING AND REPLACING SONGS IN A FILM PRIOR TO RELEASE

Especially in the case of lower- or medium-budget films, the producer will often want to replace an existing song score prior to the film's release. There can be many reasons for such a move, but it will usually result from a producer's initial decision to try to get the cheapest composer possible because of initial budgetary constraints. If the score doesn't work, or if the final cut of a film convinces a producer that it has a real chance in the marketplace if it has some well-known songs, the producer may decide to try to get additional songs as replacements for the music in certain scenes. Considering that the music budget may have already been depleted, the producer will many times go to record companies or publishers with whom it has worked before and try to get permission to use certain songs and master recordings at reduced prices. The producer may also contact a music consultancy service that deals in film music licensing on a daily basis and give them the assignment. Depending on the relationship between the producer or music consultant and the record company or music publisher, reduced-rate deals are many times achieved within hours.

PROMOTIONAL TELEVISION PROGRAMS

Some film companies will film the premiere of the motion picture as well as its premiere party for promotional purposes. On occasion, a company will make a television program and distribute it to stations around the country as well as the Internet to stimulate interest in the film. Since such promotional shows do help the motion picture and expose the songs in the film, film companies many times ask music publishers for either free or minimal-fee synchronization licenses. These requests are handled on a case-by-case basis, with many of the agreements containing "most favored nations" provisions (e.g., if one song receives a fee, all other songs will receive the same fee, or if one song gets a larger fee than any other, all songs will receive that larger fee). In negotiating such agreements, you should remember that even though there is no or only a minimal up-front synchronization fee payable, the vehicle is really for promotional purposes only and should be dealt with in that spirit. Your position in these negotiations may also determine whether the motion picture company feels that you are a person or company that it can work with on future projects, a factor that can never be minimized.

NONPROFIT FILMS AND FREE USE OF MUSIC

On occasion, when a film is produced on behalf of a certain cause with all profits contributed to the promotion of that cause, the producer will ask music publishers and record companies for free licenses. If the project and its goals seem worthwhile, most publishers and record companies will charge either nominal fees or no fees at all. Often such agreements are on a "most favored nations" basis, which guarantees payment to all songwriters and publishers if anyone else gets paid.

SCREEN CREDIT

Virtually all motion picture producers will give screen credit for the use of pre-existing songs in motion pictures. This credit is almost always included during the crawl at the end of the film. The publisher is seldom mentioned, though the film *Chicago* provided a full-frame credit to Unichappel Music. The film producer usually affords credit only to the title of the song, the writers, and, if a pre-existing master recording is used, the name of the record company and the recording artist. Additionally, if a recording artist makes a new version for release on a soundtrack album, the credits will include such information. In a field where credit provisions are important, it is vital to provide for a correct line credit in the license itself so that the proper information on the screen is assured. Credit in advertisements for the film is almost unheard of, but does occasionally occur at the film producer's option particularly if the song is a current hit or the artist is well known.

MUSIC CUE SHEETS AND THEIR IMPORTANCE

After a motion picture has been produced and a final version has been edited, the producer will prepare a music cue sheet that lists all the music used in the film, including how each song was used, its timing in seconds, the identity of the writers and music publishers and their performing rights affiliation, and if pre-existing master recordings have been used, the identity of recording artists and record companies. Considering the amount of music used in most films, this cue sheet is usually completed soon after the theatrical release, but depending on the producer and available staff, it can be longer.

Some music cue sheets contain specific scene explanations and dialogue details, but most contain only chronological information on the titles, writers, publishers, performing rights affiliation, master recording information, timing (20 seconds, two minutes, etc.), and generic usage (visual vocal, background music, etc.). At the fringe of the industry are low-budget companies that do not even bother to type a cue sheet and others that do not even know what a music cue sheet is.

Because ASCAP, BMI, SESAC, and GMR use these cue sheets to determine how music is used, who owns the music, and how royalty payments should be made when a film is shown on television, it is essential that the writer and publisher secure a copy and review it closely. Because a motion picture uses so much music in so many ways (visual vocals, background vocals, background instrumentals, opening and closing credits, etc.), it is not unusual for mistakes to be made on cue sheets, whether it be a false timing, a mislabeling of a song's use, or an incorrect identification of the writer and publisher. By looking over a copy of the cue sheet, the writer and publisher can correct any inaccuracies before the producer distributes the cue sheet to the performing rights organizations. In addition, since cue sheets are circulated throughout the world by ASCAP, BMI, SESAC, and GMR, and in addition by music publishers who send them to their subpublishing representatives in foreign countries, who then register them with their local performing rights organizations, a correct cue sheet is the key to receiving what you are due. Table 8.2 illustrates the format and the type of information that should be on a cue sheet.

MUSIC CUE SHEET

Table 8.2

TITLE OF FILM: FILM COMPANY NAME:

NAME OF COMPOSER: U.S. RELEASE DATE:

No.	Selection	Composer	Publisher	How Used	Time
1.	Film Company Logo	Name (ASCAP)	Film Company Publishing Co. (ASCAP)	Bkg. Inst.	0:10
2.	Main Title Theme	Name (ASCAP)	Film Company Publishing Co. (ASCAP)	Bkg. Inst. (Opening Credits)	1:40
3.	Beach Scene	Name (ASCAP)	Film Company Publishing Co. (ASCAP)	Bkg. Inst.	2:45
4.	Existing Hit Song	Name (BMI)	Outside Publishing Co. (BMI)	Bkg. Vocal	0:35
5.	City Landscape Scene	Name (ASCAP)	Film Company Publishing Co. (ASCAP)	Bkg. Inst.	1:12
6.	Existing Hit Song	Name (ASCAP)	Outside Publishing Co. (ASCAP)	Visual Vocal	0:47
7.	Existing Hit Song (Master Licensed from Warner Bros. Records)	Name (BMI)	Outside Publishing Co. (BMI)	Bkg. Vocal	1:15
8.	Car Chase Scene	Name (ASCAP)	Film Company Publishing Co. (ASCAP)	Bkg. Inst.	2:24
9.	Existing Hit Song (Master Licensed From MCA Records)	Name (ASCAP)	Outside Publishing Co. (ASCAP)	Bkg. Vocal (Closing Credits)	3:30

GETTING SONGS INTO FILMS

Music publishers play an important role in convincing film producers to use past hit songs in their movies. The successful ones promote their catalogues by means of sampler albums, catalogue lists, and songbooks. These samplers range from CDs containing 30- to 40-second excerpts of a publisher's main songs to massive print catalogues with accompanying full-song CDs. "Idea books" suggest certain titles for certain scenes and contain separate listings of a publisher's catalogue by songwriter, recording artist, era, or genre of music. Virtually all companies also promote their catalogues and new releases via e-mail and via their websites.

When record companies promote the use of their recordings with producers, they also help the songwriter and publisher. Important too are good working relationships with music supervisors, independent music consultants, film agents, and the heads of the music departments of Los Angeles-based motion picture companies.

WEBSITES

Web sites have become extremely valuable in the areas of information and promotion, because film producers, directors, and music supervisors are able to gain immediate online access to a music publisher's catalogue via their computers, smartphones, or other devices. Many of these sites provide not only song title, writer and recording artist information but also give the potential user the ability to sort the catalogue by, among other things, type of music, lyric content and message, time period, and chart activity. Additionally, many sites enable the film licensing staff to request the use of a particular song via an online license request.

Whether one is a songwriter, music publisher, or record company executive, it is also vital to know what pictures are in development, in pre-production, in production, or in post-production (both *Hollywood Reporter* and *Variety* keep track of productions filming in and outside the United States), since contact with producers to suggest ideas can help. Many music publishers are able to secure the script of a film from the producer or music supervisor and give specific suggestions for the use of compositions as either background music or visual vocals for use in individual scenes. Film companies appreciate constructive promotion—not the shotgun approach of suggesting every song in one's catalogue for a particular film.

PRODUCERS AND THE SELECTING OF SONGS

Prior to making the final choice, many producers select a large number of possible songs and secure quotations from music publishers. Usually a list of only about 15 to 25 songs will be given to the people clearing (i.e., getting permission to use) the music, but many times a producer may express interest in anywhere from 30 to 50 compositions, even though only 10 to 15 uses are actually needed. There have even been cases of producers getting fee quotes for up to 150 different songs for a 10- to 12-song picture. If a director or music supervisor has a specific song in mind for a particular scene but the fees quoted by the music publisher are too high for the music budget of the film, it is sound business practice to have commitments on a number of alternate, less costly songs. If the song is being used as a visual vocal, however, the producer does not have the luxury of waiting until post-production for actual music selection and will usually secure price quotes for only a few preferred compositions.

Most of the major film production companies know which publishers are flexible in their pricing policies and are easy to work with, as well as those publishers whose licensing policies conform with those of the producer. Many film producers also have extensive music libraries and reference materials that they review when making selections. The publishers who continue to be successful in the promotion of songs for motion pictures, however, are those who continually promote their catalogues, because personnel changes at many film companies make it vital to let people know what you have. Good working relationships with the people at the various studios cannot be overemphasized.

RECAP

Considering the ever-increasing global market for films and that market's importance to musical compositions, knowing how to negotiate a motion picture license is one of the cornerstone responsibilities for anyone who is responsible for ensuring that songs continue to earn money. It can be a tricky business and one filled with complexities, but it is an area that, if handled professionally and correctly, has the potential of generating enormous amounts of income and exposing songs to millions of people.

THE SONG WRITTEN FOR A MOTION PICTURE

One of the most difficult types of song to write, for any lyricist or composer, is the song specifically written for a movie. The writers of these songs usually fall into one of three categories. The first is the professional songwriter living in Los Angeles, New York, or another city where films are produced. The second type is the writer/recording artist. The third type is the successful record producer who is also a writer. The difficulties of breaking into this field are greater for the nonperforming writer, who must not only write quickly but also evoke the specific feeling that a director wants for a scene. The writer/artist, on the other hand, is many times hired for film work more because of past or current record success ("name value") and less as a result of a knowledge of the intricacies of writing for film. Emergence of successful record producer/writers into this field is due primarily to their experience and ability to select, write, and produce a hit contemporary sound.

BREAKING INTO THE BUSINESS

With few exceptions, for songwriters to have any chance of getting into this field, they must live in an area that is a film-producing center. Otherwise, it is very difficult to build the relationships and contacts necessary for not only the first break but also continuing assignments.

THE SONG FOR FILM—FROM START TO FINISH

A successful writer (or the writer's agent) gets a call from a director or music supervisor, is told that a film is in production, and is asked whether he or she wants to write a song for the film. If the writer says yes, either a script of the movie or video of the scene is provided, or the basic story line of the film is read over the phone. If the writer is a lyricist, they will discuss who the composer of the music should be (many times it is the underscore composer). The writer will then be given direction and suggestions as to the "feel" of the song as well as the emotions and thoughts needed in the lyrics and the music. The director normally already has in mind a model song, which he or she has probably "temp tracked" to the particular scene in order to simulate the type of feeling needed. The writer will then be informed of the deadline for submission and will write the song and present it in "demo form" to the director or music supervisor. At this point, it is very common for the director to ask for a rewrite or, in some cases, to reject the song. After the song is rewritten and accepted, the recording artist enters the picture. A recording session has to be booked subject to a particular artist's availability. At the session, sometimes multiple versions of the same song will be recorded to see which one fits best into the movie. The writing of the song, the presentation of the demo, the rewrites, and the recording session are all under strict time limits (sometimes as short as one week), as the film is usually in its final post-production phase, with final prints of the film due for release to movie theaters on a specific date.

As opposed to the above scenario, some film producers use a cattle-call approach whereby many writers are asked to submit songs for a project. Sometimes fees are paid to the writers for their submissions; at other times, song submissions are on a totally speculative basis.

THE "SONG WRITTEN FOR A FILM" CONTRACT

When a producer hires a composer or lyricist to write a song for a film, the compensation as well as the rights of all parties are set forth in a commissioning agreement. These contracts typically state that the producer employs the composer or lyricist to write a song within a stated period of time in accordance with certain ideas and instructions supplied by the producer. A due date for a demo record is set forth in the agreement, and the producer almost always reserves the right to make any changes. Upon delivery of the song, the writer receives an initial fee (e.g., $25,000 for a song, $7,500 for the lyrics, etc.) as well as a guarantee of additional future compensation in the form of songwriter royalties, which is either in the body of the agreement or attached as a separate schedule (e.g., 50% of mechanical income earned from record and CD sales as well as download income; a set rate for sheet music; 50% of any synchronization income from the uses of the song in a television series, other motion pictures, video games, ringtones, or commercials). The writer also normally receives screen credit for the composition. In consideration for the writing fee, the writer usually grants all rights to the producer (with the exception of his or her share of royalty income) under an employee-for-hire or work-for-hire contract.

Writer Services. The songwriter is employed by the film producer to write a new and original song (or songs) for the motion picture. The contract will specify whether the writer is being hired to write a complete song or to provide lyrics to new or already-composed music. In some cases, the contract will be a joint agreement among the producer, the composer of the music, and a separate lyricist. The "work" will be written in accordance with such ideas and instructions as the producer may supply to the composer and lyricist and will be suitable, in the producer's opinion, for use in the film.

Starting and Completion Dates. Because of the time constraints of the post-production phase, the starting date is usually the day the contract is signed. As shown in the two examples here, the completion date may be fixed or open-ended.

EXAMPLE 1. "The composer shall deliver the song to the Producer in the form of a demonstration record and lead sheet on or about March 16, 2018. Producer shall have the right to require Composer (or Lyricist) to make any changes, modifications, additions, or deletions that the Producer desires and that all such changes are to be without additional compensation to the Composer (or Lyricist)." The writing time in this contract was ten days, as the agreement was signed on September 6, 2018.

EXAMPLE 2. "The term of the Writer's employment shall commence as of the date of the Agreement (December 10, 2017) and shall continue until completion of all services required by the Producer including any services required in connection with changes or modifications during the recording and dubbing of the work." The term of this contract is open-ended, as it runs from the date of the signing of the agreement through the date when the recording and dubbing are complete.

Writing Fees. The amount of the fee paid to a writer depends on whether a complete song (or songs) or just lyrics are being contracted for; whether the song is to be used as the theme song, as a visual vocal, or as background; the music budget of the film; whether the film is being produced by a major studio, a large independent company, or a smaller independent; the writer's stature and past film song success; whether the writer is also the artist who will perform the song in the movie and his or her success as a performing artist; the negotiating power of the writer's agent or representative; and the current industry practice as to the range of fees being paid to writers for film songs—the going rate.

Fees can range from $1,500 for the lyrics to one song to in excess of $300,000 for a complete song if the writer is also the performing artist. All of the fees paid are nonrecoupable (i.e., cannot be deducted from royalties) and nonreturnable (i.e., the producer cannot ask for the money back if he or she does not like the song).

For a reasonably successful nonperforming writer (or writing team), the range of fees might be as follows:

$7,500 to $10,000 for a lower-budget quality film from a major studio

$12,500 to $15,000 for songs in subsequent films (assuming the first film did reasonably well)

$25,000 to more than $50,000 for a song for medium- to higher-budget films (assuming the writer has had a number of previous film credits)

$50,000 to in excess of $100,000 for the theme song to a major film for an established film songwriter

Obviously, if one or more of the writer's past film songs has been a major hit, won an Academy Award, or been nominated for any other award (Golden Globe, Grammy), the writer's song fee for subsequent films will be affected positively.

EXAMPLE 1. "In full consideration of all rights granted by Writer to Producer, Producer agrees to pay to Writer $25,000 payable within 10 days after the execution of the Agreement" (theme song for a medium-budget major release).

EXAMPLE 2. "$1,500 payable promptly following delivery of the lyrics to the Producer" (lyrics to one song for a new writer).

EXAMPLE 3. "$60,000 payable at $30,000 upon the commencement of the services and an additional $30,000 upon the completion of all services" (theme song for a major film release written by established writers).

Screen Credit. Songwriter screen credit is a negotiable item. Some major writers and writer/artists are able to negotiate a spot in the film's opening credits. Most song credits, however, appear in the film's closing credits (the credit roll); even here some writers are able to negotiate a single-frame card credit, separate from all of the other songwriter credits.

EXAMPLE 1. "Writer shall receive credit in the end titles of all positive prints of the film. Credit is conditional upon the performance of all the provisions of this contract and that the song is actually used in the film as released. Credit shall not be given in any form of advertising."

EXAMPLE 2. "Composer shall receive appropriate credit on the screen in size, style of type, and placement in the picture as the Producer, in his sole discretion, may determine. Credit shall read "music and lyrics by [Name of writer] in connection with the song title."

As an example of the type of bargaining position that some major writer/artists have as to credit, *Saturday Night Fever* (1978), *Gangs of New York* (2002) and *Skyfall* (2012) showed a writer screen credit in the opening credits of the film. In *Saturday Night Fever* the full-frame credit read "Original Music by Barry, Robin, and Maurice Gibb," and listed the songs "How Deep Is Your Love," "Night Fever," "Staying Alive," and "More Than a Woman," as well as the recording artists, the Bee Gees. The closing credits of the film listed all of the songs again as well as any other outside songs, writers, and artists (Kool & the Gang, Rick Dees, KC and the Sunshine Band, etc.). In *Gangs of New York*, U2 received a full-frame credit for "Hands That Built America" and Adele received full frame credit as a performer and co-writer for "Skyfall," the theme song to the James Bond movie of the same name.

Grant of Rights. The grant of rights is of the broadest nature possible in order to allow the film producer unlimited ownership of all aspects and ingredients of the film. The following clauses indicate the broad nature of the rights that the writer gives to the film producer:

EXAMPLE 1. "Composition is specifically ordered or commissioned by the Producer for use as part of a motion picture entitled [Name of Picture] and is a 'Work Made For Hire.' Producer is the author and composer for all purposes and the owner of all right, title, and interest, throughout the world, for all purposes, without condition, restriction, or limitation subject only to royalty compensation as set forth herein."

EXAMPLE 2. "Producer shall own all rights of every kind in and to the results and proceeds of Artist's services hereunder, including copyright and exploitation in any and all media throughout the universe."

EXAMPLE 3. "The complete, unencumbered, exclusive, and worldwide rights which vest in producer hereunder shall include, but shall not be limited to, motion picture, synchronization, mechanical, performing, and dramatic rights, and all other rights of every kind, nature, and description, whether now known or hereafter to become known or come into being."

The film producer will normally retain the right to change or adapt the song as well as to add music or lyrics to it. Also, the writer normally grants the producer the right to use the writer's name, likeness, and biography in the advertising and exploitation of the film for all time.

Songwriter Royalties. The contract, regardless of whether it is a "work made for hire" agreement or a regular songwriter-publisher agreement, will always set forth all of the areas where the songwriter receives royalties: among others, mechanical royalties from download, record, and CD sales; a set rate for sheet music sales; 50% of any synchronization income from the use of the song in a television series, other motion pictures, or commercials; ringtone royalties; performance royalties (ASCAP, BMI, SESAC, GMR, foreign societies); and foreign royalties.

Exclusivity. Practically all film songwriting contracts are nonexclusive and the writer is free to continue other projects or write for others during the term of the services agreement. This nonexclusivity is conditioned, though, by clauses stating, for instance, that the writer "will not render any outside services which would prevent the work (the film song) from being completed within the time period specified in the contract."

Publishing. Most contracts provide the producer with 100% of the publishing rights and income of the composition. This is particularly true if the producer is a major studio or large independent. Most film studios and movie production companies have their own publishing arms, and most songs written for a film are assigned to the studio's publishing company. Music-publishing income is part of the consideration for the writer's services fee, and it is therefore not the norm for writers in this area to retain any of their own publishing. There are writers, though, who because of their past success in film or other areas are able to share in a film song's publishing income either through a co-publishing or administration agreement or through some form of participation agreement. The same applies to well known writer/artists.

Writers sometimes are able to retain the publishing on songs if they are employed by a medium-size or small film-production company. Many of these companies do not have music-publishing companies as part of their operation, and some do not understand the short- or long-term earnings that can be generated by a film song. In those cases, it is not unusual for a writer to keep the copyright as well as the publishing income that flows from that copyright.

Originality. The writer will always guarantee that the song is totally original for the film, is not based in whole or in part on any other composition, and does not infringe upon the copyright of any other composition or the right of any other party. A certificate of authorship will also be provided by the writer as well as any other documents that the producer requires for proof of ownership.

Use or Nonuse of the Song. The producer of the film will usually have no obligation whatsoever to use the song in the film or to exploit the composition in any way.

Performance Royalties. The writer will receive his or her writer performance royalties directly from the performing rights organization of which he or she is a member. If a situation arises where a performing rights society is unable to license a user for various reasons, then the writer should try to negotiate with the producer some form of continuing royalty payment for the use of the song. Without such a "safeguard" provision, the producer may be able to license the song without compensation to the writer. The same considerations are true with respect to the publisher's share of performance income if the writer has been able to negotiate a co-publishing agreement with the film producer.

THE WRITER/RECORDING ARTIST AGREEMENT FOR CREATING AND RECORDING A COMPOSITION FOR A MOVIE

When the songwriter is also a recording artist and is not only creating the song for the motion picture but also performing it both in the film and on the soundtrack album, the composing agreement will cover, among other things, not only the writing aspects and mechanical royalty issues but also the areas of recording procedures, recording costs, artist royalty percentages, advances, and any restrictions placed on the record company distributing the soundtrack by the record company to which the artist is signed.

The following represents the basic format of this type of agreement, which is many times a 7- to 10-page "short form" agreement rather than the much longer score agreement.

Basic Project Information: The title of the film, plus the names of the director, the stars appearing in the film, the identity of the distributing film company, and the projected release date are mentioned.

Cooperation: The writer/artist agrees to cooperate with the reasonable requests and instructions of the film company. In most cases, the writer/artist agrees to make any reasonably requested changes not only to the composition but also to the master recording, until a satisfactory composition and recording is delivered to the film company.

Record Company Waiver: The writer-artist acknowledges the right of his or her current record company to the exclusive recording services of the artist and agrees to cause the record company to grant a written waiver of the exclusivity provisions to allow the film company to hire the writer/artist to record the composition for use in the film and soundtrack album.

Publishing Company Waiver: If the writer/artist is signed exclusively to a music publisher, the writer/artist will also secure a waiver from the music publisher to allow the writing of the composition for the film project. This waiver is vital because most film companies demand all or a portion of the copyright in the newly created composition (although this is not always the case), and this transfer of rights would not be possible if a writer is signed to an exclusive music publishing contract under which all compositions written are owned by the publisher.

Work-for-Hire: The writer/artist will agree that the newly written composition is a work-for-hire and that the copyright (or a portion thereof) is assigned to the film company. The film company will also secure the right to utilize the composition in the motion picture and in advertisements, trailers, and other promotions, as well as to distribute the film on video.

Samples: There will be a warranty by the writer/artist that there are no samples of any pre-existing material in the composition and master created for the film.

Use: The actual placement of the composition and master in the film will usually be mentioned. For example, if the use is to be over the end credits, such will be referenced. The actual timing of the usage in the film will not be mentioned since this may not be determined until the final distribution cut.

Co-Ownership: Many successful writer/artists are able to retain 50% of the copyright in the music publishing rights, with the film company securing the other 50%. If this is the case, the agreement will specify the ownership percentages of the new composition. Even though it is not the norm, certain very successful writer/artists are able to retain 100% of the copyright and publishing rights.

Administration: If the writer/artist is able to retain a portion of the publishing, the film company will many times jointly allow the writer/artist's music publisher to administer the composition throughout the world. If the writer/artist's publishing company is able to secure co-administration rights (where each party represents, licenses, and collects royalties for its respective share of the composition), the film company usually places some restrictions on the writer's publishing representative. For example, if there is a matching folio containing compositions from the motion picture, the film company will reserve those rights for its affiliated print company or third-party licensee. In addition, there is many times a restriction placed on the writer's publishing company to grant synchronization licenses for use of the composition in other films, television programs, or commercials for a specified period of time after the release of the motion picture without the film company's permission. For example, a sample clause might dictate that no synchronization licenses may be granted for two years after the release of the film without the film company's consent. Such a provision ensures that the film company that paid for the creation of the composition will not be faced with any competing uses or other licenses that can detract from the composition's impact in the theatrical version and home video version of the film.

Controlled Composition Clause: The composing agreement will always contain acceptance by the writer/artist of the controlled composition clause provisions of the recording agreement for the soundtrack album, which dictate, among other things, the amount of mechanical royalties that will be paid for the sale of the soundtrack album or singles. In many cases, the provisions will be attached as an exhibit. In other cases, there will be a specific reference to what the mechanical rate is (for example, 100% statutory rate at the time the recording is completed or released, a 75% statutory rate with no possibility of reduction, a 75% statutory rate with a 12-composition album cap, 100% statutory with a 12 composition cap, 100% statutory for downloads, etc.).

Rights and Restrictions of the Various Record Companies: Considering that most well-known artists who record songs for motion pictures are signed exclusively to record labels, negotiations always take place between the film company and/or the record company releasing the soundtrack album and the artist's current record company. In this regard, the soundtrack record label may secure the right to put the recording on the soundtrack album but might only be able to release it as a single with the permission of the artist's record label. In many cases, the artist's label may be able to include the master on its next studio album or any "greatest hits" album, but with the proviso that such will not occur for one year from release of the film in the United States (unless, of course, the film company agrees to the contrary that a sooner release may occur). Other times, the master recorded for use in the film may be included on both the soundtrack album and the artist's album with virtually no restrictions.

Fees: When a film company is dealing with a very successful writer/artist, the fees will be substantial. In many cases, there is a so-called "all-in" lump-sum recording fund which covers not only the creative fee for writing the composition and for being the recording artist and producer of the composition, but also all the costs of recording the master (studio, tape, engineers, musicians, vocalists, equipment rentals, and mixing costs). When this all-in fee approach is used, there is also usually a negotiated sum designated as the creative fee for composing the composition (for example, $60,000 of the $200,000 recording fund being the songwriter fee).

There are many variations as to how the monies are paid, but the norm is to pay a portion on the signing of the agreement with the writer/artist, and the remainder is paid when the composition and master recording have been delivered to and accepted by the film company.

Artist Royalty: The agreement will also specify what the artist royalty will be and will, many times—since the percentage royalty is pro-rated depending on the number of other artists and masters on the soundtrack album—guarantee a minimum percentage below which the artist's rate will not go. For example, if the overall artist royalty for the album is 15% of the suggested retail list price (which will be divided by all the individual masters on the album), many agreements provide that each artist will not receive less than 1% to 1.5% per individual master on the album. This type of so-called "floor" arrangement is usually inserted into the agreement only when it is requested by the artist's representative.

As in all record contracts, the artist royalty for top-line normal retail sales will be reduced for certain categories (such as record clubs, foreign, mid-price, budget, and single sales) and recorded configurations (new technology devices), and it will be subject to other deductions (such as packaging charges, free goods, discounts) and reserve policies (to cover returned albums and singles). Because there is a real complexity to the many interlocking and interrelated provisions of the recording agreement and how they impact on an artist's royalties and rights, it is essential to include in the film agreement as much definitive information as possible on how royalties are to be calculated.

Advances: If there is an advance paid to the artist that is recoupable from the artist royalties, no royalties will be paid until the advance has been recouped by the record company. Royalties will begin to flow to the artist after the advance has been recouped. Artist advances, however, are not recouped from the artist's songwriter/ music publisher royalties, because these mechanical royalties will be paid through, regardless of whether the artist's recording artist advance has been recouped.

Accountings: Royalties will be paid either 45 to 60 days after the end of every quarter or 45 to 60 days after the film company receives royalties from the record company distributing the soundtrack album. There will be audit right provisions (usually no audit more than once in any 12-month period) and other clauses that dictate a specified time to make an objection to a royalty statement.

Credit: Songwriter and performer credit will be guaranteed in the film (almost always in the closing credits) and, if the artist is signed to another record label, that label many times will receive on-screen credit as well. Credits may also be guaranteed for certain ads for the soundtrack album and, on occasion, for ads for the motion picture, but all this is negotiable.

LIFE AFTER THE MOTION PICTURE RELEASE (WHERE THE REAL MONEY IS MADE)

Just as with songs used in television series, movie songs can have a substantial financial life well beyond the initial synchronization or writing fee. Table 8.3 gives examples of the dollar figures a successful movie song can earn. The following sections review the revenue-producing areas listed in the table.

INCOME FOR A SUCCESSFUL MOVIE SONG

Table 8.3

$25,000	Synchronization and video buy-out fee
$800,000	U.S. radio/television/streaming performance royalties for a hit single
$18,200	"A" side single U.S. download/record sales (200,000 copies)
$45,500	U.S. album sales (500,000 copies)
$7,500	Foreign theatrical performances
$4,000	Academy Awards Show performance in Best Song category
$4,000	Grammy Awards Show performance in Best Song category
$20,000	Sheet music and folios
$7,000	Initial television broadcasts of the film on pay and network television
$250,000	Commercial
$2,000	Ringtones
$10,000	Video games
$22,000	Foreign "A" side single sales
$55,000	Foreign album sales
$900,000	Foreign radio and television performance royalties for a hit single
$15,000	Miscellaneous royalties
$2,185,200	Writer and publisher royalties

MOTION PICTURE HOME VIDEO LICENSING

Because the market for home video is enormous throughout the world—with major motion pictures selling between 400,000 and 20 million units—DVDs, Blu-ray, videodiscs, downloads, and other home video configurations are a major source of revenue for film companies even though the numbers are not what they once were.

One-Time Buy-Out. All of the major and smaller motion picture companies demand that the music publisher or writer accept a one-time buy-out fee for all DVD, Blu-ray, download, video cassette, and other home video rights, regardless of the actual number of units that may be sold or distributed in the future. The video buy-out is part of the synchronization license fee paid to the music publisher for use of the song in the film.

Royalty per DVD or Disc. When the home video market was in its inception, many licenses provided for an actual royalty for each cassette sold. The royalty paid for the use of a composition was based on either a set monetary rate (usually from 6¢ to 8¢ per song) or a percentage of the wholesale or retail price of each video, shared on a pro-rata basis by all songs contained in the video. The pro rata sharing was sometimes based on the duration of each song in relation to the aggregate timing of all songs or music on the video or, alternatively, the duration of the song in relation to the duration of the entire motion picture. This approach, however, is unacceptable to all motion picture companies in the U.S. and is not used.

Elimination of Songs Because of Home Video Policies. Because of the "video buy-out or nothing" policies of motion picture companies, if a publisher does not agree to a buy-out payment for home video distribution, the song will not be used even though it may be right for the movie. A film's director, writer, or music supervisor has little or no influence to change the film distributor's video policy, and if a publisher or songwriter holds out for a per-unit royalty and the motion picture company's policy is one of video buy-outs only, a replacement song will virtually always be used.

Deleting Songs from Home Video Releases. Even after a song has been included in the theatrically distributed version of a film, if a motion picture company cannot negotiate an acceptable video buy-out contract with a music publisher or songwriter, it may choose to take the song out of the home video version. Because video rights are now negotiated at the same time as the synchronization license, such a situation occurs only with older movies (where licenses did not provide for home video), films that had per-video royalty rate guarantees, and films that had "to be negotiated in the future" home video provisions.

DVD AND BLU-RAY ONLY LICENSING

With the advent of DVDs and the special features and bonuses included with the home video version of motion pictures, scenes that were deleted from the theatrical version and the songs used in those scenes many times appear on the DVD version. Certain compositions are also played during the main menu of the DVD. As with the theatrical version, there will be a synchronization and video fee payable upon release of the motion picture to the home video market.

HIT SINGLES FROM MOTION PICTURES

A significant source of income for the composer, lyricist, and publisher of movie songs is the hit single. And considering that a soundtrack album can contain multiple successful singles, the monies that can be made in this area can be extraordinary.

Mechanical Royalties. The song's publisher many times licenses the song to a record company for the statutory royalty for every download, record, and CD sold. In many other cases, the rate will be 75% to 85% of statutory for physical product with 100% of statutory for digital product. If other recording artists cover the song, the mechanical license can bring in hundreds of thousands of dollars long after the song's initial popularity. Think of the many recordings over the years of Henry Mancini's "Moon River," from the 1961 film *Breakfast at Tiffany's.*

ASCAP, BMI, SESAC, and GMR Royalties. U.S. radio and TV performances as well as streams of a movie song can add hundreds of thousands of dollars of royalty income if the song becomes a hit record, becomes a standard, and is recorded over the years by many artists in addition to being used in other films or television programs. It is not unusual for such a song to earn from $20,000 to more than $100,000 per year in writer/publisher catalogue performance royalties long after the movie's release.

Foreign Performance Royalties. For movie songs, the foreign market can represent a substantial revenue area for writers and publishers, particularly since American product is the staple of many countries' theaters as well as radio and television programming. In fact, in the area of 700 million dollars is forwarded to ASCAP, BMI, SESAC, and GMR for foreign performances each year. For songwriters with a song in a film, the areas that can generate foreign performance royalties include radio, television, cable, audio and audiovisual streaming services, wired music, and live performances as well as income generated by theater performances of the film. Table 8.4 gives examples of the type of writer foreign performance royalties that can be generated during the initial year of chart activity for two successful "A" side film singles.

THE MOTION PICTURE SOUNDTRACK ALBUM

When a film studio decides to release a soundtrack album, the studio (or its music representatives) will either go to its affiliated record label or to the star's label (if he or she is a recording artist) or shop the project to an interested record label. The record company will usually provide an advance to the film studio to put the album together (negotiate licenses, new song costs, masters, etc.). The agreement would grant the record company the right to manufacture, advertise, and sell the soundtrack album and singles with artist royalties (negotiated) of 16% of retail pro-rated to all artists who have masters on the album. The artists would need exclusivity waivers from their record companies to appear on the album. Single releases would be scheduled (e.g., 10 weeks prior to the film release), with the album release set for no later than three weeks before the picture opens. Music videos would be released with each single and they would contain actual footage from the film with the costs of the videos being shared by the studio and the record company. The type of film credit would be negotiated (usually in the closing credits), and royalty statements would be issued semi-annually. In practically all cases, the film studio would be the copyright owner (a work for hire) of the new songs and masters.

HIT SONGS FROM FILMS: FOREIGN RELEASE

Table 8.4

Country	Society	Song A	Song B
Australia	PRA	$22,040	$32,575
Austria	AKM	$6,400	$7,425
Belgium	SABAM	$6,256	$9,245
Canada	SOCAN	$20,500	$38,000
England	PRS	$52,760	$80,000
Finland	TEOSTO	$1,664	$2,500
France	SACEM	$2,060	$35,500
Germany	GEMA	$16,400	$22,400
Holland	BUMA	$17,280	$12,432
Hong Kong	CASH	$556	$1,200
Italy	SIAE	$3,260	$18,000
Japan	JASRAC	$3,366	$12,000
Norway	TONO	$1,270	$1,850
South Africa	SAMRO	$1,450	$1,250
Spain	SGAE	$2,244	$6,780
Sweden	STIM	$5,670	$7,420
Switzerland	SUISA	$2,970	$3,200
Other Countries		$4,235	$8,525
Totals:		$170,381	$300,302

When the studio wants to use a pre-existing master recording, they would negotiate a fee (e.g., $50,000) for the nonexclusive right to use the master in the film for the worldwide period of copyright in the sound recording, as well as to reproduce the master for downloads, DVDs, Blu-ray, etc. for home use sale of the film and for the soundtrack album. An album royalty and screen credit would be negotiated, as well as the right to use the artist's name for advertising and other purposes.

As to pre-existing songs as well as newly written songs, the music publisher will usually license the U.S. mechanical rights to their songs for the minimum statutory rate of 9.1¢. If there are a large number of songs on the album, the record company may ask all song owners to agree to a maximum aggregate mechanical royalty cap on each physical record (e.g., from 11 to 14 compositions multiplied by either statutory or 75% of statutory) that would be divided equally among all songs, or a 75% statutory rate for each song.

TELEVISION COMMERCIALS PROMOTING THE FILM

Virtually all films use television commercials to advertise the theatrical release and to increase box office receipts. Although extremely expensive (with some marketing budgets running from ⅓ to ½ of a film's cost), this method of multimillion-dollar promotion is a necessity in today's marketplace. Payments are occasionally made for the use of songs in those commercials, but normally these rights are given without charge as part of the license to include the song in the film. The motion picture producer virtually always gets the right to include the "in context" use of the song in any trailers, television commercials, airline promos, or other advertising media. If, however, the song is being used differently than it was used in the film (for example, being used as thematic background throughout the entire commercial), additional fees are negotiated. Occasionally, a film producer will also use a song that is not in the motion picture as part of the advertising campaign for the film. In these cases, a fee of between $12,000 and more than $150,000 will usually be charged. Performance monies may also be available for television motion picture promo performances.

SHEET MUSIC FOLIOS

Motion picture songbooks continue to generate excellent sales, and classic movie songs such as "Happy," "The Way We Were," "My Heart Will Go On," "Moon River," "Mrs. Robinson," "Purple Rain," and "As Time Goes By" are contained in countless non–motion picture folios. Such theme folios generally earn royalties of between 10% and 20% of the retail selling price, with the aggregate amount divided equally among all copyrighted compositions. For example, if a particular book containing 50 songs had a retail selling price of $12.95, each song might receive 2.6¢ for each folio sold. If the folio concentrates on one film exclusively, there may be an additional royalty percentage paid (for example, an extra 5%, similar to a "personality folio" rate). Single sheet-music editions are also an important source of income and exposure for certain songs, as the number of different configurations that can be distributed by a knowledgeable print company are many and varied. For example, one print company successfully distributed an Oscar- and Grammy-winning song in versions for piano and voice, piano solo, easy piano, big-note piano, piano duet, organ solo, high voice and low voice, handbell choir, easy concert band, regular concert band, jazz ensemble, vocal solo with jazz ensemble, and chorus.

MOTION PICTURE SONGS IN COMMERCIALS

The advertising industry provides a very lucrative outlet for successful movie songs. Casablanca's "As Time Goes By" (a song made famous by its inclusion in a movie) has been used in the television advertising campaigns of countless products, including Ciara Perfume, AT&T's Personal Computers, and American Express. Other film songs used in commercials include the *Rocky* theme for United Healthcare, "Stayin' Alive" for Chick-fil-A, "Hungry Eyes" for Applebee's restaurants, "Car Wash" for American Express, "Love Story" for GE Profile Appliances, "The Pink Panther" for Heineken, "Born Free" for T-Mobile and Ragu Sauce, and "Help" for Mercury cars. If the writer and publisher license their composition through ASCAP, BMI, SESAC, or GMR for radio and television broadcasts of the commercial, additional royalties can be generated. And since commercials are now being included on home videos as well as in movie theaters and on mobile phones, another lucrative area is opening up for movie songs used in commercials.

ROYALTIES FROM MOTION PICTURE THEATERS

In most countries outside the United States, motion picture theaters are required to pay royalties to the local performing rights society (GEMA in Germany, SACEM in France, PRS for Music in England, SOCAN in Canada, APRA in Australia and New Zealand, JASRAC in Japan, IMRO in Ireland etc.) for the music used in films. The writer's share is then distributed by the foreign society to the writer's U.S. society, which will then pay the American composers and songwriters. The publisher's share of such fees is usually sent to the publisher's local representative or subpublisher in each foreign country. The subpublisher then remits the royalties (less its administrative percentage) to the American publisher. Royalties for music publishers who do not have foreign representatives are handled the same way as the writer's share of performance monies.

The fees (tariff) paid by movie theaters to foreign performing rights organizations are usually based on a percentage of the theater's box office receipts (from .02% to 3%, depending on the country), the number of seats in the theater, the number of screenings per week, as well as whether the theater is in the city or the country. Some countries also have a lump-sum minimum alternative payment to the percent tariff with others giving discounts to members of the local national cinema federation. In certain countries, the societies allocate shares of revenue to non-music rights-holders, such as scriptwriters. Most domestically produced motion pictures do not earn a great deal of money from theaters outside the United States, but for those songs contained in motion pictures with worldwide appeal the monies can be substantial. For example, blockbuster films can generate well over $750,000 in aggregate writer and music-publisher foreign theatrical royalties for all the music uses.

TELEVISION BROADCASTS OF THE MOTION PICTURE

Broadcasts of the movie on subscription or pay television, basic cable, pay per view, video on demand, audio visual streaming services, and over-the-air free television stations will generate performance royalties.

FILM SONGS USED IN TV PROGRAMS

Since many television series use well-known film songs either as background music or visual vocals, this area, because of the synchronization, video fees, and performance royalties, can be extremely valuable for the motion picture song. Some examples are "The Star Wars Theme" played as the finalists on *American Idol* go to see *Star Wars: Episode III*, "Footloose" sung on *Will & Grace*, "Moon River" from *Breakfast at Tiffany's* being sung by Peg Bundy while dancing with Al at an expensive restaurant in *Married with Children*; and "Over the Rainbow" (*The Wizard of Oz*) played at a high school reunion attended by Mulder and Scully in *The X-Files*.

FILM SONGS USED IN OTHER MOTION PICTURES

The inclusion of a film song in another motion picture allows that song to earn income in all the ways that apply to its original use. Some examples of motion picture songs used in other films include "Live and Let Die" in *Shrek the Third*, the score to "Hell's Angels" as background to scenes from the film's theatrical premiere in *The Aviator*, "Theme from 'A Summer Place'" played in the background as Julia Roberts and George Clooney talk in a casino in *Ocean's Eleven* and "Alfie" played in the background while Michael Douglas and Glenn Close have a drink in *Fatal Attraction*.

MISCELLANEOUS SOURCES OF INCOME

In addition to the areas previously mentioned, other sources of income for the motion picture song include off-Broadway, touring, and Broadway musicals such as *Frozen*, *Kinky Boots*, *Aladdin*, *The Producers*, *The Lion King*, and *Beauty and the Beast* (for a flat weekly fee or pro-rata sharing of a percentage of the weekly box office receipts); karaoke and sing-along (usually licensed at the statutory mechanical royalty rate with additional fees for the reproduction of lyrics); lyric reprints in magazines, novels, and nonfiction books (for a flat fee); published screenplays such as Woody Allen's *Hannah and Her Sisters*, which contained portions of the songs "The Way You Look Tonight" and "Bewitched" (normally for a flat fee); video jukeboxes (a small synchronization fee and a set penny rate per month for each machine); greeting cards (for a percentage of the wholesale price, a flat fee, or a set penny rate, with additional monies due if the music is played); computer, trivia, and board games (buy-outs, negotiated royalties or a percentage of the statutory mechanical rate depending on the timing of the song); recording artist videos (for a specific penny royalty, percentage of the wholesale price, or one-time buy-out fee); and interactive singing dolls and toys (licensed at a negotiated rate). In addition, another source of worldwide revenue is the use of movie themes as ringtones (e.g., "The Pink Panther Theme" and "Theme from Halloween").

DRAMATIZING A SONG INTO A MOTION PICTURE OR TELEVISION PROGRAM

On occasion, if the story line of a composition is strong, or the subject matter unique, there might be interest by a producer, a third party, or one of the copyright owners to try to turn the song into a motion picture or television production. In these cases, the agreement to secure the necessary rights is usually structured as an option agreement with various payments triggered upon the achievement of certain specified events or criteria. The following will summarize some of the approaches in this area; an area which can be extremely valuable if, in fact, the motion picture or television vehicle is actually produced and commercially distributed.

Initial Option Period and Extensions. In most cases, the interested producer (which can be a music publisher or songwriter or other third party who believes in the viability of the project) will receive an option to purchase the necessary motion picture, television, and other ancillary rights for a set amount of money which is normally nonrecoupable. This initial period can last for a period of months or years depending on the bargaining power of the parties. The rights granted by the option will be exclusive and will many times be for a period of one year.

There will usually be an option to extend the duration of the initial exclusive period for an additional period of time (e.g., six months, one year, etc.) for the payment of an additional fee to the copyright owner of the composition, which is, in most cases, the music publisher. There also may be an additional payment, sometimes called a "setup bonus," if the owner of the option is able to receive an initial commitment from a film company, television production company, or broadcast/cable entity with such bonus being paid upon commencement of the script or upon the optioning of the "spec script" by a producer or other party.

Purchase Price. Once a firm commitment has been secured from a film or television company and the project is going ahead, the producer will exercise its option to acquire the property and will pay the copyright owner(s) of the composition the purchase price.

The purchase price will usually be structured with different price points dependent on the type of project going forward. For example, there may be a set price depending on whether the production is a theatrical motion picture, a made-for-TV film, or a television series, with further monetary distinctions made if the broadcaster is a network, cable, or Internet streaming service. In this regard, the payment is many times made at the start of principal photography of the project.

Rights Granted. The primary exclusive rights granted will be those related to the creation and production of an initial motion picture or television program, as well as any allied rights throughout the world or universe. The rights granted will also include the right to produce additional film or television programs based on the composition or original production and will include the rights to use all characters, story lines, dialogue, and scenes.

In addition, the producer will receive the right to utilize the composition as the theme to the project (e.g., opening or closing credits) as well as in the project as the producer elects. Other rights granted include, but may not be limited to, broadcast, transmission, exhibition and distribution, advertising and promotion, merchandise derived from the project and the right to use the title of the composition.

Synchronization Fees. If the project goes forward, there will be synchronization fees payable to the music publisher (and songwriter) if the composition is actually utilized in the film or television series. In most cases, the actual fees will be spelled out in the agreement (rather than in a "to be negotiated in good faith" clause) with set dollar amounts on an episode-by-episode basis if a television series and a one-time payment if a motion picture or made-for-TV movie. In context and out-of-context promo uses (such as trailers, advertising, etc.) will also be negotiated.

Profit Participation. If the project is a movie or series, there can be profit participation based on the adjusted gross income of the producer. The participation percentage is usually not large (e.g., 2%–5%) with an important part of the negotiation being the definition of "adjusted gross" revenue and how it is calculated, an area which is complex and which has created a certain amount of litigation.

Television Episode Royalties. In addition to the synchronization fee for each episode using the composition, there will also be a so-called rights fee, which recognizes the underlying dramatization rights to the composition, for each episode produced and broadcast.

Consultancy Fees. In some agreements, the music publisher and/or songwriter may be guaranteed a consultancy fee. For a television series, this would be on an episode basis and for a film, it may be a one-time fee.

Spin-Offs, Remakes, Prequels, and Sequels. If there is a spin-off, remake, prequel, or sequel made by the producer, there will be additional fees payable to cover compensation for these additional projects based in some way on the contents of the original production. For example, the purchase price payment, episode rights royalty, and profit participation might be structured between 25% and 50% (but can be more) of the amounts paid for the original project; the actual amount being negotiable, depending on the bargaining power of the parties.

Other Clauses. There will also be provisions with respect to assignment, warranties, representations, and indemnities, as well as error and omissions (E&O) coverage for the music publisher and writer under the producer's policy.

Long Form Agreement. Since the initial document is many times a short form agreement (3 to 5 pages), there will be language which provides that the parties intend to negotiate a long form agreement in good faith but with the understanding that the signed short form will be a binding agreement between the parties.

MOTION PICTURE UNDERSCORE

A spaceship approaches Pandora and the land of the Na'vi.

The Hobbits journey through Middle-earth to destroy the One Ring.

A young wizard on his magical broomstick triumphs in a bewitched Quidditch match.

A great white shark slides through a seemingly peaceful, moonlit ocean.

The indestructible ocean liner collides with an iceberg.

A young boy and a small alien take off into the sky on a bicycle.

All the above scenes are good by themselves, but they have been made memorable because of the music associated with them. They are prime examples of underscore fulfilling its purpose. Whether the score is dramatic, soothing, romantic, comedic, or foreboding, it is a part of the fabric of any motion picture.

The world of the feature film underscore composer is not only one of the most creatively stimulating and financially rewarding areas of music, it is also one of the most demanding in terms of musical expertise and training, conducting experience, and discipline in the meeting of rigorous deadlines. It is also a business where multimillion-dollar investments as well as the professional lives of all those involved in a motion picture wait in hopeful expectation at the end of the filmmaking process for the magic of the musical score—the glue that holds much of the motion picture together.

HISTORY OF THE FIELD

During the early to middle years of Hollywood (the 1930s through 1950s), the great names of orchestral scoring included Erich Korngold (*The Adventures of Robin Hood*), Franz Waxman (*Sunset Boulevard*), Max Steiner (*Gone with the Wind*), Alfred Newman (*Wuthering Heights*), Bernard Herrmann (*Citizen Kane*), Miklos Rozsa (*Ben Hur*), and Dimitri Tiomkin (*High Noon*). In addition, many of the great names of the pop and musical theater world of the time (the Gershwins, Cole Porter, Jerome Kern, Harry Warren, Johnny Mercer) were also involved with songs for film as well as scores.

Commencing with the 1960s and continuing into the 2000s, a new era of giants emerged on the scene, including John Williams, Henry Mancini, James Horner, Alex North, Elmer Bernstein, Maurice Jarre, Jerry Goldsmith, Bill Conti, Ennio Morricone, James Newton Howard, Howard Shore, Alan Silvestri and Hans Zimmer, among others. Of this new generation of composers, many were classically trained and able to conduct symphony orchestras as well as arrange and orchestrate for any type of musical instrument under the sun. Others achieved scoring success after making the transition from the pop music world. This latter category of writers includes, among others, Trent Reznor of Nine Inch Nails (*Girl With the Dragon Tattoo*, *The Social Network*), Johnny Greenwood of Radiohead (*There Will Be Blood*, *The Master*, *Phantom Thread*), Randy Newman (*Meet the Fockers*, *Toy Story 2*), Stewart Copeland of the Police (*Wall Street*, *Rumblefish*), Danny Elfman of Oingo Boingo (*Batman*, *Spider-Man*), Karen O of Yeah, Yeah, Yeahs (*Where the Wild Things Are*), Mark Knopfler of Dire Straits (*The Princess Bride*) and Marc Shaiman (*A Few Good Men*, *Sleepless in Seattle*). Still others are composers who work in both the symphonic world and the movie world (e.g., John Corigliano, Elliot Goldenthal, and Tan Dun) and others such as Michael Giacchino (*Lost*, *Medal of Honor*, *Call of Duty*) come from the television and video game world.

THE FEATURE FILM SCORE CONTRACT

The contract that a composer signs with a major studio or independent production company is standard in some areas yet completely negotiable in others. Three of the primary factors affecting whether a standard or nonstandard contract is finally settled upon are the stature and past success of the composer, the size of the music budget, and the knowledge, power, and stature of the composer's agent negotiating the deal. The following clauses form the basis of any scoring contract in the world of movies.

Summary of Basic Provisions. The basic areas covered in every motion picture scoring contract relate to the types of services to be performed by the composer, the length of time during which they are to be completed, the fee for those services, how that fee is to be paid, transportation and living expenses, screen as well as all types of advertising credit, the ownership of the copyright, composer, and artist royalties for uses of the music outside of the film, and the handling of performing rights payments.

Composer Services. The scorer is hired to compose all of the underscore music (and in some cases, individual songs) for the film as well as to arrange and orchestrate the score; to conduct an orchestra to record the work; to produce, supervise, and edit the recording of the score; and to deliver the final, fully edited and mixed master recording in accordance with the film's post-production schedule. Additionally, the composer is required to consult with the producer of the film not only on the recording budget but also on the placement of the music in the motion picture and the "feel" that the music should have.

Starting and Completion Dates. Although the time frame allowed a composer to create the score for a film varies depending on whether the composer is involved in the film from inception (rare), involved in the film commencing with the post-production period (the norm), or involved with the film as a replacement for another composer whose score has been thrown out by the producer at the last minute, the standard amount of time allotted composers to compose and record a full background score for a major film ranges between four and 12 weeks. Factors affecting the time frame include the amount of music needed as well as the complexity of the instrumentation desired. The actual duration of many contracts, however, can be significantly shorter if the picture is behind schedule, over budget, or being released sooner than the studio originally planned. Any of these factors can compress all post-production aspects of the film (composing, recording, editing, dubbing, sound effects, etc.) and can force a composer to "spot," score, and record a major motion picture in a two- to three-week period. These post-production "crunches" are particularly true for summer and Christmas releases—the two times of the year when the film studios jockey for position for success in the peak ticket-buying seasons. Although the "duration of services" clause will vary based on the particular studio or production company contract being used, the following clauses are representative:

EXAMPLE 1. "Composer shall commence services on January 4, and complete all of the services as expeditiously as possible in accordance with the post-production schedule of the movie." This clause is somewhat open-ended, and the writer must stay aware of the film's post-production schedule in order to write, record, and deliver the master recording on time.

EXAMPLE 2. "Services are to be commenced on the 'spotting date' of the picture and completed within 12 consecutive weeks from that date." This contract gives the composer a definite period of time in which to write and record the score.

EXAMPLE 3. "Services to be commenced upon the signing of the Composer-Production Company agreement with delivery to the Producer of the complete recorded score, the original manuscripts of the score, and all musical orchestrations and arrangements of the score, by no later than [date]." The time allotted to composing and recording the score in this type of contract depends on the date the contract is signed versus the "no later than" delivery date arrangement.

It is also important to include in these contracts a provision that covers the composer's compensation if the producer requires his or her services beyond the specific number of weeks set forth in the agreement. For example, a contract might specify "$10,000 a week in additional compensation."

Composing Fees and Packages. The composing fees paid to a feature film composer vary considerably, depending on the past success and stature of the composer; the amount of music needed in the film; the type of music required (electronic, orchestral or both); the total budget for the film; the total music budget, including the cost for licensing pre-existing outside songs or master recordings; whether the film producer is a major studio, a major independent, or a minor player in the film world; the size of the orchestra needed to record the score; whether the composer is contracting to bear all or most of the costs of music (a package) or only negotiating the composing fee; whether the film is intended for wide distribution or only a limited release; the standard fees paid by a particular studio versus the fees of other studios; and the skills of the individuals on both sides of the negotiation fence—the studio and the composer's agent. Depending on many of the above factors, composing fees can range from $10,000 for a lower-budget film to in excess of $1,500,000 for a big-budget studio release using the services of a well-known composer.

The following examples illustrate three variations of composer compensation:

EXAMPLE 1. $105,000 payable as follows:
1. $35,000 upon the signing of the contract or the commencement of spotting (i.e., the composer, director, producer, and music supervisor watch the film and discuss where the music should be).
2. $35,000 upon the commencement of the recording of the motion picture score.
3. $35,000 upon completion of all composer services as well as timely delivery of the master recording to the producer. The master recording has to be acceptable to the producer.

EXAMPLE 2. $1,100,000 payable as follows:
1. $350,000 upon commencement of services;
2. $350,000 upon commencement of the recording;
3. $390,000 upon completion of all services and delivery of the master;
4. $10,000 upon execution of the agreement.
5. Orchestration to be paid separately at $80.00 per page.

EXAMPLE 3. Combination fee plus package totaling $650,000 payable as follows:
1. $150,000 upon commencement of services;
2. $150,000 upon completion of the recording;
3. $150,000 upon completion of services and delivery and acceptance of the master;
4. $50,000 upon execution of the agreement and;
5. $150,000 as an electronic package fee.

One of the considerations that dictates the amount of the fee negotiated in the composer-studio contract is whether the composer is assuming responsibility for all costs of his or her efforts, or is solely contracting for composing and conducting services. If one is contracting for the whole package, all items that the composer is agreeing to furnish (as well as all exclusions) should be specifically spelled out in the contract in order to prevent situations where the composer ends up losing money because of unknown (at the time of signing) or significantly higher costs of some of the undertakings. Some obvious items that should be excluded include the licensing cost of any music not written by the composer, any reuse, new use, or supplemental market fees and other residual type payments generated under union agreements, any rescoring or re-recording costs required for creative reasons, after the delivery of the master recording, that are outside the control of the composer and lyricist and vocalist expenses. Items covered under the package may include, without limitation, costs of musicians, instruments, programmers and samplers, mixing and sweetening costs, conductors, orchestrators, copyists, payroll taxes, studio costs, tape, IATSE costs, arrangers, and all related costs for the electronic and orchestral portions of the work, among other items.

These "all in" package deals should not be taken by any composer inexperienced in budgets and music production costs. They are attractive though to some film companies and do provide composers new to the film field with an opportunity to break into the business, in addition to providing knowledgeable scorers with an opportunity for fees not within the capacity of other scorers. A composer package of $75,000 "all in" for a lower-budget quality film may generate only a minimal profit to a composer, but it does accomplish the goal of achieving a feature film credit.

Box Office/Award Bonus Provisions. Occasionally, based on the stature of the composer, or in cases of limited composing and music budgets, particularly in the independent film area, bonus provisions involving domestic and foreign box office results as well as composer award nominations are sometimes able to be negotiated.

For example, if the film were to gross $75, $100, $150, $200, and $250 million dollars in U.S. domestic box office receipts, the composer would be paid an additional $150,000 upon reaching each level. Or if the film were to reach $200, $300, or $400 million in worldwide grosses, the composer would be paid an additional $75,000 at each level. For independent features, you would negotiate significantly lower gross receipts and composer payments. For example, the receipts might start at $10 or $20 million domestic gross receipts and move up from there.

On the award front, you might have an award bonus provision of $20,000 if the score is nominated for a Golden Globe or Academy Award with an additional amount allocated for a marketing campaign prior to the final results. Winning the award could generate an additional fee.

Screen Credit. The type and placement of screen credit for a composer is a negotiable item. A separate card will usually read "Music by [the composer's name]." The credit can be in the main titles and of the same size as the star, the producer, writer of the screenplay, or director, or it can be at the end of the film in a size somewhat less than the other principals. Most well-known composers are able to negotiate the inclusion of their names in all paid advertising (newspapers, magazines, etc.), as well as on soundtrack albums and all printed publications (sheet music, song folios, songbooks, etc.). Most contracts normally exclude the composer's name in all advertising of the movie on screen, radio, or television, any special advertising or award or congratulatory ads (e.g., the star gets nominated for an Academy Award and the studio takes out an ad in the *Hollywood Reporter* or *Daily Variety*), or any teaser advertising.

Somewhat related to this provision is the "name and likeness" clause, which gives the motion picture producer the right to use the composer's name, likeness, and biographical information for the advertising, exploitation, distribution, and exhibition of the film throughout the world for all time. A number of "proven success" composers are able to dictate that likenesses and biographical material must be approved by the composer before any use by the film company.

Songs/Publishing/Masters. If the composer is asked to write a song separate from the score or asked to expand an existing cue to a full length song, additional compensation should be negotiated. In cases where lyrics are being added to existing score, normally no additional compensation is paid. A portion of the music publishing, in appropriate situations, should be negotiated for.

In cases of low fee/low budget independent films, negotiations are sometimes conducted whereby the composer not only gets rights to the publishing but also ownership of the masters. The composer would, of course, grant all the necessary rights the filmmaker needed to distribute the film worldwide and in any media forever.

Amount of Music. Many contracts do not specify the total number of minutes of score that a composer must write. These contracts assume certain durational amounts typical of feature films and leave it to the composer and producer to determine at the spotting session how much music is to be written and where it is to be placed in the picture. A sample clause might read, "The Composer contracts to compose, conduct, etc. all of the original music required by the Producer." Other contracts, however, actually specify a minimum number of minutes of music to be scored. "Composer agrees that the Score shall contain a minimum of thirty (30) minutes of original music" or "the music shall be approximately sixty (60) minutes in length and shall be of a high-quality and professional nature" illustrate two examples of such clauses.

Exclusivity. Most film agreements state that the composer's services are nonexclusive but on a 1st priority basis for most of the engagement with exclusivity during a portion of the term normally during recording until completion. Other agreements specify the services as exclusive during the entire term.

Transportation and Expenses. Most composers either live or have accommodations in the cities where the primary movie production and recording facilities are located. For certain motion pictures, though, the producer will require the composer to travel. The following examples of "transportation and expenses" clauses give a feel for what is possible in this area.

EXAMPLE 1. "$1,500 a week while away from Los Angeles for hotel, meals, local transportation, and phone (accommodations and expenses), as well as first-class round-trip transportation for the Composer and spouse."

EXAMPLE 2. "Studio shall furnish Composer reasonable living expenses while on site in the amount of $1,000 per week. Such amount is provided on a nonaccountable basis and is in lieu of company furnishing composer's meals, lodging, and other normal living expenses. For any period of less than one week, the weekly rate will be prorated."

EXAMPLE 3. "Round-trip coach class transportation plus the cost of reasonable lodging and meals."

Ownership of the Copyright. Practically all score agreements are employee-for-hire or work-made-for-hire agreements; that is, the musical score is created at the specific request of and under the direct supervision of the film producer. For the all-inclusive composing and services fee, the composer "grants to the producer all rights, title, and interest throughout the world in perpetuity, in and to the work and the recordings." By this grant, the producer owns the worldwide copyright for the entire term of copyright protection. Under an employee-for-hire contract, the producer (the movie studio or production company) becomes the author pursuant to the U.S. Copyright Law and the composer does not have the right to recapture the U.S. copyright at the end of the 35- to 40-year period provided for under that law. Any specific rights to the music that the composer may retain must be stated in writing and signed by all parties.

The typical grant-of-rights provision signed by composers gives the studio the exclusive right to publish the composition, to make and sell sound recordings, to execute all licenses regarding the use of the work, to change the work, to combine the work with other works, and to transmit the work by any means now available or to be available in the future. Through this grant, the studio becomes the owner of all rights of copyright and is usually free to assign or license those rights to others. This clause is normally of the broadest nature possible, and it is not unusual to see the inclusion of phrases such as "all other rights of any nature whatsoever," "perpetual and unlimited rights," or "any rights throughout the entire universe whether now or hereafter existing" in the film scoring contract. Employee-for-hire agreements are very different from standard songwriter-publisher agreements, where the songwriter assigns the copyright to the publisher but retains the right to recapture the U.S. copyright at the end of 35 or 40 years.

The primary composer compensation rights, in addition to the composing and services fee, set forth in most score contracts include all or most of the royalties as set forth in the standard songwriter agreement, including the right to receive performance royalties from domestic and foreign performing right organizations, mechanical royalties, sheet music and folio royalties, foreign royalties, and synchronization royalties.

Membership in a Performing Rights Organization (PRO). The composer must be a member in good standing of a performing rights society as well as any other applicable labor organization, guild, or union that may have jurisdiction.
There are more than 100 performing right societies in the world, with two of the largest, ASCAP and BMI, located in the United States. For U.S. composers, the contract will state either ASCAP, BMI, SESAC, or GMR, depending on the writer's membership or affiliation. For foreign society composers (e.g., PRS for Music, SOCAN, SACEM, APRA, IMRO, SIAE, GEMA, etc.), the decision as to whether the film score is licensed in the United States by ASCAP, BMI, SESAC, or GMR is usually based on the composer's preference, and contracts involving foreign composers should be clear on this point. Performing right societies provide to most screen composers the bulk of their life-of-copyright income, and it is essential that a screen composer maintain a membership in a performing rights organization.

In recent years, the performing rights clause in film and television scoring contracts has undergone some major changes due to pressure from the U.S. television networks, the local television industry, and the cable television industry as well as audio visual streaming services. Although the clause specifically states that "the composer shall receive the writer's share of royalties for public performances of the score and musical compositions," additional provisions have been added to many film and television scoring agreements to address the scenario of what happens if "a broadcasting station (or other user) does not have a current valid license agreement with ASCAP, BMI, SESAC, or GMR" "if it is unlawful for the performing right society to issue a license," or "if a network, local, or cable television station requires a direct license of the public performing rights."

Many of these "what if" clauses initially left it to the producer to negotiate the performing right fees without specific compensation to the composer. More recent variations of the clause provide that the producer and composer shall negotiate "in good faith" the performing right payment in the event that licensing does not occur under the auspices of ASCAP, BMI, SESAC, or GMR. The main result of many of these clauses, if they become effective, is that the composer will not receive any continuing performance royalties other than the initial composing fee as well as the possibility of some "good faith" negotiated fees in the future. If a composer is going to agree to such a clause, he or she should at least try to negotiate a fee of 50% of whatever the motion picture company negotiates, plus some type of specific dollar figure as a continuing performance royalty payment for all future television and all other types of broadcast uses. As the foreign performing rights area is one of the film composer's most important sources of income, any clause should also be clear as to how these royalties would be handled. Legal advice is recommended for anyone negotiating this type of clause.

Disposition of the Score. The producer has no obligation to accept the finished score, to use the score in the picture, to promote or exploit it, to release it on a soundtrack album, or even to release the picture. Further, the producer may request certain changes, deletions, or additions to the finished score prior to accepting it. If these changes are requested because the composer did not consult with the producer on the score or because the score is technically deficient in any way, then the composer pays the cost of the changes. In almost all other cases, the producer pays the cost for any such requested changes.

It is rare for a producer or director to throw out a fully written score because the producer or director doesn't like it or it doesn't fit the picture, but such circumstances do occasionally happen even for major composers. When it does occur, the original composer may be allowed to revise the original score or come up with a new score, or the producer may hire another composer to write and record an entirely new score. Even if the initial composer's score is not used in the picture, he or she does get paid for the work that is completed. Obviously, the composer's reputation and possible future work could be jeopardized by a producer's rejection of a score, and composers usually try to accede to the producer's thoughts and ideas throughout the entire post-production process.

Warranties. The warranty clause states that the composer is free to enter into the agreement, that the music will be entirely original, that the composer's services and skills are unique and of the highest caliber, and that he or she can grant all rights in the music (including the copyright) to the film's producer. Under the re-recording restriction clause, the composer agrees not to conduct, produce recordings, or re-record the motion picture score for anyone else for a stated period of time (three to five years normally) commencing from the date of the delivery of the score and master recordings to the producer. The warranty clause and re-recording clause assure the producer not only that the body of work being contracted for is free from plagiarism but also that the composer is prevented from making recordings of the score for other companies that could be in competition with the producer's recording of the score.

Instructions and Requests of the Producer. The composer agrees to comply with all of the producer's reasonable instructions and requests, to compose the score to the best of his or her ability, and to consult with the producer as to the style, content, and all other elements of the score. In addition, the composer agrees to meet with the producer or the producer's representatives for approval of the recording budget. All costs of the recording are the producer's responsibility and not the composer's. If the composer contracts to assume some or all costs of the recording and other music costs, the contract will specifically set forth all of the areas covered by the composer's "all in" fee.

The amount of instruction and direction given to the composer depends on the filmmaker. Some producers are "hands on" individuals who give very specific instructions as to where music should go and what it should feel like. Other producers look to the composer to capture the filmmaker's view as set forth in the discussions at the spotting session.

Suspensions and Terminations. The producer has the right to suspend the running of time of the composer's agreement based on disability, force majeure, or default. Although these are negotiable items and vary by contract, there are certain industry standards and definitions in effect.

Disability. The composer's ability to compose or perform services is interfered with because of the composer's mental, physical, or other disability.

Force Majeure. The preparation, production, or completion of a film is interrupted owing to reasons beyond the producer's control: fire, accidents, weather, labor disputes, acts of God, laws or governmental orders, shortages or an inability to obtain materials or labor, and the death or disability of a principal member of the cast or the director are a few such reasons.

Default. The composer's failure, refusal, or neglect to compose or perform any of the duties set forth in the composer's agreement with the producer.

In order for a producer to suspend a composer, some contracts specify that written notice be given to the composer within a specified period of time (e.g., one week) after the reason for suspension occurs. Other contracts, however, have no specific notice requirement, and a suspension is deemed to be in effect if a default or disability continues for a certain number of days. In a force majeure situation, the producer will notify the composer of the suspension, and the contract will remain in abeyance until the production again commences. During the suspension, no fees are paid to the composer and he or she must be ready to report to work when the film resumes production. In cases of the composer's disability or default, the suspension ends at such time as the composer reports to the producer for work, provided he or she is physically able to work or has cured the default.

The producer can terminate the composer's employment for any composer default, for any composer disability that lasts for more than _____ weeks, or if a force majeure lasts for _____ consecutive weeks. The composer, on the other hand, can terminate the agreement if he or she receives no compensation for a consecutive period of _____ weeks due to a force majeure. The composer must give written notice to the producer, and the contract is terminated unless compensation is resumed within a specified period of time.

Morality Clause. The composer must conduct himself in a manner consistent with public conventions and morals and shall not commit any act that would prejudice the producer or the entertainment industry. This clause, a remnant of the 1930's film industry, still remains in one form or another in many film contracts, despite its broadness and vagueness.

Orchestration. The costs of orchestration are either included in the "composer services" provision or excluded. If at all possible, orchestration costs should be excluded from the overall composing and conducting fee, as it is a "wild card" sum that can be a very low four-figure number or a five-figure surprise. For example, if a composer negotiates a $75,000 services fee and then learns at the spotting session that the producer wants a 60-piece orchestra rather than a small ensemble, the costs of arranging for an entire orchestra as well as the copying of all of the individual instrument parts can be prohibitively expensive. The best advice to any composer or representative is to keep this figure as a separately paid item and not as an open part of the services fee. For example, a clause might read that the "Producer shall hire a third party orchestrator at a rate of $80 a page."

Infringements. In the event that any infringement or other claim is made against the producer or the publisher in regard to the musical score, any monies payable to the composer shall be withheld until a final determination is made as to the claim. Occasionally, the monies withheld must be in an amount that is consistent with the claim (e.g., if a claim is for $10,000, the producer can withhold only up to $10,000). Sometimes a clause is negotiated to provide that if the person making the claim does not file suit within a specified period of time (e.g., one year) after the claim letter is received or bond posted, all monies withheld by the producer must be released to the composer.

Notices and Governing Law. All notices, payments, statements, or other documents are made in writing and are sent either by personal delivery, telegram, email, fax, or registered or certified mail. The laws of the relevant state govern the agreement, and any modifications or changes in the agreement must be in writing and signed by all the parties.

Assignment. The producer can assign the entire agreement, at any time, to any party. The composer, on the other hand, cannot assign or transfer any part of the agreement without the written consent of the producer. On occasion, the producer will allow the composer to assign his or her royalties (e.g., as collateral for a bank loan), but the composer is never allowed to assign the actual composing services to another party. On the other hand, the composer may request that the producer remain liable for any continuing obligations (e.g., royalty payments derived from exploitation of the score) even though the agreement has been assigned to another company—a request that is usually not accepted by the producer.

Summary Composer Deals. The following two composer deals should help in putting a "full deal" into context.

1. "A" list composer "non-package" fee deal combined with an "electronic package"

Composer is hired to compose, orchestrate, conduct and arrange an original score to be completed in 10 weeks. Services to be on a nonexclusive first priority basis except during the recording session where they will be exclusive.

Composing fee will be $800,000 payable $250,000 upon commencement of services; $250,000 upon the completion of recording; $250,000 upon completion of all services; and $50,000 upon execution of the formal agreement. In addition, the Composer will receive an electronics package fee of $200,000 payable $100,000 upon commencement and $100,000 upon completion of the electronic aspects of the score. If the term of services extends beyond 10 weeks due to causes beyond the composer's control, an additional $100,000 weekly pro-rated fee will be paid. Finally, $20,000 will be paid for the music for one song separate from the score.

Producer further agrees to pay $10,000 if the score receives an Academy Award or Golden Globe nomination and an additional $15,000 if it wins either award. Further if the domestic box office of the film reaches $150, $200, and $300 million dollars (or alternatively $300, $400 and $600 million in worldwide receipts) an additional $100,000 will be paid at each plateau level.

Screen credit will be on a separate card in the opening titles with credit in all paid ads subject to customary exclusions. Use of the music in any unrelated film or in a video game will require additional compensation to be negotiated in good faith. Standard song writer royalties as well as a 10% artist and 4% producer royalty is attached as Schedule A.

Further, the final agreement will contain additional terms and conditions as have been established as precedent for Composer or are typical in composer agreements for other composers of similar stature as Composer.

2. Composer "package" deal for low budget independent feature film

Producer employs [Name of Composer] to compose, conduct, and arrange an original score for the motion picture [Title of Film] and to record, produce and deliver "film mixes" to the Producer as well as "record mixes satisfactory for inclusion in a possible soundtrack album. In addition, the Composer is to write one original song satisfactory to the producer and deliver a song master. The Term will commence on the "spotting session" date and continue until completion of all services reasonably required by the producer. The composer agrees to comply with the producer's reasonable requests and instructions and the services will be on a "nonexclusive first priority basis" except for the period commencing the recording sessions through the "mix down" of the score per the picture's post production schedule where they will be "exclusive."

The deal is a "package" where the composer will pick up the costs of most of the music recording and production, excluding the costs of licensing outside music, travel and living expenses, lyricists and vocalists, "reuse" and "new use" supplemental market fees, among other items. The fee will be $60,000 payable $20,000 upon commencement of services; $25,000 upon completion and delivery to the satisfaction of the producer and $15,000 upon execution of the formal agreement and certificate of authorship. An additional $10,000 will be paid for the "song" package payable promptly upon the delivery of the master satisfactory to producer and the publishing will be split 50/50.

Songwriter/composer royalties as well as artist/producer soundtrack royalties are set forth in Exhibit A and the producer agrees to pay the composer an additional $20,000 when the film reaches $20 and $40 million dollars respectively in U.S. box office receipts.

The work shall be a "work made for hire" and the composer waives all "moral rights." In addition, screen credit of "Music by [Name of Composer]" will be on a single frame in the opening credits with the composer agreeing not to re-record the score for anyone other than producer for a period of 5 years except with producer's written consent. Any music composed for the film and not used will revert to the Composer.

SOURCES OF INCOME: THE UNDERSORE COMPOSER

The various sources of income for the composer of the underscore are listed in Table 8.5.

SOURCES OF INCOME: THE UNDERSCORE
Table 8.5

$250,000	Composing, arranging, and conducting fee
$200,000	Foreign theatrical and other performance royalties for a major box office film (first year)
$18,000	Initial U.S. cable television run (multiple broadcasts) over one year
$8,500	Network television broadcast of the film (50 minutes of music)
$45,000	U.S. and foreign television performances of the film (five-year period)
$45,500	Soundtrack album (U.S. mechanical royalties for 100,000 units sold and 10 tracks)
$$567,000	Total composer fees and royalties

COMPOSING, ARRANGING, AND CONDUCTING FEE
When a motion picture company commissions a composer to write music for a film, factors affecting the fee paid include the overall budget of the film; the budget for all music uses (underscore, new songs, pre-existing songs, record company and recording artist fees); the amount of score needed for the film and whether it is electronic, orchestral, or both; the size of the orchestra required; whether the composer is undertaking a "package deal" or contracting only for the composing, arranging, and conducting; whether the film is produced by a major company and intended for large-scale distribution or is scheduled for only limited theatrical release; the composer's past film credits and successes; the stature and bargaining power of the composer's agent; and whether the composer is able to retain a portion of the copyright to the score and publisher's share of income for his or her own publishing company.

Although the composer's fees vary depending on the many factors listed, the following represent some ranges for motion picture fees and packages in various scenarios:

1. "A" level composer: $750,000 to $1,000,000 plus fee. Separate package fee of $100,000–$200,000 for electronic elements of the score (if applicable).
2. Midrange successful composer: $300,000–$500,000 fee for a major studio film plus electronic package of $20,000–$30,000 (if applicable).

3. Entry level composer for a major studio film: $100,000–$250,000 fee.

4. Independent and low budget features: $10,000–$50,000.

5. Packages can range from $300,000 to well over $1,500,000 depending on the mix of electronic and orchestral elements. For independent features, $100,000–$300,000 would be a representative range for package deals.

FOREIGN THEATRICAL AND OTHER PERFORMANCE ROYALTIES

The fees received from foreign performing right societies constitute one of the largest sources of income for U.S. film composers (see Table 8.6 for an example of the kind of money that can be generated from a successful film). As U.S. films remain exceptionally popular in foreign countries, the total license fees collected by these societies for U.S. composers are substantial. The top countries for film income include the United Kingdom, Italy, France, Germany, the Netherlands, Japan, and Australia. Two of the biggest movie box office countries, China and India, produce minimal composer foreign royalties.

THE COMPOSER'S FOREIGN PERFORMING RIGHTS ROYALTIES FOR THE INITIAL RELEASE YEAR OF A MAJOR BOX OFFICE FILM

Table 8.6

Country	Society	Composer's Foreign Royalties in USD
Australia	APRA	$20,000
Austria	AKM	$800
Belgium	SABAM	$1,250
Canada	SOCAN	$4,100
England	PRS	$32,500
Finland	TEOSTO	$850
France	SACEM	$75,125
Germany	GEMA	$38,010
Holland	BUMA	$800
Hong Kong	CASH	$1,480

Italy	SIAE	$48,265
Japan	JASRAC	$3,250
Norway	TONO	$1,210
South Africa	SAMRO	$650
Spain	SGAE	$3,950
Sweden	STIM	$4,250
Switzerland	SUISA	$4,100
Other Countries		$12,500
Total:		$253,090

To appreciate the size of these performance monies and how they translate into substantial dollars for U.S. film composers, a brief analysis of the English society (PRS for Music) should be of interest. PRS, founded in 1914 and covering the United Kingdom, and many Commonwealth countries, had total 2016 revenues of £626 million and distributed approximately £528 million, after payment of operating costs, to composers, lyricists, songwriters, and music publishers. In the United Kingdom alone, PRS collected £9.8 million from cinemas, with much of that money going to U.S. film composers through distribution from PRS to ASCAP, BMI, SESAC, and GMR.

As to the monies paid to composers, songwriters, and publishers for showings of a movie in foreign movie theaters, some of the formulas used by foreign performing right organizations include fees based on a percentage of revenue from ticket sales, a fee based upon occupied seats, a percentage of net receipts, a percentage of gross box office receipts, a lump-sum payment for smaller theaters, a percentage of gross box office receipts with a guaranteed minimum payment, a country versus urban theater calculation, and a seating capacity of the theater taking into account the ticket price, among others. Though the licensing formulas vary by country, a rough guide is 1% of the box office of foreign country movie theaters. Bear in mind that many foreign societies take off both administrative/operating costs as well as, in many cases, social and cultural deductions prior to forwarding any theater monies to the U.S. performing right societies, deductions that can be substantial.

To put the timing of foreign royalty distributions into perspective, Table 8.7 illustrates the U.S. payment dates from one U.S. society for the score of a 2017 film that played in many foreign movie theaters.

U.S. DISTRIBUTION OF FOREIGN MONEY FOR A 2017 FEATURE FILM RELEASED IN MANY FOREIGN COUNTRIES

Table 8.7

Country	U.S. Distribution Dates
Argentina	August 2018, February 2019
Australia	November 2017, February, May, August 2018
Britain	November 2017, February, May, August 2018
Canada	February, May, August, November 2018
Denmark	February, August, November 2018
France	February, May, November 2018
Germany	February, August, November 2018
Italy	August 2018, February 2019
Netherlands	August, November 2017, February, May 2018
Sweden	August, November 2017, February, May 2018
Spain	February, August 2018
Switzerland	November 2017

The foreign monies that can be earned by film composers many times surpass all of the writer income that is received from all types of U.S. performances. These monies are earned regardless of how well a film has performed at the box office in the U.S., as many a domestic box office failure has generated in excess of $100,000 in writer foreign performance royalties. Blockbuster films have been known to generate in excess of $1,000,000 in foreign theatrical royalties alone.

In the United States, ASCAP, BMI, SESAC, and GMR do not license movie theaters for the music used in films. This nonlicensing status of U.S. theaters was the result of the 1948 Alden Rochelle court decision, which ruled against ASCAP's practice of licensing movie theaters as well as the then-exclusive nature of ASCAP writer and publisher agreements. Although the decision only affected ASCAP, BMI agreed to be bound by the judgment, and henceforth no U.S. movie theater has paid performance royalties for the performance of music in films, despite the Alden Rochelle licensing objections having been corrected many decades ago. The nonlicensing status of the music in films when shown in movie theaters is set forth in both the ASCAP Articles of Association as well as the ASCAP Consent Decree and the affiliation Agreements of BMI and SESAC.

U.S. CABLE, NETWORK, AND LOCAL TELEVISION PERFORMANCES

The largest source of continuing royalty income for most score composers is the quarterly performance payments received from ASCAP, BMI, SESAC, and GMR. Motion picture composers can and have earned well in excess of $500,000 in television performance royalties for a single successful film over the full term of copyright. And even if a film is not a success at the box office, substantial television performance earnings are still possible, since ASCAP, BMI, SESAC, and GMR do not distinguish in their royalty payments between high- versus low-budget films, box office successes versus box office failures, initial airing versus repeats, or brilliantly composed music versus pedestrian scoring. A screening of the top-grossing film of all time would be paid the same as moviedom's biggest failure, provided that both films were shown on the same cable, local, or network television station, or streaming service with all other factors being equal (i.e., Nielsen rating, time of day, bonus structure in place, etc.). It is important to note that the audiovisual streaming service royalties are insignificant compared to traditional network, local, and cable TV performances.

Table 8.8 estimates the performance royalties for a successful composer with multiple films in distribution both theatrically and on television. The following two examples of the U.S. television performance earnings for the writer and publisher of the underscore for an individual film over a 10-year period should help to place this area into some perspective. Although no two pictures are alike in terms of the amount of music or specified distribution areas, many films do earn well in the U.S. television area.

U.S. PERFORMANCE ROYALTIES FOR A COMPOSER WITH MULTIPLE FILMS IN DISTRIBUTION

Table 8.8

Period	Areas	Royalties
Year 1	Network TV	$18,000
	Cable/Pay TV	$22,000
	Local TV/Streaming	$8,000
	Foreign	$179,000
	Total Royalties	$227,000

Year 2	Network TV	$16,000
	Cable/Pay TV	$35,000
	Local TV/Streaming	$12,000
	Foreign	$150,000
	Total Royalties	$213,000
Year 3	Network TV	$7,000
	Cable/Pay TV	$26,000
	Local TV/Streaming	$9,000
	Foreign	$70,000
	Total Royalties	$112,000

SOUNDTRACK ALBUMS

Although quite a few score soundtrack albums are released each year, most of them are geared to a selective audience and many of them appear on specialty labels. Therefore, the sales are usually not significant. Many of these albums are not motivated by the same considerations as those prevalent in "song" soundtrack albums: such as securing a Top 10 single chart activity to help sell the motion picture during its initial theatrical release. Some score albums do sell very well, though, particularly if the score is for a blockbuster motion picture or if there are one or two hit songs on the album.

A sample soundtrack score album contract where the composer is the artist (i.e., conductor of the orchestra) might read as follows: An artist royalty of 10% of the suggested retail list price (20% of the wholesale price) for sales through normal retail channels in the U.S. less packaging deductions, applicable taxes, and artist royalties due any other participating artist on the album. A percentage will also be deducted for the actual conversion cost involved (repaying the musicians according to union regulations for using the film music on a recording, mixing costs, mastering costs, etc.). The same record company deductions, reserves against returns, exclusions, and so on, of a typical recording contract would also be included. A producer royalty (e.g., 4% of the suggested retail list price) would also be negotiated and would be pro-rated based upon the number of selections on the album by other artists and producers. If the record company decides that a live album is necessary (the music is reorchestrated, rescored, and re-recorded), the compensation to the composer/conductor would include the union scale payments for each element of the composer's work. An album credit provision would also be negotiated. A sample clause might state that the composer would receive front cover and label credit of "music composed by [Name of Composer]" if at least 50% of all of the total selections were composed by him. Otherwise, it would be at the producer's discretion on the back cover.

For album sales, the statutory mechanical publisher and writer royalty would apply unless voluntarily reduced by the music publisher or composer; for example, a record company might demand that a maximum cap on mechanical royalties per album be agreed to as a condition of the album being recorded and released. Soundtrack score albums should also be reviewed in the context of contract provision changes being negotiated in the regular album area (for example, the elimination of any "new media royalty deductions" as well as packaging and container deductions for downloads and Internet sales, etc.).

CONCLUSION

Having a song in a motion picture or composing a score for a film can open up unlimited opportunities and create a lifetime annuity for writers and music publishers. From hit records, broadcast radio and streaming services, the Academy Awards, commercials, ringtones, and dolls, toys and greeting cards to television themes, foreign motion picture theater performances, other motion pictures and television series, video games, Broadway shows, and soundtrack albums, the financial life of the movie song and the motion picture music score can last well beyond the Hollywood premiere.

CHAPTER 9

MUSIC, MONEY, AND COMMERCIALS

From Bob Dylan's "Forever Young" for Chevy Trucks, Lady Gaga's "Just Another Day" for Samsung, Imagine Dragon's "Thunder" for Microsoft, Gershwin's "Rhapsody in Blue" for United Airlines, ELO's "Livin' Thing" for Volkswagen and NVDES' "Turning Heads" for Apple iPhone X, music is advertising.

THE ADVERTISING AGENCY AND HOW IT WORKS

THE PHONE CALL FROM THE ADVERTISING AGENCY

AGENCY: Hi, this is Bill Smith from [name of agency] in New York. I'm calling because one of our clients would like to use a song that you publish in an upcoming advertising campaign.

PUBLISHER: Glad to hear that. Can you give me the name of the song, the product, and details of the campaign?

AGENCY: The client is [car company] and the song we would like to use is [title of song]. For your information, we are also going to use the [name of recording artist] record of the song during the commercial.

The campaign will be for the United States for one year, and we'd like to have two additional options to extend the license for one year each. The media will be all television plus Internet, with an option to broadcast the commercial on radio. Since we might also want to expand the territory for the commercial to Canada, certain countries in Europe, Japan, and Australia, we'd also like to get separate option fee quotes for Canada, Europe, Japan, and Australia. And we'd appreciate a fee quote if we were to use the commercial on a worldwide basis if we decide to do that type of global campaign plus a quote for the product's website, as well as e-mail, print, and on-hold phone use. We'd also like to have the right to distribute the commercials to smartphones, cell phones, and other handheld personal digital devices, as well as to place the commercial in video games. In addition, we would like to have industrial rights (including but not limited to dealer showrooms, auto shows, trade shows, and internal in-store/retail, jumbotrons), rights to B-Roll usage (including the right to mention the song title and the artist's name) for entertainment programs and other broadcast outlets as well as newspapers and magazines. We also need an option for video-on-demand. It's our client's policy that the song can't be licensed to another car company or to any automotive parts products during the term, and your agreement to this competitive product restriction is essential.

PUBLISHER: Auto commercials rarely hurt hit songs, and since there is no change of lyrics, the use seems acceptable. I would appreciate it, though, if you could send me a copy of the storyboard so I can get an idea of how the commercial will look and how the song will actually be used. I'll then be able to give you the fee quotes that you need.

AGENCY: I'll e-mail you the storyboard within the hour, but I must ask you to keep the concept confidential and will send you a brief confidentiality agreement prior to e-mailing you the story board.

PUBLISHER: I definitely will, and I'll get back to you later today with prices.

ANOTHER ADVERTISING COMMERCIAL REQUEST VIA E-MAIL

AGENCY: Please see the below specifics with respect to the use of the Composition entitled "[Title of Song]" for use in our client's commercial:

Product: Smartphone.

Use Type/Length/Number of Spots: Background vocal and visual vocal/one thirty (30) second and one fifteen (15) second spot including revisions, remakes, cut-downs, versions, lifts, and edits of the commercial.

Media: All forms of broadcast media; industrial media (limited to trade shows, keynotes/conventions, corporate videos and product-sponsored events); cinema; in stores; Internet (online and online advertising including but not limited to the product's website, Facebook, YouTube, press and/or promotional websites, product owned channels, (all uses being in-context solely as edited into the television commercial).

Territory: The world and universe.

Term: Paid Media: Four (4) months; Non-Paid Media (industrial, Internet, PR): Four (4) months.

Option To Extend Term: An option to extend the initial Term for an additional two (2) months.

Exclusivity: Total exclusivity (including Internet) for four (4) months (specifically excludes use in motion pictures, television programs, or video games which are all permitted as exceptions to the grant of exclusivity).

Initial Fees: Composition: $_____;

Master Recording: $_____.

Option Fees: Composition: $_____;

Master Recording: $_____.

We look forward to your response as well as any questions that you may have.

Sincerely,

[AGENCY REPRESENTATIVE]

Whether the owner of a song is the sponsor, agency, jingle writer, production company, music publisher, or a rock, hip hop, country, pop or Latin superstar, the advertising business can be a valuable source of income for both the songwriter and publisher. Since an understanding of how music is licensed in this industry is necessary to appreciate the use of music to promote consumer products and to understand the financial ramifications, the following sections examine many of the business and legal decisions that lead to getting songs into commercials.

THE ADVERTISING AGENCY AND ITS USE OF MUSIC

When an advertising agency produces a commercial, it has the option to use music in a number of ways. In many cases, the advertising agency hires a composer, lyricist, or production company to create a new song specifically for the commercial (e.g., "I Won't Drift Away" for AT&T, or "This Bud's for You" for Budweiser).

Other times, a hit song may be needed to identify an important trait of the product (such as "Satisfaction" for Hilton Hotels, "Takin' Care of Business" for Office Depot, "Like a Rock" for the dependability of a truck, and "Everything Is Beautiful" for a shiny wood finish), convey a certain message (such as "Don't Stop Believin'" for Nissan, "We Won't Get Fooled Again" for Dish, "With a Little Help from My Friends" for Wal-Mart, "I've Had the Time of My Life" for United Healthcare, "I'll Be There" for an insurance company, "Let's Spend the Night Together" for a hotel chain, and "Stand by Me" for a credit card buyer's protection program), or create a specific mood (such as "On the Road Again" for Passat, "Goin' to the Country" for Geico Motorcycle Insurance, and "Sweet Caroline" for Hyundai). The agency may use the melody of a popular song and create new lyrics or change the original lyrics slightly to fit the advertising message (as in "Gilligan's Island" theme for Applebee's, "YMCA" for Diet Dr Pepper, "What the World Needs Now" for Dove Bars, and "Love and Marriage" for Fruit & Fiber cereal).

At other times, an instrumental version of a song will be used (e.g., "Spirit in the Sky" for Lyft, "Take Me Home, Country Roads" for Google Home, "Singin' in the Rain" for GE, and "As Time Goes By" for American Express Buyer's Insurance), or if the song was originally an instrumental (e.g., "Rocky Theme" for AT+T, "Love Story" for GE Appliances, "Pink Panther Theme" for Heineken and Owens-Corning, or the "Chariots of Fire Theme" for sponsors such as Nike, Nissan, and Duracell batteries), the instrumental is performed with no changes. Agencies may also use a combination of the above alternatives in a campaign for a certain product, such as the use of "Secondhand Rose" instrumentally and with new lyrics in separate AT&T commercials, and "Lean on Me" for Chevrolet trucks, both instrumentally and with the original lyrics.

The client or agency may also want a hit recording used in the commercial (e.g., Bruno Mars' "Just The Way You Are" for Estée Lauder, or Led Zeppelin's "Rock and Roll" for Cadillac) or a new version of a past hit song (e.g., Cher and Future singing "Everyday People"), may want a successful recording artist to sing the new lyrics for a hit song (such as Elton John with "Sad Songs" for Sasson and Aretha Franklin with a version of "Rescue Me" for Pizza Hut), may contract with a hit songwriter/recording artist to create and perform advertising jingles for a particular product or may hire a hit songwriter/recording artist to sing the jingle in commercials (e.g., Brad Paisley for Nationwide). The agency may also decide to take instrumental music from a production music/background music library or use a work not under copyright protection (i.e., a song in the public domain).

THE IMPORTANCE OF THE ADVERTISING AGENCY

When an agency is hired to create a radio, television, or Internet commercial, it must first be decided whether the campaign demands a new song or whether the advertiser wants to use a past or present hit song. On occasion, the client may request a certain song for its overall marketing theme. In most cases, though, the advertising agency and its creative department not only develop and sell a specific campaign but also suggest the music to be used—a responsibility whose importance cannot be overemphasized, since the choice of the right music or advertising lyric is essential to getting consumers to recall the commercial and brand name when they're choosing a product to buy.

THE JINGLE

If a campaign requires new music, the advertising agency consults with its client concerning the theme and direction of the campaign as well as about the overall creative budget, including the music budget. The agency, if it does not have an in-house music department, then usually hires a jingle-production company that specializes in advertising music to write a song and produce a demonstration recording tailored to the planned commercial. Such a jingle-production company is normally a self-contained unit that can (through its staff writers, producers, and in some cases, ownership of recording studios) write the jingle and produce a finished demo.

The agency and its client are then able to hear a reasonable facsimile of the commercial and, if it is what they are looking for, proceed to a finished version. If an agency has an in-house music department with a staff of songwriters, lyric creators, and producers, it will often develop and produce many of its clients' jingles without going to third parties.

Another alternative is to contact an independent songwriter, explain the theme of the campaign, and hire the writer to create the jingle. Having his or her own production facility is many times essential for a composer to secure the commercial assignment, unless the composer has a successful track record for writing hit songs or a reputation in the jingle business as a successful commercial writer. Alternatively, the agency can go to a production music house or library for already created music or purchase the exclusive or nonexclusive advertising use rights to a past or present hit song.

CREATION OF A JINGLE AND THE MONIES THAT CAN BE EARNED

The fees payable to a writer for creative services related to the writing of a radio or television jingle can range from minimum compensation to well over $250,000. The amount of compensation depends on the type of campaign being planned (e.g., national, local, Internet, test), the music budget, and whether the writer is an independent contractor unaffiliated with an advertising agency or a jingle production company, is signed to a production company or owns his or her own firm, is an employee of the advertising agency, has a hit song that the agency wants to use, or is a successful writer/recording artist who will create and perform advertising music.

THE INDEPENDENT WRITER

When an agency contacts an independent writer, the fees for writing a jingle may range from a few hundred dollars to a few thousand dollars, depending on the music budget and the extent of the campaign being planned. If the agency is dealing with a superstar, however, the total creative fees can easily range from $500,000 to millions if a multiple-year arrangement is involved.

THE JINGLE PRODUCTION COMPANY

It is common for the writer to own, or be signed to, a jingle production company. In such cases, the fee paid by the advertising agency to this one-source operation includes the monies for the creation of the jingle, the costs of the recording studio, the arranger's fee, and the salaries of the musicians and singers who perform at the session. Based on the wide range of services and expertise provided by these production companies, the amount of money paid by the agency is much greater than that paid to an individual jingle writer. For example, the value of a 30-second commercial to a production company can range from $5,000 to well over $50,000, depending on whether the commercial is to be aired in local markets or is the centerpiece of a national campaign.

THE WRITER AS EMPLOYEE OF AN ADVERTISING AGENCY

A number of advertising agencies have in-house writers and production staffs whose primary job is to create and produce much of the music needed for their radio and television commercials. These writers receive a salary for creating jingles and normally assign the rights to their music to the agency as part of their employment agreement. The employee/writer will normally receive no other monies for creating a jingle, with the possible exception of performance royalties from his or her respective performing rights organization and, if so negotiated, songwriter royalties if the jingle becomes a commercially released recording or is used in a manner other than as part of an advertising campaign (e.g., from a television set or radio in a scene from a movie or a television series episode, as a sample in a released recording, in a video game, in a songbook or album featuring advertising songs, etc.). Owing to the costs involved, however, very few agencies are large enough to support in-house writing and production staffs.

HIT SONGS USED IN COMMERCIALS

Though many commercials use music or songs written specifically for the advertising campaign, an increasing trend is the use of past or present hit songs to sell a product. By using a hit song, the agencies attempt to capitalize on the instant recognition of the song and the recall of the product because of its identification with a familiar song.

The fees paid by advertising companies for the use of popular songs in commercials can exceed $1,000,000 for a one-year use in a national campaign, with the normal range being from $125,000 to $300,000. The amount of the fee depends on, among other considerations, the past and present popularity of the song, the type of media campaign being planned, the territory involved, the nature of the product or service being advertised, the music budget, the number of songs being used in the commercial, the past unavailability of a song for commercials, whether master recording rights (the original hit record version) are also being secured, whether total advertising exclusivity as opposed to product exclusivity is being requested (e.g., a prohibition against any other advertising use of the song vs. restrictions only for competing consumer goods), whether present or future promotion of the song might be diluted because of the commercial tie-in, the importance of the song to the message of the campaign, and whether the agency wants to alter the original lyrics.

For example, fees will be higher for a song that has stood the test of time and has become a recognizable standard regardless of genre than they will be for a one-time hit that has lost some or much of its original popularity. Fees will also be higher for a campaign that will include television, radio, and the Internet, rather than a campaign that is broadcast on the Internet and radio only. Fees will be higher if the territory of the commercial campaign is the world or North America rather than the United States only. Fees will be larger if the product is a well known national brand with a large advertising budget rather than a regional product with a limited advertising budget. Larger fees will be charged if there is more than one commercial using the song being shown as part of the campaign (unless the other commercials are only shorter edits, cut-downs or lifts of the main commercial). A higher fee will be charged if the hit song has never been used before in a commercial or if the songwriter has been very restrictive in the past as to licensing for commercials. And a larger fee will usually be charged if the product being advertised is undesirable.

PERMISSION TO USE A HIT SONG IN A COMMERCIAL

When an advertising agency wants to use a hit song in a commercial, it will contact the music publisher of the song for permission and, if the composition is available for licensing, negotiate a fee for a specified term with options.

In most cases, an agency will use a song only for a limited campaign (normally one year or less), but many songs have become so vital to a product and its success that they have been used for years (e.g., Led Zeppelin's "Rock and Roll" for Cadillac, "When You Wish Upon a Star" for Disneyland, "Fly Like an Eagle" for the U.S. Postal Service, "Rhapsody in Blue" for United Airlines, "Anticipation" for Heinz Ketchup, "Like a Rock" for Chevy, and Henry Mancini's "Pink Panther Theme" for Owens-Corning). By obtaining an option to continue to use the song (always at an increased fee), the agency and its client are assured that, if a campaign is successful, they can continue to use the song in the commercial for a pre-established fee, an option that may be vital if the song has become inherently identified with the product or if the campaign has been a success. Obviously, since many agreements provide for only two options, re-negotiations do occur when the commercial is very successful and the advertising agency and sponsor want to extend the term past the time period specified in the initial agreement.

If an agency wants to secure the master recording rights to a popular song (i.e., the actual hit recording), it must contact the record company that owns those rights, as the music publisher can only grant rights to use the musical composition, not a specific recording. For example, if an advertising agency wants to use the Rolling Stone's recording of "Satisfaction," the Frank Sinatra version of "That's Life," the Led Zeppelin version of "Rock and Roll," or any other hit recording, the agency must conduct separate negotiations with both the record company (for the existing recorded performance) and the music publisher (for the song contained on that recording). Because of the double negotiation and double fees inherent in this type of situation, licensing a well-known song and hit record for a single commercial can be extremely expensive (combined fees from $400,000 to more than $800,000 per year are not unusual), and this approach is normally reserved for major advertisers with large media budgets.

Because of the expensive nature of using both the hit song and recording that made the song famous, many agencies will only secure rights to the song and re-record another version of the song for use in the commercial (sometimes with the original recording artist if the artist is out of the re-recording restriction period of the record contract). Sometimes the agency will use a lesser-known master of the song if it works in the context of the commercial. The plus side to this approach is that it substantially reduces the out-of-pocket production costs of the commercial. Another possible plus side is to have the song recorded by a new artist with a contemporary style that may better appeal to the audience that the agency is trying to reach. The minus side is that people won't hear the hit recording they are used to hearing when they think of the song. Agencies also have to be careful when they re-record a hit song to make sure that the new version does not sound so much like the original hit recording as to constitute an infringement of the artist's rights, since there has been litigation in this area.

TIME LIMIT FOR FEE QUOTES

In almost all cases, the fee quote given to the advertising agency has a time limit and is not open ended. For example, many confirmations from the music publisher or record company will state that the fee quote is valid for 30 days. At the expiration of the agreed upon period, if the commercial has not gone forward, the agency will have to make another request to keep the quote in effect.

MOST FAVORED NATIONS PROVISIONS

In most commercial agreements, the music publisher will ask for a most favored nations clause to be inserted into the agreement to make sure that if an existing master recording is being used that the publishing fee will receive the benefit of, and be equal to, the master fee if it is higher than that quoted for use of the composition. The clause is also used when there are multiple songwriters and publishers on a composition to make sure that all will be sharing proportionally in the final fee regardless of the fact that one writer or publisher may have quoted a lower fee than the others.

ADVANTAGES AND DISADVANTAGES OF A HIT SONG BEING USED IN A COMMERCIAL (FROM A PUBLISHER'S AND WRITER'S POINT OF VIEW)

Some music publishers and writers feel that any identification with the selling of a consumer product can damage the future earning potential of a copyright, as it may hinder additional new recordings or other uses. Some also feel that any advertising connection is anathema to the integrity of a song. With this in mind, a number of writers and publishers deny all requests to use a song in a commercial, regardless of the amount of money being offered or the product being promoted. In some cases, permission is granted but the fees quoted are extremely high to ensure that, if the song is used, a premium will have been paid by the advertising agency to compensate for the use or for possible loss of projected future income. In others, the fees charged are higher than usual if the songwriter or music publisher feels that the specific product identification or terms of the agreement might adversely affect either future advertising uses by other sponsors or future promotion of the original work. Finally, in cases where the songwriter, estate, lawyer, music publisher, or other authorized representative feels that the product is not right but does not want to give a flat refusal, permission may be granted but the fees will be so large that an agency and its client will find it economically impossible to go ahead with the planned campaign.

On the other hand, many music publishers and songwriters realize that the exposure generated by a national advertising campaign, especially if the lyrics are not being changed, will generate additional opportunities and uses for a song by stimulating interest in cover recordings by other artists and reintroducing it to a new audience, including motion picture and television producers and video game developers. A large lump-sum payment to the publisher and writer for the use of a song in a commercial is also a primary consideration. If one is being offered between $150,000 and $1,000,000 for a one-year use in a major campaign, it is pure fantasy to think that economics may not have some influence in the final decision. The nature of the product being advertised, how the song is used in the context of the commercial, the current annual income generated by the composition from other uses, the remaining copyright life of a composition, whether the song or its future earnings potential might be hurt by the use, whether songwriter approvals have to be secured, and the nature of any lyric changes are all considerations that can either make or break a negotiation.

JINGLES (SONGS WRITTEN FOR COMMERCIALS)

THE JINGLE WRITER AND THE ADVERTISING AGENCY

You hereby grant to our client [Name of Sponsor] all the right, title, and interest throughout the world in and to the musical composition entitled [Title of Song] written and composed by [Writer's Name] for use in the following commercial: [Title of Commercial].

The above language is standard (in one form or another) in many jingle contracts. The writer of the music or lyrics traditionally assigns virtually all rights to the agency or sponsor. In most cases, the rights sold are all-inclusive, with the exception that some writers retain their right to receive royalties from ASCAP, BMI, SESAC, and GMR for performances of the commercial on the Internet, radio, or television, and songwriter royalties if the song is recorded and released to the general public or used in a video game, DVD, film, television series, or as a ringtone or ringback.

Some of the more important rights transferred by the writer to the agency or client are:

The right to register a claim of copyright to the composition in the name of the advertising agency or client

The right to use the composition in all forms of advertising and merchandising

The right to alter, expand, adapt, and edit the composition

The right to use, publish, perform, broadcast, reproduce, and exploit the composition by any means

Considering the many possible uses of music, many writers also negotiate a songwriter's agreement that guarantees them a share of income generated by nonadvertising uses. For most jingles, however, such other uses rarely occur, and a writer's income is usually limited to the writing fee and possibly royalties from the performance rights organizations for broadcasts of the commercial.

THE AGENCY AND THE PRODUCTION COMPANY

Since most jingle writers are signed to commercial production companies that handle all aspects of the making of the jingle, the advertising agency will usually contract with the production company instead of with the individual writer. The contract language is similar to that used in the writer-agency jingle contract, except that the production company warrants to the agency that it, not the songwriter, owns all rights to the jingle (the writer having already assigned his or her rights in the jingle to the production company). In all contracts in which a jingle is sold to an agency, the writer and production company also agree to indemnify the agency and the client against any liability, losses, and expenses, including reasonable attorneys' fees, arising out of the use of the musical composition in the commercial. Occasionally, the indemnity is limited to the amount of money actually paid by the agency to the writer or production company.

THE WRITER/RECORDING ARTIST JINGLE AGREEMENT

When an agency is interested in having a successful writer/recording artist write and perform a song created specifically for a product, the agreement will usually cover the following areas in one form or another.

Services: The writer will agree to create a two- to three-minute demo recording on or before a specified date. If the client accepts the song, a fully mixed and engineered recording will be made and delivered according to a set timetable, many times with a separate 30- and/or 60-second version/edit of the long version. In this regard, the writer/artist will agree to make any changes reasonably requested by the agency or that are mutually agreed upon. The contract will further state that the agency or client may create 15-second, 30-second or any other versions or cutdowns of the recording depending on the needs of the campaign.

Ownership: The contract will state that the song and the recording were made pursuant to a "work made for hire" agreement with copyright in the name of the client.

Non-acceptance: If the agency decides not to use the song and recording, it will assign all rights back to the writer/artist. In some cases, the agency will provide that the song or demo cannot be exploited for a specified period of time after delivery or receipt of the notice that the song will not be used.

Acceptance: If the song and recording are accepted by the agency, the client and agency will almost always have the exclusive right to use the song and recording in any manner with respect to the advertising of the product in any and all types of promotional campaigns.

Fees: Although there are a number of variations in this area, there will be an initial fee paid within a certain number of days after the first demo is provided to the agency. If the agency decides to go forward, an additional fee will be paid to cover the next set of recording costs that will result in the final master. The final creative fee will be paid within a set number of days after the delivery of the final professional recording which will be used in the commercial.

Restrictions: On occasion, the writer/artist may be asked not to provide services to a campaign for a competing product during an agreed upon period of time (e.g., one year, six months, etc.) after the signing of the jingle agreement.

Royalties: The writer will usually be entitled to receive performance royalties from his or her performing rights organization (ASCAP, BMI, SESAC, GMR) for streams, broadcasts, and other performances of the commercial. If the agency or client do not have a publishing company, the writer's company may be also able to claim the publisher's share of performance royalties. There also may be additional royalties negotiated (if a nonadvertising version of the song used in the commercial becomes a hit record, is downloaded from iTunes, is included in a scene in a motion picture or television series episode, etc.) but this is subject to renegotiation.

Waiver of Exclusivity: If the writer/artist is signed to a music publisher or record company, these companies will have to waive their exclusivity rights with respect to the song and recording used in the commercial. In such a case, both the music publisher and the record company may take a portion of the creative fee payable as consideration for waiving their rights to the jingle and recording.

For example, the publisher and record company might ask for 50% of the fee and allow the writer artist to keep the remainder. Or if the writer or artist is in an unrecouped advance position, they may take a portion of the fee and use it for recoupment purposes. There are many variations in this area including using the entire fee as income under the respective publishing and recording artist agreement and distributing the monies according to the terms of the agreements.

NEGOTIATING WITH AN ADVERTISING AGENCY FOR A HIT SONG

This will confirm our agreement pursuant to which (Publisher) grants to (Advertiser) the right, license, privilege, and authority to record, at its own expense, the copyrighted musical composition entitled (the Composition) and to use recordings of the Composition in commercials (the Commercials) advertising the products and/or services of Advertiser, subject to the applicable conditions contained herein.

When an agency commissions the writing of a new song for a commercial, it usually acquires all rights in the jingle for its client. The agreement for a hit song, however, is much less encompassing, as it is purely a license that permits the agency to do certain things during a specified period of time under certain conditions, with a termination of all rights after the agreement is over. (Table 9.1 shows some hit songs used in TV commercials.) The following sections explain the more important issues that occur during such negotiations.

HIT SONGS USED IN TV COMMERCIALS

Table 9.1

Song Title	Product	Genre
Theme from *Cheers*	Michelob Ultra	TV Theme
"Tomorrow"	Entresto	Broadway Song
"Rock Around the Clock"	Subway	1950s Rock 'n' Roll
"Fly Me to the Moon"	E*Trade	Standard
"Lose Yourself"	iTunes	Hip Hop Hit
"Rocky Theme"	United Health Care	Film Theme
"Bibbidi-Bobbidi-Boo"	Toyota	Film Song
"Under Pressure"	Coca-Cola	Rock Hit
"Dream On"	Super Bowl	Pop Hit
"Theme to 'A Summer Place'"	Toyota	Movie Theme

"Take My Breath Away"	Gain Detergent	Pop Hit
"Old Time Rock 'n' Roll"	Guitar Hero	Classic Rock
Theme from *The Odd Couple*	Subway	TV Theme
"Work It"	iPod/iTunes	R&B/Hip Hop Hit
"Higher And Higher"	Total Toothpaste	Soul Classic
"Purple Haze"	Pepsi	Classic Rock
"Let's Get Down"	Campbell's	Hip-Hop Hit
"Blue Skies"	HP	Standard
"I Want to Be Free"	Coca Cola C2	Rock Hit
"Shaft"	Burger King	Movie Theme
"Tonight, Tonight"	Mountain Dew	Broadway Song
"Your Cheatin' Heart"	Pepsi Edge	Country Classic
"Tax Man"	H&R Block	Classic Rock

PARTIES TO THE AGREEMENT

In most cases, the advertising agency gets permission directly from the copyright owner of the hit song, which is usually the music publisher. Occasionally, the songwriter or music publisher has previously signed an administration, collection, or representation agreement, whereby a larger music publisher, law firm, manager, music industry agency, or other representative has been given the authority to negotiate licenses for the commercial exploitation of a particular hit song or catalogue of songs. In that case, the advertising agency will contract with the administrator, who is acting on behalf of the song's original copyright owner.

COPYRIGHT OWNERSHIP

Ownership of the existing song is never transferred to the agency, as the agreement is merely a license of certain specified rights. On the other hand, if the agency creates new lyrics for the song, the agency will usually copyright the new material for its client, and the owner of the hit song will usually have no rights to the newly created lyrics.

DURATION OF LICENSE

The term of the commercial license is usually one year for a national campaign plus a number of options (normally one to three additional one-year options at the election of the advertising agency). As marketing campaigns take on many variations, however, the term requested by an agency can be for a day, a number of days. a week, a number of weeks, a month, a few months, a year, multiple years, or any combination thereof. For example, a license can be for a one-day test in one or two cities with options for up to three one-year periods on a national basis if the test results in positive consumer reaction; it can be for one month, as in the case of Christmas campaigns, or for a few days or a few weeks, as with Mother's Day, Father's Day, Fourth of July, Easter, Labor Day, Memorial Day, or Thanksgiving Day promotions.

EXCLUSIVITY VERSUS NONEXCLUSIVITY (COMPETING PRODUCT VERSUS TOTAL EXCLUSIVITY)

Unless total advertising exclusivity is requested, the music publisher will not be restricted from licensing the song to other advertisers during the duration of the commercial agreement. The agency contract will, however, contain language prohibiting the use of the song in connection with commercials that promote competing or related products. This is called "product exclusivity." For example, if a song is licensed for a car commercial, the same song may not be given to another automobile maker but can be simultaneously licensed for use in a commercial promoting soda, smartphones, Internet services, television sets, hamburgers, or dish detergent under a nonexclusive, noncompetitive product license. Some of these noncompetitive clauses are very broad and restrictive (e.g., restricting a song used in a pie commercial from any type of food product or for a song in a beer commercial being used in connection with any type of beverage), and some are very limited (e.g., restricting a song used in a perfume commercial from use in a campaign for another perfume, but not from ads for cosmetics). If the fee paid for the song is very low, there may be no product restrictions at all.

If the campaign is a major one or if the identification of the hit song with the product is considered vital to the promotion, the agency may request total advertising exclusivity. Such exclusivity, however, is rare, because the additional fees payable to the music publisher and songwriter for taking the song entirely off the market are usually prohibitive. Fee quotes from $250,000 to over $1,000,000 are not unusual for one year of total exclusivity. An agency may also lose interest in a song if it discovers that the song is currently being used in another product campaign or has recently been so used. The same considerations come into play when a master recording of a song is being chosen.

GRADUATED EXCLUSIVITY PROVISIONS IN COMMERCIALS

On occasion, an agency may request total "all product" exclusivity for advertising purposes for only a limited period of time rather than total exclusivity during the entire period that the commercial is airing or being streamed. For example, an agency may agree and/or request that the total "all product" exclusivity provision last for only between three and six months from first air date or other authorized exploitation date of the commercial even though the license term for the advertising use agreement of the composition is for one year.

This type of approach will ensure that the agency/sponsor will receive the full impact of the composition being taken "off the consumer product advertising commercial market" for the important initial period of the advertising campaign but which will also reduce the licensing costs since total "all product" exclusivity can be very expensive if it is effective for the entire term of the license.

These types of limited total exclusivity understandings will many times include a prohibition for use of the composition in trailers for motion pictures, television programs, and video games, since, in some respects, this type of use is part of an advertising campaign for a product (although unrelated to the consumer product campaign). Recognizing the need for publishers to be able to license compositions in the normal course of business for nonadvertising consumer product uses, the agency will almost always allow the composition to be licensed for use in a motion picture, television series, video game or other standard licensing area (e.g., the composition or master recording being used in a scene in a motion picture); the only prohibition being its out-of-context use in the advertising or marketing campaign of the film, television, video game, or other project.

Once the limited total exclusivity period has ended, the "competing product" exclusivity aspect will be the only licensing prohibition attached to the composition. For example, if the client is a computer hardware company involved in the smartphone area and the term of the license agreement is for one year (with the first six months containing a total exclusivity guarantee), once the second six-month period begins, the only restrictions placed on the songwriter or music publisher licensing the composition would be to not license the composition in an advertising commercial for any competing computer hardware products including smartphones and related devices (depending on what is included in the definition of the competing product category).

Once again, as in most areas of the music licensing business, the actual deal terms depend upon the bargaining power of the parties negotiating the agreement, the sponsor's need for a particular composition or master recording, the availability of viable alternatives, among other factors, and the quality of representation on both sides of the negotiation. It should be noted that these same conditions apply to the master recording of the composition if the agency wants to use the original master recording as opposed to recording its own new version.

RIGHT OF FIRST REFUSAL

Although not common, some agreements give the agency's client the right to be notified by the music publisher of the composition used in a campaign if a request to use that same composition is received for use in an ad campaign by another product even if the other product is not in a competing category. For example, even if a composition is being used in an automobile commercial and the only restriction on licensing is product exclusivity related to cars or automobile products, if a request is received for a soap commercial, the publisher would be obligated to notify the agency of the new request.

Under this scenario, the current client of the ad agency would have the right to elect to pay the publisher an additional license fee to have the publisher either deny the new request or deny the request and add the new request's product category to the current product exclusivity categories.

Under this type of right of first refusal clause, the agency and its client would have to make its decision within a short period of time after being notified so that the publisher could know whether it could go forward with the new request. If the agency decides to exercise its refusal rights, then a good faith negotiation fee would be payable to the publisher to compensate it for not being able to license the composition to the noncompeting product. The fee negotiation with the client–current agency of the existing commercial will be a very short one (e.g., 24 to 36 hours) to prevent the publisher from losing the possible new use because it can't respond with a fee quotation in a timely manner.

NUMBER OF COMMERCIALS

The agency contract will specify the number of commercials that will use the song (e.g., "one 30-second television and Internet commercial, one 15-second television and Internet commercial, and one 30-second radio commercial" including edits, versions and variations) or, if undetermined at the time the contract is signed, a maximum number (e.g., "one 60-second commercial with up to three 20-second edits, cutdowns, or lifts" or "one 60 second commercial with unlimited edits, lifts, and tags").

PAYMENT OF FEES

The initial fee is usually paid upon signing the agreement or within a short time, such as 10 days. Any option payments are paid upon the commencement of the option period or within a few days thereafter (e.g., "Within 10 days after the option is exercised or within five days after the option period commences").

EXERCISE OF OPTIONS

The advertising contract will be structured so that the agency is the party that decides whether or not an option is picked up. This is accomplished by written notice prior to or by the last day of the current contract period (e.g., "in the event that the agency wants to extend the license agreement for an additional one-year period, it must notify the music publisher of its option exercise at least 10 days prior to the expiration of the current period of the term"). If the agency does not exercise such option rights, the license agreement expires and no further use of the commercial (other than the agency's right to submit the commercial for advertising industry award shows or other agreed-upon exceptions) may be made after the current period expires.

TERRITORY

The territory requested for a major advertising campaign is usually the United States of America, its territories, possessions, and commonwealths, but depending on the potential consumer base for the product, Canada may also be included for an additional fee. Another common approach is to define the territory as North America which will include the United States, Canada and Mexico. Since the Internet is almost always included as part of the media use, the territory for this one area will be many times listed as worldwide. If the product has a regional base, or the planned campaign is designed as a test, or the product is new and the campaign is in a limited introductory stage, the licensed territory may be only one city, one state, a number of cities or states, or any variation thereof. For example, the territory may only be for the city of Baltimore, for the state of Illinois, or for one identified shopping mall in Los Angeles or Atlanta. If the initial territory is limited but the product has national potential, the agency will usually require options for expanded territories. For example, a campaign may be tested in a number of geographically related cities or states (e.g., Los Angeles, San Diego, and San Francisco, or New York, New Jersey, and Pennsylvania) and, if successful, expanded into other regions (Phoenix, Seattle, and Las Vegas, or California, Washington, and Oregon). Or the territory may be defined as geographic areas covering no more than a certain percentage of the U.S. population (e.g., 10%, 20%, etc.) with options extending the commercial into areas covering a larger percentage (e.g., 30%, 50%, 75%, 100%). When a commercial finds consumer acceptance, the agency wants to be able to broadcast the commercial in areas other than those specified in the original license and the variations requested are numerous. Therefore, options for additional media and territories are prevalent in contracts for limited-market or test commercials.

At times, the use of a song in specific foreign countries or throughout the world will also be requested, but this usually occurs only in the case of internationally accepted products (such as Apple, Google, Microsoft, Pepsi-Cola, McDonald's, Budweiser, BMW, or Coca-Cola). The addition of foreign countries is usually handled on an option basis unless the agency and sponsor want to make a guaranteed up-front commitment. For example, an agency may license the hit song in the United States and Canada for one year with three one-year options and also have the right to extend the use into the United Kingdom for a set fee, into all of Europe for another fee, into Japan for a separate fee, into other selected countries for an additional fee, and for the entire world for yet another fee. There are usually time limits as to when these various options can be exercised by the agency, the specifics of which are subject to negotiation between the music publisher, songwriter, and advertising agency.

MEDIA

Television, Internet, and radio are the standard media requested, but depending on the thrust of the campaign, print uses (for example, lyrics of the composition used in magazine ads, on billboards or in the commercial itself) may also be included in the license. Many agreements will also specifically refer to streaming Internet via the product's YouTube, Facebook, Twitter, and other social media pages. Additionally, with commercials being used on motion picture home videos, in motion picture theaters during previews, and on mobile phones, smartphones, and other digital devices, rights for home and personal video and theater promos, may also be negotiated. Other areas that might be included are industrial (internal, sales conferences, showroom displays, in-store, jumbotrons, trade shows, in-stadium and places of public assembly) as well as B-Roll usage and electronic press kits. Because some agencies also use the hit song as part of their in-store or Internet promotions (reduced price or free CDs, downloads, or giveaways), extra monies may be paid to the music publisher and songwriter for such "point-of-sale non-record store outlet" promotions. For example, an agency may secure an option to distribute up to 50,000 downloads of the song used in the commercial for a one-month period at any time during the license term for either the U.S. statutory mechanical royalty rate or, if acceptable to the writer and music publisher, a reduced mechanical rate. Or there might be a promotion that offers free downloads to the consumer on a redemption basis, depending on whether or not a customer has a winning bottle cap or other instant winner code/number on the inside packaging of a product or website, among other ways, to win.

Certain advertising uses of music may be restricted to use in shopping malls, in-house training sessions, or at sales conventions, the fees for such uses being reduced accordingly. E-mail uses may also be requested. In addition, some agencies may request an option for "in-game" advertising whereby ads may be put into video games (similar to product placement licenses) or digitally inserted into online video games.

Because of the importance of music to certain advertising campaigns, a number of websites devoted to the product will feature the songs and recordings which have been or are being used in the actual commercials. One example is the Lincoln MKS official website which featured the songs "Under the Milky Way" performed by Sia, "Major Tom (Coming Home)," recorded by Shiny Toy Guns, and Cat Power's version of David Bowie's "Space Oddity." All the commercials could be played on the site and there was information on each song and the artist. In addition, the site also featured a "making of" section which had performance clips as well as artist interviews.

FOREIGN COUNTRIES

Because many songs have international appeal, a substantial number of commercial requests come from advertisers in countries outside the United States. Most of these requests pertain to English-speaking territories, but Germany, France, Italy, and Japan can also generate substantial income from such uses. In such cases, the writer or publisher's representative in the foreign country (the subpublisher) may handle the negotiations after either consulting with or getting approval from the U.S. copyright owner but if the commercial is originating in the United States, the U.S. publisher will usually negotiate the agreement (many times after receiving input from its foreign subpublisher in the applicable territory. In the case of a change of lyrics or a foreign-language version being used, the U.S. publisher will virtually always have approval rights. On occasion, the U.S. publisher (on behalf of itself and the songwriters) will negotiate directly by means of e-mail or telephone with the foreign ad agency and bypass its local subpublisher, but this approach depends on the terms and conditions of the foreign subpublication agreement that controls the song. Because the foreign subpublisher many times is more familiar with what fees the market can bear in its territory than the U.S. publisher, who may be thousands of miles away, the actual negotiations are many times handled by the subpublisher, with either input or approval from the U.S. publisher. Performance royalties can also be earned since many foreign country performing rights organizations (e.g., APRA in Australia, PRS in the United Kingdom, etc.) do pay writers and publishers for commercial uses.

RESTRICTIONS ON SONGWRITER/RECORDING ARTISTS

When an agency pays a well-known writer/performer substantial monies for the use of a song, it may also request a prohibition on the licensing of any other song in the writer's catalogue in conjunction with a competing product during the term of the commercial license agreement. Such catalogue restriction clauses are not common and are totally negotiable, with any prohibition dependent on, among other things, the amount of compensation being paid, if the writer/artist's performance is being used in the commercial, and whether the writer/artist has control over the use of his or her songs and recordings, since in many cases a third-party music publisher controls the songs and a record company controls the recordings of the writer/artist's performances of those songs.

RESTRICTIONS ON FIRST BROADCAST USE BY ANOTHER PRODUCT

Since agencies do pay substantial fees to use hit songs in commercials, some will request that the music publisher not license the song to another advertiser for use in a commercial for a product campaign that will be streamed or broadcast in advance of the initial airing of its television, Internet, or radio commercial. Such a request is understandable and may be acceptable, provided that the restriction does not encompass a substantial period of time, that the fee is large enough to compensate for possible loss of other advertising income, and that the publisher is not prohibited from entering into noncompeting product license agreements during the restricted period for commercials that will be broadcast after the expiration of the nonbroadcast period.

LYRIC CHANGES OR INSTRUMENTAL USES

If the lyrics of the hit song are to be revised by the agency to fit the theme of the commercial (e.g., "My Girl" becoming "Coffee" for Lavazza Coffee, "Groovin'" being changed to "Reuben" for a Subway sandwich promotion, "Fame" becoming "Shorts," and "Leave It to Beaver" becoming "Leave It to Cargo" for Old Navy, "Shaft" becoming "Shaq" for Burger King, and "I'm A Soul Man" becoming "I'm A Bic Man" for Bic razors), or if entirely new lyrics are to replace the original lyrics, the exact nature of the lyric revisions or new lyrics will always be specified in the license agreement so that no misunderstanding will arise between the agency and the music publisher or songwriter as to what was intended and agreed upon prior to the commercial's being on the air. If the composition will be used instrumentally and without the original lyrics, or both instrumentally and with new lyrics in separate commercials, that will also be indicated in the body of the contract. Specificity in this area cannot be overemphasized for the protection of all parties to the license agreement; the more concrete and exact a contract is, the less likely that there will be a lawsuit. It is also very common for a publisher to charge more for the commercial use of a song when a lyric is changed than when it is not.

CONFIDENTIALITY AGREEMENTS

On occasion, the advertising agency will ask the music publisher to sign a confidentiality agreement before the agency sends the publisher copies of the storyboard or provides specifics as to the type of marketing campaign and the actual content of the commercial being planned. If such an arrangement is requested by the agency, it usually occurs immediately after a quote for the composition has been given by the publisher, but, in some cases, this arrangement may be requested when the agency contacts the music publisher to ask for the use of a composition and explains the general nature of the use.

The confidentiality agreement can take many forms but, in most cases, it is a short document. In the agreement, the music publisher acknowledges that, in the course of the development, pre-production, production, or post-production of the commercial, the publisher may learn certain information relating to the products of the client, the advertising plans for the product, and the contents of the commercials relating to the advertised product. In this regard, the music publisher and its employees or affiliated companies agree not to disclose any portion of such information to any third parties without obtaining the prior written consent of either the advertising agency or the client.

Some of the guarantees that may be agreed to by the music publisher, if such a confidentiality agreement is requested or demanded by the advertising agency, are:

That it will not provide anyone with the storyboard, script, advertising copy or other elements used in the development or production of the commercial;

That it will not allow any third parties to view, exhibit, or inspect the commercial prior to the actual broadcast or commercial distribution of the commercial;

That it will not disclose the fee;

That it will not disclose the content of the advertising commercial prior to the initial broadcast or distribution date of the commercial; and

That it will not authorize the release of any promotional or publicity materials about the music publisher that mention the commercial or the services rendered by the music publisher in relation to the commercial.

PERFORMANCE RIGHTS

The agreement for a hit song is similar to a television synchronization license in that the advertiser/client (like the producer of a television series) is given the right to include the composition in the commercial, with the streaming, broadcast, or performance of that composition being conditioned on a streaming service, radio, or television station's having a valid performing rights license from ASCAP, BMI, SESAC, GMR, or some other person, firm, corporation, or association (including the music publisher) duly empowered to grant such rights on behalf of the copyright owners.

ALTERNATIVE COMPENSATION PACKAGES

A number of sponsors are also funding or contributing to the touring costs of major artists and, as a result, arrangements are many times made to include either concert footage or the artist's songs in advertising commercials for the sponsor's product. In these cases, the commercial licensing fees may be different from the standard advertising agreement since the fee for the use of a song or a performance is made in a different manner. This concept also appears in a number of other variations where the writer/artist receives compensation (which may be nonmonetary in the case of promotion benefits) that may not fit into the format of the traditional advertising commercial license agreement.

PERFORMANCE ROYALTIES FOR ADVERTISING MUSIC

Most music used in commercials is written specifically for the product being promoted. When the agency or sponsor has not bought out the broadcast rights for a jingle, performance royalties can be earned but are usually insignificant unless the advertising campaign lasts many years. Nonetheless, most of the large advertising agencies have had in-house music publishing divisions for many years, and there is a growing trend for even small agencies to set up music publishing companies to collect this source of income.

In the case of hit songs used in commercials, however, substantial monies can be made. All that is needed is information on the advertising field, experience with the rules and regulations of the performing rights organizations with respect to commercial payments, and reasonableness in one's negotiating position with the agency or sponsor. A single phone call or e-mail, if handled correctly, can result in hundreds of thousands of dollars in immediate income, as well as additional dollars in back end performance royalties.

CONCLUSION

Whether one is writing original music and lyrics for an advertising agency, a production music house, or a music library, or has previously existing songs or scores used in a commercial, advertising can be a lucrative area for writers and music publishers. For many, today's world of advertising music is not the "sell out" of years ago but rather another way of exploiting one's music and making money.

CHAPTER 10
MUSIC, MONEY, AND PERFORMANCES

The performing rights area—the world of ASCAP, BMI, SESAC, and GMR in the United States, and foreign country societies throughout the rest of the world—represents, for most songwriters, film, and TV composers and music publishers, the greatest source of continuing royalty income. Throughout the world, writers and publishers receive in the area of $7 billion in royalties from this right of copyright each year, yet very few understand what the right is, where these royalties come from, which organizations negotiate and collect them, how these organizations compute royalties, how the services offered by these organizations compare with one another, how one may leave one organization to join another, and how you can remove your works. Considering that performance royalties continue well beyond the lives of many writers (life of the author plus 70 years in many cases), knowledge of this area is a necessity for anyone involved in any aspect of music. Though the royalty figures do vary for any given type of use based on many factors, Table 10.1 sets forth the type of monies that can be earned in this field.

PERFORMING RIGHT ROYALTIES FOR VARIOUS TYPES OF USES

Table 10.1

Type of Performance	Writer and Publisher Royalties
Number One Billboard pop song of the year	$2,400,000
10 minutes of underscore per episode on a network television series airing for 10 years	$1,656,000
Theme song for a network television series on the air for five years	$460,000
Song performed on primetime network television	$7,000
Hit song used in a commercial with a two-year broadcast run	$400,000
No. 1 pop chart single	$1,400,000
No. 10 pop chart single	$500,000
No. 50 pop chart single	$90,000
15 minutes of underscore on each episode of a television series airing for one year	$44,000
One performance of a primetime network television series theme song	$2,000
A major popular song's lifetime of copyright earnings	$7,500,000
Jingle performance on network television	$50
Production company logo	$50
Worldwide foreign performances of a Top 10 chart hit	$1,600,000
One college radio performance	6¢
Foreign performances of the underscore from a Number One worldwide blockbuster movie	$1,000,000

THE PERFORMING RIGHT

Despite its name, the musical composition performing right has nothing to do with artists or performers. It is a right of copyright that is set forth in the U.S. Copyright Law, as well as the laws of most countries, and that applies to the payment of license fees by music users when those users perform the copyrighted musical compositions of writers and publishers. This right recognizes that a writer's creation is a property right and its use requires permission as well as compensation. Performances can be songs heard on a terrestrial radio station, an audio streaming service, or a digital jukebox; underscore in a television series; or music performed live or on tape at a Las Vegas show, an amusement park, a sporting event, a major concert venue, a local rock 'n' roll, country, or jazz club, or a symphonic concert hall. Performances can be music channels on an airplane, music at a convention, or music on hold on a smartphone. Music users (those who pay the license fees) include the major television networks, U.S. local television and radio stations, pay cable services (HBO, Showtime), basic cable (USA Network, MTV, VH-1, A&E), online services, concert halls, streaming services, websites, the hotel industry, colleges and universities, nightclubs, bar and grills, theme parks, and many others. In short, in most situations where music is played (with the exception of the home), a user is paying a license fee, an organization is collecting those fees, and writers and publishers are being paid royalties for the performances of their copyrighted works.

In the United States, this right's primary recognition came as part of the 1909 Copyright Act, with further definition under the 1976 Copyright Revision Act. The right covers the nondramatic performance of copyrighted musical works. It does not involve dramatic rights, also known as grand rights, where performances of a composition are licensed directly by the copyright owner. Dramatic, or grand rights, include works being performed in musicals (the live theater), operas, ballets, and so on. Compositions, though considered dramatic in the context of their original theater or opera setting, are generally under the nondramatic right when performed individually on radio or television. In the United States, four performing rights organizations (PROs) negotiate license fee agreements with the users of music and distribute those fees back to the writers and publishers whose music and lyrics are being performed. The organizations are the American Society of Composers, Authors, and Publishers (ASCAP), a nonprofit writer and publisher membership association founded in 1914, Broadcast Music, Inc. (BMI), a nonprofit broadcaster owned corporation organized in 1939, SESAC, a for profit corporation originally founded in 1930, and Global Music Rights (GMR), a for-profit corporation established in 2013. It is important to note that music publishers also negotiate fees for the compositions they represent for certain media. As the vast majority of the license fees in this area are either ASCAP or BMI, the primary focus of this chapter will be on those two organizations.

PRO SAMPLE STATEMENT

Media	Performances	Writer or Publisher Royalty
TV per Program	148	$2,500
Commercial Radio	289,800	$163,000
College Radio	3,395	$118
Satellite Radio	707	$2,100
Network TV	200	$1,800
Local TV	128	$900
Cable TV	40	$1,000
Public Broadcasting	80	$50
Digital Jukebox	43,500	$100
Ringback Tones	30,000	$200
Theme Parks	16,000	$450
Commercial Jingle	1,100	$520
Sports League	10	$120
Aircraft	1,500	$30

Live Concerts
  Headliner
  Opening Act
	
	44
	20
		
		$1,400
		$110

Streaming Services (Apple, YouTube, Pandora, Tidal, Spotify, etc.)	430,000 18,000,000 350,000 65,000,000 350,000 40,000	$100 $4,000 $90 $50,000 $35 $3

Audiovisual Services (Netflix, Amazon, Hulu, Apple, etc.)	2,000,000 2,000	$166 $0.40
Background Music Services	380,000	$65

U.S. PERFORMING RIGHTS ORGANIZATIONS: OVERALL VIEW

It is important to note in reading this chapter to keep in mind that all four U.S. PROs—ASCAP, BMI, SESAC, and GMR—are very different in nearly every aspect of their operations. The U.S. PROs have different ownership and organizational structures (association, corporation, nonprofit, profit, etc.), payment methodologies, payment formulas, bonus provisions for successful radio, streaming, and television compositions, royalty categories, both for type of use (theme song, score, visual vocals, audio-only performances, etc.) and category of user (traditional and satellite radio, television, streaming services, live performance venues, background music services, etc.). Each PRO utilizes different membership and affiliation agreements as well as rules and procedures which contain, among other things, different resignation and termination procedures and dates, withdrawal of works provisions, royalty payment systems, allocation of revenue procedures, dispute resolution and recourse provisions, and change of payment practices.

The basic similarity among all four is their overall role in negotiating license agreements with the users of music for the performance of their writer's and publisher's works, collecting the license fees attributable to those agreements, and distributing royalties to their writers and publishers.

ROYALTIES, CONSENT DECREES, LITIGATION, AND LEGISLATION

All writers and publishers need to be aware of the substantial role and effect that government, litigation, and legislation have had, and continue to have, on U.S. PRO royalties.

In the case of ASCAP and BMI, they have been under consent decrees with the government since 1941 for alleged anti-trust abuses. These decrees regulate to a certain extent how these organizations operate and function both in the licensing field as well as in their relationships and responsibilities to their writers and publishers. Under the decrees, federal rate courts were established where in situations where ASCAP or BMI and a user could not come to an agreement on what a "reasonable license fee" for the use of a PRO's music was, either party could go to court, have a trial, and have a judge decide what the license fees should be in any given area. From a writer and publisher point of view, past decisions, particularly as regards the online/digital audio and audiovisual streaming services, have not been good as far as license fees or the resulting royalties from those fees.

As to SESAC and GMR, the two smaller U.S. PROs, they are not under consent decrees with the government or currently under any government oversight. SESAC did, though, in its settlements of anti-trust litigation brought against it by both the local radio and television industries, agree to mandatory arbitration when negotiated license fee agreements cannot be reached. In addition, SESAC agreed to not interfere with any of its writers' and publishers' efforts to issue direct licenses to users. GMR, however, is completely unregulated and, in many cases, is the exclusive licensor of its writers' and publishers' works-issues which resulted in anti-trust litigation between the radio industry and GMR.

Issues continue to develop as to the interpretation, length, and necessity of the consent decrees, and the viability of alternative rate setting mechanisms, among others. Litigation as well as legislation also play a role in the amount and type of royalties that writers and publishers receive.

THE ORGANIZATIONS AND HOW TO JOIN

ASCAP

The American Society of Composers, Authors, and Publishers is an unincorporated membership association formed in 1914 by writers (composers and lyricists) and music publishers. ASCAP's charter members included Victor Herbert, John Philip Sousa, Jerome Kern, and Irving Berlin, among others, and its total membership in its first year of operation was 170 writers and 22 publishers. The society has a board of directors of 12 writers and 12 publishers, who are elected for two-year terms by the membership. The president of the society is a member of the board as well as chosen by the board and has traditionally been a writer member. The basic principles that govern the society are that members similarly situated should be treated alike, that revenues collected from a particular area are to be distributed to performances in that area, and that distributions are to be made on an objective basis. ASCAP has in the area of 700,000 writer and publisher members and has been subject to a consent decree with the U.S. government since 1941.

To be eligible to join ASCAP as a full writer or publisher member, it is necessary to have either one commercial recording (CD, album, download, digital file, etc.) of a song written or published by the prospective member, commercially available printed sheet music of the composition, a program from a concert or recital hall listing the composition, or evidence of a performance of the composition in an ASCAP-licensed medium (a letter from a club, radio, or television station confirming the performance, a cue sheet from a film or television producer, or a broadcasting station or a website performance) listing the composition with writer and publisher information included. Once the writer or publisher meets the eligibility requirements, an application must be completed and forwarded to ASCAP for election to membership. If a writer is also a publisher, a separate publisher application needs to be completed. For publisher memberships, it is also necessary to clear with ASCAP the prospective company name to make sure that the name is not currently being used by another U.S. or foreign publisher. Applying online can be done at www.ascap.com.

The month in which a writer or publisher is elected determines the extent of any retroactive royalty payments. The following 2017 election chart shows the retroactive period covered by each election:

Writer Elections	Retroactive Crediting Date
January–March 2018	April–June 2017 performances
April–June 2018	July–September 2017 performances
July–September 2018	October–December 2017 performances
October–December 2018	January–March 2018 performances

Publisher Elections	Retroactive Crediting Date
January–March 2018	July–September 2017 performances
April–June 2018	October–December 2017 performances
July–September 2018	January–March 2018 performances
October–December 2018	April–June 2018 performances

BMI

Broadcast Music, Inc., is a corporation organized in 1939 by members of the radio broadcasting industry, with which writers and publishers affiliate. Ownership now also includes television broadcasting companies. Publisher affiliation was available from inception, with writer affiliation commencing in 1950. BMI has a board of directors consisting of 13 executives associated with companies in the broadcasting field and one BMI employee who is the president. BMI has more than 800,000 affiliated writers and publishers, and has been under a consent decree with the U.S. government since 1941.

The eligibility requirements to become affiliated with BMI as a writer or publisher are basically the same as those set forth for ASCAP, with the addition of affiliation available to a writer whose work is likely to be performed on radio, television, etc.

Once the writer or publisher meets the eligibility requirements, an application for writer or publisher affiliation must be completed and returned to BMI. Publisher names must be cleared for use with BMI prior to the application being completed. Affiliation takes effect upon the writer or publisher signing the contract and BMI countersigning the document. If a writer does not have a publishing company, BMI will pay the full publisher share to the writer.

TYPES OF LICENSE AGREEMENTS

The most common type of license agreement signed by users with ASCAP and BMI is the "blanket license." This license allows a user (a radio or television station, for instance) to perform any works in the ASCAP or BMI repertory during the term of the license for a specific negotiated fee. This unlimited access to repertory includes all of the past works of writer and publisher members or affiliates, as well as the works written by such members or affiliates during the entire term of the license agreement with ASCAP or the writer and publisher affiliation agreement with BMI. The license also covers the works of writers who are members of foreign societies (PRS, SOCAN, APRA, etc.). The blanket license allows a user to perform the copyrighted works of writers and publishers without worrying about infringement litigation (performing copyrighted works without permission), the administrative recordkeeping of what is being performed, or the identity of the correct parties to be paid and what the payment is to be. Blanket licenses are negotiated agreements in which the license fee paid by the user can be, among others, a flat dollar fee, a per-subscriber or gross revenue fee, a fee based on net receipts from sponsors, a fee based upon intensity of music usage, or based on such other objective factors as the number of full-time students for universities, the seating capacity and the types of equipment used in nightclubs, and live entertainment expenditures for hotels. License agreements have a maximum term of five years.

A "per program license," on the other hand, is a license for the entire repertory of a specific PRO with payment—a percentage of program revenue—made only for programs that contain that specific PRO's repertory, which is not directly licensed by the writer or publisher copyright owner. Since ASCAP and BMI writer and publisher agreements are "nonexclusive" based upon the provisions of their respective consent decrees with the government, they have a right to negotiate "direct licenses" with users (broadcasters, etc.) or "source licenses" with program producers for the use of their musical compositions thereby bypassing the ASCAP or BMI license entirely. Under the per program license, stations also pay an incidental music fee for music uses not contained in specific programs and ambient uses in local news programs. The core provisions of this license were set by the court decision *U.S. v. ASCAP/Application of Buffalo Broadcasting* (S.D.N.Y. 1993).

Two additional types of licenses are the "adjustable fee/carve out blanket license," which is a blanket license whose fee can be subsequently reduced by the number of direct or source licenses a user negotiates and a "through-to-the-audience license" with a fee that takes into account the "value of all performances made pursuant to the license including all further transmissions by users with an economic relationship to the licensee." A good example of the latter are the network licenses when a television network (ABC, CBS, NBC) broadcasts its programming to all of its affiliated stations. This network license would cover all music on the network programs broadcast by those stations with no further license required by the affiliated stations.

With the online/digital world no longer considered "new media" requiring separate PRO licenses in many situations, most traditional media PRO licenses now cover retransmissions or simultaneous streaming on websites, webcasts, multicasting, and programming supplied by stations via mobile, wireless, or any other digital platform on a through-to-the-audience basis. For strictly Internet music users, separate PRO licenses apply.

Most licenses are negotiated by the PROs on an industry-wide basis with entities representing the members of specific industries. These include the Radio Music Licensing Committee (RMLC) for traditional radio, the Television Music Licensing Committee (TMLC) for local television stations, the NCTA—the Internet and Television Association for Cable Television Operators, the American Hotel and Lodging Association (AHLA) for every segment of the hotel industry, and the National Association of College and University Business Officers (NACUBO) for colleges and universities, among others.

Finally, any entity or individual who has an exclusive right to license a work(s) (as opposed to a PRO under restrictions) can negotiate with users any type of license agreement agreed upon by the parties. Without such an agreement, the user cannot perform the composition and would be subject to a copyright infringement action if they did so.

DIRECT LICENSE ADMINISTRATION SERVICES

Both ASCAP and BMI have business units to handle the administration of direct licenses entered into between their publishers and digital services. The units collect, process, and match performance information as well as distribute royalties pursuant to each PRO's distribution policies and rules. They do not negotiate license fees.

WRITER AND PUBLISHER CONTRACTS AND TERMINATION DATES

One of the most important provisions of any contract is the termination provision—the clause and rules that govern how you can leave an organization in order to join another. In the performing rights area, these provisions not only control whether a writer or publisher can leave but also whether one can remove their works from one organization and place them with another. Over the years, there have been many major writer and publisher switches—some due to advances, guarantees, bank loans, and other financial incentives, some due to significant outpayments by one organization over another for the same type of use, some due to an organization's rules and regulations which significantly affected earnings, some because of the difference in payments between writers and publishers, some because the staff and services are better elsewhere, some based upon personal relationships, some based on philosophy, some based on the inability to correct a problem or understand a problem or solve a problem, some based on inadequate surveys of performances which determine payment, and some just to make a change. Regardless of the reason, it is essential you know each organization's termination/resignation provisions as well as the rules, regulations, and policies affecting continued payment as well as the ability to remove works.

When a writer or publisher joins ASCAP, affiliates with BMI or SESAC, or contracts with GMR, they fill out an application and sign a contract, which is a legally binding agreement that sets forth the specific contractual obligations, duties, and remedies of all parties. Contracts have changed over time, so always be aware of the most recent PRO contract as well as the significance of any changes.

The ASCAP agreement is the same for both writers and publishers and gives the society the right to license the nondramatic public performances of the member's works. The agreement also grants ASCAP the right to enforce and protect the rights of public performance, to prevent infringement of such works by litigation, and to have all of the rights and remedies for enforcing the copyrights as well as the right to sue under such copyrights. The agreement is subject to the provisions of ASCAP's 2001 consent decree with the government (the Second Amended Final Judgment), as well as the Society's Articles of Association, the Compendium of Rules and Regulations and Policies Supplemental to the Articles, the Membership Agreement, the Rules, Regulations and Policies adopted by the Board of Directors, ASCAP's Survey and Distribution System: Rules and Policies and the Board of Review Rules of Procedure. The agreement also states that the board of directors must consist of an equal number of writers and publishers, and that the royalties distributed must be divided into two equal sums for division to writer and publisher members. The agreement is nonexclusive, which means the writer or publisher retains the ability to directly license their works to a user.

The ASCAP agreement is a continuing year-to-year agreement that gives a writer or publisher the right to resign from the society any year. A specific form needs to be completed and signed and notice provisions based on a writer or publisher's date of election to ASCAP must be adhered to. Advance written notice must be sent no more than six months nor less than three months before the effective resignation date. For instance, writers and publishers elected to ASCAP membership in January,

February, or March of any year must give notice between October 1 and December 31 of the prior year for the resignation to be effective on April 1. The resignation notice dates for April, May, and June ASCAP elections of any year would require notice between January 1 and March 31 for an effective resignation on July 1. July through September elections would require notice between April 1 and June 30 with an effective date of October 1 and October through December elections require notice between July 1 and September 30 for an effective date of January 1.

The contracts that most writers and publishers sign with BMI are the same, but provisions can be negotiated provided the writer or publisher makes such a request and has the bargaining power to effect a change. Although most initial affiliation agreements are not negotiated, many successful writers and publishers renegotiate the provisions prior to any extension of the contract.

The BMI agreement specifies a relationship of ordinary contracting parties with all disputes to be submitted to the American Arbitration Association in New York; the agreement grants to BMI all of the rights you own to publicly perform and to license others to perform anywhere in the world in any and all media. It also appoints BMI as one's true and lawful attorney to restrain infringements of and/or to enforce and protect the rights granted hereunder. The agreement is nonexclusive whereby the writer and publisher retain the right to directly license their works to others and is subject to all the provisions of the BMI consent decree.

Most BMI writer agreements are for a period of two years and continue thereafter for additional terms of two years each, unless they are terminated by either party by registered or certified mail at least three months (some specify 60 days) prior to the end of a term. For example, if a writer signed a BMI contract on June 30, 2018, the contract would run until June 30, 2020, and continue to renew for additional two-year periods (June 30, 2022; June 30, 2024; June 30, 2026) unless terminated. A writer could terminate by giving registered or certified notice to BMI no sooner than six months prior to June 30, 2020, or any two-year term after that, and no later than three months (some older contracts specify 60 days) prior to June 30, 2020, or any two-year term after that.

Most BMI publisher agreements are for a period of five years from the date of signing and continue for additional periods of five years each, unless terminated by either party by registered or certified mail not more than six months or less than three months prior to the end of a term. If a publisher misses the termination date, the contract extends for an additional five-year period. For example, if a publisher signed a contract on June 30, 2017, and wished to terminate the contract sometime afterward, notice would have to be given no sooner than six months prior to June 30, 2022, and no later than three months prior to June 30, 2022. If these termination dates were missed, the contract would extend to June 30, 2027.

Some of the types of BMI deals negotiated in the past by certain writers and publishers include year-to-year, six-month, quarterly, or monthly agreements. For writers who own their own publishing companies, agreements are sometimes negotiated where the duration of the writer and publisher agreements are the same and coterminous (beginning and ending on the same days) and have the same termination notice requirements.

ROYALTY ASSIGNMENTS/BUYOUTS OF WRITER ROYALTIES

For many years, royalty assignments of writer royalties as well as "buy outs" of writer royalties were rare primarily based on the internal policies and philosophies of the U.S. PROs. In today's world, that situation has changed completely as all the PROs now accept assignments of royalties to third parties. In many cases, there are specific conditions that must be met for the assignment to be accepted and be effective.

In the case of ASCAP, the Articles of Association generally prohibit the assignment of royalties except as the board of directors may provide by regulation and even then, the assignments are subject to ASCAP's review and approval. The approved assignments include assignments to corporations 95% owned by one or more writer members, irrevocable assignments of deceased writer royalties, irrevocable and revocable assignments of living writer royalties under certain conditions, assignments related to repayment of a line of credit, loan, or advance, and assignments to provide a security interest to a financial institution, among others.

BMI recognizes an assignment of royalties to a third party in certain circumstances, including to lending institutions or other person or entity who makes a bona fide loan of a specific sum of money which is intended to be repaid, in whole or in part from BMI royalties. BMI also will accept certain irrevocable permanent assignments of royalties to a third party who purchases a writer's royalty income stream. Assignments can be limited to only compositions in a catalogue as of the time of the assignment or current catalogue works plus new works that are put into the catalogue or only works set forth on a specific schedule of copyrights.

As to SESAC and GMR, they both accept assignments in specific types of cases.

DIRECT LICENSING

The ability of a copyright owner to directly license a work to a music user and bypass the PRO is a settled issue with ASCAP, BMI, and SESAC. Language in both the ASCAP and BMI consent decrees guarantee the right of any member or affiliate to directly license their works to a user. SESAC, as it is not under a consent decree with the government, incorporates the following language in its writer and publisher affiliation agreements that insures the right to directly license: "Publisher retains the right to issue nonexclusive licenses directly to any third person for the public performance in the U.S., its territories and possessions, of any work subject to this agreement." The PROs cannot interfere in any way with this right or the ability to exercise this right.

Language as to the ability to direct license as well as the effect of a direct license has been standard in many types of industry license agreements, including work-for-hire and employee-for-hire contracts for many decades. A sample clause might read:

The performing rights in this Composition, to the extent permitted by law, shall be assigned to and licensed by the applicable PRO with said organization authorized to collect and receive all monies earned from the public performance of the Composition and to pay the Writers and Publishers directly. If to the extent it is unlawful for the PRO, or any of its affiliates, to issue small performing rights licenses or the applicable performing rights organization does not from time to time, for any reason whatsoever, maintain a regular system of collecting performance fees and/or a third party licensee (i.e., a television network, independent television station, digital music service, etc.) requires direct licensing of such rights, Company and Publisher shall have the right to directly license their respective shares of the public performance rights in the Composition to such third parties. If the Company or Publishing Designee receives a distribution of earned public performance fees from any source that does not make a separate distribution directly or indirectly to Publisher, then Publisher shall be entitled to receive its portion of such fees and Writer shall be entitled to receive the Writer's share of such fees.

Additional variations of a direct license clause are as follows:
Licensee desires to obtain from Publisher a blanket license for all necessary performance, reproduction, and distribution rights militated by the delivery of programming embodying Publisher's catalogue and Publisher is willing to grant such right to license on a nonexclusive basis.

The right to publicly perform and to authorize others to perform the Composition by means of a media entity not licensed by ASCAP, BMI, or SESAC is subject to clearance of the performing right either from the Licensor or from any other duly authorized licensor acting for or on behalf of Licensor subject to good faith negotiations in accordance with established industry customs and practices.

An issue in many agreements is what happens to the writer's share when a copyright owner, usually the music publisher, directly licenses a work to a user. Clauses range from "payments to be made based upon the prevailing PRO rates for the specific use," "compensation to be negotiated in good faith," reasonable fee," "fee subject to arbitration," "a complete buyout with no further compensation," or "50% of any license fee received."

CONSIDERATIONS IN MAKING A DECISION

Because the four U.S. performing rights organizations are organized differently, have entirely different payment formulas, owners, contracts, and philosophies, and collect substantially different amounts of money from all types of media, the decision as to which one a writer and publisher should join or affiliate with should not be taken lightly, as millions of dollars in royalty income can be at stake if the wrong decision is made. Two of the most important considerations in this decision should be which organization will best protect your copyrights over their entire copyright life and which organization will compensate you best, both in the short term as well as the long term, for U.S. and foreign performances of your works.

The primary areas that need to be considered include the length of a writer's or publisher's contract and the procedures to terminate that contract if one wants to leave, fairness and equality of treatment in the distribution of royalties, the actual dollar amounts paid for every type of use (scores, themes, visual vocals, etc.) in all relevant media (television, radio, streaming services, etc.), recognition of the value of all of a writer's and publisher's copyrights whether they be new or old works, procedures whereby each organization changes its payment rules, dispute resolution procedures, the bonus systems in place, relationships with foreign performing rights organizations, maximum and accurate collection of foreign income, among others.

Although many writers at the start of their careers fail to appreciate the importance of this decision, it represents one of the most important ones they will ever make, as it will affect performance royalties for the life of the copyright of a composition. Mistakes can be costly in this area, and it is far better to learn the basics at the start of one's career rather than midway or at the end.

The good news is that you can move from one PRO to another as long as you follow the resignation and termination rules and procedures. Whether you can move one's past works to the new PRO is an entirely different story.

ASCAP AND BMI INCOME AND DISTRIBUTIONS

The starting point for how much an ASCAP or BMI performance is worth is the total revenue that comes into each organization. Table 10.2 sets forth the total domestic and foreign receipts of ASCAP and BMI, as well as the total royalty distributions each year to writers and publishers. The table also illustrates the substantial growth of this field over the past decades. In the case of ASCAP, the figures are exact, as detailed annual financial statements are issued to the membership. In the case of BMI, recent years reports are precise with estimates given for years when BMI did not issue financial statements to its affiliates. The BMI year, as opposed to the ASCAP January-through-December year, runs from July 1 of one year through June 30 of the following year. For instance, BMI reported in September of 2017 receipts of $1.13 billion and $1.023

billion in distributions for their 2016–2017 year, whereas ASCAP's 2017 revenue was $1.144 billion with $1.007 billion in distributions. The operating costs for both ASCAP and BMI are in the area of 12–13%. SESAC and GMR, as they are privately held, do not issue financial statements to their writers and publishers.

ASCAP AND BMI RECEIPTS AND DISTRIBUTIONS

Table 10.2

Year	ASCAP Receipts	ASCAP Distributions to Members	BMI Receipts	BMI Distributions to Affiliates
2016	$1,059,000,000	$904,000,000	$1,060,000,000	$931,000,000
2015	$1,014,849,000	$867,365,000	$1,013,000,000	$877,000,000
2014	$1,002,596,000	$883,543,000	$944,000,000	$814,000,000
2010	$935,281,000	$844,641,000	$917,000,000	$789,000,000
2009	$995,118,000	$862,960,000	$905,000,000	$788,000,000
2008	$933,607,000	$817,803,000	$901,000,000	$786,000,000
2006	$785,475,000	$680,267,000	$779,000,000	$676,000,000
2000	$577,157,000	$480,304,000	$501,000,000	$417,000,000
1992	$389,979,000	$312,029,000	$280,000,000	$230,000,000
1982	$186,974,000	$152,340,000	$120,000,000	$100,000,000
1972	$69,467,000	$52,899,000	$40,000,000	$30,000,000

COMPONENTS OF ASCAP AND BMI INCOME

The primary job of ASCAP and BMI is to negotiate license fee agreements with the users of music for the nondramatic performance of copyrighted works and to pay those fees back to writers and publishers based on the performances of their compositions. Knowledge of the sources making up each organization's total income is important, as it relates directly to the royalties paid for music and lyrics in any area.

DOMESTIC

In the domestic area (U.S. users of music), the largest single source of revenue comes from television, with radio in second place and general (concert halls, nightclubs, hotels, etc.) and background music operations third. The remainder of each organization's total income comes from the symphonic and concert field, new media uses, and interest on investments. Using ASCAP as a guide, since it does publish specific financial figures, the society's 2015 year-end financial statement is illustrative of where a PRO's money comes from. For that year total receipts were $1,014,849,000 which included $348 million from television (network, local cable, etc.), $174 million from radio stations, $131 million from the general licensing area, $56 million from new media and $6 million from the symphonic and concert area. To illustrate comparative growth, the 1972 ASCAP year of $69 million in receipts showed $33 million from television, $18 million from radio, $8 million from the general licensing area, and $314,000 from the symphonic field.

FOREIGN

In recent years, one of the greatest areas of income growth for both ASCAP and BMI has been the royalties received from foreign performing rights organizations. The reasons for this growth have primarily been due to the ever-increasing popularity of the U.S. repertory overseas as well as the substantial increase in the number of radio and television stations as well as digital services in foreign countries. For certain years, exchange rate fluctuations can affect the amount of incoming foreign money. Every major country of the world has a performing rights society that collects for ASCAP and BMI writers and publishers when their works are performed in the foreign territory. These societies forward those monies to ASCAP and BMI, which in turn distribute them to their members or affiliates. Through agreements with these foreign societies, ASCAP and BMI also collect for foreign writers and publishers whose works are performed in the U.S. and forward those monies to the particular society of which the foreign writer or publisher is a member.

In 2016, ASCAP received approximately $300 million from foreign societies for foreign performances of its writers' and publishers' works. BMI's 2016–2017 foreign receipts figure was $294 million. By contrast, in 1987 ASCAP's foreign collections totaled $50 million, with BMI's at approximately $30 million. Considering that most major music publishers collect performance money directly from foreign societies through local subpublishers, most of the foreign money received and distributed by ASCAP and BMI is writer money. The top countries sending performance money to the U.S. are Britain (PRS for Music), Germany (GEMA), Japan (JASRAC), Italy (SIAE), France (SACEM), Canada (SOCAN), Netherlands (BUMA), Australia/New Zealand (APRA), Spain (SGAE), Sweden (STIM), and Switzerland (SUISA), among others.

SPECIAL DISTRIBUTIONS

An important element of the ASCAP and BMI annual income figure is whether any area (television, radio, foreign, streaming services, etc.) received a "special distribution" of past monies in that year. These "special distributions" represent distributions to writers and publishers outside the regular quarterly distributions and are usually the result of a settlement or court decision regarding a user's past fees to ASCAP or BMI.

The important thing about these distributions is that they usually involve a substantial amount of additional money for performances on which ASCAP and BMI have already paid. Most writers and publishers consider this "found money," even though it may have taken years of negotiation or litigation to finalize the distributions. It is important for every writer and publisher to stay informed of these retroactive settlements or decisions in order to ensure that they are distributed by the writer's or publisher's organization, based on the specific criterion of the past performances covered by the settlement, court decisions, or voluntary agreement.

Although this criterion may seem obvious, it has not been universally followed by some in the past. For any "special distribution," the factors that you must be aware of are the total amount of the retroactive settlement, the total amount being distributed to writers and publishers, the past performance years being paid on, and the types of performance and medium sharing in the distribution. A few examples of "special distributions" include year 2000, 2001, and 2002 ASCAP total distributions of $120 million for settlements in the cable area; 1992 ASCAP distribution of $19 million from a settlement agreement with the NBC television network for performances occurring during the years 1977–1991; ASCAP distributions in 1985 and 1987 of $14 million and $43 million respectively from local television stations for the years 1979, 1980, and 1984–86 and a 2009 distribution for AOL performances, commencing April 2005, and Clear Channel performances, starting from March 2008; 2011 distributions for 2003–2011 iTunes performances and July 2008–December 2009 YouTube performances; 2015 distribution of Netflix performances from January 2013–June 2015; and BMI special distributions in 1985, 1986, and 1990 of local television monies for the performance years 1979–87, a 2007 distribution of 2002–2005 MTV monies, a 2009 distribution of CBS Television Network and Turner Broadcasting cable and satellite fees dating back to 2006 performances, a 2010 distribution of retroactive Internet royalties for YouTube and MySpace, a 2015 distribution for the 4th quarter of 2013 performances on Pandora and Spotify and the year 2013 and the first two quarters of 2014 on YouTube, 2017 distributions for 2011–2013 Apple Music performances and first quarter through third quarter 2016 performances on Tidal, Vevo, and Groove Music.

As many of the license agreements being made by ASCAP and BMI concern new types of users and some involve retroactive payments for prior periods of time, writers and publishers should stay aware of all new agreements made in order to make sure that they get their fair retroactive share of any past-due monies received by ASCAP or BMI from a user.

INTERIM FEES

Of increasing importance to the amount of royalties being paid to writers and publishers are the situations where users and the performing right organizations are not able to reach final agreements on what license fees should be for a particular period of time. The result of not being able to negotiate a final agreement has been that many users (the television networks, the local television industry, the pay and basic cable industry, etc.) as well as ASCAP and BMI have litigated the matter or gone to a rate court in order for third parties (judges or magistrates) to set what the fees should be in a given area. In many of these cases, the user continues to pay at the old agreement rate or pay an "interim" court-set rate, pending the final outcome of the trial or hearing and all of its appeals. The court-set rate, arrived at after a hearing, can be significantly different than prior fee deals as many factors are taken into account including changed economic circumstances, loss or gain of market share and music use. In interim fee cases, many years or decades can elapse before final license fees for an area are determined and paid.

ADVANCES/GUARANTEES/LOANS/ON ACCOUNT PAYMENTS/OTHER FINANCIAL TRANSACTIONS

Similar to practically every other area of the music business, advances, guarantees, loans and other types of financial inducements and arrangements have been an integral part of the U.S. performing rights organization business. Prior to the formation in 1939 of BMI, there was no competition for songwriters and composers as the only U.S. society was ASCAP, a situation common to practically every other country of the world where only one society is the norm. Once BMI was formed, competition for U.S. repertory commenced.

At the time of its founding in 1939, BMI made a number of arrangements for the movement of existing ASCAP catalogue as well as for the placement of all new writer catalogues. Major efforts were also made in the signing of writers and publishers in genres of music currently becoming popular in the U.S. In the 1960s, BMI was successful in offering significant advance and guarantee deals to many ASCAP film and television composers resulting in a significant loss of major writers and market share for ASCAP. Commencing 1971, ASCAP countered by signing over the next three decades many successful R&B writers and writer/artists as well as many successful pop and rock 'n' roll writers and artists and film and television composers. BMI countered over the years with significant writer and publisher signings.

SESAC, never a force in this world since its founding in 1930, came into its own in the 1990s with the selective signing of a number of major ASCAP and BMI pop writer/artists and successful television composers including their past catalogues. Global Music Rights, commencing in 2013 employed a similar approach as to the signing of major radio writers and their catalogues from ASCAP and BMI.

In many of the aforementioned situations, advances, guarantees as well as other types of financial arrangements played a role in the switch (see other factors in the Contract and Termination Date section).

The competition continues to this day, not only for the superstar radio songwriters and film and television composers but also for writers and composers of significance as well as new bands and artist/writers of every genre. Repertory is everything in the U.S.—what each PRO has determines its license fees which, in turn, determines what each PRO can pay its writers and publishers. The songs and scores that a PRO has in its repertory determines negotiating value and licensing value. In short, the future of each organization is in the repertory it has, the repertory it keeps, and in the repertory it adds. The size and scope of its repertory also affects its collections from foreign societies—a major source of money for U.S. writers and publishers.

Financial transactions can take many forms including an advance against all future royalties until recouped, a single or multi-year guarantee of a certain amount of money regardless of whether you earn it or not, nonrecoupable signing or retention bonuses, contractual agreements to pay a certain percentage above what other PROs are paying, matching payments on split works, partial quarterly recoupments so that some money continues to flow through to the writer or publisher as well as many other variations. Hardship and financial need advances are also considered based on need as well as money projected in the system for a writer's or publisher's repertory. Loan arrangements from banks vary and use the writer or publisher applicable catalogue earnings as well as income projections (chart songs, television series, foreign box office film success, etc.) in projecting the amount of the loan as well as repayment provisions.

It is important to note that in cases where a writer leaves one U.S. PRO and joins another PRO and is unable to move his or her past catalogue to the new PRO, all of a writer's foreign country incoming performance distributions for all past works will now be forwarded by the foreign society to the writer's new PRO regardless of whether the new PRO has the right to license those works in the U.S. This switch can have a major recoupment factor for the writer's new PRO as many advances and other financial arrangements are recoupable from both domestic and foreign incoming distributions. In many cases, particularly with successful radio writers and film and television composers, this can mean hundreds of thousands of dollars or millions of dollars in distributions.

PAYMENT DATES AND METHODS OF PAYMENT

ASCAP

ASCAP pays its publishers for U.S. performances approximately five-and-a-half months after the end of each three-month performance quarter, with writers being paid shortly thereafter. A performance statement is issued with each check, and it includes the titles of performed compositions, ownership percentages, performance types, number of plays, media, television episode titles and dates, film titles, duration, credits, and royalty dollars. The following chart illustrates the payment dates for 2017 performances and can be used as a general guide to ASCAP payments.

Performances	Publisher Payment	Writer Payment
January–March 2017	September 2017	October 2017
April–June 2017	December 2017	January 2018
July–September 2017	March 2018	April 2018
October–December 2017	June 2018	July 2018

ASCAP distributes royalties for foreign performances of ASCAP writer and publisher works in February, May, August, and November of each year. Each distribution covers a specific number of countries, time periods, and areas of performance (television, radio, cinema, general, etc.). Performance statements listing all performed titles in each country are issued along with the payments. For example, a sample ASCAP statement might list 50 countries with some of the statement descriptions as follows: United Kingdom (PRS), radio (July–Sept '17), general (July–Sept '17),or Canada (SOCAN), cinema film (January–March '17), television (January–March '17).

ASCAP writers have the choice of receiving their quarterly royalties either on a "Current Performance" basis or an "Averaged Performance" plan (an updated version of the old Four Funds system). The Current Performance plan (the plan on which most writers receive royalties) distributes in one check 100% of the monies due a writer for a three-month performance period. For example, if a writer's radio, television, and wired music performances totaled 8,000 performance credits for a quarter and the value of one credit for that quarter was $8.95, the writer would receive a check for $71,600. The Averaged Performance plan of distribution, on the other hand, calculates each writer's quarterly distribution by taking into account a writer's recent activity as well as a writer's royalty distributions over time.

It is important for every ASCAP writer to know what plan of payment he or she is on, as one's method of payment does have an effect on one's domestic royalty distributions. For example, if a writer who was averaging $2,500 a quarter in royalties on the Averaged plan has a major chart song, or becomes the composer for a network television series with many minutes of music in each episode, the short-term royalty checks for the new activity would be far less than what would have been paid if the writer were on Current Performance, the reason being that only 20% of each averaged check is based on a writer's most recent quarter of activity. The remaining 80% of each check involves five- and 10-year averages of a writer's quarterly distributions.

On the other hand, if an averaged writer was making in the area of $15,000 to $20,000 per quarter and had little or no current activity, the writer's distribution would still remain good for quite some time, as 80% of that writer's payment is based on a five- and 10-year average of his or her past performance dollar values. All new writers are on Current Performance.

The Averaged Performance Plan's writer's checks have three elements in their computation. Twenty percent of each check is based on the most recent performance quarter's credits times the current performance dollar point value for that quarter times 20%. For example, if a writer had 2,500 performance credits in the first quarter of the year 2017, the first computation would be as follows: 2,500 × $8.95 credit value × 20% = $4,475. Similarly, 60% of the check is based on the averaged dollars over 20 performance quarters. In this example, the computation would be 2Q2012 through 1Q2017 quarterly credits × each quarter's Current Performance credit value, divided by 20 × 60%. The remaining 20% of the check is based on averaged dollars over the past forty quarters. In this example, you would take each quarter's credits for the period second quarter 2007 through first quarter 2017 and multiply them by each quarter's current performance point value, then divide by 40 and multiply by 20%. The total of all three computations would result in the writer's check received for the first performance quarter of the year 2017. Though percentages can change, in the area of 77% of the Averaged Performance payment is based on five- and 10-year averages, with 23% based on the most recent quarter's credits. A writer can switch from the Averaged Performance plan to the Current Performance plan or vice-versa by giving notice prior to October 1 of any year, and the switch will take effect the first distribution of the next year (January).

Both types of writer distribution plans serve a purpose, depending on a writer's long-term past and current activity, as well as the writer's financial needs both now and in the future. Practically all ASCAP writers, once on Current Performance, remain on Current Performance throughout their entire membership. Advice as to which payment plan is best for you should always be sought from knowledgeable representatives. All ASCAP foreign royalty distributions are paid to writers as reported by the foreign society and have nothing to do with a writer's domestic choice of distribution.

Publishers are paid the full value of their quarterly statement credits in one check. For instance, if a publisher's catalogue generated 50,000 performance credits in a quarter and the value of one publisher credit for that quarter was $8.95, the publisher's check would be for $447,500.

BMI

BMI pays its writers and publishers for most domestic U.S. performances approximately five-and-a-half months after the end of each three-month performance period. Performance statements are issued with each check. The following 2017 performance periods and their payment dates are representative of payments.

Performance Quarters	Writer and Publisher Payment
January–March 2017	September 2017
April–June 2017	January 2018
July–September 2017	March 2018
October–December 2017	June 2018

BMI makes four foreign performance distributions each year and includes them along with their domestic distributions. Foreign performance statements are issued covering specific countries, time periods, and types of performances and media.

ASCAP AND BMI PAYMENT PHILOSOPHY AND RULES

The payment philosophy and payment rules for the two main U.S. licensing organizations are entirely different for every medium licensed (radio, television, background music services, live performances, streaming services, etc.), as well as for every type of performance (theme songs, underscore, visual vocals and instrumentals, jingles, logos, etc.). In addition, the bonus criteria and add-on monies for successful songs on traditional and satellite radio and streaming services as well as for all music in highly rated television programs is also entirely different. Understanding each organization's underlying philosophy and payment practices is a necessity for understanding your royalties, past, present, and future.

ASCAP

As previously mentioned in the contracts section, ASCAP's philosophy and rules are set forth in seven documents. The Weighting Rules outline the limits that govern ASCAP's board of directors in weighting performances. As all types of performances have different crediting weights (3%, 12%, 60%, 100%), which translate into royalties, these limits are important in defining the relationship between types of performances. The Weighting Formula contains the specific weights for each type of performance as well as other rules affecting the value of performances in any licensed area (television, radio, etc.). The Writer's Distribution Formula explains the two types of payment plans available to writers (current performance and averaged), and the Publisher Distribution Formula explains the publisher's method of payment. The Articles of Association describe the obligations of writer and publisher membership, the procedures used for complaints and protests, the eligibility standards for membership, the voting process used to elect the board (any member who has performance credits in the latest available survey year preceding the election gets one vote; additional votes are based on the number of credits each member has during that year, with a maximum of no more than 100 votes for any member), and many other items. The Compendium contains the rules and regulations adopted by the ASCAP Board as well as administrative policies and practices which supplement the Articles.

In general, ASCAP distributes the license fees collected from a specific area on the performances occurring in that area. For example, radio license fees are paid to radio performances, television fees to television performances, streaming service fees to online performances, etc. The dollar value of a performance is determined by the amount of license fees collected in that area, the amount of ASCAP performances in that area during a three-month period, the different types of performance, and the relationship of that area's license fees to the license fees of all other areas. Writer and publisher payments are made according to the results of census (100% pickup) or sample surveys of performances in each of the areas licensed. Pursuant to a "follow the dollar" philosophy, licensees are surveyed in proportion to their fees to ASCAP.

The values for every type of performance are set out in percentage terms in the Weighting Formula (100% for a feature performance, 60% for theme songs, etc.). Payment formulas using these percentages arrive at the number of credits for a particular type of performance. The number of credits generated by a performance varies based on the medium in which the performance occurs (e.g., radio, television, cable), the type of performance (visual vocal, underscore, theme song, jingle), and the economic significance of the station (the amount of license fees paid). The total of all writer or publisher credits in a quarter are then divided by the total amount of money available for distribution in that quarter to arrive at the dollar value of one credit. A writer or publisher's quarterly credits are then multiplied by that dollar value to arrive at the writer or publisher quarterly royalty check. For instance, if six million ASCAP writer performance credits are generated in a quarter from all feature performances, underscore, theme songs, logos, promos, and jingles, and the writer money available for that distribution is $60 million, the value of one writer credit for that three-month period will be $10.00 ($60 million ÷ six million credits). If a writer has 20,000 credits for all of the compositions in his or her catalogue, for instance, the writer check would be $200,000. The reason, incidentally, that ASCAP uses weights for different types of performances rather than specific dollar amounts on a printed schedule is that it is impossible to know in advance of each quarter precisely how many ASCAP performances there will be in that quarter or what the exact distributable income will be for that quarter.

In the radio area, all feature uses of songs (regardless of their past performance history) are treated equally when performed on the same station or service, with the exception that works that generate more than a certain number of radio or streaming service feature performance credits (hit songs, major catalogue songs, etc.) in a quarter are given an extra bonus payment. In the television area, all types of performances are given specific crediting weights, which translate into dollars. For highly rated shows, additional monies are paid to the themes, underscore, and feature performances contained therein because of their increased value to the repertory. Certain songs that have a substantial history of past performances receive additional crediting (money) when they are used as underscore or in commercials.

BMI

For decades, BMI payment rules were set forth in BMI payment schedules which were issued periodically with each new schedule replacing certain provisions of the older one. These schedules listed dollar and cent values for certain types of performances in specific media (e.g., $5.00 for a full feature performance on television, $1.00 per station for a theme song, etc.) and general statements as to performance areas which had no dollar and cent figures attached to them. Prior to each distribution, voluntary additional monies were added to certain types of performance (e.g., "for this quarter only, TV network primetime feature uses are increased by 110%, theme payments are increased by 30%, morning and afternoon rates by 160%, and other network rates by 100% with radio earnings plus 20%) and bonus monies were added to radio performance based on current activity as well as prior performance history.

Commencing with July 2004 radio performances and October 2007 television performances, BMI replaced all of the dollars and cents per performance figures and quarterly voluntary add-on payments with a payment schedule taking into account the total license fees from an area and the current as well as past performance history of songs in the radio area and increased payments for certain performances of songs in television series, added bonus payments for frequently performed themes, and eliminated all time-of-day factors in favor of the number of viewers watching a show.

PAYMENT CHANGES

Both ASCAP and BMI periodically change their methods of payment, and any change can have a substantial effect on a particular writer or publisher's current and future earnings. This chapter needs to be read in light of the possibility that the system and payments in effect when you joined ASCAP or became affiliated with BMI could very well be different in the days, months, or years after you join. Only with some knowledge of past payment practices and philosophies can a writer or publisher make an informed decision with respect to which organization to join or affiliate with, as well as what to anticipate for the future.

With ASCAP, the ASCAP Board of Directors must approve any change in the Weighting Rules and the Weighting Formula, and all ASCAP members must be notified of such a change. Prior to 2001, notification to the Justice Department and sometimes a U.S. District Court hearing were necessary, but the 2001 ASCAP consent decree removed these provisions.

The following examples illustrate the financial ramifications of payment changes. Television underscore was credited by ASCAP with a 20% payment for three minutes of music in 1960, with subsequent changes over the years to 25%, 27.5%, 30%,

36%, 42%, 48%, and 60% in 2005. A 50% payment for 14-week primetime network television theme songs was instituted in 1983, with all themes increased to 60% in 2005. The theme rate prior to 1983 was 10%. Jingles were increased from a 1% payment in 1960 to a 3% payment in 1982. Different payments, depending on time of day of performance, were put into effect in 1973 for network television performances. An increase in payment for frequently performed radio songs was introduced in 1992 and in 1994. A system of payment premiums (royalty add-ons) for highly rated television shows was commenced with fourth quarter 2004 performances. Audio streaming service (Pandora, Spotify, etc.) bonuses were introduced for fourth quarter 2014 performances and a classic song bonus took effect with second quarter 2015 performances.

With BMI, all payments are subject to change at any time. Examples of some of these changes include the institution of a bonus system for songs in 1977; and a 1977 "Network A" background music increase from 12¢ per minute per station to 22¢ with an increase again in 1984 to 36¢ per minute per station. In 1980 BMI began paying on commercial jingles on an experimental basis. The entire bonus system for radio songs and "million performance works" was substantially changed in the 1987 schedule with a whole-scale revision again in 2005. The television payment system was again significantly changed with June 2008 payments, where time-of-day factors were eliminated, duration became a part of every performance royalty computation, and a new theme bonus was added. A "Streaming Hits Bonus" took effect with first quarter 2015 performances.

Bear in mind that any change by ASCAP, BMI, SESAC, or for that matter, any foreign performing right organization (PRO), in their valuing of a specific type of performance can have an effect on all other types of performances. So pay attention to all PRO payment changes, as they can, and many times do, affect the monies you receive.

CO-WRITTEN COMPOSITIONS

ASCAP and BMI writers can collaborate on compositions with each other even though they are members or affiliates of different organizations. In cases where an ASCAP writer and a BMI writer co-write a song, the publishing interest of the ASCAP writer must be placed in an ASCAP publishing company and the BMI writer's publishing interest placed in a BMI publishing company. Each writer-publisher pair will receive royalty payments from its respective performing right organization. The same arrangement would occur if ASCAP or BMI writers co-wrote a song with a SESAC writer. Each publisher's share must match its corresponding writer's share. For example, if an ASCAP and BMI writer have a 75%–25% writer split on a song, the ASCAP publisher would have 75% of the publishing and the BMI publisher 25%. In this example, ASCAP would pay 75% with BMI paying 25%.

REMOVAL OF WORKS

Both ASCAP and BMI have specific rules as to the removal of works by a writer or publisher for future licensing as they have guaranteed in their license agreements that a user can perform all works in the PRO's repertory when the license was signed as well as all works created during the term of the license. With ASCAP, one of the primary provisions relates to whether there are any license agreements still in effect as of the time of the effective date of the writer or publisher resignation. The works remain with ASCAP until each existing license expires. At BMI, a primary contract provision allows works to be removed at the end of the writer affiliation contract (normally every two years) and at the end of the publisher affiliation contract (normally every five years), assuming valid termination notices have been sent. With the exception of some older contracts, all BMI contracts now have licenses in effect clauses. Specific licensing issues arise (i.e., the ability to license) if only a portion of a work is removed from one organization and placed with another performing right organization (i.e., only the writer share is moved without the corresponding publisher share). Further, the rules in this area do change based upon the introduction of new contract language into agreements as well as PRO internal policy decisions. Contract termination provisions and knowledge of PRO internal policy provisions regarding removal of works is essential for any writer or publisher.

BENEFITS AND SERVICES

In addition to their primary role of licensing, collection, and distribution, the PROs provide many other services to the music industry and the public at large. Some of these additional activities include a series of band and new-writer showcases throughout the U.S. and in foreign countries. These showcases are heavily attended by music industry executives looking for new talent. Other activities include music business and creative-writing workshops, film scoring and musical theater workshops, grant and scholarship programs for high school and college music students and others exhibiting excellence in music, book and article awards, sponsorships of regional music business conferences and songwriter associations, online index searches, which provide information on the millions of songs in the their repertories, and benefits such as health, instrument, and studio insurance, music instrument, prescription, and merchandise discounts, credit unions and bank loan programs, e-mail marketing platforms, and website building tools, among others. Both organizations also spend a great deal of time and effort in the legislative area, ensuring that the rights of creators are protected, represented, and expanded.

PERFORMANCE SURVEYS

One of the most important aspects to consider when joining or affiliating with a PRO is what types of performance surveys they employ. This is the starting point for every royalty calculation: was your performance picked up when it was performed on network television, a pay cable channel, a local over-the-air radio station, an online audio or audiovisual streaming service, a major league baseball park, a large or small concert venue, etc.

Surveys in this area can be either a census where every performance is picked up and reported or a sample where only a portion of all performances is used to represent the universe of all performances in that specific media (e.g., one surveyed performance is blown up to represent 10 performances)

For many years, this was a major difference between the PROs as in some areas of performance (local television, radio, live performances, etc.), substantial differences occurred as to the size of surveys being employed. That issue these days is academic, as practically every important area of performance is a census 100% pickup basis or a substantial sample. The PROs employ many technological innovations in this area including pattern recognition technology to assist in the identification and matching process. Keep in mind that with the advent of the Internet, the PROs now license and process trillions of performances across all media. Further, in the digital space where the license fees are small compared to the number of performances occurring on each service or platform, the PROs do have performance thresholds for the payment of royalties.

ASCAP PAYMENTS AND PAYMENT RULES

In general, the value of every ASCAP writer and publisher performance is determined each quarter by looking at the total amount of money that is available for distribution in that quarter, the specific monies available from each licensed medium (radio, cable, network television, live performances, etc.), the total number of ASCAP performances during that three-month period, the types of those performances (underscore, themes, visual vocals, jingles), and the areas where each type of performance occurred (pay cable, network or local television, radio, wired music, websites, airlines, etc.).

Each type of performance generates a certain number of performance credits, depending on the payment formula (i.e., theme) and the medium (i.e., radio) where the performance occurs. All performance credits for all writers and publishers are totaled each quarter and divided by the total amount of income available for distribution that quarter. The resulting figure is the dollar value of one credit. Each writer's and publisher's total performance credits are then multiplied by that dollar value to arrive at a writer's or publisher's quarterly royalty check.

To use a simple example for illustration purposes, if during the first performance quarter of 2018 (January–March) a writer received a performance statement showing a total of 10,000 radio credits, 4,000 network television credits, 1,000 local television credits, 500 cable credits, and 500 streaming service credits for seven songs, the total of this writer's quarterly credits would be 16,000. In the same three-month period, all other ASCAP writers generated a total of 6,984,000 performance credits for their works. The total number of writer credits to be paid on in that quarter would therefore be seven million. If $70 million was available for distribution to writers in that quarter, the value of each credit would be $10.00 ($70 million ÷ 7 million = $10). The writer with 16,000 credits would receive a check for $160,000. Publisher payments are arrived at in the same way.

TYPES OF PERFORMANCES AND THEIR VALUES

The seven basic types of performances that ASCAP pays on are feature performances, theme songs, underscore, jingles, promos, logos, and copyrighted arrangements of public-domain works. Each of these types is given a specific weight, which in turn determines its value. The weights are set forth in percentage terms and are contained in the ASCAP Weighting Formula. The highest-weighted performance is a feature performance (100%); all other types of performances receive different weights relative to this 100% weight. Since how a performance is weighted is one of the primary factors determining its value, every writer and publisher should be familiar with all of the ASCAP performance weights. Any composition can receive any of the various percentage weights depending on how it is used in a program. Weights and their values can change, so it is essential to be aware of what the current ASCAP percentages are for each type of use.

EXAMPLE 1. A writer writes a song that is recorded and performed on radio or sung on camera by an artist on a television show. This is a "feature performance" and receives 100% crediting. The same song is used in a product commercial and receives 5% crediting. The song is next used as underscore for a made-for-TV movie and receives 20% crediting per minute of duration. Finally, the song is used as a theme song for a network primetime television series and receives 60% crediting for all airings on network, local, and cable TV. Despite the fact that the same song is being used throughout this example, the payment for that song would be different in each situation discussed, because how a composition is used determines payment.

EXAMPLE 2. An instrumental composition is used as the theme for a feature film. Because of the film's success, the composition is released as a single and becomes a Number One chart record. Years later, the composition is used in a car commercial and is also chosen as the theme for a syndicated television series. The crediting weights for this composition would be 20% per minute of duration when the movie is shown on television, 100% when the composition is performed on radio or as a visual instrumental on television, 12% when it is used in a commercial, and 60% when it is used as the theme for a television series.

WEIGHTS

The following definitions and ASCAP crediting weights cover most of the types of performances that occur on radio and television. The list is not all-inclusive or definitive, as there are not only crediting variations on many of the weights specified, but also some weights do change; still, the list should cover the performances of most writers and publishers.

Feature Performance. "Any performance which is a principal focus of audience attention and which constitutes a musical subject matter on a radio or television program and is not a performance as a theme, jingle, background cue, or bridge music."

100% crediting for a song on the radio of any duration.

100% crediting for a song on television 60 seconds in duration.

100% crediting for a "qualifying work" of any duration up to one minute with any duration over one minute to be computed on a per second basis up to a maximum of 200% for the entire use.

200% maximum crediting for a non–"qualifying work" song with a duration of two minutes. Any duration less than two minutes is computed pro rata on a per second basis.

Themes. "A musical work used as the identifying signature of a radio or television personality or of all or part of a radio or television program or series of programs."

60% crediting for a theme song for a television series

20% crediting for each minute of duration of a theme for a feature film, movie of the week, or miniseries, or 60% regular theme crediting, whichever is higher.

Separate compositions, used as the opening theme and as the closing theme, each receive full theme crediting.

Underscore. "Mood, atmosphere, or thematic music performed as background to some nonmusical subject matter being presented on a radio or television program."

20% crediting per minute of duration for underscore to television series, specials, movies of the week, and feature films.

50% crediting for a hit song (qualifying work) used as underscore to a television program or film.

20% per minute crediting for a hit song (qualifying work) used as underscore if the durational payment would be greater than 50%.

Advertising Music. "Jingle shall mean an advertising, promotional, or public service announcement containing musical material (with or without lyrics), where (a) the musical material was originally written for advertising, promotional, or public service announcement purposes; or (b) the performance is of a musical work, originally written for other purposes, with the lyrics changed for advertising, promotional, or public service announcement purposes with the permission of the ASCAP member or members in interest; or (c) the performance is of a musical work, originally written for other purposes, which does not have at least 300 feature performance credits recorded in ASCAP's radio and television surveys during the five preceding fiscal survey years."

3% crediting for any work originally written for advertising purposes.

5% crediting for a song written for nonadvertising purposes.

12% crediting for a past hit song used in a commercial with no change in the original lyrics. The song must be a "qualifying work" to receive this crediting.

For any song written specifically for a commercial (a jingle), the crediting is 3%. For any song or instrumental composition not originally written for advertising purposes (an album cut, a song from a film, a series theme song, a hit song, etc.), the crediting can be 3%, 5%, or 12%, based solely on the song's past history of performances. If the lyrics are changed for any nonadvertising song (e.g., a hit song with new advertising lyrics), the credit is 3%, regardless of the song's past performance history.

Copyrighted Arrangements. "Works in the public domain for which an arrangement has been made and such arrangement has been copyrighted."

Many copyrighted arrangements receive either 2% or 10% crediting, but the credit can go as high as 100%, based upon such factors as a new title and lyrics, a transference from one medium to another, the extent of creative treatment and original musical characteristics as well as being identifiable as a set piece apart from the public-domain source music. The performance royalties for these works will be paid to the new arranger and the arranger's publisher, and not to the original writers or publisher of the public-domain song. Increased copyrighted arrangement crediting up to 100% is made by ASCAP via submissions reciting the reasons requesting such increased crediting with a review, if requested by a member, by the ASCAP Special Classification Committee, which then makes a determination of whether increased crediting should be given to the work. Increased crediting for public-domain works is also important because many record contracts pay mechanical royalties based on the crediting the work receives from ASCAP (50%, 100%, etc.).

Qualifying Works. A qualifying work is any composition that, because of its history of feature performances on radio and television, receives additional crediting and royalties when it is used as underscore, cue, or bridge music, or in a commercial.

For a song to qualify for the highest qualifying work crediting status (i.e., 50%), the work must have a total of 40,000 radio and television feature performance credits since October 1, 1959 (approximately $358,000 using recent credit values), and 10,000 of those feature performance credits must have occurred within the five latest survey years, with no more than 3,000 credits from any one survey year counting toward that total, provided, however, that when a work accumulates 300,000 radio and television feature performance credits, it is a qualifying work without any other test.

50% crediting for a qualifying work used as underscore to a television series or feature film.

12% crediting for a qualifying work used in a commercial. The extent of the crediting is based on a song's history of feature performances.

3% crediting for a qualifying work used in a commercial with the original lyrics changed to fit the advertising message.

The entire concept of qualifying works is important for all lyricists, composers, and publishers, as it provides additional crediting (and money) to works with a significant history of past performances when they are used as underscore, in commercials, or as short features on television. Instead of receiving the regular television underscore crediting of 20% per minute, or the jingle crediting of 3% or 5% or the pro-rata payment for feature performances of songs of less than one minute on television, these songs could receive a 50% crediting payment if they were used as underscore of a very short duration in a television show, 12% in an advertising commercial or 100% for an under-one-minute visual vocal.

PAYMENT FORMULAS/WEIGHTS INTO DOLLARS

The ASCAP percentage crediting weight for each different type of performance is one of a number of factors in the royalty formulas that ASCAP uses to arrive at the dollar value of a performance. Once the calculations for each of these formulas are completed, the resulting figure is the total number of credits for an individual performance. For example, a network television visual vocal may generate 140 total writer and publisher credits, a theme 90 credits, a radio performance 5 credits, and 20 minutes of basic cable television underscore 80 credits. The number of credits generated by a single performance depend on the medium, the type of use, the broadcasting stations' weight in terms of the size of their license fees to ASCAP, the frequency at which the station is surveyed by ASCAP, and whether the performance is a 100% census pickup or a sample pickup. Once the credits for an individual performance are computed, those credits are then multiplied by a dollar value to arrive at the worth of that performance. Performance credits are the figures that are reflected on all ASCAP writer and publisher statements.

For radio, local television, and cable performances, the payment formula takes into account the weight of the station airing the performance (the median station weight is one), the use weight of the performance (e.g., feature, theme, underscore, jingle), the strata multiplier for the medium in which the performance occurs (i.e., the number given to each surveyed medium that relates the license fees and credits of that medium to the license fees and credits of all other surveyed media), and the time of day of the performance for network, local and cable TV. In the case of network television performances, a hook-up weight (i.e., the number of individual stations carrying the broadcast) replaces the station weight number of the other formulas.

A look at a performance on three different license fee "pop" radio stations illustrates how these factors come together to arrive at a payment:

Station Weight		Use Weight		Strata Multiplier		Total Credits
1	×	100% ×	×	30	=	30
.28	×	100%	×	30	=	8.4
.06	×	100%	×	30	=	1.8

If the dollar value of one credit was $8.95 in this quarter, the writer payments would be $268.50, $75.18, and $16.11, respectively.

RADIO

For many decades, the ASCAP payment system for radio performances was that all feature songs, regardless of their stature or history of performances, were paid the same if they were similarly situated. For example, if Irving Berlin's "White Christmas" or Stevie Wonder's "Superstition" and the newest ASCAP song by the newest ASCAP writer were all performed on the same radio station back-to-back, the crediting for each song would be the same.

AUDIO FEATURE PREMIUM (AFP)/THE RADIO BONUS

Commencing with performances fourth quarter, 1991, ASCAP significantly changed the way successful radio songs were paid. A "radio award" system was put into place where additional monies were added to every radio performance credit as soon as a song generated 5,000 feature radio credits in that quarter.

For example if the value of one credit was $4.00 and a song generated 3,000 feature radio credits, the writer or publisher payment would be $12,000. But if the song generated 8,000 feature credits, its basic earning would be $32,000 (8,000 × $4.00) plus an additional 25–40% on top of that figure.

Commencing with fourth quarter 1993 performances, the "awards" system was replaced by the "Radio Feature Premium," which was basically a three-tier extra payment radio system whereby songs that generate more than a certain number of feature radio credits in a three-month period receive additional performance credits, which translate into additional dollars. The initial three qualifying tiers were: 2,500–2,999 credits in a quarter; 3,000–3,999 credits in a quarter, and 4,000 or more credits in a quarter. As a song reaches each one of these tiers, additional performance credits are added to each song's total radio credits in that quarter. All of a song's credits in all medium (TV, wired music, etc.) are then totaled and multiplied by a per-credit dollar value (e.g., $8.95 per credit) to arrive at a writer or publisher royalty.

Effective fourth quarter 2014 performances, the RFP was renamed the Audio Feature Premium (AFP) system and included satellite radio and audio streaming services in the bonus structure.

A good example of how this tier system works is by looking at this nine-month (three quarters) writer or publisher earnings chart of a Number One crossover pop hit:

Dollar Amount	Credits	
$75,484	8,434	(network, cable, and local television)
$3,759	420	(wired music)
$348,190	38,904	(radio)
$143	16	(theme/background ads on radio)
$130,741	14,608	Tier 1
$143,370	16,019	Tier 2
$150,431	16,808	Tier 3
$852,118	97,630	

Of the total $852,118 writer share, the tier add-on monies of $422,542 represented more than a 100% addition to the radio monies. It is important to note that these tier level criterion numbers can change each quarter (e.g., 2,500 radio credits can be lowered to 2,000 radio credits or raised to 5,000 credits) and can be applied to different genres of radio performances (pop, country, Latin, etc.) with different qualifying tiers for each genre. For example, the bottom end qualifying credit tier for a country chart song could be lower than the qualifying credit tier of a pop song.

A few more summary examples should help to show the significance of the AFP bonus given to the quarterly performed songs. The analysis looks at a one quarter distribution of three "pop" songs—one a major hit, the other a minor hit and the third a song which did not qualify for a bonus. The value of one credit in the examples is $8.95.

	Song Genre	Regular Credits	Premium Credits	Total Credits	Royalty
1	Pop	9,500	21,500	31,000	$277,450
2	Pop	3,700	1,500	5,200	$46,540
3	Pop	1,400	0	1,400	$12,530

CLASSIC SONG BONUS

In addition to the Audio Feature Premium, ASCAP also has a Classic Song Bonus which adds additional monies to songs which have accumulated 300,000 past radio and television feature performance credits and which do not have high levels of radio and television feature performances in the most recent four survey quarters (i.e., have not received an AFP bonus in the last four quarters). This bonus can add significant monies to "standards" as well as qualifying past hit songs.

Radio Survey. All writer and publisher payments from radio are made on the basis of large sample surveys of performances of U.S. radio stations. Each time a broadcast performance is picked up in the radio survey, multipliers are included in the payment formula to blow up that performance to a figure that approximates a national census of that song's performances. All radio stations are categorized by geographic area, by type of community within that geographic area, and by the amount of revenue (license fees) that the particular station pays to ASCAP. The survey is a scientifically designed random (based on mathematical probability), stratified (licenses are classified into groups that have common characteristics), and disproportionate (depth of the sample varies with the amount of the fees paid by licensees) survey set up by independent survey experts and is constantly being reviewed as to its effectiveness. Radio information is received via a number of sources including electronic data, fingerprinting, and station logs and tapes. To make distributions even more precise, there are separate survey and distribution groupings of pop, country, urban contemporary, religious, classical, Latin, world music, and jazz formats.

Network Television. Performances on the ABC, CBS, and NBC television networks (as well as Fox, CW, and My "networks") are surveyed on a census basis (i.e., a 100% pickup). The main rules in effect as of 2017 that affect the value of network performances are the following:

Time of Broadcast. ASCAP has four time-of-day factors that affect the value of performances on television. For Monday through Sunday programs aired between 7:00 p.m. and 12:59 a.m., a 100% payment is made. For programs airing between 1:00 p.m. and 6:59 p.m., a 75% payment is made. For programs airing between 7:00 a.m. and 12:59 p.m., a 50% payment is made. For programs airing between 1:00 a.m. and 6:59 a.m., a 25% payment is made.

To figure out the value of any performance on network television, one needs to determine what the evening 100% rate is and then reduce it to a 75%, 50%, or 25% payment depending on whether the composition was broadcast on an afternoon, morning, or overnight show. For example, if the payment for prime-time evening underscore were $170 per minute, the afternoon underscore rate would be $127.50 per minute (i.e., 75% of evening), with the morning payment at $85 per minute (i.e., 50% of the evening rate) and the overnight rate at $42.50—assuming, of course, that the same number of network stations were carrying each show. For PBS, 100% crediting applies to 7:00 a.m. to 12:59 a.m., and 25% crediting for 1:00 a.m. to 6:59 a.m.

Length of Performance. For feature performances of a song that is a qualifying work (40,000 feature performance credits, etc.), full credit is made regardless of the song's duration up to one minute. A song can be three seconds long or one minute long and still receive 100% crediting. For a nonqualifying work (most visual vocals and visual instrumentals on television), the payment is computed on a per-second basis pro-rata to 100% crediting for a 1 minute performance. For example, a 30-second feature would be credited at 50% of a 100% payment whereas a one minute feature would be paid a full 100% crediting. This per-second proration continues up to a duration of two minutes with no additional crediting for any seconds or minutes beyond two minutes.

There is no durational requirement for themes. A theme can be five seconds long or two minutes long, and full payment is made in either case. Underscore is paid on the basis of its duration. For example, if a one-hour program has 60 minutes of underscore, full payment will be made for all 60 minutes of music.

Network Hook-up. The hook-up weight is the number of network stations carrying the broadcast. ASCAP hook-up values are in 10-station increments. A hook-up of 200 or more stations is given a weight of one; a hook-up of 190–199 stations is given a weight of .949. If 180 to 189 stations are carrying a broadcast, the weight is .9, and so forth.

NETWORK PAYMENT FORMULAS

As we have seen, the ASCAP formula for valuing any type of performance takes into account the weight of the broadcasting station, the use weight for the type of performance, the strata multiplier for the medium in which the performance takes place, the feature multiplier add-on to all television performances, and the time of day (the when, where, and how). Bonus credits and money are added where applicable. The result of all of these factors is the total number of credits generated by a performance. Once all performance credits are determined for all performances, the total is then divided by the total amount of money available for that distribution to arrive at the value of one credit. All of a writer's or publisher's credits are then multiplied by that dollar credit value to arrive at a writer's or publisher's royalty check. The following are a number of examples setting forth the network payment formulas. The factors that can change are the strata multiplier, the dollar value of one credit, and any use weight changes. The example is a primetime ABC, CBS, or NBC program broadcast on 200 stations with three minutes of underscore and one theme with an $8.95 value for one credit. If the network strata or the credit value for a quarter was different than the figure used in the chart, those numbers would be substituted in the following formula.

For all television uses (features, underscore, theme songs, etc.), an additional amount would also be added to the network payment formula if the show had a high Nielsen rating. An additional theme bonus factor would also be added each quarter for primetime themes—a bonus which significantly increases the value of such themes. The regular writer and publisher combined payment formulas prior to the add-ons are as follows:

Strata	Use Weight	Station Weight		Credits		Credit Value		Dollar Value
140	x .60 (underscore)	x 1	=	84	x	$8.95	=	$752.00
140	x .60 (theme)	x 1	=	84	x	$8.95	=	$752.00

LOCAL TELEVISION

ASCAP conducts a census survey of performances on local television stations (a 100% pickup) of all network series, i.e., series originally on network television and now being aired on local television stations (e.g., *Everybody Loves Raymond*) all first-run syndicated series (e.g., *Star Trek: The Next Generation* and *The Simpsons*), and all theatrical films and made-for-TV movies. Locally originating programs (news, sports, public affairs, etc.) are surveyed on a sample basis. The value of performances on each of the census stations reflects the license fee income from that station. For example, a theme or underscore performance on the Number 1 fee-paying station would be worth more than the same performance on the Number 2 station.

As for the local television stations being surveyed on a sample basis, performances picked up there are worth substantially more than the local census station performances, because one "sampled pickup" represents many other performances of the same work on other stations. One element of the payment formula for local television performances, the station weight, takes into account the license fees of a particular station as well as the frequency of the survey sampling on that station.

To illustrate the computations, take an example of a former network television series being performed on three census stations. The series has nine minutes of underscore and separate opening and closing theme songs. The series airs once a week in primetime during a 12-week quarter; all 36 performances would be logged on the three census (100% pickup) stations. The writer computations and royalties might look like the figures in Tables 10.3 and 10.4. In the local area, the four time-of-day factors applicable to network television (100%, 75%, 50%, 25%) apply to the computation of all royalties.

UNDERSCORE ROYALTY ON THREE REPRESENTATIVE TELEVISION STATIONS

Table 10.3

		Census Station 1		Census Station 2		Census Station 3
Strata multiplier		150		150		150
Underscore weight	×	.20	×	.20	×	.20
Minutes	×	9	×	9	×	9
Census strata/ station weight	×	.15	×	.1	×	.004
Airings/pickups	×	12	×	12	×	12
Credits		486		324		12.96
Value of 1 credit	×	$8.95	×	$8.95	×	$8.95
Total		$4,349.70		$2,899.80		$115.99

THEME MUSIC ROYALTY ON THREE REPRESENTATIVE TELEVISION STATIONS

Table 10.4

		Census Station 1		Census Station 2		Census Station 3
Strata multiplier	×	150	×	150	×	150
Theme weight	×	.6	×	.6	×	.6
Census strata/ station weight	×	.15	×	.1	×	.004
Airings/pickups	×	12	×	12	×	12
Number of themes	×	2	×	2	×	2
Credits		324		216		8.64
Value of 1 credit	×	$8.95	×	$8.95	×	$8.95
Total	×	$2,899.80	×	$1,933.20	×	$77.33

The composer in this case would make a total of $7,365.49 in underscore payments and $4,910.33 in theme payments for the 12-week broadcast run of the program. These computations do not take into account the "add-on premium" monies paid to highly rated shows.

In recent years, local television station royalties have been less of a factor in many composers' earnings as many stations have opted for "per program licenses" rather than blanket licenses and many older series are being syndicated on low license fee stations thereby substantially reducing the writer and publisher royalties on these types of shows.

HIGHLY RATED SHOWS BONUS PAYMENTS/TELEVISION PREMIUM

Commencing with fourth quarter 2004 performances, additional payments are made for theme, underscore, and feature performances in top-rated TV series and cable. The television premium currently applies to highly rated series on primetime network, daytime network, primetime cable and satellite television, daytime cable and satellite television, and local television stations.

These "premium" add-on monies are designed to compensate writers and publishers for their contribution to the success of hit shows. The highest add-ons are allocated to the top-rated shows with lesser add-ons given to the next tier of successful shows. All other shows are paid at the regular quarterly theme, score, and feature rates. To give you an example of how these premiums work, the following is a hypothetical showing possible values for a top-tier, medium-tier and non-tier primetime network television show. The writer and publisher combined theme payment would be $2,000 for the top rated show, $1,700 for the mid-tier show and $1,500 for the-non-tier show. One minute of score would be $400, $340, and $300 respectively with a one-minute feature at $1,700, $1,600, and $1,500. Keep in mind that the tier numbers and the specific dollar premium add-on to each tier and type of use can and do vary by performance quarter.

CABLE

ASCAP conducts a census (a 100% pickup) of performances on all general entertainment services (HBO, Showtime, the Movie Channel, Cinemax, USA Network, Comedy Central, Lifetime, Arts & Entertainment, TCM, FX, the Nashville Network, Nickelodeon, TNT, etc.). The use weights as well as the time-of-day factors are the same as for all other areas of television.

The strata multipliers in the cable field were, for many years, significantly lower than those for network or local television, primarily because cable license fees to ASCAP were significantly lower than those paid by the networks or by the local television industry. Consequently, the payments for most uses were lower. Due to settlements between ASCAP and the primary elements of the cable industry in 2000, 2001, and 2002 (Viacom, HBO, Turner, local originations, etc.), cable fees and distributions have significantly increased and cable revenues to ASCAP now significantly exceed those of local and network television combined.

The royalty formula for all cable performances is the same as network or local. The strata multiplier × station weight × time-of-day factor × use weight = credits. Tier 1, 2, or 3 television premium bonuses are then added for highly rated shows.

As cable, both basic and pay, is the media where most programming occurs, the following gives you an idea of the types of combined writer and publisher royalties prior to bonuses being generated in this area. The example includes a primetime series with one feature performance (100% crediting), one theme song (60% crediting) and one minute of score (20% crediting) on three different license fee paying systems with a credit value of $8.95.

Strata	Station Weight	Time of Day	Use Weight	Total Writer/ Publisher Credits	Total Royalty
85	.44	100%	100%	37.4	$334.74
			60%	22.4	$200.48
			20%	7.5	$67.12
85	.25	100%	100%	21.25	$190.19
			60%	12.75	$114.11
			20%	4.25	$38.03
85	.04	100%	100%	3.4	$30.43
			60%	2	$18.26
			20%	.68	$6.07

AUDIOVISUAL STREAMING SERVICES

Due to Rate Court decisions as well as subsequent license fee negotiations emanating from the effects of those decisions, the license fees as well as the resulting songwriter, composer, and music publisher royalties in this area have been, to date, minimal. This applies to the streaming services Netflix, Hulu, Amazon, Apple, and others.

In computing royalties in this area, ASCAP uses the type of use distinction (score, theme, feature, etc.) but does not apply a time-of-day factor nor does it at this time have a premium bonus structure as it does for television.

MUSIC AND LYRICS IN ADS, PROMOS, AND PSAS

With ASCAP, there are many different aspects of music in advertisements including TV commercials, radio commercials, network promos, short and long form infomercials, public service announcements and movie trailers.

ASCAP processes television ads and PSAs reported by Competitrack, the digital monitoring system, on a census survey. A work registration must be on file and an advertisement claim form must be completed that includes information on whether it's a commercial or PSA, the first air date, the title, the ASCAP ID, the product name, and the Competitrack ad code. In addition, an MP3 of the work or a link to a website containing the musical work must be attached. There are submission deadlines for TV claims.

The network promos are processed based on information submitted by the networks. For radio ads, PSAs, short form infomercials, movie trailers, non-network promos and TV ads not monitored by Competitrack, ASCAP relies solely on Soundmouse fingerprint technology to identify music. Information needed includes the audio or library file name track title, the ISWC number, the ASCAP work ID, and the writer and publisher names. There are submission deadlines to Soundmouse. All of this area is surveyed on a sample basis.

Long form commercials (longer than 5 minutes) are processed in the same manner as other program performances (cue sheets, etc.). Claims have to be submitted in order to be paid and there are deadlines for submission.

Music in short infomercials is credited as advertising announcements with all performances of musical works within a long infomercial credited at 40% of the otherwise applicable credit.

PAYMENTS

Effective with performances beginning October 1, 1993, ASCAP put into effect three separate payment categories for music and songs in commercials. Prior to this date, five separate categories were in effect. The crediting percentages are 3% for works written specifically for commercials or for other works (album cuts, etc.) that were not written specifically for commercials and that do not have at least 300 feature performance credits recorded in ASCAP's radio and television surveys during the five preceding survey years. For works that were not originally written for commercials and that have at least 300 feature performance credits in radio and television over the most recent five years but that do not meet the credit test of a "qualifying work," the percentage payment is 5%. Finally, for qualifying works, the percentage payment is 12%. The 12% payment applies to most hit songs as well as standards being used by advertisers in their campaigns. Songs qualify under this category if they have at least 40,000 past radio and television feature credits since October 1, 1959, and have 10,000 radio television feature credits during the most recent five years toward which total not more than 3,000 credits shall be counted for any such year. Any work that has 300,000 or more radio television feature performance credits automatically qualifies for the 12% crediting and the work does not need to meet the 10,000 credit/five-year criterion applicable to most qualifying works.

In determining the actual payments for songs or music in commercials, one needs to remember that all of the rules affecting other types of performances (network time-of-day factors, etc.) also apply to commercial music. Additional provisions limit the number of royalty payments for a jingle that is performed more than once on the same station during a two-hour period. ASCAP also employs jingle subsamples in the local television, radio, and cable area. These subsamples of performances (a percentage of the regular surveys in these areas) result in all surveyed jingle performances being given multiples in the radio area and in the local television area to arrive at the final value of a performance.

For major product campaigns being broadcast primarily on network and local television, commercials using a hit song with no change in the lyrics can earn in excess of $100,000 in writer and publisher earnings over the space of one year. For campaigns lasting many years, the amounts can be substantial.

LIVE PERFORMANCES

ASCAP conducts a census survey (100% pickup) of all songs performed in the 300 largest concert tours and festivals in the United States, as well as all songs at a dozen or so selected venues (Madison Square Garden, Radio City Music Hall, Hollywood Bowl, American Airlines Arena, etc.). Song use information is gathered from set lists and usually is split 90% to the headliners and 10% to the opening act. The split between one headliner and two opening acts would be 90/5/5, and a co-headliner split would be 50/50. Tours are ranked according to total revenue, and payments reflect the economic value of each tour. ASCAP relies on the data from Pollstar, which includes box office revenue, dates, venues, headliners and opening acts. Once the eligible concerts are identified, the box office revenue is allocated to headliners and opening acts. The live concert survey is a separate distribution pool with the distributable revenue from live concert licensees paid only to writers and publishers with live concert performances in the survey.

For songs in these tours, the songwriter and publisher per song royalties can be substantial ranging from less than $100 for a number of minor concerts to over tens of thousands of dollars per song for a major tour.

ASCAP also has a program of payment for small venues not included in the live concert survey. The OnStage program allows writers to notify ASCAP of their live performances via Member Access. Based on the license fees of the establishment, payments, though small, will be made. ASCAP does have submission deadlines in order for royalty payments to be made to a writer's direct deposit account.

Live tour payments commenced in 1993. The Symphony Concert, Recital, and Educational Survey covers licensed symphony orchestras and serious concert artists on a census basis, as well as all works performed in licensed educational institutions that pay the guest artist or ensemble $1,500 or more. Other educational institutions' concerts are surveyed on a sample basis. Some of the fees from other live performances not covered by these surveys are distributed as a surrogate on the basis of all performances on television and all feature performances on radio. ASCAP also has an ASCAP Plus Awards system for writers of children's music, concert music, jazz, and musical theater where monetary awards are given by an independent panel of music experts. This program recognizes writers whose works are substantially performed in media not surveyed by ASCAP or whose works have a unique prestige value.

PER PROGRAM DISTRIBUTIONS

In the local television area, stations either have blanket or per-program licenses with ASCAP. A station with a per-program license pays a license fee only for each program using ASCAP music that is not otherwise licensed (direct or source license) in an amount that is dependent on that program's ad revenues.

Under the blanket license, local stations pay license fees without regard to the specific musical content or revenues of any particular program. Since specific license fees can be allocated to specific television programs under the per-program license, ASCAP distributes the fees from each specific program to the writers and publishers with music contained in that program.

THE INTERNET

ASCAP Internet licenses are based upon, among other things, revenue and traffic, and they cover individual sites and aggregators as well as other new business models. Internet distributions to writers and publishers commenced in 1997 with license fees determined by industry wide agreements, standard form agreements, multiple interim and final Rate Court decisions and orders as well as settlements of litigation.

THE BMI PAYMENT SCHEDULE

As previously mentioned, BMI for many decades issued periodic payment schedules listing minimum dollar and cent rates for radio and television performances with voluntary add-on payments made each quarter to increase the base rates. In addition, various types of bonus systems were in place for radio performances which took into account past cumulative performance histories and current activity. A detailed history of these systems and their payments can be found in previous editions of this book. The basic structure of the current BMI payment system commenced with third quarter 2004 performances in the radio area and with television performances starting fourth quarter 2007.

THE CURRENT RADIO PAYMENT SYSTEM

Effective with performances July 1, 2004, BMI put into effect a system of commercial radio payments based upon three categories—the Current Activity Payment, the Hit Song Bonus, and the Standard Bonus with songs eligible for payment under one, two, or all three of the categories.

The Current Activity Payment. All radio-performed works in a quarter are eligible for this payment. A unique royalty rate is calculated for each work based upon the license fees of the stations performing the work, as well as the number of times the work was performed on those stations. Most of the radio monies distributed each quarter are in the Current Activity fund and represent the base royalties that all performed songs receive in a quarter.

The Hit Song Bonus. Works that are performed more than 95,000 times in a quarter are eligible for additional royalties and receive a pro-rata portion of an allocation by BMI of the distributable radio revenue for these types of songs. The amount of extra money is based on a song's actual number of current performances; works with higher quarterly counts earn more Hit Song royalties than works with lower counts. Based upon the genre of the song, the license fees of the station as well as other factors, this bonus also applies to hit songs with a lower threshold of quarterly performances.

The Standards Bonus. Songs that have a cumulative history of 2.5 million commercial radio station performances and have a minimal number of current quarter performances are classified as "standards" and are eligible for this bonus in that quarter. An amount of money is allocated by BMI to be distributed on a pro-rata basis according to the actual number of cumulative historical commercial radio performances for each eligible work in combination with that work's performances in the current quarter. Works with the higher combination of cumulative historical and current quarter commercial radio performance counts earn larger standards royalties than those with the lower combination of such performances.

BMI has also recently begun to pay on short duration radio performances (less than 60 seconds) on certain stations using audio pattern recognition technology. These short duration detections do not count toward Hit Song or Standards Bonus eligibility criterion.

ADDITIONAL CRITERIA FOR PAYMENT

BMI also uses supplemental criteria (other than or in addition to the three new bonus factors) to establish increased valuation for certain works performed on U.S. commercial radio stations. A small additional allocation from the amount available for distribution each quarter (including general licensing and other funds) may be used for this purpose.

RADIO PAYMENT EXAMPLES

The following chart illustrates sample BMI writer or publisher distribution figures for songs reaching certain quarterly performance levels. As with past BMI radio payment schedules, these dollar figures will vary by performance quarter due to the fluctuation of the amounts of money BMI puts into the funding of the current activity pot, the hit song bonus pool, the standards bonus pool, and the "supplemental criteria" pool among other factors. Though most songs will earn royalties from one or possibly two of the payment categories (Current Activity or Current Activity and Hit Song Bonus), some songs are able to earn money from all three payment categories (i.e., a song with more than 2.5 million cumulative historical performances that also qualifies for a Hit Song Bonus) in a quarter.

Performances	Current Activity	Hit Song Bonus	Standards Bonus	Total Royalty
1,000,000	$300,000	$425,000	-	$725,000
950,000	$185,000	$400,000	-	$585,000
570,000	$140,000	$325,000	-	$465,000
520,000	$65,000	$100,000	-	$165,000
375,000	$45,000	$60,000	-	$105,000
320,000	$125,000	$200,000	-	$325,000
160,000	$28,000	$25,000	$7,500	$60,500
110,000	$15,000	$20,000	$15,000	$50,000
85,000	$19,000	-	$7,000	$26,000
50,000	$11,000	$18,000	-	$29,000
35,000	$5,000	-	$1,000	$6,000
22,000	$4,000	-	-	$4,000
1,200	$250	-	-	250$
150	$60	-	-	$60
2	$0.26	-	-	$0.26

TELEVISION: TYPES OF PERFORMANCE

The three most common types of performances on television are feature performances, theme songs, and underscore/background.

Feature Performance. "A performance of a work which is the focus of audience attention at the time of the broadcast." Cue sheets list them as a Visual Vocal (VV) or Visual Instrumental (VI).

Theme. "A performance of a work regularly associated with a television program and identifies that program to the viewer when used as the opening and/or closing theme music." Theme credit is given only when a work is used in multiple episodes of a TV program.

Background Performance. "A performance of a work used as a dramatic underscore to a scene where the music is not the focus of audience attention yet nonetheless is used to set the mood of the scene." These works are generally background instrumental music are noted on cue sheets as BI. A song where lyrics are audible, even though there may be some dialogue in the foreground of the scene, is a background vocal performance.

For purposes of clarification, a television program is defined as an audiovisual production that is broadcast on over-the-air, cable, or Internet television with a duration typically greater than 15 minutes.

TELEVISION PAYMENTS

Commencing with performances October 1, 2007, BMI significantly changed the way they paid for music on network television. They eliminated the specific base rate performance payments (e.g., $0.71 per minute of score per station, $3.50 per station for a primetime theme song) as well as the four time-of-day factors that had been in place for decades and replaced it with a three-category payment system coupled with a factor reflecting the television audience measurement of a show as well as the duration of every type of use. By 2014, the same rules that initially applied to network TV were also in effect for premium and basic cable and local TV with digital services added later. The three payment categories are:

Current Activity Payment. A unique royalty rate based upon the available license fees available that quarter, is calculated for each performance taking into consideration the duration of the use, the weighted royalty value for each usage type (feature, theme, score) as well as the Nielsen audience measurement numbers of the program. The substantial majority of the amount available for distribution each quarter is used to make Current Activity payments.

Super Usage Payment. Performances of songs (Background Vocal, Visual Instrumental, and Visual Vocal Usages) with a continuous duration of one minute or greater are Super Usages. The royalty rate for these uses are higher than those of a feature performance with a duration of less than one minute.

Theme Music Bonus Payment (Network Television Stations Only). Based on the importance and recognizable aspect of the theme song to a show, BMI increases the payment for certain themes that receive a minimum number of quarterly network performances. The current qualifying numbers are 2,000 quarterly performances for ABC, CBS, and NBC, 1,700 performances for Fox, 700 performances for the CW network, and 150 for Univision.

A good example illustrating these numbers is an ABC show which airs 10 times in a quarter with 200 stations carrying each broadcast. The result, 2,000 performances. BMI allocates a portion of the amount available for distribution each quarter for each television network for this bonus. Each eligible theme performance in that quarter receives a pro rata portion of this bonus fund according to the actual number of its quarterly performances. Themes have to qualify anew each quarter for this bonus.

As to the weighted royalty value of each type of music use, score (background music) carries an index of 1 with themes and features given an index above 1. Further, the duration of a theme (opening and closing) is taken into account in all network theme payments. For example, a long duration opening and closing theme which qualified for the Theme Bonus would be paid higher than a short duration opening and closing theme which qualified for the Theme Bonus and had the same number of performances. The audience measurement factor would also affect the final theme payment.

Based on this new system, there can be a wide range of payments for network themes, features, and score with one of the primary factors being the number of people watching the show—the Nielsen Audience Measurement. In the case of themes, duration now also plays a significant role. You could have a very short theme use on a network show with few performances in a quarter and receive in the low hundreds of dollars whereas a long opening and closing theme having over 2,000 performances in a quarter all with high viewership could generate in excess of $3,000 or more in writer and publisher money.

LOCAL TELEVISION

For local television programming, BMI employs a combination of a census survey (100% pickup) of certain types of programs and a sample survey of other types of programs. Any network series that goes to syndication, any series that is made for first-run local television syndication, and any feature film or television movie of the week is covered by a census survey of performances. For all original programs produced only for a particular local television station, BMI employs a sample survey of performances whereby a performance on a local station is multiplied by a statistical multiplier based on the ratio of stations logged to stations licensed. The rates on blanket stations are weighted to reflect the license fees paid by a station or group of stations. This field is the same for all areas of television, namely a Current Activity payment, a Super Usage payment, and an Audience Measurement factor.

It should be noted that per-program license fees are separated from blanket fees, and royalties are arrived at by calculating the fee associated with the individual program and applying the relationships between the various use types. Fees are distributed only to those writers and publishers who have works on the specific program.

CABLE

In the pay cable and basic cable network area (e.g., HBO, Showtime, MTV, USA Network, Lifetime, Discovery, etc.), BMI receives its program information from cue sheets from cable networks, program producers and distributors, and other outside data sources and pays out on a census basis. The rates are determined each quarter by applying the amount of license fees collected from each cable network against the payable performances using the methodology of all other areas of television, namely, a Current Activity payment, a Super Usage payment and an Audience Measurement factor.

The following chart gives examples of the current BMI calculations for a Super Visual Vocal on a highly rated network primetime series as well as the same type of performance on a medium pay cable channel and a local television station. The royalty figure represents a writer or publisher distribution.

Media	Count	Timing	Your %	Current Activity	Super Usage	Royalty
Network	199	2:20	100%	$1,300	$640	$1,940
Cable	10	2:20	100%	$65	$32	$97
Local	62	2:20	100%	$40	$20	$60

MUSIC AND LYRICS IN COMMERCIALS

"[A] Commercial Jingle is a work (either pre-existing or specifically written for an advertisement) used to advertise a product and/or service." BMI pays for music contained in commercials for compositions greater than 5 seconds when appearing in nationally broadcasted commercial jingles on networks, cable networks, and local television on a limited basis. Performance data comes through Competitrack and payments are calculated on the time of day of the performance and the number of jingles aired in a quarter.

To receive payment, a BMI commercial jingle form needs to be completed including a copy of the commercial, a copy of the synch license where applicable, the title used in the commercial, the title of the commercial spot, the product, the ISCI number, the writer's name and affiliation as well as share, the publishing company, information and whether it was an original composition or adapted from an existing work.

LIVE PERFORMANCE PAYMENTS

Royalty payments are calculated for each BMI licensed work used in the opening and headliner's acts for all dates on the 300 top grossing tours. Tour payments began in 1996 and are based on set lists, solicited from headliners and opening acts performing at those events. Royalty payments are calculated for each performed work based primarily on the license fees collected from the tour or event. As with ASCAP, songs in major tours can earn substantial monies in distributions. The concert royalty split is 90% to the headliner and 10% to the opening act. BMI also distributes the license fees it receives from professional sports teams and leagues to songs played during those games.

BMI uses radio and television performances as a proxy for the distribution of a portion of its other live performance money. Licensed concerts in the symphonic and classical world are also paid on a census basis.

INTERNET

In addition to the form agreements as set forth on its website, most of BMI's major agreements in this area have been either negotiated or Rate Court set. Internet distributions to writers and publishers began in 1998.

SESAC

SESAC is a performing rights organization founded in 1930 by the Heinecke family and incorporated in 1931. It was originally known as the Society of European Stage Authors and Composers and concentrated on classical and gospel music. Prior to 1970, only publishers joined SESAC. In 1992 SESAC was sold to a group of investors. It was sold again in 2012 to the private equity firm Rizvi Traverse with a subsequent sale in 2017 to the investment firm the Blackstone Group. In 2015, SESAC purchased the mechanical rights organization the Harry Fox Agency, from the National Music Publishers' Association (NMPA), enabling SESAC to license both the performance right and the mechanical right, a practice it had discontinued in 1992. SESAC licenses primarily all of the same users that ASCAP and BMI license and has reciprocal agreements with foreign societies for the collection of its writers' and publishers' performances outside the U.S. As SESAC is a for profit corporation, it does not release its financial income including revenue, distributions, operating costs and profits to its writer and publisher affiliates. Reliable estimates though place their annual revenues in the $250 million to $300 million range.

AFFILIATION AND CONTRACTS

As opposed to ASCAP and BMI where anyone can join if they meet the minimal qualifications of membership or affiliation, one has to be invited by SESAC to affiliate as a writer or publisher and they do not accept unsolicited affiliation applications. SESAC does have a standard writer and publisher agreement, which can be modified through negotiation. The writer and publisher contracts grant to SESAC on a nonexclusive basis the "right to perform publicly and to license to others to perform publicly, the writer's and publisher's works throughout the world by any means or through any medium now known or thereafter devised. The affiliate retains the right to issue nonexclusive licenses directly to any third party." The term of the writer agreement is three years, with automatic renewals for three-year periods on the same terms and conditions as the original agreement if not terminated by the writer. The publisher contract runs for a period of three years, with automatic renewals for additional three-year periods if not timely terminated. Writers and publishers can terminate these agreements by giving written notice by certified mail, return receipt requested, at least three months but not more than six months prior to the expiration of the current period of the term. SESAC contracts prior to the late 1990s were five-year publisher and three-year writer agreements automatically renewable. Works are able to be removed from the SESAC repertory at the end of the writer and/or publisher contract (normally every three years), assuming an effective termination notice has been sent. Always check for contract changes.

PAST PAYMENTS

For many years, SESAC paid writers and publishers based primarily on the position a song reaches on the Adult Contemporary, Black/Urban, College Alternative, Country, and Top 40/CHR singles charts, with other payments made on the basis of nationally released and distributed album cuts in the areas of Rock, Latin, Jazz, Christian, and Inspirational. In the case of chart singles, SESAC had a formula giving a writer and publisher a specific amount when a song reaches a particular position, with additional amounts called "post-chart payments" paid in subsequent years. Chart payments were distributed in four quarterly installments commencing with the calendar quarter during which a song enters the trade paper charts. The record release payments were distributed similarly. All payments were subject to change by SESAC at any time without prior notice.

CURRENT PAYMENTS

In television, SESAC licenses all the broadcast networks, the cable networks, local broadcast, and syndicated TV as well as public television and pay-per-view, on-demand services and audiovisual streaming services. The basic television royalty formula is the following: Station Count × Use Type × Weight × Duration × Time of Day Weight = Credits. Total credits are then divided by the television license fees available for distribution resulting in a Value Factor. Credits are then multiplied by that Value Factor to arrive at a writer or publisher royalty distribution. Time of day weights for weekdays are 100% crediting for 7:00 p.m.–10:59 p.m., 75% for 11:00 p.m.–1:59am, 25% for 2:00 a.m.–5:59 am, 50% for 6:00 a.m.–3:59 p.m. and 60% for 4:00 p.m.–6:59 p.m. Weekends are 100% crediting for 12:00 p.m.–11:00 p.m., 75% for 11:00 p.m.–1:59 a.m., 25% for 2:00 a.m.–5:59 a.m. and 50% for 6:00 a.m.–11:59am. Audience measurement may replace time of day in the future.

In radio, SESAC licenses broadcast radio, public radio (NPR, etc.), satellite radio, and Internet radio. The basic payment formula is the number of performances plus a Bonus Factor where applicable equals a certain amount of credits. Total credits are then divided by the radio license fees available for distribution resulting in a Value Factor. Credits are then multiplied by that Value Factor to arrive at the royalty check. Bonus payments are given to songs which reach certain performance levels on radio and vary by quarter as well as by radio format/genre.

The formulas for satellite radio, Internet radio, and background music services (Muzak, Music Choice, DMX, etc.) are the same as traditional radio.

The following are some examples of how SESAC statements reflect radio performances on a Top 40, Adult Contemporary, and Modern Rock station. Their formula takes into account the radio format, the format weight, the BDS Audience and the Value Factor. Bonuses also come into play.

Format	Detects	Total Audience	Credits	Value Factor	Royalty
Top 40	2,500	80,000	12,000	.03	$1,200
AC	9,000	47,000	70,000	.06	$14,000
MR	3,300	155,000	24,000	.035	$2,800

SESAC's television value weighting system for themes, score, and feature performances are set out in percentage terms relative to each other. Features are credited at 100% with themes at 60%, score at 16.67% per minute, jingles, promos and logos at 3.5% and copyrighted arrangements of public domain works at 15%. Feature performances on television 31 seconds or longer are credited at 100% with duration of 16 to 30 seconds and 1 to 15 seconds receiving 50% and 25% respectively. There is a maximum payment of 12 feature performances per hour.

Though payments do vary by quarter as well as because of changes in the payment formulas, some recent representative writer or publisher ABC, CBS, or NBC primetime network television payments are $1,117 for a feature performance, $186 for one minute of score and $1,341 for the opening and closing themes to a show. For a Fox series, the figures would be a combined $1,115 total for the opening and closing themes, $155 for one minute of score and $929 for a feature performance.

Live performance payments are made for all size venues across the United States and are weighted according to venue size/seating capacity. Performances are multiplied by the venue weight to arrive at credits. License fees are then factored in to arrive at a royalty payment for the show. SESAC relies on Pollstar for concert information and affiliates providing information on the venue name, address, size, dates of performances and songs performed through the online live performance notification system.

SESAC performance statements are categorized by Network TV, Cable TV, Monitored Radio, Satellite Radio, Background Music, Digital Media, Live Performances and International. In the radio area, song title, share, source, and earnings are listed with television listing the show/production title, composition title, air date, share, use, duration, and day part of the performance.

It is important to note that all the aforementioned payment practices as well as royalty values are subject to change at any time without prior notice. The royalty distribution system does not modify or amend the affiliation agreements with the affiliation agreement terms superseding the distribution system.

PAYMENT DATES

SESAC royalty payments for domestic performances are made approximately 90 days following the end of the calendar quarter in which a performance occurs. For example, first quarter performances are distributed three months later in June. Second quarter performances would be paid at the end of September, and so forth. Further, SESAC also has an accelerated system of monthly radio royalty payments as long as an affiliate has signed up for direct deposit. For example, radio performances occurring in January would be paid around April 30, with February performances paid on May 31. Foreign royalty payments are paid no later than 180 days after the close of the calendar quarter in which these royalties are processed. For example, royalties received from foreign societies between January 1 and March 31 would be distributed on or about September 30 of that year.

GLOBAL MUSIC RIGHTS (GMR)

Global Music Rights (GMR), founded in 2013, is a joint venture between Azoff Music Management and Madison Square Garden Entertainment. It is a for-profit corporation formed as an alternative to the traditional performing rights model. Global's business model is to contract with a select group of successful songwriters, songwriter/artists and their publishers to represent their performing rights on an exclusive basis. Their initial business plan involved the signing of major radio writers and writer/artists as well as their catalogues from ASCAP and BMI with various inducements including a guarantee of paying more than they were receiving from ASCAP and BMI for performances of their works and that they would negotiate higher license fees in the future than those previously negotiated by ASCAP and BMI as well as those set by the Consent Decree Rate Courts.

AGREEMENTS

Though GMR contracts are negotiated agreements between the parties, there are a number of provisions that are contained in numerous agreements, which should give an idea of the basic agreement contractual provisions that writers and publishers sign.

As opposed to ASCAP, BMI, and SESAC agreements that are nonexclusive, GMR has the exclusive right to license the writer's and publisher's works as well as the exclusive right to collect the writer's and publisher's share of performance monies. As ASCAP and BMI writer and publisher contracts are normally not co-terminus (ending on the same date) and subject to "licenses in effect" provisions, there is a request/requirement that prior works be moved to GMR at the first contractual publisher termination date. Further, GMR is authorized to directly license works in specific situations.

The term of the agreement is normally five years but can be longer or shorter depending on the negotiation. No rights are given to GMR as to synchronization, mechanical, or dramatic rights or any Neighboring Rights or artist-related rights relating to sound recordings. The agreement also authorizes GMR to represent the writer before the U.S. Copyright Office, the Copyright Royalty Board, or any other agency regarding the performance right and can negotiate, enforce, or withhold and restrict licensing of the works.

LICENSES

The primary license that GMR offers music users is a blanket license. As of this time, they do not offer a "carve-out blanket license" nor a per program license nor any of the other types of licenses that ASCAP, BMI, or SESAC offer. As they are not under a consent decree with the government, as ASCAP and BMI are, nor any other regulatory oversight or restriction, performing any of their compositions without a license subjects the user to a copyright infringement lawsuit.

ROYALTY PAYMENTS AND STATEMENTS

GMR has a fixed per-play royalty for radio, a rate card for television performances, and a digital per-stream payment in the online world which can periodically be changed. As opposed to ASCAP, BMI, and SESAC, there are no bonuses above their basic rate structure and duration is currently the primary payment factor for all types of television uses with the exception of themes which receive a higher rate. Time of day factors also come into play in the television area. License fees and the total number of plays or performances are primary factors in arriving at the value of any performance. Keep in mind that as GMR is a new entrant into the PRO field, their payment schedules are new and should be considered a "work in progress."

Statements are issued four times a year and remitted approximately three to four months after a performance quarter. Statements reflect the number of performances and royalties in the areas of Broadcast Radio, Satellite Radio, Digital Services, Television and Other with a summary sheet showing top earning songs, earnings by media, and a radio airplay analysis graph, among other items.

As to foreign country performances, GMR has an arrangement with PRS for Music to collect writer performance monies and remit them, based upon the contractual GMR/writer agreement, either directly to the writers or to GMR for distribution. All foreign performance royalties are paid the quarter after the money is received by GMR and are included as part of the regular quarterly distribution. Except when specifically contracted for, foreign writer royalties are not used for recoupment purposes. As with the other U.S. PROs, publishers normally collect their foreign royalties either directly from foreign societies or via subpublishers.

PRO COMPETITIVE PAYMENTS

This chapter has given you the basics of the current ASCAP, BMI, SESAC, and GMR payment systems and policies that apply to the majority of performed compositions as well as the special rules and rates that apply to hit songs on radio and streaming services, major catalogue songs, film and television themes, scores and songs on highly rated shows, and other specific "royalty add-on/bonus" concepts. The payments made to the category of "special works" can be significantly higher than the payments made to compositions not in those special categories. Further, payments do vary between ASCAP, BMI, SESAC, and GMR and can vary significantly by performance quarter, by genre of music, by media and type of use, by radio, audiovisual, and streaming service bonus schedules as well as by specific writer and publisher contracts and arrangements, among other factors. That is why it is essential to have some knowledge of past payment practices and philosophy if one is to understand current payments as well as the direction of payments in the future. It is essential to always check with each PRO as to their current value system, payment rules, and actual values for each area of performance.

CHART SONGS—WHAT THEY EARN

Successful single releases are the mainstay of the programming for many U.S. radio stations and once a single is a success, it will continue to earn royalties for decades. Table 10.5 estimates the U.S. performing rights earnings for a major across-the-board chart song during its first 12 months of release. Table 10.6 gives an example of what the U.S. songwriter and publisher earnings might be for the same song decades later. Table 10.7 gives a breakdown of the areas that generate income for a very successful writer's total catalogue of songs. The chart assumes a currently active writer with one Top 20 chart song during the year as well as a back catalogue of five significant chart songs. Finally, Table 10.8 gives a range of figures of the U.S. writer or publisher earnings for various chart songs during the first year of release. The figures in the tables are intended as a reference guide and not as a guarantee. Some songs will earn less than the figures stated, others more, because of the many variables affecting a particular song or writer including the license fee of a station, the particular genre of music, the bonus structure involved and the basic payment for the use, among others.

Always keep in mind that ASCAP, BMI, SESAC, and GMR have very different radio payment schedules in addition to differences in the amount of money they collect. There will always be a difference in royalties between ASCAP, BMI, SESAC, and GMR for the very same song and for the very same number of performances. Always keep in mind that payments and values change in each organization sometimes with no or very little notice and that the royalties you were used to one day may very well be very different at a later date.

MAJOR POP CHART SONG EARNINGS

Table 10.5

	Radio	Television	Wired Music and Other Uses	Total
Quarter 1	$360,000	$40,000	$1,000	$401,000
Quarter 2	440,000	32,000	2,500	474,500
Quarter 3	240,000	20,000	2,000	262,000
Quarter 4	120,000	8,000	1,500	129,500
Writer/ Publisher Total	$1,160,000	$100,000	$7,000	$1,267,000

The figures as set forth in these tables are intended to show the substantial sums of performance money that can be earned by chart writers and publishers. One big hit can provide literally a lifetime of earnings for the writer as well as the beneficiaries of his or her estate. The tables also illustrate why successful copyrights are so valuable to a publishing company and why the prices to buy an existing publishing operation are high. And considering that the foreign earnings can equal or surpass the U.S. earnings, the figures of some chart songs as set forth in the tables can be doubled for a major worldwide hit.

EARNINGS FOR A PAST HIT SONG

Table 10.6

Year	Radio	Television	Wired Music	Total
Year 18	$40,000	$4,000	$1,500	$45,500
Year 19	51,000	4,600	1,300	56,900
Year 20	42,500	3,500	5,200	51,200
Year 21	52,800	6,800	3,200	62,800
Year 22	33,000	3,300	1,200	37,500
Writer/Publisher Total	$219,300	$22,200	$12,400	$253,900

MAJOR WRITER ANNUAL EARNINGS

Table 10.7

	Radio	Television	Wired Music	Total
Quarter 1	$190,000	$ 40,000	$ 2,700	$232,700
Quarter 2	115,000	35,000	3,600	153,600
Quarter 3	100,000	12,000	1,900	113,900
Quarter 4	140,000	36,000	2,800	178,800
Writer/Publisher Total	$545,000	$123,000	$11,000	$679,600

CHART SONG EARNINGS BY POSITION OVER ONE YEAR

Table 10.8

Top 100	Adult Contemporary	Country	R&B	Writer or Publisher Total		
1	1	1	1	$300,000	–	$1,000,000
1	1	–	–	275,000	–	900,000
1	10	–	–	250,000	–	600,000
1	–	–	–	225,000	–	500,000
5	–	–	–	150,000	–	300,000
10	–	–	–	90,000	–	250,000
20	–	–	–	65,000	–	150,000
30	–	–	–	50,000	–	100,000
50	–	–	–	25,000	–	80,000
90	–	–	–	5,000	–	25,000
–	–	1	–	300,000	–	750,000
–	–	5	–	150,000	–	400,000
–	–	10	–	75,000	–	250,000
–	–	20	–	40,000	–	100,000

Note: Individual songs may earn more or less than the ranges set forth in this chart, because most charts reflect a combination of performance factors.

FUTURE CHANGES

The performing rights area is a field which is currently undergoing many changes. It is essential that writers, publishers, and representatives stay informed of all new changes (payment formulas and schedules, bonus structures, surveys, type of use values, methods of doing business, contracts, etc.) if they are to understand this field and make intelligent decisions. As we have seen, in many cases payments can be changed at any time without notice to the writers and publishers being affected. Court decisions, legislation, as well as, international developments also have an effect in this area. Try to use history as a guide to the future of payments and direction in this area. Always check the ASCAP, BMI, SESAC, and GMR websites for up-to-date payment as well as other information (ASCAP.com, BMI.com, SESAC.com, and globalmusicrights.com).

CHAPTER 11
MUSIC, MONEY, AND BROADWAY

BROADWAY

Broadway and touring productions, a $2.5 billion business in the United States, represents, for composers, lyricists, and songwriters involved in the field, a significant source of royalties and in the case of a hit, a lifetime annuity. Each year, Broadway produces many new musicals in addition to revivals of musicals from the past. Most of these shows never recoup their financial investment but when a *Hamilton*, *Beautiful: The Carole King Musical*, *Wicked*, *Jersey Boys*, *The Lion King*, *South Pacific*, *Phantom of the Opera*, or *Mamma Mia!* succeeds, the financial returns can be staggering both for investors as well as creators and other royalty participants.

TYPES OF BROADWAY MUSICALS

Musicals can take many forms with the particular form many times dictating the type of contract and royalty structure received by composers, lyricists, and songwriters as well as the music publishers involved. The most common types of musicals are a new show with original music and lyrics (*Hamilton*, *Kinky Boots*, *Cats*), a "catalogue/jukebox musical" which uses pre-existing songs (*Beautiful: The Carole King Musical*, *Mamma Mia!*, *Motown: The Musical*, *Rock of Ages*, *Jersey Boys*, *American Idiot*) and shows that combine new compositions with pre-existing works. In many cases, an additional royalty participant will also be involved in cases where the show is adapted from a work in another media such as a book, feature film, television program, or comic book (*Frozen, Aladdin, SpongeBob SquarePants: The Broadway Musical, School of Rock, Rocky, Doctor Zhivago, The Lion King, Beauty and the Beast, Spider-Man: Turn Off the Dark, The Addams Family, Dirty Dancing*). This latter category sometimes uses the originally composed music as well as lyrics, other times uses entirely new compositions or utilizes a combination of both old and new.

WEEKLY COSTS OF A BROADWAY MUSICAL

The starting point for most royalty calculations is the weekly operating costs of the musical. These costs are many and determine whether the show is making money, losing money, or breaking even on a weekly basis. Most Broadway musicals' weekly operating costs are in the area of $400,000–$750,000 but some shows are known to exceed $1,000,000 in a week.

WEEKLY EXPENSES OF A BROADWAY SHOW

Table 11.1

EXPENSES

Salaries	Theater Costs
Cast	Rent and administration
Chorus	Box office and mail staff
Musicians and conductor	Theater staff
Crew	Payroll taxes
Stage manager	Union pension and welfare
General manager	Air conditioning
Press agent	Theater expenses
Wardrobe and dressers	Tickets
Extra stagehands	Transportation
Equity vacation pay	
Star vacation pay	

Publicity	Miscellaneous
Television	Office expense
Newspaper	Legal
Photo and signs	Accounting
Printing and promotion	Payroll taxes
Press expense	Insurance
Television residuals	Local taxes
Subway and misc. advertisements	League dues
Group sales	Pension and welfare
	Miscellaneous

Departmental	Royalty Payments
Electrical	Writers
Props	Director/choreographer
Costume	Producer's fee
Carpenter	Other royalty
Rentals	Participants

A representative breakdown of the costs associated with a musical with weekly running expenses of $600,000 are as follows: Physical Production ($49,000 for carpentry, electrical, etc.), Salaries ($132,000 for cast, general manager, stage manager, press agent, music director, musicians, etc.), Re-Occurring Fees ($11,000/ music coordinator, technical supervisor, etc.), Taxes and Benefits ($40,000/ union pension and welfare benefits, etc.), Rehearsals and Casting ($1,000/ studio rental), Advertising and Promotion ($120,000/ artwork, television media, marketing, photography, print media, website, etc.), Theater Venue Expenses ($190,000/fixed weekly theater charges, theater share, local musicians and crew, etc.), General and Administrative Expenses ($20,000/legal, accounting, payroll expenses, office charges, insurance, etc.), Royalties ($35,000/author, producer, director, choreographer, music supervisor, original venue royalty, etc.) and Miscellaneous ($2,000).

It is important to note also that there is a huge amount of money expended prior to the show's "opening night" and first week's operating costs. Those are the figures involved when you hear that a musical costs $10 million to $20 million in investors' money just to get the show to the Broadway opening. This is the total amount that investors need to recoup prior to the musical returning a profit.

These costs include any option fees paid (book writer, lyricist, composer), possible image and likeness royalties, fees payable to the organization that initially presented the production, scenery, props, costumes, sound, creative fees (lighting, sound, costume and scenic designers, musical supervisor, dance music arranger, orchestrator, choreographer, director, etc.), production fees (general manager, casting directors, production managers, accounting, legal, etc.), rehearsal salaries and fees, theater rental, hauling and storage and general and administrative costs (executive producer and production consultant fees, office operating costs, payroll service, insurance, etc.). In some cases, the theater itself has to be reconstructed which can lead to additional costs over and above those related directly to the musical.

THE BROADWAY COMPOSER AND LYRICIST
In this world of multimillion-dollar investments, enormous profits, and equally enormous losses, the book writer, composer, and lyricist of a Broadway musical can earn unbelievably large amounts of money during the New York run, as well as for many years after the final curtain goes down on Broadway. In fact, the Broadway show does not necessarily have to be successful for the songwriters to make money. In some cases (depending on the quality and appeal of the songs in the show), the composer and lyricist may receive substantial long-term royalties from exploitation of the compositions in other areas, even if the original Broadway production is not terribly successful or, in a few cases, a total failure. Although the emphasis of this chapter is on the musical aspects of the Broadway show, the authors do not mean to lessen the role or importance of the book writer/librettist in any manner, since without that individual's contribution the Broadway musical would not exist.

SOURCES OF INCOME FOR THE BROADWAY COMPOSER AND LYRICIST
Innumerable potential sources of both immediate and long-term income are available for the writers of Broadway musicals. The following list represents the most significant:
Option payments from the show's producer
The advance based on the amount of capitalization for the show
Out-of-town pre-Broadway performances
The Broadway opening and New York run
The Broadway show cast album
Hit singles and cover records
U.S. touring productions during and after the Broadway run
Radio, Internet, and television performances of songs from the show

The motion picture sale: (a) The soundtrack album; (b) Television performances of
the film; and (c) Foreign performances of the film in theaters

Stock, amateur, and foreign theatrical productions

Television and radio advertising commercials using songs from the play

Television performances of the play

Advertising commercials promoting the play

The Tony Awards telecast

The Academy Awards telecast (if the play is made into a motion picture)

The Grammy Awards telecast (if songs from the play become hit records)

Home video/DVD/downloads/pay-per-view/video-on-demand

Ringtones and video games

Uses of songs from the play in motion pictures unrelated to the Broadway musical

Uses of songs from the play in television series

MUSIC LICENSING AGREEMENTS

There are three basic contracts or license arrangements that cover most situations on
Broadway. They are (1) the Dramatists Guild of America (DGA) Approved Production
Contract (APC), (2) royalty pool arrangements and (3) Fixed-Dollar royalty shows.
Variations of these are found in practically all Broadway productions, from original
shows, to revivals, to "catalogue musicals."

DGA/APC

The Dramatists Guild of America is a professional association of playwrights,
composers, lyricists, and librettists for the stage. As part of its role, the DGA provides
model contracts for all levels of production (Broadway, touring companies, amateur,
etc.) and gives advice to members on how their contracts compare to industry
standards. The "model contracts" are very comprehensive and are designed to make
sure creators receive fair compensation as well as retain significant control over their
works. They cover every important area including advance payments, option periods,
copyright ownership, royalty adjustments, production rights, and subsidiary rights,
among others. The APC contract deals with what happens to productions before,
during, and after they are produced.

OPTION PAYMENTS

When a theatrical producer becomes interested in a specific property for production
on Broadway, that producer normally acquires an option to produce the play from the
book writer, composer, and lyricist. This option agreement guarantees to the producer
the exclusive rights to produce the play and specifies an agreed-upon period of time
to find interested investors and actually produce the musical. Because most Broadway

productions take months, if not years, to reach the stage, the Dramatists Guild requires the producer to pay the author, composer, and lyricist of the musical certain minimum payments from the time that the agreement is signed to the point where the show is actually produced. In this way, the writers are ensured a certain amount of income prior to the show's opening. These option payments are deductible from capitalization advance payments and, provided production costs have been recouped, from up to 50% of future royalties due the writers. It should also be stressed that the Guild's compensation standards are only minimums, and depending on a writer's past success record and bargaining power, these option payments can be negotiated upward.

The option payments stipulated by the Dramatists Guild to be shared among the writers are as follows:

First Option Period. $18,000 for the 12-month period after the effective date of the contract, which is payable upon signing.

Second Option Period. $9,000 for a second 12-month option period, payable prior to the end of the first year.

Third Option Period. $900 per month for a maximum of 12 months during the third year.

ADVANCE PAYMENTS

In addition to the option payments, the producer will also pay to the book writer, composer, and lyricist the following aggregate advance payments:

- 2% of the capitalization of the musical, payment to be made on the first day of full-cast rehearsal but in no event later than five business days before the initial first-class performance (i.e., a live stage production in a regular evening bill in a first-class theater in a first-class manner with a first-class director and cast)
- 2% of any additional capitalization contributed to the musical, payment to the writers to be made within 10 business days after the producer has received such monies

The total sum of these two advances is reduced by 2%, and that net amount is then payable to the writers. The aggregate advance payment need not be in excess of $60,000, regardless of the amount of capitalization secured by the producer to put on the musical.

Capitalization, for purposes of the advance payment calculation, is defined as the amounts contributed by investors in order to pay production costs and obtain an ownership interest in the venture producing the musical, plus a percentage of certain loans secured by the producer but not including, among other items, security bonds and other union or theater guarantees, option payments to the writers, and certain advertising, promotional, and press-related costs. As with the option payments, these advance payments are deductible from up to 50% of future royalties due the writers of the musical once the production costs of the musical have been recouped.

PRE-BROADWAY PERFORMANCES

Most Broadway musicals tour a number of weeks or months prior to their New York openings. In this way, the show can be "tried out" before live audiences and any changes, new songs, replacements, or fine-tuning that may be necessary can be made before the Broadway opening. In some cases, the out-of-town run results in only minor changes; in others, entire scenes and musical numbers are discarded and replaced. In some instances, the pre-Broadway run will be the end of the line for the show, since disastrous out-of-town reviews have been known to close some musicals even before the Broadway opening. The out-of-town pre-Broadway run can be as little as a few weeks (for example, three weeks each in Boston, Philadelphia, and Washington), a few months (two months in Chicago or Toronto), or as long as one year. In addition, some musicals will open in cities outside the United States such as London before coming to Broadway.

Pursuant to the provisions of the Dramatists Guild contracts, the book writer, composer, and lyricist of the musical are guaranteed a set fee for the first 12 out-of-town performances, and varying percentages (depending on whether or not a show has recouped its costs) of the gross weekly box office receipts for all subsequent pre-Broadway out-of-town, New York preview, and regular performances. The actual minimum aggregate royalties to be divided among the librettist, composer, and lyricist are:

Initial 12 out-of-town performance weeks and each week of preview performances, pre-recoupment: $4,500 for each full performance week

Thirteenth and subsequent performance weeks, pre-recoupment: 4.5% of the gross weekly box office receipts until the official press opening in New York or the end of the week during which all production costs have been recouped, whichever is earlier

Post-recoupment performances: 6% of the gross box office receipts, starting with the week after the show has recouped its investment

THE BROADWAY OPENING

After the out-of-town pre-Broadway run, the musical normally enters New York for previews. Once the musical opens, the writers are guaranteed a minimum royalty of 4.5% of the weekly gross box office receipts until the show's costs have been recouped, and 6% of such receipts thereafter. For example, a hit musical on Broadway will usually take in from $700,000 to $2,000,000 per week in ticket sales. If the writers were sharing the Guild's post-recoupment minimum of 6% (2% each to the composer, lyricist, and book writer), the weekly writer royalties would range from $14,000 to $40,000 each. And by multiplying this figure by 52 weeks, each writer would receive from $728,000 to $2,080,000 in annual royalties from the Broadway run of the show alone—if they are receiving the minimum royalty set by the Dramatists Guild. Successful writers can and do negotiate better royalty arrangements because of their past history of hits and stronger bargaining power.

BROADWAY WRITER ROYALTIES

To illustrate the minimum royalty provisions and what they mean in actual dollars for the composer and lyricist, let us consider a play that opens on Broadway as a smash hit and runs for four years. The book writer, composer, and lyricist are each receiving the 1.5% pre-recoupment and 2% post-recoupment share of the gross weekly box office receipts under their Guild contract. The musical is sold out for the first year with an average of $1,000,000 in weekly receipts, and recoupment of costs is achieved at the end of the year. In the second year, it averages $900,000; in the third, $750,000; and in its final year on Broadway, $600,000. Under this scenario, the book writer's, composer's, and lyricist's weekly royalties from the Broadway run of the show would be computed as follows for each writer:

First year:

$ 1,000,000	Average weekly gross box office receipts
× 1.5%	Writer royalty (pre-recoupment)
$ 15,000	Weekly royalty
× 52	Weeks in one year
$ 780,000	*Annual writer royalties*

Second year:

$ 900,000	Average weekly gross box office receipts
× 2%	Writer royalty
$ 18,000	Weekly royalty
× 52	Weeks in one year
$ 936,000	*Annual writer royalties*

Third year:

$750,000	Average weekly gross box office receipts
× 2%	Writer royalty
$ 15,000	Weekly royalty
× 52	Weeks in one year
$ 780,000	*Annual writer royalties*

Fourth year:

$ 600,000	Average weekly gross box office receipts
× 2%	Writer royalty
$ 12,000	Weekly royalty
× 52	Weeks in one year
$ 624,000	*Annual writer royalties*

COPYRIGHT OWNERSHIP

It is important to keep in mind that the copyright ownership of intellectual property is very different in the theater world than in most other areas of entertainment. To quote the DGA, "The Author [book writer, composer, and lyricist] shall retain sole and complete title, both legal and equitable, in and to the play and all rights and uses of every kind except as specifically herein provided. Further all contracts for the publication of the music and lyrics of the play shall provide that the copyright be in the names of the composer and lyricist." In recent years though, there have been exceptions to this long standing practice—namely motion picture and television studios where musicals are being made from feature films or television series where all of the original music was written under "work for hire" agreements or where "work for hire agreements" are a company's business norm when hiring writers to create original compositions.

ROYALTY POOLS AND OPERATING PROFITS

The most common type of formula being used on Broadway today is the "royalty pool" arrangement whereby all royalty participants (for example, music and lyric writers, book writer, director, choreographer, underlying rights owner, producer, etc.) share in an agreed-upon percentage of the weekly operating profits of the musical with certain guaranteed minimum per-point royalties. The total amount of money in the royalty pool is based on a show's operating profits, which is the difference between the Gross Weekly Box Office Receipts (GWBOR) and the actual weekly running expenses of the show.

For example, a show grossing $1.25 million in GWBOR with operating costs of $700,000 would have operating profits of $550,000. If the royalty pool percentage for this show was 35%, the royalty participants would receive a total of $192,500 (35% of $550,000) with the investors receiving $357,500 (65% of $550,000).

Once the royalty pool percentage of GWBOR is set, all royalty participants are assigned points in the pool and distributions are made based on the number of points each participant has. If there were a total of 20 points and the composer and lyricist had 3 points each with the remaining 14 points allocated to all other royalty participants, the royalty split on $192,500 would be $28,875 to the composer, $28,875 to the lyricist and $134,750 payable to all others.

In addition, there is a minimum royalty (sometimes referred to as a "point") that must be paid to all royalty participants if the show is not running a weekly profit (i.e., it is breaking even or operating at a loss). This royalty is based on a set dollar value for each royalty point that a participant has in the pool. If the minimum per point value was $500, each party would multiply their points by $500 and that would be their respective royalty for that week. Finally, the royalty pool percentage can be increased once a show achieves 110% to 125% full investor recoupment of total capitalization. For example, it can go from a 35% pool to a 40% pool. This minimum royalty clause ensures that the royalty participants will receive some compensation during periods when the show is trying to find an audience, is struggling, or is just in a temporary "down" period. Occasionally, royalty participants may forego or reduce these minimums if it helps to keep the show open.

Royalty calculations and payments are normally paid after each four week performance period commonly referred to as a "cycle."

FIXED-DOLLAR SHOWS/COMBINATION WITH ROYALTY POOL

In situations where the Broadway show is using pre-existing songs, the producer sometimes may try to negotiate a specified weekly dollar payment (e.g., $600 per song per week). Under such a plan, the producer does not have to deal with a percentage of box office receipts formula or a royalty pool. Whether the show is a hit or a flop, the figure remains the same. These payments are normally based on an eight performance week and are reduced proportionally if there are less than eight.

In the case of so called "Catalogue Musicals," many times two formulas will be used. Well-known songs and songs integral to the story may be paid on a royalty pool basis or a percentage of box office receipts calculation (as in the DGA/APC discussed above) whereas other songs in the show receive Fixed Dollar weekly amounts. Obviously, this is an area for negotiation as it can have a significant effect on the amount of royalties a songwriter and his or her music publisher receive especially if the show is a hit.

Since it often takes years to develop a musical for presentation as a first run commercial production, the agreement for use of a pre-existing song in a musical will provide for a development period. For example, an agreement might read that the producer will have two (2) years to have the musical open on Broadway or other first run venue. During this period, the right to make theatrical use of the compositions often will be exclusive to the producer for live theatrical use and there will be a payment made to secure these rights (sometimes in the form of an advance, recoupable from future royalties).

Since you never know how long it is going to take to fully develop a theatrical musical, to say nothing of securing the necessary financing, the producer usually has an option to extend the development period for an additional period of time (one year, two years, etc.) with payment of an additional advance to the composers and lyricists (and/or music publisher, if applicable).

It should also be noted that, depending on the amount of money being paid for the commitment to be able to use the composition or compositions in the "to-be-developed musical," the rights may or may not be exclusive since exclusivity ties up the composition for use in this area for a period of time with no guarantee that the show will actually be produced. Thus, the money being paid can be a very important issue when the producer introduces the concept of "exclusivity" into the negotiations as opposed to "the nonexclusive right to use the composition" in the show. For example, a license might read "Licensor grants Licensee the nonexclusive, limited right during the term and territory to use and perform the composition in live dramatico-musical performances of the specific production. Licensor may grant others the right to use the composition in other live stage productions."

GRAND RIGHTS SONG LICENSE AGREEMENT

When a producer wants to use a pre-existing composition in a musical, the negotiated agreement between the copyright owner (usually the music publisher or administrator) and the producer is referred to as a Grand Rights License Agreement. (The term "grand rights" is used to distinguish dramatic performances, i.e., those within a musical play or other dramatico-musical work, from nondramatic or small right performances, which are performances without any dramatic element (that is, no book, staging, costumes, dramatic gestures, etc.) that are most often licensed through a performing rights society. This eight- to ten-page agreement grants the live stage rights (Grand and Dramatic) to the producer for a specific Broadway or off-Broadway production. The publisher grants an "exclusive option" to present an initial first class (or second class) production in the United States and Canada within a specified period of time usually with advances paid if option periods are involved. If the producer presents the required number of public theatrical performances, the producer will have "vested" and will have the right to license additional productions throughout the territory.

The royalty structure for the pre-existing composition can either be a fixed dollar amount per week, a royalty pool arrangement with a minimum weekly guarantee, or a GWBOR formula pursuant to the Dramatists Guild APC contract. The producer will also negotiate a subsidiary rights clause with specified fees and royalties if the production is licensed for presentation in motion pictures, radio, television, cast albums, or any other audio or audiovisual format. The producer also has the right to arrange the composition provided it does not alter the fundamental character of the composition. Warranties and dispute resolution procedures are also set forth in the agreement.

WRITING A NEW SONG FOR A MUSICAL

The basic structure for this type of agreement is as follows:

As to services, the writer is hired to compose the music and lyrics to one song for the new musical. Composer is to deliver the composition according to an agreed-upon schedule and revise upon request. The producer, in the case of a non-work-made-for-hire situation, acquires the sole and exclusive license to use the song in any and all versions, productions, etc., of the musical as well as the writer's name and likeness, right of publicity and promo rights on a nonexclusive basis. If the song is included in the official opening night, the producer's rights will be perpetual. Further, if the song is used, the producer can place it on cast albums and merchandise and has the right to embody the composition in a motion picture, television, or other audiovisual adaptation. If the song is not used in the Broadway opening or a first class production within a certain period of time, all rights will revert back to the writer except for any intellectual property elements in the song owned by the producer. A creative writing fee would be negotiated (e.g., ⅓ upon signing the agreement, ⅓ upon delivery of a final version and ⅓ if the song is included in the full draft of the script) along with royalty clauses either reflecting the APC percentages, a royalty pool, or some other arrangement as well as all customary composer and lyricist shares of subsidiary rights income as set forth in Article XI of the Dramatists Guild Approved Production Contract (APC). Credit, warranty and indemnification clauses, among others, would also be negotiated.

UNDERLYING RIGHTS AGREEMENT

The underlying rights agreement is negotiated when a producer wants to make a musical from a pre-existing work. Obvious examples are musicals based on motion pictures. Considering that practically all of the original music in a film (score and songs specifically written for the film) are written under work-for-hire contracts, the underlying rights owner (the studio, for example) already controls all rights in the work including the music. The underlying rights/copyright owner normally receives a royalty percent equal to the composer, lyricist, or book writer under the APC contract and is normally in the area of 2% of the GWBOR with a possible increase upon recoupment.

This agreement grants a license to produce and present one dramatico-musical play based upon the motion picture entitled [Name of Motion Picture] and upon the original screenplay upon which the play is based. The Grant of Rights includes the worldwide live stage dramatico-musical rights in and to the property and all component parts of the property including without limitation the unrestricted right to adapt, translate, change, rearrange, interpolate in, add to (including the addition of music and lyrics) and subtract from the property all in the Producer's sole discretion. In addition, the Producer has the right to engage persons to write or revise the play based on the property and compose music and lyrics for the play in accordance with the provisions of the overall agreement. The Producer also has the right to exploit the publication, mechanical reproduction, synchronization and small performance rights in the separate music and/or lyrics of the play. The underlying rights owner many times has the right to approve the musical's book writer, composer, and lyricist and also participate in a share of the Subsidiary Rights proceeds.

It is important for any composer, lyricist, or songwriter who created works under a work-for-hire agreement for the feature film now being made into a musical to determine what royalty structure will govern their compositions if used in the final Broadway production. The possibilities include the Dramatists Guild pre- and post-recoupment percentages, a royalty pool participation, a creator's Schedule A royalty addendum attached to the original work-for-hire agreement, or some other arrangement.

THE MOTION PICTURE AS A BROADWAY MUSICAL

A musical based upon a previously released motion picture is a formula that many times spells success on Broadway. *Frozen, Young Frankenstein, The Lion King, Monty Python's Spamalot, The Producers, Beauty and the Beast, Hairspray, The Lord of the Rings, The Little Mermaid, Legally Blonde, Dirty Dancing, Mary Poppins, Thoroughly Modern Millie, Saturday Night Fever* and *Little Shop of Horrors* are only a few of the shows that entered the world of theater with a built-in audience of millions of moviegoers.

Under the copyright law, such a musical would be a derivative work of the motion picture copyright and as such the stage producer would need a license to use the underlying work. Based on the APC contract royalty minimums of 4.5%–6% (pre-recoupment/post-recoupment) of the gross box office receipts to the composer, lyricist, and book writer, the underlying rights owner (i.e., the movie studio) would try to negotiate an amount equal to the other three participants (i.e., 6% to 8% rather than 4.5% to 6%). The same equal sharing would be the case in a royalty pool situation as well as for all subsidiary rights. Based upon the box office success of the film, additional compensation may be negotiated.

THE TELEVISION SERIES AS A BROADWAY MUSICAL

Although it is not common, Broadway musicals can also be based on television series with all of the royalty provisions that apply to the motion picture of a Broadway musical applying here as well. An example of this is *The Addams Family*, which opened in 2010, and the 2017 *SpongeBob SquarePants: The Broadway Musical*.

ROAD PERFORMANCES DURING AND AFTER THE BROADWAY RUN

Many successful shows have national touring companies that play selected cities throughout the United States and Canada during and after the Broadway run. For example, *The Lion King* opened on Broadway in November 1997 to rave reviews and capacity audiences. More than twenty years later, it was still grossing over $2 million per week on Broadway with many more millions being generated by 25 global productions. Another example is Wicked, which opened on Broadway to standing ovations and million dollar weekly grosses. Years later, the national touring production set the record for the highest grossing week in touring history with a take of $3.2 million at Washington D.C.'s Kennedy Center. And whether it's *Mamma Mia!*, *Jersey Boys*, *Movin' Out*, *Hairspray*, *Phantom of the Opera*, or *The Producers*, the same is true for successful Broadway musicals.

WEEKLY COSTS OF A SHOW ON THE ROAD

One of the most expensive projects in the entire area of Broadway musicals is to take the show on a national tour. Because of the additional costs involved (from per diems, living expenses, travel, and cartage to advertising, theater rentals, crew salaries, and the monumental costs of television commercials), producers try to organize such tours for only the most successful shows. Table 11.2 illustrates the type of monies that must be spent in taking a Broadway show on the road.

COSTS OF A BROADWAY SHOW ON THE ROAD

Table 11.2

EXPENSES

1.	Salaries	
	Cast	$ 41,000
	Chorus	$ 24,000
	Vacation and sick pay	$ 2,400
	Stage managers	$ 4,900
	Company and general managers	$ 6,000
	Press agents	$ 2,500
	Wardrobe/dressers/makeup	$ 4,600
	Production manager and supervisors	$ 1,700
	Conductor	$ 2,500
	Music coordinator/supervisor	$ 1,300
	Overtime and rehearsals	$ 2,500
	Total	$93,400

2.	Royalties	
	Author(s)	$67,000
	Director	$24,000
	Choreographer	$6,000
	Set and costume designer	$6,000
	Lighting designer	$2,300
	Sound designer	$1,500
	Total	106,800

3.	Producer's Fee	
	Total	$16,000

4.	Publicity	
	TV	$65,000
	Online advertising	$10,000
	Website maintenance	$500
	Print advertising	$4,000
	Outdoor photos and signs	$3,600
	Press agent expenses	$3,500
	Total	$86,600

5.	Departmental	
	Electrical and sound	$5,000
	Costume, hair, and makeup	$5,000
	Carpenter and props	$2,000
	Rentals	$27,000
	Company and stage managers	$250
	Maintenance reserve	$4,000
	Total	$43,250

6.	Theater expenses	
	Fixed theater expenses	$20,000
	Rent and sharing terms	$60,000
	Theater and box office staff	$16,500
	Stagehands	$32,000
	Musicians	$41,000
	Total	$169,500

7.	Miscellaneous	
	Office expense	$1,500

Legal	$600
Accounting	$600
Casting	$600
Payroll taxes	$6,000
Union benefits	$6,000
Insurance	$8,000
League dues	$550
Travel and living reserve	$3,000
Long-distance calls, photocopying	$750
Miscellaneous	$1,800
Total	$29,400
Total Weekly Expenses	**$544,950**

ADJUSTMENTS IN A WRITER'S ROYALTIES (DRAMATISTS GUILD CONTRACTS)

THE NEW YORK RUN (MINIMUM WEEKLY GUARANTEE)

In the event that, after a musical has recouped its investment, the weekly box office receipts do not exceed 115% of the weekly break-even point for the show, the combined aggregate writer royalties will be reduced to $3,000 per week plus 35% of the weekly profits for that week, rather than the normal 6% of gross royalty. If the director of the musical receives for any such week a royalty that is less than the full royalties specified in his or her contract, then the writer's percentage may be reduced on a pro-rata basis from 35% to no less than 25%. If this formula of $3,000 per week plus percentage of the profits takes effect, the total royalty may not exceed the normal 6% post-recoupment amount.

TOURING SHOWS (MINIMUM WEEKLY GUARANTEE)

In the weeks before the touring costs are recouped, if the weekly box office receipts do not exceed 110% of the weekly break-even point, the writers shall receive an aggregate $3,000 plus 25% of the weekly profits. As with the Broadway run, the total royalty shall not exceed the pre-recoupment 4.5% rate. After recoupment of costs has been achieved, if the 115% weekly break-even point is not exceeded by the box-office receipts, the writers will share a guaranteed $3,000 plus 35% of the weekly profits, but shall not earn more than the equivalent of the 6% weekly post-recoupment royalty. As on Broadway, the 35% can be reduced to not less than 25% if the director is not receiving full royalties during a particular week. During any week that a musical (whether it be on Broadway or on tour) suffers a loss, the writers will share a combined $3,000 fixed royalty and will not be paid on a percentage basis.

BROADWAY SHOWS PRODUCED UNDER NON–DRAMATISTS GUILD CONTRACTS

Since shows written by non–Dramatists Guild members are produced without using the Guild's Approved Production Agreement, there are a number of arrangements in addition to the "Fixed Dollar Shows" previously discussed that may be made between the parties involved in such a musical. The following section explains some of the more prevalent approaches in these agreements.

PERCENTAGE-OF-RECEIPTS ROYALTY

Most Broadway musicals use a percentage of the weekly box office receipts in determining how much the composers and lyricists of a show will receive. In the case of songs written by a number of writers (e.g., a show with a number of pre-existing compositions) each song may receive a pro-rata share of the agreed-upon percentage (e.g., 15 compositions sharing 3% equally, increasing to 4% upon recoupment or 110% recoupment of the investment), or each song may receive a pro-rata percentage dependent on its timing and use in the play (e.g., each song getting its proportionate durational share of 70 minutes of music). On the other hand, if the same writers have written all the songs in a play, those writers will receive the entire percentage. Depending on the negotiating power of the writers, these percentages usually range from 4% to 6%, with well-known Broadway musical writers receiving more. Obviously, if a show is grossing $900,000 a week, the difference between a 4% and 6% royalty ($36,000 vs. $54,000) can be substantial.

One interesting variation of the formula for the pro-rata sharing of royalties by different writers occurred in the musical *Sugar Babies*, which had a lengthy run on Broadway and on the road. Twenty songs (including such standards as "Don't Blame Me," "I Can't Give You Anything but Love," and "On the Sunny Side of the Street") shared in a percentage of the box office receipts according to whether the use was music and lyrics, music only, or lyrics only. Under the formula, the total royalties due all writers and publishers were divided in half, with 50% being attributable to lyrics and 50% to music. Each song shared in one or both funds according to its use.

TOURING SHOWS WITH GUARANTEES

A fairly common variation of the percentage-of-receipts royalty occurs when a successful musical is touring the country under arrangements that guarantee the play a certain amount of money each week, regardless of actual ticket sales. Under such arrangements, both the producer and the theater/presenter receive a guaranteed amount. Then the overage is shared by the producer and theater on a percentage basis (e.g., 60% to 80% to the producer and 20% to 40% to the theater).

If the writers are receiving their royalties based on a percentage-of-receipts formula, their royalties are based on the monies received by the producer and not those to which the theater is entitled. Suppose, for example, that the box office, after the deduction of certain expenses, brings in $1,000,000 in one week. The guarantee arrangement allocates the first $300,000 per week to the producer and the next $100,000 to the theater; the remainder ($600,000) is shared, 75% to the producer and 25% to the theater. The writers' 6% royalty comes out of the producer's combined guarantee and share of the remainder:

Producer	
$300,000	Guarantee
+450,000	75% of $600,000
$750,000	Total
× 6%	Writer royalty
$45,000	Writer royalties

Theater	
$100,000	Guarantee
+150,000	25% of $600,000
$250,000	Total

TOURING SHOWS VERSUS THE BROADWAY PRODUCTION

In certain situations, the touring version of the musical will be different from the Broadway version because of costs limitations and timing restrictions (e.g., the need for the musical to be an hour and fifteen minutes). For example, a show being performed in Las Vegas might not contain the songs and scenes of the show on Broadway since the playing time of the musical has to be reduced. In these cases, certain compositions may be dropped from the production, resulting in a loss of royalties for the songs deleted.

OFF-BROADWAY TO BROADWAY TO OFF-BROADWAY

It is possible for a show that originates off-Broadway to transfer to Broadway because of its success and after the Broadway run is over, transfer back to off-Broadway. An example of this is the Tony Award–winning *Avenue Q*, a reminder that the life of a stage musical doesn't have to end after the off-Broadway or Broadway run.

SECONDARY PERFORMANCES/BROADWAY MUSICALS

In addition to the Broadway run and the first class touring productions, another lucrative source of income for the author of a musical play is the secondary performance market. This market includes stock, amateur, and professional productions, as well as certain types of productions in cities such as Atlantic City, Las Vegas, Reno, Lake

Tahoe, and Branson. Because of the nature of the licensing in this area, the author of the play will provide the company licensing the musical with all elements that may be needed for the play to be produced in the secondary market. The licensing agent may also elect to create its own materials, with the approval of the authors, to make the play more attractive to partners who are interested in performing the play.

The licensing agreement is usually exclusive and will last for a specified period of time. The territory can be the United States and Canada or for the world. The licensing agent will take a commission on the productions that it licenses with the remainder being split between authors and the producer of the first class production pursuant to the subsidiary rights sharing formula.

Advances payable upon the signing of the licensing agreement are the norm with additional advances many times payable upon recoupment of the initial advance.

Included in the secondary performance agreement are credit provisions as well as language stating that no changes shall be made in the play including any change to the characterizations, time, place, or gender of the characters without the permission of the authors. The licensing agent will also agree not to license secondary performances of a play in a city in which there is a first-class touring production.

SUBSIDIARY RIGHTS AND THE PRODUCER

In order for the producer of a musical to share in the income generated from the cast album, a motion picture sale, the home video market, commercial uses (such as games, dolls, T-shirts, souvenir programs and toys), stock performances (including university resident theaters and dinner theaters), amateur performances by nonunion actors, concert tour versions, and theatrical performances in certain foreign territories, it must present the musical in one of the following ways:

UNITED STATES

1. One of the following series of consecutive paid public first-class performances in the United States: 10 previews plus the official press opening in New York City; five previews plus the official press opening and five regular performances; five out-of-town and five preview performances plus the official press opening (provided there are not more than 42 days between the last out-of-town performance and the first preview performance); or five preview performances and the official press opening in New York, if the play has been produced previously by someone other than the current producer and the show has substantially the same cast and scenic designs of the prior presentation.

2. Sixty-four paid out-of-town performances occurring within 80 days of the initial performance.

3. Sixty-four performances as outlined above in arenas or auditoriums if—because of the nature of the play, its size, or complexity of the production—playing in traditional first-class theaters would not be feasible or desirable.

UNITED KINGDOM

If the play is initially produced in London, there must be 21 consecutive performances in London. If the play is initially produced outside of London, there must be 64 performances within 80 days after the first performance, with such performances taking place either totally outside London or partly outside and partly in London.

AUSTRALIA AND NEW ZEALAND

There must be 21 consecutive first-class performances, including an official press opening.

PRODUCER'S SHARE OF SUBSIDIARY RIGHTS UNDER DRAMATISTS GUILD CONTRACTS

If the producer has achieved the above criteria, the producer and the investors who financed the play will be allowed to share in the revenue derived from subsidiary rights according to three alternative formulas, as set forth in Table 11.3. Unless the producer and the writers of the musical jointly select Alternative III at the signing of the production contract, the producer can choose either Alternative I or Alternative II on or before midnight on the first day of rehearsal at which the producer requires all cast members. If the producer does not give such notice, the writers may select the plan for the producer by giving both the producer and the Dramatists Guild notice on or before midnight of the next business day following the first rehearsal date. If both the producer and the writers fail to choose an alternative, then Alternative III will automatically apply.

Because subsidiary income from a Broadway musical can be substantial, many producers keep a show open even though losses are being incurred just to make sure that they become entitled to a share of this potentially valuable future source of income.

THREE ALTERNATIVE FORMULAS FOR SHARING SUBSIDIARY RIGHTS REVENUE

Table 11.3

Type of Right	I	II	III
Media productions (television, soundtrack albums, motion pictures, home video, etc.)	50% in perpetuity	same	30% in perpetuity

Stock and ancillary performances (equity stock, resident theaters, dinner theaters, concert tour versions, opera versions, etc.)	50% for the first five years/25% for the next 5 years	30% for 36 years	30% for the first 20 years/25% for the next10 years/20% for the next 10 years (total of 40 years)
Amateur performances (English-language versions using nonprofessional actors)	25% for 5 years	0%	same as for the stock above
Revival performances	20% for 40 years	same	same
Commercial use products (wearing apparel, toys, games, figures, dolls, souvenir books and programs, etc.)	(a) 10% of the gross retail sales of goods sold at the theater (not to exceed 50% of the producer's license fee)	same	same
	(b) 50% of the producer's net receipts from sales in other locations	same	same
	(c) Rights extend during the period in which producer retains the right to produce the play in a territory and for no more than five years after said rights have expired for contracts entered into prior to the expiration date	same	same

PRODUCER'S RIGHT TO SUBSIDIARY INCOME UNDER NON–DRAMATISTS GUILD CONTRACTS

Since writers who are not members of the Dramatists Guild do not use the guild agreement, the right of a producer to share in the many subsidiary sources of income that flow from the musical is negotiable in such cases. While many of these contracts are based on principles outlined in the Dramatists Guild Approved Production Contract, the actual terms are subject to the negotiating expertise and bargaining power of the parties.

LIFE AFTER BROADWAY (WHERE THE MONEY IS MADE)

For many songs from musicals, the real money comes from sources other than the Broadway run or the national and foreign touring productions. Granted, a handful of writers make millions of dollars from live theatrical performances, but the major royalties for many writers come from the sale of hit records and CDs, downloads and Internet streaming, radio and television performances of the songs from the show, commercials, motion pictures using Broadway songs as theme or background music, the theatrical release and television broadcasts of the motion picture, sheet music and folios, option and acquisition payments for the production of the musical as a film, television broadcasts of the show, cover recordings, home video, ringtones and video game use, and the Tony Awards show. Because of the importance of this "non-live theater income" and what it means to the financial well-being of a songwriter and music publisher, the following sections review how the money is made and what you must know to make it.

HIT SINGLES FROM BROADWAY SHOWS

One of the most lucrative sources of income for the composer and lyricist of the Broadway musical is the hit single, since Number One songs can generate in excess of $300,000 in CD and download sale income, and more than $1,000,000 in traditional radio, streaming services, and television performance royalties. In addition, because of the mass exposure that hit singles receive, a number of important areas are opened up such as commercials, movies, and television series, which can generate hundreds of thousands of dollars in short- and long-term income for the writer and music publisher.

TOURING PRODUCTIONS

Since the composer/lyricist compensation is many times based on a royalty pool arrangement, there is usually a minimum dollar compensation guarantee provided for with respect to each four-week performance period regardless of the operating profits of the show for each particular accounting period. For example, the producer might guarantee each of the authors $4,000 without regard to how the show is performing financially during a particular accounting period.

MECHANICAL ROYALTIES

There will also be a mechanical royalty for sales of the cast album and single tracks taken from the show. For example, these songwriter/music publishing royalties are many times paid at the statutory rate with a song cap for albums and a full 100% statutory rate for digital downloads. In the United States, the statutory mechanical rate is 9.1 cents per composition (or 1.75 cents per minute if the composition is over 5 minutes in duration). For a show in which the music is primarily in the form of songs or other individual numbers, the statutory rate would be paid on each number so that the 9.1 cents basic rate would apply to each number of 5 minutes durations or less, and 1.75 cents per minute for numbers in excess of 5 minutes duration. For a show in which the music is continuous, the 1.75 cents per minute basic rate may be applied to the entire work. In either case, it is common in the U.S. for the record company to propose adjustments to limit the total mechanical royalties paid on physical copies (e.g., CDs, vinyl, etc.). To put this income source into perspective for a successful show, the total cast album sales for the 2015 musical *Hamilton* are in excess of 1,400,000 with over 700,000 of those digital.

It is important to note that this source of income, in addition to physical recordings and permanent downloads, also includes limited downloads, interactive streaming, ringtones, paid locker services, purchased content lockers, mixed service bundles, limited offerings, and music bundles.

For sales outside the United States, mechanical royalties will be paid in conformance with the rules and regulations of the applicable foreign country society (many times a percentage of the wholesale or price to the dealer with respect to albums). For example, in the UK, the physical product rate is 8.5% of the purchased price to the dealer with an 8% of gross revenue rate for permanent downloads.

The above mechanical rate calculations will also apply if the musical is made into a film or television production and there is a new soundtrack album or tracks released from these new versions of the play. These royalties can be significant especially in the area of musicals made into motion pictures. For example, the soundtrack sales in the United States alone for *Les Miserables* and *Rock of Ages* were over 650,000 and 320,000 respectively. Doing the math, the monies that can be earned can be substantial especially since the mechanical royalties from digital sales will be at statutory as opposed to any reduced statutory controlled composition rate provided for in the soundtrack agreement. This does not even take into account the individual track sales which can be significant.

MOTION PICTURE RIGHTS TO THE MUSICAL

If the musical is made into a theatrical motion picture, the composer and lyricist will often be entitled to share in a percentage of the actual purchase price received by the producer from the film company. In most cases, this will equate to a small percentage of the final budget of the motion picture. There is usually a floor and a ceiling to the amount and there also may be a continuing participation in the backend profits of the motion picture company provided for. Obviously, the negotiations in this area are complicated because of the various formulae and/or practices of the particular film company, industry understandings, court cases, and the terms of the signed contract with respect to the definition of what constitutes backend profits and the calculation thereof.

In many cases, there is a separate synchronization fee payable for each composition being put into the movie; especially when dealing with pre-existing compositions not written for the play. If this is the case, there is usually an agreed-upon fee specified in the initial rights agreement so there is certainty for all parties as to the cost rather than a "to be negotiated in the future" provision.

THEME PARKS, ICE SHOWS, AND OTHER LIVE VERSIONS

These types of shows are licensed on either a one-time flat fee (sometimes with additional payments if the version continues to run for a set period of years) or on a royalty basis.

TELEVISION RIGHTS

If the musical is made into a television production, there will be a flat-fee payment to the composers and lyricists which can be based on the duration of the program. In addition, as previously discussed, the composers, lyricists, and their music publisher may receive performing right income for the individual numbers.

PERFORMANCE ROYALTIES

Performing rights organizations such as ASCAP (the American Society of Composers, Authors, and Publishers), BMI (Broadcast Music Inc.), SESAC, and GMR (Global Music Rights) license only the nondramatic performance right in copyrighted musical works and therefore are not involved in the licensing of live musical theater on the stage. This is a dramatic performance right reserved for licensing by the copyright owner who in most cases is the Author (book writer, composer and lyricist) or the music publisher in the case of pre-existing songs. But if the musical is broadcast on television (network, local, cable, etc.) or songs from the show are played on the radio or performed in other licensed media, writer and publisher performance earnings from performing rights organizations can prove substantial over the life of the copyright. It's not unusual for a major hit song to generate well over 1 million dollars in writer and publisher earnings during its initial chart activity period let alone many millions of dollars more over the composition's copyright life.

To put this area into perspective, total combined annual receipts of the three U.S. performing rights organizations ASCAP, BMI, and SESAC are in excess of $2.5 billion with combined television and radio license fees accounting for over $1 billion of that total. In addition, approximately $700 million represents primarily writer money coming in from foreign countries for performances of U.S. writers' works with an additional $300 million collected from the general licensing and live nondramatic performance area. Successful musical compositions from the theater share significantly in the distributions from all major and minor licensed media as well as income from all distribution channels.

As successful musicals have a worldwide market, performance royalties from foreign countries can be substantial, particularly if there is a feature film version of the show or recordings of individual songs released. Foreign country performing rights organizations (i.e., PRS for Music in the U.K., SOCAN in Canada, APRA in Australia/New Zealand, SACEM in France, IMRO in Ireland, SIAE in Italy, etc.) not only license television, radio, live, and Internet performances (among others), they also license movie theaters for all of the music contained in films being shown in their territory. This latter income source can prove substantial for musicals made into feature films as most foreign country performing rights societies license movie theaters on a percentage of box office gross receipts (1% as an average) less certain administrative, social, and cultural deductions.

BROADWAY SHOW MUSIC IN COMMERCIALS

Another source of income for the Broadway song is its use in radio or television commercials advertising consumer products. Since the fees for such commercial use can be substantial (e.g., from $125,000 to more than $1,000,000 per year for well-known songs), this area can represent a major source of potential income for the writer and his or her publisher. Some examples of Broadway show songs used in commercials are "Tomorrow" from *Annie* for Entresto, "Rich Girl" (Gwen' Stefani's adaptation of "If I Were a Rich Man" from *Fiddler on the Roof*) for Pepsi/iTunes and "Tonight, Tonight" from *West Side Story* for Mountain Dew and Intel.

TELEVISION AND INTERNET COMMERCIALS PROMOTING A BROADWAY MUSICAL

Because television and the Internet are such important mediums, virtually all Broadway musicals use television commercials to advertise their presence and promote ticket sales. Although extremely expensive, this method of promotion has, in many cases, had spectacular results. On occasion, payments are made for the use of songs in these commercials, but normally such rights are given without charge because of the promotional nature of the spots.

TELEVISION PERFORMANCES OF SONGS IN THE PLAY

Each year, the Tony Awards show is presented on network television to an audience of millions of viewers. During this annual presentation, there are three basic situations where Broadway show music is used, and for which composers and lyricists receive ASCAP, BMI, SESAC, and GMR performance royalties. They are:

Staged production number. Actual production numbers from the shows that were nominated for Best Musical of the Year.

Background music used while Tony winners accept their awards. Music is ordinarily played while the award winners walk to the stage for their acceptance speeches. In addition, instrumental music is performed to introduce the celebrities who act as presenters.

Song medleys. During the course of the evening, there usually is a production number that contains songs from either past or current Broadway shows.

The writers of music performed on the Tony Awards show are paid by ASCAP, BMI, SESAC, and GMR according to the duration of music used, the number of uses during the show, the number of television stations carrying the program, how the song is used, whether bonuses are applied, and the song's past performance history.

TELEVISION PERFORMANCES OF THE PLAY

A number of Broadway musicals have been televised in their entirety, normally at the end of or after their New York run. Such televised performances represent an additional source of income for the songs used in a Broadway show, since there are up-front synchronization right payments as well as the ASCAP, BMI, SESAC, and GMR nondramatic performance royalties. Payments in this area are much smaller than those negotiated when a musical is produced as a theatrical feature motion picture. Because there is a possibility that a televised version of a musical might hurt the sale of motion picture rights or injure the potential box office for either the Broadway run or road performances, such television performances are not that common.

THE BROADWAY SHOW CAST ALBUM

At one time, the Broadway cast album was a significant source of income for the writers and publishers of a musical. Such past successes as *My Fair Lady* and *The Sound of Music* sold millions of copies worldwide, and shows such as *Hair, South Pacific, Hello, Dolly!, Jesus Christ Superstar,* and *Fiddler on the Roof* further added to the reputation of the Broadway cast album as a financial gold mine. In recent years though, with the exception of *Hamilton,* Broadway show albums have not generated the sales and enthusiasm that they had in the past. Of course, there have been a number of very successful records such as *Jersey Boys, The Lion King, Evita, A Chorus Line, Grease, Rent, Funny Girl, 42nd Street, Cats, Les Miserables, Mamma Mia!* and *Phantom of the Opera,* but the cast album, as a genre, has not shown the international consistency and mass appeal that were once expected of a hit Broadway musical.

Record Contract Royalties. In most cases, the producer of the Broadway musical will negotiate the record contract for the original cast album. Where the writers have the requisite bargaining power, however, they may retain the right to make the agreement themselves. Pursuant to the terms of the recording contract, the record company will usually agree to pay a royalty based on a percentage of the retail selling price of 90% to 100% of all albums sold. The writers of the show and the play's producer normally share this record royalty; many times on a 60% to the authors and 40% to the producers split. All recording costs and advances are deducted from any monies due the writers and producer before the record company makes any royalty payments. For example, if a Broadway cast album cost $400,000 to produce and a $50,000 advance is also given, no royalties will be distributed until all the recording costs and advances have been recouped by the record company.

MOTION PICTURE SOUNDTRACK ALBUMS

If a Broadway musical has been produced as a major theatrical feature film, the motion picture soundtrack album can generate substantial mechanical and performance income for the writers and publishers of the original Broadway production. For example, *Dreamgirls* went to Number One and *Chicago* went to Number Two on the charts; *Oklahoma!* was on the trade paper album charts for more than 300 weeks, *The King and I* and *South Pacific*, more than 250 weeks, and *The Sound of Music*, more than 230 weeks. *Hairspray, Rent, Fame*, and *Hair* also did well. As with the "live" Broadway cast album, mechanical royalties for physical albums may be paid either at the statutory rate or, if negotiated downward, at 75% to 85% of the statutory rate for a 12- to 13-song album. Downloads will be paid, in most cases, at the statutory rate. In addition to mechanical royalties, a royalty percentage (similar to that received by a recording artist) of 1% to 4% is many times negotiated for the writers and publishers of the songs contained on the album.

SUCCESSFUL COVER RECORDS

One of the best examples of the lasting popularity of some Broadway songs is Barbra Streisand's *The Broadway Album*, which contained songs spanning over five decades of theatrical history, from *Show Boat* (1927) to *Sunday in the Park with George* (1984). The album's sales of more than 3 million copies in just a few months of 1985 proved that, with the right combination, theater songs will always earn money. In 1993, Streisand did it again with her *Back to Broadway Album*, which went to Number One on the charts in its first week of release. Additionally, countless Broadway songs continue to be recorded by artists of all genres.

COVER SINGLES

Broadway show songs can and do have a life of their own as hit singles outside of the musical and long after the show has closed. One example is Gwen Stefani's 2005 chart single "Rich Girl" (based on "If I Were A Rich Man" from *Fiddler on the Roof*), which earned substantial royalties for the original writers from performances, single and album sales, samples, a national commercial, ringtones, and all the other ancillary income generated by a hit song.

SHEET MUSIC FOLIOS

Even though the print business has not been as profitable as it once was, Broadway-oriented theme books continue to generate good sales. The standard royalties for such folios are between 10% and 15% of the retail selling price; all copyrighted compositions normally share equally in the aggregate amount. If the folio concentrates on one play exclusively, an additional royalty percentage may be paid (e.g., an extra 5%, similar to a "personality folio" rate). Individual print configuration for compositions in the play can also be good sellers.

ROYALTIES FROM MOTION PICTURE THEATERS

In most countries outside the United States, motion picture theaters are required to pay royalties to the local performing rights society for the music used in films. The writer's share of such monies is distributed by the local society to either ASCAP, BMI, SESAC, or GMR, which then pays the U.S. composers and lyricists. The publisher's share of such fees is normally distributed to the publisher's local foreign representative, who then remits the appropriate share to the U.S. publisher. Most countries charge theaters a percentage of the total box office receipts, but some base fees on the number of seats in each theater as well as other factors. Most domestically produced motion pictures will not earn a great deal of money from theaters outside the United States, but for those Broadway musicals that become motion pictures with worldwide appeal, the monies can be substantial. In fact, $100,000 to $300,000 in combined writer and publisher theater performance royalties is not unusual for hit films.

BROADWAY SONGS USED IN TELEVISION PROGRAMS

Because many television programs use well-known standards either as background music or sung by a person on camera, this area can be extremely valuable for the Broadway song in terms of performance, synchronization, and home video income (e.g., $11,000 for an all-television license, $9,500 for a video license, synchronization option payments, mechanical income from soundtrack albums, ASCAP, BMI, SESAC, and GMR performance income, etc.), as well as re-exposure to millions of people.

BROADWAY SONGS USED IN MOTION PICTURES

Another extremely lucrative source of income is the inclusion of Broadway show songs in motion pictures as theme, background music, or visual vocals. Because of the various royalty-generating media involved in motion pictures (e.g., the initial $15,000 to over $60,000 synchronization fee, performance income from television broadcasts of the film, soundtrack album sales, royalties from theaters exhibiting the film in foreign countries, ringtones, video game uses, and performance and mechanical royalty income from hit records taken from the show), this area can mean hundreds of thousands of dollars to the writer and music publisher. One example is Prince Charming singing "One" from *A Chorus Line* in the film *Shrek the Third*.

THE BROADWAY MUSICAL AS A MOTION PICTURE

Even though the heyday of the Broadway musical as a major motion picture is over, for those musicals that are transferable to film, the profits can still be substantial. The motion picture sale can take a number of different turns and encompass a number of areas, but virtually every agreement will encompass most of the areas that follow.

Payment for the Rights. The motion picture company will pay a negotiated fee (e.g., from $1 million to more than $10 million) for the rights to produce a motion picture based on the musical. Obviously, the final compensation is based on the success of the show on Broadway and on the road, the conviction of the producer that the show can be successfully made into a commercial film, whether the film will have international appeal, and what is given up by the writers in other areas of the agreement.

Percentage of the Proceeds from the Film. The producer, writers, and music publishers are many times given a percentage of the net monies earned by the motion picture after the break-even point for the film has been reached. A number of different formulas are used in this area depending on the company producing the film, and each is extremely complicated. For example, break-even for a film company normally includes the recoupment of a multiple of the direct costs of making the film, fixed deferred payments (as opposed to deferred income based on how well the film does), a production fee for the film's producer, overhead fees to the producer equal to a set percentage of the production costs, supervisory fees to the film company financing the production, and the bank interest on the money needed to produce the film.

Fees for Remakes or Sequels. The film's producer will usually be given the right to produce a remake or sequel, provided a specified fee ($250,000 and above) is paid within a certain number of days after principal photography has begun. If additional compensation based on a percentage of the net earnings was received on the original film, the same formula or a percentage thereof would also be received for the remake. As for sequels, the fees paid and percentages are many times more than those that would be payable for a remake of the original film.

Fees for Television Films or Series. In addition to the motion picture, sequel, and remake rights, the film producer will also try to negotiate for television rights to a made-for-TV movie or series based on the play if the theatrical film is actually produced. In the event that the television version is released theatrically outside the United States, a further payment may be due (usually the equivalent of or more than the television fee). If a television series is based on the play (including a spin-off based on characters in the play), additional fees will be due, dependent on, among other factors, the running time of the series. In addition, many contracts provide for payments of negotiated fees (sometimes based on a percentage of the initial fee) for each rerun of the program up to a certain limit.

HOME VIDEO/DVD/BLU-RAY/DOWNLOADS/VIDEO-ON-DEMAND

At one time, home video income meant something only if the Broadway play was made into a feature film. Now, however, home video versions are being made of actual live stage musicals. As in the television series and motion picture area, there are a number of different ways to license songs for home video (e.g., the one-time buy-out for all sales, the roll-over advance or set dollar amount for a set number of units, and the per-unit royalty or penny-rate-per-song formula).

NON-CAST ALBUMS OF THE BROADWAY MUSICAL

There has been a recent trend by record companies to produce new recordings of a show with performers who were not in the original production. This trend has not only affected older shows such as *Carousel*, *South Pacific*, and *Showboat*, but has been extended to newer musicals as well. Such an approach takes the Broadway album out of the sometimes limited "cast album" category and puts it into the mainstream record-buying market.

CATALOGUE MUSICALS

A popular form of contemporary musical is the show using the individual songs of a successful writer or writer/artist with a story structured around them, called catalogue musicals or sometimes jukebox musicals. Some examples are *Mamma Mia!*, based on the Abba catalogue of songs, *American Idiot* (songs of Green Day), *Million Dollar Quartet* (songs recorded by Elvis Presley, Johnny Cash, Jerry Lee Lewis, and Carl Perkins), *Come Fly With Me* (songs sung by Frank Sinatra including the Sinatra recordings), *Unchain My Heart* (songs recorded by Ray Charles), *Movin' Out*, which uses Billy Joel compositions, *Smokey Joe's Café*, based on the catalogue of Jerry Leiber and Mike Stoller, *Love, Janis*, an off-Broadway production based on the life of Janis Joplin, *We Will Rock You* from Queen, *Tonight's the Night*, based on Rod Stewart songs, *Saturday Night Fever* from the Bee Gees, *Taboo* using Boy George compositions, *All Shook Up* featuring Elvis Presley songs, *Good Vibrations* based on the Beach Boys' catalogue, *Lennon* with songs by John Lennon, *The Boy from Oz* playing Peter Allen songs, *Jersey Boys* featuring songs recorded by Frankie Valli and the Four Seasons, *Ray Charles Live!* using songs recorded by Ray Charles, *Ring of Fire* based on the recordings of Johnny Cash, and *The Times They Are A-Changin'* using Bob Dylan songs. Though the songs in this type of show may have a guaranteed appeal (most being past hit songs), a good lesson to remember is that songs themselves will not save a show if the book or other elements do not measure up to the audience's expectations.

Even though many jukebox musicals concentrate on a specific artist or songwriter, there are opportunities for other songs to be used in such a play even though they were not associated with the primary focus of the play. For example, *Jersey Boys*, which focused on music recorded by Frankie Valli and the Four Seasons, used additional well known songs from the era (for example, "Earth Angel" and "I'm in the Mood For Love") as did the Frank Sinatra–centered musical "Come Fly With Me," which used

Dave Brubeck's "Take Five." In addition, a musical which is based on a concept album can also include songs from other albums recorded by the artist (such as Green Day's *American Idiot*–based Broadway musical which also used material from their *21st Century Breakdown* album in addition to all songs on their *American Idiot* album).

These type of shows are handled in a number of ways including the royalty pool, the percentage of gross box office receipts, and the fixed weekly dollar amount royalty arrangement.

DEVELOPING A JUKEBOX OR CATALOGUE BROADWAY MUSICAL

The Beginning. When a producer has enough funding and backing to begin development of a so called jukebox or catalogue musical (i.e., a theatrical play which focuses on the existing songs of one writer or group of writers and/or recording artists), the producer will contact the music publisher(s) who owns the copyright to the compositions for approval to use the compositions in the production. In cases where the songwriter owns these so called "grand rights," the songwriter will be the party contacted. This same scenario will occur if the potential theatrical musical is based on a pre-existing motion picture or other audio visual work.

Development Agreements. If after reviewing the concept, storyline, and/or script of the play, the publisher decides that it wants to go forward with the project, it will sign an option agreement (known as a development agreement) which will allow the producer to perform the compositions in readings, workshops, and other developmental productions of the play as well as, many times, regional or not-for-profit theater presentations.

Time Limitations. Under the terms of the development agreement, there will be a negotiated time period within which the producer has to open the official production of the play from the signing of the agreement (e.g., two years, three years, etc.). If a first class production is not presented within the time period agreed upon, and if an extension is not negotiated, the agreement will terminate and the producer will no longer have the rights to use the compositions in the play.

Advances. In many of these agreements, the publisher will receive an advance upon the signing of the agreement and additional advances when certain options, if applicable, are exercised and once the play has its official first class opening; such monies to be recoupable against royalties payable to the publisher for theatrical performances of the play.

There are a number of variations in this area. For example, there might be an advance due if either a 29-hour Actor's Equity Reading or an Actor's Equity

Workshop or development production occurs. An additional advance might be paid if an out-of-town try-out production is mounted. An advance might be due in the event that the producer is awaiting the availability of either a Broadway, West End, or other theater, a director, or a star.

In addition, the advance may only be recoupable from 50% (rather than 100%) of the royalties that are payable to the publisher or songwriter. There also may be a guarantee that the publisher or writer will not receive less than the weekly minimum guarantee under a net operating profits royalty pool arrangement. Once again, it should be stressed that there are time limits in these development agreements for certain agreed-upon events to happen which trigger advances. If the time limitations are exceeded, the rights may revert to the publisher or writer unless an extension is agreed to, a negotiation that may result in triggering another advance or payment.

Licensing Restrictions. In most of these development agreements, there will be certain restrictions placed on the publisher with respect to licensing the compositions being licensed to other projects (similar in concept to the competing product restrictions that are contained in an advertising commercial agreement). In effect, the publisher will agree not to license the same composition to a live musical theatrical production which is substantially similar to the style and concept of the current development project which has a storyline and plot based upon the lyrics of the composition and music thereof (e.g., a *Mamma Mia!*–type of production). On occasion, this restriction can extend to any competing type of similar production in any media, including motion pictures, but that is a subject of negotiation, bargaining power, and the amount of money being paid.

In virtually all of these licenses, the competing project restriction relates to multiple compositions being licensed by one publisher and/or writer (e.g., four compositions) and is not usually applicable to a single composition unless that composition is essential to and identified with the subject matter of the play.

Additionally, the publisher will be allowed to license the composition or compositions to any other play which is not a *Mamma Mia!* type of production, provided that the other play is a dramatic play and not a musical, although music may be a part of such play and local nonprofit productions such as school or small community plays.

The noncompeting play restriction will last through the term of the development period and, if applicable, any option periods and then through the New York City or West End of London opening or tour and will continue until a negotiated period of months after the conclusion of the first class commercial run of the play.

Most Favored Nations. Since most compositions being used in these developmental projects are paid at the same rate and under the same terms as all other compositions being licensed for the musical (either on a percentage of the weekly gross box office receipts or on a royalty pool basis…there being exceptions to the rule when certain compositions are paid on a flat fee weekly or monthly regardless of the box office receipts or royalty pool calculations), it is standard for there to be a most favored nations clause guaranteeing such equality of financial/royalty compensation treatment in these type of agreements.

Branding. In the event that the songwriters allow their names in the title and in connection with the branding, advertising, and promotion of the play, there may be an additional royalty due which is based on a percentage of the box office receipts. For example, an additional 1% of the gross box office receipts might be payable for these "outside of the normal play royalty" rights.

Song as Title to the Play. In the event that the title of a composition in the play is used also as the title of the musical, an additional royalty will be due. This royalty is many times calculated as an additional composition which shares in the aggregate song royalties due for performances of the play. For example, if there were 15 compositions in the production, the aggregate song royalty due for a particular accounting period (e.g., a week a month, etc.) would be divided by 16 rather than 15 with the composition being used as the title being paid twice.

Exclusivity. In certain cases, the producer may request exclusivity which will totally restrict licensing opportunities in the musical theater area. This is not common, but because of the potential loss of licensing opportunities by taking a group of songs totally "off the market," the agreement will many times give the publisher or writer a percentage share of the net profits of the play. This is in addition to any box office receipts or royalty pool royalties. For example, a 1% to 3% sharing in the net profits might be provided with respect to income related to the original production and the same or a lesser amount with respect to subsequent productions.

Obviously, the definition of net profits is extremely important in this scenario since it is essential to know how such amount is to be calculated. At a minimum, there should be language in the agreement which provides that it shall be consistent with prevailing industry customs and practice at a minimum and there should be a most-favored-nations reference to make sure that the definition is as favorable in substantive terms or the same as any other net profits participant. Accountings as to net profits should be on at least a quarterly basis and should match the accounting requirement given to all other parties who are participating in this type of income.

Approvals. Depending on the bargaining power of the parties, the songwriters' role in the production, and whether the songs were the inspiration for and/or an integral part of the creation of the production, the songwriters may have approval rights over the principal cast, director, choreographer, book writer, and replacements. The songwriters may also have approval rights over changes in the music and lyrics (non-substantive changes may be accepted provided that they do not change the original meaning of the lyrics or are merely new orchestration and arrangements of the original music). In all cases, there will be a time limitation in which the songwriters must either approve or disapprove with nonresponse being usually deemed approval.

Opening Night Tickets/Travel and Living Expenses. For the opening of the first U.S. commercial production as well as, in many cases, the initial opening in New York, Los Angeles, London (or other designated major cities), it is common that a certain number of complimentary tickets for house seats to be available for the writers as well as, if applicable, opening night party passes.

In addition, first class airline tickets, first class hotel accommodations for a specified number of nights, and a per diem may be provided. In some cases, the producer will request that the writers use their best or reasonable efforts to attend the openings and participate and/or assist in the promotion of the musical play. Again, this is all dependent on the capitalization of the production (e.g., multi-million dollar investment, less than that, etc.), stature of the songwriters, contribution to the production, and bargaining power.

House Seats. It is standard for agreements to provide that a certain number of house seats will be available for purchase at regular box office prices with respect to commercial productions of the musical. Many times the house seats will be in certain rows of the theater (e.g., 4 to 12 in the center section of the orchestra) and on a specified hour hold basis (e.g., 48 to 96 hours) for regularly scheduled performances (some exceptions being during the Tony Awards voting season or when there are sold out theater party dates).

Merchandise. There are many formulas in this area of commercial use products, which include toys, games, dolls, clothes, books, souvenir programs, posters, mugs, and all kinds of items which relate to and are identified with the actual production. Included as well can be characters from the production. Many of the calculations distinguish between in-theater and outside-theater sales. As an example, sales of merchandise in venues outside of the theater might generate a pro-rata royalty of 25% to 50% of net receipts (net receipts being calculated as gross income paid to the producer less all taxes and customary cost incurred in the creation, manufacture, and sale of the merchandise). As to sales which occur in the theater where the play is being performed, the royalty might be a pro-rata share of 10% of the gross retail sales.

It should be noted that the image and likeness rights of the songwriters of the compositions used in the play are not included in these grants of commercial use merchandising rights and the use of such rights by the producer will be subject to a separate negotiation including approval mechanisms and additional compensation, if granted.

Cast Albums. Negotiations will usually occur relating to royalties from any cast album or tracks therefrom. In this regard, there are mechanical royalties which will be due the songwriters and music publishers for the sale of digital and physical product, the rates being statutory for digital in most cases and either statutory with a cap or a reduced statutory rate with or without a cap for physical sales.

In addition, and depending on the bargaining power of the parties, there might be an additional participation royalty based on a percentage of the net royalties to the show's producer after recoupment of recording costs and other standard record company contractual deductions.

It should be mentioned that if a songwriter is also the producer of the album or individual track, there will also be a producer royalty negotiated which is typically based on a percentage of the retail or wholesale price of the recording.

Credit. If the production is based on the musical works of one writer or group of related co-writers, then it is standard for the writers to receive credit in all programs of the production. There is usually a provision guaranteeing that there will be space for a biography of reasonable length for the primary writers. In addition, there might be a clause which provides that the writers will receive credit in all advertising with some exceptions.

Royalties. The development agreement will also detail the composer and lyricist royalties that the writers will receive for not only development productions, but also first class productions of the musical. For example, the agreement may provide for composer/lyricist royalties based on 4% to 5% of the gross weekly box office receipts for first class productions and a percentage of that for development productions. In virtually all cases, an alternative royalty pool formula will also be provided for (i.e., a royalty based on a percentage of weekly or monthly net profits with a minimum guarantee) since this latter approach has become more of the norm in many cases.

CONCLUSION

Musical theater: expensive to get into, difficult to write, and many times very costly to get out of. But for the composers and lyricists of hit new musicals and past successful shows, and songwriters and music publishers of pre-existing compositions used in "catalogue" musicals and dramatic plays, the theater can be a significant source of income.

Though Broadway hits are "where the money is," there are many examples of shows that never recouped their initial Broadway investment but have lived on for decades in stock, regional, resident, dinner, university, concert, amateur, and foreign country performances, providing continuing royalties to all those involved. The size and scope of those royalties though are most often determined by the original contract signed. Contracts and licensing arrangements can be, and are, very different based on the type of show, the particular music use and the negotiating tactics, knowledge, experience, and bargaining power of the respective parties. Good advice: know your contracts, your license agreements, and definitely know and understand the field you are dealing in. Without that knowledge, fame and fortune may very well be fleeting—if it comes at all.

CHAPTER 12
MUSIC, MONEY, AND VIDEO GAMES

VIDEO GAMES

Video games represent a major worldwide entertainment revenue area. And for songwriters, composers, music publishers, and artists, this interactive area has become a major new source of exploitation and revenue whether it's "breaking new bands," re-mixing a standard, using a previously existing track, composing a new score, or re-cutting an "old" film score. In the nonlinear world of the video game, music can literally be placed anywhere, serving a multitude of purposes depending on which direction the player goes. Many of the most successful types of games are those that involve dance, general adventure, first-person shooter, racing, sports, war, fantasy, fitness, and most importantly, multiple sequels to a popular game. A successful franchise is the name of the game in this area of entertainment.

Video games are normally created by independent developers who then contract with a video game publisher to distribute the game and many times to help finance its creation. In some cases, the publisher and the developer are one and the same entity and handle all aspects of the game under "one roof." Because of the sophistication of games for consoles, PCs, and portable devices, as well as the costs of console development (all various models and upgrades of Sony PlayStation, Microsoft Xbox and Nintendo, among others), video games have become very expensive to produce, with some exceeding the $20 million mark. In addition, the development process can last for years. Other types of games—cell phone, mobile device, and online games, for instance, as well as "expansion packets," "enhancements," and add-ons to current games, can be produced at a considerably lower cost.

TYPES OF VIDEO GAME MUSIC

As in the feature film area, music in a video game can be either a pre-existing song or record (the original or a remix), a new song written for the game as well as another project (an upcoming album), a score or song written specifically for the game or a pre-existing film or television score recut for a game.

As to the song and record area, the *Grand Theft Auto* franchise features many different genre radio stations in its cars, ranging from Blondie to N.W.A, from Guns N' Roses to Tito Puente. The *Gran Turismo* franchise has compositions from all over the world to match the many countries and autos involved in the world of car racing. The *Guitar Hero* and *Rock Band* games use well-known rock songs as well as masters from groups such as Metallica, Guns N' Roses, the Rolling Stones, and Pearl Jam. A number of artists are also releasing new songs in video games prior to the artist's album release. Other games are based on a personality (e.g., 50 Cent, Eminem, the Beatles) or a group of artists (e.g., *Def Jam Vendetta*) and showcase songs and records within the story of the game. Some video games allow you to remix your own version of songs, whereas others let you personally customize the game by inserting your own songs into a game. For some games released in foreign countries (e.g., France, Germany, etc.), local songs and artists are sometimes substituted for the original songs and records of the U.S. version of the game.

In the score area, composers are in some cases using full orchestras—just as they would in a feature film (e.g., Michael Giacchino's separate scores to *The Incredibles* feature film and *The Incredibles* video game). Other games utilize electronic scores via digital workstations (synthesized instruments, music samplers, etc.) with still others combining both orchestral and electronic elements.

SONGS IN VIDEO GAMES

When a producer wants to use a pre-existing song in a video game, the license normally covers the following areas:

Game, Song, and Master Description. The request for the composition will give the game title, describe the overall nature of the game, how the song or master will be used (e.g., being played from an automobile stereo) and information on the title, songwriter, publisher, and percentage controlled. The actual timed length may be stated or the language may say "up to the entire length of the composition." The contract may also state that there can be more than one rotation. Some agreements provide for use in cross-sell trailers in other games or as part of promotional broadcast features such as "making of" programs.

Mashups and Mixes. With respect to those games that allow the player to create mashups of the songs in the game, some games have restrictions and other games have very few restrictions in the license as to which songs can be combined or grouped together (or what the nature of the remix can be) since the point of many of these games is to take full advantage of interactive gameplay and the choices that can be made. This is a negotiable area with respect to the type of license requested and issued.

A variation of the "timing and use" clause for a DJ-type game would be "up to a full composition, which may be edited itself or otherwise combined or grouped together with other licensed compositions to produce an interactive gameplay computer software audio mix."

There are certain games that allow the users to rearrange, sample, augment, play back, and share the compositions using various ways including looping, editing, changing, instrumentation, sampling, real-time remixing, or adding additional musical elements and sound effects. These rights as well as post-game share issues such as users being able to transmit gameplay videos of the compositions on approved content distribution sites (e.g., Facebook, YouTube, etc.) with embedded links to purchase the compositions on iTunes or Amazon, or via other digital music distribution channels—all have to be negotiated. The ability of the game producer to use and share gameplay motion-capture of a user playing a game track on approved content distribution sites are other issues that may be addressed depending on the type of game involved.

Obviously, the more leeway that users have to manipulate any composition licensed to the game, the more protections will be required by the music publisher/ copyright owner of the licensed composition to protect the original composition from liability based on what the game player may add as well as restrictions that will prevent the game player from changing the inherent nature of the licensed composition (including any surrounding audiovisual content) in a manner that is unacceptable.

Description of the Configuration. Some descriptions are very broad and others are very specific. For example, some agreements include language covering all software programs or other electronic products in any format or platform that is designed for use with computers. Others refer to any existing electronic devices as well as any that may be developed in the future. Many also indicate the type of distribution medium on which the game may be distributed. For example, the contract may mention all current and future game platforms and formats including Sony PlayStation 4 Pro, Microsoft Xbox One, Nintendo 3DS XL, PC, Windows, all digital media platforms and mobile operating systems including but not limited to iOS and Android platforms, mobile handheld, smartphones, tablet computers and other app enabled devices, mobile, Web, Web-connected television, the Internet, social networking services, CD ROM, DVD, mobile phones, magnetic diskettes, optical disks, and PDAs, as permitted distribution media. Others will be less specific or provide that distribution will not be limited to only the areas mentioned.

Online Versions. If the game is available online, the agreement will have language that permits the transmission of the game over telephone lines, cable television systems, cellular telephones, satellites, and wireless broadcast "as well as any other service or method now known or hereinafter invented for the delivery or transmissions of such digitized product enabling interactive use."

Fees. The fee paid to music publishers for the use of a song in most video games (*Grand Theft Auto, Madden NFL, Call of Duty*, etc.) is a one-time buyout synch license regardless of how many units of the game are sold. The fees can range from $2,500 to $10,000 but can be higher or lower depending on, among other key factors, the stature of the song, its importance to the particular game, whether it's a new band or an established act, etc. The fee normally is on a "most favored nations" basis with other songs in the game as well as with the master recording.

SALES PLATEAU BONUSES/PER-UNIT ROYALTIES

Certain types of music-intensive games (*Guitar Hero, Rock Band, DJ Hero, Dance Central*, etc.) pay royalties on a per-unit basis or dependent upon the game reaching certain specified sales plateau levels. Many times, these type of arrangements are made on a most favored nations basis with all other songs used in the game. The following is a good example of a per-unit royalty deal: 0 to 500,000 units sold, 1 cent per unit; 500,001 to 1,000,000 units sold, 1.3 cents per unit; 1,000,001+ units sold, 1.5 cents per unit. These types of deals are normally accompanied by an advance against a certain amount of units, ($11,000 advance on 1 million units) and are paid pro-rata according to the publisher's share of the composition. The master recording is usually treated similarly.

An example of a "sales plateau" deal would be:

$7,000.00 to put the song into the game (synch fee)

$5,000.00 at 350,000 units sold

$6,000.00 at 500,000 units sold

$4,000.00 for every additional 250,000 units sold thereafter.

If the video game in both of these examples sold 2 million units, the publisher/writer synch fee royalties would be $26,500 in the per unit royalty example and $42,000 in the sales plateau example.

Another variation of the royalty formula game has the per-unit royalty decreasing as more games are sold. An example of this type of approach is a game producer agreeing to pay a set penny rate for each unit sold (e.g., 3.5 cents up to 1,000,000 sales) with a reduction after the game exceeds those initial thresholds. (3 cents from 1,000,000 to 3,000,000 units and then reduced upon exceeding that threshold). There is a floor below which the royalty cannot go below regardless of the number of sales (e.g., an agreement that the per unit royalty will not be reduced to (less than 2 cents).

DOWNLOADABLE CONTENT (DLC) ROYALTIES

Even if your song is not included in the original version of the game, a significant amount of royalties can be earned if the song is chosen as downloadable content. This may also be referred to as "add-on content" in some agreements. The synch fee royalties in this area are normally based on a percentage of revenue received by the game publisher each time the particular song is downloaded into the game, and in many cases, there is an advance against royalties involved. The following are some examples of DLC deals:

1. 20% of net revenue (on a pro-rata basis based upon 100% ownership). "Net Revenue" shall mean amounts actually received by the game publisher for the download of the composition, less third party distribution fees actually paid.
2. 15% of the actual retail price per digital download with an advance of $5,000 for songs downloaded into Tier 1 of the game. For compositions downloaded into Tier 2 of the game, 9% of the actual retail price per digital download on the first 100,000 units with an increase to 15% for all units sold afterward with an advance of $3,000 (all pro-rated for ownership less than 100%).

BUNDLED CONTENT

In many cases, packs of songs are sold as a download rather than individual tracks. If a song is "bundled" in such a download pack, the revenue received from the download of the entire pack is equally divided between the songs for purposes of calculating the royalties for each song. These packets of tracks are sold in multiples (3, 6, 10, etc.) at varying prices ($2.99, $6.25, $14.99, $24.99, etc.).

Export Keys. Certain games will allow the player who possesses the game to receive through purchase of the export key a duplicate copy of a composition as downloadable content for use solely in sequel games. There will be a separate royalty paid for this type of use which can be calculated as the greater of cents per composition or a percentage of the retail selling price of the export key divided by the number of recordings which are exportable pursuant to the export key. There will usually be an advance to the publisher if this option is exercised.

License and Rights. A broad grant of rights by the music publisher might read as follows: "The music publisher grants to the video game publisher or developer the nonexclusive, worldwide right, license, privilege, and authority to make arrangements and orchestrations of the song for its recording purposes, excerpt portions of the song for incorporation into the game, record, produce, and affix the song in timed relation or synchronization with sequences, reproduce, manufacture, sell, license, and exploit the song in the game on all platforms and in any and all media, transfer and memorialize the game to other platforms, and utilize excerpts for advertising and promotion of the game."

Term. Some agreements have a set term (such as five years, seven years, 10 years, etc.) during which the song can be used in the video game. If there is a set term, the video manufacturer will many times have the right to sell off its inventory of games for a period of time once the term is over. Other licenses last for as long as the video game is in distribution. For example, the term might be "life of the game (this second version only)," or it might be "commercial life of the game" or "perpetual commencing on the date of first commercial exploitation of the program." Others state that the term is for the life of copyright of the composition.

Territory. The territory of distribution is usually the world.

Song Lyrics. As part of the license agreement, the game producer will, in many cases, have the right to request that the music publisher that controls the existing composition provide lyrics. Included in the grant of rights may be the right to use the lyrics in connection with the game, its packaging, and advertisements subject to any negotiated limitations.

Companion Products. Many game producers receive the right to release the compositions used in the video game in companion products such as an audio CD, download, or separate DVD release of the game. Sometimes fees are actually set in the agreement (for example, 100% or 75% reduced statutory rate for a CD), and other times there is a good-faith negotiation provision as to the ultimate fee that will be charged for the applicable companion product.

Editing. The producer many times has the right to edit for timing and looping purposes. Certain agreements also provide for the right to edit objectionable language or lyrics.

Collateral Materials. Many agreements provide that the video distributor can use the composition in its advertising, promotional, and marketing materials related to the video game. This may include internal and external sales meetings, conferences and seminars, in-store promotions and demonstrations, DVD trailers, online promotional trailers and nondownloadable audio streaming, and even advertising over closed-network college campuses as long as the use is in context. Such promotional usage does not include out-of-context uses or other types of advertising campaigns such as network, cable, or satellite television, radio or theatrical.

Credit. Most contracts provide that credit for the composition be given on the inside of the video game packaging. Credit may also be placed in the manual for the game or actually in the digital format of the game. If there is a master recording also licensed, the notice will usually contain the name of the record company and the name of the recording artist in addition to the composition information. Credit is also many times included on the game's website.

Website of a Game. A number of game producers will feature the music used in the game on the official website with appropriate credits. In some cases, there might be a streaming music player or jukebox that will allow the user to listen to a 30-second clip of the song. There is also many times information on where to purchase the music either online or from a physical location and, in some cases, the download can occur directly from the site. There may also be links to the artist's website, as well as album cover displays and information on the artist. Many of these items may also be featured on the video producer's site.

Other Provisions. Notice, applicable law, audit, warranty, and indemnification provisions are similar to most other license agreements.

CONSOLE AND STREAMING GAMES

More and more games are becoming interactive (dance, singing, playing, etc.) and have both a console version and a streaming version. Due to the streaming aspects of the game, the requests have become more complex due to the multiple platforms and rights involved. The following represents many of the areas that will be involved in such a license.

PLATFORMS

Any gaming console, device, or software on which an interactive experience can be played, now known or hereafter devised, including:

- All mobile platforms including but not limited to IOS, Android, and Windows mobile devices (i.e., smartphones, smart glasses, smart watches, tablets, etc., including iPhone, iPod, iPad, Samsung Galaxy, Amazon Kindle, etc.).
- All connected TVs and screens, set top boxes and digital media players including Amazon Fire, Samsung, Sony, Android TV, Apple TV, Roku, Google Cast, etc.).
- All console platforms as well as their respective media delivery service (including PS3, PS4, Xbox 360, Xbox One, Wii, WiiU, Switch, PSP, PS Vita, DS, 3DS, Steam, PSN, Xbox Live, etc.).
- All computer and similar technologies including PC and Mac.

DELIVERY METHODS FOR STREAMING:

- Interactive streaming (the end user chooses which composition to play)
- Non-interactive streaming (the composition is chosen for the end user)
- Offline playback (the end user can access the catalogue offline with tracking data submitted to the servers).

COMPOSITION USES:

- In menus, in-game scenes (interactive use), and for all platform procedures.
- With the recording's lyrics (subject to the music publisher's approval) as part of in context marketing and demonstrations at trade shows, e-sports events, gaming award shows and live game demo shows.

DURATION OF THE USE:

- The composition can be used in looping, random, or repetitive play.
- As a preview (in the game's menus and/or in the stores where streaming is made available to end users).
- In a short version (up to two minutes thirty seconds).
- Up to its full version.
- As an excerpt (verse + chorus, up to forty five seconds).
- As a playable sixty second preview (for the streaming game).

EDITING

The composition and its lyrics can be edited for inclusion in the game for timing, ESRB rating, and other gameplay purposes (i.e., for transition purposes between compositions in the different gameplay modes such as pitch shift time stretch for intros and outposts and instrument layering levels, etc.) with the game producer being authorized to make arrangements and orchestrations.

FINANCIAL TERMS

A. *Primary Video Game.* An advance based on 100% of the publishing rights which is recoupable from all royalties. A per-song penny royalty payable on the number of copies of the game sold less returns. There may be a reserve to cover returns which will be released within a number of months.

B. *Streaming Video Game.* An advance usually provided if the composition is utilized in this aspect of the game. As to the actual streaming royalty, there can be a number of alternative formulas depending on how the revenue base is structured. The following are examples: 1. Advertising Net Revenue: These royalties are derived from access by users of the composition as part of the streaming game which is subject to the display of advertising. The royalty is a percentage of net ad revenue and is based on the number of plays of a particular composition compared to the total number of songs played by the end-users in this ad-supported aspect of the game. There may also be a per composition minimum royalty amount. Advertising Net Revenues can mean any revenues received by the game producer from in-game advertising net of actual third party billing and/or distribution fees, VAT or other sales taxes. 2. Subscription Net Revenue: These royalties are derived from that aspect of the streaming game that can be accessed by end-users in exchange for the monies that they pay as part of a subscription service. Again, the actual royalty calculation is a percentage of the subscription revenue based on the number of plays per composition compared to the total number of compositions played by end-users. There can also be a guaranteed penny per stream rate involved in the formula. Net revenues will be revenue received from the subscriptions less third party billing and distribution fees, VAT, or other sales taxes and returns. 3. Non–Revenue Generating Uses: For non–revenue generating uses (e.g., for demonstration, charitable and promotion purposes), there may be a fraction of a penny royalty provided on a per stream basis. 4. All of the streaming rates will be on a most favored nations basis with all recordings and compositions which are made available on the service.

PERFORMANCE ROYALTIES
Depending on the game, the royalties may include monies due for performances of the composition.

USER GENERATED CONTENT (UGC)

Many games allow the end users to share short videos which include the composition to which they are performing or dancing. The end users can elect to save the video on their cloud accounts and/or share or post the video on approved sharing media. There is usually a restriction on downloading the videos since they can only be shared as a stream unless an offline saving functionality is approved.

MOBILE GAMES

Mobile games represent a huge segment of the video game industry and are many times downloaded from an app store or pre-loaded into a mobile device. These games take many forms including rhythm games, games that turn your phone into a musical instrument or turn your speech into rap or involves karaoke and/or the creation of duets with well-known artists via a split screen among many other types all of which use music in some form or another. These games use various forms of economic models including free-to-play, pay per download, subscription and share of advertising, among others.

The following represents some of the basic terms and fees for the apps and social online "casual" games:

1. $4,000 to the publisher based upon a 100% share with timing of up to 5 minutes over multiple uses. For every million downloads, 25% of the fee will be paid to publisher. Use involves in game gameplay, menus, and videos with the world as the territory. As to advertising, the artist's name and photo can be used.

2. A voice or instrument app for mobile devices which includes the lyrics of the song and/or the original master or a re-recorded version. For streamed songs, the royalty rate shall be 25% of the actual selling price of the song to the end user with a negotiated floor price and a most favored nations clause with all other songs in the app. For downloaded songs, the royalty shall be 25% of the actual selling price of the song to the end user with a floor. Advances are given for both the instrument version as well as the voice version with additional advances provided if the song is a current chart hit. Accountings are quarterly.

3. A variation for certain types of mobile games provides a one-time fee with a term of a certain number of years and the territory being the world. The media for these games is normally social media networks, the Internet, iPhone, iPad, mobile, and wireless devices, etc.

SUMMARY VIDEO GAME DEALS

The following two licenses should help in putting all of the provisions of a license in context:

1. *First Person Adventure Game.* Song, either as an instrumental or vocal version, can be used in all versions, episodes and supplements of the game. Fee is $5,000 for 100% share as well as worldwide rights. As to media, any and all home entertainment gaming platforms now known or hereafter created, whether tangible or intangible as well as all online services or online social networking sites and any of the foregoing successors and predecessors.

   The type of use will be background up to a full use as well as multiple uses within the game with the term of the license being 10 years.

2. *Dance Game.* Publisher grants Producer, its successors and assigns, the nonexclusive license to use the composition in the video game [Title of Video Game] which may be distributed via software programs or electronic products or services in any format and/or platform which allow the end user to manipulate the presentation of the content of the product or program during its use. Territory is the world with a term of seven (7) years and a sell off period of one (1) year following expiration of the term. Composition can be used in its full or short version and lyrics can be

displayed. Song can also be used in the auto dance application which allows users to share short videos with the help of their platform camera.

Royalty rate will be $.03 per sale if song is used in the main game with a most favored nations clause with all other songs and an advance of $_____ recoupable against future royalties. If the song is used in streaming, there will be an additional advance paid and a streaming royalty of 15% of the advertising net revenue. Royalties are to be paid quarterly.

VIDEO GAMES BASED ON TELEVISION SERIES

An increasing source for video games is the hit television series. This type of game is developed, in most cases, well after the series has become a hit on network, local, or cable television, and the demographics as well as the interactive possibilities are studied carefully prior to development. *Teenage Mutant Ninja Turtles*, *South Park*, *The Walking Dead*, *Lost*, *CSI: Crime Scene Investigation*, *Deadliest Catch*, *Doctor Who*, *24*, *The Sopranos*, and *The Simpsons* are good examples of this type of new media exploitation.

VIDEO GAMES BASED ON MOVIES

Feature films represent a popular source for video game development with some games released simultaneously or shortly before or after a feature film's release (e.g., *Avatar*, *The Lord of the Rings*, *King Kong*, *Harry Potter*, *The Incredibles*, *Spider-Man*, *Star Wars Episode III: Revenge of the Sith*, *Batman Begins*, *Pirates of the Caribbean*), and others developed and released years after the film (e.g., *The Godfather*, *Dirty Harry*, *Scarface*). In some cases, sequels are made to a movie game even though no sequel to the movie was ever made (i.e., a new game based on the original characters of the movie). Some studios, as owners of the underlying right (the movie copyright), license the development of the game to an outside company for a royalty percentage of the video game sales. Other video game projects are produced by the game division affiliated with the film studio copyright owner (normally a conglomerate such as Disney, Warner Bros., Paramount, Universal, etc.), or jointly with an outside game publisher or developer.

In many cases, video games based on feature films do not use the same music as used in the film. In other cases, though (i.e., John Williams' scores to the Star Wars films; Howard Shore's scores to the Lord of the Rings trilogy, the theme to *The Godfather* film), much or at least some of the original film music is used and re-cut with the rest of the score consisting of newly composed music.

VIDEO GAME UNDERSCORE CONTRACT PROVISIONS

The contract that a writer signs to compose underscore for a video game is many times similar to the motion picture underscore contract. It covers the type of services to be performed, the length of time to complete, the fee, credit, copyright ownership, and royalty provisions. Some sample contract provisions follow:

Composer Services/Time Frame.

The Composer is hired to compose, arrange, orchestrate, conduct, record, edit, and deliver such original material as may be required for incorporation into the video game entitled [Title of Video Game] in a form specified by Producer and delivered in a timely manner in accordance with the instructions and directions of producer. Alternatively, Composer must participate in pre-production development, thematic and creative meetings, and deliver on schedule. If the masters or score are not satisfactory, Composer agrees to re-arrange, re-record, or write new music until reasonably satisfactory to Producer.

Contracts normally specify services are nonexclusive but on a first priority basis or specify a certain time frame where services are exclusive.

Grant of Rights/Copyright. The music is almost always a "work-made-for-hire" specifically ordered and commissioned for the game. The company becomes the "author" of the music and owns "without limitation, throughout the universe and in perpetuity, all right, title, and interest whether now known or hereafter devised" without any obligation to pay the composer any compensation except as explicitly provided in the contract.

Package Deals. Most video game composer deals are packages, either electronic or a mix of orchestral and electronic, where the composer assumes most of the costs of composing, producing, and recording the music with certain exclusions paid by the video game company. Occasionally, non-package fee deals do occur but they are many times reserved for top tier film composers working on well-known game sequels. The size of the package fee varies based on the number of minutes of music required and how much orchestral music is involved, as well as the stature of the composer, among other factors.

Some examples of "package" language are as follows:
To compose and package 60 minutes of electronic score including all costs incurred in the recording and delivery of the master but excluding the following costs: _____

To compose and package a score of 80 minutes of score, comprised of 50 minutes of electronic music and 30 minutes of orchestral score. Included in the package are all costs related to musicians, singers, recording studio costs, copying, orchestration, mixing, dubbing, editing, cartage, etc. Exclusions are as follows: _____

Most video game exclusions are very similar to those in feature film scoring contracts. Some of the more common ones are licensing of music not composed by the composer, re-scoring if required for creative reasons outside of the composer's control after delivery of the masters, vocalists, and lyricists if requested by the company, mag stock and transfers, etc.

Fees. Fee deals are fairly rare in the video game area, an area reserved normally for top-tier film composers. Fees range between $350,000 to $1.5 million for a superstar composer—roughly $4,000 to $20,000 a minute in per-minute terms. In these cases, the video game company will pay for the orchestral recording out of a separate budget. There are some packages in this top tier where the composer covers the recording costs but the fees vary based upon the amount of orchestral elements required. Composers in this tier retain their full writer's and record royalties.

For mid-tier composers, package deals range from $100,000 to $400,000. The package fees increase based on the stature of the composer, the number of minutes of music required, and the number of orchestral elements required, and range in the area of $2,000 a minute with a high of $5,000 a minute.

For entry-level composers, package deals start in the area of $1,200 a minute for an electronic score and increase depending on whether some live musicians are also used.

Composers generally record out of their home studios and use a few live musicians to supplement the electronic score. In general, major games normally require 60 to 120 minutes of music including stems. Finally when negotiating fees, one needs to consider both the rate per minute as well as the overall fee to determine exactly the nature of the composer compensation package.

Payments are many times tied to the composer reaching certain "milestones" but occasionally have language similar to feature film contracts.

A sample of a number of actual deals follow:
$140,000 payable ¼ upon execution of the agreement;
¼ upon delivery of the first milestone;
¼ upon delivery of the second milestone;
¼ upon completion, delivery, and approval.

$500,000 payable:
$100,000 on commencement of services;
$100,000 upon delivery of 10 cues;
$100,000 upon delivery of 20 cues;
$100,000 upon delivery of 5 additional cues;
$100,000 upon delivery of the full 35 cues and completion of all delivery requirements.

$160,000 total combined orchestral/electronic mix payable $50,000 upon execution of the agreement, $60,000 upon the recording of the orchestral portion of the score, and $50,000 upon completion, delivery, and approval of the masters.

$40,000 payable ⅓ upon execution of the agreement, ⅓ upon approval of the electronic demos, and ⅓ upon completion, delivery, and acceptance of the master.

Composer will compose, orchestrate, sequence, record, and mix approximately seventy-five (75) minutes of music for the game at a price of $1,000 per minute, for a total amount not to exceed $75,000 without Developer's or Publisher's prior written approval. The milestone and delivery schedule, payments and payment dates are as follows: $15,000 on the execution of this agreement; $12,000 on Developer's or Publisher's written acceptance of 15 minutes of music; $12,000 on written acceptance of an additional 15 minutes of music (total of 30 minutes); $12,000 upon written acceptance of an additional 15 minutes of music (total of 45 minutes) and so forth.

As part of these deals, the Developer or Publisher may request minor alterations to the music or possibly some additional music which the composer will many times complete for no extra fee. An additional fee should be negotiated if through no fault of the composer, a substantial amount of changes are requested or if the company asks for substantial additional new music above the amount contracted for. Specific completion dates for each milestone will also be set forth (i.e., January 1, April 1, July 1, etc.) and the payments will be made assuming the work is developed and delivered in a form acceptable to the Developer or Publisher. After delivery of each milestone, company will have a certain number of days to review the material to see if it conforms to the technical and commercial requirements. If they object, the composer will have a specified number of days to correct.

Screen Credit. Credit in the form of "Music Composed By [Name of Composer]" is normally set forth in the credit section of the video game, in the manual, and on the website per "the company's standard policy."

Composer Royalties. The ability to earn "outside the game" backend royalties varies with many companies attaching a schedule which includes the standard royalties of performing rights, print, mechanical royalties, 50% of all synchronization fees, foreign, etc. Other companies may allow the composer participation in the ASCAP, BMI, SESAC, and foreign society royalties and no other royalty sources. In total "buyout" situations, no royalties are due with composer compensation limited only to the initial creative/package fee.

For uses of the score or theme in other video games owned or distributed by the company or in sequels, no additional fees are normally paid. But if the music is used other than in those limited situations, additional fees should be negotiated.

In situations where soundtrack albums are released, normal record contract provisions should apply, including artist and producer royalties, if applicable. For example, a clause might read, "Ability to use the music in any and all current or subsequent versions of the Game in any medium now known or hereafter discovered with no obligation to Composer other than those expressly set forth in this Agreement."

Additional contract provisions. Many of the additional video game composer contract provisions are very similar to those of a feature film contract. They include image and likeness rights, no obligation to use the music, re-record restrictions for a number of years, royalty statement dates, audit rights, termination provisions, representations and warranties, indemnification, remedies against both the composer and the employer, preparation of the cue sheet, governing law, transportation, and living expenses, assignments and the certificate of authorship. Based on the nature of this industry, confidentiality clauses are extensive as well as strict.

CHAPTER 13
MUSIC, MONEY, AND DIGITAL MEDIA

Digital media and traditional media, once separate in focus, influence, contracts, licensing and fees, are now, in most instances, intertwined when dealing with the business of songs and records. And though traditional media is still producing the lion's share of royalties, the monies from digital distribution have been increasing significantly each year. In the world we are in, you have a combination of the old rates, concepts and laws applying in some cases with other areas being subject to the negotiation of completely new rates based upon new business models, laws, considerations, private and industry wide negotiations, court decisions, royalty board and tribunal decisions and developing industry practices. And in many cases, you have the combination of both.

RIGHTS

The basic activities involving music on the Internet are streaming (both interactive and noninteractive) and downloading (unlimited, limited, conditional, tethered, etc.) and involve the two separate copyrights of the musical composition and the sound recording. The song copyright generates income for the songwriter, composer, and music publisher, whereas the sound recording copyright generates revenue for the label, the artist, the producer as well as background vocalists and musicians. A synchronization right is also involved when songs and recordings are used in audiovisual programming (feature films, television series episodes, webisodes, etc.). Each of these rights involve separate negotiations either through collection societies or by individual parties or organizations and, in the case of sound recordings, are further subdivided into whether the use is noninteractive or interactive.

THE LAWS

The primary laws governing music use on the Internet are the Sound Recording Act of 1971, the 1976 Copyright Law, the Audio Home Recording Act of 1992, the Digital Performance Right in Sound Recording Act of 1995 (DPRA), the Sonny Bono Term Extension Act of 1998, the 1998 Digital Millennium Copyright Act (DMCA), the 2002 World Intellectual Property Organization treaties (WIPO), and the Copyright Royalty and Distribution Act of 2004, among others. In addition, Copyright Royalty Board decisions, ASCAP and BMI rate court decisions, and other PRO litigation as well as negotiated agreements between music publishers, record companies, and digital services play a major role in the licensing fees and terms of the online world.

THE SONG

When a song is played on a website, the site must have a performance license from ASCAP, BMI, SESAC, or GMR (depending on which PRO controls the song) or obtain a direct license from the copyright owner (usually the music publisher). These licenses are either negotiated or court set. Without such a license and assuming no exemption, the website can be liable for copyright infringement.

When a song is "downloaded" (a copy is made or stored), a license must be acquired from the copyright owner (the publisher usually) or the owner's agency (e.g., the Harry Fox Agency, etc.). Based upon the compulsory license provisions, the royalty to be paid is the statutory rate in effect at the time of the download (i.e., 9.1 cents or 1.75 cents per minute of playing time or fraction thereof if larger in 2018–2022).

THE RECORDING

The 1995 DPRA Act and the 1998 DMCA Act created a limited public performance right for the digital performance of sound recordings over cable, satellite, and by webcasters. When a sound recording is played In the applicable digital media, different royalties and negotiations apply depending on whether the use is interactive or noninteractive.

SOUNDEXCHANGE

One of the most important royalty collection organizations for recording artists and record companies, as well as vocalists and musicians who sing or perform on sound recordings is SoundExchange, a tax exempt organization incorporated in 2003 whose primary purpose is the collection, administration, and distribution of the limited digital performance right for sound recordings—a right that resulted in $952 million in collections and $884 million in distributions to artists and record companies in 2016, as well as hundreds of thousands of dollars to individual successful artists. This is an audio only right as SoundExchange is not involved with audiovisual transmissions or downloads of any nature.

As to the performing rights aspect of sound recordings, the right that was enjoyed by musical compositions (ASCAP, BMI, SESAC, etc.) was nonexistent for sound recordings as no performance royalty existed in any medium for the performance of records. That changed in 1995 with the passage of the Digital Performance Rights in Sound Recordings Act (DPRSRA), which provided for a limited right when sound recordings are publicly performed "by means of a digital audio transmission." The 1998 Digital Millennium Copyright Act of (DMCA) included webcasting as a category of performance applicable to this limited performance right. This new right applied specifically to satellite radio services (e.g., Sirius XM), Internet radio (e.g., Pandora), cable television audio music channels (e.g., Music Choice), and certain business establishment services (e.g., Muzak, DMX). Over-the-air broadcast radio remained exempt.

It is important to note that the statutory license as set forth in Sections 112 and 114 of the Copyright Act applies only to noninteractive services. The right to perform copyrighted sound recordings for on-demand services (interactive services such as Spotify) remains with the copyright owner (normally the record label) and is a negotiated agreement between the label and the music user. If the parties cannot come to an agreement on the fee, the sound recordings cannot be streamed. These deals can make many forms including a percentage of gross, net, or ad revenue, a per-stream rate, an equity stake in the business, advances and guarantees, a trade-off of services (e.g., free advertising or increased usage of a company's catalogue) or a combination of these and other elements. All royalties received by the record company from voluntary negotiated licenses are usually paid to recording artists based upon the specific provisions of each artist's recording agreement.

RATES AND TERMS OF THE STATUTORY LICENSE

The rates and terms of the sound recording statutory license are set by the Copyright Royalty Board (CRB), an administrative body created by Congress. Sound Exchange has been to date the sole entity designated by the CRB to collect royalties paid by the services operating under the statutory license. Any service that complies with the statutory and regulatory conditions may obtain a license via federal statute without having to negotiate directly with the copyright owner for the rights to those recordings.

There are a number of requirements a webcaster must comply with in order to be eligible for this "compulsory license." They include no advance notice of what is being played and they cannot play more than three songs from a particular album, including no more than two consecutively, within a three-hour period. Nor can they play four songs by a particular artist, including no more than three consecutively during the same period (this is referred to as the "sound recording performance complement"). Other restrictions involve archived programming, looped programming, and the number of times a webcaster can repeat programs during a certain period of time. The service must also file a Notice of Use of Sound Recordings under the statutory license with the Copyright Office and comply with the all the requirements of Sections 112 and 114 of the Act. Services can also negotiate licenses directly with noninteractive services if they so choose and not be bound by the statutory rates or requirements.

As the rates decided by the CRB translate into the royalties that artists and labels receive, the following represents a summary of the main royalty formulas of this billion dollar right:

1. For the years 2016–2020 webcasting area, the rate in 2016 for commercial subscription services is $0.0022 per performance with commercial nonsubscription services at $0.0017 per performance with subsequent years adjusted by increases or decreases in the Consumer Price Index. Different rates apply for noncommercial webcasters and smaller webcast transmissions.

2. For the years 2018–2022, the CRB rates for the digital performance of sound recordings for Sirius XM's satellite radio service are 15.5% of gross revenue and 7.5% of revenue for the cable and television music services provided by Music Choice and Muzak.

Most licensees in this area forward to SoundExchange on a monthly basis a Statement of Account reflecting a licensee's calculation of the payments due and reports of the use of recordings including the title of the track, the featured artist, the ISRC identification number (International Sound Recording Copyright) or album name and the audience measurement reflecting the actual total performances of each sound recording—a "per play per listener" factor. SoundExchange then matches the recordings with their database of known recordings (well over 30 million sound recordings and 20 million unique ISRC numbers) to determine the entitled parties to be paid. As to each services license fees, they are generally allocated on a pro-rata basis where each sound recording performed on that service generates the same amount of money per track, regardless of the commercial success of the track. For example, if the license fee from a service was $10,000 and there were 100,000 performances, each performance would be worth 10 cents. The operating costs for SoundExchange over recent years have been in the area of 4.6% to 5.3% and are taken off the top prior to distributions being made.

ARTIST AND RECORD COMPANY PAYMENTS

Royalty distributions are allocated 50% to sound recording copyright owners (normally the record label), 45% to featured artists, and 2.5% each to nonfeatured musicians and nonfeatured vocalists with the latter two funds being administered by the American Federation of Musicians (AFofM) and the Screen Actors Guild–American Federation of Television and Radio Artists (SAG-AFTRA) respectively. As to the Feature Artist 45% allocation, the royalties are generally allocated on a pro rata basis unless all the members of a featured artist (band, duo, etc.) instruct SoundExchange as to a different split. Statutory royalties are typically paid 45 days following the end of the month in which the liability accrued.

LETTERS OF DIRECTION FOR PRODUCERS AND OTHER "CREATIVE PARTICIPANTS"

Though record producers, mixers, remixers and engineers cannot join SoundExchange directly, they can share in an artist's SoundExchange royalties as SoundExchange does accept letters of direction (LODs) from artists who wish to share some of their performance royalties with those who were part of the creative process of the record. In many cases, the producer percentages are actually set forth in the artist/producer agreement. These monies can prove substantial for successful albums. For example if an artist has an "all in" 16% royalty and the producer has a 4% royalty, the producer could receive 25% of the SoundExchange Feature Artist royalties with a letter of direction.

The "Feature Artist" letter of direction cannot be used to direct payments to labels or any person or entity not directly involved in the creative process. The LOD form contains the name and legal name of the artist, the effective date, the name and address of the payee, information on the specific sound recording and track name and the percentage of the Featured Artist share being given to the "creative participant." LODs are revocable as they are solely an accommodation to the artist.

FOREIGN COUNTRY ROYALTIES

Throughout the world, the right that SoundExchange handles would be considered a "Neighboring Right" which stems from the 1961 Rome Convention for the Protection of Performers, Producers of Phonograms, and Broadcasting Organizations legal provision that performers and the producers of sound recordings, among others, must receive equitable remuneration for broadcasting and communications to the public. In excess of $2 billion is generated annually by this right with SoundExchange representing close to 50% of the worldwide collections.

SoundExchange has reciprocal agreements with all of the major foreign country collective management organizations (PPL in the UK, Re:Sound in Canada, GVL in Germany, PPCA in Australia, etc.) that handle this right on behalf of U.S. artists and record companies who designate SoundExchange as their agent. The problem is that this is a reciprocal right only between countries and if one country limits the right, as the U.S. does with terrestrial radio being exempt from the performance right, foreign countries will not collect in their territory for U.S. performances on their own terrestrial radio stations—a situation costing U.S. artists and record companies many millions of dollars in royalties. The result is that SoundExchange is dealing primarily with digital radio collections and distributions in these reciprocal arrangements. SoundExchange does not charge an administrative fee for distributing foreign monies and you must be a member as well as complete an International Mandate form for these collections.

CONTRACTS

In order to receive digital performance royalties from SoundExchange, you must register as a Feature Artist or Sound Recording Copyright Owner. One can also join SoundExchange as a member, which provides additional benefits as well as the ability to collect foreign monies. To receive U.S. digital royalties though, one does not have to be a member but rather just needs to register with SoundExchange.

Joining SoundExchange as a member does have additional benefits which are not available to those who only register. These include international collections, lifestyle and industry discounts and savings, advocacy, and insider access and information. Membership is free. The Performer agreement designates SoundExchange as its agent to collect the digital public performance royalties exclusively during the term as well as the authority to negotiate and represent someone in governmental proceedings and audits (rate proceedings, etc.). The term of the agreement ends December 31 of each year with the ability to resign with 30 days prior notice to December 31. The Sound Recording Rights Owner Agreement is similar in most respects to the Performer Agreement.

ADMINISTRATION OF DIRECT LICENSES

A number of record labels have negotiated direct deals with streaming services thereby bypassing the statutory license and its requirements. SoundExchange is available to administer the growing number of these direct licenses. In fact, of the $952 million in collections in 2016, statutory royalties totaled $822 million with the remainder from nonstatutory licensing arrangements between sound recording copyright owners, settlement administration and foreign collective management organizations.

STATEMENTS

As opposed to statements in the musical composition performance world (ASCAP, BMI, SESAC, etc.) where numerous different factors determine the value of any type of performance, SoundExchange statements are relatively easy to understand as all performances on an individual licensed service are worth the same and there are basically only four primary sources of revenue.

In the case of a record company or featured artist statement, the front page monthly summary sheet lists five (5) earnings by license type, the Top 10 artists and earnings attributable to those artists for a record company, and the Top 10 Titles and their earnings. For example:

U.S. Earnings by License Type

Adjustments: $8,000, Webcasting: $ 68,000, Satellite Radio: $14,000, Cable Radio: $3,500, Business Establishment Services: $240.

Top 10 Artists (record company)

Artist 1: $36,000, Artist 2: $14,000, Artist 3: $12,000…Artist 10: $275

Top 10 Performances (feature artist or record company)

Track 1: $21,000, Track 2: $18,000, Track 3: $14,000…Track 10: $1,100.

For record producers with a Letter of Direction from the artist, there will also be a category of Payments Received from Third Parties (the Artist). Year-to-date royalty summaries are also included for the five (5) different license types and foreign earnings are also included where applicable. A corresponding spreadsheet includes all details by services and all performances.

PURCHASE OF CMRRA

In 2017, SoundExchange added a new dimension to its business when it formed SXWorks as a subsidiary when it purchased CMRRA, the Canadian Musical Reproduction Rights Agency, a music licensing collective that represents music publishers and administers the majority of songs recorded, sold, and broadcast in Canada. SXWorks offers administration and back office services for publishers to support multiple licensing configurations and to accurately track, report, and compensate rights owners and creators for music usage.

PRE-1972 RECORDINGS

Prior to 1972, no federal copyright protection existed for sound recordings. Congress rectified that situation with the Sound Recording Act of 1971 which extended copyright protection to any recordings that were fixed on or after February 15, 1972. Pre–February 15, 1972, recordings though remained subject to the protection afforded by state laws. Based on the effective date of the federal law, streaming services (Sirius XM and Pandora), took the position that no performance royalties were due for the performances of pre-1972 recordings on their services.

A number of lawsuits were filed against Sirius XM and Pandora by the major labels in the California and New York State courts and by the 1960s group "Flo & Eddie" (who later founded the Turtles) in the federal courts of California, New York, and Florida. Initial decisions were favorable to the labels and to Flo & Eddie, resulting in significant settlements for the past (and some future) uses of pre-1972 recordings. Subsequent decisions in the Flo & Eddie litigation by the New York Court of Appeals, affirmed by the 2nd Circuit Court of Appeals and the Florida Supreme Court, reversed that trend by ruling that New York common law has never recognized a right of public performance for pre-1972 recordings and that in Florida, no public performance right exists for sound recordings recorded and released prior to February 15, 1972. Ongoing litigation in these cases as well as others continue with many millions of dollars at stake. As there is no federal statute involved, the laws in each state control. The California statute, incidentally, grants the copyright owner of pre-1972 sound recordings exclusive ownership to February 15, 2047.

DIGITAL DOWNLOADS: SOUND RECORDINGS

For any sites that allow digital downloads (permanent or conditional), a license must be secured from the copyright owner of the recording (usually the record company) as the right to make and distribute copies of a sound recording is not covered by any compulsory license and must be negotiated with the record company.

SUBSCRIPTION: SOUND RECORDINGS

In cases of subscription on demand streaming or subscription permanent downloads, the negotiated agreements between digital distributors and the labels include among other agreements, a percentage of the subscription revenue, a percentage of the net and a 50/50 split (all reduced by agreed upon deductions).

SYNCHRONIZATION: SONGS AND SOUND RECORDINGS

Synchronization Royalties. As in other areas, when a composition is put into an audiovisual program on the Internet (i.e., an episodic series, a movie, etc.), a synchronization license needs to be negotiated and a fee paid.

ASCAP, BMI, SESAC, AND GMR INTERNET LICENSES

The four U.S. performing rights organizations negotiate separate license agreements with Internet music users. In the case of ASCAP and BMI, if an agreement cannot be reached as to what the music fees should be for a service, or for that matter, what actually needs to be licensed on a site (a stream versus a download, for instance), a rate court judge decides all issues and fees after a trial of the facts. These rate courts (the federal court in the Southern District of New York) are mandated by the ASCAP and BMI Consent Decrees with the U.S. government and have dealt in recent years with license fee issues and interim and final fee orders involving many of the major players in the industry including AOL, AT&T, Verizon Wireless, YouTube, MobiTV, Yahoo and RealNetworks, among others. The decisions in this area have come up with a number of license fee formulas including a percentage of gross revenue figure (less customary deductions) taking into account a Music Use Adjustment factor (total number of hours that users stream music versus the total of all hours on a site), a percentage of gross revenue for noninteractive streaming and on-demand streaming, different percentages of revenue figures based on the music intensity of the programs and flat fee deals, among others. In addition to the judicial setting of fees, there have also been numerous voluntary agreements entered into by the U.S. PROs and the major users in this area.

ASCAP, BMI, and SESAC also have standard industry form licenses that authorize Internet sites and services to perform all of the works in each organization's repertory (songs, scores, etc.) regardless of the file format. These Internet licenses do not authorize the reproduction or distribution of the music or sound recordings, or the public performance of the sound recordings.

DOWNLOADS AND ONLINE SUBSCRIPTION SERVICES

There are numerous legitimate digital music sites and services that provide:

Full (Permanent) Downloads. 1) Time-limited downloads (which time out or become inaccessible after a set period of time or when a person's subscription is not renewed or runs out). 2) Use-limited downloads (which have certain restrictions attached to them, including limitations on the transfer of a recording to multiple devices, limitations on the number of times you can burn a recording, or limitations on the number of times you can listen to a recording).

There are other sites that only distribute full downloads and CD burns without any need for a paid subscription to use the service. There are other sites that are purely subscription-based and offer only on-demand streaming of music without any download availability. And there are other online services that offer full downloads, temporary downloads, on-demand streaming, transfers to portable music players, and CD burns on a subscription basis.

There are numerous variations as to how these sites operate, the services they provide, and how much they charge. For example, there might be a 49¢, 79¢, 99¢, or $1.29 single-track download cost; a $4.99, $8.00, or $9.99 album download cost; a $6.99, $8.95, or $9.95 per-month unlimited music streaming option; or pay on-demand radio service, as well as many other variations as to pricing and services offered.

Some sites offer the ability to get the lyrics to compositions; others enable the consumer to look at or download the album cover artwork; others provide personal playlists; others feature videos; and some give in-depth artist profiles.

Since every company is looking for a business model that works not only for them but for the consumer as well, variations relating to prices charged for music, restrictions imposed, and services offered continue to change and evolve.

Pre-loaded Music Files. A number of these online music services provide the subscriber with a key (sometimes called a "decryption key") that allows the subscriber to decrypt a music file that has been preloaded into a computer or other digital device. These preloaded files, which are digital files that contain a sound recording of a composition, are then accessed by the consumer through the use of the decryption key, which is provided once it is established that the user has the right to such access via a subscription or other license agreement.

Digital Downloads (Known as Permanent Digital Downloads or PPDs). Record companies in the United States have been using a notice of compulsory license when notifying music publishers of their intention to offer digital downloads of songs. In the notice, the record company names the song to be downloaded as well as the identity of the songwriters and music publishers, identifies the recording artist performing the song, gives the names of the officers and directors of the record company, and provides an expected distribution date of the digital phonograph delivery ("DPD") of the song (for example, "from time to time after [date]"). Because these requests come in the form of a compulsory license, the digital download will be licensed and paid at the statutory rate unless the music publisher approves a different rate.

The current statutory rate for permanent digital downloads of a composition is 9.1¢, or 1.75¢ per minute of playing time or fraction thereof, whichever amount is larger. Per the Copyright Royalty Board, this statutory mechanical rate is effective through 2022.

Since record companies are able to pass along the digital mechanical licenses to online music services, these services are able to use the authority of these DPD licenses to download music. In these cases, the online music service pays royalties to the record company that owns the master recording being downloaded which, in turn, pays the music publisher, who then pays the songwriter or the music publisher licenses through an agent such as the record company will pay the agent who will then pay the publisher who will pay the songwriter his or her share of the royalties.

ON-DEMAND STREAMING AND LIMITED DOWNLOADS (SUBSCRIPTION SERVICES)

2008 CRB Ruling on On-Demand Streams and Limited Downloads. On November 24, 2008, the Copyright Royalty Board/Copyright Royalty Judges affirmed the provisions of a settlement agreement between the National Music Publishers Association ("NMPA"), the Nashville Songwriters Association International ("NSAI"), the Songwriter's Guild of America ("SGA"), the Recording Industry Association of America ("RIAA") and the Digital Media Association ("DIMA").

This settlement provided for a compulsory statutory royalty scheme covering both on-demand streams and limited downloads (sometimes called tethered or time-out downloads); two areas of Internet music distribution for which there were no established statutory royalty rates for musical compositions.

Services Covered. In addition, there are different musical composition rates depending on the type of service and type of offering. For example, there are different royalty calculations depending on whether the service is offering:

standalone nonportable streaming only,

standalone nonportable mixed use,

standalone portable,

bundled service, or

free nonsubscription/ad-supported services.

The standalone nonportable subscription-streaming only is a service through which one can listen to sound recordings only in the form of interactive streams and only from a nonportable device to which streams are transmitted while the device has a live network connection.

The standalone nonportable subscription–mixed use is, except as provided for below in the bundled subscription service, a service where one can listen to sound recordings either in the form of interactive streams or limited downloads but only from a nonportable device to which streams or downloads are originally transmitted. The standalone portable subscription service is one where the end user can listen to sound recordings in the form of interactive streams or limited downloads from a portable device.

The bundled subscription service is one that has one or more products or services as part of a single transaction without pricing for the subscription service separate from the products or services with which it is made available (e.g., when a user can buy a portable device and one-year access to a subscription service for a single fee).

The free nonsubscription/ad-supported service is a service that offers licensed activity free of charge.

2012 CRB Royalty Rates and Additional Services Covered. In 2012, an additional five types of subscription service were added to the compulsory statutory royalty scheme. They are:

• paid locker,

• purchased content locker,

• limited offering,

• mixed service bundle, and

• music bundles.

The paid locker service is a subscription service where the end user pays a fee which provides continuous access for Internet connected devices to recordings purchased previously by the end user.

The purchased content locker service is one that is offered for free to purchasers of permanent digital downloads, ringtones, or physical records from a qualified seller (or is otherwise in possession of phono-records of sound recordings prior to the user's first request to have access to the sound recordings by means of the service) that allows the purchaser access to digital versions of the purchased content from an Internet connected device at no incremental charge above the otherwise applicable purchase of the PPDs, ringtones or physical recordings.

The subscription-based limited offering is a service that offers a very limited catalogue of music such as music of a particular genre or from a limited playlist or a service that offers streams of preprogrammed playlists.

The mixed bundle service is one that provides the sale of permanent digital downloads, ringtones, locker services, or limited offerings together with a nonmusic product (such as a mobile phone or Internet service) for one price.

The music bundles subscription service is one which provides for the sale of two or more of the following products together for one price: physical records (e.g., CDs, LPs), permanent digital downloads, or ringtones.

Under the 2012 statutory rate formula, there were also a number of variables involved in the actual calculations for a particular service and offering including the revenue of the applicable service, the costs of content, numbers of subscribers, performing rights license fees paid to ASCAP, BMI, SESAC, and GMR as well as the aggregate number of plays of all musical compositions during the applicable royalty accounting period.

As to the formula itself, the actual royalty was arrived at by taking the greater of (a) the applicable percentage of the service's revenue (e.g., 10.5% for most services and either 12% or 11.35% for others) or (b) the lesser of (i) the service's record label master recording royalty payments (with different percentages applied whether the licenses were pass through or non–pass through) or (ii) a set per subscriber monthly amount (e.g., $.50 in the case of standalone nonportable subscriptions-streaming only services and $.80 for standalone portable mixed use).
Once this figure was arrived at, the cost of the royalties paid to performing rights organizations was deducted.

The actual royalty pool to be shared by all musical compositions was under this complex formula then calculated as the greater of the above result or the per subscriber minimum for the particular type of service (e.g., $.15 per subscriber per month in the case of a standalone nonportable subscriptions–streaming only service, $.30 for standalone, portable subscriptions–mixed use, and $.25 for bundled subscription services).

The royalty pool was then calculated on a monthly basis and royalties were distributed quarterly to the publishers of the compositions used based on the activity of each composition in relation to the activity of all other payable compositions.

2018–2022 CRB Ruling and Royalty Rates. In 2017 there was a hearing and trial before the Copyright Royalty Board to determine new rates for the years 2018 through 2022 in which all the interested parties (NMPA/NSAI, Apple, Spotify, Google, Pandora, and Amazon) all explained their recommendations and submitted separate proposals to the judges. On January 26, 2018, the CRB announced its rate determinations.

Summary of Changes. In effect, the topline rates for streaming were raised from 10.5% of a service's revenue to 15.1% over the five year 2018–2022 period. The CRB simplified how royalties were calculated, removed caps on the Total Content Cost (the royalties that are paid to record companies to stream the master recordings), included "greater of" language in place of the "lesser of" language contained in the 2012 CRB ruling resulting in songwriters and music publishers getting the greater of the service revenue percentage and the monies paid to the record companies/content owners (rather than the lesser of), increased the royalty ratio which composition owners receive versus what the master recording owners receive, provided for a late fee for nontimely payment of royalties and established discount rates for family and student subscription plans. As in the past, payments to the performing rights organizations for the performance right are deducted from the calculation to arrive at the final mechanical streaming royalty payable to music publishers and songwriters.

Actual Royalty Rates. The rates for the five (5) year period from January 1, 2018, through December 31, 2022, for the various services are as follows.
- In 2018, 11.4 percent of revenue or 22.0 percent of total content cost
- In 2019, 12.3 percent of revenue or 23.1 percent of total content cost
- In 2020, 13.3 percent of revenue or 24.1 percent of total content cost
- In 2021, 14.2 percent of revenue or 25.2 percent of total content cost
- In 2022, 15.1 percent of revenue or 26.2 percent of total content cost

ROYALTY CALCULATION STEPS
The following represent the steps that are taken to arrive at the actual mechanical royalties that are paid for interactive streaming, limited downloads, and other services mentioned above.

STEP 1:
All-In Royalty. The initial step is to calculate the royalty rate that applies to the type of offering being provided by the digital service. This number will be the greater of

the applicable annual percent of revenue of the service (e.g., 11.4%, 12.3%, 13.3%, 14.2%, and 15.1%, depending on the year) and the applicable percent of the total cost of content (TCC) to license the master recordings (22.0%, 23.1%, 24.1%, 25.2% and 26.2% depending on the year). This is referred to as the All-In Royalty.

STEP 2:

Subtracting of Performance Royalties. The next step is to subtract the total amount of public performance royalties of musical works that either has been or will be paid by the service pursuant to public performance licenses for use of the musical works.

STEP 3:

Payable Royalty Pool. The payable royalty pool is the amount payable for the reproduction and distribution of all musical works used by the service for a particular offering during the applicable accounting period. This amount is the greater of the result in Step 2 above and the subscriber-based royalty floor (if any) from the calculation described below.

STEP 3 ADDITIONAL CALCULATION IF SUBSCRIBER-BASED SERVICE:

Subscriber-Based Services. There are subscriber-based royalty floors for use when calculating the final amounts of the Payable Royalty Pool arrived at via Step 3 above. The floors are based on the type of offering that the service is providing to the subscriber and can be very different ranging from 15 cents to 50 cents per subscriber depending on the offering.

The different types of service with their respective royalty floors are:

1. Standalone Nonportable Subscription—Streaming Only: When the subscriber can listen to sound recordings only in the form of interactive streams and only from a nonportable device to which such streams are originally transmitted while the device has a live connection, the subscriber-based royalty floor for use in Step 3 is the aggregate amount of 15 cents per subscriber per month.
2. Standalone Nonportable Subscription—Mixed: This type of service is when the subscriber can listen to sound recordings either in the form of interactive streams or limited downloads but only from a nonportable device to which such streams or downloads are originally transmitted. The subscriber-based royalty floor for use in Step 3 is the aggregate amount of 30 cents per subscriber per month.
3. Standalone Portable Subscription Service: When the subscriber can listen to sound recordings in the form of interactive streams or limited downloads from a portable device, the subscriber-based royalty floor for use in Step 3 is the aggregate amount of 50 cents per subscriber per month.
4. Bundled Subscription Service: This is a service that offers its subscribers one or more other products or services as part of a single transaction without pricing for the subscription service providing licensed activity separate from the products

or services with which it is made available (e.g., a case in which a user can buy a portable device and one-year access to a subscription service providing licensing activity for a single price). The subscriber-based royalty floor for use in Step 3 is the aggregate amount of 25 cents per month for each user who made at least one play of a licensed musical work during such month. For information, this type of user is referred to as an "active subscriber."

In summary, the following are the subscriber-based royalty floors:

Service	Monthly Per-Subscriber Royalty Floor
1. Standalone Nonportable Subscription— Streaming Only	15 cents
2. Standalone Nonportable Subscription—Mixed	30 cents
3. Standalone Portable Subscription Service\	50 cents
4. Bundled Subscription Service	25 cents

STEP 4:

Per-Work Royalty Allocation. The per–musical work royalty is arrived at by dividing the royalty pool determined in Step 3 by the total number of plays of all musical works during the applicable accounting period (other than promotional royalty rate plays). This results in a per-play allocation. This result is then multiplied by the number of plays of each individual musical work.

ADDITIONAL PROVISIONS:

Play Definition. A "Play" is defined as an interactive stream or limited download of 30 seconds or more, except a track that lasts in its entirety under 30 seconds and the user streams the entire 30 second duration of the track.

Student Plans and Family Plans. A student plan is a discounted subscription available on a limited basis by a service. A family plan is a discounted offering which can be shared by two or more family members for a single subscription price. A student plan account is treated as 0.50 subscribers per month and a family plan account is treated as 1.5 subscribers per month (both pro-rated for users who only subscribe for part of a month or who might have been part of a free trial).

Overtime Adjustments. The regulations provide for increased royalty crediting for musical works that are contained on master recordings that are longer than

5 minutes in length. As to these compositions, there will be an adjustment in the number of plays as follows:

5:01 to 6 minutes—Each play = 1.2 plays

6:01 to 7 minutes—Each play = 1.4 plays

7:01 to 8 minutes—Each play = 1.6 plays

8:01 to 9 minutes—Each play = 1.8 plays

9:01 to 10 minutes—Each play = 2.0 plays

For playing times of greater than 10 minutes, .2 will continue to be added for each additional minute or fraction thereof.

Promotional and Free Trial Offerings/Certain Purchased Content Locker Services. There will be no royalties for the following:

a. Promotional Offerings of audio-only interactive streaming and limited downloads of musical works that the service offers to the end users in context of a free trial or other promotion for which the service receives no monetary consideration;

b. Free trial offerings for which the service receives no monetary consideration; and

c. Purchased content locker services for which the service receives no monetary consideration.

Accounting Information. As to the actual royalty statements from the various services, they are required to provide sufficient information as to how the royalty pool and per-play allocations were determined, the type of licensed activity involved, the number of plays of each musical work that is the basis of the per-work royalty allocation as well as whether and how a minimum royalty or subscriber-based royalty floor does or does not apply.

Late Payments. A service will pay a late fee of 1.5% per month or the highest lawful rate, whichever is lower, for any payment received by the copyright owner after the due date.

Music Bundles. The statutory mechanical royalty rate for a packaged music bundle is the rate provided for by the CRB for each configuration of the bundle (e.g., physical recording and downloads at either 9.1 cents or 1.75 cents per minute of playing time or a fraction thereof, whichever amount is larger), and ringtones (24 cents).

SHARING IN ADVERTISING REVENUES FOR USER GENERATED CONTENT

In addition to receiving performing rights royalties through ASCAP, BMI, SESAC, GMR or through a direct agreement with a digital service, writers and publishers also have the option, depending on the service, of sharing in the advertising revenue of ads surrounding the videos containing the videos of their compositions. Since this is an option, the music publisher must agree to monetize such uses (the other alternatives are to send a takedown notice if the publisher deems the use as infringing or without authorization or elect to allow the use of a composition in a video but elect not to monetize and have ads surrounding the video).

A primary example in this area is YouTube's policy toward sharing of advertising revenue. YouTube differentiates between two types of user-generated content: one being where the user video has the composition being sung or performed by the person posting the content without using the original record company master recording, and the other is the user video that uses the original master recording that was commercially released by an artist's record company.

In the case of a user video that does not use the commercially released record company sound recording (e.g., where the video features the user actually performing a composition), YouTube will pay the music publisher fifty percent (50%) of the net advertising revenue related to ads surrounding the video. This ad sharing revenue can be reduced by any compensation that YouTube might pay the user who uploaded the user video to the website with the provision that the percentage of ad revenue payable to the music publisher of the composition cannot be less than thirty-five percent (35%) of the net revenue.

The other type of user-generated content video is one which contains the original pre-existing sound recording (e.g., a video where the user may be dancing to it, lip-synching the composition rather than actually singing it, etc.). In this scenario, the music publisher will receive fifteen percent (15%) of the net advertising revenue generated by the ads surrounding the video.

It should be noted that if there is more than one publisher that owns or controls the composition being used in the video, the payments will be shared on a pro-rata basis based on the percentages of control. Additionally, if there is more than one composition contained in the user video, the net ad revenue will be divided evenly based on the number of compositions in the video before determining the pro-rated share due each publisher.

It should also be mentioned that there are certain restrictions that are agreed to with respect to a publisher agreeing to monetize the use of a composition in a user video, the primary one being the digital service agreeing to not permit the placement of an advertisement in connection with a composition that suggests that the publisher, writer, or artist is associated with or endorses such advertisement of any product or service, or to suggest a tie-in between a particular composition or artist, on the one hand, and an advertisement, product, or service, on the other.

SUBCRIPTION, CLOUD, AND LYRIC SERVICES

This type of service allows end users to download copies of musical content acquired from legitimate sites to multiple computers or devices and re-access copies of such previously acquired content. These can also be a paid service that allows users to back up and access their content collections remotely, stream content via a subscription service, and access lyrics to the musical compositions covered by the service.

Other Services. The cloud service agreement can also have other components attached to it such as a music subscription service and a lyric access service.

The subscription service will be a full-track, on-demand, portable, unlimited streaming service for digital music, audio-video and related content, with cached and offline playback. The devices covered will be all hardware devices now known or hereafter devised including personal computers, telephones, smartphones, tablets, home audio, video, or audio/video consumer electronic devices (e.g., set top boxes, Internet connected A/V receivers, Internet connected televisions, DVD players, Blu-ray players, and gaming consoles), digital player devices, and automotive platforms.

CLOUD SERVICES

Songwriter/Publisher Royalties. The royalties payable to the music publisher will depend on the number of music-only or music video downloads or streams containing music from a songwriter's or music publisher's catalogue in relation to the aggregate number of downloads and streams of all musical compositions and music videos accessed by users of the service during a particular month.

Royalty Payment Calculations. One representative formula has royalty payments to the music publishers based on the greater of an agreed-upon percentage of the aggregate cloud service fees that the provider receives from its users, or a minimum penny rate per cloud service user.

Number of User Devices Able to Access Music. The cloud service allows the user to download the masters, music videos, or ringtones, containing the compositions to a certain number of devices. One example is up to ten (10) computers or devices (e.g., a portable music player, tablet, or mobile/smartphone) which are owned by the user.

Term of the Agreement. The term is many times for a one year period with automatic one year renewals unless a termination notice is sent by the publisher to the service within a specified number of days prior to the end of the then-current period of the term (e.g., at least 30 days prior to the applicable expiration date of the applicable contract period). The term can also be for multiple years as well, depending on the negotiations between the parties, advances or other payments, bargaining power, and needs.

Territory. Because the publisher is based in the United States and controls repertoire for licenses originating in its own country, the territory is many times limited to the United States, and its territories and possessions. Expansion of territories so that an agreement covers the United States and Canada or the world is a discussion that continues to take place but the question always is whether a publisher in the United States can, or even it would like to, authorize a license for other territories considering the rights of subpublishers and societies outside the United States.

Other Provisions. The remainder provisions are fairly similar to those in other types of agreements including warranties, governing law, restrictions, notice clauses, and audit rights (which always become more complicated when a third party such as a record company is responsible for distributing the publishing royalties and not the service itself).

STREAMING (NONINTERACTIVE)

LICENSED RIGHTS
The Web licensee will receive the right to transmit the composition as an audio stream via the Internet on certain approved sites as well as the right to digitally encode, reproduce, archive, and make copies of the composition for the streaming purposes allowed under the license.

LICENSE FEES AND SERVICES
Many streaming sites offer a number of different types of services (e.g., streaming while connected to the Internet, streaming cached stations without a simultaneous live connection, streaming a paid subscription service, portable device streaming, on-demand streaming, conditional downloads with on-demand streaming, etc.).

Because of the variety of choices, sites offer a number of different types of songwriter/publisher royalty structures for streaming depending on the type of service the consumer has selected (e.g., $.00025 for basic streaming, $.0003 for premium subscription, among many others). There are also royalty plans that pay the music publisher and songwriter a percentage of subscriber receipts or advertiser revenue (e.g., from 4% to 15%) and some that guarantee that the royalty will be the greater of a set penny rate per stream or a pro-rata percentage of receipts.

PERFORMANCE RIGHTS
As with interactive streaming, most licenses provide that the streaming can only occur if the transmission is licensed by ASCAP, BMI, SESAC, or GMR in the United States

or other applicable performing rights society outside the United States. This will ensure that the songwriter and music publisher will also receive performance royalties from the streaming.

Term. The term is usually limited in duration (e.g., 1 to 3 years).

Restrictions. Many of the licenses contain the following types of limitations or restrictions:

The audio streams can only be transmitted to the users directly or by using a link to a Web page without a charge being made to the user for accessing the stream.

No downloads or electronic storage on a device or system will be available to the end-user.

The end-user will not be able to alter, distort, mutilate, or otherwise modify the master recording or composition.

Nothing in the rights granted can be used to imply sponsorship or endorsement of the website or Web page or of any product or service contained on the site or page.

Credit. A credit line for the composition and master recording will appear on the Web page or other place where users are able to select the audio streams. Credit guarantees usually provide for information on the following:

Composition Title

Songwriter

Publisher

Recording Artist

Record Label

Server Location. There is a specific warranty as to the location of the servers (e.g., "servers are located in the United States").

Accountings. The streaming royalties are paid on a calendar year quarterly basis (i.e., ending March 31, June 30, September 30, and December 31 of each year), with payment of royalties to the music publisher made 45 days later. Audit rights are available.

PODCASTING

Podcasting enables computer users to download broadcast or streamed program files so that the shows or material can be accessed and listened to in the future. Since there are a number of rights involved including downloading, clearance with the copyright owner of the composition (usually a music publisher) and the recording (usually a record company unless the artist owns the master) is essential. In addition, since performance rights are also involved, licenses should be secured from the appropriate performing rights society ASCAP, BMI, SESAC, or GMR.

RINGTONES/MASTERTONES/MOBILE AND SMARTPHONES

On October 16, 2006, the Register of Copyrights issued an opinion that the compulsory licensing provisions of the U.S. Copyright Law apply to most ringtones and mastertones, and that record companies or other firms are allowed to use statutory mechanical licensing procedures and rates to license musical compositions for use in these areas.

Pursuant to a ruling made by the Copyright Royalty Board in October 2008, for every mastertone made and distributed in the United States, the statutory royalty rate payable to music publishers for each composition is 24 cents. In 2017, this rate was re-affirmed by the Copyright Royalty Board as effective through 2022.

RINGBACKS/OTHER USES/MOBILE, SMARTPHONES, AND OTHER DIGITAL DEVICES

Even though mastertones are licensed at the statutory rate in the United States, there are other types of music uses on smartphones and other digital devices such as ringbacks that are not covered by the Copyright Royalty Board established rates.

Because of the enormous worldwide popularity of this area, a large number of companies have entered the market to provide ringbacks and other nonstatutory uses of music for smartphones and other digital devices. Although the contracts vary from company to company or from music publisher to music publisher many of the following areas will be covered.

Term. The duration of the agreement will usually extend for a period of from one to three years. Occasionally there may be an automatic extension unless the music publisher gives notice prior to the expiration of the term or a good faith negotiation clause once the term is over, but, in most cases, the term will end as of a set date unless the parties mutually agree to an extension.

Territory. Most companies will try to secure a worldwide license so that there are no territorial restrictions as to where they can provide music to mobile phone users. The majority of U.S. music publishers, however, limit the territory to the United States, its territories, possessions, and the Commonwealth of Puerto Rico, or to the United States and Canada. It should be mentioned that many publishers use the services of the Harry Fox Agency in the U.S. and CMRRA in Canada for licensing in this area (rather than license directly). In cases where the territory is limited (for example, the United States), the ringtone company will have to make arrangements in other countries (e.g., Canada, the United Kingdom, France, etc.) with the representative of the publisher in those territories if it wants to sell musical ringtones and ringbacks outside the original licensed territory.

Royalties. The royalty structure is somewhat negotiable, but the current industry-wide royalty in the United States is often the greater of 10¢ to 20¢ (the "floor") for each completed download of a composition to a digital device, or 10% to 12% of the price to the consumer or of all monies earned and/or received by the ringtone company from all forms of exploitation of the composition authorized and permitted under the agreement. For example, if the 10¢/10% formula is used and the ringback was sold to the consumer for $1.99, the royalty to the songwriter/music publisher would be 19.9¢ (the higher of 10¢ or 10% of $1.99). If the ringback cost the smartphone customer 90¢, the 10¢ minimum royalty would be paid because 10¢ is greater than the 9¢, which would be paid under the 10% of 90¢=9¢ formula.

Some agreements also change the floor, depending upon the price of the ringtone to the consumer. For example, if the ringback costs the customer $1 or less, the floor might be 10¢. If the price of the ringback is more than $1, the floor might be increased to 12.5¢ or 15¢.

There are also agreements that do not use percentage-based royalties or minimum per-transaction royalty floors. Such agreements guarantee a set royalty per download, regardless of what the consumer is paying. Rates vary, but one example in this area is 30¢ being paid to the music publisher for ringbacks. It should also be noted that many recording artist and producer agreements contain provisions concerning payments for ringbacks including how the calculations for ringbacks are computed.

Co-Written Compositions. In the case of co-written compositions where there are multiple songwriters with different publishers, the royalty will be shared on a pro-rata basis based on each company's percentage of control. For example, if there are two writers with two separate publishers, each controlling 50% of the composition, the 10¢/10% royalty will be shared equally. Occasionally, higher royalties are paid for special promotions or tie-ins, such as mobile phones being sold with the hit song from a new motion picture included as the ringback.

Most Favored Nations Clauses. Many agreements contain provisions that guarantee that if another music publisher receives a higher royalty rate (or higher fixation fee, if applicable), the higher royalty rate or fee will be automatically raised, effective as of the date that it was given to the other publisher. For example, if a publisher is receiving a 10¢ per song ringback download royalty, and the ringback company signs a contract with another publisher at an 11¢ rate, the 10¢ rate will be increased to 11¢ as of the effective date that the new rate is given. The same increase would occur if one publisher received a 12% royalty while others had contracts that provided for a 10% rate.

It should be mentioned that most favored nations clauses many times not only relate to the money aspects of the agreement (e.g., royalty rate, fixation fee, advances excluding overall catalogue advances) but may, if so negotiated, apply to other material terms of the agreement such as territory or duration of the term as well.

Compositions Controlled. Most agreements start off with a schedule of approved compositions that are actually attached to the agreement. Then as the smartphone company selects new compositions to be added to the list of available ringbacks, it will contact the music publisher for approval. In some cases, the publisher will agree to respond in a set number of days or within a reasonable time after the request by the ringback company, but most agreements do not have these types of mandatory response periods.

Advances. Some agreements provide for an advance payable on the signing of the agreement. The amount of such payment, which will be recoupable from all royalties due in the future, is totally negotiable.

Rights Granted by the Music Publisher. The language varies from agreement to agreement and is sometimes very broad and other times very limited, depending on the negotiations and bargaining power of the parties. Virtually all agreements (other than some short-term movie or other tie-in agreements, which may be exclusive) are nonexclusive, so that the music publisher can grant the same rights to multiple mobile phone, smartphone, and mobile device companies. Some contracts state that the company can create monophonic- or polyphonic-only ringback sound recordings of the music to the composition; others state that they can create ringback sound recordings of the compositions in MIDI, WAV, ADPCM, or similar downloadable and transmittable digital data formats; and others refer to excerpts of pre-existing sound recordings where the ringback is the actual master recording featuring the artist who originally performed the song. There are numerous definitions and ways of describing the rights being granted, and the above are just examples.

Virtually all licenses exclude print rights to the lyrics of the compositions being used. Other restrictions in the agreement include karaoke rights, synchronization rights, and the right to use the song to promote any products or services. These areas, however, may be included for additional fees if the parties agree to have such restricted uses included.

Additionally, the license with the music publisher for the musical composition does not include sound recording rights to masters since these rights must be secured from the record company that owns the master containing the artist's performance.

Agreements also give the company the right to distribute the composition over the Internet (or any successor global computer network) or over regional wireless transmission networks for transfer to smartphones or other individual communications devices of consumers for their personal uses.

Performance Rights. Many licenses provide that public performances of the compositions are subject to the ringtone company securing appropriate licenses from the applicable performing rights organization (for example, ASCAP, BMI, SESAC, and GMR in the United States). This will ensure that performance royalties are paid to the songwriters and music publishers of the compositions used. If the territory includes countries outside the United States as well, the agreement is subject to the rights of and licensing by the various performing rights societies outside the United States (e.g., SOCAN in Canada, PRS for Music in the United Kingdom, etc.). Some ringtone/ringback companies also license the performing rights directly from the music publisher and songwriter, usually on a percentage basis. Based on an ASCAP Rate Court decision involving Verizon, no performance right exists in a transmission of a ringtone to a phone. On the other hand, based on a separate ASCAP Rate Court decision involving AT&T, there is a licensable performance right when a consumer goes to a site to preview ringtones.

Timing. There is usually a restriction that the mobile phone ringback cannot play for more than a specified period of time.

Royalty Accountings. The ringtone company sends royalty statements and royalty payments to the music publisher within 45 days after the end of each calendar quarter. The actual statement will include all royalty-bearing transactions on a country-by-country, title-by-title basis including the number of transmissions, downloads, or deliveries of each composition.

Audit rights are provided so that the music publisher can verify royalty statements and royalties. Some agreements provide for the audit costs to be paid by the ringtone company if the audit reveals an error of 5% or more in the royalties paid for the period being audited. If an audit uncovers monies that are due, some agreements provide for such royalties to accumulate interest at "prime rate" or some other agreed upon formula. The publisher many times has to give at least 30 days notice to the ringtone company that it intends to conduct an audit and there are usually provisos that any audit will be done during normal business hours and at the place where the company keeps its books and records.

Other Provisions. Many agreements provide for an obligation on the part of the ringtone/ ringback company to take all reasonable action to secure and maintain protection of the compositions by encryption or otherwise in conformance with copyright laws. Many provide that compositions cannot be licensed to any party that is engaged in piracy or any unauthorized uses of musical compositions. Other contracts guarantee that no promotional use on the ringtone/ringback company's website shall be presented as an endorsement or commercial advertisement for the ringback service.

There are also indemnification clauses that deal with claims and breaches, notice provisions which dictate how the ringtone/ringback company and music publisher put each other on notice (mailing, faxing, e-mailing, etc.), governing law provisions (New York, California, etc.), and clauses that give a party a certain amount of time to cure a breach or alleged breach of its obligations or representations under the agreement (for example, a 30-day period to cure a breach or alleged breach after notice has been given by the other party).

MASTER RINGTONES/MASTER RINGBACKS

When the actual master recording is used as the ringtone or ringback, the copyright owner of the artist's recording (which, in many cases, is the record company) receives a separate royalty that is shared by the artist according to the terms of the recording agreement. Master royalties in this area vary, but record companies receive from 30% to 40% of the price of the ringtone to the consumer.

RINGTONES WITH VIDEO

If the master ringtone or ringback includes video aspects (such as a ringtone using a portion of the recording artist video or another type of audiovisual file when a call or other communication is received), the royalty paid to the music publisher is often larger than it would be for audio alone due to the additional rights being granted by the music publisher or songwriter.

RINGTONES/FOREIGN COUNTRIES

In territories outside the United States, ringtone licensing for compositions is many times handled by the various mechanical and performing rights societies in each territory. Because ringtones are a global income source, the following represents how two foreign territory organizations handle the licensing of ringtones. PRS for Music in the UK (formerly PRS and MCPS) has a composite license for both the performance and mechanical license of 12% of revenue for ringtones with a 10 pence per file minimum and 15% of revenue for ringback tones as well as polyphonic tones with a 15 pence minimum per file. The license requires quarterly accountings and includes the following rights:

the right to copy the musical work in order to create the ringtone;

the encoding of the file onto a server;

any copies created in transit to the consumer; and

the copy of the file delivered to and held by the consumer.

Another example is Australia where AMCOS (the mechanical right society) and APRA (the performing right society) license compositions. The APRA tariff for truetones (the actual recording is being used) is 2.2% of the retail price or 3.3 cents whichever is higher with the AMCOS rate at 11% of retail or 15 cents whichever is greater. There is also an "upload fee" which is client-specific and is charged on the first occasion a work is reported as a ringtone.

APPLICATIONS (APPS)

Because of the wide variety of apps for smartphones, computers, and other digital devices, and the use of music in many of them, this entire area has not only become an extremely valuable source of income but also an effective method to promote known songs and introduce new material to the general public.

For example, there are artist-based apps, music streaming apps (streaming and downloading), karaoke apps, song lyric apps, music engagement apps, music creation apps that assists users in creating music, music branding apps, and touring apps, among many, many others.

In many cases, a number of songs and recordings are pre-loaded and there is many times a link to a site (such as iTunes) so that a particular song can be purchased via download.

The term of the agreements are usually from two to three years but can be longer. Occasionally, there are automatic renewals of one year unless notice to the contrary is given. The territory is either for the United States, the United States and Canada, or for the world.

The distribution of the app is usually for digital media platforms and all gaming platforms, including existing and future formats of wireless and mobile devices, home consoles, and handheld formats, PC/Mac formats and online games with multi-player online capability via the Internet as well as any wireless transmission network or other media now known or created in the future.

The use of how and in what context the music is being used in the app will be described and there will usually be a confirmation that the agreement is for this app and this app alone.

There are a number of ways that royalties can be structured for these mobile game apps. In fact, some agreements contain alternative computation formulas with the music publisher receiving the greater of the results. Most apps base royalties on a percentage of the retail price or on net revenue and range from 15% to 50%. For example, the music used might be entitled to 20% to 25% of the retail price paid by the consumer for the download from the game or app store. In this regard, there are usually minimum retail prices described for various possible rates (e.g., 1 track for $0.49, 2 tracks for $0.99, 6 tracks for $2.99, etc.) with all songs in the multi-track sale receiving their pro-rata share of the income.

In many of these licenses, there are certain items deducted from the receipts (commissions charged by the app store owner, sales taxes and credit card transaction fees) but there are also minimum royalty payment guarantees for each composition used in many licenses (e.g., $0.08, $0.10, etc.).

As an illustration, a smartphone app might be designed to allow a user to sing along with a well known song or master recording. To facilitate the performance, the lyrics to the song scroll in timed relation to the audio performance. The user sings into the microphone/headphones of the mobile device with scores being based on rhythm and pitch evaluation (among other possibilities). In such a case, if the retail price of the app is 99¢ for a one song download and the publishing royalty is 50% of the net revenue generated by the transaction, the actual royalty might be 17¢ because both the app store and the app developer will take a percentage of the monies prior to the calculation of the actual music publisher royalty. For example, the app store might charge a fee for its services of 30% of the retail price (99¢ x 30% = 69¢) and the app developer might charge a fee of 50% of the remainder (69¢ x 50%= 34¢). The music publisher would then receive 50% of the 34¢ in net revenue under such a scenario which would result in a 17¢ per song royalty for the app usage. It should be noted that if a price to the user covers two songs rather than one as used in our example, the publisher royalty would be shared on a pro-rata basis between the songs paid for, subject to any per song minimum guarantees.

In virtually all these apps, royalties will be paid on a most favored nations basis so that all publishers and the songwriters they represent will get the benefit of the highest royalty rate paid. These clauses usually include the monies payable to the record company for the use of the master recording as well and just not the monies payable for the musical composition used in the app. Accountings are many times on a quarterly basis.

In addition, there are usually provisions that allow the potential consumer to see in-context snippets of the game using screenshots with short portions of songs (e.g., 30 seconds or less sound excerpts) without payment of royalties but such provisions must be agreed to by the publisher. The same is true, subject to the publisher's approval, for online and in-store promotional videos/trailers, in-app song previewing (streaming only without download capabilities) and in-store promotions and gift cards.

Video Sharing Apps. There are certain apps that are designed to allow users to use compositions in short videos that they are able to store and also share with others on the official app website. Many of these app developers have blanket agreements with publishers and they usually provide a royalty structure on a most favored nations basis.

The publisher will grant the app user the right to preview the composition so he or she can decide if they want to use the composition in their video and, if they so elect, to incorporate it in the video and permit others to save the video in their storage clouds and share the videos with public or private audiences via the app's website as well as approved e-mail or messaging services (e.g., "MMS") or third party social platforms (e.g., Facebook, Instagram, Twitter, etc.).

Use of the composition may be limited to a specific duration (e.g., not in excess of thirty (30) seconds) and restricted to the version contained on a commercially released recording by a record company that has also signed a use agreement with the app company. The territory can be the world or the U.S. depending on the publisher's rights. The term may be for a year with automatic renewals unless notice to the contrary is given or for a set period of time (e.g., three years, etc.). It should be noted that if the agreement covers a large number of compositions and/or writers under a blanket catalogue arrangement, there are many times certain compositions that are restricted because of approval rights with a separate schedule detailing the titles and/ or writers. And there may be take-down rights provided to the publisher if there are certain songwriter relations concerns, loss of rights to a composition, or legal claims issues.

As to royalties, one formula being used provides the music publisher with royalty compensation equal to that of what us being paid to the applicable record company that owns or controls the master recording of the performance of the composition.

Since, in many cases, public performing rights are excluded from the grant of rights by the publisher, an agreed-upon percentage will be deducted from the royalties payable to the publisher for the synchronization and exploitation rights if such share is being collected by or allocated to the writer and publisher's performing rights organization.

Because of the large number of ways that apps use music and the primary and/ or secondary focus points of the app, there are a number of areas that should be considered and addressed when negotiating a license depending on the type, initial concentration, and further ability of the app to give users additional ways that they can use or distribute their experience as well as whether the user can add user-generated context into the mix and distribute such to other people (including what those additional users can do to or with the content that they receive and whether the creator/copyright owner of the original source material has a voice and income participation in what happens to the original song and/or recording on which everything was based).

Issues To Review. The following represent some of the issues that should be raised and questions asked depending on the nature of the app and the rights being requested.

1. Can users interact with the music and, if so, how?
2. Can users' performances or interactive activities be recorded and distributed via certain or unlimited media?

3. Is the music being used audio-only or is there an audiovisual aspect?

4. Does the app feature full or partial compositions?

5. Are the original lyrics able to be altered?

6. Is the melody or instrumental recording able to be changed?

7. What is the revenue model? Is it percentage of revenue based or a set royalty per use? How is revenue defined? Are there minimum per-use royalty guarantees ?

8. Is the music file subject to user-generated content and, if so, what are the controls and restrictions as to what the initial user (and any subsequent user) can do?

9. Is there any advertising tie-in to a commercial product involved?

10. Are the files totally portable so that they can be transferred to any device or medium, or are there restrictions?

11. Can the Internet files be restricted only to users in the territory of the license ("geo-gating")?

12. What security measures are in place to protect the rights of the writers and publishers of the compositions?

DIGITAL JUKEBOXES

Unlike jukeboxes that play actual physical CDs, this system uses digital recordings that are transmitted digitally from a central database or server to the individual jukeboxes around the country.

Grant of Rights. The music publisher gives the digital jukebox company the nonexclusive right to copy the compositions on the company's database and to digitally transmit them to the jukeboxes for performance or for storage on the hard drive of the digital jukebox so that they can be played when selected. Sometimes the compositions are pre-loaded in the digital jukebox with future compositions being downloaded via the Internet.

Royalties. The music publishing royalties that are payable are based on the number of times that a composition is actually played on each jukebox. One established formula provides for a payment of one-half cent ($0.005) each time the song is played. This royalty, however, is not a performance royalty since these rights are normally reserved for licensing through the performing rights organizations. There may also be a one-time payment of the U.S. statutory mechanical rate (without regard to playing time) when the initial recording of a composition is put on the server (sometimes known as a "fixation" fee).

There is usually a most favored nations provision in all of these agreements which guarantees that all music publishers and songwriters will receive the same royalty and get the benefit of the highest royalty paid.

Performance Rights. These rights are normally reserved for licensing through ASCAP, BMI, SESAC, and GMR in the United States, and are not covered by the digital jukebox agreement (other than to say that the digital jukebox company will secure performance rights licenses from the applicable performing rights organization).

Term and Territory. The term is many times from one to three years with the territory being limited to the United States (including its territories and possessions) or the United States and Canada.

Excluded Rights. Unless agreed to the contrary, audiovisual or synchronization rights are excluded from the license. Karaoke, print, merchandising, artist likeness, and derivative rights as well as the right to use any composition to promote products or services (including being part of a game or contest) are also not permitted. Additionally, there will be a guarantee that the selection of a song by a customer will not trigger any advertising (either audiovisual or audio-only) unless the music publisher has agreed to such in advance.

RECORD COMPANY CONTRACTS

RECORDING ARTIST ROYALTIES FOR DOWNLOADING MASTER RECORDINGS

With respect to how a recording artist gets paid for a permanent digital download of a recording, there are a number of variations depending on the royalty language of the recording artist agreement (e.g., retail royalty based on the retail price, wholesale price, net profit percentage, etc.), the price of the download (99¢, $1.29, etc.), the fees taken by either the retailer or the download service (20%, 30%, etc.), and whether there is an aggregator involved, among other items. The following represent some summary variations of the calculations.

One variation is computed on the basis of the wholesale price of the download. Assuming an artist has a 15% royalty and the retail price to the consumer is $1.29, a representative calculation would look as follows:

$1.29	Retail Price
× 70%	Wholesale Price Equivalent
$0.91	Wholesale Price
× 15%	Artist Royalty Percentage
$0.137	Actual Artist Royalty

Another variation based on a 99¢ retail price follows:

$0.99	Retail Price
– 20%	Combination Digital Distributor/Retailer Fee
$0.79	Net Income to the Record Company
× 15%	Artist Royalty Percentage
$0.12	Actual Artist Royalty

A third variation is where the artist's royalty is based on a percentage of the record company's net profits (rather than on the retail or wholesale price of the download). Assuming that the royalty split is 50/50 (which is negotiable), there will be deductions relating to the fees charged by the digital service provider and the aggregator (if applicable) as well as music publishing mechanical royalties, among other items.

LICENSED MASTERS/DOWNLOAD ROYALTY CALCULATIONS

There are other interpretations as to how artist royalties from downloads should be calculated which treat the entire sale as part of a license to a third party rather than a direct sale to the consumer. Under this type of classification, third-party license income would be, under many agreements that do not specifically deal which Internet sales or activity, shared on a 50/50 basis between the record company and the recording artist.

This type of formula is more favorable to the recording artist since the calculation is not based on the artist's physical record sale royalty (e.g., a percentage of either the wholesale price to the dealer or suggested retail price to the consumer) but on an equal sharing of the record company's net receipts from the download sale (e.g., 50% of the monies received by the record company in the prior example). There are many variations in these types of royalty calculations but the artist royalties are virtually always substantially higher if the "masters licensed" basis is used rather than the wholesale or retail price based royalty formula (known as the "regular retail channels" sales formula).

It should be noted that there is litigation with respect to this entire area of whether artist download royalties should be calculated on a "master licensed" or "regular retail channels" basis since legal interpretation as to which type of formula correctly applies in a particular situation may depend on the precise wording of the agreement, legal precedent, and whether digital distribution was even contemplated (or in existence) at the time an agreement was signed or an amendment negotiated, among other items. Legal counsel in all such matters is advised because of the complexities involved.

WEBSITE OWNERSHIP AND CONTROL

Most contracts specify that the artist owns the website (domain name) bearing his, her, or the group name. But there are some companies that take the position that the URL (Uniform Resource Locator) is something that should be owned by the record company and not by the artist (at least for a specified period of time). All the rights and obligations of the record company as well as the artist should be specifically listed in the contract so there is no confusion as to what can transpire on an artist site. Some items that need to be negotiated include who has access to the e-mail list of the site, who is allowed to sell merchandise, and who has the right to download from the site. Other items include the right to "link" to other sites and the right of a company to use the artist's name on other websites. Artist manager contracts should also be reviewed because managers, in some cases, own or co-own the name of the group.

According to many recording artist agreements, the record company has the right to create, host, and maintain Internet sites that relate to the recording artist and the recordings produced under the artist agreement. Because there may be a number of possible Internet sites and domain names available for a recording artist, the record company will usually want control over the official site or primary website, which many times will feature the Uniform Resource Locater (URL) containing the artist's actual name (e.g., "www.artistname.com") or a close variation of such name.
In many cases, the costs of maintaining and developing of such sites are treated as recoupable advances under the recording artist agreement.

If the recording artist owns a website when the recording agreement is signed, the artist may give the record company rights to enable the company to further enhance, develop, and maintain the existing site, especially if it is to become the official site for the artist. Outside of the official or primary websites (which may also be called cybersites), the recording artist will usually have the right to register and maintain other sites that concentrate on other career aspects, such as touring, acting, and merchandising. As to these alternative sites, the artist may have to guarantee that there will be a hyperlink to the so called official record company-maintained site, that the unofficial site will not be listed as the official site, and that the names of the official site and the alternative site will not be confusingly similar.

The actual look and feel of the website can be vitally important, because it becomes a reflection of the artist's image and persona. Consequently, almost all agreements provide for consultation with the artist and, in some cases depending upon bargaining power, consent by the recording artist regarding all important aspects of the site.

As to the content of the official website, both the record company and recording artist may create and contribute material that will be used on the site. After the term of artist agreement is over, the record company will have the right to use the materials it created and the artist will many times have the right to use the items which were created or supplied by the artist. Some agreements also provide that the record company will be able to continue to use materials created by the artist on its sites, and other agreements guarantee that the record company will stop using the artist-created materials after written notice from the artists.

As to the creation of websites, some agreements provide that the record company will create an official artist website within a certain period of time after the artist agreement is signed or, at the latest, within a certain time period (e.g., 90 to 180 days) after the release of the artist's first album. If the website is not created within the agreed-upon time period, the artist will usually have the right to own, develop, and host the official website. If this occurs, the record company will many times have the right to include a hyperlink to other websites operated by the record company that include references to the recording artist, or feature or contain recordings of the artist.

Some of the services the record company may be required to provide in its construction and maintenance responsibilities are development of the navigational structure, digitization and encoding of audio files, engagement of hosting services, creation of hyperlinks, registration with search engines, creation of guest books, chat rooms, and other discussion forums, posting of touring dates and other related information, and establishing marketing and publicity activities to promote traffic to the artist's website.

Once the active term of the recording artist agreement is over, the issue of who owns the URL to the official website is very important, because most times the URL is the artist's actual name or a very close variation. There are a number of variations in this area but, if the record company is the party who registered the URL to the official site, the artist many times has the right to send the record company a written notice that the rights to the domain name should be transferred to the artist. Depending on the contract, this request can be sent to the record company at any time after the active term of the artist agreement ended (with some contracts stating that the notice can't be sent until 6 to 12 months after the end of the agreement). When this occurs, the record company will give the artist the rights to the domain name for future use but will usually condition the transfer of rights on the artist, including hyperlinks on the new artist site as well as a guarantee that the record company will be able to use a domain name for its own site which is reasonably similar to the name of the recording artist.

WEBSITE MERCHANDISE SALES

The record company many times has a nonexclusive right to sell artist-related merchandise (such as T-shirts, posters, photos, stickers, etc.) on the official website or other artist sites that are maintained by the record company. If the record company has the right to sell such online merchandise, there is many times a 50/50 split of the net income. And these monies are usually paid to the artist regardless of whether or not the artist has recouped all advances paid under the recording artist agreement. Some of the items that may be deducted from gross income to arrive at the net are manufacturing costs, advertising and promotion expenses directly related to the online merchandise, and shipping, packaging, and postage.

CONCLUSION

Digital media and distribution represents an integral part of music licensing and royalties for songwriters, publishers, artists, and record companies. On the record side, substantial income is being generated whereas on the songwriter/music publisher side, there remains a significant gap as to appropriate compensation. Much of this field is evolving via litigation, arbitration, legislation, voluntary negotiations between the parties, Copyright Royalty Board determinations, new business models, and international agreements and treaties.

CHAPTER 14
MUSIC, MONEY, AND FOREIGN COUNTRIES

At one time most U.S. writers did not earn most of their income in foreign countries. That situation has changed. The money is there, and if one knows the market, it can be extremely important to the songwriter, composer, or writer/performer. There are many parallels to doing business in the United States, but each foreign country has its own rules and its own distinct way of licensing music, collecting royalties, and protecting copyrights. It is vital that a songwriter or composer and his or her music publisher select the right foreign representative, since it is virtually impossible to handle and promote one's music or lyrics adequately thousands of miles away without the assistance and expertise of competent local personnel, as well as some understanding of local rules.

OVERVIEW

In a business that is becoming at once more global and more complicated, we now face a new world of legal and financial issues: fluctuating exchange rates, local music publishers sharing monies earned from songs they do not own, income being lost because local collection societies have not been given the proper information, foreign translators receiving a portion of a U.S. writer's royalties, statutes of limitations for claiming royalties, mechanical income being based on a percentage rather than set dollar rates for downloads and record sales, multiple year delays in the transmittal of royalties, U.S. writers and publishers of songs used in films and television programs receiving nothing because music cue sheets have not been registered, royalties being lost from live tours because set lists have not been supplied, motion picture theater royalties based on box office receipts and other factors, and complicated formulas for keeping track of what songs are being used and how much should be paid. Dealing effectively with music in countries outside the United States is not for the novice.

This chapter explains the major things that one must know when negotiating for foreign representation, including:

The role of the subpublisher and the factors that go into choosing the right one

The duration of the agreement

The information that must be supplied for effective representation

The importance of daily or weekly contact

Advances and guarantees

Cover recordings and local-language versions

CD, DVD, and home video sales; television series, commercials, and motion pictures

Download, streaming, and ringtone rates

Foreign collection society rules, regulations, and deductions

ASCAP, BMI, SESAC, and GMR's relationship with foreign performing right societies

Retention rights if a song is recorded by a foreign artist

Fees charged by foreign representatives for handling U.S.-originated songs and catalogues

Extensions based on nonrecoupment of advances or failure to deliver enough commercially released recordings

Keeping track of what has already happened thousands of miles away or, in the case of Australia and other countries, one day into the future.

THE ROLE OF THE SUBPUBLISHER

The role of the foreign subpublisher is, in most respects, the same as that of a music publisher in the United States. For example, its services include protecting copyrights, registering songs with the local mechanical and performance collection societies, promoting new uses, collecting royalties, auditing royalty statements from record companies, video distributors, and other users of music, negotiating licenses, and suing infringers.

ADMINISTRATION VERSUS PROMOTION

As with U.S. publishing companies, certain foreign publishers are known for their administrative abilities, others for their promotion capabilities, and still others for a combination of the two. In choosing a subpublisher, therefore, a writer or publisher has initially to decide what he or she is looking for and then select the subpublisher that best fits those needs. For example, a major writer/recording artist with international stature may only want to make sure that monies earned from his or her self-contained recordings and performances are properly collected in each territory. In such a case, a subpublisher known for its administrative abilities would be the ideal choice, because local promotion is not an important consideration. On the other hand, if a writer or publisher is looking for cover records by local artists or local territorial exploitation of new uses, the selection may be a subpublisher noted for its strong relationships with local record, television, video game, and film producers in its territory.

WORLDWIDE REPRESENTATION VERSUS TERRITORY-BY-TERRITORY AGREEMENTS

Another choice to be made is whether or not you want to commit your catalogue to one company for the entire world (such as through an overall agreement with a company that has fully staffed offices in all major territories) or select foreign representation on a country-by-country basis, depending on specific needs and expectations in each particular territory. One advantage of going with a worldwide company (besides the daily communication and transmittal of information that occurs between offices) is that, if there is a problem a few thousand miles away, one can always try to resolve it with personnel working in the company's U.S. headquarters. This immediate access by local telephone or appointment rather than dealing by means of e-mail, fax, letter, or staying up half the night to talk to someone during business hours in a foreign territory can be very important.

On the other hand, there is always the fear that one's catalogue might not get the personal attention that it deserves when affiliation is with a major worldwide conglomerate that owns or administers hundreds of thousands of songs. In addition, as in any multinational business, a company may have effective personnel in one country and an inefficient office in another country. Because of these problems, a number of writers and publishers feel that choices should be made on a territory-by-territory basis; in some cases, that means that one's foreign representatives will be a combination of worldwide U.S.-based companies and local independent firms. For example, you might have one major in certain territories, another major in others, and a number of local independents in territories where you feel you can get better service from a nonmajor. A third alternative is to allow an independent U.S. publisher with which you have a good relationship to represent your songs overseas through its subpublishers in each area of the world. Through such a relationship, a writer or publisher who does not know the foreign market can use the expertise and experience of a U.S. company to select and communicate with its own network of independent foreign affiliates.

There are no hard and fast rules in this area, as all decisions are predicated on one's knowledge (or lack thereof) of each country outside the United States. Obviously, if you do not have a good grasp of the foreign music market, it may be safer and easier to let a U.S.-based company with offices in foreign countries represent your songs. But if you do have some knowledge of the foreign market (or don't mind taking the time or incurring the expense to learn), picking and choosing on a territory-by-territory basis may be advantageous, depending on your specific needs in each separate territory of the world.

THE SUBPUBLISHING AGREEMENT

The agreement whereby a writer, writer/performer, writer/producer, or U.S. music publisher grants the right to represent musical compositions in countries outside the United States is known as a "subpublishing agreement." Because of the ever-increasing importance of foreign countries to the earning power of U.S.-originated compositions, and the many positive and negative consequences that can occur owing to how one deals with the relationship created by this type of contract, it is a document that should not be taken lightly. With this in mind, the most important provisions of foreign subpublishing agreements are reviewed here.

TERM

Decades ago, it was not uncommon to commit an entire catalogue to a foreign representative for the life of copyright of each composition controlled by the subpublishing agreement. Thus many standards are still currently controlled overseas by companies for the full term of copyright protection through agreements that were signed 60 or 70 years ago. The standard duration of subpublishing agreements in today's market, however, is normally from three to five years, with three years being the minimum accepted by many foreign royalty collection societies. The term of an agreement is one of the many negotiable items contained in any subpublishing agreement, variations of the term are based on the amount of advances given, retention rights for local cover recordings or procured uses, the right to collect "pipeline" royalties (monies earned prior to the expiration of the term of the subpublishing agreement but not yet paid by the music user until after the end of the term), the right to collect monies earned prior to the commencement of the term, released-album guarantees, extensions if advances have not been recouped, rules of local performing rights societies, suspensions due to breaches, and extensions based on the nonachievement of guaranteed earnings plateaus.

ROYALTY PERCENTAGES

The compensation received by the foreign representative is always based on a percentage of the monies generated by the songs controlled by the agreement. For example, if a U.S. publisher enters into a subpublishing agreement with a foreign publisher for the territory of France, the French subpublisher would receive a percentage of the royalties earned by the compositions from CD sales, downloads, streams, television and radio broadcasts, advertising commercials, motion picture and video game uses, ringtones, and other exploitation that actually occurs in France. The standard fees fall within the 10% to 25% range, but if a writer/artist is a superstar with a worldwide audience and guaranteed international album and single releases, the fees may be as low as 5%, since the subpublisher's role is merely to administer and properly register the songs, issue licenses on the artist's recordings, and collect monies generated by the artist. If a certain catalogue is successful enough to generate uses and income by its very nature (e.g., that of a television- and movie-oriented company with successful worldwide series or films), the fees chargeable by subpublishers may be in the 10% to 15% range, since these catalogues virtually guarantee substantial television, theatrical, and soundtrack album income. If a catalogue does not have such guaranteed income-producing music, however, the fees charged by a local subpublisher will usually be in the 15% to 25% range.

LOCAL COVER RECORDINGS

If promotion of the U.S. catalogue is one of the reasons for selecting a certain subpublisher, most agreements will provide that the subpublisher may retain a larger percentage of the income that is generated from a local recording or other use secured in the particular foreign country (a "cover record"). For example, if the fee on a CD or other recording that originated in the United States is 10% to 20%, that fee may be raised to between 30% and 40% for income generated by a single or album recorded and released by a foreign recording artist. Some agreements provide that if a local recording is secured, the subpublisher's percentage on all versions of the song contained on that cover record will be increased. Since this type of provision can be somewhat unfair if the original U.S. version is a major hit, this is something that one must guard against, unless the local version becomes a major hit in a foreign territory where the U.S. version is not generating substantial income already. If one signs with a worldwide company, it is often specified that if there are to be increased percentages for local cover records, such increases shall only apply to the territory in which the cover record is released (or becomes a hit, if applicable) and not to all countries controlled by the agreement.

INCREASED FEES FOR COVER RECORDS (MECHANICAL VERSUS PERFORMANCE INCOME)

Many of these "increased cover version percentage" clauses relate to mechanical income only (i.e., the sale of CDs, downloads, and other audio recordings). This is a royalty-generating area that is fairly easy to monitor, since royalty statements from record labels indicate earnings by specific record number and recording artist. Some contracts, however, allow the subpublisher to take an increased fee on radio and television performance income generated by the cover version of the song as

504 **MUSIC, MONEY, AND SUCCESS**

well—an inclusion that is extremely hard to monitor, since performing rights societies do not account separately for different broadcast versions of the same song. When performance income is included in the subpublisher's increased percentage on cover recordings, one formula that is used to compute the performance income due the cover record versus the original version is based on a ratio of the mechanical income derived from the cover record to that derived from the original. For example, if total mechanical royalties during a period amounted to $100,000, with the local cover record accounting for 40% of that amount, 40% of the performance income on all versions of the song would go to the cover record and 60% to noncover recordings. In such a case, if $100,000 in performance income was earned on a song and a subpublisher was entitled to retain 40% of cover record income and 25% of noncover income, its share of performance income would be computed as follows:

Performance Income	Subpublisher Fee	Monies to Subpublisher	Monies to U.S. Publisher
$40,000 (40%)	40% (cover record)	$16,000	$24,000
$60,000 (60%)	25% (noncover)	$15,000	$45,000

PRINT

The U.S. publisher usually receives either 12.5% to 15% of the marked retail selling price on printed editions of all compositions, or 50% of the subpublisher's net income. In many cases the print area is not a major source of income, but sizable monies can be earned from songwriter personality folios or specialized editions such as a folio from a hit album or theme-based packages such as a "best of Broadway" folio.

COMPOSITIONS CONTROLLED BY THE AGREEMENT

The compositions controlled by the agreement may comprise:

The entire catalogue of a U.S. publisher

All songs written by a certain writer or writer/artist

Selected compositions

An individual hit song

Entire Catalogue. In the event that an entire catalogue of compositions is being represented, many agreements contain the following language:

Publisher grants to Subpublisher the following rights in and to all the musical compositions listed on Schedule A as well as any and all musical compositions currently or hereafter owned or controlled by Publisher during the term of this Agreement.

In effect, the U.S. publisher is assigning its entire catalogue (including all future songs acquired during the term) to the subpublisher for representation in a specified foreign territory. In an age where publishing companies are bought and sold on an almost weekly basis, however, many publishers exclude major catalogue acquisitions from the subpublishing agreement, since such large infusions of compositions (and the income generated from them) are usually not contemplated during the negotiations leading up to the signing of a foreign representation agreement. For example, if a U.S. company with 70,000 songs buys another publishing company with 50,000 songs, the subpublisher of the acquiring company would normally be required to renegotiate the terms of its agreement with the acquiring publisher if it wanted to represent the 50,000 songs that were bought. In most cases, however, a reasonable number of new songs are expected to be added every year to a catalogue, and such compositions written in the normal course of business (e.g., by staff writers signed exclusively to the U.S. company) would normally be represented by the subpublisher at no further cost.

Writer/Artist Compositions. When dealing with the catalogue of a writer/performer, the standard agreement will relate to all songs written by the writer/artist or all songs written by the artist that are contained on that artist's commercially released albums.

Individual Hit Songs. On occasion, if a song becomes a hit in the United States and there are no foreign commitments, a number of subpublishers will contact the U.S. publisher for representation of that one song exclusively. In virtually all such cases, advances will be paid for the rights being transferred, the amount dependent on whether the song is scheduled for release in a particular foreign territory, the past success of the recording artist in that country, the influence of the record company releasing the single or album in the foreign territory, and the adaptability of the song for local cover recordings and other local income-generating uses. If one enters into a number of these single-song deals with a number of different subpublishers for separate countries, it can get quite time-consuming and burdensome trying to keep track of what each subpublisher in each foreign territory is doing with the song. It is often wise, therefore, if one has established a successful relationship with a particular foreign publishing company in the past, to use that firm for future single songs, or at least give that subpublisher the opportunity to match any advance or other terms offered by another company in the same territory.

ADVANCES

Since negotiation bidding in foreign countries can be very competitive, depending on the catalogue or songs being offered, advances are the norm if a catalogue or song is likely to generate income in the subpublisher's territory. For example, monetary advances in the six- or seven-digit range are not unusual, depending on the catalogue and territory involved. The amount of the advance being offered should not be the only factor considered in choosing a foreign representative, however, as the company's integrity, reputation for administration and promotion, personnel, royalty rates, retention rights, and duration of the agreement must all be factored in the "good deal" versus "bad deal" equation. Many writers or publishers will go with the offer that contains the largest up-front payment, but poor administration and inadequate promotion may ensure that the advance is the last money that will ever be seen. If a deal looks too good to be true, one should be wary; companies are not charities that give money away to worthy individuals or causes. And don't underestimate a firm just because it is in a foreign country or its representatives do not speak proper English. No subpublisher stays in business by making bad deals or losing money. In most cases, they know their market and how it works much better than you do.

HOW ADVANCES ARE PAID

Depending on the type of subpublishing agreement being entered into, the advances payable to the U.S. writer or music publisher can be structured in a number of different ways, including:

A one-time payment upon signing (e.g., $20,000 upon execution of the agreement).

Specified advances at the start of each one-year period of the subpublishing agreement (e.g., $10,000 upon signing and $10,000 on each one-year anniversary date of the term of the agreement).

Advances upon the release of each album featuring the writer/performer, with reductions depending on the number of songs controlled on each such album (e.g., $50,000 upon the commercial release of each album in the territory, provided the writer/artist has written or controls at least 80% of the compositions on the album). Under this type of guaranteed-percentage control clause, if the guarantee is not met, then the advance is reduced proportionately. For example, if the writer/artist guarantees that 100% of each album will be written by the artist and the subpublisher agrees to pay $100,000 for such an album, an album on which only 80% of the songs are written by the artist would receive a reduced advance of $80,000.00 ($100,000 × 80% = $80,000).

Advances upon recouping all or a specified percentage of the previous advance (e.g., $100,000 upon recouping 80% of the previous $100,000 advance).

Advances on local chart activity (e.g., $5,000 if a song reaches the Top 20 on the local trade paper charts, $10,000 if it achieves Top 10, and an additional $10,000 if the song becomes Number One). Advances in this area are predicated usually on 100% control of a particular song, with pro-rata reductions in the event that there are co-writers whose share is not controlled by the subpublishing agreement.

Advances based on a company's acquisition of other U.S. catalogues (e.g., a mutually agreeable advance in the event that the U.S. publisher acquires a major company for representation).

Advances based on actual earnings in the foreign territory (e.g., in the event that $50,000 is earned during the initial one-year period of the term, an additional advance of $50,000 will be paid to the U.S. publisher).

INFORMATION THAT MUST BE SUPPLIED TO THE FOREIGN REPRESENTATIVE

Certain basics must be adhered to concerning the type of information that should be supplied to one's subpublisher to ensure that proper registration can be made, licenses issued, and monies collected for uses of the songs controlled by the subpublishing agreement. Foremost is correct information as to the title of the composition, the songwriter's identity (plus authorship percentages if there are co-writers), performing rights affiliation of the songwriters and music publishers, and the publisher's control percentages if there is more than one copyright owner or administrator. For example, if you are a music publisher and you own only 33.33% of a particular song because two other songwriters have collaborated with your writer (both of whom are signed to different publishers), it is vital that the foreign representative be given all the facts. If the basics are not provided to one's subpublisher in a correct format, there will be no guarantee that foreign earnings will be remitted for uses outside the United States. And even if those earnings are eventually remitted after mistakes have been rectified and proper identification has occurred, delays may have sapped a good portion of the interest or other investment income that could have been achieved had the royalties been transmitted and received in a timely manner.

In addition to the creation and ownership information referred to above, the U.S. music publisher or other representative should submit the following to the foreign subpublisher:

All record and release information on the compositions so that mechanical royalties and performance royalties can be collected for the compositions that have been commercially released in the territory. This information should include the date of the recording's initial release in the United States, release information in other territories, and record label identification, as well as the title of the album, album number, configuration information, and the recording artist's identity.

Copies or files of recordings released on major labels that are likely to be released in foreign territories. It is advisable to send one's subpublisher at least one copy of each recording released in the United States that contains a composition controlled by the subpublishing agreement.

If the songs have appeared in any U.S.-produced television series or motion picture, copies of the music cue sheets prepared by the producer of the series or motion picture must be sent to the subpublisher for registration with the local performing rights society. If this is not done, performance royalties due from television broadcasts or motion picture theater showings are likely to be either delayed or lost forever.

If a writer-artist is doing a live concert tour in a foreign territory, the U.S. publisher should secure a set list of all songs being performed at each venue and send these lists to the foreign subpublisher so that it can notify the local society of the performances and receive concert royalties.

Certain foreign territories need lead sheets and lyric sheets of the compositions to be able to make effective registrations with their local collection societies. If published sheet music of a composition is available, it should be sent to the foreign subpublisher.

AT-SOURCE ROYALTY PAYMENTS

A number of subpublishing agreements contain what is referred to as "at source" royalty language. This means that there will be no extra charges or deductions from royalties passing from one foreign territory to another before being remitted to the United States.

An example of such language is as follows:

All royalties payable shall be based on gross income received at the source and shall not in any way be reduced by any charges including, but not limited to, any sublicensees granted by Subpublisher except only for:

1. Those fees and commissions paid by the Subpublisher to the performing rights societies, mechanical license societies, and other collection agents in the territory; and

2. Payments made by the Subpublisher for any "value-added" taxes and other taxes, if any, required to be deducted in the territory.

The inclusion of this language will prevent a foreign company from double-deducting its fees on monies earned in portions of the territory covered. For example, if an agreement covers the separate countries of Germany, Austria, and Switzerland, with all monies remitted to the United States by the German office of a subpublisher, such language will prevent the German affiliate from deducting fees that may have already been deducted by the Austrian or Swiss affiliate that actually collected the monies. Without such an "at source" provision, the Austrian company could take its 20% and forward 80% to the German office, which in turn might deduct an additional 20% from the 80% before remitting the remainder to the U.S. publisher. Under such a system, the U.S. publisher would receive 64% of the monies earned in Austria (e.g., $100 × 80% = $80 × 80% = $64), rather than the 80% that it should have received under an 80/20 agreement with at-source language.

Another value of such an at-source provision is that it will dictate the maximum terms of any agreements between U.S. companies with foreign branch offices or wholly owned affiliates in other countries and ensure that contracts between such related companies in foreign territories are at an "arm's-length" basis. For example, if a writer/publisher signs an 80/20 at-source worldwide subpublishing agreement with a U.S. company that has 75/25 subpublishing agreements with its foreign affiliates, 80% of the monies earned in a foreign country would be remitted to the U.S. for payment to the writer, regardless of the foreign affiliate's entitlement to a 25% share according to its contract with the U.S.-based parent company. In these cases, the U.S. company would usually split the 20% with the foreign subpublisher.

RIGHTS GRANTED TO THE FOREIGN REPRESENTATIVE

The U.S. writer or publisher will, in most cases, grant the following rights in and to the musical compositions to the subpublisher:

Mechanical Rights. The right to issue mechanical licenses and collect royalties for the manufacture and distribution of records, CDs, downloads, and other audio recordings is always granted to the foreign representative. If these rights are not given to a local representative, mechanical royalties will many times be remitted by the local mechanical collection society to the Harry Fox Agency in New York for distribution to its publisher members.

Performance Rights. The local foreign representative is given the right to register the songs with the performing rights society in the territory and collect the publisher's share of income earned by performances of the songs on the streaming services, radio, and television as well as in hotels, restaurants, discos, elevators, live concerts, and motion picture theaters. The writer's share of that performance money, however, is remitted by each local society directly to ASCAP, BMI, SESAC, or GMR (depending on the writer's U.S. affiliation) and is not paid to the foreign subpublisher. ASCAP, BMI, SESAC, or GMR, in turn, will remit the songwriter or composer monies directly to the writer in each organization's foreign royalty distributions.

If a publisher does not have a representative in a foreign territory collecting its performance income, the publisher's share of any foreign earnings is forwarded directly to ASCAP, BMI, SESAC, or GMR in the United States for distribution. A U.S. publisher that does not have a foreign representative registering songs and collecting monies in its territory, though, takes an unwise risk that all monies earned in a foreign country will not be remitted to the U.S. The foreign market is complicated and intricate, and the only way for a company to ensure that monies are being handled and accounted for properly is to have someone in a foreign country looking after its affairs.

AUDIOVISUAL RIGHTS

Television and Motion Pictures. The U.S. publisher normally gives the foreign representative the right to issue synchronization rights to include songs in television shows and motion pictures that originate or are filmed or produced in the specific territory controlled by the subpublisher. For example, the subpublisher in Germany usually is able to issue a synchronization license for the use of a composition in a motion picture or television program produced in Germany but will not be able to issue a license for a film or television program produced in the United States or any other country outside of Germany.

Home and Personal Video. Whether or not to grant home video rights to the subpublisher for projects produced outside the foreign territory represented by the subpublisher but distributed within that territory is a major decision that must be faced by the U.S. publisher. As for motion pictures produced in the United States, the film producer will always demand that the U.S. publisher grant home video rights on a worldwide basis via a one-time nonroyalty buy-out basis. Under such a grant, there is no money paid to the foreign representative. As with motion pictures, most producers of U.S. television series do not want to pay each foreign subpublisher royalties for video sales in foreign countries and demand worldwide licenses—a one-time buy-out fee for all home video sales that is payable to the U.S. publisher. The same is true for video games. The subpublisher, however, is usually given the right to negotiate home video licenses for audiovisual projects produced in the foreign territory, at least with respect to sales in that particular territory.

Recording Artist Videos. Because many of the songs on music videos are written or controlled by the recording artist, the record company will virtually always have a provision that grants it the worldwide right to manufacture and distribute short or long home video versions of the artist's performances. As for songs written by outside writers, the record company will have to negotiate a separate agreement with the publisher of each song, with, in most cases, a worldwide license granted on a per-unit royalty or buy-out basis. As in the film area, it is rare that a subpublisher would be allowed to negotiate a separate video license for this product for sales in its territory.

Commercials. Occasionally the right to include a song as part of a commercial produced and broadcast in a foreign territory is given to the subpublisher, but many times such a right is retained by the U.S. publisher. If this right is granted to the subpublisher, it is usually conditional upon the subpublisher's receiving approval for each particular request (usually after having sent the U.S. publisher all details concerning the use, including the name of the product, type of campaign, duration of license, and whether the lyrics will be changed). And even in cases where the subpublisher has total control over the granting of a commercial license, these rights will still be subject to any specific restrictions contained in the underlying songwriter's contract under which the U.S. publisher secured its rights.

Print. The right to include the songs in folios or to manufacture and distribute sheet music or other print uses (including lyric only requests) is virtually always included in the rights being granted.

RIGHTS RESERVED BY THE U.S. PUBLISHER

Depending on the bargaining power of the parties, it is not uncommon for the U.S. publisher or writer to exclude the following areas from the rights given to the foreign subpublisher:

Dramatic or literary rights (e.g., motion pictures, television shows, video games, or books based on the story line of the song or using characters created by the writer and appearing in the song)

Commercials, political campaign uses, and endorsements

Grand rights (the right to use a song in a stage musical or live theatrical drama)

Ownership of the copyright

All other rights that are not specifically granted by the terms of the subpublishing agreement

ROYALTY PAYMENT DATES AND AUDIT RIGHTS

As in almost all publishing agreements, royalties will normally be accounted for twice a year, with semiannual payments and statements sent to the U.S. music publisher between 45 and 90 days after December 31 and June 30 of each year. On occasion, a subpublisher will be able to pay on a quarterly basis. The terms and conditions pertaining to audit rights are similar to those contained in U.S. publishing agreements (at least 30 days' notice, conduct of the audit being during normal business hours, restrictions on how many times one can audit, etc.).

RETENTION RIGHTS

Most foreign subpublishers will try to provide that, regardless of the termination of the agreement, they will retain some or all of the following rights for a period of time:

Pipeline Monies. This right enables the subpublisher to collect monies that have been earned during the term of the agreement but that were not yet received at the time the agreement expires. For example, if the expiration or termination date is June 30 and a hit record comes out in May, the record sales and performance royalties will not be paid until long after the June 30 date. The subpublisher will want to collect and take its fee on all activity that occurred during its period of representation. The U.S. publisher usually concedes this negotiable item, especially if the subpublisher has not been able to collect monies earned prior to its representation because a prior subpublisher had similar retention rights. In addition, if large advances have been paid to the U.S. publisher, the subpublisher will many times be given the right to collect such accrued earnings if the advance has not been recouped. If, however, no advances have been paid, there may be a total cutoff of all rights upon expiration of the agreement.

If retention of such so-called pipeline monies is granted to a subpublisher, a time limit on such rights (such as 6 to 18 months) is often demanded by the U.S. publisher to prevent a pipeline collection period from being entirely open ended. Additionally, guarantees that the terminated subpublisher will not have administration rights during the collection period ensure that the new foreign representative will have all necessary rights to represent the song or songs. In another variation of the right to pipeline money, all collection rights are terminated, but the new subpublisher must pay the prior representative its contractual fee (e.g., 10% to 25%) for all such monies earned during the prior term but not paid until after expiration of the agreement. Since the new subpublisher is doing accounting and other administrative work under such a scenario but paying the full subpublisher's fee to another party, the U.S. publisher may have to give its new representative an additional percentage (e.g., 5% to 10%) as compensation, which will reduce the monies being remitted to the United States.

Retention Rights If Advances Are Unrecouped. If advances paid to the U.S. publisher have not been recouped, the foreign subpublisher may have the right to extend the agreement for a specified period of time, thus giving it a better opportunity to recover its advances. It is advisable for the U.S. publisher to place a time limit on such retention of the catalogue, as it would be very unwise to leave such rights open-ended. If such an extension is necessary, it is preferable for the U.S. publisher to provide for an additional retention period only if the foreign representative has not recouped a specified percentage of all advances, such as 75% to 90% rather than 100% of all past advances. In addition, such recoupment and extension clauses are often based on monies earned but not yet paid prior to the termination date, as good-faith estimates can be made as to the amount of money that is in the pipeline. Many times, the U.S. publisher has the right to repay advances (or repay a percentage of the unrecouped balance such as 115%) to cause recoupment.

Retention Rights on Guaranteed Albums. If advances are paid upon the release of albums (in the case of a writer/performer), the subpublisher will normally have retention rights to the songs on any such album that is released in the last six months or one year of the agreement. Such a provision is fair, because royalties generated by the album will not be received by the subpublisher until four to nine months after chart activity. Thus it is reasonable, if the subpublisher has paid an advance for it, to retain the right to receive earnings derived from its use. After all, if an album is released one day before the expiration of the subpublishing agreement and an advance is paid upon such release, the foreign representative will have no way to recoup its money unless the contract is extended for the songs on that album.

Retention on Local Cover Records. In many cases, the subpublisher will retain the right to administer a composition if a local cover record has been released during the term of the agreement. The same applies to other uses (e.g., local film and television uses) generated by the promotion efforts of the foreign subpublisher. There are many variations on this theme, such as retention only if the cover record becomes a hit, reaches a certain trade paper chart position, earns in excess of a certain amount of money, or is actually secured by the subpublisher (rather than a "fall in" without any effort), with the usual retention period being from one to three years after either the release of the record or the termination of the agreement.

For example, one such clause might read:
With respect to any Composition which is embodied on an "A" side of a single cover record which attains a chart position of 40 or better in the official French singles chart during the term hereof, Subpublisher shall retain its rights to said Composition for an additional one (1) year period after expiration of the term.

FOREIGN PERFORMING RIGHTS SOCIETIES

All major countries have a performing right society that licenses the copyrighted works of its own nationals as well as U.S. writers and publishers. A number of these societies also administer the right in certain other countries and territories where a small society or no local society exists. As many U.S. writers and publishers receive the majority of their income from foreign sources, Table 14.1 lists many of the primary societies of the world. Each of these societies has its own rules and procedures for the distribution of money to its own members as well as to foreign societies. Some of these rules are similar to those in the United States; others are very different. Societies deal with each other through signed negotiated reciprocal agreements.

ORGANIZATION AND DISTRIBUTION RULES

A look at four societies should be of help in understanding the royalties that come to writers and publishers from foreign countries. PRS for Music administers the right in Great Britain as well as other overseas territories, with SOCAN covering Canada, APRA covering Australia and New Zealand, and SACEM covering France and a number of territories.

FOREIGN PERFORMING RIGHT SOCIETIES

Table 14.1

Albania—ALBAUTOR	Netherlands—BUMA
Algeria—ONDA	Nigeria—MCSN
Argentina—SADAIC	Niger—BNDA
Armenia—ARMAUTHOR	Norway—TONO
Australia—APRA	Panama—SPAC
Austria—AKM	Paraguay—APA
Azerbaijan—AAS	Peru—APDAYC
Barbados—COSCAP	Philippines—FILSCAP
Belgium—SABAM	Poland—ZAIKS
Belize—BSCAP	Portugal—SPA
Bosnia and Herzegovina—SQN	Romania—UCMR-ADA
Brazil—UBC/SICAM	Egypt—SACERAU
Brunei—BeAT	El Salvador—SACIM
Bulgaria—MUSICAUTOR	Estonia—EAU
Canada—SOCAN	Finlan—TEOSTO
China—MCSC	France—SACEM
Chile—SCD	Georgia—GCA
Columbia—SAYCO	Germany—GEMA
Conga—SONECA	Great Britain—PRS
Cost Rica—ACAM	Greece—AEPI
Cuba—ACDAM	Guatemala—AEI
Czech Republic—OSA	Honduras—AACIMH
Denmark—KODA	Hong Kong—CASH
Dominican Republic—SGACEDOM	Hungary—ARTISJUS
Eastern Caribbean—ECCO	Iceland—STEF
Korea—KOMA	India—IPRS
Latvia—AKKA-LAA	Indonesia—WAMI
Lithuania—LATGA-A	Ireland—IMRO
Macau—MACA	Israel—ACUM
Republic of Macedonia—ZAMP	Ecuador—SAYCE
Malawi—COSOMA	Italy—SIAE
Malaysia—MACP	Jamaica—JCAP
Mauritiu—MRMS	Japan—JASRAC
Mexico—SACM	Kazakhstan—KaZAK
Moldova—ASDAC	Kenya—MCSK
Montenegro—PAM CG	Russia—RAO
Morocco—BMDA	Serbia and Montenegro—SOKOJ
Mozambique—SOMAS	Singapore—COMPASS
Nepal—MRCSN	Slovak Republic—SOZA

Slovenia—SAZAS
South Africa—SAMRO
Spain—SGAE
Suriname—SASUR
Sweden—STIM
Switzerland—SUISA
Taiwan—MUST
Thailand—MCT
Trinidad & Tobago—COTT
Turkey—MESAM/MSG

Uganda—UPRS
Ukraine—UACRR
United Kingdom—PRS
Uruguay—AGADU
Uzbekistan—GAIUZ
Venezuela—SACVEN
Vietnam—VCPMC
Zaire—SONECA
Zambia—ZAMCOPS
Zimbabwe—ZIMRA

All of these societies are governed by a board of directors consisting of writers and publishers elected by the membership and pay out all license fees collected after expenses of the operation are deducted. In all cases, separate pools of license fees are set up from each licensed area for distribution to writers and publishers who have performances in each area, with the payment split allocated 50/50. Distributions are made quarterly by SOCAN, PRS for Music, and APRA with bi-annual distributions at SACEM, and all use a combination of census and sample surveys of users for distribution purposes. All these societies make live performance (concert) and movie theater distributions. The distribution rules for each society are precise, with no preset fees or minimum amounts in any payment formula.

In the case of SOCAN, most tariffs are set by the Copyright Board of Canada. SOCAN's revenue comes primarily from television, cable, and radio, followed by general and concert, online streaming, and satellite radio. In the area of 20–25% of their domestic revenue is forwarded to ASCAP, BMI, SESAC, and GMR due to the performances of U.S. repertory.

In the radio area, most of which is tracked on a census basis, songs that are less than one minute receive one credit with songs with a duration of 1:00–6:59 receiving four credits each. The total number of credits in a quarter are then divided by the money available for distribution in the radio pools to arrive at a dollar credit value. In the television area, there is a Broadcast Pool (terrestrial) and a Non-Broadcast Pool (cable) where duration, type of use and in the case of the Broadcast Pool, a Time of Day factor, determine payment. Each performance receives one credit for each second of duration with the theme (both opening and closing) and feature performances credited at 100% and score at 60%. Any performances in the Broadcast Pool that air between 2:00 a.m. and 5:59 a.m. receive 5% of the normal credit. The formula for payment is Duration × Type of Use × Station Weight (license fee) × Time of Day × Number of Performances × Credit Value = Royalty. The Cinema tariff takes into account the number of seats in a theater with all monies paid out based on duration, number of performances, and type of use as reflected on the film cue sheet.

APRA, the Australasian Performing Right Association, has five distribution pools reflecting monies from Free to Air TV, Subscription TV, Broadcast Radio, Cinema, and Concerts. In Free to Air TV, one credit is given for each second of duration with Feature Music credited at 100%, Themes at 75%, Score at 50% and Ads at 7.5%. Time of Day factors also come into play with 6:00 p.m.–10:30 p.m. performances credited at 100%, 6:00 a.m.–6:00 p.m. at 30% and midnight to 6:00 a.m. at 10%. The formulas for Subscription TV are the same but no Time of Day cutback applies. In Broadcast Radio, one credit is given for each 15 seconds up to 1 minute with songs with a duration of 1 minute and 1 second to 5:59 receiving 12 credits each. Live concerts are paid similar to radio but with songs in excess of 1 minute being awarded 12 credit points each. For cinema performances, 1 credit is given for each second of duration with Type of Use factors applied. For online streaming services, 1 credit is given for each 15 seconds of duration up to 1 minute with songs in excess of 5:59 receiving 12 credits each. For Video-On-Demand, 1 credit is given for each second of duration with Type of Use factors also considered. As to Live Concerts, distributions are made on the basis of reported set lists.

SACEM, the French Society, represents music as well as other rights including literary works, dramatic works, and visual arts, among others. In the television area, duration of the use is the primary payment factor which is then revised by the coefficients of Type of Use and the day and hour of the performance. As to Type of Use factors, pop song videos, instrumental or vocal pop songs with a visual performer presence receive a coefficient of 8, dramatic serials and series a 5.75, music in commercials and feature films a 5 with other types below that. Time of Day factors apply to Monday through Saturday performances with a separate category for Sundays and holidays. The coefficients are 1, 1.2, 1.5, 1.7, 2, 3, and 4 with the primetime segment of 7:00 p.m.–9:30 p.m. receiving the 4 and the period after midnight receiving the 1. In the cable area, channels are categorized as Generalist, Thematic, or Foreign. The radio area contains many different sectors (national, private, etc.) with the duration in seconds of the work the primary factor for nationwide radio stations, and duration, musical diversity, and the promotion of local repertoires all factors considered in local radio.

PRS for Music, the UK Society, is the home of the Performing Right Society (performances) and the Mechanical-Copyright Protection Society (mechanicals). On the performance side, PRS licenses national, local, and international radio stations as well as online and digital radio stations on a census pay-for-play basis with duration as the primary payment factor. Representative samples as well as analogy are also used when necessary. Television is also paid on a pay-for-play basis with some sampling involved when appropriate. Royalties are determined by the annual revenue of the station, the amount of music used, and the duration of the use. In television, the 6:00 p.m.–11:00 p.m. primetime period is paid at two times the rate for all other time periods. In the live performance area, various calculations apply including a set royalty for small licensed venues, a "busker" payment for performances in underground station designated areas, a 3% of box office receipts for pop concerts with royalties distributed on a per-second basis and a fixed administrative cost and accelerated royalty payment for large concerts. Royalties are also paid from set lists of DJ licensed venues and festivals. Cinema royalties are based on box office receipts and the duration of all music uses set forth on the film's cue sheet.

In the online world, music services need licenses for both the musical work and the sound recording. As to the musical work, both the performing right and the mechanical right need to be cleared by the service. PRS has license agreements with UK-only domestic online music services that provide streaming, downloads, and ringtones. These licenses cover both the performance right and the mechanical right and royalties are split between those two rights according to the use. The MCPS PRS mechanical/performance split for downloads is 75%/25% with on-demand streaming at 50/50, interactive webcasting at 25/75 and ringtones split ⅔-⅓. As to multi-territory licensing across Europe, PRS licenses only those works it has been mandated to license across those territories. The PRS license excludes most of the works represented by the major music publishers who have set up their own "special purpose vehicles" in combination with specific societies to license those rights.

PAN EUROPEAN MULTI-TERRITORY LICENSING

As Europe is by far the largest royalty contributor to U.S. writer and publisher royalties (close to 70% of all incoming foreign distributions), it is important to have a basic understanding of how the digital online world of music is licensed and distributed. For traditional media (terrestrial radio, television, etc.) licenses are negotiated by the collection societies in each country on a territory-by-territory basis—in short, a society in one country cannot issue a license in another country. Licenses are negotiated only for users and performances occurring within its territory. For writers and publishers who are members of a specific country's society, they receive royalties directly from that society for licenses and performances in that country with performance monies from other countries being handled by reciprocal/bilateral agreements between the societies in each country.

The online/digital world, though, involves transmissions and activity across multiple territories thereby necessitating multiple negotiations and licenses with every collection society in every territory the activity covers. Further, in the online world in Europe, there is both a mechanical right as well as a performance right in any form of online distribution so a user would have to deal with both the mechanical and the performance organization in every country in order to do business. Complaints to the European Commission from the user communities started in the year 2000 resulting in a number of EU directives and recommendations issued to facilitate the clearance of rights on a multi-territory basis and increase competition among collection societies. A major problem in implementing changes in this area was that writers and publishers in Europe assign on an exclusive basis both the mechanical right and performance right directly to the local societies thereby making it difficult to withdraw works from the societies. The only exception is PRS for Music in the UK, where the performance right is assigned to PRS but the mechanical right is assigned to the music publisher.

The major music publishers, unhappy with the low amount of royalties emanating from the societies' mobile and digital licensing efforts, wanting accelerated payments and more transparency, and desiring more control over their works, among other factors, commenced a withdrawal of the mechanical licensing rights from the European societies for the Anglo-American repertory that they controlled. This repertory included all the works of writer members or affiliates of ASCAP, BMI, SESAC, SOCAN, PRS, APRA, SAMRO, and IMRO. The publishers formed individual joint venture "special purpose vehicles" (CELAS, PAECOL, DEAL, PEDL, IMPEL, ARMONIA, ARESA, SOLAR, etc.) with a specific society or societies (PRS, GEMA, SACEM, SGAE, SIAE, etc.) to negotiate terms and license agreements with the ad-supported and subscription streaming services, download retailers, etc., on a multi-territory basis. ASCAP, BMI, and SESAC signed nonexclusive representation agreements with these societies allowing them to also represent the matching performing rights for online and mobile licensing on a multi-territory basis in Europe. Online services in Europe henceforth need to negotiate licenses with these "special purpose vehicles" if they wish to use the Anglo-American repertory on their services as well as each local country collection society for the use of local repertory.

MECHANICAL ROYALTIES

As in the United States and Canada, mechanical royalties are payable for the distribution of physical audio recordings in foreign countries. As opposed to the United States and Canada, where the rate is expressed as a penny rate, the mechanical royalty provisions in other territories are usually expressed as a percentage of either the retail selling price (RSP) or the published price to the dealer (PPD) or a percentage of revenues with penny minimums. Under such formulas, all compositions on a particular album or other recording share in the aggregate royalties calculated under the percentage computation. Table 14.2 provides information on how mechanical royalties are arrived at in selected foreign territories.

FOREIGN MECHANICAL ROYALTY RATES (PARTIAL LIST)

Table 14.2

Country	Mechanical Rate
United Kingdom	8.5% PPD
Japan	6.0% RSP

Austria, Belgium, Denmark, France, Germany Italy, Netherlands, Norway, Spain, Sweden, Switzerland	9.009% PPD
Australia	8.7% PPD
Canada	8.3¢

There are mechanical right societies in virtually all territories that license recordings and collect income. Table 14.3 identifies some of those organizations and the territories of representation.

FOREIGN MECHANICAL RIGHT SOCIETIES (PARTIAL LIST)

Table 14.3

Society	Territory
AMCOS	Australia
SABAM	Belgium
CMRRA	Canada
SODRAC	Canada
MCSC	China
NCB	Denmark, Finland, Sweden, and Norway
GEMA	Germany
CASH	Hong Kong, Macau
SDRM/SACEM	France
JASRAC	Japan
SIAE	Italy
STEMRA	Netherlands
SAMRO	South Africa
SGAE	Spain
SUISA	Switzerland
MCPS	United Kingdom

Unlike the U.S., where the performing right society and the mechanical right society are separate entities, in many countries the performing right society is also the mechanical right society (e.g., GEMA in Germany) or is a combination of two societies jointly working together (e.g., PRS for Music/MCPS in the UK or APRA/AMCOS in Australia).

RINGTONES

As in the United States, mobile phone ringtones (MPRT) represent another source of income. The MPRT rates charged by the societies are usually a percentage of the price to the consumer or subscriber revenue (e.g., 10%, 12%, etc.) and are often split between performing and mechanical rights.

DOWNLOADS/STREAMS/SUBSCRIPTION SERVICES

In most foreign countries, specific licensing arrangements have been established regarding the mechanical/reproduction right and the performance/communication right for downloads and streams. Rates, in the main, are decided by copyright boards or copyright tribunals in each territory or via voluntary agreements.

In the UK, PRS for Music offers a joint license covering both the performance and mechanical right. The fees are the greater of a percentage of revenue figure or on a per song rate. Downloads are 8% of gross revenue with a 5 pence minimum for one track and reduced minimums for tracks of two or more in a bundle. PRS has various online music licenses involving download and streaming services with classifications of subscription, pay-per-use, free-to-consumer, and advertising, among other factors taken into account. For services that provide on-demand streaming, permanent downloads, and webcasting and have annual revenues of less than 200,000 pounds, PRS has a specific number of pounds annual blanket fee depending on the revenue class of the service. A number of major agreements in this area are under nondisclosure restrictions.

In Canada, online music tariffs are established by the Copyright Board of Canada either mandatorily or at the request of an interested party. Depending on the type of service, royalties are payable to the collective societies SOCAN, for the performance/communication right and CSI, the joint venture of the mechanical/reproduction right societies CMRRA and SODRAC. The rates for various types of online music tariffs are as follows:

Permanent and Limited Downloads: 8.91% of revenues with minimum fees of 3.6 cents per track in a bundle of 13 tracks or more or 6.6 cents per track otherwise payable to CSI; Non-interactive, Semi-interactive and Interactive webcasts 1.49% of revenues payable to CSI with a $100 minimum and 5.3% of revenues payable to SOCAN for semi- and interactive webcasts with a $100 minimum; hybrid webcasts 3.13% of revenues with a $100 minimum to CSI and 3.48% of revenues with a $100 minimum to SOCAN. In the category of Permanent Downloads of Music Video, they generate 5.64% of revenues with minimums to SODRAC. For Semi-interactive or Interactive webcasts of music videos, 2.99% of revenues with a $100 minimum goes to SOCAN.

In Australia, digital music service providers pay APRA/AMCOS for the communication and reproduction rights at a rate of 9.9% of the retail price for single track music downloads as well as bundles and albums and 8.8% of the retail price for music video downloads with minimums. There are also various types of online licenses depending on what type of service and offerings are being provided.

CONCLUSION

In a world of ever-expanding markets and opportunities, the foreign marketplace can be for many a major revenue source. To get what you are due, it is essential that you know which organizations are collecting for you and how they are distributing money for the performances of your work.

CHAPTER 15

MUSIC, MONEY, AND PUTTING IT ALL TOGETHER

The $4 million income chart as shown in Table 15.1 is not a dream; it represents a very real scenario for a songwriter who is able to put it all together. Since the chart reflects many of the separate income-producing areas discussed in the book, this chapter summarizes how those areas can come together to create the multimillion-dollar income that people dream of.

In the following illustration, we will assume that the songwriter has a 50/50 co-publishing agreement with a music publisher (i.e., the songwriter is entitled not only to his or her full songwriter's share of income but also to 50% of the income reserved for the music publisher) and is a recording artist with a Number One radio hit, 100,000 download-selling single as well as a 200,000 unit-selling album (100,000 of which are digital downloads). Based upon the artist's success, the artist is asked to score a feature film which does very well worldwide and a television series based on the film which leads to a Broadway musical years later. The opportunities that present themselves and the monies that can be earned as a result of having a hit are not exaggerated; given the right set of circumstances and the right songs, the results shown here are real and, in some respects, even less than what can be earned.

POTENTIAL SONGWRITER/PUBLISHER/RECORDING ARTIST GROSS INCOME

Table 15.1

$9,100	U.S. single sales (100,000 downloads)
$200,200	U.S. album sales (200,000 copies)
$4,000	Interactive streaming mechanicals
$900,000	U.S. radio and TV performances
$60,000	Streaming royalties
$11,000	Foreign single sales
$250,000	Foreign album sales
$700,000	Foreign radio and TV performances
$25,000	Sheet music, folios and print
$200,000	Commercial
$20,000	Television series all media license
$40,000	Motion picture use
$4,000	Foreign theatrical film performances
$624,000	Broadway show
$15,000	Video game synch fee
$30,000	Video game royalties plus advance
$1,000	Ringtones and ringbacks
$600	Lyric reprint in a novel
$40,000	Toys, dolls and greeting e-cards
$3,000	Karaoke
$225,000	Motion picture scoring fee
$300,000	Foreign theatrical score royalties
$35,000	U.S. television score royalties
$30,000	Internet and miscellaneous
$3,726,900	Total writer and publisher royalties

$20,000	Motion picture sound recording master use
$281,475	Recording artist royalties (digital/physical sales)
$25,000	Interactive streaming royalties
$50,000	SoundExchange artist royalties
$12,000	SoundExchange producer royalties
$4,115,375	Total gross income

MECHANICAL ROYALTIES (DIGITAL AND PHYSICAL)

Assuming that all download, CD, vinyl, and other audio recording sales occurred in the United States and the record company agreed to pay the songwriter/artist and music publisher the statutory mechanical rate (rather than a 75% physical product controlled composition reduced rate) for the single and up to 11 compositions on the album, the writer and publisher royalties would be as follows:

100,000	Singles downloaded
× .091	Statutory rate
$9,100	Writer and publisher royalties

200,000	Albums sold
× .091	Statutory rate
$18,200	Royalties for one song
× 11	Songs on album
$200,200	Total album royalties

If additional hit singles were taken from the album, additional royalties would be earned. But for purposes of this illustration, we'll hold the mechanical royalties due from sales of the initial single and album to $209,300 ($9,100 + $200,200) in aggregate songwriter and publisher income. Since the writer would receive 75% of these monies (i.e., 50% as songwriter and 25% as co-publisher) and the publisher 25%, the final sharing of earnings would be:

$156,975	Songwriter/Co-Publisher
$52,325	Publisher

Outside the United States and Canada, mechanical royalties are primarily based on a percentage of the dealer price (with some countries on a retail price basis).

U.S. PERFORMANCE ROYALTIES

The "A" side single reaches Number One on the pop charts and crosses over to other trade paper charts. It is one of the most heavily broadcast songs of the year on both traditional radio as well as satellite (Sirius XM) and earns $600,000 in writer performance royalties. The same amount is earned as publisher royalties, which results in the following monies being remitted to the songwriter:

$600,000 Writer royalties

+ 300,000 50% Co-publisher royalties

$900,000 Total performing right domestic royalties

RECORDING ARTIST ROYALTIES

The computations in Table 15.2 assume that the writer as recording artist had a $150,000 fund to record the album, had a 15% album retail price royalty rate, a 15% artist download single rate, a 25% album-only packaging deduction, no producer-royalty deduction, payment on 95% of physical recordings sold (which includes free goods), and $120,000 in recoupable video, independent promotion, and publicity costs.

ALBUM ROYALTY

Table 15.2

$14 CD retail price

× 25% Packaging deduction

$3.50 Dollar deduction

$14 CD retail price

− 3.50 Packaging deduction

$10.50 Royalty base

× 15%	Royalty %
$1.575	Artist royalty
× 95,000	Album sales (100,000 x 95%)
$149,625	Artist royalties

ALBUM DOWNLOAD RECORDING ARTIST ROYALTIES

$9.99	Album Retail Price
– 20%	Digital Distributor Fee
$7.99	Net Income To Record Company
× 15%	Recording Artist Royalty Percentage
$1.198	Actual Recording Artist Royalty
× 100,000	Album Downloads
$119,850	Artist Royalties

SINGLE TRACK DOWNLOAD ROYALTY (REGULAR RETAIL CHANNELS FORMULA)

$0.99	Retail Price
– 20%	Digital Distributor Fee
$0.99	Net Income To Record Company
× 15%	Artist Royalty Percentage
$0.12	Actual Artist Royalty
× 100,000	Album Downloads
$12,000	Artist Royalties

Certain recording artist agreements may provide for a 50/50 sharing between the artist and the record company of the record company receipts as to downloads (known as a "licensed master" calculation) but, for the sake of this calculation, the "regular retail channels" artist royalty formula is being used.

Final Calculations:

$269,475	Album royalties
+ $12,000	Single track royalties
$281,475	Total royalties gross income
– 150,000	Recordings costs
– 50,000	Video costs
– 70,000	Promotion/publicity costs
$ 11,475	Final royalty check

STREAMING ROYALTIES: SONGS AND SOUND RECORDINGS

Though streaming royalties for most songs represent a minor royalty source, hit songs can generate substantial royalties from Spotify, Pandora, Apple, YouTube, and other online interactive and noninteractive streaming services due to the audio-only bonus provisions of ASCAP and BMI as well as other PRO's payment formulas. Major hit songs can generate, in many cases, between $50,000 to well over $100,000 in combined writer and publisher streaming earnings if they reach the quarterly bonus threshold criterions for each service. Based on the nature of these services, bonuses take effect only after many millions of quarterly performances occur. For any performances below those criteria, royalties are minimal. Keep in mind also that each PRO sets their own qualifying performance threshold for bonus payments.

As to sound recordings being performed on noninteractive sites, SoundExchange distributes all statutory license royalties 50% to the owners of the sound recordings, 45% to the featured recording artist, and 2.5% each to the background musicians and vocalists on the recording. Based on a letter of direction, the artist can share the artist royalties with the record producer. The license fees from interactive services are normally negotiated directly between the record company and the service and are normally paid by the record company to the recording artist based on the provisions of the artist's recording agreement.

COMMERCIAL USE

Because the song's message is positive and the melody is strong, the music publisher receives a request from a major soft drink company for use in its television, Internet, and radio campaign. After two weeks of negotiations, an agreement is reached that will allow the advertiser to use the song for one year as part of its campaign in the

United States. Since the agency intends to re-record the composition with a slight change of lyrics to fit the theme of the commercial, the advertiser has to license only the underlying musical composition and not the hit recording, which would have necessitated a separate license from the record company that owned the master. The fee for the initial year is $200,000, with the songwriter receiving 75% (i.e., $150,000) under the terms of the co-publishing agreement. Under the commercial license agreement, the advertiser also has options to extend the term of the contract for two additional, successive one-year periods for increased fees of $220,000 and $250,000 respectively. If all options are exercised, a total of $670,000 will be generated under the advertising use contract.

$200,000	2018 fee
$220,000	2019 fee
$250,000	2020 fee
$670,000	Total commercial fees

Under the writer's songwriter and co-publishing agreement, 75% of the $670,000 (or $502,500) will be remitted in royalty income to the songwriter, with the music publisher retaining $167,500.

MOTION PICTURE USE

A few months after the song reaches Number One on the charts, a motion picture producer requests the right to use the composition in a scene that has a hit song playing from a jukebox in the background while two characters discuss a bank robbery plan in a bar. For the synchronization right to include the song in the film, the buy-out grant for home video distribution, and all the other rights that normally appear in a motion picture license, the music publisher charges the film producer a fee of $40,000, 75% of which will be paid to the writer by the publisher. Since the hit record is also being used in the scene, the film producer also contacts the writer/artist's record company and, after negotiations have been concluded, agrees to pay the record company an additional $40,000 for the use of the master recording. Since the writer/performer is entitled to receive 50% of any licensing income per the terms of the recording artist agreement, $20,000 of the $40,000 fee will be the artist's share from the master recording license.

Additionally, the composition and recording are put on the film's soundtrack album, which sells 250,000 royalty-bearing copies and generates $22,750 in gross mechanical income as well as master recording license royalties for use of the artist's hit recording. When the film is shown in theaters outside the United States, performance royalties will also be generated for the songwriter and music publisher via the foreign societies affiliated with the writer's U.S. performing rights organization. And when the motion picture is broadcast on television in the United States or in foreign countries, or streamed on the Internet, additional writer/publisher performance royalties will be generated for years into the future.

TELEVISION SERIES USE

The script for a television series calls for a nightclub performer to sing a contemporary hit song during a particular scene. The music coordinator for the series calls the publisher and requests price quotes for a worldwide, life-of-copyright, all-media excluding theatrical synchronization license (which includes a personal/home video buy-out). The publisher negotiates a $20,000 all-in synchronization fee for the song's use in the television series. The songwriter, through the co-publishing arrangement, receives 75% of these monies and will also receive performance royalties from either ASCAP, BMI, SESAC, or GMR when the series episode is actually broadcast in the United States or streamed on the Internet. If the series is distributed to and broadcast in countries outside the United States, the local performing rights society will license the television performance, collect royalties, and send the writer's share to ASCAP, BMI, SESAC, or GMR in the United States for distribution. Because the music publisher's share of foreign performance income is usually collected by a subpublishing representative in each country, such monies are usually distributed by the local subpublisher directly to the U.S. publisher, which will in turn pay the songwriter his or her 50% co-publisher interest. If there is not a subpublisher in the foreign broadcast territory, the publisher royalties will be distributed by the local society to ASCAP, BMI, SESAC, or GMR in the United States for distribution.

FOREIGN MECHANICALS AND PERFORMANCES

Because the market outside the United States is, for an increasing number of songwriters, becoming more and more important, those album and single sales can easily double the income generated in the United States. Since, other than in Canada (which like the United States calculates physical product mechanical royalties on a set penny basis), the computations depend on the country of sale, the percentage used in the particular territory, and the price basis on which the percentage is applied, computations can be somewhat complex. Suffice it to say that the monies can be substantial. Subpublishers will normally collect mechanical income and remit such to the original publisher in the United States. The Harry Fox Agency and CMRRA also have reciprocal relationships with many mechanical rights societies throughout the world to ensure collection of royalties in cases where there is not a subpublisher. Because

ASCAP, BMI, SESAC, and GMR have relationships with the other performing rights societies around the world, performances of U.S.-originated compositions are licensed by those societies on behalf of the U.S. writers and publishers. ASCAP, BMI, SESAC, and GMR in turn, provide the same service for foreign writers and music publishers when their compositions are broadcast or otherwise performed in the United States.

THE BROADWAY MUSICAL

Although Broadway is a very specialized field, some songwriters are able to transfer their skills into that area. The songwriter in our illustration has composed the music to songs for a musical that finally secures the multimillion-dollar backing needed for a show to get to Broadway. The reviews are good, and the show grosses an average of $800,000 per week during the initial year of its Broadway run. The songwriter is being paid under a Dramatists Guild contract rather than a royalty pool arrangement and, as the only composer of the songs that appear in the musical, is entitled to ⅓ of the 4.5% prerecoupment gross box office receipts royalty (with the book writer and lyricist sharing the remaining 3%). Assuming the musical opens during the initial week of January, plays 52 weeks during the year, and still has not recouped its investment by December 31 of that year, the writer will receive $624,000 in royalty income for the year on Broadway.

$800,000	Weekly box office receipts
× 1.5%	1/3 Prerecoupment royalty
12,000	Weekly composer royalty
× 52	Weeks
$624,000	Annual composer royalty

MOTION PICTURE UNDERSCORE

Based on the writer's success in the songwriting field, as well as some prior experience and training in composing and orchestrating for film, the songwriter is hired by a motion picture producer to compose a contemporary-sounding music score for a major studio film. The negotiated composing fee is $225,000. The film is released, becomes a worldwide hit and generates substantial performance money from all the major countries in the world. After its theatrical release, the film is aired twice on network television in the United States. Within a few years, the writer and publisher receive a total of $300,000 from foreign performing rights societies and $35,000 from a U.S. performance society for the two network television airings.

ADDITIONAL INCOME-PRODUCING AREAS

In addition to the sources mentioned previously, a number of other income-generating opportunities can open up for the songwriter because of a hit song or hit record. For example, a novelist might include a portion of the lyrics to a composition in the scene of a best-selling novel; a video game producer may use the song; a phone app might feature the song; a video jukebox company may include the record company's artist video on its machines; a producer might license a song for use in a hologram; a karaoke manufacturer may select the song for use in its product line; a "how to," exercise, or other special-interest video distributor may select the composition or hit recording for use in a home video project; a sheet music manufacturer might sell single sheets of the song and include it in a varied number of folios or other print arrangements or "how to play" lessons; a telephone company may ask for a cell phone ringtone or ringback license; an interactive video manufacturer may choose the song to be featured in one of its home or personal video programs; a digital jukebox distributor may license the audio for use on its machines; a theme park might use it as part of a ride or attraction; a film company might use the song in its promo campaign for a new motion picture; a baseball player may select the song to be played when he walks to the batter's box; a clothing company may want to put the lyrics on a pair of jeans; a major greeting card company may select it for a musical e-card; and a doll manufacturer may select the song as part of the doll's singing repertoire—all of which generate additional year-in and year-out income for the songwriter and music publisher. Many of these opportunities continue to occur during the copyright life of a composition (e.g., a song may be used in a number of different television programs, motion pictures, video games, and commercials, and contained on a number of different albums or single releases); with each new use, relicensing generates new revenue.

Subscription services represent a growing source of income. These services include an unlimited listening of songs for a monthly fee (either on an interactive or noninteractive basis), a specific download fee, a limited number of burns for a fee, transfers to portable devices, various price structures based on options of use (specific range of streams and downloads, both time and nontimed, permanent and nonpermanent), and many more.

CONCLUSION

The list of ways that a song, score, or master recording can earn money is never-ending and constantly changing. Knowing how these many opportunities are licensed, the money that can be made, and how they all fit together can ensure a long and profitable career.

CHAPTER 16
MUSIC, MONEY, AND THE BUYING AND SELLING OF SONGS

s the continuing emergence of new technology enlarges the boundaries of the entertainment industry, the ownership of musical compositions has become more and more valuable, not only to the major conglomerates, Internet companies, indies, and startups, but also to any company creating programming for the general public or who needs and/or values content. Hit songs and film and television scores earn large amounts of money from their use on CDs or vinyl; in audiovisual projects such as motion pictures, television series, video games, Blu-rays, DVDs, and home or personal video; in royalty-bearing downloads; on smartphones and other mobile devices; as ringtones; and in an unlimited number of other entertainment-related distribution vehicles—print, karaoke, interactive media, Broadway, off-Broadway and regional musicals, subscription services, computer games, merchandising, digital and video jukeboxes, commercials, music boxes, lyric reprints in novels and nonfiction books, holograms, and so on. With all this activity, ownership of compositions can make a substantial impact on a writer's income or a company's bottom line.

This chapter reveals the inside information on how these acquisition and sale agreements are structured, how one arrives at the dollar multiple used in the final purchase price of a song or catalogue of songs, how a presentation to a buyer should be structured, where the major danger points in any purchase-and-sale negotiations are, and what areas the buyer should look at to determine whether or not to acquire a catalogue at the asking price. Whether the seller is a songwriter with one hit song, a songwriter/recording artist, a record producer with songwriter and/or publishing rights, heirs to a deceased writer's estate, or a publishing company with hundreds of thousands or millions of copyrights, and whether the buyer is a publishing company, investment firm, management company, digital service, bank, hedge fund, or successful recording artist or producer, this chapter details how the deals are made.

OVERVIEW

When buying or selling music-publishing catalogues, as in any acquisition, a number of areas must be analyzed before closing the sale. First, we will look at a few of the basic concepts.

PURCHASE OF ASSETS

In the majority of acquisitions, the buyer acquires only the assets of the seller (an "asset sale") and not the corporation or other legal entity that owns the musical compositions (a "legal entity sale"). The right to use the music publisher's name or names is virtually always transferred to the buyer, and the legal entity is usually retained or dissolved by the seller. In cases where the transfer does not occur, there normally is a restriction on the use of the name by the seller for a specified period of time; for example, the selling company may agree not to use its publishing company name for five years from the date the compositions are sold. On occasion, the buyer will actually use the prior name as representative of the compositions being acquired (especially if there is substantial goodwill involved or the name has an established worldwide identity) through the use of a "doing business as" designation, but in most cases the former name will be retired and all songs will be transferred into the publishing affiliates of the acquiring entity.

THE PURCHASE PRICE

The actual purchase price of the acquisition is almost always based on a multiple of the average annual net earnings of the selling company over the most recent three to five fiscal or calendar years. For example, if an acquisition occurs in 2019, it would normally be based on a multiple of the net income for either the period 2016–2018 or 2014–2018. In many respects, taking the five-year basis is safer for the buyer, because the longer the period considered, the less likely it is for an isolated event (such as from a one-time chart record, audit recovery, litigation settlement, or major commercial use) to have a disproportionate effect on the overall net income. A three-year period can be acceptable, however, if the buyer is able to discount such income fluctuations.

Sometimes a lesser period (such as the two most recent years or, in some cases, even the most recent one year period) will give the buyer a better idea as to where the catalogue's earnings are going. Occasionally, a buyer may also be offered the possibility of acquiring all or a portion of the publishing rights to a catalogue with little or no earnings history (as in the case of a new recording artist/songwriter with a current album in the Top 10 and a Number One single); instead of using past earnings as a guideline, the buyer will have to predict future earnings on the chart activity and project earnings on future not-yet-released albums and singles—a somewhat tricky proposition, even with experience.

CALCULATION OF NET INCOME (CASH VERSUS ACCRUAL BASIS)

The "net income" of a catalogue (which is the basis of the purchase price computations) is virtually always defined as gross royalty income received by the selling company, less all royalties payable to songwriters and other third parties. Two methods are used to calculate the net income: the cash basis and the accrual basis. Under the cash basis formula, the buyer takes the gross royalty income received by the seller during a particular period and deducts the amount of songwriter and other third-party royalties actually paid out during that period. For example, if $7 million was received in 2018 and $2,500,000 was paid to songwriters and other royalty participants in that year, the net income would be $4,500,000.

The more reliable method, however, and the one that gives the buyer a truer reflection of the worth of a publishing catalogue, is the accrual basis of net income computation. Under this method, the buyer takes the gross earnings received during a year and deducts the income actually paid to songwriters and other third-party royalty participants during that year, plus royalties that will be paid out in the future from that income. For example, publishers normally pay songwriters their royalties for income received between January 1 and June 30 of each year, within 45 to 90 days after June 30 (from August 15 to September 30). Royalties payable to the songwriters on income received during the July 1 through December 31 period, however, would be paid out between February 15 and March 31 of the next year. Under the cash method, the royalties payable from the July 1 through December 31 period would not be reflected in the calculation of net income for the year being considered, since they would be payable on a date outside that period. What the buyer would be getting with the cash method is a computation based on income received during a specified year, less the royalties payable from income received from a prior year (e.g., songwriter royalties payable from July 1 through December 31 of the previous year), plus the royalties that were actually paid out for income received during the first six months of the year being considered. Under the cash net income basis, the seller could have a poor income period for the final six months of one year and a very successful succeeding year, and the resulting net income for the successful year would look artificially high, because the buyer would be deducting royalties paid from a low-income period (the last six months of the prior year) and only one royalty payment from the first six months of the successful year. The accrual basis, by taking into account the gross income received less the royalties actually paid or due to be paid on that income, will always give a more realistic view of what a catalogue is actually worth during a particular year. The five-year net income figures may look as follows:

Year	Gross Income	Less Royalties Paid or Due	= Net Income
2014	$10,000,000	$4,000,000	$6,000,000
2015	$8,000,000	$3,500,000	$4,500,000
2016	$11,000,000	$5,000,000	$6,000,000
2017	$12,000,000	$5,500,000	$6,500,000
2018	$14,000,000	$6,000,000	$8,000,000
Totals	$55,000,000	$24,000,000	$31,000,000

$31,000,000	Aggregate 5-year net income
÷5	Number of years considered
$6,200,000	Average annual net income

SALARIES AND OTHER COSTS OF DOING BUSINESS

In most cases when an acquisition is being contemplated by an existing music publisher, the costs of running the catalogue (salaries of employees and benefits, rent, lease commitments on the premises, postage meters, photocopying, microfilm copying, document retrieval systems, executive contracts and golden-parachute clauses, expense accounts, catalogue promotion costs, copyright registration fees, demonstration recording sessions, subscriptions, etc.) are usually not considered, because most large publishers can incorporate an acquired catalogue into their existing system without major cost additions. Granted, there are increased costs for the acquiring party if the catalogue being bought is a large one, but with the ability of computers, and dependent on the quality and experience of the personnel currently employed by the buyer, the extra costs may not be substantial. If the acquiring company is not a functioning music publisher or if it only has a small staff that is unable to handle a large catalogue, the extra costs related to the acquisition and future management of the company (especially if the buyer wants to hire all or some of the seller's personnel and absorb the salary and social costs related thereto) are often considered in the computation of the purchase price. Under these circumstances, the seller may reject such factors, but they the buyer may consider them when formulating a final offer.

PURCHASE PRICE MULTIPLES

Once an average annual net income figure is calculated, the buyer and seller will negotiate a multiple to be placed on such earnings to arrive at a final purchase price. For example, if a multiple of five were used in the above illustration, the price would be $31 million, and if a multiple of 10 were used, the acquisition would cost $62 million. In recent years, multiples have been in the 8 to 18 range, but can be higher or lower depending on a number of factors, including the nature of the rights being acquired, including whether it is an acquisition of music publishing rights, songwriter royalties, passive income rights, termination rights, etc., the remaining copyright life of the compositions being purchased on a country by country basis, the costs of borrowing the money related to the acquisition, the loss of income from other investment areas in which the purchase price could have been used, anticipated return on capital, the need of the seller to dispose of its publishing assets, the value of owning musical compositions to other divisions of the buyer, whether the buyer has a network of wholly owned or affiliated publishing companies around the world into which the catalogue can be integrated, the relative worth of the U.S. dollar to foreign currency (which can either lower or raise future receipts), the current state of the industry, the existence of new technologies that may enhance the use of the catalogue, whether the catalogue represents a broad range of musical compositions or has a concentration in only one type of music, whether there are other bidders, and the anticipated ability of the buyer to promote the catalogue in new areas effectively, along with the additional monetary returns projected from those promotion efforts.

THE PROSPECTUS: ITS FORM AND CONTENT

The prospectus is the initial document forwarded to all potential buyers when a music publishing company or catalogue of songs is up for sale. The document can range in length from three to five pages for a small catalogue with few compositions to a small book of 200 to 400 pages or more for a major publishing operation. Though varying greatly in length and focus, the basic information contained in this document is similar for most sales, and the prospectus is normally sent only to a limited number of potential buyers—those entities that are known to be seriously interested and capable of financing the acquisition price. A confidentiality letter that mandates that any information disclosed is not be communicated to outside parties or used against the selling company is also usually sent to each prospective purchaser for signature.

BUSINESS SUMMARY

The first item in the prospectus is a brief history of the company being sold and its place within the entertainment industry. Items discussed include a company's prior acquisitions of other publishing companies, principal places of business, number of employees, and the total number of compositions (both copyrighted and uncopyrighted) controlled by the company. If the list of prospective buyers includes nonmusic entities, a brief primer on the main sources of music publishing income will also be given.

FINANCIAL INFORMATION

Income statements are given for the most recent three- to five-year period. In addition, annual projections for the future are sometimes provided, especially if there are current commitments or activity that will result in substantial future monies (e.g., if a publisher has a Number One song on the charts but has not yet been paid for CD sales, downloads, Internet streams [both noninteractive and interactive], or radio and television performances). The income statements list the gross revenues of the company, royalty or other contractual payments to third parties, advances and other costs, overhead, and net income (referred to as the "net publisher's share"). A more detailed revenue statement of the primary revenue-producing areas of performing rights payments, mechanical income, synchronization fees, print royalties, other miscellaneous fees, and foreign collections is also provided. The detailed area analysis lists specific dollars received by generic royalty source, as well as the percentage of the company's total income provided by each song revenue area.

Type of Revenue	2018 Revenues	% of Total
Performance rights fees	$2,814,000	42.0
Mechanical license fees	$1,608,000	24.0
Synchronization fees	$234,500	3.5
Print fees	$201,000	3.0
Other fees	$33,500	.5
Foreign earnings	$1,809,000	27.0
Total revenues	$6,700,000	100.0

LISTING OF TOP-EARNING COMPOSITIONS

A separate chart of the publishing company's top-earning songs is always included. The chart is usually compiled either as a listing of the top 25, 50, 100, or 500 songs in the catalogue or by all songs earning in excess of a certain annual amount ($25,000, for instance). These charts will usually reflect each composition's earnings over a period of years in order to give the prospective buyer an impression of how the catalogue has performed over the years. These composition listings include songs, television and film themes, and underscore.

NET INCOME AND EARNINGS HISTORY CHARTS

Although gross income figures are of interest to a prospective buyer, of utmost importance are the net income amounts. It is one thing to know how much in gross earnings is being generated by a catalogue of songs, but without knowing how much money is payable to third parties from such income (e.g., songwriter royalties, co-publisher royalties, etc.), it is impossible to determine what the catalogue is really worth in net profit terms. In effect, a buyer is not only purchasing an income stream but, more importantly, a stated amount of money that is left over as pure profit after all royalty participants have been paid. Because of the importance of net income as opposed to gross income, the seller will always provide the buyer with summary charts for a number of recent years detailing gross income receipts, royalties that were payable from such receipts, and net income that remained after royalties were paid.

Company Compositions (January 1, 2015–December 31, 2018)

Title	Revenues
#1 (song)	$749,321
#2 (song)	$621,483
#3 (TV series)	$368,501
#4 (song)	$314,238
#5 (feature films)	$219,452
#6 through #48 (misc.)	$1,548,000
#49 (song)	$28,556
#50 (TV series)	$21,750
#50-Song total:	$3,871,301

Depending on the sophistication of the seller's books and records, as well as the time and effort expended in putting together the financial aspects of the prospectus, the net income charts can be presented in a number of formats. From the buyer's perspective, the more specific the information presented the better. For example, if the seller is able to provide annual summaries of income by source (CD sales, downloads, noninteractive streams, interactive streams, public performance income, television and motion picture synchronization income, commercial fees, sheet music and folio revenues, home video, theatrical royalties, etc.), separated into U.S.-based and foreign-generated income less songwriter royalties paid or payable from that income, and with final net income figures on each category, the buyer will have an easier time digesting the numbers and formulating its offer, thus improving the chances of the negotiations being concluded quickly. The more information that is provided by the seller at the start of negotiations, the better it will be for all parties, because the more questions that are answered during the initial stages of negotiation, the more likely it will be that the talks will proceed smoothly. It is always better to give a potential buyer exactly what it needs up front rather than to provide incomplete information that will have to be filled in at a later date—a rule of thumb that should always be kept in mind when putting together any prospectus or catalogue information package for potential purchasers. An example of a one-year income chart is set forth in Table 16.1.

This type of net income analysis should be prepared for each one-year period being presented by the seller to the prospective buyer. The income charts can be very specific (e.g., a listing of the names of all record companies that have paid the seller any monies, rather than just one line that includes all aggregate record company monies), but regardless of the amount of detail provided, the charts represent the minimum amount of information that should be provided by the selling company to the prospective purchaser.

2018 INCOME CHART/EARNINGS HISTORY

Table 16.1

A.	United States Source	Gross Receipts	Royalties	Net Income
1.	Mechanicals (CD and download sales)	$2,000,000	$1,400,000	$600,000
2.	Synchronization (television, motion pictures, commercials, video games, home video)	$700,000	$400,000	$300,000
3.	Performances (ASCAP, BMI, SESAC, GMR)	$1,200,000	$200,000	$1,000,000
4.	Print	$140,000	$75,000	$65,000
		$4,040,000	$2,075,000	$1,965,000

B.	Foreign Source	Gross Receipts	Royalties	Net Income
1.	Mechanical	$750,000	$400,000	$350,000
2.	Synchronization	$100,000	$60,000	$40,000
3.	Performances	$600,000	$100,000	$500,000
4.	Print	$20,000	$8,000	$12,000
		$1,470,000	$568,000	$902,000

C.	Summary Source	Gross Receipts	Royalties	Net Income
1.	Mechanicals	$2,750,000	$1,800,000	$950,000
2.	Synchronization	$800,000	$460,000	$340,000
3.	Performances	$1,800,000	$300,000	$1,500,000
4.	Print	$160,000	$83,000	$77,000
		$5,510,000	$2,643,000	$2,867,000

CURRENT CONTRACTS

The prospectus will include summaries of all current contracts to which the selling company is a party, including all songwriter and recording artist agreements as well as all co-publishing, income participation, or administration agreements with songwriters or other publishing companies. These contract summaries can prove invaluable to the prospective buyer, as they not only contain an overview of the seller's current business activities and commitments but also can provide clues to future but currently unrecognized revenues.

FOREIGN SUBPUBLISHING AGREEMENTS

The prospectus will include a listing of all agreements the company has entered into with foreign subpublishers. Foreign revenue sources include performance fees, synchronization and mechanical fees, print payments, and all other payments due the copyright owner. Information provided for each subpublishing agreement includes the name of the subpublisher, the duration of the agreement, the territories covered by the agreement, advances plus unrecouped balances (if any), royalty rates, extended rights for cover recordings or new uses secured, and accountings. Any special contractual provisions are also explained. For example, a representative schedule might look as follows:

Subpublisher	Territory	Term	Retention Rights
(Name of company)	France	3 Years (1/1/18–12/31/20)	None
(Name of company)	United Kingdom	3 Years (7/1/18–6/30/21)	If a local cover recording is secured and reaches the Top 100 on the trade paper hit singles charts, the song will be retained until 6/30/23.
(Name of company)	Japan	3 Years (4/1/18–3/31/21)	None

FUTURE COMMITMENTS

The prospectus will also detail future financial commitments under existing agreements that will be assumed by the buyer if the acquisition is consummated. These may be installment payments due for prior acquisitions, weekly or monthly advances due songwriters currently under contract, and any number of other obligations required pursuant to the terms of the agreements being sold. A representative schedule follows:

Payee	Type of Agreement	Term	Advances Due
(Name of songwriter)	Exclusive songwriter	one year plus two one-year options (7/15/18–7/14/19, 7/15/20–7/14/21, 7/15/22–7/14/23)	Year 1: $3,000 monthly; Year 2: $3,500 monthly; Year 3: $4,000 monthly
(Name of songwriter/ recording artist)	Exclusive songwriter/ copublishing	one album plus three options for three additional albums, commencement date 3/1/18; one album released	$50,000 per year plus an additional $75,000 for each album recorded by the songwriter on a major record label containing at least 10 songs written by the songwriter

THE LETTER OF INTENT/SHORT-FORM COMMITMENT-TO-SELL AGREEMENT

Because formal acquisition agreements are quite lengthy and very time-consuming to negotiate, many prospective buyers, after having reviewed the initial prospectus but before any due diligence investigations are commenced, will request that the seller sign a binding short-form agreement that will require it to sell the catalogue (and guarantee that the buyer will acquire the catalogue), provided certain terms and conditions are satisfied. These short-form commitment letters (which range from five or six pages, excluding exhibits, to more than 25 pages) are essential for the prospective buyer, who may spend tens of thousands of dollars during its investigation of the assets being acquired, to ensure that the acquisition will be consummated. These short-form letters also afford the prospective buyer certain rights either to terminate the negotiations or to reduce the purchase price if certain elements are not what they were warranted to be (e.g., if the seller has substantially overstated its income, if certain litigation matters were not disclosed in the prospectus, if the terms of various songwriter agreements were misrepresented, if future outgoing advance commitments to songwriters have been understated, if the rights to certain important compositions have been or are being lost in the near future). They can also be very important for the selling company, as they provide security that a prospective buyer will not back out of the deal if all the information contained in the prospectus is correct.

Although these short-form commitment letters vary in length and in format, the following provisions are usually contained in all such documents:

DESCRIPTION OF ASSETS BEING SOLD

A general statement of what is being acquired (such as "all musical compositions currently owned by _____ Music") is always included. Any exceptions to the general statement (e.g., all songs written by a certain writer, any song that has not been recorded and released, any song that has not earned any income) will also be stated. If available, a list of the compositions being acquired will be attached as an exhibit to this commitment letter.

EARNINGS HISTORY

An earnings history of the catalogue (containing gross receipts, royalty obligations, and net income figures) will be attached as an exhibit, and the seller will warrant that such figures accurately reflect the income received from the songs being sold during the periods reflected.

PURCHASE PRICE

The actual purchase price payable for the catalogue (e.g., $45 million, $6.5 million, $350,000) will be referred to in the short-form agreement. In most cases, the actual net earnings multiple used by the buyer to arrive at the purchase price will also be included (e.g., eight times the average annual net earnings) so that all parties know how the purchase price is being calculated.

Payment of the Purchase Price. The actual method of payment will be specified, whether it is a one-time payment or an installment sale over a period of years (e.g., the total purchase price of $4 million being payable upon full execution of the formal purchase agreement or $2 million payable upon signing with $500,000 plus interest payable upon the first, second, third, and fourth one-year anniversaries of the signing of the agreement). Any "hold back" amounts that can be used by the buyer to satisfy any claims that might occur after the acquisition date will also be specified. For example, the contract might state that $1 million of the $4 million purchase price might be withheld for a period of four years to protect the purchaser from any claims that might be lodged against any of the compositions being sold.

Reduction or Increase in the Purchase Price. Since a buyer's interest in and commitment to pay a certain sum for a catalogue is based on how much the various songs have earned in the past, should it be discovered that the income history has been overstated, the buyer will usually provide that it can either get out of the agreement or reduce the purchase price accordingly. For example, the buyer might include a provision that if the annual net income figures have been overstated by 2% (or any other negotiated percentage), it will have the option to cease negotiations and terminate the offer. In the alternative, the buyer may elect to proceed with the agreement at the same multiple, an approach that would ensure acquisition of the catalogue but at a lower price. The seller, on the other hand, might demand that if its net income figures were inadvertently understated, the purchase price should be increased, an issue which should be addressed in the short-form commitment letter and not held for future discussion during the negotiations of the long-form, formal purchase agreement.

Minimum and Maximum Purchase Price Options. Occasionally, a seller may demand that if the purchase price falls below a certain stated amount because of adjustments in income figures resulting from the buyer's due diligence investigations, the sale agreement may, at the seller's election, not be consummated. The buyer, on the other hand, may demand that if adjustments in the seller's favor raise the purchase price to an amount in excess of the maximum figure that the buyer is willing to pay, the buyer can cancel the agreement.

Additional Purchase Price Reductions. If the acquisition begins with a binding letter of intent or memorandum of understanding ("MOU") with legal and financial due diligence to commence after signing, there may be buyer protective provisions introduced that will give the buyer certain rights to reduce the purchase price depending on what is uncovered in the due diligence.

Considering that many larger-scale acquisitions take months to close, the buyer may ask for the right to reduce the purchase price if the earnings of the catalogue do not maintain a certain level during the period from the signing of the letter of intent/MOU to the actual closing date when the agreement is signed. For example, there might be a clause that provides that if the net publisher's share of income generated by the catalogue does not achieve a certain dollar figure on an annualized basis during this period, the price can be reduced by the product of the shortfall and the multiple that was used to determine the purchase price.

For example, if the purchase price was based on the financial assumption that the catalogue had an annual net publisher share of $1,000,000 over the past three years and the net publisher share for the calendar quarter during the due diligence period was only $200,000 ($800,000 on an annualized basis), the buyer might try to secure a reduction in the purchase price under such a scenario. Since all calendar quarters are not equal, the seller would argue that such quarterly income was not representative of a full year's earnings and, depending on the exact language of the agreement, there would either be a discussion or an automatic reduction.

Holdback Amounts and Escrow Accounts. In most acquisition agreements, there is a percentage of the purchase price that is held for a period of time to cover any liabilities that might occur from a third party claim or a breach of warranties by the seller or the underlying agreements and the compositions being sold. The actual holdback amount usually ranges from 10% to 20% of the actual purchase price but can be more or less depending on the circumstances of the particular deal. For example, if the total acquisition price is $10 million, from $1 million to $2 million might be held. The actual amount is the product of negotiation, bargaining power, the results of due diligence, potential claims, and the condition of the assets being acquired.

The next aspect is the length of time that these holdback monies can be held by the purchaser. The norm is between one and three years depending on how comfortable the purchaser is with the results of its due diligence investigation and the potential liabilities that may have been uncovered as well as the extent of the warranties or guarantees given by the seller.

In some cases, a portion of the holdback amount will be released progressively if no claims have been received. For example, 25% to 50% of the holdback might be paid out to the seller if no claims have been received during the first year, second year, etc. but this is purely negotiable as many times the amount is held for the entire holdback period.

In many cases, there is a separate third party escrow account established into which the holdback monies are deposited. The escrow account may or may not accrue interest and, on occasion, is invested in safe securities. In other cases, the purchaser will hold the holdback amount in its own accounts and distribute it according to the terms of the acquisition agreement.

If there is a third party escrow agreement, there is also negotiation as to what the escrow agent needs to release the monies (e.g., signatures from both the seller and buyer, other defined and confirmable facts, etc.) and what procedures have to be taken if the buyer and seller do not agree as to the release of monies (e.g., court order, arbitration, mediation, final judgment, etc.).

WARRANTIES

Included in the short-form commitment letter are a wide range of warranties and representations by the seller, including statements that it owns the rights to the compositions, that they are freely assignable to the purchaser, that they do not infringe on any other compositions, that there are no "key man" clauses in any songwriter's contract that would force the buyer to hire certain employees of the seller in order to acquire the compositions, that the summary financial figures submitted represent actual earnings and do not include advances or other nonearned income, that the seller has paid proper royalties on all income received, and that, except as disclosed in the short-form agreement, there are no existing, pending, or threatened claims against the seller or any of the compositions being sold.

First-Tier versus Second-Tier Compositions. In some acquisition agreements, there is a distinction between what are known as first-tier and second-tier compositions. First-tier compositions are those that are significant earners as well as, in many cases, moderate earners. Some agreements define first tier as all compositions that represent 70% to 80% of the aggregate catalogue earnings over a period of time. Sometimes the definition covers every composition that has earned over a stated dollar figure (e.g., $5,000, $10,000, $20,000, etc.). Second-tier compositions are those that don't fit under the first tier category.

The importance of the two distinctions relates to the warranties and the amount of time that the seller's warranties and indemnification stay in effect. Since the buyer wants the seller's representations and warranties to remain as long as possible after the closing date of the agreement, the purchaser will concentrate on this aspect in its negotiations. Because the second tier compositions may be less important money-wise as a portion of the actual purchase price being paid, a buyer may allow the warranties to lapse sooner than those for the first tier compositions.

On occasion, the buyer will also allow the seller's warranties to be based on the seller's knowledge with respect to the second-tier compositions (the word "knowledge" and what it means and to whom it applies being a highly negotiated definition) as opposed to the stricter warranties on the first-tier compositions, which many times are without any (or very limited) qualification. Since the second-tier compositions, by their definition, are less important in the purchase price calculations considering they represent, in many cases, lesser-earning titles, there also may be a less intensive due diligence investigation devoted to such titles especially in the case of an acquisition of a large catalogue where time is an element unless a particular composition was a major or decent earner at one time but has not achieved such level of earnings in the more recent accounting periods being analyzed.

Limitation of Liability in Acquisition Agreements. Depending on the bargaining power of the parties negotiating an acquisition agreement, there may be limits put on the seller's liability in the event that there are breaches of the representations and warranties given by the seller which occur after the agreement has been signed and the ownership of the compositions transferred to the buyer. An example of this is an infringement claim being received by the buyer on a song that was acquired.

In many cases, there is no limitation as to the seller's liability for damages if an infringement is actually established (either through a final adverse court judgment or settlement). For example, if there is an adverse final judgment of $500,000 against the buyer related to a composition it acquired, the seller will be liable for the entire $500,000. In other cases where the seller has the requisite bargaining power, there can be a limit placed on the seller's liability regardless of the actual loss, costs, or damages resulting from the claim. For example, if the purchase price for a catalogue is $4 million, the seller might argue for a limitation of $3 million as its maximum financial exposure. Or the seller might secure an agreement from the buyer that the liability will not exceed the amount of the actual purchase price. For example, if the seller received $2 million dollars for the catalogue as the purchase price, the seller would not be liable to the buyer for any damages in excess of the actual purchase price.

Another tack by the seller to limit liability is to try to negotiate an end date to the warranties and guarantees made in the acquisition agreement. For example, the seller may request that its warranties will only last for a stated number of years (e.g., 3 years, 5 years, 10 years, etc.) after the acquisition agreement is signed so that it will have no liability if a third party claim is received after the agreed upon end date. A third way for a seller to limit liability is to establish what is known as a claim basket. Under this type of provision, the indemnifying party will have liability related to a breach of warranties or representations only to the extent that the aggregate amount of all losses related to the breach exceeds a specific negotiated amount (the "basket"). For example, a clause might read that the seller will only be liable for losses over $25,000, etc. with the buyer absorbing any losses less than the basket figure. If the basket scenario is agreed to, the buyer may insist that if the basket threshold is exceeded (e.g., if the claims amount to $100,000) that the seller be liable retroactive to dollar one of the losses.

This entire area is subject to the negotiation between the parties and is all part of the give and take related to such.

SUBPUBLISHING AGREEMENTS

Attached as an exhibit to the commitment letter is a summary of all existing foreign subpublishing agreements, including information on the territories covered, the royalty percentage retained by the foreign publisher, the term of each agreement, and retention rights, as well as whether any advances were received or are due in the future.

INCOME CUTOFF DATE

Because it is usually somewhat impractical to determine how long the buyer's various investigations of the assets being acquired will take, and the length of time that will be expended in the negotiation of the long-form formal acquisition document, a specific cutoff-of-income date will be contained in the short-form agreement. In effect, the parties will agree to a specific date (usually at the end of a calendar quarter or semiannual period) on or after which the buyer will be entitled to all income receivable from the catalogue. Under such a provision, any monies received prior to the cutoff date will remain the seller's property (subject to the payment of royalties to songwriters and other royalty participants), and any monies received on or after the cutoff date will be the property of the buyer (again subject to the payment of all royalty obligations related thereto).

A sample clause might read:
All royalties, income, or other earnings of any nature, kind, or description in respect of the Compositions received on or after January 1, 2019, regardless of when earned, shall be the sole and absolute property of the Buyer. If any such sums are received by the Seller or any of its affiliates on or after that date, they shall transmit the same immediately upon receipt to the Buyer.

DEFINITIVE CLOSING DATE

To prevent negotiations, investigations, and drafting of the formal purchase agreement from continuing for an unlimited period of time, the seller and buyer will normally agree on an outside closing date (the date that the final agreement is actually signed and the catalogue of songs is transferred). If negotiations are still continuing as of that date, either party may have the right to terminate the agreement. In most cases, however, this right is never exercised, as an extension of time is usually agreed to; but it does put pressure on the parties to get things done as quickly as possible.

INVESTIGATING THE ASSETS BEING ACQUIRED

After the potential buyer has reviewed the seller's prospectus, and usually after both parties have either entered into a short-form commitment letter or the prospective purchaser has signed a confidentiality letter, the buyer will conduct both a financial audit of the income figures and a legal inquiry into the assets being acquired. This "due diligence" investigation can take only a few days with respect to smaller catalogues and up to months when the seller is transferring substantial numbers of copyrights. Because the conduct of the buyer's due diligence investigation and the nature of what it uncovers is one of the most significant aspects of any acquisition (as the findings will not only determine the final purchase price but also whether or not the acquisition is consummated), the following sections review many of the areas of discovery.

FINANCIAL DUE DILIGENCE

After analyzing the gross and net income summary sheets provided by the seller in its prospectus, the buyer's auditors will conduct a number of examinations not only to test the validity and accuracy of the figures represented but also to determine whether the seller's books and records were kept in conformance with generally accepted accounting practices. The auditors will examine actual royalty statements received from music users such as record companies, video distributors, and print companies; remittances from performing rights societies including ASCAP, BMI, SESAC, GMR, and direct licensing; and the royalties that the seller has distributed to songwriters in conformance with the agreements by which it (or any predecessor-in-interest) acquired ownership in the compositions. In addition, inquiries will be made to determine whether correct exchange rates were used with respect to foreign income receipts, whether monetary advances were treated as earned income, whether there exist any unrecouped balances on advances received by the seller, whether income taxes were paid, whether the seller used an accrual or cash basis in matching costs with revenues on its income schedules, whether any extraordinary one-time payments were included, and whether any income related to periods outside the years being used as the basis of the purchase price was received during and included in the basis period figures.

With this general overview, a number of the more important areas can now be reviewed in greater detail.

Songwriter and Other Third-Party Royalty Obligations. Since all musical compositions have royalty obligations related to income received for their use, a primary concentration of any audit is to make sure that all songwriters were paid their appropriate share of royalties. For example, a songwriter is normally due 50% of all monies received from the sale of records, CDs, and downloads of his or her songs; 50% of all income received by the publisher from television, motion picture, and home video uses; 50% of income or a set penny rate for sheet music; and 50% of income or a percentage of the wholesale price of folios. In addition to songwriter obligations, there may be other royalty participants such as a successful songwriter's wholly owned publishing company that shares in all income receipts, a recording artist who may share in a portion of the income from a particular composition, another publisher that may have co-ownership rights, and so on, all of which must be analyzed and checked to determine whether such parties were paid proper remittances. Obviously, if net income is based on gross earnings less all royalties due on that income and the seller has incorrectly calculated its royalty obligations, the net income must be revised to reflect those inconsistencies and the purchase price adjusted accordingly. For example, in the event that the seller lists a song as having earned $100,000 in mechanical download royalties but has paid the songwriter only $40,000 as his or her 50% share, the net income on this song would be listed in the prospectus schedule as $60,000. Because of the mistake, the buyer would reduce the $60,000 to $50,000, as the songwriter should have been paid an extra $10,000. Thus, rather than the buyer's paying a purchase price multiple on an inflated net income figure (e.g., 8 × $60,000 = $480,000), the buyer would apply its multiple on the contractually correct figure (e.g., 8 × $50,000 = $400,000). In addition, if the songwriter were signed to a co-publishing agreement, the royalty percentages would have to reflect the terms of such an agreement (for example, the writer might be entitled to 75% of certain income rather than 50%).

Extraordinary Out-of-Period Audit Recoveries. In the normal course of business, audit recoveries will be received from record companies and other music users on a periodic basis. Such audits are a way of life and, as received by the seller, will be also received by the buyer. Because these normal audit recoveries, which always relate to monies that should have been paid in prior periods, are standard in the publishing business, most are treated as legitimate income received during the purchase price base period. In the case of substantial recoveries that relate to a number of out-of-period years, however, the buyer usually demands deletion of such income. For example, if $50,000 from an audit was received in 2018 for album sales and income that should have been remitted in 2013 (a period not part of the base years on which the acquisition multiple is being applied), the buyer would naturally object to such receipts being included in the purchase price computations or, at least, request a discounting of such larger-than-usual audit recoveries.

Special Performing Rights Distributions. For many decades, performing rights organizations have distributed royalties over and above their normal quarterly remittances that reflected positive adjustments in past license fees paid by certain music broadcasters. These "special distributions," normally the result of retroactive settlements with a user, or favorable court decisions regarding the past fees of a user, represent monies that should have been paid in the past. Because these monies are reflected on a music publisher's income reports during the year they are received (with no reference to when they should have been received), all or a portion of such special distribution income may relate to periods prior to the years on which the purchase price multiple is being applied. Considering that some of these distributions are substantial and can dramatically alter the price being paid for a catalogue, this area represents a main focus of a buyer's financial due diligence game plan. This same principle applies to negative adjustments to income that has been received in the past by the seller.

Litigation and Settlement Recoveries. Because litigation and settlements are part of the business of publishing, any recoveries from industry-wide or individual law suits or settlements must be analyzed since this type of income is included in the earnings of the catalogue being acquired. If these recoveries represent one-time payments which will not occur again, the buyer may want to delete (or reduce) the monies from the earnings on which the purchase price multiple is being applied.

Advances. Because all music publishing acquisitions are based on earnings, the financial due diligence investigation will concentrate a portion of its inquiries in discovering whether advances were received by the seller and treated as earnings in its prospectus. In the music industry, it is fairly common for a music publisher to receive an advance from a music user or other licensee, which can be recouped from royalties earned in the future. For example, if a subpublisher in Germany wants to represent a U.S. publisher's catalogue in Germany, the amount of any advance being offered may be an important part of a U.S. publisher's agreeing to such representation. The due diligence investigation is designed to uncover the existence of such advances and determine what portion of any advances were earned back during the purchase price basis periods. Obviously, if an advance of $100,000 was received in 2018 and only $29,000 was actually earned in that year, the purchaser would want to apply the price multiple only on the $29,000 in earnings and not on the full $100,000. In addition, financial due diligence will also determine what portion of any advance remains unrecouped, since the buyer will not receive any income from the party that paid the advance until full recoupment has been achieved.

Matching Income with Royalty Obligations. As previously discussed in the analysis of cash versus accrual basis accounting, one of the main examinations centers on the matching of income received during a particular year with the royalty obligations that are due on that income. For example, if $40,000 was received by the seller for download, CD, or other mechanical royalty sales of a specified composition, the buyer's auditors will review the royalty provisions of the underlying songwriter's agreement, determine what percentage of receipts should have been paid to the songwriter, and then match their conclusions with the amounts that the seller actually remitted to the writer. In the event of any discrepancy, an adjustment will be made in the seller's net income figures, which will then be reflected in the purchase price computation.

Pipeline Income. An extremely important part of financial due diligence is the buyer's analysis of how much money has been earned by the compositions being acquired but has not yet been received by the seller. This type of information and its accuracy can sometimes make or break a deal. For example, because many royalty sources pay the music publisher monies months after they are actually earned, if there has been substantial recent performance and sales activity on the catalogue, the resulting earnings will be payable to the buyer, which makes the acquisition more attractive. On the other hand, if a catalogue's earnings are diminishing or if major chart activity royalties have already been received and there is not much money in the pipeline that will be payable to the buyer after the acquisition takes place, the buyer may reduce or revise its offer.

LEGAL DUE DILIGENCE

In conjunction with the buyer's financial specialists, the buyer's attorneys will simultaneously conduct their own due diligence investigation of the rights being acquired. This due diligence can be handled by examining hard copies of documents, going into a secure Internet data room, or a combination of both. Considering the complexities of the music industry, the types of agreements entered into, and the domestic and foreign laws that control the rights of the parties in this area, legal due diligence is an extremely time-consuming matter that requires sophisticated expertise and is best left to seasoned professionals. Because of the size of many of the catalogues being purchased and the impossibility of checking all agreements on each of the songs being acquired within a limited amount of time, the primary focus of efforts is normally on the compositions that earn substantial amounts of money each year (the "top earners"), with a secondary focus on songs with moderate earnings and a test-basis focus on the remaining compositions.

Included in the legal due diligence investigation are a review and analysis of the copyright registrations of each composition; the underlying terms of the agreements through which rights were initially acquired from the songwriters or other copyright owners; the completeness of all song files; securement of renewal rights; validity of chain of title to the compositions; existence of any liens or mortgages; restrictions on licensing for certain media; pending, threatened, or existing litigation; past lawsuits and settlements that may have an effect on future rights; the terms and duration of all license agreements and foreign subpublishing commitments; actual and possible reversion and termination rights in and to the compositions; royalty provisions of songwriter and other third-party income participation agreements; assignability of the compositions; existence of any "key man" clauses; and a wide range of other issues related to ownership, duration of rights, impediments, restrictions including songwriter approvals over uses, transferability, and future promotability of the compositions being acquired.

COPYRIGHT PROTECTION AND MUSICAL COMPOSITIONS.

The 1909 Copyright Act, the 1976 Copyright Revision Act, and the 1998 Sonny Bono Copyright Act form the basis of a music publisher's ownership and control of compositions, as well as the duration of that ownership. Without knowing the basics of the 1909, 1976, and 1998 laws and what effect they have on a specific catalogue, a prospective buyer could easily overpay or a seller undersell in any given purchase-and-sale transaction involving musical compositions.

Copyright Considerations in a Sale. In looking at a catalogue, one has initially to determine the term of copyright years remaining on any given composition in the catalogue. Most of the major acquisitions concluded over the past 10 years have involved publishing companies containing a combination of old copyrights (those written prior to January 1, 1978), new copyrights (those written on or after January 1, 1978), and works for hire (primarily film and television background music scores written during both periods). The 1909, 1976, and 1998 laws treat all of these works differently as to the duration of the "copyright monopoly." Although this area is a complex one, some basic rules should be borne in mind.

Works Written Prior to January 1, 1978. Under the 1909 law, these compositions had a U.S. copyright life of 28 years from registration or publication, plus an additional 28 years of copyright protection if a renewal was applied for on a timely basis. Under the 1976 and then the 1998 law, any work still in its first term of copyright received a renewal term of an additional 67 years rather than 28 years. For works already in their renewal term, an additional 39 years of copyright protection was added by the new laws to the 56-year duration provided by the old law—in effect, giving songs 95 years of protection in the United States.

Works Written Commencing January 1, 1978. For compositions written on or subsequent to January 1, 1978, the duration of U.S. copyright protection lasts for 70 years after the death of the composer or author of a composition, a revision that brings domestic protection in line with the laws of many foreign countries.

Works Made for Hire. Most motion picture and television background music scores and themes are "works made for hire" and vest the copyright in the employer rather than the creator. A written agreement between the creator and the employer specifying that the work is a work made for hire is necessary. Under the 1998 law, the term of copyright for this type of work is 120 years from the writing of the composition or 95 years from its publication, whichever terminal date is earlier. The 1909 law treated these works similarly to all other music copyrights (28-year term plus 28-year renewal), with the exception that only the employer had the right to apply for the renewal.

Uncopyrighted and Unpublished Pre-1978 works. Under the 1998 law, if a composition was written prior to 1978 but was neither published nor registered for copyright before that date, the applicable term of copyright protection became the life of the writer plus 70 years, with a guarantee of at least 45 years of protection.

Countries Outside the United States. Pursuant to the laws of a majority of countries throughout the world, the term of copyright lasts for the life of the writer plus a minimum of 70 years, a factor that in many cases provides for identical copyright protection for compositions written on or after January 1, 1978, in countries outside the United States and in the United States.

Copyright Searches. So that the buyer knows exactly what has been registered in the U.S. Copyright Office on all important compositions, it may request a search of all copyright records that will provide a listing of all registrations, renewals, songwriter and copyright-owner information, assignments, conflicting claims, identity of assignors and assignees of rights, mortgages, liens, security interest agreements, notices of use, registration corrections or amendments, and any and all other documents that have been recorded and the dates thereof. Owing to the expense of such a procedure, the search is normally done on only the top-earning compositions, with test searches performed on certain selected compositions, but depending on a buyer's concerns or the lack of complete information contained in a seller's files, searches may be done on substantial numbers of compositions in the catalogue. Because the documents registered in the Copyright Office are the basis of the rights being assigned to a buyer and can have profound effects not only on the duration of rights and full enjoyment of such rights but also on a purchaser's ability to receive a fair return on its investment, inquiries in this area are of the utmost importance.

SONGWRITER AGREEMENTS

A review will be made of all underlying agreements whereby the seller or any predecessor-in-interest acquired the rights to the musical compositions being sold. In this regard, particular attention will be made to the provisions detailing the nature of the rights granted, the term of such rights, whether copyright renewal has been secured, restrictions on how a publisher can exploit the compositions, royalty participation, assignability of the rights, and advances that may be due. Since innumerable variations may be contained in songwriter agreements, nothing can be taken for granted even if the seller has warranted that all agreements are "form contracts." For example, one contract may provide that any assignment of rights be conditioned on the songwriter's approval or that any sale of a composition can be made only if it is part of a sale of substantially all of a publisher's assets; another might have restrictions as to how a song can be licensed; another may call for certain reversion rights if a recording is not secured within a specified period of time; and another may provide for certain restrictions on the fees chargeable by collection agents or foreign representatives.

SUBPUBLISHING AGREEMENTS

Because income from territories outside the United States can be substantial, the buyer will also analyze all of the seller's commitments in foreign territories so that a determination can be made as to the availability of administration and exploitation rights in and to the catalogue overseas. For example, the buyer will produce a country-by-country schedule that includes the term of each agreement, whether there are any retention rights after expiration of the contract term, royalty percentages retained by the subpublisher for all types of income, and any other clauses that may affect the rights of the buyer with respect to future exploitation of the acquired assets and the ability to change representatives in a particular territory.

FUTURE OBLIGATIONS

The legal due diligence inquiry will also concentrate on all existing agreements that have some form of future commitment that will be assumed by the buyer. For example, if the seller has a large number of songwriters or other third parties under contract to whom weekly, monthly, yearly, or bonus activity advances are due (some of which are guaranteed versus optional), the seller needs to know the exact nature of such obligations in order to formulate effectively its acquisition price and the terms related thereto.

GUARANTEED FUTURE RECEIPT OF INCOME COMMITMENTS

Another reason for an exhaustive review of all of the seller's current agreements is to determine the nature and amount of income that may be due the seller from third parties after the acquisition has been finalized. For example, there may be guaranteed advances from foreign subpublishers, or print companies, option payments due from advertising agencies for the use of songs in commercials, predetermined fees for home video releases after certain sales plateaus have been achieved, guaranteed performance income from television and motion picture synchronization licenses, forthcoming releases of songs in the catalogue, future motion picture, television series, advertising commercial and video game commitments, and any number of other income-generating guarantees, including litigation (including class action or industry suits) that will benefit the buyer after control of the catalogue has been assumed.

EXPIRING AGREEMENTS, REVERSIONS, AND TERMINATIONS

One of the most vital inquiries involved in any purchase-and-sale agreement has to do with the analysis of all agreements and related compositions that generated income during the base period years and that either terminate or expire at some time in the near future. For example, certain top-earning compositions may have created substantial earnings during the period on which the purchase multiple is being applied, but a review of the seller's rights to such compositions might reveal that a number of those compositions will be lost to the seller because of the expiration of underlying contracts (such as an administration agreement expiring two years after the effective acquisition date), termination rights (such as a writer or estate reclaiming the final 39 or 20 years of extended U.S. copyright or recapturing rights after 35 years), foreign reversions, failure to secure renewal rights, compositions entering the public domain, and any number of other actual or potential reasons. Obviously, if a buyer is paying a multiple of 6, 8, 12, 16, or 18 on earnings (with different multiples being placed sometimes on different portions of the catalogue) during a specified period for compositions that it is going to lose, adjustments on such income (and, in some cases, total deletion) will be demanded in the final negotiations that determine the actual purchase price. One of the worst things that can happen in this entire field is for a buyer to acquire very important income-generating compositions for a substantial price and then find out that it controls the rights to those compositions for only a short period of time or, even more disastrous, that it doesn't control the rights at all. Because of the enormous amounts of money being paid for music publishing assets and the value of continued ownership of those assets after acquisition, investigations conducted in this area are the crux of any buyer's due diligence inquiries.

COMPANY VERSUS ASSET SALE

Most acquisition agreements involve the sale of compositions and, if there are active songwriter agreements, the agreements themselves and the services of the songwriters signed under those contracts. In some cases, however, the seller is not only selling the musical composition–related assets but the legal entities as well.

These type of company plus assets transactions are more complex than purely buying copyrights (since the buyer might be held liable or responsible for matters unrelated to the compositions and underlying rights agreements) and the following are just some of the many additional areas that have to be investigated by the buyer and its due diligence team.

For example, the following areas of inquiry (and these are by no means all-inclusive) will be reviewed in due diligence:

- Certificates of organization formation (depending on the entity) and bylaws;
- Minutes of stockholder directors and other executive meetings;
- Lists of current and former subsidiaries;
- List of jurisdictions in which the seller does business;
- List of entities in which the seller owns an interest plus terms;
- An explanation and backup for all short or long term debt or other financial commitments;
- Copies of UCC financing statements;
- Lines of credit;
- Loan or other financing agreements either with third parties or intercompany;
- Letters of legal counsel to auditors relating to possible claims;
- Employee contracts including guaranteed bonus or other incentive payments;
- Employee benefit plans, including profit sharing, pension, or retirement as well as present and future funding responsibility;
- Leases and ownership documents regarding property if such is being acquired;

- Federal, state, local, and foreign tax returns;
- Audits, both actual and threatened;
- Actual or pending tax litigation;
- Trademark, service mark, and trade name registrations and issues;
- Domain registration issues;
- Descriptions of current employee responsibilities, compensation, and severance issues;
- Insurance policies;
- List of bank accounts and signatories; and
- Past budgets and current budget with projections.

THE FORMAL PURCHASE AGREEMENT

In most cases, the formal acquisition-and-sale agreement will be negotiated while the financial and legal due diligence investigations are taking place. By taking such an approach, the buyer and seller will be assured that the actual signing will occur within a reasonable time after the due diligence reports have been finalized and negotiated. In some cases, however, the formal agreement will be prepared only after the results of the inquiries have been completed and any disputes arising from the inquiries have been resolved. This formal document, which is rarely less than 30 pages without exhibits, and can be hundreds of pages with exhibits, will recite, in expanded language, most of the elements contained in the short-form commitment letter and will also contain a number of other detailed provisions covering not only what was found in the due diligence inquiries but also additional clauses dealing with a number of possible occurrences.

Some of the major areas that are covered in virtually all music publishing acquisition-and-sale agreements are as follows:

A description of the assets being acquired.

The purchase price and how it is to be paid.

The effective closing date on which the buyer will take over the catalogue.

The effective date on which the buyer will be entitled to receipt of income from the catalogue.

Warranties and representations by the selling company (e.g., that the songs are original, that the songs being acquired are validly owned by the seller; that there are no infringement claims; that all songwriter agreements are in full force and effect; that none of the compositions have been lost to public domain; that the seller has not made any untruthful statements; that there are no advances or other payments due third parties except as disclosed by the seller; that all compositions will be owned for a guaranteed period of time; that no efforts have been made to accelerate the collection of income prior to the closing date; that there are no "key man" clauses in any agreement; that all tax returns have been duly filed by the seller; that there are no tax liens, security interests, or other impediments on the catalogue; that the seller has not declared (nor intends to declare) bankruptcy; that there are no finder's fees payable (and, if so, such are the obligation of the seller); that all songwriter or other contractual royalties have been properly paid by the seller for all monies that it received; and that all necessary corporate, partnership, or other legal action (including consents and resolutions) have been taken to assign the assets validly to the buyer).

- A specific transfer of rights, including any trademarks, in cases where the name of the seller's publishing companies are sold to the buyer. If the company names are not being sold or if there are any future restrictions on the seller either entering the music publishing business or using the former company names, such will also be provided for.

- The date on which all files and other catalogue information will be transferred to the buyer (usually on the closing date or within a few days afterward).

- In the event that there are unrecouped songwriter advances, whether the seller or buyer will get the benefit of any earnings that will be applied to reduce the outstanding advance balances.

- A guarantee by the seller that it will cooperate with the buyer for a certain amount of time after the closing to assist in the integration of the compositions into the buyer's system as well as answer questions or inquiries that might arise.

- Formulas and procedures that may reduce the purchase price in the event that the acquisition is an installment payment purchase or if there is a holdback of part of the price to be used by the seller in the event that certain warranties and representations are breached.

- A confidentiality understanding restricting the buyer and seller from disclosing to the press or other third parties (except for accountants, tax advisors, attorneys, or governmental agencies) the dollar terms and other sensitive provisions of the sale agreement.

- The governing state or national law in the case of disputes or interpretation of the terms of the acquisition agreement.

- The wording of the press release.

THE AFTERMATH OF THE ACQUISITION AGREEMENT

Once the acquisition has been signed by both the buyer and the seller, the initial event that occurs is the transferring of all files, computer programs, accounting books, records, correspondence, outstanding advance balance lists, sheet music and folios, demo recordings, file copy phonograph records, tapes, CDs, and digitized copies of released recordings, and every other item that will give the buyer complete information on the catalogue of songs purchased as well as all of the information it needs to effectively administer the catalogue in the future. Occasionally, the seller will retain certain royalty information in cases where it still has to process royalties to songwriters for income received prior to the closing date, but the seller will only keep such records for a short period of time to fulfill its obligations.

Simultaneous with the transfer of files and records, the buyer will, among other things, file the assignment of copyright in and to all the compositions acquired in the U.S. Copyright Office; notify ASCAP, BMI, SESAC, Global Music Rights, and any other performing rights representative in the United States of the change of ownership in performing rights; notify the Harry Fox Agency, if applicable, of the change of ownership of mechanical rights; notify all other organizations and companies that pay royalties of its rights to receive monies due the seller; and send all applicable claim information to its foreign subpublisher representatives so that reregistration can be effected to ensure that all monies earned outside the United States will be collected by or on behalf of the purchaser.

Additionally, the business and legal affairs, copyright, royalty, licensing, and financial departments of the buyer will go through the files and issue informative memos about the new catalogue to other departments (e.g., option exercise dates for songwriter agreements, contract summaries for agreements that have not been briefed by the seller, royalty rates, unrecouped advance balances, copyright renewal dates, restrictions on licensing songs to motion pictures, television series, commercials, video games, stage productions, or other media, advance due date schedules for active songwriters, minimum delivery obligations, infringement claims that have to be pursued, audits that have to be conducted, outstanding pending licenses that have to be followed up on, license requests which have to be answered) so that the new songs can be integrated into the buyer's catalogue administration and management systems. The buyer will also make sure that all prior and current registrations reflect correct ownership, writer, and administration information to ensure the correct flow of income and licensing information.

BUY-BACK PROVISIONS

Although very uncommon, an acquisition agreement may contain provisions that allow the seller to re-purchase a portion of the catalogue that was sold. The reacquisition will always be of a minority interest only (e.g., 15% as in the case of Time Warner's sale of the Warner Music Group recorded music and Warner/Chappell music publishing catalogues), with the option election having to be exercised within a certain amount of time after the sale was completed (e.g., within three years). The price is usually set by a predetermined multiple of earnings or, in the case of the Time Warner transaction, an amount equal to 75% of the then-estimated equity value of the 15% interest being reacquired but not less than a pro-rata share (i.e., 15%) of the original buyer's equity purchase price reduced by a pro-rata share of cash distributions. A buy-back option may also occur if the original buyer enters into a merger agreement with another major music entity within a certain period of time after the sale.

TERM PLUS REVERSION ACQUISITIONS

On occasion, although uncommon, an acquisition may have a specified term to it rather than a life of copyright assignment of rights. For example, a publisher might buy a catalogue for life of a copyright but with a proviso that there will be a reversion right to the seller at the end of a stated period of time if the catalogue achieves certain prenegotiated financial results. For example, if a seller has a certain reluctance as to selling the catalogue, a deal might be structured that will provide the seller the ability to get the catalogue back in a certain number of years provided the buyer's long-term financial expectations have been met. As an illustration, the buyer might agree that if after a set date (e.g., 25 years, 30 years, etc.) the catalogue has earned at least 150% of the purchase price that was paid for the catalogue, that there will be either a full or partial reversion of the rights acquired.

Another area where such specified term acquisitions occur involves U.S. termination rights, since it is not uncommon for a publisher to acquire these termination rights for a set period of time (e.g., 10 years, 15 years, etc.) with a reversion to the songwriter subsequent to such date. The value in this type of approach is that, regardless of the fact that the rights being acquired have a limited term, the writer may feel more comfortable in selling the rights knowing that at some point in time they will revert back. Obviously, in these cases, the purchase price paid by the buyer will be less than if the acquisition was for life of copyright because of the shorter rights term.

INCOME PARTICIPATION

Although rare, a seller may also retain an income participation in the net publisher's share of income earned by the catalogue in the future. Obviously, in such a case, the multiple paid by the buyer would only relate to the share of earnings from the assets being bought (e.g., on 90% of the net if the seller retained a 10% net income interest in the catalogue).

ACQUISITION EARN OUT PROVISIONS

A number of acquisitions have what is known sometimes as an "earn out" provision as an incentive for the seller to sign the deal. This type of clause can also work in a negative manner when a buyer is paying a premium but, in most cases, it represents a positive approach which rewards the seller if the value of the catalogue holds up or conforms to the future monetary projections of the seller, meets the expectations of the buyer, or even exceeds the earnings on which the purchase price was based.

In most cases, the parties agree on a specified annual average net publisher share of income that they feel is sustainable (e.g., $25,000, $200,000, $1,200,000, $20,000,000, etc.) or which should be earned to justify the amount of the purchase price. Obviously, this is part of the negotiations between the buyer and seller with both usually having different views as to what the final number should be.

Once the agreed upon net publisher share ("NPS") figure is agreed to (and this figure may be defined in a number of ways depending on whether the sale is of the publishing interests, includes writer royalties, pertains only to songwriter royalties, an income stream, or any combination thereof), the parties will formulate what happens once the actual earnings are finalized for future periods. This NPS figure (NPS many times defined as income received by the seller less royalty obligations, but this has a number of variations depending on the bargaining power and set up of the parties) is sometimes referred to as the "threshold," but terminology is not that important as the details are in the definition.

First of all, a set calculation period will be determined (e.g., two years, three years, etc.) since most of these earn-out provisions have a limited time frame. In many cases, the calculation period starts and ends at either a quarterly or semi-annually accounting period since this fits in with many royalty distribution periods but can be different depending on negotiations (e.g., two years from the signing of the acquisition agreement).

The next key is what happens if the NPS goal is achieved, exceeded, or not met during the time period provided for in the acquisition agreement. When this is determined, the next issue involves the ramifications for the seller and buyer, which could be positive, negative, or of no consequence whatsoever, depending on what the parties have agreed to.

In some cases, if the average annual NPS or threshold during the agreed-upon period has met the targeted monetary figure, the buyer may agree to pay an additional purchase price agreed upon in advance. This is sometimes referred to as a "Floor Additional Purchase Price." In addition, if the agreed upon NPS threshold is exceeded (e.g., if the targeted and desired NPS number was $300,000 and the catalogue averaged $350,000 in NPS during the negotiated calculation period), then the buyer might pay an additional purchase price based on either a prenegotiated figure or on a figure which is based on a multiple of the difference between the threshold figure and the excess amount (e.g., in the above case, $50,000).

If this formula is used, there is many times an overall cap on the amount payable by the buyer under this type of Additional Purchase Price scenario. For example, a clause might read that the extra purchase price payable cannot exceed $_____ regardless of the result of the calculations.

On occasion, if the acquired catalogue does not perform to the expectations of the parties, there might be some negative provisions inserted into the agreement (or, if there is a futures agreement that is part of the acquisition agreement), which will give some financial relief to the buyer considering its financial investment.

For example, if the buyer and seller agree contractually that the catalogue will produce income at a certain level for a specified period of time and such does not happen, the buyer might be able to recoup a certain amount or percentage of the purchase price from the royalties payable to the seller as songwriter or add an additional nonpayable but recoupable advance to the futures agreement. There are many variations in this area but the point is that earn out provisions (which are normally positive or of no consequence to the seller) can work the other way as well.

Obviously, if the acquisition does not have a futures aspect (e.g., a writer being signed to an exclusive songwriter or songwriter/co-publishing agreement which controls songs written in the future) or that both publishing and songwriter interests are being acquired 100% for a one-time purchase price, with no hold-back to cover the eventuality that a catalogue might not perform monetarily as expected, recovery by the buyer of an adjusted lower purchase price based on such nonperformance criteria may be difficult since there may be no assets to utilize for the debit adjustment.

COMPOSITIONS ACQUIRED IN THE FUTURE

On occasion in acquisitions that relate to songs of one writer or group of writers, there may be provisions which give the purchaser the right to acquire additional existing compositions controlled by other publishers which may revert to the songwriter seller during a certain specified time in the future. For example, an agreement might state that if other songs revert to the selling party during a period of ten (10) years after the sale, the acquiring company will have the right to make those songs part of the original acquisition provided certain agreed upon acquisition payments are made.

There are many variations in this area but they all include an agreed upon multiple of the net publisher's share of income generated by the newly acquired compositions over a period of time with reductions if these songs cannot be owned by the purchaser for a guaranteed amount of time. Sometimes these arrangements are on a guaranteed firm commitment basis where the purchaser must acquire the compositions, and other times on an option basis where the acquired publisher has the right to acquire or not acquire.

DIVESTITURE OF ACQUIRED ASSETS

It has become somewhat common in recent years for a music publishing company, depending on its size and market share, to be required to divest itself of some of the music assets that is has acquired in order for it to buy additional catalogues of musical compositions. This sale of assets is many times dictated by the anti-trust or competition authorities in various countries of the world as a condition for the acquisition to be approved. For example, if, as a result of an acquisition, the market share of a company becomes large enough in a particular territory or territories to be deemed monopolistic or afforded a dominant, anti-competitive position in relation to other publishing companies, it may be required to sell a portion of the assets that were acquired to competitors. In certain instances, this may entail selling off the rights to certain portions of the acquired catalogue on a worldwide basis and, in others, on a specific territory-by-territory basis.

MERGERS

There has been a recent trend for companies to merge, as opposed to a company buying another company or its assets. In evaluating the worth of the companies being merged, which has a direct effect on who controls the merger and whether or not the shareholders approve, the procedures and due diligence inquiries that take place in an acquisition apply in the same manner to a merger.

SECURITIZATION

An alternate way for writers and writer/artists to raise a large amount of cash without actually selling their songs and/or masters is securitization. David Bowie was one of the first to use this financing method. Securities are issued at a fixed interest rate and are backed by future royalties of a writer's or writer/artist's catalogue. In return, the writer or writer/artist receives ready access to a substantial amount of cash; in short, a loan repaid from royalties. In order to qualify for this type of financing, the catalogue must have a consistent royalty history and, if it is a small catalogue, it would usually have to be bundled with other catalogues to be eligible. Some of the upsides of this arrangement, as opposed to selling or taking a loan from a bank, are that the party doing the securitization retains the copyrights to the songs or masters (assuming the bondholders have been paid back at the end of the term) and may have lower administration costs, certain estate planning benefits, and a nonrecourse loan (one that does not require a personal or corporation guarantee). There are downsides, however, including possible sale of the catalogue if earnings do not achieve the financial returns guaranteed to the bondholders. Securitization is also available to music publishers.

As with acquisitions and mergers, the same due diligence investigative process and considerations apply since the prospective bondholders will need to know the past and current basis of the catalogue's earnings, as well as the prospects of future income and growth. Because of the complexities involved, one should investigate this approach thoroughly as it is definitely not for everyone.

U.S. TERMINATION RIGHTS

When acquiring U.S. termination rights under Section 203 or 302 of the U.S. Copyright Act, there are a number of factors that need to be addressed as the issues that come into play are many times not as straightforward as purchasing a catalogue when you receive rights and income from the asset immediately.

This comment is made not only if one is the current publisher to whom the termination notice has been sent, but also the representatives of the writer (or writer's estate if the writer is deceased) who has sent the notice as well as any third party publishers who might be interested in buying these rights once termination actually takes effect.

For example, under a normal sale agreement, there is a closing date when the buyer takes ownership and administration of the compositions plus all the income related to the compositions being acquired and there is not a gap as to when the rights actually vest in the buyer. As an illustration, the acquisition agreement may state that the transaction will close on January 1, that the purchase price will be paid upon or within a few days of signing and that all income received on or after January 1 (regardless of when earned) will be the property of the buyer (subject, of course, to any royalty obligation to songwriters, etc.).

In the area of U.S. termination right acquisitions, however, the scenario can be somewhat different and all parties need to understand the dynamics of not only the law, but of the financial and business realities related to these types of transactions.

Since a termination notice can be sent to the current publisher up to 10 years prior to the effective termination date, if the current publisher and terminating writer decide to negotiate an agreement under which the publisher would retain those termination rights, the publisher will be acquiring rights that it will not get the benefit of until a number of years into the future, a factor that the representatives of the writer need to also understand. For example, if a notice is sent in for a composition or group of compositions in 2017 with an effective termination date of 2027, if the publisher and writer enter into an acquisition agreement to acquire those termination rights in 2018, the actual benefit to the current publisher will not be realized until 2027 (nine years into the future).

In this type of scenario (which is not uncommon because of the 10 year maximum and 2 year minimum termination notice window provided under the U.S. Copyright Act), the current publisher might be paying the writer (or writer's estate, if deceased) an acquisition payment for which it gets no immediate benefit (other than the knowledge that it has secured the future US termination rights and that it will continue to represent the compositions in the United States after what would have been the effective termination date specified in the written notice). Because of this, a multiple of past earnings is not always used in isolation to arrive at a purchase price (unless the price is staggered and payable as individual compositions revert in the future, e.g., $_____ payable in 2020 when certain compositions terminate, $_____ payable in 2027 when other compositions terminate, etc.).

In many cases, therefore, because of the lag in the signing of the purchase agreement and the date that the acquiring publisher is actually getting the benefit of the administration of and income from such rights, a discounted cash flow analysis is used to arrive at a purchase price for the U.S. termination rights.

Another interesting aspect of acquiring and valuing U.S. termination rights is that one has to examine and segregate U.S. generated income only on a composition-by-composition basis in any analysis of past earnings that form a primary basis of how one projects the future income that is being bought. This is the case since the original publisher's right to continue to license and collect outside the U.S. income is not lost when rights are terminated under Sections 203 or 302 since the termination only relates to the U.S. Thus in evaluating past earnings as a guide to the future, the potential buyer must remove any foreign-based earnings from the figures being analyzed (although such nonterminable income can definitely become a factor in the negotiations as to how a final acquisition agreement is achieved and the terms thereof).

Since the current publisher retains certain income streams in the U.S. regardless of the termination (such as mechanical income derived from licenses issued prior to the effective termination date, as well as performance income from audiovisual licenses issued prior to termination), these retained use income streams have to be factored into the equation as well since this represents income which is not being lost.

In addition, since many of these acquisitions cover musical compositions written by a writer over an extended period of time due to exclusive agreements with publishers or writing compositions for different publishers, there will many times be staggered reversion dates depending on when each composition was copyrighted, published, or assigned to the original publisher. Thus a group of compositions might be reverting in 2021, another group in 2025, and another group in 2027, and so on. In any analysis, therefore, the acquiring publisher must factor in when the income stream and rights being bought will actually be received, as well as what income will be lost if the rights are not acquired and go to another publisher and the dates such income will be lost.

In a world of complexities, fluctuating market projections, and expectations (whether justified or not), it should be emphasized that one of the bargaining advantages that a writer's current publisher has over a potential outside buyer (who cannot sign an acquisition agreement until the date that a composition has actually reverted) is that the current publisher still retains rights to the composition or compositions outside of the United States since foreign rights are not affected by any U.S. termination. The termination right relates to the territory of the U.S. only.

In this regard, the current publisher can, if it elects, change the foreign income splits more in favor of the writer as part of the deal to secure the U.S. rights. For example, if a writer's original agreement provides that foreign subpublishers have the right to take a 15% fee on income received in foreign territories, the current publisher might reduce the fee to 10% or 5%, which would ensure that more royalties would be sent back to the U.S. (with the songwriter's share of these royalties being increased). Or if the writer has a 50/50 deal with the publisher, it might be changed to a 60/40 sharing of income arrangement in the writer's favor. There are innumerable variations in this area and the above two are only included to illustrate the fact that the current publisher can do things to benefit the writer contractually that a third party publisher who does not control the foreign rights cannot.

Another advantage that the current publisher has is that it can offer the writer an advance on the songwriter's future catalog earnings (both foreign and domestic) or, in some cases, even offer to buy such royalties if the writer or the writer's estate is interested.

ASSIGNMENTS OF WRITER ROYALTIES

Another way that songwriters and composers generate current income is through the assignment or sale of specific or all royalty income streams. These transactions take many forms with the two most common being (1) an assignment of royalties to a third party (e.g., a lending institution, a particular person or entity, etc.) as a loan using one's royalties to repay the loan and (2) an irrevocable assignment of a writer's income stream (i.e., performances, mechanicals, etc.) via a purchase agreement with a third party or the writer's current publisher. It should be mentioned that these agreements come in all shapes and sizes since a songwriter may elect to assign only a portion of his or her royalties (e.g., a sale of nonperformance songwriter income while retaining the songwriter's share of performance income) rather than all writer royalties. Or a writer might sell 50% of his or her songwriter royalties and keep the other 50%, etc. It is very advisable that any writer contemplating these types of agreements be advised by competent tax, business, and legal counsel as the effects, particularly in cases of an outright sale of all future royalties, can be significant to both the buyer and the seller.

For many types of songwriter and composer income streams, assignments or sales are permitted with very few restrictions. Because of the issues that may arise (terminations, rights of heirs, capital gains versus ordinary income, etc.) reference should always be made to the copyright law, estate law as well as the tax code in any of these transactions. In the area of performance income (ASCAP, BMI, SESAC, GMR) though, there are additional requirements as well as restrictions that need to be dealt with and considered as each organization has their own rules on assignments as well as sales.

As a member of ASCAP, a writer is subject to the Articles of Association as well as Rules and Regulations of the Society. The Articles state that royalties shall not be sold or otherwise disposed of except as the board of directors may from time to time provide by regulation. The board has approved certain forms of assignments, both revocable and irrevocable subject to ASCAP's review and approval. These include an assignment of royalties to a corporation 95% owned by one or more writer members, an irrevocable assignment of a deceased writer's royalties as long as all successors consent, irrevocable and revocable assignments of a living writer's royalties to a spouse, children, and parents, a family limited partnership, or a living trust for the repayment of an advance, loan or lien.

There is an additional form of irrevocable assignment of writer royalties approved by ASCAP for writers who have earned a significant of amount of income with specific requirements to be met for approval.

BMI recognizes assignments of writer royalties to third parties in certain circumstances, including to a lending institution or other person or entity who makes a bona fide loan which is to be repaid from BMI royalties. They will also accept certain irrevocable permanent assignments of royalties to a third party who purchases a writer's royalty income stream. SESAC also accepts assignments of royalties as does

GMR. Since rules and regulations in this area do change, one needs to consult with the applicable performing rights organization for up to date information.

As with any acquisition, the same due diligence procedures followed in a publishing catalogue sale should be adhered to in a writer income stream assignment or sale.

CONCLUSION

Whether a buyer's interest stems from the seizure of an investment opportunity, a desire to increase current market share, or a realization that its current ability to compete in a world of multinational communication conglomerates necessitates the acquisition of copyrights or additional copyrights, and whether the seller is motivated by a desire to monetarily capitalize on a valuable asset or a need for substantial cash infusion to fortify other divisions, the music publishing business represents an investment that rarely disappoints either the buyer or the seller.

CHAPTER 17
MUSIC, MONEY, LAWYERS, MANAGERS, AND AGENTS

C reative talent and skill are one thing; it is quite another to take that talent and skill and make them successful. That is the role of managers, lawyers, and agents. The very best ones can take you to the top both professionally and financially. The worst ones can take everything you have and leave you with nothing. Decisions and advice as to contracts, image, direction, and financial planning are some of the most important things that a creator must deal with. It is the job of these representatives to make the right decisions and do what is best to achieve the short-term and long-term goals of an artist's career.

LAWYERS AND THEIR ROLE

In a world of complex deals, the role of the attorney in the careers of songwriters and recording artists has significantly increased. In fact, in many cases, it is the lawyer who, through his or her industry connections, experience, and reputation, is the person responsible for securing the initial interest from a music publisher or record company. For example, the attorney many times is the person who makes contact by sending a recording of compositions for review and who suggests the overall terms of an agreement if the publisher or record company shows interest. And in instances where the attorney is called upon to negotiate and finalize an agreement that has been initiated by another, the ability to close the deal expeditiously and on the best terms possible is vital.

In a world of extremely complex contracts and business relationships, where one word in a 100-page agreement can mean the difference between financial security or bankruptcy, selection of an attorney is one of the more important choices that has to be made. It is even more important in today's entertainment industry, where the lawyer not only has to know the legal ramifications of a particular word, sentence, clause, or paragraph in an agreement (as well as how all the parts interrelate with one another) but must also have a thorough grasp of the practical, business, and financial ramifications of what is being agreed to by the songwriter, composer, or recording artist. This dual role of attorney and business advisor cannot be overemphasized, as it represents the crux of the lawyer's role in today's industry.

LAWYERS' FEES

Lawyers' fees can be structured in a number of ways in the music and entertainment industry depending on, among other things, the policies of the attorney or law firm involved, the nature of the services being rendered, whether or not the attorney secured the interest of the company desiring to sign the writer or writer/artist, whether the representation relates to the negotiation of one contract or a series of agreements, whether the attorney is handling all of a client's legal affairs or has just been retained for a single negotiation, whether the attorney is being brought in by either a client or law firm to handle only a specialized aspect of the agreement or to conduct all aspects of the particular negotiation, and whether the writer or writer/artist is a known quantity who is financially stable or is at the beginning of his or her career, with little money to spend for legal representation.

In most cases, the monetary compensation received by the lawyer is based on a set hourly rate, a retainer plus hourly rate, a flat prenegotiated dollar amount, a percentage of the advances or advances received under the agreement, a percentage of the earnings generated under the agreement, or a combination of some of the above methods.

Hourly Rates. Many law firms have a policy that charges to a client are based on a set dollar figure per hour of work done. For example, in the entertainment industry, fees can easily range from $200 to $750 per hour for attorneys, with less being billed for paralegals and other assistants. Law firms also charge their clients for increments of each one-hour period of representation on a pro-rata basis. If a particular lawyer charges $300 per hour, a phone call or negotiation that lasts for 15 minutes or less will normally be billed at $75 (e.g., ¼ of $300). In addition to the attorney's individual time, much of the research is given to paralegals or first-year associates, with an appropriate reduction in the hourly rate. All actual out-of-pocket costs such as copying charges, fax bills, telephone charges, messenger bills, overnight mail charges, court filing fees, courier bills, secretarial overtime, and so on will be billed to the client, as the hourly fee does not include such costs, also known as disbursements.

Because a number of items make up the monthly bill, they are either listed separately or categorized on the client's statement. For example, specific messenger fees may be itemized on a daily basis (e.g., $15 on 6/24, 6/26, and 6/29) or may be lumped into one aggregate figure (e.g., $56 in messenger fees for the month of June). In contrast to the categorization of disbursements, however, the fees charged by individual lawyers are always listed separately. A billing might read:

Attorney Name	Rate	Hours	Total
Primary negotiating partner	$400	7	$2,800
Secondary research attorney	$250	10.5	$2,625
Research paralegal	$100	6.5	$650

Depending on the particular law firm and history with the client, the monthly bills may include very general or very specific descriptions of the services rendered during the billing period. For example, the legend on the bill can be as general as "negotiation of recording artist agreement with _____ Records" or as specific as "telephone call to _____ re: Paragraph 17.05 of the proposed recording agreement with _____ Records" or "meeting with _____ of _____ Records re: warranty paragraphs." The generality and specificity of a bill depend on the business practices of the law firm and the needs of the client, and they should be discussed when entering into the attorney-client relationship so that all parties know what is to be expected of them. Law firms, however, do maintain exact records of their expenses and time, and can usually give the client as much detail as desired.

Retainers. Certain clients pay an overall monthly or yearly fee to a law firm, from which actual hourly charges billed during a particular year will be deducted. For example, a client may pay a law firm a guaranteed $1,000 per month, which keeps that law firm constantly available for legal advice during the year. This arrangement is similar to having someone "on call," with any actual charges incurred during a particular month or year being deducted from the prepaid retainer. This type of arrangement is common between lawyers and clients who have continuing legal needs throughout the year.

Flat Fees. A fairly common arrangement when an attorney is negotiating a single agreement for a client (e.g., an exclusive songwriter's agreement, a recording artist agreement, a record producer agreement) is the flat fee. Under this type of arrangement, the lawyer tells the client in advance how much the negotiation and representation will cost regardless of the amount of time expended. For example, the attorney may quote the client a $7,500 "all in" figure, and that amount will be the final fee payable whether the attorney spends 10 hours or 50 hours in finalizing the agreement. These flat-fee arrangements many times do not include out-of-pocket disbursements such as telephone, copying, and messenger services, and this issue should be discussed with the lawyer at the time one is entering into such an arrangement.

Percentage of Earnings. In addition to the hourly and flat-fee arrangements, some lawyers are also entitled to a percentage of the client's income under the agreement that is negotiated. Occasionally, these percentage arrangements apply only to the initial advance received under the agreement being negotiated (e.g., 5% of the advance due the writer upon signing of the agreement). At other times, the percentage applies only to advances that are paid during the term of the agreement. And at still other times, the percentage applies to all income generated by the agreement, regardless of whether the monies are earnings or advances, or whether the monies are payable during the term of the agreement or afterward.

For example, if an attorney's percentage is 10% of the initial advance and there is a $100,000 signing advance payable to the writer or recording artist, the attorney will be entitled to $10,000 upon execution of the agreement, with no further payments due. If the attorney's percentage is based on all advances received by the writer or artist during the term of the agreement and the client is guaranteed $100,000 per year in advances over a five-year period, then the attorney will receive $10,000 each year for five years (i.e., 10% of each $100,000 payment). In the case where the client and attorney agree that the attorney will be entitled to a percentage of all advances and earnings generated by the agreement regardless of when received, the attorney will receive his or her percentage of income as long as the particular songwriter or recording artist earns royalties from either all compositions written during the term of the songwriter's agreement or, if applicable, recorded during the artist agreement. For example, if a songwriter writes a hit song during the term of the agreement and it becomes a well-known standard earning $50,000 to $100,000 per year over its copyright life, the attorney who negotiated the agreement would continue to receive the agreed-upon percentage for as long as the composition earns income.

Such percentage arrangements take on many forms and do not necessarily mean that the client will not be charged an hourly fee or a flat rate for the negotiation and finalization of the particular agreement; that entitlement may be in addition to the actual legal fees charged for the services rendered. As with any representation relationship, it is advisable to clarify the financial aspects of the arrangement so that all parties realize what the potential monetary ramifications are in advance.

COSTS AND DISBURSEMENTS

In addition to the actual legal fees, other specified costs are usually charged to the client. For example, costs for third-party courier and messenger service, outside copying services, filing fees, deposition transcripts, and court reporters will all be charged. In addition, a number of other "in house" charges will also be included on the bill, such as reproduction charges, outgoing faxes, document preparation charges if specialists are needed, long-distance telephone charges, computerized research, and secretarial overtime, plus meal and travel allowances if late night work is required.

MANAGERS AND THEIR ROLE

Managers take on many jobs and faces. They can range from a full-scale controller of an artist's life and a comprehensive all-service person or company acting in conjunction with an artist, to a financial adviser and money caretaker, to a minor player attending to various aspects of an artist's career. Managers are exceptionally important for most artists, as they advise them on all aspects of their career, including recording contracts, booking agents, the venues and dates they should be or are performing, the choice of a public relations firm and program, and the entire game plan for the artist's career. They also bring in accountants and financial advisors for the handling of all of the money generated by the commercial exploitation of that artist.

The reason that most artists take on a manager is to make them successful, to handle all of their business in an orderly fashion, to respond to their needs, and to do everything possible to promote their careers. Managers look for artists that they can make successful and, of course, from whom they can derive income. Some of the qualities that an artist should look for in a manager are the ability to listen to what the artist is about and to perceive what the artist's actual talent is. The ability to communicate is also important, particularly where the artist and manager disagree as well as in the area of what needs to be done to prepare the artist for the marketplace. The manager should also be cognizant of all aspects of the business side of the entertainment industry and be able to bring in the best team possible to make the artist's career both a creative and financial success. The team includes a competent staff with not only the ability to handle all of the specific duties necessary but also good working relationships with agents, accountants, attorneys, record companies, publishers, producers, and P.R. agents, among others—all of whom will work in conjunction with the manager to further the success of the artist's career.

To be effective, managers should have a relatively small number of artists that they are handling, as each artist needs a good deal of time and attention. Managers do not have to have a major track record or large offices to succeed for an artist.

Many managers have small operations with a roster of two or three artists, with some of them signed to a major or independent label and the others unsigned developing acts. Other managers may have one successful act and one new band that is being promoted for a record deal. Still others may have no signed acts but still do a spectacular job in furthering an artist's career. And there are the major managers and management companies with numerous clients, some successful and others not, some formerly successful and others about to break big. The question whose answer all artists need to feel secure with is, "Is my manager dealing effectively with all of the parties and entities that are necessary to make me a success, and is my manager achieving the goals that have been set?"

MANAGER'S CONTRACTS

Although many managers do not have written contracts with their clients but only "handshake" understandings, it is always advisable to have a written contract spelling out the aspects of the manager-client relationship. A written document is not only good during the years the relationship is working but also important for both parties at times when things are not going well or at such time as the artist takes the final step of firing the manager. One common situation in this industry involves new artists hiring a manager who, through a good deal of hard work, achieves success for the artist. Because of the success, the artist may look around for another manager to take him or her to the next step, be advised by others to make a change, or receive offers from other managers to make a change. With or without a contract, lawsuits may occur. But with a signed contract, all of the parties will at least know the full extent of their obligations and whether or not those obligations were fulfilled.

Most management contracts specify the income areas on which a commission will be charged. Although this is a negotiable item, many contracts specify a percentage of all income generated by the artist. One of the important items that must be resolved is whether the contract specifies a commission on the artist's gross income or net income. Gross income includes the total of all income coming in, whether or not such items as attorney fees, marketing costs, recording costs, and so on will reduce the figure. Net income is the total amount of money after certain deductions are made. Net income contracts should include a specific definition of what is and what is not included in the net figure. Obviously, it would be to an artist's financial benefit to have a net figure contract. For a manager, a gross figure contract would be more financially rewarding.

The duration of most managerial contracts is for a specific number of years (three to five years), with others based on the artist's continuing involvement with a particular deal (a recording agreement, for instance) that the manager has negotiated. An agreement with a new band may be for one year, with four consecutive options on the part of the manager and a renegotiation of the entire contract after five years. For successful artists, the annual option to renew or terminate the management agreement might be at the election of the artist. Other contracts give both parties a mutual option to terminate. In reality, you could have a situation where a new artist is signed by a manager, becomes successful, and then demands renegotiation in the middle of the contract term. Some managers will renegotiate at that time; others will renegotiate only at the end of the five-year contract term. Termination by the artist can result in a negotiated settlement of a single payoff, a continuing involvement by the manager in deals already set up, or a declining-percentage arrangement whereby the artist continues to pay the manager a percentage of income but reduces that percentage each year over a stated number of years.

For artists taking on a manager, it is many times good to have particular goals set forth for each option period. If the manager does not meet those goals in any option period (e.g., sign the artist to a recording deal no later than second option period), then the artist is able to terminate. It is also advisable to have a "no assignment of contract" or "key man/person" clause in the agreement. The last thing an artist normally wants is for his or her contract to be assigned to a different management company or to be stuck with a management company when the person who signed them leaves. Artist consent should be required in either of these situations.

It is important that every artist-manager contract have a clause stating that "the artist has carefully reviewed all of the contract provisions with an attorney and is fully aware of all the consequences and provisions of the agreement," since if a relationship breaks down, the client may charge that the contract is unconscionable, that he or she was not represented by legal counsel (or not represented by competent counsel), that he or she was naive and taken advantage of when the contract was signed, and that the contract is therefore null and void.

MANAGER'S FEES

The commission that a manager normally charges runs between 10% and 25%, with 15% to 20% being the norm. Variations on these percentages usually pertain to gross or net definitions and any areas that are specifically excluded from commissions. For example, one manager may charge 20% on all income exclusive of monies received for recording costs, tour support, and the writer's performing rights income, whereas another manager might charge 15% of all gross income received plus any expenses that the manager incurs that are directly related to the business of the artist's career. Most managers do take their commission on all advances, merchandising, and tour earnings; some take it also on recording costs and other items. If a manager wears many hats, as many of them do, it is important for an artist not to be charged commissions on the nonmanagerial roles of the manager. For instance, the artist should not be charged a commission fee on top of the fees that come in when the manager is acting in another role.

Also, if the artist had income from ventures or careers prior to the manager's arrival (a prior record deal, for example), compensation from those projects should be specifically excluded from gross or net compensation formulas used to calculate the manager's fees.

It's always good for all parties to remember that the music business is a tough one and managers need leeway in their efforts on behalf of an artist. They are the ones on the front line and should be given enough latitude to do their job.

AGENTS

The primary job of an agent is to find and book work for the artist, including live performances, television shows, and movie deals. Booking agents work with promoters to figure out how to sell the dates for a particular artist, how to get guaranteed commitments for that artist, and how to advertise an artist's concert dates. A primary job of the agent is to make sure all contracts are in order and that promoters provide accurate attendance figures and accountings. The fee charged by agents depends on the agent's track record and what he or she can achieve for the artist. Fees are normally between 5% and 10% of what the agent books, but can be negotiated lower for a major act.

Film and television agents, on the other hand, represent score composers, theme writers, and songwriters whose work is primarily used in the movies and on television. The role of these agents is to get their clients work, and to represent them in negotiating their film and television deals.

Agent contracts vary; some agents espouse handshake deals, and others use signed contracts. The contracts in this field take many forms but normally cover only the writer's career in the film, television, and soundtrack world. The commissions usually charged are between 10% and 15% of the negotiated deal. The contract normally covers the items that are commissionable (e.g., writing fee, mechanical royalties, writer publishing income, etc.) and the areas that are not (e.g., performance right royalties, nonfilm and television projects, etc.), as well as the legitimate business expenditures to be charged to the client in furtherance of his or her career. Some contracts also contain provisions whereby the writer can terminate the agreement upon written notice if the agent does not procure a legitimate job offer within a certain period of time.

CONCLUSION

There are many individuals and companies involved in one's career including attorneys, agents, managers, business managers, bankers, investment advisers, mortgage brokers, media specialists, image consultants, financial planners, etc. All play a role in the success or failure of a writer or artist. And whether you use the services of only one of these "specialists" or you use them all (or more), you have to understand what each of them do and their cost. Always ask questions, always require sufficient answers, and always stay involved in your career. Success can be short-lived or last well beyond a lifetime. Good advisers are one of the main keys to success.

CHAPTER 18

MUSIC, MONEY, AND BREAKING INTO THE BUSINESS

Being a songwriter, a recording artist, or both is similar in many respects to any other business. Talent, professionalism, commitment, persistence, connections, luck, finding the right vehicle to get people to notice you, being in the right place at the right time, knowing the behind-the-scenes realities of how things work, having the right people behind you, and being with the right company are all part of the formula for becoming successful. And even though the music and entertainment industry is one of the most unpredictable fields in terms of who makes it and who doesn't, it is a world that has certain rules that have to be learned, as well as certain approaches and routes that have proven to increase your chances of breaking in. It is very rare indeed in this business for anyone to make it without years of working hard, networking, and making the right moves.

SOCIAL MEDIA PLATFORMS/MUSIC WEBSITES/ INTERNET

If you are a writer/artist or songwriter, one of the most common ways to have your music heard or your presence and/or brand recognized is through one of the many music-related websites and/or social media. There are many variations in this area as to whether or not there will be any compensation for downloads, streaming, or CDs and/ or vinyl sold from retail sites and, if so, how much. The submission agreements must be read carefully, but the Internet is a significant vehicle because it reaches millions of people. Creating your own website (including podcasting, downloads, streaming, and merchandise sales, song information, upcoming performances, branding ideas, reviews, etc.) can be a great promotional and marketing tool as well as a way to build up a fan base both locally and throughout the world.

In this area, there are a number of music related social media platforms and websites which, among other things, offer new bands the opportunity to showcase new recordings in addition to providing forums, blogs, classifieds, podcasting opportunities, and tour information. Other sites feature videos. Some sites charge for listings and others do not. Some sites provide writer and artist profiles, and others offer either paid or free downloads depending upon the directions of the artist. Others offer daily and weekly rankings based on the number of streams requested as well as reviews by visitors to the sites. Other sites provide for financial support from fans on an investment basis (e.g., individual tracks, albums, extras, credit thank-yous, co-ownership, participation in designated income streams, and any number of other variations), with some opportunities being short term, others being long term, others giving people insights into the creative process with no ownership interest, or anywhere in between.

Certain sites and social media platforms are sampled and monitored by both major and independent record companies (as well as television, motion picture, app, and video game music supervisors) because they have gained a reputation for featuring the best of undiscovered and unsigned artists. Being featured, highlighted, or discussed in blogs can also raise awareness about a writer's and artist's work.

Obviously, one of the problems with social media platforms and the Internet is that there are so many sites and it can be very difficult not only to attract people to your site or to your music but also to figure out which of the outside sites really have the audience (and, if applicable, assets) to have a real impact on your career (whether such impact is creative, financial, or both). YouTube, Twitter, Facebook, Instagram, Snapchat, and LinkedIn are some of the primary social media network sites or platforms with impact but one has to continue to monitor and research the marketplace in this area since it is a quickly changing world. These as well as other sites have many music sharing applications including the ability to upload and sell your songs and videos and create a musician or songwriter profile, as well as join groups with similar interests or tastes. It is vital that you understand the meaning of any agreement that you sign or any commitments that you may have to make to have your music or video appear on social media platforms and websites.

INFORMATIONAL AND REFERRAL SITES AND APPS

Because of the multi-faceted nature of certain sites or apps, the ability of being heard, recognized, or accessed has greatly expanded if your music is featured. For example, the availability of "Listen on _____," "Buy on _____," "Access lyrics on _____," "Video on _____," "Merchandise available on _____," "Interviews on _____," "How the songs or recordings were created and/or developed on _____," "Share with _____," etc. are just some of the choices that people interested in your music have. Taking advantage of such opportunities and capabilities is essential to securing and engaging an audience for your music as well as you as a creator, regardless of the competitive odds.

CO-WRITING SONGS WITH WRITERS WHO HAVE PUBLISHING DEALS

One of the best ways for a new writer to break in is to co-write a song or songs with a writer who is currently signed exclusively to a music publisher. By getting involved with such a writer, your name and your talent will be exposed to music publishers who will promote your work because of their relationship with your co-writer. If their efforts are successful, it could also lead to you being offered an exclusive songwriter's contract.

Your co-writer's publisher will usually try to publish your share of the song since it will be spending the same amount of money and expending much of the same effort on promotion that it would were it the sole publisher of the song. In fact, some exclusively signed songwriters have provisions in their publishing contracts that obligate them to use reasonable efforts to sign any co-writer. As an independent co-writer, the decision is up to you. It may give you the opportunity of being with a good promotion and administration-minded publisher.

BEING IN A PERFORMING GROUP

One of the best ways to succeed in today's market is to be a performer or part of a group. Your songs will be performed before audiences, some of which may be A&R people from publishers or record companies. And if the group is signed to a record deal, your songs will have a guaranteed outlet to the general public. Also, since many of the large music publishers are signing groups (and their writers) and financing elaborate demo sessions (or actually recording a finished album) in the hope of negotiating a recording artist agreement with a major label, writing for a performing band increases the odds for success.

By being with a band, you will also be able to create that finished sound that is many times needed when you submit demo recordings of your songs—an advantage that many writers, unless they own sophisticated home recording equipment and have the know-how to use it, do not possess. One has to be careful, though, when using one's band on a demo being submitted to a music publisher, that the version is not so unique that the publisher will not see the value of the song itself and its potential for other artists.

SUBMITTING SONGS TO MUSIC PUBLISHERS

At one time, music publishers had staffs that listened to unsolicited song submissions sent in by songwriters. Even though most of the submissions were rejected, it was a viable way for a songwriter to be heard. Because of an increased number of infringement suits against publishers by writers claiming that the melodies, lyrics, or ideas of their submitted songs were used without authorization or copied by others, as well as the growing cost of "errors and omissions" insurance for publishers and record companies, most established music publishers will not accept unsolicited CDs, files, or other recordings.

Such reticence on the part of the music companies to listen to new material from unknown writers is an unfortunate development, because it reduces the chances for writers without track records to get their songs heard. However, because of the ease of filing a lawsuit (whether legitimate or not) and the substantial cost of defending against even the most outrageous claims, most companies have chosen to review songs only from people they know or who have been referred by a person or firm that they know or trust. Regardless of this trend to play it safe legally, there are still some publishers who listen to unsolicited material, and it is best to call and find out about a particular company's policy before sending your demo recording.

DEMO RECORDINGS

For publishers that do review songwriters' demos, one has to remember to follow a number of important rules with respect to any submission. Of major importance is that the demo sound professional. This does not mean that one has to spend thousands of dollars in studio time and musicians, as home recordings with the right equipment can many times successfully convey what is needed. One should also not try to show off instrumental virtuosity on a demo if you're trying to showcase the song as opposed to you as an artist; the publisher is listening to the structure of the song as opposed to how a finished recording might sound. If you have an interesting arrangement or some important licks that really help sell the song, then include them on the demo.

It is also absolutely essential to get into the song as quickly as possible without a long instrumental introduction, which may test the listener's patience.

A good approach is not to try to overwhelm the publisher's A&R staff with 10 or 20 songs, because most company personnel do not have the time or patience to go through the entire catalogue of a writer's unpublished works. Pick three of your best songs (with the most commercially appealing or appropriate, depending on the needs of the recipient, at the start of the recording), as most professional listeners will form their opinion after the initial two or three songs and, many times, after the first verse and chorus of the first composition.

You should also provide the lyrics for each song with the names of all co-writers, their authorship shares, whether they are affiliated with another music publisher, and whether they are members of ASCAP, BMI, SESAC, GMR, or a foreign society. The writer's name, phone number, e-mail address, and website, if applicable, should be listed, along with any worthwhile reviews or credits. If you have had songs previously recorded or used in television shows, feature films, or commercials, it is best to include that information even if the songs may be owned by another publisher. The whole point is to give a company a reason to listen, and anything you can realistically add to who you are and what you have done can only help the first impression.

SONGWRITER CONFERENCES

One way to increase your exposure to the music industry and get to meet people actually in the business is to attend as many songwriter conferences as possible. Most of these one-, two-, or three-day meetings have panel discussions on the various business and legal aspects of music as well as creative seminars about writing, performing, and song reviewing. Besides the educational value of such conferences, you will get a chance to talk with other writers and industry executives whose only reason for being there is to help aspiring writers or performers. In fact, many well-known executives or creators who are virtually impossible to contact under normal circumstances are easily accessible during such conferences. And since the atmosphere is usually casual and receptive to the exchange of ideas, these conferences can be the perfect place to make connections, compare notes, ask questions, get advice, and most importantly, give you a sense that you belong to an industry that many times seems only a dream.

ASCAP, BMI, and SESAC are instrumental in organizing, sponsoring, or lending their support to these conferences, and a call to either organization should give you a good idea of what is scheduled for your area. In addition, trade publications, websites, the entertainment section of your local newspaper, and the various songwriter organizations throughout the country are all valuable sources of information concerning forthcoming music industry seminars.

SHOWCASES

For bands and singer/songwriters, one of the best opportunities for discovery is to be asked to play in one of the major showcase events held throughout the country. Many songwriter associations and music business conferences have a series of live band and writer showcases at their annual events; as these events are attended by industry executives from many major and independent companies, the opportunity can be a good one.

ASCAP, BMI, and SESAC have showcases for most types of music and performances in Los Angeles, New York, and Nashville and occasional showcases in other cities. Practically all showcase participants are chosen through submission guidelines or through ASCAP, BMI, and SESAC representatives actually seeing the band or writer perform. Some of the most successful bands in the country have been signed as new bands from these showcases.

ATTORNEYS

One of the most effective ways of getting an introduction to a music publisher or record company is through entertainment lawyers, since many have connections with music publishers and record companies, both major and independent. They usually have negotiated agreements with such companies on behalf of their clients, have represented the company itself, or have in some respect had a relationship with the company that enables them to submit a recording. The good music attorneys also have a real knowledge of each company from top to bottom and can usually contact the right person for a particular project—an asset that can not only save time but also give the agent or writer/performer a better than even chance of being heard by the right people. In addition, whether the response is positive or negative, an answer will normally be given more quickly if a known entertainment lawyer is involved.

Submissions from a lawyer are many times looked on differently, especially if the attorney has a good reputation or other clients with the company. Sometimes the person who submits a project can matter as much as the project itself.

Because most music attorneys are fairly selective and have strong feelings about what they feel is saleable, a writer's presentation must be very strong to get an attorney involved, especially if you expect the attorney to do the initial work on a reduced-rate or percentage basis prior to a deal being secured. Obviously, if you have a track record of some prior success, the entertainment lawyer may have an easier time deciding whether to represent you when there is no commitment, since a sales pitch to a record company or music publisher can be more easily presented if based on your past success and future potential. If you are an unknown quantity and not a performer or part of a band, however, convincing a lawyer to represent you on a speculative basis can be difficult unless your recordings and songs are extremely commercial or the attorney really believes in you and is willing to take a chance.

RECORD PRODUCERS

Because record producers are many times at the end of the process of selecting what songs are recorded by an artist and what songs are actually put on an album, having a producer listen to your songs is as good as (and sometimes better than) having the actual artist hear them. As in the case with many music publishers though, submitting a song to a producer is not an easy task. Because of the potential lawsuits that may come from listening to or having had access to submitted songs, many producers are even more careful than large publishers. Still, a number of them will talk to writers with an introduction from a lawyer or acquaintance, and persistence is vital in this area.

If a writer has done the homework (knowing who is producing what artist, what types of songs are being recorded, whether the artist did well with the last album or whether a change of direction is needed, the concept of the next album, whether the producer is a writer or has a stable of writers whose songs are used or is looking for some new blood, etc.) and has a professional demo recording and good songs, getting to the right producer is a possibility.

MANAGERS

As with entertainment lawyers, many managers have an ongoing entrée to the music publishers and record companies. Being signed with the right manager can almost guarantee the proper exposure of your songs to those who make the real decisions in the music industry. Good managers, though, are very selective in their choice of whom they represent, since they try to keep their roster of clients small and are paid not on an hourly basis but on a percentage of the monies earned by their clients. Because managers are normally responsible for all expenses and do not make any money unless their clients have some success, their decision whether to sign a writer is based on a combination of both financial and creative factors—a combination that many times does not bode well for the newcomer.

AGENTS

In many respects, agents fall into the same category as managers, in that they usually have good contacts with publishing and record companies and receive compensation based on their clients' earnings. Consequently, most agents accept only writers, artists, or writer/performers who they feel are promotable for paying jobs and will not waste their time by signing you just for the sake of having another person under contract. An agent who sees your potential and feels a real interest in your development can be a real stepping-stone to getting recognized, since agents can expand your horizons into other areas, such as writing for motion pictures and television.

Because agents are as specialized as any other professional in the entertainment industry, it is wise to contact only agents who concentrate in the field that you are pursuing or, if you are established, the area into which you want to expand. An agency that specializes in securing television and motion picture assignments for composers may not specialize in securing a live one-week stand at a local music club. It is extremely important to find out the direction and expertise of particular agents, since contacting the wrong one without doing your homework will be a waste of time for all involved.

MUSIC VIDEOS

Because of the widespread popularity of music videos as well as the ability to produce audiovisual performances with home equipment at reasonable prices, video presentations of a writer or writer/performer have given creators a new dimension for promoting their work. One of the values of a video is that publishers or record companies do not have to go and see a writer/performer to decide whether they are interested in pursuing a contractual relationship, as they can get a good feel by watching the video. And if there is interest after reviewing the video, they can then go see the performer in person.

A video can be especially valuable to a performer who does not live close to Los Angeles, New York, or Nashville. And because most of the major music publishers are now looking for writers whom they can develop as recording artists, a good video may not only help sell the song but also display the performance potential that many publishers are looking for. An exciting video can be a valuable asset to an artist's website or to an artist's reputation on social media and can be used as an entrée to other websites and platforms, and to many of the cable television stations in your area, as most public-access stations are always looking for new programming to round out their broadcast schedule.

CABLE TELEVISION

With the emergence of public-access cable channels throughout the United States, the songwriter/performer has been given an inexpensive vehicle to expose his or her music and talents to the general public and to those that make the creative business decisions that run the entertainment industry.

ASCAP, BMI, AND SESAC

ASCAP, BMI, and SESAC can be valuable resources and referral services for new writers and artists, as these organizations have people on staff who listen to recordings, go to clubs to hear performers, and generally give advice to thousands of writers every year. On occasion, they can also provide a writer or artist with a referral to music publishers who might be looking for the type of music that the writer is writing and record companies whose focus is similar to the artists. Also, these organizations' showcase series are some of the most successful in the country.

PBS/NPR RADIO STATIONS

A number of music-related programs affiliated with public broadcasting feature songs and recordings by newer or noncommercial writers and artists. Because of the industry respect for the independence and taste of those responsible for selecting music for these programs (which many times include unreleased demos by unsigned acts), having your recording broadcast can lead to television series, motion picture, and video game use possibilities, as well as record contract interest because of the professional entertainment audience who may be listening. A number of these stations also make their programming available simultaneously over the Internet or via podcasts, which can add extra exposure.

INTERNET RADIO

Because of the noncommercial nature of the music being streamed or broadcast on many Internet radio stations, this vehicle represents another opportunity to have your music heard. Many of these stations are very open to new artists.

PAYING TO GET YOUR SONGS PUBLISHED

One of the most important things to remember is that legitimate music publishers do not charge songwriters to publish or record their songs. Many companies do recoup a certain percentage of their direct costs (such as copyright registration fees, the making of lead sheets, and the costs of a demo recording session) from a writer's future royalties, but this occurs only if a song earns money. The writer should never be asked to pay any monies up front for these services.

FINDING THE RIGHT PUBLISHER

If a writer has friends or acquaintances in the music business, they will normally be able to give some advice as to who the good publishers are. Whether these comments are based on actual experience or "on the street" rumors or hearsay, if you trust the person you're talking to, it can be a step in increasing your information about who to contact and who to stay away from. Also, never underestimate your own intuition (especially after you have talked with various companies and their personnel); many times, you are the best judge as to whether there is a rapport, good support staff, and a real commitment toward your creative direction.

Another consideration that must be addressed is the type of songs that you are writing and whether they fit into a particular publisher's current catalogue. For example, if you write country music, it may not be advisable to submit your songs to a publisher who deals only in theater or motion picture music, unless it has a separate branch office in Nashville promoting country music. Conversely, if you write rock, a Nashville publisher may not be the right company to promote your song, unless it has a Nashville pop division as well as a staffed pop office in Los Angeles or New York. The same common sense applies if you are a hip-hop writer or if you create tracks. It is always helpful to look at the trade paper charts for all genres, as they will give you a good idea of who the successful publishers are in your field. Many of these trade magazines also have year-end issues that list the top publishers, artists, producers, and record companies in each type of music, which is a valuable way to narrow your focus.

Even though a company may not be currently hot in a particular category of music, it may be trying to get into that field or may have a prior successful track record in that field and might be looking for new writers, as opposed to buying into expensive deals with recording artists, writer/performers, or producers currently successful in that genre. A writer should always try to find out whether the company is serious in its intentions to expand its base and has the requisite staff to compete successfully in the new area before committing one's song and future.

Other important things to look for are the business, legal, and creative experience of the people working at the company, its promotion abilities, whether it has availed itself of the many advances in computer technology, the quality of its foreign representatives, its connections with motion picture, video game, and television companies, its relationships with record producers and recording artists, whether there are any such artists or producers on staff, its success in licensing songs for commercials, and its reputation as a responsive and innovative organization.

DIFFERENT TYPES OF PUBLISHERS

Music publishers come in many forms, shapes, and sizes, and all have particularly attractive qualities to offer to a songwriter or writer/artist. Major companies (sometimes affiliated with a record company and sometimes not) are usually full-service operations with experienced personnel in all aspects of music and business. Some of these companies are primarily interested in acquisition (buying other existing companies). These companies are bottom-line financial investment entities and may serve some writers or publishers interested in getting the highest short-term offer possible. Other companies, though major operations, try to service not only their old copyrights but also their new ones. Some of the major companies have a philosophy of buying into success and chart activity, whereas others try to develop what they have as well as what will generate their business in the future.

Most motion picture and television production companies have affiliated music publishing operations to control and administer the music used in their products. Some of these companies are among the most successful at signing and promoting new writers and artists regardless of whether their music is film- or television-oriented. Others are primarily collection agencies administering film and television copyrights throughout the world.

Many record producers also have their own publishing companies, either in conjunction with a major company or by themselves. A number of these companies are fully staffed organizations that sign new writers as well as writer/producers. Although very selective, these companies offer an opportunity for a writer or artist to be considered for any project the producer is involved in.

Most music publishers are what is referred to as "independent" in that they are not owned by large conglomerates, motion picture companies, television producers, or record companies. Their primary or sole source of income is from the commercial use of the songs in their catalogues, and their main thrust is the protection and promotion of the music they control without having to deal with any of the company policies that may be dictated by a firm's non–music publishing divisions. And even though these independents may not have the instant access to an affiliated motion picture, television, or record company, they can be very effective (depending on their reputation and promotion capabilities) in getting songs recorded or placed in theatrical films and television series, commercials, and videos. The selling point that most of these companies use is that they represent a more hands-on and personal approach to the writer and are usually very accessible to songwriters.

FILM AND TELEVISION

The film and television field is one of the more difficult areas to break into. Many of the composers in this field have a background of symphonic or classical training at a university or conservatory. For many years, the ability to compose and orchestrate for, as well as to conduct, a full orchestra was a necessity to working on many feature films and episodic television (one-hour drama shows, particularly). Changes in the musical tastes of producers and the public, the high costs of studio orchestra recording, and the low cost of professional home studios have enlarged the possibilities in this field for contemporary songwriters, as many shows look for a "current" sound similar to what is being played on radio. Writers formerly associated with the record field have written some of the most successful films and television series.

This field is particularly difficult to break into if one is not living in or near the major production cities. It is possible to get your first credits elsewhere (college films, small independent films for limited release, documentaries, webisodes, etc.) and then bring those credits with you to Los Angeles, New York, or any other city which has major production facilities.

Initially, every composer must compile a good demo whether as a file, CD, DVD, or other acceptable presentation format. These demos, usually more costly than songwriter demos, must show an ability to compose creatively and to create an interesting and experienced "sound." These demos range from full-blown orchestral scores to one-person electronic scores. Once a demo is completed, it should be forwarded to composer agents, music departments of studios and production companies, and the Los Angeles film and television departments of ASCAP and BMI. A composer's credits should also be enclosed. The likelihood of gaining entry with one of these recordings is slim, but it is worth a shot. The demo can also be used as a work sample that can be given to working composers with whom you come into contact as well as anyone else you may meet in the industry. One needs also to organize and catalog their music libraries for ease of presentation and licensing.

One of the best ways of breaking into television and motion pictures is to be accepted in the ASCAP or BMI film and television scoring workshops. These annual workshops are held in Los Angeles, where up-and-coming composers attend instructional sessions on the creative and business sides of film and television music, and finish the course by scoring, conducting, and recording a session. ASCAP, BMI, or the writer can then send these finished demo recordings to music departments, agents, and well-known composers who may be in need of new composers. For talented new composers, ASCAP and BMI are both excellent referral services if one's work is top-notch.

Some of the ways in which composers have broken into television and motion pictures include:

Composing cues for more senior or successful composers who may have a series or film and who, due to time restrictions or the amount of music involved, look for new writers to compose some of the cues, usually in the style of the principal composer. Quite a few television series, both network as well as original shows for local and cable television, have used this approach.

Orchestrating cues for established composers who have a specific film or television project. Many new composers get these assignments through contact with the main composer or because they have sent demos or are known to film and television agents, production and studio music departments, independent film producers, and college and university music departments. Orchestration for these projects is one of the best learning experiences that a composer can have.

Ghostwriting for other composers. Ghostwriting involves composing a score for another composer for a series or film but not receiving any credit for the work. Although the composer does gain composing experience, the credit as well as all royalties normally go to another person or to the main composer. This is a practice not encouraged by many in the industry.

For songwriters, one's publisher as well as one's agent can be instrumental in gaining an entrance into the field. Although many songwriters do not have orchestral training, the proliferation of electronic scores have put less emphasis on training and more on the contemporary sound. Some successful songwriters who have composed for major films have done so by creating basic scores and then hiring orchestrators to develop the themes and write the full film scores.

The most important thing that a new composer must do is to connect with as many people as possible in the film and television community. One needs to join organizations, attend conferences, and stay up on what film and television music currently sounds like. It is important also to study filmmaking and be familiar with the terms used in the business. As in most areas of the music business, a certain amount of luck and being in the right place at the right time is necessary. But you must have the skills and knowledge to take advantage of any break.

MUSIC SUPERVISORS

For independent artists and new bands particularly, connection with a music supervisor is a possible way to get your songs into film and television projects. Music supervisors are individuals (or companies) hired by film and television producers to choose the music to be used in their productions. Many times they are open to listening to new material as many productions, particularly independent ones, are looking for new music and sounds. Budgets also come into play as independents normally do not have the money to get well-known songs and masters and therefore are looking for a less expensive music option. Music supervisors normally reside in or near the cities of major production (e.g., Los Angeles, New York) and can be accessed via industry and trade publications.

VIDEO GAMES

Many of the major video game developers and publishers have in-house music departments that choose much of the music used in their games. These individuals are very open to new band and artist material and should be contacted with product. Other companies rely on outside music supervisors who are hired on a per-project basis. In the area of scoring, composers need the same skills as are necessary in film and television in addition to understanding and dealing with the nonlinear aspect of game scoring.

DEMO REVIEWS IN PRINT AND ONLINE PUBLICATIONS

There are a number of music-oriented sites or publications that review and rate demo recordings submitted by writers or writer/performers. Because many of these sites and publications are accessed and/or read by music industry and A&R executives, a favorable review can assist in securing some initial interest to at least give a writer some credibility that will help open the door.

CONCLUSION

With more and more songwriters, composers, and artists trying to make it, the competition as to who succeeds is more intense than ever. Staying focused, believing in yourself, doing the research, using all the tools available, having good representation or sound support group, making the right choices, acting like a professional, using social media, and knowing how the business works are all essential to getting your talent recognized and your career started.

CHAPTER 19

GUIDE TO MUSIC INDUSTRY ORGANIZATIONS

There are many organizations that serve the needs of various sectors of the music industry, and they can be of great help to professionals and newcomers alike. The following national organizations are among the most important.

ACADEMY OF COUNTRY MUSIC (ACM)

WWW.ACMCOUNTRY.COM
The Academy of Country Music is a nonprofit organization founded in 1964 to promote and increase the market for country music, with membership open to any creative or business professional whose work is related to country music. The organization conducts seminars, charity events, and showcases and produces the Academy of Country Music Awards show.

5500 Balboa Blvd.
Suite 200
Encino, CA 91316
Phone: 818-788-8000
E-mail: info@acmcountry.com

AMERICAN FEDERATION OF MUSICIANS (AFM)

WWW.AFM.ORG

The American Federation of Musicians of the United States and Canada is the largest organization in the world representing professional musicians. The union negotiates agreements for its musician members and provides significant benefits including health care and pensions, among other options.

West Coast Office:
3220 Winona Avenue
Burbank, CA 91504
Phone: 323-462-2161

New York Headquarters:
1501 Broadway
Suite 600
New York, NY 10036
Phone: 212-869-1330

Nashville Office:
11 Music Circle North
Nashville, TN 37203
Phone: 615-244-9514

Legislative Office:
5335 Wisconsin Ave. N.W.
Suite 400
Washington, DC 20015
Phone: 202-274-4756

SAG-AFTRA

WWW.SAGAFTRA.ORG

SAG-AFTRA is a diverse union representing over 160,000 recording artists, actors, broadcast journalists, and other professionals in television, radio, sound recordings, commercials, non-broadcast/industrial programming, and Internet and digital programming.

New York:
1900 Broadway
Fifth Floor
New York, NY 10023
Phone: 212-944-1030
E-mail: aftrany@aftra.com

Los Angeles:
5757 Wilshire Boulevard
Seventh Floor
Los Angeles, CA 90036
Phone: 323-954-1600
E-mail: losangeles@aftra.com

Nashville:
1108 17th Ave. South
Nashville, TN 37212
Phone: 615-327-2944
E-mail: nashville@aftra.com

COUNTRY MUSIC ASSOCIATION (CMA)

WWW.CMAWORLD.COM

The Country Music Association, founded in 1958, is a not-for-profit trade organization with 6,000 members whose purpose is to promote country music in the United States and overseas. It produces the CMA Awards show, and the International Country Music Fan Fair. Membership is available for companies and individuals who are directly or substantially involved in the industry.

35 Music Square East
Suite 201
Nashville, TN 37203
Phone: 615-244-2840
E-mail: info@cmaworld.com

DRAMATISTS GUILD, INC.

WWW.DRAMATISTSGUILD.COM

The Dramatists Guild, founded in 1920, has a membership of 6,000 playwrights, composers, and lyricists whose works are performed on the live stage. Its members are able to utilize the protections of the Guild's various production contracts and procedures for verification of box office royalty statements, as well as many other services.

1501 Broadway
Suite 701
New York, NY 10036
Phone: 212-398-9366

GOSPEL MUSIC ASSOCIATION (GMA)

WWW.GOSPELMUSIC.ORG

The Gospel Music Association was founded in 1964 and has as its purpose the promotion, encouragement, and support of all forms of gospel and religious music. It provides educational and resource materials to its members, organizes Gospel Music Week, and produces the Dove Awards.

4012 Granny White Pike
Nashville, TN 37204
Phone: 615-242-0303
E-mail: info@gospelmusic.org

HARRY FOX AGENCY

WWW.HARRYFOX.COM

The Harry Fox Agency, Inc., was established in 1927 by its corporate parent, the National Music Publishers Association, Inc., to provide an information source, clearinghouse, and monitoring service for licensing musical copyrights. The Agency represents more than 44,000 American music publishers and licenses a large percentage of the uses of music in the United States on records, tapes, CDs, downloads, ringtones, interactive streams, the Internet, and imported phono-records. Additionally, the Harry Fox Agency handles the collection and distribution of royalties derived from the uses of copyrighted musical compositions pursuant to the licenses issued, as well as the auditing of the books and records of licensees utilizing copyrighted musical compositions pursuant to the licenses issued. It also represents its publisher principals in the collection, distribution, and monitoring of royalties earned under the Audio Home Recording Act.

40 Wall Street
Sixth Floor
New York, NY 10005
Phone: 212-834-0100
E-mail: clientrelations@harryfox.com

NASHVILLE SONGWRITERS ASSOCIATION INTERNATIONAL (NSAI)

WWW.NASHVILLESONGWRITERS.COM

NSAI is a not-for-profit trade association founded in 1967 that is dedicated to professional and aspiring songwriters in all fields of music and works to protect and further the rights of all songwriters. NSAI is one of the largest songwriter organizations in the United States, with a membership of 5,000, and concentrates in the areas of legislation, education, and recognition of the song and songwriters.

1710 Roy Acuff Place
Nashville, TN 37203
Phone: 615-256-3354 or 800-321-6008
E-mail: reception@nashvillesongwriters.com

NATIONAL ACADEMY OF RECORDING ARTS & SCIENCES (NARAS)

WWW.GRAMMY.COM

NARAS is a not-for-profit organization formed in 1957 to represent the interests of the creative and technical people in the recording industry. It has more than 16,000 members, produces the Grammy Awards show, and is at the forefront of issues involving the recording industry and its members. The NARAS Foundation is involved in the archiving and preservation of sound recordings, Grammy in the Schools, and MusiCares. In its educational mission, NARAS provides scholarships, annual grants for research and educational projects, workshops, publications, and a career handbook.

National/Los Angeles Office:
3030 Olympic Boulevard
Santa Monica, CA 90404
Phone: 310-392-3777
E-mail: losangeles@grammy.com

Nashville:
1904 Wedgewood Avenue
Nashville, TN 37212
Phone: 615-327-8030
E-mail: nashville@grammy.com

New York:
104 West 40th Street
Suite 400
New York, NY 10036
Phone: 212-245-5440
E-mail: newyork@grammy.com

Other Chapters: Atlanta, Chicago, Florida, Memphis, Pacific Northwest, Philadelphia, San Francisco, Texas, and Washington, DC

NATIONAL MUSIC PUBLISHERS ASSOCIATION (NMPA)

WWW.NMPA.ORG
NMPA is a trade organization founded in 1917 representing American music publishers and their songwriting partners. Its mission is to protect, promote, and advance the interests of creators. NMPA promotes legislation for increased copyright protection for musical works in the United States and throughout the world, provides comments on regulatory proposals to the respective entities promulgating them such as the Copyright Office, and supports legal action on various copyright and music industry issues when deemed necessary in the interests of its members.

975 F St. NW
#375
Washington DC 20004
Phone: 202-393-6672

PERFORMING RIGHTS ORGANIZATIONS

ASCAP (AMERICAN SOCIETY OF COMPOSERS, AUTHORS, AND PUBLISHERS)

WWW.ASCAP.COM

New York:
1900 Broadway
New York, NY 10023
Phone: 212-621-6000

Atlanta:
950 Joseph E. Lowery Blvd. N.W.
Suite 23
Atlanta, GA 30318
Phone: 404-685-8699

Los Angeles:
7920 W. Sunset Boulevard
Third Floor
Los Angeles, CA 90046
Phone: 323-883-1000

Miami Beach:
420 Lincoln Road
Suite 502
Miami Beach, FL 33139
Phone: 305-673-3446

Nashville:
Two Music Square West
Nashville, TN 37203
Phone: 615-742-5000

Puerto Rico:
Ave. Martinez Nadal
c/Hill Side 623
San Juan, PR 00920
Phone: 787-707-0782

London:
4 Millbank
Second Floor
London, SW1P 3JA
Phone: 44 20 7439 0909

BMI (BROADCAST MUSIC, INC.)

WWW.BMI.COM

New York:
7 World Trade Center
250 Greenwich Street
New York, NY 10007
Phone: 212-220-3000
E-mail: newyork@bmi.com

Los Angeles:
8730 Sunset Boulevard
Third Floor West
Los Angeles, CA 90069
Phone: 310-659-9109
E-mail: losangeles@bmi.com

Nashville:
10 Music Square East
Nashville, TN 37203
Phone: 615-401-2000
E-mail: nashville@bmi.com

Miami Beach:
Phone: 305-673-5148
E-mail: miami@bmi.com

Puerto Rico:
1250 Ponce de Leon Avenue
San Jose Building
Suite 1008
Santurce, Puerto Rico 00907
Phone: 787-754-6490
E-mail: puertorico@bmi.com

GLOBAL MUSIC RIGHTS

WWW.GLOBALMUSICRIGHTS.COM

Atlanta:
3340 Peachtree Road NE
Suite 570
Atlanta, GA 30326
Phone: 404-261-5151

Los Angeles:
1100 Glendon Avenue
#2000
Los Angeles, CA 90025

London:
84 Harley House
Marylebone Road
London NW1 5HN, United Kingdom
Phone: 44 20 7486 2036

SESAC

WWW.SESAC.COM

Nashville:
35 Music Square East
Nashville, TN 37203
Phone: 615-320-0055

Atlanta:
Suite 111
Atlanta, GA 30318
Phone: 404-897-1306

Santa Monica:
2150 Colorado Avenue
Suite 150
Santa Monica, CA 90404
Phone: 424-291-4750

Miami:
1221 Brickell Ave.
Miami, FL 33131
Phone: 305-534-7500

New York:
961 Joseph Lowery Blvd. NW
152 West 57th Street
57th Floor
New York, NY 10019
Phone: 212-586-3450

London:
67 Upper Berkeley St.
London W1H7QX
England
Phone: 44 020 7616 9284

RECORDING INDUSTRY ASSOCIATION OF AMERICA (RIAA)

WWW.RIAA.ORG

RIAA is a record company trade association founded in 1952 whose purpose is the improvement of the music and recording industry. Efforts focus on the areas of prevention of counterfeiting, bootlegging, record piracy, and related problems. RIAA is also the body that certifies Gold, Platinum, Multiplatinum, and Diamond sales awards.

1025 F Street N.W.
10th Floor
Washington, DC 20004
Phone: 202-775-0101

SOCIETY OF COMPOSERS & LYRICISTS (SCL)

WWW.THESCL.COM

The main focus of the SCL is the education, promotion, and support of film and television composers and songwriters. The SCL, founded in 1983, conducts workshops for writers and filmmakers on the creative, financial, and practical benefits of music in film. Membership is open to professionals and new writers as well as film and television business personnel.

8447 Wilshire Boulevard
Suite 401
Beverly Hills, CA 90211
Phone: 310-281-2812

SONGWRITERS GUILD OF AMERICA (SGA)

WWW.SONGWRITERSGUILD.COM

The SGA is a voluntary association of songwriters founded in 1931 whose membership is open to published and unpublished writers and estates of deceased writers. The Guild's services include reviews of songwriter contracts, music publisher audits, group medical and life plans, catalogue administration, a copyright renewal service, an estate administration service, workshops, and a royalty collection plan. The Guild's popular songwriters contract sets minimum royalty rates for various uses of a song, requires publishers to return songs to writers if a recording has not been made within 12 months, provides a sliding scale of percentages for sheet music, and contains a publisher audit clause and an assignment of a song to a publisher clause that cannot exceed 40 years or 35 years from the date of first release of a recording, as well as other favorable songwriter provisions. The Guild is also active in legislative and judicial areas. In 1999, the National Academy of Songwriters became part of SGA.

Brentwood, TN:
210 Jamestown Park Road
Suite 100
Brentwood, TN 37027-7570
Phone: 615-742-9945
E-mail: nash@songwritersguild.com

Hollywood, CA:
6430 Sunset Boulevard
Suite 705
Hollywood, CA 90028
Phone: 323-462-1108
E-mail: la@songwritersguild.com

SOUNDEXCHANGE

WWW.SOUNDEXCHANGE.COM

SoundExchange is an independent not-for-profit performing rights organization created to collect and distribute royalties to sound recording copyright owners, featured artists, and to SAG-AFTRA and AFM on behalf of background musicians and vocalists from digital audio transmissions. The DPRA of 1995 and the DMCA of 1998 granted performing rights in sound recordings for certain digital and satellite transmissions. The royalties generated by the compulsory license created by these acts are administered, collected and distributed by SoundExchange. SoundExchange is governed by a board of artist and label representatives. Royalty sources include satellite radio, digital cable, direct satellite TV, webcasts, and simulcasts from radio.

Reciprocal agreements have been negotiated with foreign collection societies.

733 10th St NW
10th Floor
Washington, DC 20001
Phone: 202-640-5858
Fax: 202-640-5859

U.S. COPYRIGHT OFFICE

WWW.COPYRIGHT.GOV

Register of Copyrights
Copyright Office
Library of Congress
101 Independence Avenue SE
Washington, DC 20003
General questions: 202-707-3000

CHAPTER 20

SAMPLE CONTRACTS

When entering into any agreement that involves your music, it's important to consult a knowledgeable entertainment attorney or other qualified representative. However, for your information, we have provided a sampling of the types of contracts that may be presented to you in conjunction with deals for:

- Motion Picture License (use of a song in a motion picture)
- Television Series License (use of a song in a television series)
- Advertising Commercial License (use of a song in an advertising campaign)
- Video Game License (use of a song in a video game)
- Digital Download License (use of a song as a download)
- Mechanical License (use of a song on a CD or other physical audio recording)

MUSICAL COMPOSITION SYNCHRONIZATION-USE LICENSE (MOTION PICTURES)

This musical composition synchronization-use license agreement ("Agreement"), dated as of _____, is hereby acknowledged and entered into by and

between _____ ("Licensor"), of _____,
and _____ ("Licensee"), of _____,
effective as of the date set forth under Schedule A, attached hereto and, by this
reference, incorporated herewith, which shall dictate and govern, in the event of any
conflicts between it and the main body of this Agreement.

1. The musical composition(s) (collectively or individually, hereinafter referred to as
   the "Composition") subject to this Agreement, as well as the individual name of each
   credited songwriter per each Composition (individually or collectively, hereinafter
   referred to as the "Writer"), as well as Licensor's sole percentage of ownership and/
   or control of said Composition (as an undivided interest in and to the copyright of
   the Composition), are all as specifically set forth under Schedule A.

2. The motion picture being produced, owned and/or controlled by Licensee and
   covered by this Agreement is specifically set forth under Schedule A ("Motion
   Picture").

3. The term of this Agreement is specifically set forth under Schedule A ("Term"). Upon
   expiration of the Term, if any, Licensee shall have no rights to the Composition in
   or in connection with the Motion Picture, unless otherwise provided for hereunder.

4. The territory covered by this Agreement is set forth under Schedule A ("Territory").

5. The number and type(s) of use(s) and correlating timing(s) of the Composition
   subject to this Agreement as performed in the soundtrack of the Motion Picture
   (individually or collectively, hereinafter referred to as the "Use"), are set forth under
   Schedule A. Accordingly, Licensee warrants and represents that said Use is final and
   accurate.

6. Grant of Rights: Conditioned upon Licensee's full and continuing compliance with
   all of the terms, covenants and conditions hereunder, and further subject to and in
   consideration of the non-refundable sum set forth under Schedule A, representing
   Licensor's sole percentage of ownership and/or control of said Composition (which
   is payable upon execution and delivery hereof), Licensor hereby grants to Licensee,
   its successors and assigns, the non-exclusive, limited right, license, privilege and
   authority to:

   a. reproduce the Composition, in synchronism or in timed-relation with the
      Motion Picture, but not otherwise, and to make copies of said reproductions for
      distribution thereof into and throughout the Territory;

b. publicly perform for profit or non-profit and authorize others to so publicly perform the Composition, solely as synchronized in and as part of the Motion Picture, to audiences in motion picture theaters and other places of public entertainment where motion pictures are customarily exhibited ("Theatrical") in the United States, its territories and possessions (the "USTP"), and elsewhere throughout the rest of the Territory, subject to the provisions of paragraph 8 hereunder, including the right to exhibit the Motion Picture into such theaters and such other places of public entertainment, as well as the so-called "non-theatrical" markets, with the understanding and upon the condition that exhibition of the Motion Picture in the USTP by means of any forms of television and/or via the Internet for any purpose whatsoever shall be subject to the provisions of paragraph 7 herein below, to the extent applicable; and

c. exhibit, reproduce, transmit, distribute, perform and exploit, and to authorize others to so exhibit, reproduce, transmit, distribute, perform and exploit the Composition, solely as synchronized in and as part of the Motion Picture as a whole and substantially in its entirety (specifically, such grant of rights excludes any and all re-uses in or as part of web-isodes, behind-the-scenes footage, best-of programs, or any other variations thereof, including bonus content, unless otherwise provided for hereunder), by means and/or methods of only those certain audio-visual media, as expressly set forth under Schedule A, subject to and in accordance with the terms, conditions and limitations set forth hereunder.

i. In-Context Trailers: Exhibition in trailers produced for the advertising and exploitation of the Motion Picture, limited to the licensed media granted hereunder, provided that the Composition shall not be used for any such purpose other than as used in the Motion Picture (i.e., in-context only, as synchronized originally to picture for the portion or portions of the Motion Picture embodying the Composition and used in such trailers).

ii. Out-of-Context Trailers: Exhibition in so called "out-of-context" trailers produced for the advertising and exploitation of the Program, limited to the licensed media granted hereunder, subject to the terms and conditions hereunder as well as the additional fee set forth under Schedule A.

iii. Film Festival Exhibition: Any and all exhibition to/for public or private audiences for non-commercial purposes, limited to said exhibition at so called "Film Festivals" and/or "Film Markets" only (as such terms are commonly accepted in the entertainment or phonograph record industries), as well as the right to authorize said exhibition to others accordingly, subject to the terms and conditions hereunder.

iv. Theatrical Exhibition: Any and all exhibition to/for public or private audiences, for commercial or non-commercial purposes, and the right to authorize others to so exhibit the Motion Picture, at theaters and other places of public entertainment where motion pictures are customarily exhibited, subject to the terms and conditions hereunder.

v. Video on Demand (VOD): Any and all means of exhibition via VOD capabilities, regardless of the end-user's receiving device, for which such end-users pay a fee to a service provider to gain, at the user's discretion, viewing access to content from a certain broadcasting entity, subject to the terms and conditions hereunder.

vi. All TV Media: Any and all means of exhibition on any and all television media, including without limitation, free television, basic cable television, pay television, satellite television, "VOD," "DBS," "CATV" and closed-circuit-into-homes television, subject to the terms and conditions hereunder.

vii. Streaming Internet: Any and all means of exhibition on the Internet, but specifically limited to streaming, non-downloadable content only, subject to exhibitor complying with current public performing rights requirements of the respective portion of the Territory, if any, including the probability of a valid and authorized performing rights license in place, subject to the terms and conditions hereunder.

vii. Streaming Wireless: Any and all means of exhibition via personal and/or traditional home media and wireless devices, but specifically limited to streaming, non-downloadable content only, subject to exhibitor complying with current public performing rights requirements of the respective portion of the Territory, if any, including the probability of a valid and authorized performing rights license in place, subject to the terms and conditions hereunder.

ix. Electronic Sell-Through ("EST"): Any and all means of exhibition via manufactured copies within a digital/electronic, non-tangible end-product, or any other similar forms thereof, whether now known or hereafter devised ("EST"), so long as such EST contains the Motion Picture as a whole and substantially in its original entirety (specifically, said grant of rights excludes any and all re-uses, clips or otherwise, in or as part of web-isodes, behind-the-scenes footage, best-of programs, or any other variations thereof, unless otherwise provided for hereunder); and, subsequently, the right to sell, lease, license or otherwise make EST of the Motion Picture embodying the Composition available to the public to own as audio-visual content intended primarily for personal or home use, as such terms are commonly accepted in the entertainment or phonograph record industries, subject to the terms and conditions hereunder.

x. Videograms: Any and all means of exhibition via any and all tangible audio-visual devices, such as videocassettes, videodiscs, and similar contrivances, whether now known or hereafter devised ("Videograms"), provided such Videograms contain the Motion Picture as a whole and substantially in its original entirety (specifically, said grant of rights excludes any and all re-uses, clips or otherwise, in or as part of web-isodes, behind-the-scenes footage, best-of programs and/or any other variations thereof, unless otherwise provided for hereunder); and, subsequently, the right to sell, lease, license or otherwise make said Videograms of the Motion Picture embodying the Composition available to the public to own as audio-visual content intended primarily for personal or home use, as such terms are commonly accepted in the entertainment or phonograph record industries, subject to the terms and conditions hereunder.

1. Public Performance: The right to publicly perform and to authorize others to publicly perform the Composition as recorded in the Motion Picture is subject to the following:

a. each television and/or Internet media entity in the United States, its territories & possessions ("USTP") that is licensed to exhibit, broadcast or transmit a public performance of the Motion Picture ("Media Entity") must comply with the established public performance license protocol at the time of said public performance in its portion of the Territory, if any, including the probability of securing a valid license from the American Society of Composers, Authors and Publishers ("ASCAP"), Broadcast Music, Inc. ("BMI"), SESAC, or GMR, whichever may be applicable;

b. the right to publicly perform and to authorize others so to publicly perform the Composition as recorded in the Motion Picture by means of a Media Entity not in compliance with the established public performance license protocol at the time of said public performance, including the probability of a current public performance license with ASCAP, BMI, SESAC, or GMR, whichever may be applicable, is subject to prior approval of said public performance right from Licensor or from any other duly authorized licensor acting for or on behalf of Licensor, all subject to good faith negotiations in accordance with established industry customs and practices;

c. with respect to any public performance of the Motion Picture embodying the Composition in locations outside of the USTP, Licensor and Licensee duly understand that the laws, customary practices, rules, regulations and/or any correlating fees already established in such location of the Territory outside of the USTP at the time of said public performance shall dictate and govern; and

d. Licensee agrees to furnish Licensor with a music cue sheet of the Motion Picture within thirty (30) days after the first public exhibition of the Motion Picture at which admission is charged (except so-called "sneak" previews).

2. Screen Credit: If the Composition is contained in the Motion Picture, as first commercially released to the public, screen credit shall be given to the Writer and/ or Licensor in the end title credits of the Motion Picture among credits for all other "outside" (i.e., pre-existing) compositions and master recordings licensed for synchronization-use and, thereby, performed in the soundtrack of the Motion Picture, in the same manner and size of type used to accord said screen credit for outside, licensed music. No casual or inadvertent failure to execute and deliver screen credit provisions herein shall be deemed a breach of this Agreement, so long as Licensee uses good-faith efforts to cure any such non-performance in a timely manner, upon the receipt of a written notice of said non-performance from Licensor.

3. Reservation of Rights: Licensor reserves all rights not expressly granted to Licensee under this Agreement; accordingly, said granted rights are expressly non-exclusive, unless otherwise provided for hereunder. In addition:

a. this Agreement does not authorize or permit any use of the Composition not expressly set forth herein, including but not limited to the right to: (i) make any changes to the Composition other than to shorten the Composition utilizing a continuous portion thereof; (ii) utilize the Composition in any device now known or hereafter devised intended for reproduction of sound-alone or audio-only; (iii) to use the story of the Composition, or any excerpt thereof, in the Motion Picture; and/or (iv) make any changes in the original lyrics or in the fundamental character of the Composition;

b. for any avoidance of doubt, this Agreement grants rights only in such licensed media (as set forth under Schedule A) which embody the Motion Picture as a whole and as substantially or generally released and in a linear format only; specifically, this Agreement does not grant any rights to use the Composition, whatsoever, in any and all: (i) interactive, non-linear, non-sequential and/or all such similar future devices, now known or hereafter devised, that provide a user with the ability to manipulate, alter or change at-will, the Motion Picture's audio or visual content in any manner whatsoever (as examples only, but not limited to, sequence of scenes, actors' dialogues, music and/or any other audio, visual or audio-visual element in and to the Motion Picture); or (ii) any device that is programmed in such a manner as to permit a user to manipulate the Motion Picture's images and/or audio material in a non-linear progression, whether now known or hereafter devised; for the purposes hereof, the inclusion of "chapter stops" or other addressable locator codes of any kind shall not be deemed to constitute non-linear manipulation; notwithstanding the foregoing, so called editor's and/or director's cuts, special versions for the visually and/or hearing impaired or other similar alterations are hereby excluded from the provisions herein; and

c. all "derivative work" copyrights and "collective work" and/or "compilation" copyrights (as those terms are respectively defined in the United States Copyright Act) in and to the Composition as a result of Licensee's exercise of its rights hereunder, shall belong to, and be exclusively owned by, Licensor.

4. Licensor's Warranty and Indemnification: Licensor warrants only that it has the legal right to grant the rights specified hereunder. Licensor shall indemnify and hold Licensee harmless against any third party claims, liabilities, losses or damages actually incurred by Licensee as a result of Licensor's breach of this warranty, but in no event shall the total liability of the Licensor hereunder or otherwise exceed the consideration received by it hereunder. This Agreement is given and accepted without any further warranty, representation or recourse.

5. Licensee's Warranty and Indemnification: Licensee will indemnify and hold harmless Licensor from any and all claims, liabilities, losses and damages arising from any breach of Licensee's warranties, representations or covenants under this Agreement, or in any way resulting from or connected with Licensee's use of the Composition in any manner not approved nor granted by Licensor hereunder.

6. Assignment: This Agreement is binding upon and shall inure to the benefit of the respective successors, assigns and/or sub-licensees of the parties hereto. Notwithstanding anything contained herein to the contrary, Licensee may transfer its rights under this Agreement, provided Licensee remains liable for any failure on the part of its assignee(s) to comply with any and all sections under this Agreement.

7. Conditions Precedent: The non-exclusive rights granted to Licensee hereunder shall be of no force or effect until Licensor receives from Licensee the consideration specified under Schedule A and/or until this Agreement is fully executed by Licensee and Licensor. In addition:

a. Licensee shall be solely responsible for obtaining all requisite consents and permissions from any and all co-publisher(s) of the Composition and/or any owner(s) of the master recording embodying a performance of the Composition, if applicable, and shall be solely responsible for paying any and all payments, fees, royalties and other sums required to be paid, if any, for such consents and permissions.

8. Choice of Law: This Agreement is being entered into and shall be construed in accordance with the laws of the State of _____, as if it were entered into and wholly executed in the State of _____. All judicial proceedings brought against a party with respect to this Agreement or any related document shall be brought in any state or federal court of competent jurisdiction in the County of _____ in the State of _____. By its execution and delivery of this Agreement, each of the parties accepts, for itself and in connection with its properties, generally and unconditionally, the exclusive jurisdiction of the aforesaid courts.

9. Entire Agreement: This Agreement wholly sets forth the entire understanding between the parties hereto and no modification, amendment, waiver, termination or discharge shall be binding unless confirmed by a written instrument duly signed by the party to be charged therewith. This Agreement may be executed in one or more counterparts, each of which shall be deemed an original (including signatures delivered by facsimile or "pdf" formats), all of which together shall constitute a single agreement. If any part of this Agreement is adjudicated as invalid or unenforceable, it shall not affect the validity of any remaining provision or condition within the balance of this Agreement.

IN WITNESS WHEREOF, the parties have caused the foregoing to be executed as of the date first set forth above.

AGREED TO AND ACCEPTED: AGREED TO AND ACCEPTED:

_____   _____
("Licensor")   ("Licensee")

By_____   By_____
An Authorized Signatory   An Authorized Signatory

Federal Tax ID#:

Schedule A

A. Motion Picture: _____

B. Composition: _____

C. Writer: _____

D. % Owned/Controlled: _____

E. Publisher(s): _____

<u>Initial Use</u>

F. Use Description: _____

G. Territory: _____

H. Term: _____

I. Licensed/Granted Rights: _____

J. License Fee/Consideration: _____
(Licensor's pro-rata share of the 100% license fees)

K. MFN: _____

L. Option(s): _____

M. Screen Credit: _____

N. Special Terms/Conditions: _____

All payments, royalties and other consideration shall be sent directly to:

_____

IN WITNESS WHEREOF, the parties have caused the foregoing to be executed as of the date first set forth above.

AGREED TO AND ACCEPTED: AGREED TO AND ACCEPTED:

_____   _____

PUBLISHER   PRODUCER
("Licensor")   ("Licensee")

By_____   By_____
An Authorized Signatory   An Authorized Signatory

Federal Tax ID#:

MUSICAL COMPOSITION SYNCHRONIZATION-USE LICENSE (TELEVISION)

This musical composition synchronization-use license agreement ("Agreement"), dated as of _____, is hereby acknowledged and entered into by and between _____ ("Licensor"), of _____, and _____("Licensee"), of _____, effective as of the date set forth under Schedule A, attached hereto and, by this reference, incorporated herewith, which shall dictate and govern, in the event of any conflicts between it and the main body of this Agreement.

1. The musical composition(s) (collectively or individually, hereinafter referred to as the "Composition") subject to this Agreement, as well as the individual name of each credited songwriter per each Composition (individually or collectively, hereinafter referred to as the "Writer"), as well as Licensor's sole percentage of ownership and/ or control of said Composition (as an undivided interest in and to the copyright of the Composition), are all as specifically set forth under Schedule A.

2. The individual linear, audio-visual program being produced, owned and/or controlled by Licensee and covered by this Agreement is specifically set forth under Schedule A ("Program").

3. The term of this Agreement is specifically set forth under Schedule A ("Term"). Upon expiration of said Term, if any, Licensee shall have no rights to the Composition in or in connection with the Program, unless otherwise provided for hereunder.

4. The territory covered by this Agreement is set forth under Schedule A ("Territory").

5. The number and type(s) of use(s) and correlating timing(s) of the Composition subject to this Agreement as performed in the soundtrack of the Program (individually or collectively, hereinafter referred to as the "Use"), are set forth under Schedule A. Accordingly, Licensee warrants and represents that said Use is final and accurate.

6. Grant of Rights: Conditioned upon Licensee's full and continuing compliance with all of the terms, covenants and conditions herein, and further subject to and in consideration of the non-refundable sum set forth under Schedule A, representing Licensor's sole percentage of ownership and/or control of said Composition, as provided hereunder (which is payable upon execution and delivery hereof), Licensor hereby grants to Licensee, its successors and assigns, the non-exclusive, limited right, license, privilege and authority to:

a. reproduce the Composition, in synchronism or in timed-relation with the Program, but not otherwise, and to make copies of said reproductions for distribution thereof into and throughout the Territory; and

b. exhibit, reproduce, transmit, distribute and exploit the Composition, and to authorize others to exhibit, reproduce, transmit, distribute and exploit the Composition, solely as synchronized in and as part of the Program as a whole and substantially in its entirety (specifically, such grant of rights excludes any and all re-uses in or as part of web-isodes, behind-the-scenes footage, best-of programs, or any other similar bonus content, unless such re-uses are otherwise provided for hereunder), by means and/or methods of those certain media, as specifically set forth under Schedule A and further defined hereinbelow, but not otherwise, subject to and in accordance with the terms, conditions and limitations set forth hereunder.

i. In-Context Trailers: Exhibition in trailers produced for the advertising and exploitation of the Program, limited to the licensed media granted hereunder, provided that the Composition shall not be used for any such purpose other than as used in the Program (i.e., in-context only, as synchronized originally to picture for the portion or portions of the Program embodying the Composition).

ii. Out-of-Context Trailers: Exhibition in so called "out-of-context" trailers produced for the advertising and exploitation of the Program, limited to the licensed media granted hereunder, subject to the terms and conditions hereunder including the additional fee set forth under Schedule A.

iii. Free Television: Any and all means of exhibition on standard or so called "free" television, subject to the terms and conditions hereunder.

iv. Basic Cable/Satellite Television: Any and all means of exhibition on basic cable/satellite television (including DBS), for which subscribing members of the public pay a standard fee to a service provider to gain viewing access to content from groups of certain broadcasting entities, but otherwise do not pay a premium fee for such content transmitted, subject to the terms and conditions hereunder.

v. Pay Cable/Satellite Television: Any and all means of exhibition on pay cable/satellite television (including DBS) for which subscribing members of the public pay a premium fee to a service provider to gain viewing access to content from a certain broadcasting entity, subject to the terms and conditions hereunder.

vi. Video on Demand (VOD): Any and all means of exhibition via VOD capabilities and access, regardless of the end-user's receiving device, for which such end-user pays a fee to a VOD service provider to gain, at the user's discretion, viewing access to audio-visual content, subject to the terms and conditions hereunder.

vii. All TV Media: Any and all means of exhibition on any and all television media, including without limitation, free television, basic cable television, pay television, satellite television, "VOD," "DBS," "CATV" and closed-circuit-into-homes television, subject to the terms and conditions hereunder.

viii. Streaming Internet: Any and all means of exhibition on the Internet, but specifically limited to streaming, non-downloadable content only, subject to Licensee and/or Program exhibitor complying with current public performing rights requirements of the respective portion of the Territory, if any, including the probability of a valid and authorized performing rights license in place, subject to the terms and conditions hereunder.

ix. Streaming Wireless: Any and all means of exhibition via personal and/or traditional home media and wireless devices, but specifically limited to streaming, non-downloadable content only, subject to Licensee and/or Program exhibitor complying with current public performing rights requirements of the respective portion of the Territory, if any, including the probability of a valid and authorized performing rights license in place, subject to the terms and conditions hereunder.

x. Videograms: To reproduce and/or fixate the Composition in synchronism or in timed-relation with the Program, but not otherwise, and to make copies of said reproductions and/or fixations thereof for distribution via manufactured copies within any and all tangible audio-visual devices, such as videocassettes, videodiscs, and similar contrivances, whether now known or hereafter devised ("Videograms"), so long as such copies are of the Program as a whole and substantially in its original entirety (specifically, said grant of rights excludes any and all re-uses, clips or otherwise, in or as part of web-isodes, behind-the-scenes footage, best-of programs, or any other similar bonus content, unless otherwise provided for hereunder); and, subsequently, the right to sell, lease, license or otherwise make said Videograms of the Program embodying the Composition available to the public to own as audio-visual content intended primarily for personal or home use, as such terms are commonly accepted in the entertainment or phonograph record industries, subject to the terms and conditions hereunder.

xi. Electronic Sell-Through: To reproduce and/or fixate the Composition in synchronism or in timed-relation with the Program, but not otherwise, and to make copies of said reproductions and/or fixations thereof for distribution via manufactured copies within a digital/electronic, non-tangible end-product, or any other similar forms thereof ("EST"), so long as such copies are of the Program as a whole and substantially in its original entirety (specifically, said grant of rights excludes any and all re-uses, clips or otherwise, in or as part of web-isodes, behind-the-scenes footage, best-of programs, or any other similar bonus content, unless otherwise provided for hereunder); and, subsequently, the right to sell, lease, license or otherwise make said digital/electronic, non-tangible end-product of the Program embodying the Composition available to the public to own as audio-visual content intended primarily for personal or home use, as such terms are commonly accepted in the entertainment or phonograph record industries, subject to the terms and conditions hereunder.

xii. All Media Excluding Theatrical: Any and all means of exhibition on all media now known or hereafter devised, excluding only theatrical exhibition, but including, without limitation, via free television, basic cable/pay television, satellite television, VOD, closed-circuit-into-homes television, the Internet, personal and/or traditional home media and wireless devices, Videograms, EST, so-called "non-theatrical exhibition" (including common carriers) and any similar media or method of distribution now known or hereafter developed, subject to the terms and conditions hereunder.

xiii. All Media: Any and all means of exhibition by way of any and all means of media whatsoever, whether now known or hereafter devised, subject to the terms and conditions hereunder.

xiv. Option(s): Only if set forth under Schedule A, Licensor grants to Licensee the right to such Option(s), any one or more of which may be exercised, if at all, by Licensor's receipt of Licensee's written notice on or before the expiration date of the Option(s), respectively, accompanied by the specified payment thereof.

7. Public Performance: The right to publicly perform and to authorize others to so publicly perform the Composition as embodied in the soundtrack of the Program as granted hereunder is without prejudice to the rights of any regional and/or local organizations and/or societies authorized to oversee public performance rights vis-à-vis the obligations of public exhibitors and/or broadcasters throughout the Territory, where said obligations may be required by prevailing custom or practice, law or regulation in that portion or country of the Territory. Furthermore and for any avoidance of doubt:

a. each television and/or Internet media entity in the United States, its territories & possessions ("USTP") that is licensed to exhibit, broadcast or transmit a public performance of the Program ("Media Entity") is obligated to comply with the established protocol for securing public performance rights at the time of said public performance, if any, including but not limited to an authorized license in place from the American Society of Composers, Authors and Publishers ("ASCAP"), Broadcast Music, Inc. ("BMI"), SESAC, or GMR, whichever may be applicable;

b. any Media Entity in the USTP not in compliance with the established protocol for securing public performance rights at the time of said public performance, if any, including but not limited to an authorized license in place from ASCAP, BMI, SESAC, or GMR, whichever may be applicable, is subject to curing such non-compliance either with Licensor or any other duly authorized agent acting for or on behalf of Licensor, subject to good faith negotiations in accordance with established industry customs and practices; and

c. If applicable, Licensee agrees to furnish Licensor with a music cue sheet of the Program within thirty (30) days after the first airdate or broadcast of the Program.

8. Reservation of Rights: Licensor specifically reserves unto itself all rights of every kind and nature except those specifically granted to Licensee on a non-exclusive basis hereunder. For any avoidance of doubt:

a. his Agreement does not authorize or permit any use of the Composition not expressly set forth hereunder, including but not limited to the right to: (i) make any changes to the Composition other than to shorten the Composition utilizing a continuous portion thereof; (ii) utilize the Composition in any device now known or hereafter devised intended for reproduction of sound—alone or audio-only; (iii) to use the story of the Composition, or any excerpt thereof, in the Program; and/or (iv) make any changes in the original lyrics or in the fundamental character of the Composition, unless otherwise provided for hereunder;

b. this Agreement grants rights only in such licensed media (as set forth under Schedule A) which embody the Program as a whole and as substantially or generally released and in a linear format only; specifically, this Agreement does not grant any rights to use the Composition, whatsoever, in any and all: (i) interactive, non-linear, non-sequential and/or all such similar future devices, now known or hereafter devised, that provide a user with the ability to manipulate, alter or change at-will, the Program's audio or visual content in any manner whatsoever (as examples only, but not limited to, sequence of scenes, actors' dialogues, music and/or any other audio, visual or audio-visual element in and to the Program); or (ii) any device that is programmed in such a manner as to permit a user to manipulate the Program's images and/or audio material in a non-linear progression, whether now known or hereafter devised; for the purposes hereof, the inclusion of "chapter stops" or other addressable locator codes of any kind shall not be deemed to constitute non-linear manipulation; notwithstanding the foregoing, so called editor's and/or director's cuts, special versions for the visually and/or hearing impaired or other similar alterations are hereby excluded from the provisions herein; and

c. all "derivative work" copyrights and "collective work" and/or "compilation" copyrights (as those terms are respectively defined in the United States Copyright Act) in and to the Composition as a result of Licensee's exercise of its rights hereunder, shall belong to, and be exclusively owned by, Licensor.

9. Licensor's Warranty and Indemnification: Licensor warrants only that it has the legal right to grant the rights specified hereunder. Licensor shall indemnify and hold Licensee harmless against any third party claims, liabilities, losses or damages actually incurred by Licensee as a result of Licensor's breach of this warranty, but in no event shall the total liability of the Licensor hereof or otherwise exceed the consideration received by it hereunder. This Agreement is given without any other warranty by or recourse against Licensor.

10. Licensee's Warranty and Indemnification: Licensee will indemnify and hold harmless Licensor from any and all claims, liabilities, losses and damages arising from any breach of Licensee's warranties, representations or covenants under this Agreement, or in any way resulting from or connected with Licensee's use of the Composition in any manner not approved nor granted by Licensor hereunder.

11. Assignment: This Agreement is binding upon and shall inure to the benefit of the respective successors, assigns and/or sub-licensees of the parties hereto. Notwithstanding anything contained herein to the contrary, Licensee may transfer its rights under this Agreement, provided Licensee remains liable for any failure on the part of its assignee(s) to comply with any and all sections under this Agreement.

12. Conditions Precedent: The non-exclusive rights granted to Licensee hereunder shall be of no force or effect until Licensor receives the consideration specified from Licensee and/or until this Agreement is fully executed by Licensee and Licensor. In addition:

a. Licensee shall be solely responsible for obtaining all requisite consents and permissions from any and all co-publisher(s) of the Composition and/or any owner(s) of the master recording embodying a performance of the Composition, if applicable, and shall be solely responsible for paying any and all payments, fees, royalties and other sums required to be paid, if any, for such consents and permissions.

13. Choice of Law: This Agreement is being entered into and shall be construed in accordance with the laws of the State of _____ as if it were entered into and wholly executed in the State of _____. All judicial proceedings brought against a party with respect to this Agreement or any related document shall be brought in any state or federal court of competent jurisdiction in the County of _____ in the State of _____ and by its execution and delivery of this Agreement, each of the parties accepts, for itself and in connection with its properties, generally and unconditionally, the exclusive jurisdiction of the aforesaid courts.

14. Entire Agreement: This Agreement wholly sets forth the entire understanding between the parties and no modification, amendment, waiver, termination or discharge shall be binding unless confirmed by a written instrument duly signed by the party to be charged therewith. If any part of this Agreement shall be invalid or unenforceable, it shall not affect the validity of any provision or condition within the balance of this Agreement.

IN WITNESS WHEREOF, the parties have caused the foregoing to be executed as of the date first set forth above.

AGREED TO AND ACCEPTED: AGREED TO AND ACCEPTED:

_____   _____
("Licensor")   ("Licensee")

By_____   By_____
An Authorized Signatory   An Authorized Signatory

Federal Tax ID#:

Schedule A

A. Program: _____ Episode # _____
B. Composition: _____
C. Writer: _____
D. % Owned/Controlled: _____
E. Publisher(s): _____

Initial Use
F. Use Description: _____
G. Initial Airdate: _____
H. Term: _____
I. Territory: _____
J. Licensed/Granted Rights:
K. License Fee/Consideration: _____
    (Licensor's pro-rata share of the 100% license fees)
L. MFN: _____
M. Options Granted: _____
N. Special Terms/Conditions: _____

All payments, royalties and other consideration shall be sent directly to:

_____

IN WITNESS WHEREOF, the parties have caused the foregoing to be executed as of the date first set forth above.

AGREED TO AND ACCEPTED: AGREED TO AND ACCEPTED:

_____   _____
PUBLISHER   PRODUCER
("Licensor")   ("Licensee")

By_____   By_____
An Authorized Signatory   An Authorized Signatory

Federal Tax ID#:

MUSICAL COMPOSITION SYNCHRONIZATION-USE LICENSE (ADVERTISING COMMERCIAL)

This musical composition synchronization-use license agreement ("Agreement"), dated as of _____, is hereby acknowledged and entered into by and between _____ ("Licensor"), of _____ and _____ ("Agency") as agent for its client _____, (collectively, hereinafter referred to as "Licensee"), of _____ _____, effective as of the date set forth under Schedule A, attached hereto and, by this reference, incorporated herewith, which shall dictate and govern, in the event of any conflicts between it and the main body of this Agreement.

1. The musical composition(s) (collectively or individually, hereinafter referred to as the "Composition") subject to this Agreement, as well as the individual name of each credited songwriter per each Composition (individually or collectively, hereinafter referred to as the "Writer"), as well as Licensor's sole percentage of ownership and/ or control of said Composition (as an undivided interest in and to the copyright of the Composition), are all as specifically set forth under Schedule A.

2. The advertisement spot produced, owned and/or controlled by Licensee and covered by this Agreement (the "Ad Spot") shall be used to promote the individual product specifically set forth under Schedule A solely (the "Product"), and not otherwise.

3. *Term:* The term of this Agreement is specifically set forth under Schedule A ("Term"). Upon expiration of the Term, if any, Licensee shall have no rights to the Composition in or in connection with the Ad Spot, unless otherwise provided for hereunder.

4. *Territory:* The territory covered by this Agreement is set forth under Schedule A ("Territory").

5. *Use:* The number and type(s) of use(s) and correlating timing(s) of the Composition subject to this Agreement as performed in the soundtrack of the Ad Spot (individually or collectively, hereinafter referred to as the "Use"), are set forth under Schedule A (including lifts, edits and versions thereof). Accordingly, Licensee warrants and represents that said Use is final and accurate.

6. *Grant of Rights:* Conditioned upon Licensee's full and continuing compliance with all of the terms, covenants and conditions hereunder, and further subject to and in consideration of the non-refundable sum set forth under Schedule A, representing Licensor's sole percentage of ownership and/or control of said Composition (which is payable upon execution and delivery hereof), Licensor hereby grants to Licensee,

its successors and assigns, the non-exclusive, limited right, license, privilege and authority to:

a. reproduce the Composition in synchronism or in timed-relation with visual elements of the Ad Spot, but not otherwise; and

b. exhibit, reproduce, transmit, distribute and exploit the Composition, and to authorize others to so exhibit, reproduce, transmit, distribute and exploit the Composition, solely as synchronized in and as part of the Ad Spot as a whole and in its entirety, by means and/or methods of those certain media, as specifically set forth under Schedule A, subject to and in accordance with the terms, conditions and limitations set forth hereunder.

c. Option(s): Only if specifically set forth under Schedule A, Licensor grants to Licensee the right to such Option(s), any one or more of which may be exercised, if at all, by Licensor's receipt of Licensee's written notice to do so, prior to the respective end of the option term, accompanied by the specified payment thereof.

7. *Exclusivity:* Only if specifically set forth under Schedule A, but not otherwise, Licensor will refrain from any synchronization-use licensing of the Composition in any advertisement spot, whatsoever, for the identified product(s) and/or for the identified duration of time thereof, in order to meet any negotiated exclusivity granted to Licensee by Licensor hereunder.

8. *Public Performance:* The right to publicly perform and to authorize others to so publicly perform the Composition as embodied and performed as part of the soundtrack of the Ad Spot, as granted hereunder, is without prejudice to the rights of any organizations and/or societies authorized to oversee public performance rights vis-à-vis the obligations of public exhibitors and/or broadcasters throughout the world, where said obligations may be required by prevailing custom or practice, law or regulation. Accordingly:

a. each media entity in the United States, its territories & possessions ("USTP") that is licensed to exhibit, broadcast or transmit a public performance of the Ad Spot embodying the Composition ("Media Entity") must comply with the established protocol for public performance licensing in that respective portion of the Territory and at the time of said public performance, if any, including the probability of a valid and authorized license in place from the American Society of Composers, Authors and Publishers ("ASCAP"), Broadcast Music, Inc. ("BMI"), SESAC, or GMR whichever may be applicable;

b. any Media Entity in the USTP that is licensed to exhibit, broadcast or transmit a public performance of the Ad Spot embodying the Composition, but not in compliance with the established protocol for public performance licensing in that respective portion of the Territory and at the time of said public performance, if any, including the probability of a valid and authorized public performance license in place with ASCAP, BMI, SESAC, or GMR, whichever may be applicable, is subject to prior approval of such needed public performance right from Licensor, or from any other duly authorized licensor acting for or on behalf of Licensor, pursuant to good faith negotiations in accordance with established industry customs and practices;

c. with respect to any public performance of the Ad Spot embodying the Composition in locations outside of the USTP, Licensor and Licensee duly understand that the laws, customary practices, rules, regulations and/or any correlating fees already established in such location of the Territory outside of the USTP at the time of said public performance shall dictate and govern; and

d. Licensee shall deliver to Licensor a quarterly summary to indicate the total sum of Ad Spot broadcasts, with the name and address of each authorized Media Entity who so fulfilled said broadcasts; Licensee acknowledges that Licensor shall view all information within such quarterly summary to be confidential, for disclosure only, if at all and/or necessary, to Licensor's respective public performance rights representative in the subject Territory of such Ad Spot broadcast, for the purposes of resolving any discrepancies with correlating public performance royalties made from the broadcasts of the Ad Spot.

9. *Reservation of Rights:* Licensor reserves all rights not expressly granted to Licensee under this Agreement; said rights are non-exclusive, unless otherwise provided for hereunder. In addition:

a. this Agreement does not authorize or permit any use of the Composition not expressly set forth hereunder, including but not limited to the right to: (i) make any changes to the Composition other than to shorten the Composition utilizing a continuous portion thereof; (ii) utilize the Composition in any device now known or hereafter devised intended for reproduction of sound-alone or audio-only; (iii) to use the story of the Composition, or any excerpt thereof, in the Ad Spot; and/or (iv) make any changes in the original lyrics or in the fundamental character of the Composition, unless otherwise provided for hereunder; and

b. this Agreement grants rights only in such licensed media (as set forth under Schedule A) which embody the Ad Spot as a whole and in a linear format only; specifically, this Agreement does not grant any rights to use the Composition, whatsoever, in any and all: (i) interactive, non-linear, non-sequential and/or all such similar future devices, now known or hereafter devised, that provide a user with the ability to manipulate, alter or change at-will, the Ad Spot's audio or visual content in any manner whatsoever (as examples only, but not limited to, sequence of scenes, actors' dialogues, music and/or any other audio, visual or audio-visual element in and to the Ad Spot); or (ii) any device that is programmed in such a manner as to permit a user to manipulate the Ad Spot's images and/ or audio material in a non-linear progression, whether now known or hereafter devised.

10. *Licensor's Warranty and Indemnification:* Licensor warrants only that it has the legal right to grant the rights specified hereunder. Licensor shall indemnify and hold Licensee harmless against any third party claims, liabilities, losses or damages actually incurred by Licensee as a result of Licensor's breach of this warranty, but in no event shall the total liability of the Licensor hereunder or otherwise exceed the consideration received by it hereunder. This Agreement is given without any other warranty by or recourse against Licensor.

11. *Licensee's Warranty and Indemnification:* Licensee will indemnify and hold harmless Licensor from any and all claims, liabilities, losses and damages arising from any breach of Licensee's warranties, representations or covenants under this Agreement, or in any way resulting from or connected with Licensee's use of the Composition in any manner not granted nor approved hereunder by Licensor.

12. *Assignment:* This Agreement is binding upon and shall inure to the benefit of the respective successors, assigns and/or sub-licensees of the parties hereto. Notwithstanding anything contained herein to the contrary, Licensee may transfer its rights under this Agreement, provided Licensee remains liable for any failure on the part of its assignee(s) to comply with any and all sections under this Agreement.

13. *Conditions Precedent:* The non-exclusive rights granted to Licensee hereunder shall be of no force or effect until Licensor receives the consideration specified under Schedule A from Licensee and/or until this Agreement is fully executed by Licensee and Licensor. In addition:

a. this Agreement shall terminate upon notice to Licensee in the event of any material breach of the obligations hereunder by Licensee or its permitted successors and assigns or Licensee's distributor(s), providing, however, that Licensor shall have notified Licensee of its breach or non-performance in writing and Licensee fails to cure same within thirty (30) days after the sending of said notice; any termination which occurs pursuant to this paragraph shall render the use of the Composition in the Ad Spot unauthorized and Licensor shall thereupon be entitled to seek any and all legal remedies, provided, however, that Licensor shall not be entitled, by reason of any breach, to enjoin, restrain and/ or seek to enjoin or restrain the distribution of the Ad Spot whatsoever; and

b. Licensee shall be solely responsible for obtaining all requisite consents and permissions from any and all co-publisher(s) of the Composition and/or any owner(s) of the master recording embodying a performance of the Composition, if such master recording is used, and shall be solely responsible for paying any and all payments, fees, royalties and other sums required to be paid, if any, for such consents and permissions.

14. Licensee shall deliver to Licensor one (1) MPEG via CD-Rom copy or valid digital download link including Ad-ID and/or ISCI codes of the final Ad Spot produced hereunder for Licensor's archives, including all cut-downs, lifts, edits and versions thereof.

15. *Choice of Law:* This Agreement is being entered into and shall be construed in accordance with the laws of the State of _____ as if it were entered into and wholly executed in the State of _____. All judicial proceedings brought against a party with respect to this Agreement or any related document shall be brought in any state or federal court of competent jurisdiction in the County of _____ in the State of _____ and, by its execution and delivery of this Agreement, each of the parties accepts, for itself and in connection with its properties, generally and unconditionally, the exclusive jurisdiction of the aforesaid courts.

16. *Entire Agreement:* This Agreement wholly sets forth the entire understanding between the parties hereto and no modification, amendment, waiver, termination or discharge shall be binding unless confirmed by a written instrument duly signed by the party to be charged therewith. If any part of this Agreement shall be invalid or unenforceable, it shall not affect the validity of any provision or condition within the balance of this Agreement.

Schedule A

A. Subject Product of Ad Spot: _____
B. Composition: _____
C. Writer: _____
D. % Owned/Controlled: _____
E. Publisher(s): _____

Initial Use
F. Use Description: _____,
   including lifts, edits and versions thereof

G. Licensed/Granted Rights: _____

H. Territory: _____

I. Term: _____

J. License Fee/Consideration: _____

K. MFN: _____

L. Exclusivity: From _____ to _____;
provided, however, that all rights granted hereunder for all Internet, Wireless and Mobile media is done so strictly on a non-exclusive basis.

M. Option(s) and Fee(s): _____

N. Special Terms/Conditions: (i) Payment of License Fee herein is due no later than _____ (__) business days after the first exhibition of the Ad Spot in any licensed media or _____ (__) business days from the date hereof, whichever is earlier; and (ii) all uses of the Composition authorized hereunder shall be limited to in-context use only, as it is edited into the final Ad Spot for broadcast.

All payments and/or other consideration shall be sent directly to: _____

IN WITNESS WHEREOF, the parties have caused the foregoing to be executed as of the date first set forth above.

AGREED TO AND ACCEPTED: AGREED TO AND ACCEPTED:

_____   _____
("Licensor")   ("Agency")

as agent for _____
("Licensee")

By_____   By_____
An Authorized Signatory   An Authorized Signatory

Federal Tax ID#:

MUSICAL COMPOSITION SYNCHRONIZATION-USE LICENSE (INTERACTIVE/NON-LINEAR VIDEO GAMES)

This musical composition synchronization-use license agreement ("Agreement"), dated as of _____, is hereby acknowledged and entered into by and between _____("Licensor"), of _____, and _____ ("Licensee"), of _____, effective as of the date set forth under Schedule A, attached hereto and, by this reference, incorporated herewith, which shall dictate and govern, in the event of any conflicts between it and the main body of this Agreement.

1. The musical composition(s) (collectively or individually, hereinafter referred to as the "Composition") subject to this Agreement, as well as the individual name of each credited songwriter per each Composition (individually or collectively, hereinafter referred to as the "Writer"), as well as Licensor's sole percentage of ownership and/or control of said Composition (as an undivided interest in and to the copyright of the Composition), are all as specifically set forth under Schedule A.

2. Licensee is developing, producing, selling and/or distributing an interactive video game as set forth under Schedule A (the "Game") and is the subject matter covered hereunder by this Agreement, with the understanding that the Game will be manufactured for commercial sales distribution.

3. The term of this Agreement shall commence as of date set forth under Schedule A ("Term"). Upon expiration of the Term, if any, Licensee shall have no rights to the Composition in or in connection with the Game, unless otherwise provided for hereunder.

4. The territory covered by this Agreement is set forth under Schedule A ("Territory").

5. The number and type(s) of use(s) and correlating timing(s) of the Composition subject to this Agreement, as performed in the soundtrack of the Game (individually or collectively, hereinafter referred to as the "Use"), are set forth under Schedule A. Accordingly, Licensee warrants and represents that Use is final and accurate.

6. Grant of Rights: Conditioned upon Licensee's full and continuing compliance with all of the terms, covenants and conditions hereunder, and further subject to and in consideration of the non-refundable sum set forth under Schedule A, representing Licensor's sole percentage of ownership and/or control of said Composition (which is payable upon execution and delivery hereof), Licensor grants to Licensee, its successors and assigns, a non-exclusive, limited license to:

a. Use the Composition in synchronization with the Game and to make copies of the Game in the platforms specified under Schedule A for distribution into and throughout the Territory; and

b. exhibit, transmit and exploit the Composition, and to authorize others to do so, incorporated in the final version of the Game and only via any additional media specified under Schedule A ("Media"), but not otherwise.

7. Royalty: Only if applicable and specifically set forth under Schedule A, but strictly not otherwise, royalties, with respect to the distribution of units of the Production, as so permitted within the grant of rights under paragraph 6 hereinabove (the "Royalties"), shall be determined and paid as follows, with the understanding that the non-refundable sum referenced under paragraph 6 and due upon execution hereof serves as a non-returnable, recoupable advance against the number of units noted hereunder:

a. with respect to units of the Game sold, an amount specified under Schedule A shall be paid to Licensor, based upon Licensor's sole percentage of ownership and/or control of the Composition;

b. Licensee shall render to Licensor, on a quarterly basis and within forty-five (45) days after the end of each calendar quarter after the first commercial sale of the Game, a detailed written statement of the royalty due to Licensor; such statement shall be accompanied by a remittance of such amount as shown to be due; and

c. upon _____ (__) days' written notice, Licensee shall permit Licensor, Licensor's chartered accountant or certified public accountant, or any other representative of Licensor, to inspect, at Licensee's place of business and during usual business hours, all books, records and other documents relating to this Agreement; under no circumstances shall Licensor be entitled to conduct such an examination more than once during any calendar year and not more than once as to any accounting period; said statements and payments, in the absence of written objection thereto by Licensor within _____ (__) years from receipt thereof, shall constitute an account stated as to all royalties due for the period covered by such statement and/or payment.

8. Public Performance: The right to publicly perform and to authorize others to so publicly perform the Composition as embodied within the Game, as granted hereunder, is without prejudice to the rights of any organizations and/or societies authorized to oversee such public performance rights vis-à-vis the obligations of public exhibitors and/or broadcasters throughout the world, where said obligations may be required by prevailing custom or practice, law or regulation. Accordingly:

a. each media entity in the United States, its territories & possessions ("USTP") that is licensed to exhibit, broadcast or transmit a public performance of the Game embodying the Composition ("Media Entity") must comply with the established protocol for public performance licensing in that respective portion of the Territory and at the time of said public performance, if any, including the probability of a valid and authorized license in place from the American Society of Composers, Authors and Publishers ("ASCAP"), Broadcast Music, Inc. ("BMI"), SESAC, or GMR, whichever may be applicable;

b. any Media Entity in the USTP that is licensed to exhibit, broadcast or transmit a public performance of the Game embodying the Composition, but not in compliance with the established protocol for public performance licensing in that respective portion of the Territory and at the time of said public performance, if any, including the probability of a valid and authorized public performance license in place with ASCAP, BMI, SESAC, or GMR whichever may be applicable, is subject to prior approval of such needed public performance right from Licensor, or from any other duly authorized licensor acting for or on behalf of Licensor, pursuant to good faith negotiations in accordance with established industry customs and practices; and

c. with respect to any public performance of the Game embodying the Composition in locations outside of the USTP, Licensor and Licensee duly understand that the laws, customary practices, rules, regulations and/or any correlating fees already established in such location of the Territory outside of the USTP at the time of said public performance shall dictate and govern.

9. Reservation of Rights: Licensor specifically reserves unto itself all rights of every kind and nature except those specifically granted to Licensee on a non-exclusive basis hereunder. For any avoidance of doubt:

a. this Agreement does not authorize or permit any use of the Composition not expressly set forth herein, including but not limited to, the right to (i) make any changes to the Composition other than the ability to edit, cut, loop, or otherwise excerpt portions of the Composition as necessary for Game integration, utilizing continuous portions thereof; (ii) perform, exhibit or utilize the Composition in any sound-alone or audio-only device, whether now known or hereafter devised, separate from the Game; (iii) to use the story of the Composition, or any excerpt thereof, as a base foundation of and/or in the Game in any way; and/or (iv) make any changes to the original lyrics or the fundamental musical character of the Composition (unless otherwise provided for hereunder);

b. this Agreement does not authorize or permit any use of the name of the Writer in the Game or in any other way, except as otherwise provided for in paragraph 10 hereunder, including but not limited to, any means of publicity, promotions or co-promotions, so called "tie-in" campaigns, music videos or within or in connection with any other similar scenario(s), unless otherwise provided for hereunder or so granted by the Writer's authorized representative under separate agreement; and

c. all "derivative work" copyrights and "collective work" and/or "compilation" copyrights (as those terms are respectively defined in the United States Copyright Act) in and to the Composition as a result of Licensee's exercise of its rights hereunder, shall belong to, and be exclusively owned by, Licensor.

10. Credit: Licensee shall accord Licensor screen credit in the Game and/or credit via packaging inserts thereof and/or any other physical or digital Game-related materials, if such credit is accorded to other licensors of pre-existing music as performed in the soundtrack of the Game, in a size and form no less prominent than any other said music licensor, in substantially the same manner.

11. Production Costs: The entire cost of the overall production, manufacture, distribution, promotion and sale of the Game, including, but not limited to, all expenses for artwork, transport costs and/or commercial or trade advertising shall be at Licensee's sole expense.

12. Licensor's Warranty and Indemnification: Licensor warrants that it has the legal right to grant the rights specified hereunder. Licensor shall indemnify and hold Licensee harmless against any third party claims, liabilities, losses or damages actually incurred by Licensee as a result of Licensor's breach of this warranty, but in no event shall Licensor's aggregate liability exceed the amount of consideration actually paid to Licensor hereunder. This Agreement is given without any other warranty by or recourse against Licensor.

13. Licensee's Warranty and Indemnification: Licensee will indemnify and hold harmless Licensor from any and all claims, liabilities, losses and damages arising from any breach of Licensee's warranties, representations or covenants under this Agreement, or in any way resulting from or connected with Licensee's use of the Composition in any manner not approved nor granted hereunder by Licensor. Licensee further warrants and represents that it has not exploited or authorized the exploitation of, and will not exploit or authorize the exploitation of, the Composition in any way, media or context other than as licensed hereunder, as any such unauthorized exploitation constitutes infringement by Licensee

as defined under the Copyright Act, which would entitle Licensor to seek all applicable remedies thereunder.

14. Assignment: This Agreement is binding upon and shall inure to the benefit of the respective successors, assigns and/or sub-licensees of the parties hereto. Notwithstanding anything contained herein to the contrary, Licensee may transfer its rights under this Agreement, provided Licensee remains liable for any failure on the part of its assignee(s) to comply with any and all sections under this Agreement.

15. Conditions Precedent: The non-exclusive rights granted to Licensee hereunder shall be of no force or effect until Licensor receives the consideration specified under Schedule A from Licensee and/or until this Agreement is fully executed by Licensor and Licensee.

16. Copy: Licensee shall provide Licensor with _____ (__) copies of the Game for Licensor's archives.

17. Notices: The respective addresses of Licensor and Licensee for all purposes of this Agreement shall be as set forth above until notice of a new address is provided by either to the other. Any notice shall be delivered by overnight courier or certified mail, postage prepaid, return receipt requested.

18. Choice of Law: This Agreement is being entered into and shall be construed in accordance with the laws of the State of _____ as if it were entered into and wholly executed in the State of _____. All judicial proceedings brought against a party with respect to this Agreement or any related document shall be brought in any state or federal court of competent jurisdiction in the County of _____ in the State of _____ and by its execution and delivery of this Agreement, each of the parties accepts, for itself and in connection with its properties, generally and unconditionally, the exclusive jurisdiction of the aforesaid courts.

19. Entire Agreement: This Agreement wholly sets forth the entire understanding between the parties hereto and no modification, amendment, waiver, termination or discharge shall be binding unless confirmed by a written instrument duly signed by the party to be charged therewith. If any part of this Agreement is adjudicated as invalid or unenforceable, it shall not affect the validity of any remaining provision or condition within the balance of this Agreement.

Schedule A

A. The Game: _____

B. Composition: _____

C. Writer: _____

D. % Owned/Controlled: _____

E. Publisher(s): _____

Initial Use

F. Use Description: _____

G. Granted Rights/Media: _____

H. Territory: _____

I. Term: _____

J. License Fee: _____

K. Advance/Royalty Per-Unit Rate: _____

L. MFN: _____

M. Option(s) and Fee(s): _____

N. Special Terms/Conditions: _____

All payments, royalties and other consideration shall be sent directly to:

_____

IN WITNESS WHEREOF, the parties have caused the foregoing to be executed as of the date first set forth above.

AGREED TO AND ACCEPTED: AGREED TO AND ACCEPTED:

_____   _____
("Licensor")   ("Licensee")

By_____   By_____
An Authorized Signatory   An Authorized Signatory

Federal Tax ID#:

MECHANICAL LICENSE AGREEMENT
(DIGITAL DOWNLOAD)

TO:

LICENSE NUMBER:

DATE:

You have advised us, as publisher, that you wish to obtain a compulsory license to make and distribute digital phonorecord deliveries (as defined in Section 115 of the Copyright Act, and hereafter referred to as "DPDs"), of the copyrighted work listed below, under the compulsory license provision of Section 115 of the Copyright Act. The provisions hereof vary the terms of the compulsory license provision of the Copyright Act applicable to DPDs. Your making and distributing of DPDs of any such work shall constitute assent to these terms.

SONG TITLE: See Schedule A   *WRITERS:* See Schedule A

PUBLISHERS: See schedule A   *RELEASE TITLE:*

ARTIST: *RECORD LABEL:*

RECORD #:   *FORMAT:*

RELEASE: *TIME OF RECORDING:* See Schedule A

ROYALTY RATE: See Schedule A

Upon your doing so, you shall have all the rights which are granted to, and all the obligations which are imposed upon, users of said copyrighted work under the compulsory license provision of the Copyright Act, after DPDs of the copyrighted work have been distributed to the public in the United States, provided that:

1. Within forty-five (45) days after the end of each calendar quarter—or ninety (90) days after the end of each bi-annual accounting period, if Publisher has pre-approved receipt of bi-annual statements and payments—you shall account to us in detail for the number of DPDs made and distributed and not returned during said period, and shall pay us the royalties due at the same time. Such accounting shall be submitted in an electronic data format such as Excel (.xls or .xlsx), comma-separated values (.csv), or text file (.txt) to _____. A royalty template will be provided upon request.

2. This mechanical license covers and is limited to one particular recording of said copyrighted work as performed by the artist and on the DPD configuration number identified above. This mechanical license does not supersede nor in any way affect any prior agreements between the relevant parties now in effect respecting mechanical reproduction or other uses of said copyrighted work.

3. With respect to all such DPDs made and distributed and not returned in the United States, the royalty rate hereunder shall be the compulsory mechanical rate as contained in the Copyright Act that is in effect at the time such DPDs are distributed (the "Statutory Rate"). In the event the statutory rate is hereafter adjusted, then with respect to all such DPDs distributed from and after the effective date of such adjustment, the royalty rate hereunder shall be such adjusted Statutory Rate.

4. This license includes the privilege of making a musical arrangement of the copyrighted work to the extent necessary to conform it to the style or manner of interpretation of the performance involved, but the arrangement made (i) may not change the basic melody or fundamental character of the copyrighted work, (ii) shall not be subject to protection under the Copyright Act by you as a derivative work, and (iii) all copyrights and other rights in and to any such arrangement shall automatically vest in the owners of the copyrighted work upon the creation of such arrangement.

5. If more than one musical work is licensed hereunder, each such license of each such work shall be for all purposes treated as if (and deemed to be) a separate license and, without in any way limiting the foregoing, there shall be no right of offset between such licenses or otherwise in connection herewith.

6. You shall permit us, our chartered accountant or certified public accountant within _____ (__) days from the date of receipt of written notice, to inspect, at your place of business and during usual business hours, upon written notice, all books, records and other documents relating to the manufacturing and distribution of DPDs pursuant to this license. We shall have the right to make copies of such books, records and other documents as same may relate to the subject matter of this license. The cost of such audit shall be our responsibility. We shall not have the right to examine your books, records and other documents more than once per calendar year, nor once per statement. No statement rendered to Licensor by Licensee may be audited more than _____ (__) years from the date rendered.

7. In the event you fail to account and/or pay royalties to us as herein provided for, we may give written notice to you that, unless the default is remedied within thirty (30) days from the date of receipt of such notice, this license shall terminate without further notice. Such termination shall render either the making or the distribution, or both, of all DPDS for which royalties have not

been paid, actionable as acts of infringement under, and fully subject to the remedies provided by the Copyright Act. Notwithstanding revocation of the license, you shall remain liable to us for all monies previously accrued hereunder.

8. You need not serve or file the notices required by the Copyright Act.

9. The authority hereunder is limited to (i) the making and distribution of DPDs, and (ii) the making of a copy of a sound recording of the said copyrighted work on a computer file server located in the United States, its territories or possessions, solely for the purpose of distributing such DPDs. The authority hereunder does not extend to DPDs where the reproduction and distribution of a phonorecord (or the musical work) is incidental to the transmission which constitutes the DPD.

10. In the event we are required to institute any legal proceedings against you in connection with this license, in addition to any damages awarded us, we shall be entitled to our reasonable, actual outside (third party) attorneys' fees, and you shall abide by any ruling made by the Court with respect to the payment of costs and reasonable attorneys' fees in connection therewith.

11. This license sets forth the entire agreement between the parties and may only be modified or amended by means of a written amendment, designated as such and signed by both parties.

12. Neither this license or any of the rights granted to you hereunder may be assigned by you to any party, excluding wholly owned affiliated or subsidiaries of your parent company, without our prior written consent, except that you may assign this license in the course of a sale, transfer or other disposition of all or substantially all of your stock and/or assets provided such assignee shall agree to be bound by the terms and provisions hereof. We may assign this license and/or any of the rights granted to us hereunder at any time and for any reason.

13. You agree that our total liability and the total liability of the owner(s) of the copyrighted work shall not exceed, under any circumstances, the royalties paid to us pursuant to this license, so long as we have reasonable basis for purporting to grant this license on the terms set forth herein.

14. This license shall be binding upon the earlier of your execution of this agreement, or permitting the release in the United States of America of the DPD referred to above.

15. This license does not authorize the reproduction or exploitation of the said copyrighted work in any manner not specified hereunder, including, but not limited to, devices embodying sound synchronization with visual images.

16. The validity, construction, interpretation and legal effect of this license shall be governed by both the Copyright Law of the United States and the laws of the State of _____ applicable to contracts entered into and to be fully performed therein.

Accepted and Agreed To:

RECORD COMPANY: PUBLISHER:

By_____   By_____
An Authorized Signatory   An Authorized Signatory

Federal Tax ID#:

MECHANICAL LICENSE AGREEMENT—PHYSICAL

TO:

LICENSE NUMBER:

DATE:

You have advised us, as publisher, that you wish to obtain a non-exclusive mechanical license to make and distribute phonorecords of the copyrighted work listed below, under the mechanical license provision of Section 115 (c) (2) of the Copyright Act. The provisions hereof vary the terms of the compulsory license provision of the Copyright Act applicable to phonorecords. Your making and distributing of phonorecords of any such work shall constitute assent to these terms.

SONG TITLE: See Schedule A   *WRITERS:* See Schedule A

PUBLISHER: See Schedule A   *RELEASE TITLE:*

ARTIST: *RECORD LABEL:*

RECORD #:   *FORMAT:*

RELEASE DATE: *TIME OF RECORDING:* See Schedule A

ROYALTY RATE: Statutory

Upon your doing so, you shall have all the rights which are granted to, and all the obligations which are imposed upon, users of said copyrighted work under the compulsory mechanical license provision of the Copyright Act, after phonorecords of the copyrighted work have been distributed to the public in the United States, provided that:

1. Within forty-five (45) days after the end of each calendar quarter—or ninety (90) days after the end of each bi-annual accounting period, if Publisher has pre-approved receipt of bi-annual statements and payments—you shall account to us in detail for the number of phonorecords made and distributed and not returned during said period, and shall pay us the royalties due at the same time. Such accounting shall be submitted in an electronic data format such as Excel (.xls or .xlsx), comma-separated values (.csv), or text file (.txt) to _____. A royalty template will be provided upon request.

2. This mechanical license covers and is limited to one particular recording of said copyrighted work as performed by the artist and on the phonorecord number identified above. This mechanical license does not supersede nor in any way affect any prior agreements between the relevant parties now in effect respecting mechanical reproduction or other uses of said copyrighted work.

3. With respect to all such phonorecords manufactured and sold and not returned in the United States, the royalty rate hereunder shall be the compulsory mechanical rate as contained in the Copyright Act that is in effect at the time such phonorecords are distributed (the "Statutory Rate"). In the event the Statutory Rate is hereafter adjusted, then with respect to all such phonorecords distributed from and after the effective date of such adjustment, the royalty rate hereunder shall be such adjusted Statutory Rate.

4. This license includes the privilege of making a musical arrangement of the copyrighted work to the extent necessary to conform it to the style or manner of interpretation of the performance involved, but the arrangement made (i) may not change the basic melody or fundamental character of the copyrighted work, (ii) shall not be subject to protection under the Copyright Act by you as a derivative work, and (iii) all copyrights and other rights in and to any such arrangement shall automatically vest in the owners of the copyrighted work upon the creation of such arrangement.

5. If more than one musical work is licensed hereunder, each such license of each such work shall be for all purposes treated as if (and deemed to be) a separate license and, without in any way limiting the foregoing, there shall be no right of offset between such licenses or otherwise in connection herewith.

6. You shall permit us, our chartered accountant or certified public accountant within _____ (__) days from the date of receipt of written notice, to inspect, at your place of business and during usual business hours, upon written notice, all books, records and other documents relating to the manufacturing and distribution of phonorecords pursuant to this license. We shall have the right to make copies of such books, records and other documents as same may relate to the subject matter of this license. The cost of such audit shall be our responsibility. We shall not have the right to examine your books, records and other documents more than once per calendar year, nor once per statement. No statement rendered to Licensor by Licensee may be audited more than _____ (__) years from the date rendered.

7. In the event you fail to account and/or pay royalties to us as herein provided for, we may give written notice to you that, unless the default is remedied within thirty

(30) days from the date of receipt of such notice, this license shall terminate without further notice. Such termination shall render either the making or the distribution, or both, of all phonorecords for which royalties have not been paid, actionable as acts of infringement under, and fully subject to the remedies provided by the Copyright Act. Notwithstanding revocation of the license, you shall remain liable to us for all monies previously accrued hereunder.

8. You need not serve or file the notices required by the Copyright Act.

9. This license is limited to the United States, its territories and possessions and specifically excludes those phonorecords manufactured and sold in the United States for export.

10. In the event we are required to institute any legal proceedings against you in connection with this license, in addition to any damages awarded us, we shall be entitled to our reasonable, actual outside (third party) attorneys' fees, and you shall abide by any ruling made by the Court with respect to the payment of costs and reasonable attorneys' fees in connection therewith.

11. This license sets forth the entire agreement between the parties and may only be modified or amended by means of a written amendment, designated as such and signed by both parties.

12. Neither this license or any of the rights granted to you hereunder may be assigned by you to any party, excluding wholly owned affiliated or subsidiaries of your parent company, without our prior written consent, except that you may assign this license in the course of a sale, transfer or other disposition of all or substantially all of your stock and/or assets provided such assignee shall agree to be bound by the terms and provisions hereof. We may assign this license and/or any of the rights granted to us hereunder at any time and for any reason.

13. You agree that our total liability and the total liability of the owner(s) of the copyrighted work shall not exceed, under any circumstances, the royalties paid to us pursuant to this license, so long as we have reasonable basis for purporting to grant this license on the terms set forth herein.

14. This license shall be binding upon the earlier of your execution of this agreement, or permitting the release in the United States of America of the phonorecord referred to above.

15. This license does not authorize the reproduction or exploitation of the said copyrighted work in any manner not specified hereunder, including, but not

limited to, devices embodying sound synchronization with visual images.

16. The validity, construction, interpretation and legal effect of this license shall be governed by both the Copyright Law of the United States and the laws of the State of _____ applicable to contracts entered into and to be fully performed therein.

Accepted and Agreed To:

RECORD COMPANY: PUBLISHER:

By_____   By_____
An Authorized Signatory   An Authorized Signatory

Federal Tax ID#:

INDEX